SPORT IN CONTEMPORARY SOCIETY:

An Anthology

SPORT IN CONTEMPORARY SOCIETY

An Anthology

D. STANLEY EITZEN
Colorado State University

St. Martin's Press
NEW YORK

Library of Congress Catalog Card Number: 78-65246
Copyright © 1979 by St. Martin's Press, Inc.
All Rights Reserved.
Manufactured in the United States of America.
3210
fedcb
For information, write St. Martin's Press, Inc.,
175 Fifth Avenue, New York, N.Y. 10010

cover design: Tom McKeveny

cloth ISBN: 0-312-75326-8

paper ISBN: 0-312-75327-6

Preface

Most Americans are at least somewhat interested in sport, and many are downright fanatical about it. They attend games, read the sport pages and sport magazines, and talk endlessly about the subject. But even those fans who astound us with their knowledge of the most obscure facts about sport—who the opposing pitcher was when Don Larsen pitched his perfect no-hit World Series game or how many winning seasons the football team of Slippery Rock has had—do not necessarily *understand* sport.

Do sport buffs know how sport is linked to other institutions of society? Do they understand the role of sport in socializing youngsters in American values? Do they know how much racial discrimination continues to exist in American sport, and why? Do they know how often or how seldom it is really the case that sport enables its participants to rise in the American social structure? Do they know that the assumption that sport builds character is open to serious question? What about the relationship of violence in sport to the structure of society? What about the ways in which sport has perpetuated sex-role stereotypes in society? How do owners, coaches, and other sport authorities exercise power to maintain control over athletes? These are some of the issues this book examines.

There are two fundamental reasons for the ignorance of most Americans about the role of sport in society. First, they have had to rely mainly on sportswriters and sportscasters for their information, and these journalists have usually been little more than describers and cheerleaders. Until recent years journalists have rarely looked critically at sport. Instead, they have perpetuated myths: "Look what baseball did for Jackie Robinson" or "Football helped a whole generation of sons of coal miners escape the mines."

The second reason for our sports illiteracy is that sport has been virtually ignored by American academics. Only in the past fifteen years or so have American social scientists and physical educators begun to employ scientific research methods to investigate the social aspects of sport. Previously, as with sports journalism, academic research in the field of sport tended to be biased in support of existing myths. In particular the early research by physical educators was aimed at proving that sports participation builds character. In this limited perspective such phenomena as cheating, violence, and failure were, for the most part, simply ignored.

Today, however, not only academics but also a new breed of sports journalists—though the latter are still a minority—are making insightful analyses of sport's role in society. They are examining the positive *and* the negative consequences of sport. They are substituting facts for myths. Most significantly, they are documenting the reciprocal impact of sport and the various institutions of society: religion, education, politics, and economics. There is no danger that sport will suffer from such examination. On the contrary, sport is revealed as a subject far more complex and far more interesting than most of us have imagined.

This book is a collection of the writings representing this new era of critical appraisal. It includes contributions from both journalists and academics. The overriding criterion for inclusion of a particular article was whether it critically examined the role of sport in society. The praise of sport is not omitted, but such praise, as with condemnation, must be backed by fact, not mythology or dogma. (Occasionally, a dogmatic piece has been included to challenge the critical faculties of the reader.) The selection of each article was also guided by such questions as, Is it interesting? Is it informative? Is it thought-provoking? Does it communicate without the use of unnecessary jargon and sophisticated methodologies?

In short, the articles presented here not only afford the reader an understanding of sport that transcends the still prevalent stereotypes and myths; they also yield fascinating and important insights to the nature of American society. Thus, this book has several groups of potential readers. First, it is intended to be the primary or supplementary textbook for courses in the sociology of sport, sport and society, and foundations of physical education. Second, the book can be used as a supplemental text for sociology courses such as the introduction to sociology, American society, and American institutions. A third audience for this book is general readers who wish to deepen their understanding and appreciation of sport.

ACKNOWLEDGMENTS

Three colleagues have had a special impact on my interest in the sociology of sport. My initial research effort was sparked by the suggestion of Kenneth Kammeyer as we sought the solution to a research problem unrelated to sport. My interest was nurtured immensely by the inspiration and enthusiasm of Norman Yetman, with whom I worked to develop a course on sport and to investigate empirically a number of aspects of sport over several years when we both were at the University of Kansas. Finally, when I moved to Colorado State University, I had the good fortune to meet George Sage of the University of Northern Colorado, an encounter which eventually led to our collaboration on a textbook, *Sociology of American Sport*.

I also want to thank my students, graduate and undergraduate, who have contributed to my understanding of sport in social settings in a variety of ways. In particular I wish to single out the contributions of Ken Bledsoe, Don Harris, McKee McClendon, Dean Purdy, David Sanford, and Irl Tessendorf.

Contents

One

Toward an Understanding of Sport

The character of American sport has changed dramatically in the twentieth century. Sport was once primarily engaged in by persons who sought the enjoyment of physical activity and competition. Although there are occasions for this level of sport now, sport for the most part has become corrupted. The athlete's pleasure has been superseded by what brings pleasure to fans, parents, sports team owners, alumni, television, and the corporations that buy television advertising. Sport has become spectacle, big business, and an extension of power politics. This shift to what might be dubbed "corporate sport" is seen not only in the professional leagues but also in the Olympic Games, colleges, high schools, and even in children's sports. What once was regarded as play has become work. Spontaneity has been replaced by bureaucracy. The goal of pleasure in the physical activity has been displaced by extrinsic rewards, especially money.[1]

The articles selected for this book examine the current organization of sport critically and from a number of perspectives. Three quite different selections in this section serve to raise the consciousness of the reader about sport in American society. These also set the stage for the analyses of specific areas of sport found in the later sections of this anthology.

The initial selection is taken from the preface of Robert Lipsyte's perceptive book, *Sportsworld: An American Dreamland.* Lipsyte was a sports journalist for the *New York Times* and exemplifies the new breed of sports analyst. The selection reprinted here attunes the reader to the pervasiveness of sports myths and their political, economic, and social consequences for individuals and society. The questions raised about the

1

role of sport in producing failures, rationalizing failure, building character, supporting racism and sexism, and reinforcing the social class system are extremely insightful and set the stage for later selections in which these elements are discussed in greater detail.

Next is an essay by an English professor who wonders why he—and we—are so obsessed with sport. Epstein's discussion is similar to the concern shown by another academic—philosopher Michael Novak—who after watching the Dodgers lose a game on television asked:

How could I be forty years old and still care what happens to the Dodgers? How could I have thrown away three hours of evaporating life, watching a ritual, an inferior dance, a competition without a socially redeeming point? About the age of forty, almost everything about one's life comes into question. There is so little time to grasp and hold, it slides through fingers like the sand. It seems important now to concentrate. And so I asked myself: Is it time for sports to be discarded? Is it time to put away the things of childhood?

Quietly, I knew the answer. What I had just seen was somehow more important than my other work, was deeper in my being than most of what I did, spoke to me of beauty, excellence, imagination, and animal vitality—was *true* in a way few things in life are true. My love for sports was deeper than any theory that I had. The reality is better than its intellectual defense.

So I knew I had an obligation to work on this book.

I love sports, and I want to bequeath that love to my children—to that stranger with the mitt who is ten and the two girls who are eight and three. It seems a precious gift to give. But why? Why do I love sports? How can I explain it to myself, let alone to others, especially to those who are skeptical unbelievers?[2]

Novak's answer is that sport is somehow a religion, a possibility that will be examined further in a later unit. Epstein's article examines a number of other possible reasons for the strong attraction sport has for so many. He wonders: Is it the violence? Is it the competitive urge? Is it the respect for the excellence of the performers? Or is it a form of fantasy where one attempts to regain one's adolescence? His answer combines some of these elements with others. The allure of sport is found in its excellence, spectacle, clarity (we know exactly who won), and its unique function of providing a common culture—a bonding agent—for its spellbound adherents.

The final selection of this unit is by Merrill Melnick, a physical educator, who critically examines the dominant orientation of sport sociologists. He argues that the sociologists of sport must not accept sport but, rather, they should point out the inconsistencies between official rhetoric and actual practices; they should question established orthodoxies; and they should, through social criticism, work to initiate social change. As Eitzen and Sage have said in the preface to *Sociology of American Sport*:

> Our . . . goal is to make the reader aware of the positive and negative consequences of the way sport is organized in American society. We are concerned about some of the trends in sport, especially the move away from athlete-oriented activities toward the impersonality of what we term "corporate sport." We are committed to moving sport and society in a more humane direction, and this requires, as a first step, a thorough understanding of the principles that underlie the social structures and processes that create, sustain, and transform the social organizations within the institution of sport.[3]

NOTES

1. D. Stanley Eitzen and George H. Sage, *Sociology of American Sport* (Dubuque, Iowa: Wm. C. Brown, 1978), pp. 16, 18–19.
2. Michael Novak, *The Joy of Sports: End Zones, Bases, Baskets, Balls, and the Consecration of the American Spirit* (New York: Basic Books, 1976), p. xi.
3. Eitzen and Sage, *Sociology of American Sport*, p. vii.

Sportsworld

ROBERT LIPSYTE

For the past one hundred years most Americans have believed that playing and watching competitive games are not only healthful activities, but represent a positive force on our national psyche. In sports, they believe, children will learn courage and self-control, old people will find blissful nostalgia, and families will discover new ways to communicate among themselves. Immigrants will find shortcuts to recognition as Americans. Rich and poor, black and white, educated and unskilled, we will all find a unifying language. The melting pot may be a myth, but we will all come together in the ballpark.

This faith in sports has been vigorously promoted by industry, the military, government, the media. The values of the arena and the locker room have been imposed upon our national life. Coaches and sportswriters are speaking for generals and businessmen, too, when they tell us that a man must be physically and psychologically "tough" to succeed, that he must be clean and punctual and honest, that he must bear pain, bad luck, and defeat without whimpering or making excuses. A man must prove his faith in sports and the American Way by whipping himself into shape, playing by the rules, being part of the team, and putting out all the way. If his faith is strong enough, he will triumph. It's his own fault if he loses, fails, remains poor.

Even for ballgames, these values, with their implicit definitions of manhood, courage, and success, are not necessarily in the individual's best interests. But for daily life they tend to create a dangerous and grotesque web of ethics and attitudes, an amorphous infrastructure that acts to contain our energies, divert our passions, and socialize us for work or war or depression.

I call this infrastructure SportsWorld. For most of my adult life, as a professional observer, I've explored SportsWorld and marveled at its incredible power and pervasiveness. SportsWorld touches everyone and everything. We elect our politicians, judge our children, fight our wars, plan our vacations, oppress our minorities by SportsWorld standards that somehow justify our foulest and freakiest deeds, or at least camouflage them with jargon. We get stoned on such SportsWorld spectaculars as the

SOURCE: Robert Lipsyte, *SportsWorld: An American Dreamland* (New York: Quadrangle/The New York Times Book Co., 1975), pp. ix-xv.

4

Super Bowl, the space shots, the Kentucky Derby, the presidential conventions, the Indianapolis 500, all of whose absurd excesses reassure us that we're okay.

SportsWorld is a sweaty Oz you'll never find in a geography book, but since the end of the Civil War it has been promoted and sold to us like Rancho real estate, an ultimate sanctuary, a university for the body, a community for the spirit, a place to hide that glows with that time of innocence when we believed that rules and boundaries were honored, that good triumphed over evil, and that the loose ends of experience could be caught and bound and delivered in an explanation as final and as comforting as a goodnight kiss.

Sometime in the last fifty years the sports experience was perverted into a SportsWorld state of mind in which the winner was good because he won; the loser, if not actually bad, was at least reduced, and had to prove himself over again, through competition. As each new immigrant crop was milled through the American system, a pick of the harvest was displayed in the SportsWorld showcase, a male preserve of national athletic entertainment traditionally enacted by the working class for the middle class, much as the performing arts are played by the middle class for the amusement of the upper class.

By the 1950s, when SportsWorld was dominated by what are now called "white ethnics," the black American was perceived as a challenging force and was encouraged to find outlets in the national sports arena. Although most specific laws against black participation had already been erased, it took cautious, humiliating experiments with such superstars as Jackie Robinson and Larry Doby to prove that spectator prejudice could be deconditioned by a winning team. Within a few years, pools of cheap, eager black and dark Latin labor were channeled into mainstream clubs.

So pervasive are the myths of SportsWorld that the recruitment of blacks has been regarded as a gift of true citizenship bestowed upon the Negro when he was ready. It has been conventional wisdom for twenty years that the black exposure in sports has speeded the integration of American society, that white Americans, having seen that blacks are beautiful and strong, became "liberalized."

This is one of the crueler hoaxes of SportsWorld. Sports success probably has been detrimental to black progress. By publicizing the material success of a few hundred athletes, thousands, perhaps millions, of bright young blacks have been swept toward sports when they should have been guided toward careers in medicine or engineering or business. For every black star celebrated in SportsWorld, a thousand of his little brothers were neutralized, kept busy shooting baskets until it was too late for them to qualify beyond marginal work.

The white male spectator who knew few ordinary black men to

measure himself against may have had his awareness raised by watching such superior human beings as Frank Robinson, Jim Brown, Bill Russell, O. J. Simpson, and other highly merchandised SportsWorld heroes, but it also doubled his worst fears about blacks: added to the black junkie who would rip out his throat was the black superstud who could replace him as a man—in bed, on the job, as a model for his children.

By the middle of the 1970s it seemed as though the black experience in SportsWorld might be recapitulated by women. SportsWorld seemed on the verge of becoming the arena in which women would discover and exploit their new "equality." It would be a complex test of adaptability for SportsWorld. The major sports were created by men for the superior muscles, size, and endurance of the male body. Those sports in which balance, flexibility, and dexterity are the crucial elements have never been mass-promoted in America. When a woman beats a man at a man's game, she has to play like a man.

There were signs, however, that women may not embrace Sports-World as eagerly as did the blacks, profiting from that sorry lesson as well as from their own greater leverage in American society. It is no accident that Billie Jean King, while still an active player, became an entrepreneur and an important voice in American cultural consciousness while Jackie Robinson was a Rockefeller courtier almost to the end of his life.

A great deal of the angry energy generated in America through the coming apart of the 1960s was absorbed by SportsWorld in its various roles as socializer, pacifier, safety valve; as a concentration camp for adolescents and an emotional Disneyland for their parents; as a laboratory for human engineering and a reflector of current moral postures; and as a running commercial for Our Way of Life. SportsWorld is a buffer, a DMZ, between people and the economic and political systems that direct their lives; women, so long denied this particular playland, may just avoid this trap altogether.

But SportsWorld's greatest power has always been its flexibility. Even as we are told of SportsWorld's proud traditions, immutable laws, ultimate security from the capriciousness of "real life," SportsWorld is busy changing its rules, readjusting its alliances, checking the trends. SportsWorld is nothing if not responsive. Hockey interest lagging, how about a little more blood on the ice? Speed up baseball with a designated hitter. Move the football goal posts. A three-point shot in basketball. Women agitating at the college arena gates? Let 'em in. Give 'em athletic scholarships, "jock" dorms, and Minnie Mouse courses. How about a Professional Women's Power Volleyball League?

Stars, teams, leagues, even entire sports may rise or fall or never get off the ground, but SportsWorld as a force in American life orbits on.

Ah, baseball. Our National Pastime. An incredibly complex contrivance that seems to have been created by a chauvinistic mathematician intent upon giving America a game so idiosyncratic that it would be at least a century before any other country could beat us at it. And indeed it was. After a century in which baseball was celebrated as a unique product of the American character, Chinese boys began winning Little League championships, and young men from Latin America and the Caribbean began making a significant impact upon the major leagues. The highly organized Japanese, who had taken up the game during the postwar occupation of their country (perhaps as penance for yelling "To Hell with Babe Ruth" during banzai charges) were almost ready to attack again.

But SportsWorld had spun on. That other peculiarly American game, football, declared itself the New National Pastime. Baseball and God were announced dead at about the same time, but the decision against baseball apparently is taking longer to reverse, thanks in the main to pro football's colossal public relations machine. The National Football League played its scheduled games on Sunday, November 24, 1963, because its historic television deal was pending and Commissioner Pete Rozelle was determined to prove that nothing, *nothing*, could cancel the show. But that winter, NFL sportscasters infiltrated the banquet circuit with the engaging theory—quintessential SportsWorld—that America had been at the brink of a nervous breakdown after President Kennedy's assassination and that only The Sport of the Sixties' business-as-usual attitude had held the country together until Monday's National Day of Mourning unified us all in public grief.

Ten years later, though hopefully still grateful, America had grown bored with the cartoon brutality of pro football. America was boogieing to the magic moves and hip, sly rhythms of basketball, The Sport of the Seventies. We've had enough of pure violence, simulated or otherwise, went the SportsWorld wisdom, now we need something smooooooooth.

There is no end to SportsWorld theories—of the past, the present, the future—especially now that a new generation of commentators, athletes, coaches, and fans feels free to reform and recast sports, to knock it off the pedestal and slide it under the microscope, giving it more importance than ever. SportsWorld newspapermen dare to describe to us action that we have seen more clearly on television than they have from the press box, and SportsWorld telecasters, isolated from the world in their glass booths, dare to explain to us what the players are *really* thinking. SportsWorld analysts were once merely "pigskin prognosticators" predicting the weekend football scores; now they may be as heavy as any RAND Corporation futurist. Is hockey an art form or is it a paradigm of anarchy, in which case are we obligated as concerned citizens to watch it? Is tennis more than just a convenient new market for clothes and building materials and nondurable goods? What will be The Sport of the Eighties? Will no sport ever again have its own decade? Will cable television and government-regulated sports gambling and the institutionalized fragmenting of society balkanize us into dozens of jealous Fandoms?

SportsWorld, once determinedly anti-intellectual, has become a hotbed of psychologists, physicians, and sociologists questioning premises as well as specific techniques. Should lacrosse players really be eating steak before games, or pancakes? Why are the lockers of defensive linemen neater than those of offensive linemen? Does athletic participation truly "build character" or does it merely reinforce otherwise unacceptable traits? Should communities rather than corporations own teams?

But very few people seem to be questioning SportsWorld itself, exploring the possibility that if sports could be separated from SportsWorld we could take a major step toward liberation from the false values, the stereotypes, the idols of the arena that have burdened us all since childhood.

SportsWorld is not a conspiracy in the classic sense, but rather an expression of a community of interest. In the Soviet Union, for example, where world-class athletes are the diplomat-soldiers of ideology, and where factory girls are forced to exercise to reduce fatigue and increase production, the entire athletic apparatus is part of government. Here in America, SportsWorld's insidious power is imposed upon athletics by the banks that decide which arenas and recreational facilities shall be built, by the television networks that decide which sports shall be sponsored and viewed, by the press that decides which individuals and teams shall be celebrated, by the municipal governments that decide which clubs shall be subsidized, and by the federal government, which has, through favorable tax rulings and exemptions from law, allowed sports entertainment to grow until it has become the most influential form of mass culture in America.

SportsWorld is a grotesque distortion of sports. It has limited the pleasures of play for most Americans while concentrating on turning our best athletes into clowns. It has made the finish more important than the race, and extolled the game as that William Jamesian absurdity, a moral equivalent to war, and the hero of the game as that Henry Jamesian absurdity, a "muscular Christian." It has surpassed patriotism and piety as a currency of communication, while exploiting them both. By the end of the 1960s, SportsWorld wisdom had it that religion was a spectator sport while professional and college athletic contests were the only events Americans held sacred.

SportsWorld is neither an American nor a modern phenomenon. Those glorified Olympics of ancient Greece were manipulated for political and commercial purposes; at the end, they held a cracked mirror to a decaying civilization. The modern Olympics were revived at the end of the nineteenth century in an attempt to whip French youth into shape for a battlefield rematch with Germany. Each country of Europe, then the United States, the Soviet Union, the "emerging" nations of Africa and Asia, used the Olympics as political display windows. The 1972 Arab massacre of Israeli athletes was a hideously logical extension of Sports-World philosophy.

SportsWorld begins in elementary school, where the boys are separated from the girls. In *Sixties Going on Seventies*, Nora Sayre recounts the poignant confrontation of a gay man and a gay woman at a meeting. She is banging the floor with a baseball bat, and he asks her to stop; the bat symbolizes to him the oppression of sports in his childhood. But to her the bat symbolizes liberation from the restraint that had kept her from aggression, from sports, in her childhood.

By puberty, most American children have been classified as failed athletes and assigned to watch and cheer for those who have survived the first of several major "cuts." Those who have been discarded to the grandstands and to the television sets are not necessarily worse off than those tapped for higher levels of competition. SportsWorld heroes exist at sufferance, and the path of glory is often an emotional minefield trapped with pressures to perform and fears of failure. There is no escape from SportsWorld, for player or spectator or even reporter, that watcher in the shadows who pretends to be in the arena but above the fray.

Obsessed with Sport

JOSEPH EPSTEIN

I cannot remember when I was not surrounded by sports, when talk of sports was not in the air, when I did not care passionately about sports. As a boy in Chicago in the late Forties, I lived in the same building as the sister and brother-in-law of Barney Ross, the welterweight champion. Half a block away, down near the lake, the Sullivan High School football

SOURCE: Joseph Epstein, "Obsessed with Sport," *Harper's Magazine*, 253 (July 1976), 67-72.

team worked out in the spring and autumn. Summers the same field was given over to baseball and men's softball on Sundays. A few blocks to the north was the Touhy Avenue Fieldhouse, where basketball was played, and lifeguards trained, and behind which, in a softball field frozen over in winter, crack-the-whip, hockey, and speed skating took over. To the west, a block or so up Morse Avenue, was the Morse Avenue "L" Recreations, a combined pool hall and bowling alley. Life, in short, was games.

My father had no interest in sports. He had grown up, one of the ten children of Russian Jewish immigrant parents, on tough Notre Dame Street in Montreal, where the major sports were craps, poker, and petty larceny. He left Montreal at seventeen to come to Chicago, where he worked hard and successfully so that his sons might play. Two of his boyhood friends from Notre Dame Street, who had the comic-book names of Sammy and Danny Spunt, had also come to Chicago, where they bought the Ringside Gym on Dearborn Street in the Loop. All the big names worked out at Ringside for their Chicago fights: Willie Pep, Tony Zale, Joe Louis. At eight or nine I would take the El downtown to the Ringside, be introduced around by Danny Spunt ("Tony Zale, I'd like you to meet the son of an old friend of mine. Kid, I'd like you to meet the middleweight champion of the world"), and return home with an envelope filled with autographed 8-by-10 glossies of Gus Lesnevich, Tammy Maurielo, Kid Gavilan, and the wondrous Sugar Ray.

I lived on, off, and in sports. *Sport* magazine had recently begun publication, and I gobbled up its issues cover to cover, soon becoming knowledgeable not only about the major sports—baseball, football, and basketball—but about golf, hockey, tennis, and horse racing, so that I scored reputably on the Sport Quiz, a regular department at the front of the magazine. Another regular department was the Sport Classic, which featured longish profiles of the legendary figures in the history of sports: Ty Cobb, Jim Thorpe, Bobby Jones, Big Bill Tilden, Red Grange, Man o' War. I next moved on to the sports novels of John R. Tunis—*All-American, The Iron Duke, The Kid from Tomkinsville, The Kid Comes Back, World Series*, the lot—which I read with as much excitement as any books I have read since.

The time was, as is now apparent, a splendid era in sports. Ted Williams, Joe DiMaggio, and Stan Musial were afield; first Jack Kramer, then Pancho Gonzales, dominated tennis; George Mikan led the Minneapolis Lakers, and the Harlem Globetrotters could still be taken seriously; Doc Blanchard and Glen Davis, Mr. Inside and Mr. Outside, were playing for Army, Johnny Lujack was at Notre Dame; in the pros Sammy Baugh, Bob Waterfield, and Sid Luckman were the major T-formation quarterbacks; Joe Louis and Sugar Ray Robinson fought frequently; the two Willies, Mosconi and Hoppe, put in regular appearances at Bensinger's in the Loop; Eddie Arcaro seemed to ride three, four winners a day. Giants, it truly seemed, walked the earth.

All learning of craft—which sport, like writing, most assuredly is— involves imitation, especially in the early stages; and I was an excellent mimic. By the time I was ten years old I had mastery over all the big-time moves: the spit in the mitt, the fluid infield chatter, the knocking of dirt from the spikes; the rhythmic barking out of signals, hands high under the center's crotch to take the ball; the three bounces and deep breath before shooting the free throw (on this last, I regretted not being a Catholic, so that I might be able to make the sign of the cross before shooting, as was then the fashion among Catholic high-school and college players). I went in for athletic haberdashery in a big way, often going beyond mimicry to the point of flat-out phoniness—wearing, for example, a knee pad while playing basketball, though my knees were always, exasperatingly, intact.

I always looked good, which was important, because form is intrinsic to sports; but in my case it was doubly important, because the truth is that I wasn't really very good. Or at any rate not good enough. Two factors accounted for this. The first was that, without being shy about body contact, I lacked a certain indispensable aggressiveness; the second connected closely to the first, was that, when it came right down to it, I did not care enough about winning. I would rather lose a point attempting a slashing cross-court backhand than play for an easier winner down the side; the long jump shot always had more allure for me than the safer drive to the basket. Given a choice between the two vanities of winning and looking good, I almost always preferred looking good.

I shall never forget the afternoon, sometime along about my thirteenth year, when, shooting baskets alone, I came upon the technique for shooting the hook. Although today it has nowhere near the consequence of the jump shot—an innovation that has been to basketball what the jet has been to air travel—the hook is still the single most beautiful shot in the game. The rhythm and grace of it, the sway of the body off the pivot, the release of the ball behind the head and off the fingertips, the touch and instinct involved in its execution, make the hook altogether a balletic thing, and to achieve it is to feel one of the most delectable sensations in sports. That afternoon, on a deserted side street, shooting on a rickety wooden backboard and a black rim without a net, I felt it and grew nearly drunk on the feeling. Rain came down, dirt washed in the gutters, flecks of it spattering my clothes and arms and face, but, soaked and cold though I was, I do not think I would have left that basket on that afternoon for anything. I threw up hook after hook, from every angle, from farther and farther out, off the board, without the board, and hook after hook went in. Only pitch darkness drove me home.

I do not say that not to have shot the hook is never to have lived, but only that, once having done so, the pleasure it gives is not so easily forgotten. Every sport offers similar pleasures, the pleasures taken differing by temperament: the canter into the end zone to meet a floating touchdown pass, or the clean, crisp feel of a perfect block or tackle; the long straight drive or the precisely played approach shot to the green; the solid overhead; the pickup on the tricky short hop or the long ball down one of the power alleys. Different sports, different pleasures. But so keen are these pleasures—pleasures of execution, of craft completed—that, along with being unforgettable, they are also worth recapturing in any available way, and the most available way, when reflexes have slowed, when muscle no longer responds so readily to brain, is from the grandstand or, perhaps more often nowadays, from the chair before the television.

PLEASURES OF THE SPECTATOR

I have put in days on the bench, but years in my chair before the television set. Recently it has occurred to me that over the years I have heard more hours of talk from the announcer Curt Gowdy than from my own father, who is not a reticent man. I have been thoroughly Schenkeled, Mussbergered, Summeralled, Cosselled, DeRogotissed, and Garagiolaed. How many hundreds—thousands?—of hours have I spent watching sports of all sorts, either at parks or stadiums or over television? I am glad I shall never have a precise answer. Yet neither apparently can I get enough. What is the fascination? Why is it that, with the prospect of a game to watch in the evening or on the weekend, the day seems lighter and brighter? What do I get out of it?

What I get out of it, according to one fairly prominent view, is an outlet for my violent emotions. Knee-wrenching, rib-cracking, headbusting, this view has it, is what sports are really about, with sports fans being essentially sadists, and cowardly sadists at that, for they take their violence not at firsthand but at second remove. Enthusiasm for sports among Americans is little more than a reflection of the national penchant for violence. Military men talk about game plans; the long touchdown pass is called the bomb. The average pro-football fan, seeing a quarterback writhing on the ground at midfield as a result of the ministrations of Joe Green, Carl Eller, or Lyle Alzado, twitters with glee, finds his ultimate reward, and declares a little holiday in the blackest corner of his heart.

But this is a criticism that comes at sports by way of politics. To believe it one has to believe that the history of the United States is chiefly one of rape, expropriation, and aggressive imperialism. To dismiss it, however, one need only know something about sports. Violence is indubitably a part of some sports; in some—hockey is an example—it sometimes comes close to being featured. But in no sport—not even boxing, that most rudimentary of sports—is it the main item, and in many other sports it plays no part at all. A distinction worth insisting on is that between violence and roughness. Roughness, a willingness to mix it up, to take if need be an elbow in the jaw, is part of rebounding in basketball, yet violence is not. Even in pro football, most maligned of modern American sports, more of roughness than of violence is involved. Roughness raises the stakes, provides the pressure, behind execution. A splendid because true phrase has come about in pro football to cover the situation in which a pass receiver, certain that he will be tackled upon the instant he makes his reception, drops a ball he should otherwise have caught easily—the phrase, best delivered in a Southern accent such as Don Meredith's, is "He heard footsteps on that one, Howard." Although a part of the attraction, it is not so much those footsteps that fill the stands and the den chairs on Sunday afternoons as it is those men who elude them: the Lynn Swanns, the Fran Tarkentons, the O.J. Simpsons. The American love of violence theory really will not wash. Dick Butkus did not get us into Vietnam.

Many who would not argue that sports reflect American violence nevertheless claim that they imbue one with the competitive spirit. In some who are already amply endowed with it, sports doubtless do tend to refine (or possibly brutalize) the desire to win. Yet sports also teach a serious respect for craft. Competition, though it flourishes as always, is in bad odor nowadays; but craft, officially respected, does not flourish greatly outside the boutique.

If the love of violence or the competitive urge does not put me in my chair for the countless games I watch, is it, then, nostalgia, a yearning to regain the more glowing moments of adolescence? Many argue that this is precisely so, that American men exist in a state of perpetual immaturity, suspended between boy- and manhood. "The difference between men and boys," says Liberace, "is the price of their toys." (I have paid more than $300 for two half-season tickets to the Chicago Bulls games, parking fees not included.) Such unending enthusiasm for games may have something to do with adolescence, but little, I suspect, with regaining anything whatever. Instead, it has more to do with watching men do regularly and surpassingly what, as an adolescent, one did often bumblingly though with an occasional flash of genius. To have played these games oneself as a boy or a young man helps immeasurably the appreciation that in watching a sport played at professional caliber one is witnessing the extraordinary made to look ordinary. That a game may have no consequence outside itself—no effect on history, on one's own life, on anything really—does not make it trivial but only makes the enjoyment of it all the purer.

The notion that men watch sports to regain their adolescence pictures them sitting in the stands or at home watching a game and, within their psyches, muttering, "There, but for the lack of grace of God, go I." And it is true that a number of contemporary authors who are taken seriously have indeed written about sports with a strong overlay of yearning. In the men's softball games described in the fiction of Philip Roth, center field is a place akin to Arcady. Arcadian, too, is the outfield in Willie Morris's memoir of growing up in the South, *North Toward Home*. In the first half of *Rabbit Run* John Updike takes up the life of a man whose days are downhill all the way after hitting his peak as a high-school basketball star—and in the writing Updike himself evinces a nice soft touch of undisguised longing. In *A Fan's Notes*, a book combining yearning and self-disgust in roughly equal measure, Frederick Exley makes plain that he would much prefer to have been born into the skin of Frank Gifford rather than into his own.

But most men who are enraptured by sports do not think any such thing. I should like to have Kareem Abdul-Jabbar's sky hook, but not, especially for civilian life, the excessive height that is necessary to its execution. I should like to have Jimmy Connors's ground strokes, but no part of his mind. These are men born with certain gifts, gifts honed by practice and determination, that I, and millions along with me, enjoy seeing on display. But the reality principle is too deeply ingrained, at least in a man of my years, for me to even imagine exchanging places with them. One might as well imagine oneself in the winner's circle at Churchill Downs as the horse.

Fantasy is an element in sports when they are played in adolescence— an alley basket becomes the glass backboard at Madison Square Garden, a concrete park district tennis court with grass creeping out of the service line becomes center court at Wimbledon—but fantasy of this kind is hard to come by. Part of this has to do with age; but as large a part has to do with the age in which we live. Sport has always been a business but never more so than currently, and nothing lends itself less to fantasy than business. Reading the sports section has become rather like reading the business section—mergers, trades, salary negotiations, contract disputes, options, and strikes fill the columns. Along with the details of business, those of the psychological and social problems of athletes have come to the fore. The old *Sport* magazine concentrated on play on the field, with only an occasional digressive reference to personal life. ("Yogi likes plenty of pizza in the off-season and spends a lot of his time at his teammate Phil Rizzuto's bowling alley," is a rough facsimile of a sentence from its pages that I recall.) But the magazine in its current version, as well as the now more popular *Sports Illustrated*, expends much space on the private lives of athletes—their divorces, hang-ups, race relations, need for approval, concern for security, potted philosophies—with the result that the grand is made to seem small.

On the other side of the ledger, there is a view that finds a shimmering significance in everything having to do with sports. Literary men in general are notoriously to be distrusted on the subject. They dig around everywhere, and can be depended upon to find much treasure where none is buried. Norman Mailer. mining metaphysical ore in every jab of Muhammad Ali's, an existential nugget in each of his various and profuse utterances, is a particularly horrendous example. Even the sensible William Carlos Williams was not above this sort of temptation. In a poem entitled "At the Ball Game," we find the lines "It is the Inquisition, the/Revolution." Dr. Williams could not have been much fun at the ball park.

THE REAL THING

If enthusiasm for sports has little to do with providing an outlet for violent emotions, regaining adolescence, discovering metaphysical truths, the Inquisition or the Revolution, then what, I ask myself, am I doing past midnight, when I have to be up at 5:30 the next morning, watching on television what will turn out to be a seventeen-inning game between the New York Mets and the St. Louis Cardinals? The conversation coming out of my television set is of a very low grade, even for sports announcing. But even the dreary talk cannot put me off—the rehash of statistics, the advice to youngsters to keep their gloves low when in the field, the thin jokes. Neither the Mets nor the Cards figure to be contenders this year. The only possible effect that this game can have on my life is to make me dog-tired the next day. Yet I cannot pull myself away. I want to know how it is going to end. True, the score will be available in the morning paper. But that is not the same thing. What is going on here?

One thing that is going on is the practice of craft of a very high order, which is intrinsically interesting. But something as important is involved, something rarer in contemporary life, the spectacle of which gives enormous satisfaction. To define this satisfaction negatively, it is the absence of fraudulence and fakery. No small item, this, when one stops to think that in nearly every realm of contemporary life fraud and fakery have an established—some would say a preponderant—place. Advertising, politics, business, and journalism are only the most obvious examples. Fraud seems similarly pervasive in modern art: in painters whose reputations rest on press agentry; in writers who write one way and live quite another; in composers who are taken seriously but whose work cannot be seriously listened to. At a time when *image* is one of the most frequently used words in American speech and writing, one does not too often come upon the real thing.

Sport may be the toy department of life, but one of its abiding compensations is that, at least on the field, it is the real thing. Much has been done in recent years in the attempt to ruin sport—the ruthlessness of owners, the greed of players, the general exploitation of fans. But even all this cannot destroy it. On the court, down on the field, sport is fraud-free and fakeproof. With a full count, two men on, his team down by one run in the last of the eighth, a batter (as well as a pitcher) is beyond the aid of public relations. At match point at Forest Hills a player's press clippings are of no help. Last year's earnings will not sink a twelve-foot putt on the eighteenth at Augusta. Alan Page, galloping up along a quarterback's blind side, figures to be neglectful of that quarterback's image as a swinger. In all these situations, and hundreds of others, a man either comes through or he doesn't. He is alone out there, naked but for his ability, which counts for everything. Something there is that is elemental about this, and something greatly satisfying.

Another part of the satisfaction to be got from sports—from playing them, but also from watching them being played—derives from their special clarity. Sports offer clarity of a kind sufficient to engage the most serious minds. That the Cambridge mathematician G. H. Hardy closely followed cricket and avidly read cricket scores is not altogether surprising. Numbers in sports are ubiquitous. Scores, standings, averages, times, records—comfort is found in such numbers. ERA, RBI, FGP, pass completions, turnovers, category upon category of statistics are kept for nearly every aspect of athletic activity. (Why, I recently heard someone ask, are records not kept for catchers throwing out runners attempting to steal? Because, the answer is, often runners steal on pitchers, and so it would be unfair to charge these stolen bases against catchers.) As perhaps in no other sphere, numbers in sports tell one where things stand. No loopholes here, where figures, for once, do not lie. Nowhere else is such specificity of result available.

Clarity about character is also available in sports. "You Americans hold to the proposition that it is self-evident that all men are created equal," I not long ago heard an Englishman say, adding, "it had better be self-evident, for no other evidence for it exists." Sport coldly demonstrates physical inequalities—there are the larger, the faster, the stronger, the more graceful athletes—but it also throws up human types who have devised ways to redress these inequalities. One such type is the hustler. In every realm but that of sports the world *hustle* is pejorative, whereas in sports it is approbative. Two of the hustler breed, Pete Rose of the Cincinnati Reds and Jerry Sloan of the Chicago Bulls, are men who supplement reasonably high levels of ability with unreasonably high levels of courage and desire. Other athletes—Joe Morgan and Oscar Robertson come to mind—bring superior athletic intelligence to bear upon their play. And Bill Russell, late of the Boston Celtics, who if the truth be known was not an inherently superior athlete, blended hustle and intelligence with what abilities he did have and through force of character established supremacy.

Whence do hustle, intelligence, and character in sports derive, especially since they apparently do not necessarily carry over into life? Joe DiMaggio and Sugar Ray Robinson, two of the most instinctively intelligent and physically elegant athletes, brought little of either of these qualities over into their business or personal activities. Some athletes can do all but one important thing well: Wilt Chamberlain at the free-throw line, for those who recall his misery there, leaves a permanent picture of a mental block in action. Other athletes—Connie Hawkins, Ilie Nastase, Dick Allen—have all the physical gifts in superabundance, yet, because of some insufficiency of character, some searing flaw, never come near to fulfilling their promise. Coaches supply yet another gallery of human types, from the fanatical Vince Lombardi to the comical Casey Stengel to the measured and aptly named John Wooden. The cast of characters in sport, the variety of situations, the complexity of behavior it puts on display, the overall human exhibit it offers—together these supply an enjoyment akin to that once provided by reading interminably long but inexhaustibly rich nineteenth-century novels.

In a wider sense, sport is culture. For many American men it represents a common background, a shared interest. It has a binding power that transcends social class and education. Some years ago I found myself working in the South among men with whom I shared nothing in the way of region, religion, education, politics, or general views; we shared nothing, in fact, but sports, which was enough for us to get along and grow to become friends, in the process showing how superficial all the things that might have kept us apart in fact were. More recently, in Chicago, at a time when race relations were in a particularly jagged state, I recall emerging from an NBA game, in which the Chicago Bulls in overtime beat the Milwaukee Bucks, into a snowy night and an aura of common good feeling that, for a time, submerged the enmity between races; laughing, throwing snowballs, exuberant generally, the crowd leaving the Chicago Stadium that night was not divided by being black and white but unified by being Bull fans. Last year's Boston-Cincinnati World Series, one of the most gratifying in memory, coming hard upon a year of extreme political divisiveness, performed, however briefly, something of the same function. How much better it felt to agree about the mastery of Luis Tiant than to argue about the wretchedness of Richard Nixon.

In sports as in life, character does not much change. I have recently begun to play a game called racquet ball, and I find I would still rather look good than win, which is what I usually do: look good and lose. I beat the rum-dums but go down before quality players. I get compliments in defeat. Men who beat me admire the whip of my strokes, my wrist action, my anticipation, the power I get behind the ball. When this occurs I feel like a woman who is complimented for the shape of her bottom when it is her mind she craves admiration for, though of course she will take what praise she can get.

R. H. Tawney, the great historian of religion and capitalism, once remarked that the only progress he could note during the course of his lifetime was in the deportment of dogs. For myself, I would say that the chief progress in the course of my lifetime has been in the quality and variety of athletic gear. Racquets made of metal, aluminum, wood, and fiberglass, balls of different colors, sneakers of all materials and designs, posh warm-up suits, tube socks, sweatbands for the head and wrist in various colors and pipings; only the athletic supporter, the old jockstrap, remains unornamented, but perhaps even now Vera or Peter Max is at the drawing board. In any event, with all this elegant plumage available, it is a nice time to be playing ball again.

Sports can be impervious to age. My father-in-law, a man of style, seriousness, and great good humor who died a year ago in his late sixties, was born in South Bend, Indiana, and in his early manhood left the Catholic Church—two facts that conjoined to give him an intense interest in the fortunes of the teams from Notre Dame. He loved to see them lose. The torch has been passed on. I now love to see Notre Dame lose, and when it does I think of him and remember his smile.

When I was a boy I had a neighbor, a man who, after retirement, had a number of strokes. An old man and a young boy, we had in common a love of sports, which, when we met on the street, was our only topic of conversation. He once inspected a new glove of mine, and instructed me to rub it down with neat's-foot oil, place a ball firmly in the pocket, wrap string tightly around the glove, and leave it like that for the winter. I did, and it worked. After his last stroke but one, he seldom left his house. Afternoons he spent in a chair in his bedroom, a blanket over his lap, listening to Cub games over the radio. It was while listening to a ball game that he quietly died. I cannot imagine a better way.

A Critical Look at Sociology of Sport

MERRILL J. MELNICK

SPORT SOCIOLOGY AS A DISCIPLINE

The growth and development of American sociology of sport since 1965, when Kenyon and Loy first identified for the readers of the *Journal of Health, Physical Education and Recreation* the nature of the discipline, has been impressive. The past ten years have witnessed a virtual explosion in the publication of empirical investigations and some promising attempts at theory generation and model building. Important strides have been taken with respect to the description, explanation, and prediction of sport.

Changes in Sport Sociology

The establishment of a cumulative and systematic body of knowledge is well under way, and consequently it seems important, at this juncture in its history, for sociology of sport to do some stock-taking in order to see where it has been and where it is headed. This introspection is all the more important, given the ferment and change presently taking place in its parent discipline, sociology. Gary Marx (1972) has noted:

> A sociology at once more critical, and more concerned with studying immediate human problems, reaching a wide audience and granting legitimacy to a wider range of methods, has come to partly displace the concern with technique and broad theory which has characterized American sociology in recent decades [pp. 1–2].

Even the very role of the sociologist is undergoing redefinition. Gouldner (1971a) speaks of deepening ". . . the sociologist's awareness of who and what he is as a member of a specific society at a given time, and of how his social roles and his personal life affect his professional work [p. 57]." If, as Marx believes, traditional perspectives, methodologies, styles, assumptions, and masters in the social sciences and especially sociology, are being questioned, this would have important implications

SOURCE: Merrill J. Melnick, "A Critical Look at Sociology of Sport," *Quest*, XXIV (Summer 1975), 34–47.

for sociology of sport, since it has endeavored to mold itself in the image of sociology. It is for these reasons that sport sociologists Loy and Segrave (1974) are to be commended for raising some important questions about sociology of sport that must and should be answered. Their questions include:

1. What is (or should be) the primary focus of the sport sociologist?
2. What constitutes significant research problems within the context of the sociology of sport?

This paper attempts to answer these questions while posing others for the discipline's consideration. First, the dominant value orientation current within sociology of sport will be discussed. The sport sociologist as a person will then be discussed and some alternative work roles suggested. Lastly, the investigative paradigms most frequently used by sport sociologists will be looked at and an argument made for the development of new paradigms. Two such paradigms, "muckraking sociology of sport" and "humanist-existential sociology of sport," will then be defined.

Value-Free Sociology of Sport

That American sociology of sport must and should be "value-free" has been argued throughout the brief but exciting ten-year history of this academic discipline. Beginning with Kenyon and Loy's eloquent appeal for the study of physical activity as a sociological and social psychological phenomenon, the call has gone out that if sociology of sport is to gain acceptance within the academic community, its perspective or value-orientation must be a "value-free," "value-neutral," "non-normative," or "nonethical" one. To quote Kenyon and Loy (1965):

> Sport sociology, as we view it, is a value-free social science. It is not an effort to influence public opinion or behavior, nor is it an attempt to find support for the "social development" objective of physical education. . . . The sport sociologist is neither a spreader of gospel nor an evangelist for exercise. His function is not to shape attitudes and values but rather to describe and explain them [p. 25].

British sport sociologists Kane and Murray (1966) echoed similar sentiments when they wrote ". . . any serious sociological study should not concern itself with value judgments. 'Must' and 'ought' questions, cannot intrude on the presentation of material . . . [p. 112]." More recently, Loy (1972) observed:

> By nonethical is meant that sociologists as scientists are concerned with "what is" rather than "what ought to be." They are interested in social analysis, not social amelioration—in explanation not evaluation [p. 191].

Kenyon (1969) has argued that the sport sociologist ". . . who allows his personal values or social philosophy to influence his observation . . . or color his interpretations is simply engaging in bad science, by definition [p. 172]." Further Kenyon is fearful that the sport sociologist who is "value-committed" will confine his research to the study of current social problems and by so doing, forestall the development of the very knowledge upon which social action often depends. Finally, he points out that the sport sociologist who allows his research activities to be guided by a single philosophy ". . . could prevent the discovery of new and often more elegant explanatory systems [p. 172]."

None of these sport sociologists means to imply that the research process is totally devoid of value judgments. On the contrary, value judgments are implicit in the selection of research problems, research methodologies, and statistical procedures. Moreover, the very choice of the scientific method of inquiry over other methods of inquiry, such as phenomenological analysis, reflects a value bias. However, once these choices have been made, scientific objectivity, according to these sport sociologists, takes over and becomes of paramount concern if new and valid explanatory principles are to be discovered. The role that objectivity plays, according to the psychologist Clark (1967) is ". . . not in the refusal to make hypotheses, but in the rigorous assessment of the evidence accumulated for that hypothesis, so as to guard, as far as possible, against any distortion of these facts [p. 511]."

The fact that American sport sociologists regard themselves as value-free social scientists should not be surprising. Most western sociologists steadfastly maintain, with few exceptions, a similar stance. As Gouldner (1963) has noted:

> Today, all the powers of sociology, from Parsons to Lundberg, have entered into a tacit alliance to bind us to the dogma that "Thou shalt not commit a value judgment," especially as sociologists [p. 35].

According to Friedrichs (1970), ". . . Jeremy Bentham observed that the word 'ought' ought never to be used except in saying it ought never to be used . . . [p. 99]." The strict adherence to a value-free doctrine both in sociology and sociology of sport can be explained historically. The value-free conception of social science emerged during the period 1875–1900, when classical sociology was gaining acceptance in institutions of higher learning in Germany and France. The doctrine performed the important *latent* function of bringing peace within the German university by reducing intra-faculty competition for students. The possibility of a charismatic professor spouting provocative value judgments about man and society and thereby attracting a disproportionate number of students to his fold was eliminated. In addition, Weber for one ". . . feared that the expression of political value judgments in the University would provoke the state into censoring the University and would imperil its autonomy [Gouldner, 1963, p. 40]." It is apparent that, apart from any scientific consideration, the value-free doctrine served academic or professional sociology well by allowing it to maintain a low profile and gain a measure of autonomy. The well-publicized conflict between Mills and the academic sociology establishment in the 1940's and 1950's could be partially accounted for by his total disdain for value-free sociology. According to Bennett Berger (1963), Mills' "sin" consisted of being

... a political activist and a polemicist in a period when professional sociologists were more concerned with establishing their discipline as an objective science and institutionalizing it in the universities than they were with saying something important about the world and making what they said effective in the arenas of political combat [p. 3].

Thus, the value-free approach of sociology of sport can be understood by recognizing the fact that the discipline has and still is struggling to establish itself as an accredited member of the scientific fraternity. As Willhelm (1970) pointed out:

This inclination to reject social involvement by injecting the notion of value-free inquiry is ... typical of the scientific elite; it is characteristic for a social group that finally arrives, especially following what it considers to have been a hard-fought engagement to come onto the scene, to immediately sanctify its elevated status [p. 115].

There can be no argument with a value-free approach to sociology of sport, as posited by Loy, Kenyon, and others, when it refers to the norms of scientific objectivity. Scott (1972), a frequent critic of the sports establishment and "physical educators-sport sociologists," has never condemned the scentific method of inquiry in his writings. According to Scott, "... the nature of sports in American society can best be examined and elucidated by a scientific approach. However... it should be understood that science is our means, not our end [p. xvii]." What concerns Scott—and this author—most is our need to distinguish between the indispensable canons of scientific inquiry and *moral indifference*. It is when the value-free ideology, motivated principally by a concern for professional respectability, becomes a cloak for moral indifference or is used to rationalize scientific nonaccountability, that sport sociologists must stand up and take notice of their discipline's future. Gouldner (1963) has argued that where "value-free" means moral indifference, it becomes useful to those who want to neglect their public responsibilities and escape from the world. He characterizes these sociologists as ". . . living huddled behind self-barricaded intellectual ghettos [p. 43]." No one is suggesting that sport sociologists have or are planning to construct such "barricades"; however, we must guard against this happening, lest the value-free perspective make sterile our moral sensibilities and discourage us from engaging in constructive criticism. The label "social scientist" or "sport sociologist" certainly does not require us to surrender our critical impulses.

Finally, it has been suggested by a growing number of sociologists that those who hold to a value-free approach may be engaging in an exercise of self-delusion. Gouldner (1971a) has written:

> When they confine work to the demanding, misleading and unfulfillable paradigm of a value-free, high-science model, sociologists are wasting, indeed sacrificing, a part of themselves ... the notion of contaminated research presupposes the existence of uncontaminated research, and this is pure folly. All research is contaminated, for all research entails relationships that may influence both sociologist and subject [p. 96].

THE SPORT SOCIOLOGIST

There is the tacit suggestion with the value-free approach that the social scientist should set aside his personal feelings, affective states, and sentiments when engaged in scientific work. This schizoid-like characterization of the scientist was suggested by Bierstedt (1953) when he wrote:

> Science and citizenship are two different things. While a given individual may play two different roles, that of scientist and that of citizen, it is of vital importance that he not try to play them both at once. . . . To adopt another course is to prostitute the prestige of science and of a scientific reputation [p. 6].

The Sport Sociologist as a Person

I would like to suggest that what Bierstedt is calling for and what the value-free approach seems to demand is well-nigh impossible to achieve. The nonfeeling, robot-like social scientist suggested by this approach is an artificial stereotype at best. The sport sociologist is, first and foremost, a person; he has feelings, ethical and cultural preferences, some stereotypical beliefs, and probably a prejudice or two. As Willhelm (1970) pointed out:

> We must realize, however, that explicit declarations concerning a value-free activity do not in fact make activities value-free. . . . In short, it is not at all

possible for the socialized person . . . to escape values; it is only a matter of holding to one set of values rather than another [p. 119].

It would be well for the sport sociologist to study *himself* in addition to the social systems that strike his fancy. As Gouldner (1971b) has observed, the work of the sociologist is influenced at every turn by his "domain assumptions," such as "dispositions to believe that men are rational or irrational; that society is precarious or fundamentally stable; that social problems will correct themselves without planned intervention; that human behavior is unpredictable . . . [p. 31]." According to Gouldner, these domain assumptions are derived from more general "background assumptions" which he defines as ". . . affectively-laden cognitive tools that are developed early in the course of our socialization into a particular culture and are built deeply into our character structure [p. 32]." In short, background and domain assumptions are related in a significant way to the work of the sociologist and provide him with his conception of the "real" social world.

Especially interesting is Gouldner's (1971b) observation that domain assumptions are even built into scientific methodology itself. For example, he suggests that ". . . the conventional methodologies of social research often premise and foster a deep-going authoritarianism, a readiness to lie to and manipulate people: they betray a bureaucratic numbness [p. 50]." Gouldner has summarized his argument in the following way:

> When viewed from one standpoint, "methodology" seems a purely technical concern devoid of ideology; presumably it deals only with methods of extracting reliable information from the world, collecting data, constructing questionnaires, sampling, and analyzing returns. Yet it is always a good deal more than that, for it is commonly infused with ideologically resonant assumptions about what the social world is, who the sociologist is, and what the nature of the relation between them is [pp. 50–51].

Some sociologists make a specious argument when they declare that ". . . *they* [other people] are bound by society; *I* am free of it [Gouldner, 1971b, p. 54]." Strictly speaking, it is doubtful whether any social scientist can be "value-free." We are all creatures molded by social structure and culture and respond accordingly, even when engaged in the scientific enterprise. As Gouldner (1963) pointed out:

> . . . there is and can be no value-free sociology. The only choice is between an expression of one's values, as open and honest as it can be . . . and a vain ritual of moral neutrality which . . . leaves it at the mercy of irrationality [p. 51].

While there are obvious dangers in being "value-bound," it is better, according to Gouldner (1971a) to ". . . accept the dangers of a value commitment, because the risk of ending in distortion is better than beginning there, and a dogmatic and arid value-free sociology cannot be other than a myth [p. 91]."

The Sport Sociologist as Sport Critic

Friedrichs (1970), author of *A Sociology of Sociology*, described the traditional role of the sociologist when he wrote, "His is *not* the reformer's role but rather a dedication to the chaste pursuit of what *is* [p. 78]." He further stated that the task of students entering sociology during the 1950's and 1960's ". . . was to discover empirical uniformities that can be used to predict and control other empirical phenomena [p. 81]." Taking this cue, sport sociologists have gone about their work careful ". . . not to shape attitudes and values but rather to describe and explain them [Kenyon & Loy, 1965, p. 25]." Social amelioration and social evaluation are not the concern of today's sport sociologist. The acquisition and establishment of a cumulative body of knowledge *is*. While little fault can be found with the sport sociologist who chooses to follow this particular professional role, the question remains as to whether or not this is the *only* role for the sport sociologist to play. I think not. The sport sociologist as sport critic is a new professional role that has been left largely unexplored. Such a role would be consistent with traditional scholarship and ". . . the legacy of the intellectual, namely, the right to be critical of tradition [Gouldner, 1963, p. 45]." Mills (1967) offered an important observation about the role of the intellectual in society when he wrote:

> The independent artist and intellectual are among the few remaining personalities equipped to resist and to fight the stereotyping and consequent death of genuinely lively things. Fresh perception now involves the capacity continually to unmask and to smash the stereotypes of vision and intellect with which modern communications swamp us [p. 299].

He was especially critical of social scientists who ". . . censor themselves either by carefully selecting safe problems in the name of pure science, or by selling such prestige as their scholarship may have for ends other than their own [p. 302]." The net result is the acceptance of the status quo or a fantasy look into the future.

The fact that an increasing number of sociologists are calling for a review of the traditional role of the sociologist has extremely important implications for the sport sociologist. As Gouldner (1963) sees it, we are witnessing today a clash ". . . between the older heritage of the critical intellectual and the modern claims of the value-free professional [p. 45]." On the methodological front, the fact that more and more sociologists are showing a preference for ". . . the offbeat to the familiar, the vivid ethnographic detail to the dull taxonomy, the sensuously expressive to dry analysis, and naturalistic observation to formal questionnaires . . . [Gouldner, 1963, p. 47]," also has important implications for research methodology in sociology of sport. Marx (1972) raises a fundamental question when he asks:

> Should sociology be a disinterested calling pursued for purely intellectual and esthetic reasons, or should it be committed to, and involved in, solving current problems [p. 4]?

While the question implies that a choice must be made between two distinctly different approaches, probably no choice need be made. There is certainly enough room within sociology of sport to accommodate both. The point is that there *are* choices for the sport sociologist and the "intellectual and esthetic" approach that seeks out "knowledge for knowledge's sake" or the discovery of "elegant explanatory systems" is only one approach to the study of sport. The sport sociologist who chooses instead to seek out gaps between values and actual practices, who questions established orthodoxies and through his social criticism, hopes to initiate social change, would add a new and exciting dimension to the discipline.

THE DOMINANT PARADIGM IN SOCIOLOGY OF SPORT

According to Loy and Kenyon (1969):

> . . . the social significance of sport might be profitably analyzed in terms of its contribution to the functional problems of society, especially to the problem of pattern maintenance and tension management [p. 86].

More recently, Loy and Segrave (1974) reiterated the same point of view when they advised that "the best of all possible methodological worlds is of course, to utilize a complete social system model of data collection and analysis [p. 291]." Generally speaking, the investigative paradigm which has served sociology of sport most often has been one which has focused on ". . . how well sport serves the existing social system when confronted with its 'functional problems' of adaptation, attaining collective goals . . .

assuring continuity of beliefs and orientations, training, integrating, and coordinating [Hoch, 1972, p. 15]." This paradigm, developed in the United States by Talcott Parsons and Robert Merton among others, assumes an equilibrating social order and the "social system" as its basic conception of society. The task of the sport sociologist, given this paradigm, becomes one of describing, explaining, and predicting the ways in which sport contributes to society. Lee (1973) refers to it as the "managerial-bureaucratic" or "functional-systemic" paradigm in his discussion of the different ideologies present within contemporary American sociology. He describes the paradigm in the following way:

> This systemic structure, with congeries of subsystems nested within it, is usually subjected to what is called functional analysis, a concern with how the system's parts satisfy the system's and its members' needs and maintain an adequate degree of integration and balance. This usually implies the indispensability of certain functions in the maintenance of the system as an ongoing enterprise. . . . If "the system" is to persist, these needs "must" be satisfied [p. 124].

While the application of this paradigm to the study of sport groups and the interrelationships among sport, culture, and society has contributed in some important ways to the body of knowledge of sociology of sport, it remains nevertheless an ideology vulnerable to the weaknesses inherent in all paradigms. Hoch (1972) has criticized the "functional-systemic" paradigm and its followers because

> In their characteristic eagerness to manage the tensions of this society, our academic sociologists . . . completely lose sight of what kind of society this is: Does a small power elite dominate? Are the masses of poor and black people oppressed? Do the existing patterns of this society *deserve* to be managed and maintained]p. 15]?

Questions such as these raise serious doubts as to the utility of this paradigm and, at the least, encourage the sport sociologist to seek out alternatives. For the sociologist concerned with the dignity and possible autonomy of "mass man," a paradigm which places primary emphasis (Lee, 1973) on ". . . how he can be managed, led to preconceived goals, and with how the bureaucratized 'system' can be maintained and flourish [pp. 125–126]" would seem to fall short of the mark. Given this perspective of man and society, it is understandable why its adherents contend so strongly that they must be "value-free" in their scientific work. To do otherwise would reveal the paradigm's glaring insensitivity to the plight of "mass man."

Functional-Systemic Sociology of Sport as "Normal Science"

Another way of looking at "functional-systemic sociology of sport" is to see it for what it is, namely, a paradigm, or theoretical achievement that, as Kuhn (1970) stated:

> . . . was sufficiently unprecedented to attract an enduring group of adherents away from competing modes of theoretical activity. Simultaneously, it was sufficiently open-ended to leave all sorts of problems for the redefined group of practitioners to resolve [p. 10].

According to Kuhn, whenever a scientific or theoretical achievement shares these two essential characteristics, we have a paradigm, ". . . a term that relates closely to 'normal science' [p. 10]." We have a normal science wherever researchers share a similar paradigm and are ". . . committed to the same rules and standards for scientific practice. That commitment and the apparent consensus it produces are prerequisites for normal science, i.e., for the genesis and continuation of a particular research tradition [Kuhn, 1970, p. 11]."

While sociology of sport's adoption of the functional-systemic paradigm and the esoteric research it engenders can be rightfully construed as a sign of the discipline's maturity, it remains, nevertheless, a paradigm incapable of explaining all the facts with which it is confronted. It is understandable, however, why sociology of sport selected this paradigm over others, such as a conflict paradigm. Besides having descriptive value, its Parsonian character is in keeping with the theoretical proclivities of professional sociology, thus ensuring for itself a hospitable reception within the sociological community. The danger of this or any other paradigm occurs when the sport sociologist takes it for granted and feels that ". . . he need no longer, in his major works, attempt to build his field anew . . . [Kuhn, 1970, p. 19]." It is this type of laxity that sport sociologists can ill afford. Such "mopping-up" operations (Kuhn, 1970) as ". . . extending the knowledge of those facts that the paradigm displays as particularly revealing . . . increasing the extent of the match between those facts and the paradigm's predictions, and . . . further articulation of the paradigm itself [p. 24]" can seriously retard the growth and development of the discipline if pursued to the exclusion of all else. Sociology of sport is too young a discipline to become strapped to one particular theoretical orientation; a "normalized" sociology of sport would not seem in the best interests of the discipline at this point in its history. As a final thought, Kuhn's discussion of "normal science as puzzle solving" is particularly relevant to sociology of sport. The fascination of the "normal" research problem for the social scientist lies in his achieving the expected in an unexpected way. The solution, Kuhn says, of ". . . all sorts of complex instrumental, conceptual, and mathematical puzzles [p. 36]" becomes the scientist's major interest. If this be true, then it would seem imperative for sociology of sport not to engage exclusively in the exercise of puzzle-solving (Kuhn, 1970) lest it blind itself to looking at ". . . those socially important problems that are not reducible to the puzzle form, because they cannot be stated in terms of the conceptual and instrumental tools the paradigm supplies [p. 37]."

NEW PARADIGMS FOR SOCIOLOGY OF SPORT

Brown and Gilmartin (1969), after reviewing a total of 402 articles and papers that appeared in the *American Sociological Review* and the *American Journal of Sociology* during the periods 1940–41 and 1965–66, concluded that ". . . rarely encountered in our sample were intensive investigations of specific concrete social situations [pp. 289–290]." They further noted that the ". . . construction and testing of predictive hypotheses concerning the interrelations of abstract variables [p. 290]" has become the dominant sociological orientation among researchers. And finally, the authors cautioned, "If sociology is the scientific study of human social behavior, then behavior other than verbal statements of opinions and feelings warrants intensive investigation [p. 290]." Similar charges can be made with some justification against sport-related sociological research. It too is characterized by a lack of "concreteness," a concern for the abstract over the practical, and a preference for the recording of verbal statements rather than the observation of social behavior. As Loy and Segrave (1974) recently noted in an excellent review of research methodology in sociology of sport:

Nevertheless, our survey of research subsumed under the rubric of sport sociology indicates that there is a notable lack of "strictly" sociological investigations into the nature of sport [p. 290].

Given the somewhat mythical notion of a "value-free" sociology of sport, the inherent biases of the functional-systemic paradigm, the constraints imposed by a "normalized" discipline, and the research returns yielded so far, it would behoove sport sociologists to seriously consider the initiation and development of alternative value orientations and investigative paradigms. Loy and Segrave (1974) have identified three such alternatives for sport sociology. First, they see a *sociology through sport*, in which the basic emphasis is placed on testing general sociological propositions and developing sociological models and theories. Second, they identify an *action-oriented sport sociology*, devoted to the solving of practical problems and achieving a more humanistic understanding of sport. And third, they envision a *sociology of sport*, ". . . emphasizing the generation and verification of substantive theories about the significant social phenomenon of sport [p. 292]." It is in this spirit of identifying "alternatives" for the sport sociologist that the following suggestions are made.

Muckraking or "Dirty" Sociology of Sport

For those sport sociologists who believe that critical research is a necessary prerequisite for social change, muckraking or "dirty" sociology of sport may be an alternative worth considering. According to Marx (1972), muckraking sociology is a particular style of social science research which ". . . documents conditions that clash with basic values, fixes responsibility for them and is capable of generating moral outrage [p. 2]." The sport sociologist who engages in muckraking research would be primarily interested in searching out and publicly exposing misconduct on the part of prominent individuals as well as discovering scandal and incriminating evidence. For example, social issues such as drug usage in sports, illegal recruiting in intercollegiate athletics, the bureaucratic power of the National Collegiate Athletic Association, racial discrimination in professional baseball, sexism in American sports, and the effects of adult-sponsored athletic programs on pre-adolescent value systems, would be of particular interest to the muckraking sport sociologist. For obvious reasons, such a perspective would neither be especially popular among establishment-oriented sport sociologists nor among college and university officials who have traditionally encouraged, either explicitly or implicitly, a conservative "don't rock the boat" attitude from their faculties. It remains to be seen whether muckraking sport sociology with its ". . . expose, sacred cow-smashing, anti-establishment, counter-intuitive, even subversive quality . . . [Marx, 1972, p. 3]" could be practiced in an institutional setting. It would be extremely unfortunate if it could not be, because there would seem to be great value in a perspective which points out discrepancies between the abstract values of the sports establishment, such as character building, and its actual practices. By discovering and raising various social issues as a result of its probing and critical analysis of the sport institution, the sport sociologist would be performing an important educative role for the public at large.

A distinction should here be made between muckraking sociology of sport and the suggestion by Loy and Segrave (1974) of action-oriented sport sociology, mentioned earlier. For the muckraking sport sociologist, the "problems" of racism, sexism, militarism, and elitism in American sport would not be viewed as "disorders" or evidence of the breakdown of the sport institution, but rather as ". . . the products of *organized* efforts—the reality of deliberate intent . . . outgrowths of an ongoing value system which emphasizes the merits of economic gain at the expense of human dignity [Willhelm, 1970, p. 120]."

From a methodological point of view, Marx (1972) has written:

To be credible, muckraking research must respect the traditional canons of science and be judged by them, although it may not be inspired by the esthetic contemplation of ideas for their own sake or the desire to advance an abstract body of knowledge [p. 7].

One could envision the muckraking sport sociologist making much greater use of such research methodologies as participant observation, ethnography, case study, role and institutional analysis.

Muckraking sociology of sport would be no less an ideology than functional-systemic sociology of sport and would carry with it its own set of biases and domain assumptions about man and society. According to Marx, the potential pitfalls of "committed" research include:

1. The conflict in the researcher between maintaining scientific objectivity in the face of his own strong value positions.
2. The inability of descriptive documentation to add measurably to a cumulative body of knowledge.
3. The failure to *solve* social problems, thereby making muckraking research little more than shocking exposé.

In any case, for the sport sociologist who believes that expediency and social change take priority over the building of a theoretically based social science, muckraking sociology may be the answer. If, as Marx (1972) believes, the immediate value of critical research lies in its contribution ". . . to greater public awareness and more sophisticated and humane theories about social issues [p. 29]," then the sport sociologist who ventures forth into the world of "dirty" sport may have a profound effect on the future course of sport in American society.

Humanist-Existential Sociology of Sport

Closely related to muckraking sociology of sport is the humanist-existential paradigm, one of the newest and most roughly defined paradigms presently vying for consideration within academic sociology. Consequently, its biases, domain assumptions, and research methodologies, as they relate specificially to the study of sport, are still to be defined. For the present, only a brief discussion of the flavor and spirit of this unique and promising paradigm will be attempted. Lee (1973) suggests that the humanist-existential paradigm ". . . calls for a man-centered sociology in the service of human needs and goals as they are popularly defined [p. 128]." He defines an "existential humanist" as someone who deals with sociology and social science only insofar as they shed light on ". . . the current problems that impinge upon people's lives [p. xi]." Lee's ". . . intellectual focus is upon what exists and upon what is most relevant to man [p. xii]." Sociologists who assume this intellectual orientation believe (Lee, 1973) that

... first causes (or origins) and ultimate consequences, as well as absolutes and infinites, are irrelevant except as human artifacts to be considered as such. Methods and tenets useful in other sciences are to be treated as possible helpful suggestions. Techniques of research and theories must serve human understanding of man's lot [p. xii].

Sport sociologists should be wary of paradigms bearing this label, for, as Lee points out:

Just calling some methodological mumbo jumbo *humanist* does not make it relevant to human concerns. Just labeling some philosophical gamesmanship *existential* does not make it an acceptable interpretation of events [p. 129].

Whereas muckraking sociology of sport is primarily interested in searching out sport-related social issues and exposing them to an analytical process (Marx, 1972) which moves ". . . from documentation, to causal analysis, to policy suggestions, to actual policy implementation of a given piece of research [p. 23]," a humanist-existential sociology of sport would deal in a more philosophical way (Lee, 1973) with the relevant implications of ". . . social control, conflict, and exploitation, of degradation, degeneracy, creativity, and nobility and of individual, group and societal multivalence [p. 129]" as they relate to individuals involved in sport.

Besides expressing concern about those institutional problems which impinge on the athlete's life, such as loss of freedom, the sport sociologist with a humanist-existential orientation would also be interested in discovering the self-actualizing potential of the sport experience. In order to do so, he might find useful the methods of logical and phenomenological description which some sport philosophers have used (Kleinman, 1968, 1972) in order to reveal the essence of the sport experience.

Peter Berger (1963), a sociologist whose work has been instrumental in the development of a humanistically based paradigm, explains his perspective in the following way:

> . . . if there is something like a sociological anthropology, there may also be something like a sociological humanism . . . sociological understanding can be an important part of a certain sense of life that is peculiarly modern, that has its own genius of compassion and that can be the foundation of a genuine humanism [pp. 161-162].

Berger hints that he may also be a muckraker at heart when he observes:

> Before the tribunals that condemn some men to indignity because of their race or sexuality, or that condemn any man to death, this humanism becomes protest, resistance and rebellion . . . compassion can become the starting point of revolution against systems of inhumanity sustained by myth [p. 162].

To summarize, while the specific details of the humanist-existential paradigm are still to be determined, the sport sociologist whose consuming interest is in the world of men, and specifically in the social and emotional well-being of individuals involved in sport situations, should find this perspective an especially rewarding one.

THE FUTURE OF SPORT SOCIOLOGY

American sociology of sport has traveled a somewhat uneven but nevertheless exciting path over the past decade. This fledgling discipline has made rapid strides in developing a theoretical and scholarly cumulative body of knowledge. Research methodologies appropriate to the study of sport have been developed and sophisticated statistical techniques devised for data analysis. Propositions, models, and theories, some borrowed from sociology, others developed specifically for sport, are appearing with increasing frequency. As a result, certain trends have emerged which, when taken together, give sociology of sports a distinctive character at this juncture in its history. An attempt has been made to set forth some of these characteristics and to identify what might be called a "modal sport sociologist." We find that he is someone who subscribes most passionately to a "value-free" orientation; he draws a distinction between himself as a working social scientist and as a private citizen; his bias leans toward functional-systemic investigative paradigm; he views his professional task as helping to build a cumulative body of knowledge; and lastly, he is someone who is very much concerned with gaining professional respectability within the academic community.

While there can be no quarrel with the discipline's progress to date, there is an uneasy feeling which suggests that sociology of sport has become "locked into" a single paradigm that may eventually inhibit its future growth and development, its general acceptance by the public, and ultimately its value to man and society. Gouldner (1963) has observed:

> Social science can never be fully accepted in a society, or by a part of it, without paying its way; this means it must manifest both its relevance and concern for the contemporary human predicament. Unless the value relevances of sociological inquiry are made plainly evident . . . it must inevitably be scorned by laymen as pretentious word-mongering [p. 43].

In order to guard against sociology of sport becoming "pretentious word-mongering," alternative value orientations have been discussed and new investigative paradigms presented. It is hoped that these ideas will prove stimulating and provide sociology of sport with the challenge it needs if it is to mature as a discipline and realize its fullest potential for mankind.

REFERENCES

Berger, B. M. Review of *Power, politics and people: The collected essays of C. Wright Mills*, edited by I. L. Horowitz. *New York Times Book Review*, April 28, 1963, pp. 3, 50.

Berger, P. L. *Invitation to sociology: A humanistic perspective.* New York: Anchor, 1963.

Bierstedt, R. Social science and social values. In S. Koenig, R. D. Hopper, and F. Gross (Eds.), *Sociology—A book of readings.* Englewood Cliffs, N.J.: Prentice-Hall, 1953.

Brown, J. S., & Gilmartin, B. G. Sociology today: Lacunae, emphases, and surfeits. *American Sociologist*, 1969, 4, 283-291.

Clark, K. B. The psychology of the ghetto. In P. I. Rose (Ed.), *The study of society.* New York: Random House, 1967.

Friedrichs, R. W. *A sociology of sociology.* New York: Free Press, 1970.

Gouldner, A. W. Anti-minotaur: The myth of a value-free sociology. In M. Stein and A. Vidich (Eds.), *Sociology on trial.* Englewood Cliffs, N.J.: Prentice-Hall, 1963.

Gouldner, A. W. Sociology today does not need a Karl Marx or an Isaac Newton: It needs a V. I. Lenin. *Psychology Today*, 1971, 5, 53-57 and 96-97. (a)

Gouldner, A. W. *The coming crisis of western sociology.* New York: Equinox, 1971. (b)

Hoch, P. *Rip off the big game.* New York: Anchor, 1972.

Kane, J. E., & Murray, C. Suggestions for the sociological study of sport. In J. E. Kane (Ed.), *Readings in physical education.* London: Physical Education Association, 1966.

Kenyon, G. S. A. sociology of sport: On becoming a sub-discipline. In R. C.

Brown, Jr., and B. J. Cratty (Eds.), *New perspectives of man in action.* Englewood Cliffs, N.J.: Prentice-Hall, 1969.

Kenyon, G. S., & Loy, J. W. Toward a sociology of sport—A plea for the study of physical activity as a sociological and social psychological phenomenon. *Journal of Health, Physical Education and Recreation,* 1965, 36, 24-25 and 68-69.

Kleinman, S. Toward a non-theory of sport. *Quest,* 1968, 10, 29-34.

Kleinman, S. The significance of human movement: A phenomenological approach. In E. W. Gerber (Ed.), *Sport and the body: A philosophical symposium.* Philadelphia: Lea and Febiger, 1972.

Kuhn, T. S. *The structure of scientific revolutions.* Chicago: University of Chicago Press, 1970.

Lee, A. M. *Toward humanist sociology.* Englewood Cliffs, N.J.: Prentice-Hall, 1973.

Loy, J. W. Sociology and physical education. In R. N. Singer et al. (Eds.), *Physical education: An interdisciplinary approach.* New York: Macmillan, 1972.

Loy, J. W., & Kenyon, G. S. (Eds.), *Sport, culture, and society: A reader on the sociology of sport.* New York: Macmillan, 1969.

Loy, J. W., & Segrave, J. O. Research methodology in the sociology of sport. In J. H. Wilmore (Ed.), *Exercise and sport sciences reviews.* Vol. 2. New York: Academic Press, 1974.

Marx, G. T. (Ed.), *Muckraking sociology: Research as social criticism.* New Brunswick, N.J.: Transaction Books, 1972.

Mills, C. W. The social role of the intellectual. In I. L. Horowitz (Ed.), *Power politics and people: The collected essays of C. Wright Mills.* London: Oxford University Press, 1967.

Scott, J. Introduction. In P. Hoch, *Rip off the big game.* New York: Anchor, 1972.

Willhelm, S. M. Elites, scholars, and sociologists. In L. T. Reynolds and J. M. Reynolds (Eds.), *The sociology of sociology.* New York: David McKay, 1970.

■ FOR FURTHER STUDY

Avedon, Elliot M., and Brian Sutton-Smith. *The Study of Games.* New York: Wiley, 1971.

Caillois, Roger. "The Structure and Classification of Games," *Diogenes* (Winter 1965), pp. 62-75.

Coakley, Jay J. *Sport in Society: Issues and Controversies.* St. Louis: C. V. Mosby, 1978, pp. 1-14.

Edwards, Harry, *Sociology of Sport.* Homewood, Illinois: Dorsey, 1973, pp. 3-61.

Eitzen, D. Stanley, and George H. Sage. *Sociology of American Sport.* Dubuque, Iowa: Wm. C. Brown, 1978, pp. 1-57.

Fisher, A. Craig. *Psychology of Sport.* Palo Alto, Calif.: Mayfield, 1976.

Gilbert, Bil. "Gleanings from a Troubled Time." *Sports Illustrated* (December 25, 1972), pp. 34-46.

Guttman, Allen. *From Record to Ritual: The Nature of Modern Sports.* New York: Columbia University Press, 1978.

Huizinga, Johan. *Homo Ludens: A Study of the Play Element in Culture.* Boston: Beacon Press, 1950.

Lowe, Benjamin. "The Sociology of Sports—A Basic Outline." *The Physical Educator*, 28 (May, 1971), 79.

Loy, John W. "The Nature of Sport: A Definitional Effort." *Quest*, 10 (May 1968), 1–15.

Loy, John W. "A Case for the Sociology of Sport." *Journal of Health, Physical Education and Recreation*, 43 (June, 1972), 50.

Loy, John W., Barry D. McPherson, and Gerald Kenyon. *Sport and Social Systems: A Guide to the Analysis, Problems, and Literature.* Reading, Mass.: Addison-Wesley, 1978, pp. 1–64.

Luschen, Gunther. "The Sociology of Sport: A Trend Report and Bibliography." *Current Sociology*, 15 (1967), 5–140.

Luschen, Gunther. "The Development and Scope of a Sociology of Sport." *American Corrective Therapy Journal*, 29 (March/April 1975), 39–43.

Michener, James. *Sports in America.* New York: Random House, 1976.

Morford, R. "Is Sport the Struggle or the Triumph?" *Quest*, 19 (January 1973), 83–87.

Nixon, Howard L. *Sport and Social Organization.* Indianapolis: Bobbs-Merrill, 1976, pp. 5–8.

Novak, Michael. *The Joy of Sports.* New York: Basic Books, 1976.

Page, Charles H. "The Mounting Interest in Sport." *Sport and Society.* Edited by Charles H. Page and J. T. Talamini. Boston: Little, Brown, 1973, pp. 3–39.

Reid, Alastair. "The Sporting Scene: Heavy Going." *The New Yorker* (February 21, 1977), pp. 80–93.

Roberts, Michael. *Fans! How We Go Crazy Over Sports.* Washington, D.C.: The New Republic Book Company, 1976.

Saunders, E. D. "Sociology, Sport and Physical Education." Review of Sport & Leisure, 1 (Fall 1976), 122–138.

Schwartz, J. Michael. "Causes and Effects of Spectator Sports." *International Review of Sport Sociology*, 8 (1973), 25–43.

Scott, Jack. *Athletics for Athletes.* Berkeley, Calif.: Otherways, 1969.

Shaw, David. "The Roots of Rooting." *Psychology Today*, 11 (February 1978), 48–51.

Shecter, Leonard. *The Jocks.* Indianapolis: Bobbs-Merrill, 1969.

Slusher, Howard. *Man, Sport and Existence: A Critical Analysis.* Philadelphia: Lea and Febiger, 1967.

Smith, Red, Norman Podhoretz, and Thomas G. Bergin. "An Appetite for Sport." *Intellectual Digest*, 3 (June 1973), 62–63.

Snyder, Eldon E., and Elmer Spreitzer. "Sociology of Sport: An Overview." *The Sociological Quarterly*, 15 (Fall 1974), 467–487.

Snyder, Eldon E., and Elmer Spreitzer. *Social Aspects of Sport.* Englewood Cliffs, N.J., 1978, pp. 1–22.

Tarkenton, Fran. "What the Fan Wants and What He Gets." *New York Times* (January 9, 1977), p. 2S.

"How Americans Pursue Happiness." *U.S. News & World Report* (May 23, 1977), pp. 60–76.

Vander Zwaag, Harold. *Toward a Philosophy of Sport.* Reading, Mass.: Addison-Wesley, 1972.

Vander Zwaag, Harold, and Thomas J. Shechan. *Introduction to Sport Studies: From the Classroom to the Ball Park.* Dubuque, Iowa: Wm. C. Brown, 1978.

Weiss, Paul. *Sport: A Philosophic Inquiry.* Carbondale, Illinois: Southern Illinois Press, 1969.

Two

Sport as a Microcosm of Society

In the following quote, Howard Cosell argues that sport is a reflection of society:

> Once upon a time, the legend had it, there was a world that remained separate and apart from all others, a privileged sanctuary from real life. It was the wonderful world of sport, where every competition was endowed with an inherent purity, every athlete a shining example of noble young manhood, and every owner was motivated by his love of the game and his concern for the public interest. . . . The sports establishment—the commissioners, the owners, the leagues, the National Collegiate Athletic Association—would have us believe the legend. Their unceasing chant is that sport is escapism, pure and simple; that people have enough daily problems to cope with in a complex, divided, and even tormented society; and that the relief provided by sports is essential to the maintenance of an individual mental and emotional equilibrium. There is something to be said for this argument, but this hardly means that the sports establishment should be left untrammeled and that individual injustices should not be exposed. The plain truth is that sport is a reflection of the society, that it is human life in microcosm, that it has within it the maladies of the society, that some athletes drink, that some athletes do take drugs, that there is racism in sport, that the sports establishment is quite capable of defying the public interest, and that in this contemporary civilization sport does invade sociology, economics, law, and politics.[1]

Cosell's argument is also mine—sport *is* a microcosm of society. If we know how sport is organized, the type of games played, the way winners and losers are treated, the type and amount of compensation given the participants, and the way rules are enforced, then we surely also know a great deal about the larger society in which it exists. Conversely, if we know the values of a society, the type of economy, the way minority groups are treated, and the political structure, then we would also have important clues about how sport in that society would likely be organized.

The United States, for example, is a capitalistic society. It is not surprising, then, that in the corporate sport that dominates, American athletes are treated as property. In the professional ranks they are bought and sold. At the college level players once enrolled are unable to switch teams without waiting for a year. Even in youth sports, players are drafted and become the "property" of a given team.

Capitalism is also evident as team owners "carpetbag," i.e., move teams to more lucrative markets. At the same time these owners insist that the cities subsidize the construction of new stadiums, thereby making their franchises more profitable. The players, too, appear to have more loyalty to money than to their teams or fans.

Americans are highly competitive. This is easily seen at work, at school, in dating, and in sport. Persons are evaluated not on their intrinsic worth but on the criterion of achievement. As Sage has written: "Sports have consented to measure the results of sports efforts in terms of performance and product—the terms which prevail in the factory and department store."[2]

Athletes are expected to deny self and sacrifice for the needs of the sponsoring organization. This requires, foremost, an acquiescence to authority. The coach is the ultimate authority, and the players must obey. This is the way bureaucracies operate, and American society is highly bureaucratic whether it be in government, school, church, or business. As Paul Hoch has stated:

> In football, like business ... every pattern of movement on the field is increasingly being brought under the control of a group of non-playing managerial technocrats who sit up in the stands ... with their headphones and dictate offenses, defenses, special plays, substitutions, and so forth to the players below.[3]

Thus, American sport, like American society, is authoritarian, bureaucratic, and product-oriented. Winning is everything. Athletes use drugs to enhance their performances artificially in order to succeed. Coaches teach their athletes to bend the rules (to feign a foul, to hold without getting caught) in order to win. Even at America's most prestigious universities, coaches offer illegal inducements to athletes to attend their school. And, as long as they win, the administrators at these offending schools usually look the other way. After all, the object is to win, and this "Watergate mentality" permeates sports as it does politics and the business world.

These are but some of the ways that sport mirrors society. In this unit we shall examine three illustrations of how sport is a microcosm of society. The first selection, by Eitzen, shows what the structure of two major team sports—football and baseball—tells us about Americans and American society.

The second article, by anthropologist Richard Sipes, investigates the relationship between violence-prone societies and violent sports. This is a significant question. If the data show a strong positive correlation between the existence of combative sports and the incidence of war, then we have vivid proof of the link between a society's culture and its sports. More practically, if such a linkage were proven, then those interested in promoting peace would have a new target for bringing about change. They would see the necessity for changing combative sports that socialize youngsters to be combative adults to sports that are non-violent.

The next selection, excerpts from a *Sports Illustrated* series on violence, describes how brutality and physical injury are endemic to America's most popular team sport—football. These selections, by journalist John Underwood, raise important questions: Why is such a violent sport so popular? Why aren't the rules changed to provide maximum physical protection for the players? Who is responsible for the perpetuation of the brutality—the players, the coaches, the rulemakers, the officials, or the fans? The answers to these questions increase our understanding not only of football, but more important, also of ourselves and our society.

The final essay in this section, by Eitzen, investigates deviance in sport. Included in this article are discussions of cheating, drugs, violence (by players and fans), and dehumanizing practices by coaches. Each of these provide important clues about American society.

NOTES

1. Howard Cosell, "Sports and Good-by to All That," *New York Times* (April 5, 1971), p. 33.
2. George H. Sage, "Sports, Culture, and Society," paper presented at the Basic Science of Sport Medicine Conference, Philadelphia (July 14-16, 1974), pp. 10-11.
3. Paul Hoch, *Rip Off the Big Game* (Garden City, New York: Doubleday Anchor, 1972), p. 9.

The Structure of Sport and Society

D. STANLEY EITZEN

An important indicator of the essence of a society is the type of sport it glorifies. The examination of the structure of a society's dominant sport provides important clues about that society and its culture. For example, answers to the following questions will greatly inform the observer about that society: Is the sport oriented toward a group (team) or the individual? Does the outcome depend essentially on strength, speed, strategy, deception, or the mastery of intricate moves? Is the activity cerebral or physical? Is the primary goal to win or to enjoy the activity?

Let us begin by looking at what Americans consider the essence of sport—winning—to show how other societies have a different view more consonant with their culture. Sport, as played in America, is an expression of Social Darwinism—a survival-of-the-fittest approach where everyone competes to be alone at the top. Players are cut from teams even in our schools if they are not considered good enough. Tournaments are organized so that only one team or individual is the ultimate winner. Corporations sponsor contests for youngsters such as "Punt, Pass, and Kick," where winners are selected at the local level and proceed through a number of district and regional contests until a winner is declared in each category. In 1974, for instance, there were 1,112,702 entrants in the Punt, Pass, and Kick contest, and only six youngsters ended as winners.[1]

In cooperative, group-centered societies, such sporting activities would seem cruel, even barbaric, because success is achieved only at the cost of the failure of others. These societies, rather, would have sports where the object is something other than winning. For instance:

The Tangu people of New Guinea play a popular game known as *taketak*, which involves throwing a spinning top into massed lots of stakes driven into the ground. There are two teams. Players of each team try to touch as many stakes with their tops as possible. In the end, however, the participants play not to win but to draw. The game must go on until an exact draw is reached. This requires great skill, since players sometimes must throw their tops into the massed stakes without touching a single one. *Taketak* expresses a prime value in Tangu culture, that is, the concept of moral equivalence, which is reflected in the precise sharing of foodstuffs among the people.[2]

SOURCE: This essay was written for this volume.

This example demonstrates that a society's sports mirror that society. Cooperative societies have sports that minimize competition, while aggressive societies have highly competitive sports. This raises a question about the nature of the most popular American sports. What do they tell us about ourselves and our society? Let us concentrate on the two most popular team sports—football and baseball—as they are played at the professional level.[3]

THE DIFFERING NATURES OF FOOTBALL AND BASEBALL

Although there are some similarities between football and baseball, e.g., cheating is the norm in both,[4] these two sports are basically different. In many ways they are opposites, and these incongruities provide insightful clues about Americans and American society.

Two fundamentally different orientations toward time exist in these two sports. Baseball is not bounded by time while football must adhere to a rigid time schedule. "Baseball is oblivious to time. There is no clock, no two-minute drill. The game flows in a timeless stream with a rhythm of its own."[5] In this way baseball reflects life in rural America as it existed in the not-too-distant past compared to football's emulation of contemporary urban society, where persons have rigid schedules, appointments, and time clocks to punch.

The innings of baseball have no time limit, and if the game is tied at the end of regulation innings, the teams play as many extra innings as it takes to determine a winner. Football, on the other hand, is played for sixty minutes, and if tied at the end, the game goes into "sudden death," i.e., the first team to score wins. Thus, even the nomenclature of the two sports— "extra innings" compared to "sudden death"—illustrates a basic difference between them. There are other semantic differences. A baseball player makes an "error," but a football team is "penalized." The object of baseball is to get "home" while the goal of football is to penetrate deep into the opponent's "territory." In baseball there is no home territory to defend; the playing field is shared by both teams. There is no analogue in baseball for the militaristic terms of football, e.g., "blitz," "bomb," "trap," "trenches," "field general," "aerial attack," and "ground attack."

Such linguistic differences imply a basic discrepancy between baseball and football. Baseball is essentially a calm and leisurely activity while football is intense, aggressive, and violent. Football is foremost a form of physical combat, whereas baseball is one of technique. A baseball player cannot get to first base because of his strength, aggression, or ability to intimidate. His only way to get there is through skill. In football, however, survival (success) belongs to the most aggressive. Former football player George Sauer has suggested that aggression on the football field leads to success just as it gets one ahead in American society.

How does football justify teaching a man to be aggressive against another man? And how does it justify using that aggression for the ends that it has? I think the values of football as it is now played reflect a segment of thought, a particular kind of thought that is pretty prevalent in our society. The way to do anything in the world, the way to get ahead, is to aggress against somebody, compete against somebody, try to dominate, try to overcome, work your way up the ladder, and in doing so, you have to judge yourself and be judged as what you want to be in relation to somebody else all the time. Given the influence football has on young children, the immense influence it has as a socializing force in society, its impact should be rigorously examined. People learn certain values from watching football, from watching aggression, from watching it performed violently and knowing that these guys are going to get a big chunk of money if they do it well often enough.[6]

The two sports require different mentalities of their athletes. Football players must be aggressive while that is not a necessary ingredient for the baseball player. Also, baseball is a game of repetition and predictable action that is played over a 162-game schedule. The players must stay relaxed and not get too excited because to do so for every game would be too physically and emotionally draining over the six months of the season. Moreover, because the season is so long, players must pace themselves and not let a loss or even a succession of losses get them down. In football, though, losing is intolerable because of the short season (sixteen games). Thus, football players must play each game with extreme intensity. As a result the incidence of taking amphetamines ("uppers") has been much greater among football players than among baseball players. The intensity that characterizes football resembles the tensions and pressures of modern society, contrasted with the more relaxed pace of agrarian life and baseball.

One of the more interesting contrasts between these two sports is the equality of opportunity each offers. Baseball promotes equality while football is essentially unequal. This difference occurs in several ways. First, football originated among college elites and even today requires attending college to play at the professional level. Baseball has never been closely identified with college. Essentially, the way to make it in baseball is to work one's way through the minor leagues rather than by attending college (although that is one route).

A second way that baseball is more egalitarian than football is that it can be played by people of all sizes. There have been small All Star players such as Phil Rizzuto, Bobby Shantz, Pee Wee Reese, Joe Morgan, and Freddie Patek. Football, however, is a big man's game. In football the good, big team defeats the good, small team, whereas in baseball, the good, small team has an equal chance of beating the good, big team.

Baseball is also more equal than football because everyone has the opportunity to be a star. Each position has its stars. Pay is divided about equally by position. Except for designated hitters, all players must play both offense and defense. Thus, each player has the chance to make an outstanding defensive play or to bat in the winning run. Stardom in football is essentially reserved for those who play at certain positions. Only backs, receivers, and kickers score points while others labor in relative obscurity, making it possible for the "glamor boys" to score. This is similar, by the way, to American society, where the richest "players" score all the points, call the plays, and get the glory at the expense of the commoners. There is also a wide variance in pay by position in football. In 1977 the average NFL quarterback received $89,354 while the average defensive back received $47,403.

A final contrast on this equality dimension has to do with the availability of each of the sports to the masses. The average ticket price for major league baseball in 1978 was $3.98 compared to $9.67 for professional football.[7] The cheaper tickets for baseball allow families to attend and provide live entertainment for members of all social classes. Football, however, excludes families (except for the rich) and members of the lower classes because of the high prices and the necessity of purchasing season tickets.

Another major dimension on which these two sports differ is individualism. Baseball is highly individualistic. Elaborate teamwork is not required except for double plays and defensing sacrifice bunts. Each player struggles to succeed on his own. As Cavanaugh has characterized it:

Although there are teams in baseball, there is little teamwork. The essence of the game is the individual with or against the ball: pitcher controlling, batter hitting, fielder handling, runner racing the ball. All players are on their own, struggling (like the farmer) to overcome not another human being but nature (the ball). This individualism is demonstrated when the shortstop, cleanly fielding the ball, receives credit for a "chance" even if the first baseman drops the thrown ball. It is demonstrated when a last-place team includes a Cy Young Award-winning pitcher or a league-leading hitter. It is perhaps most clearly manifest in the pitcher-batter duel, the heart of the game, when two men face each other. Baseball is each man doing the best he can for himself and against nature within a loose confederation of fellow individualists he may or may not admire and respect. This reflects a society in which individual effort, drive, and success are esteemed and in which, conversely, failure is deemed the individual's responsibility.[8]

Football, in sharp contrast, is the quintessence of team sports. Every move is planned and practiced in advance. The players in each of the eleven positions have a specific task to perform on every play. Every player is a specialist who must coordinate his actions with the other specialists on the team. So important is each person's play to the whole, that games are filmed and reviewed, with each play then broken down into its components and each player graded. Each player must subordinate his personality for the sake of the team. The coach is typically a stern taskmaster demanding submission of self to the team. The similarity of the football player to the organization man is obvious. So, too, is the parallel between football and the factory or corporation, where intricate and precise movements of all members doing different tasks are required for the attainment of the organization's objective.

CONCLUSION

Sociologist David Riesman in his classic book, *The Lonely Crowd*, noted a shift in American character since World War II.[9] Prior to that war Americans were what Riesman called "inner directed," which fit the demands of an essentially agrarian society. The farmer and the small entrepreneur succeeded on their own merits and efforts. "Rugged individualism" was the necessary ingredient for success. There was the firm belief that everyone was a potential success.

But since the war the United States and Americans have changed. Rural life is replaced by living in cities and suburbs. Individuals now typically are dominated by large bureaucracies, whether they be governments, schools, churches, or factories. In these settings Riesman noted that Americans have become "other directed." Rather than an "automatic pilot" homing the inner-directed person toward his individual goal, the other-directed person has an "antenna" tuned to the values and opinions of others. In short he is a team player and conformist.

Baseball, then, represents what we were—an inner-directed, rural-individualistic society. It continues to be popular because of our longing for the peaceful past. Football, on the other hand, is popular now because it symbolizes what we now are—an other-directed, urban-technical-corporate-bureaucratic society. Thus these two sports represent cultural contrasts (country vs. city, stability vs. change, harmony vs. conflict, calm vs. intensity, and equality vs. inequality). Each sport contains a fundamental myth that it elaborates for its fans. Baseball represents an island of stability in a confused and confusing world. As such, it provides an antidote for a world of too much action, struggle, pressure, and change. Baseball provides this antidote by being individualistic, unbounded by time, nonviolent, leisurely in pace, and by perpetuating the American myths of equal opportunity, egalitarianism, and potential championship for everyone.

Football represents what we are. Our society is violent. It is highly technical. It is highly bureaucratized, and we are all caught in its impersonal clutches. Football fits contemporary urban-corporate society because it is team-oriented, dominated by the clock, aggressive, characterized by bursts of energy, highly technical, and because it disproportionately rewards individuals at certain positions.

The uniquely American sports of football and baseball, although they represent opposites, provide us with insight about ourselves and our society. What will become of these sports as society changes? Will we continue to find football and baseball so intriguing as society becomes more structured? We know that in the future American society will be short of resources. We know that its citizenry will be older and more educated than at present. We also know that society will become more urban. What will these and other trends mean for society and for sport? One thing is certain—as society changes so, too, will its sports. Does this mean that baseball and football will change? Will another sport emerge that is more attuned with the culture and structure of society? Or will baseball become even more popular as we become more nostalgic for the peaceful, pastoral past?

NOTES

1. D. Stanley Eitzen and George H. Sage, *Sociology of American Sport* (Dubuque, Iowa: Wm. C. Brown, 1978), pp. 68–69.
2. George B. Leonard, "Winning Isn't Everything: It's Nothing," *Intellectual Digest*, 4 (October, 1973), p. 45.
3. Several sources are especially important for the material that follows: Gerald J. Cavanaugh, "Baseball, Football, Images," *New York Times* (October 3, 1976), p. 2S; George Carlin, "Baseball-Football," *An Evening with Wally Londo* (Los Angeles: Little David Records, 1975); Leonard Koppett, "Differing Creeds in Baseball, Football," *Sporting News* (September 6, 1975), pp. 4 and 6; Murray Ross, "Football Red and Baseball Green," *Chicago Review* (January/February 1971), pp. 30–40; Richard Conway, "Baseball: A Discipline that Measures America's Way of Life," *Rocky Mountain News Trend* (October 19, 1975), p. 1; "Behind Baseball's Comeback: It's An Island of Stability," *U.S. News & World Report* (September 19, 1977), pp. 56–57; William Arens, "The Great American Football Ritual," *Natural History*, 84 (October, 1975), pp. 72–80; Susan P. Montague and Robert Morais, "Football Games and Rock Concerts: The Ritual Enactment of American Success Models," *The American Dimension: Cultural Myths and Realities*, William Arens (ed.), (Port Washington, New York: Alfred, 1976), pp. 33–52; and R. C. Crepeau, "Punt or Bunt: A Note in American Culture," *Journal of Sport History*, 3 (Winter 1976), pp. 205–212.
4. Cf., D. Stanley Eitzen, "Sport and Deviance," last essay of this unit.
5. Crepeau, "Punt or Bunt," p. 211.

6. Quoted in Jack Scott, "The Souring of George Sauer," *Intellectual Digest*, 2 (December 1971), pp. 52–55.
7. Tim Fedele, *Left Field*, 1 (April 1978), p. 1.
8. Cavanaugh, "Baseball, Football, Images, p. 25S.
9. David Riesman, *The Lonely Crowd* (New Haven: Yale University Press, 1950). The analysis that follows is largely dependent on Crepeau, "Punt or Bunt," pp. 205–212.

War, Sports, and Aggression: An Empirical Test of Two Rival Theories

RICHARD G. SIPES

The search for a connection between Man's "nature" and his warfare again has become a major issue during the past decade and "there appears to be a recrudescence of the idea that humans possess an instinct toward aggression and war" (Holloway 1968:33).

This paper investigates relationships which are postulated, by folk wisdom and behavioral scientists, to exist between war and fundamental characteristics of man, and between war and sports. The major hypotheses can be subsumed under two rival, mutually exclusive models: Drive Discharge and Culture Pattern.

Drive Discharge Model

(1) Instinct and Aggression: Individual and group aggressive behavior is the result of an innate drive in the individual human. This drive, although somewhat responsive to the environment, normally generates a tension in the individual. There is a certain basal level of aggression pressure in every individual and society.

(2) Aggression and War: Aggressive tension, regardless of whether the

SOURCE: Richard G. Sipes, "War, Sports and Aggression: An Empirical Test of Two Rival Theories," *American Anthropologist*, 75 (January 1973), excerpts from pp. 64–68, 70–71, and 80.

aggressive drive is innate or acquired, accumulates in the individual and society. It is like a hydraulic substance and will find an outlet in aggressive behavior of one sort or another. Warfare is aggressive action brought about at least in part by accumulated aggressive tension.

(3) War and Sports: Warlike sports serve to discharge accumulated aggressive tension and therefore act as alternative channels to war, making it less likely.

The Drive Discharge Model predicts somewhat similar levels of aggressive behavior in all societies, although the mode of expression can vary. It predicts an inverse relationship between the presence of war and of warlike sports in societies, which we should find expressed in two ways: (1) an inverse synchronic relationship should exist between societies, with more warlike societies less likely to have (or need) such sports and less warlike societies more likely to have these sports; (2) a diachronic relationship also should exist within a given society, with periods of more intense war activity accompanied by less intense activity in warlike sports and periods of less intense war activity associated with more intense sports activity. The probability of war can be reduced, according to this model, by increasing the incidence of alternative behavior similar to warfare (such as combative sports).

Culture Pattern Model

(1) Instinct and Aggression: Individual aggressive behavior primarily is learned. Although perhaps utilizing some innate characteristics, its intensity and configuration can be considered predominantly cultural characteristics.

(2) Aggression and War: There is a strain toward consistency in each culture, with similar values and behavior patterns, such as aggressiveness, tending to manifest in more than one area of the culture.

(3) War and Sports: Behavior patterns and value systems relative to war and to warlike sports tend to overlap and support each other's presence.

The Culture Pattern Model predicts dissimilar levels of aggressive behavior in different societies. It predicts a direct relationship between the presence of war and of warlike sports in societies, which we should find expressed in two ways: (1) a direct synchronic relationship should exist between societies, with more warlike societies more likely to have such sports and less warlike societies less likely to have them; (2) either no diachronic relationship at all (for no dynamic feedback is inferred by this model) or a direct diachronic relationship, if any, should exist within a given society, with periods of more intense war activity accompanied by more intense sports activity and less intense war activity associated with less intense sports activity. The probability of war can be reduced, according to this model, by decreasing the incidence of combative sports and other behavior similar to warfare.

The present study is an empirical test of these two rival models through their predictions. The predicted intersocietal synchronic relationships between sports and war are tested in a hologistic correlation study of twenty societies.

THEORETICAL BACKGROUND

Along with the idea of man's aggressive nature, and from the time of the first Olympic Game, in popular thought and learned circles, we find a recurring hope that sports and warfare might act as alternatives to each other; that possibly our intergroup problems could be resolved on the playing field rather than on the battlefield. Enough speculation on this has taken place in anthropology and allied disciplines but, with the exception of Textor (1967), Roberts, and a few others (Roberts, Arth, and Bush 1959, 1967; Roberts and Sutton-Smith 1962, 1966; Roberts, Sutton-Smith, and Kendon 1963), anthropologists have directed little objective research toward sports and almost none toward relationships between sports and war.

Instincts and Aggression

Explicit rebellion against the idea of innate behavioral characteristics in humans is traced by Marvin Harris (1968:10-12) to John Locke who, in 1690, postulated the human mind as a "white paper" at birth. At least since that time the nature/nurture controversy has been present in behavioral sciences.

Sigmund Freud viewed an instinct as a genetically programmed "chemico-physical status" which must be discharged in some fashion. Lack of direct discharge results in "tension" which can be stored and accumulated, often to be released in devious and destructive ways at a later time (Fenichel 1945:54-55, 58-61). An essentially identical "ergic tension" model is used by R. B. Catell (1965:198-204). R. W. Pickford (1941:281, 292) speaks of "impulses toward combat for possession of territory which are very deeply rooted in animals and in men." The drives irresistibly will be manifested in behavior. A. I. Hallowell (1955) uses blocked and accumulated aggression as a basic explanatory device in his analysis of Salteaux society. R. Steinmetz (1929:70) views war itself as innate. The latest and most elaborate uses of the innate drive model of aggression in animals and men are found in the works of K. Lorenz (1966) and I. Eibl-Eibesfeldt (1970).

Many researchers and theoreticians reject the idea of an innate aggression drive. R. J. Andrew (1971:54) denies the existence of long term storage or build-up of Eibl-Eibesfeldt's "central nervous excitatory potential" and of patterned searching for targets for aggression release. T. C. Schneirla and others (Asch 1952:ix; Atz 1970:178; Lehrman 1953, 1970) tend to object on other fundamental grounds, denying the validity of interspecific comparisons of behavior. M. F. Ashley Montagu (1968:ix) rejects instincts in general, saying that an appeal to them can explain everything and so explains nothing. E. Becker (1962:132) directs his criticism against the accumulable and hydraulic aspects of drive models (and these aspects can apply whether the alleged drives are instinctive or learned). He says they oversimplify and only "*seem* to describe what we are observing."

For other works on aggression and instinct, the reader is referred to R. Ardrey (1966); J. Bernard et al. (1957); A. Buss (1961); J. Dollard et al. (1939); Durbin and Bowlby (1939); E. Leach (1966, 1967); J. Masserman (1963); E. B. McNeil (1965); and J. Scott (1958).

Aggression and War

Generally, those foregoing authors who look upon aggression as an instinct also hold that it is one manifest cause of war. But one does not have to assume innateness of individual aggression to claim it as a causal factor in warfare. It is sufficient if aggression and aggression tension is present with certain operative characteristics, regardless of origin.

L. Berkowitz (1962:23); E. D. Hoedemaker (1968:71); and E. B. McNeil (1961:290) postulate learned rather than innate origins for aggressions but believe that resultant pressures and ingrained behavior patterns make war more likely. Whiting (1967:154) says child-rearing practices often lead to inhibition of direct aggression and to displacement onto alternate objects, presumably including other societies. E. D. Chapple (1970) would seem to classify aggression as an "intervening variable" between territoriality and warfare. McDougall (1964:33) says the instinct of "pugnacity" explains warfare. Ellis (1951:199); Steward and Faron (1959:325–330); J. Dollard et al. (1939:1, 190); and R. F. Murphy (1960:186) all attribute warfare to accumulated aggression tensions within the societies they studied.

Other writers reject or ignore the idea that aggression tension plays a causal role to war. S. Andreski (1968:187) says that the fact that societies must devote so much time and energy to the development of aggressive and warlike "virtues" in individuals proves these "virtues" are not innate.

He presents them as results, rather than causes, of the leaders' decisions to engage in war. J. Burton (1964:147–148) grants aggression to individuals but denies the very application of the term to nations and hence to war. Conflict theories—of which C. von Clauswitz (1911); Q. Wright (1935, 1965); J. Bernard (1949); Bernard et al. (1957); and T. Schelling (1960) are representative—seldom use the term "aggression" except in the technical military sense of initiative.

War and Sports

Freud and Fenichel (1945:485, 558) speak of the usefulness of sports as a means of "substitute discharge." N. Perrotti (1932) and R. W. Pickford (1940:132–138, 1941:282–287) probably would agree with K. Lorenz (1966:271–273) when he claims that "the main function of sport today lies in the cathartic discharge of aggressive urge . . . (especially) collective militant enthusiasm." M. Mead (1955:xxv–xxvi); G. P. Murdock (1949:90); and L. Tiger (1969:152, 216, 234, 266) all view sports as functional equivalents to war in discharging aggression tension. S. R. Rosenthal (1971), speaking of riots and war, says "RE [risk exercise] sports should replace not only the violent acts of our ancestors but the violent acts of today!"

I conducted a series of interviews with six college and four high school coaches of football and basketball in Erie, Pennsylvania, and Buffalo, New York, during February and March, 1971. They generally agreed that these sports released aggressive tension, engendered social virtues such as fair play and discipline, and reduced the possibility of warfare. These attitudes probably reflect a widely held set of professional values and perhaps would qualify as a general cultural belief in the United States.

On the other hand, S. Blanton (1942); G. Flick (1940); D. Jaeger (1939); and D. Schayes (1971) generally would ascribe to S. L. Washburn's (Tiger 1969:148) view of sports as good training grounds for combat; that is, sports are complementary to warfare rather than being alternatives. B. Rimland (1961), though, tested and found no significant correlation between the individual's level of interest or activity in sports and his success in the military.

Those physical anthropologists, psychologists, social psychologists, sociologists, and ethologists who abjure or ignore the Drive Discharge Model seldom mention sports, with one noticeable exception: Lüschen (1970:9) says that "sports are not only representative of societal norms and values . . . (they) socialize toward such patterns . . ." Neither do cultural anthropologists talk much of sports when discussing war or culture in general. It would seem, however, that a certain relationship between sports and warfare is implicit in one view of culture. "To most modern anthropologists," according to R. L. Beals and H. Hoijer (1965:279), "the patterns of a culture are held together or integrated in terms of abstractions variously known as themes, configurations, drives, or postulates." To the degree that the culture is consistent, we might expect to find somewhat similar attitudes and behaviors manifesting in different activities. We can hypothesize that such generalities as zero-sum games, indifference to suffering, bravery, aggressiveness, and the like, would apply across all the culture rather than being limited in manifestation to a single activity. Combative sports would more likely be found in warlike societies than in peaceful ones. Such sports would not be alternatives to war as much as they would be embodiments of the same theme or outlook as is war.

THE CROSS-CULTURAL STUDY

A holocultural correlation study was used to test empirically the Drive Discharge Model and its rival, the Culture Pattern Model. Specifically, the following inter-societal synchronic predictions were tested:

Drive Discharge Model: An inverse synchronic relationship between war and combative sports will be found, with more warlike societies less likely to have such sports and less warlike societies more likely to have them.

Culture Pattern Model: A direct synchronic relationship between war and combative sports will be found, with more warlike societies more likely to have these sports and less warlike societies less likely to have them.

Sample Selection and the War Variable

I used K. Otterbein's (1968) internal war study sample as a basis for my own. Otterbein used the first 628 societies listed in the Ethnographic Atlas (Murdock 1962–64) as the universe from which to draw his sample. Fifty of the sixty culture areas in the Atlas were utilized and a society selected from each. Otterbein distinguished three modes of war: internal war; external war, attacking; and external war, attacked. War frequencies in each of these modes were coded for each of his sample societies, using the categories "infrequent or never" (I), "frequent" (F), and "continual" (C). Details of his sample selection and coding methods, and definitions, can be found in his cited article.

I decided on a sample of twenty of these societies. I wanted ten relatively warlike and ten relatively peaceful societies. The best identification of a strong war orientation appeared to be a high frequency of attack on others. I ranked in random order the twenty-seven societies which had received an "F" or a "C" rating in the external war, attacking, mode. Starting with the first society, I accepted or rejected it on the basis of availability of sufficient ethnographic information in the Human Relations Area Files, State University of New York at Buffalo library, or personal library to code the sports variable. I used the first ten which qualified in this respect.

Difficulty soon was encountered in gathering ten relatively peaceful societies. Otterbein's sample contained only five which received an "I" rating in all three modes. I imposed this requirement for an "I" rating in all three modes after a preliminary investigation of the Trumai (rated "I" in internal war and aggressive external war but "F" in defensive external war) suggested that some societies may not wage internal war nor attack others primarily because they are under so much aggressive pressure from neighbors that they do not have an opportunity to seize the initiative. This appeared to be the case with the Trumai. I strongly suspect that they would wage aggressive war were they not a small, vanishing, harassed group (Murphy and Quain 1955:ix, 11; Steinen 1886:193).

Only four of the five societies coded "I" in all three modes by Otterbein could be used for the present study. The Monachi had to be rejected; although there was sufficient information to code their war activity and political system, information on sports was lacking. Rejection of twenty percent of Otterbein's peaceful societies and the necessity of locating six more means, in effect, that I have used two different samples drawn separately from the same universe. One was Otterbein's warlike societies; the other a combination of Otterbein's and my own peaceful societies. My method of selection, however, was sufficiently random and similar to Otterbein's that results would not be affected. I selected the six remaining societies in the following manner: A random list of 200 OWC Code numbers was constructed from the OWC Code (Murdock 1963). Starting with the first society so identified, I accepted or rejected it on the basis of two criteria: (1) availability of sufficient ethnographic information in the Human Relations Area Files, State University of New York at Buffalo library, or personal library to code the society, and (2) information indicating infrequent or no war activity on the part of the society. The first six so selected were used to complete the ten-society sample and can be identified in Table I by the fact that the "War" category was not coded by Otterbein. Relatively peaceful societies are not easy to find. I had to investigate 130 societies to find eleven, of which five were rejected because of insufficient information on sports in the available ethnographies.

The dependent variable, sports, was defined as a physical activity (1) engaged in primarily for amusement or recreation, (2) with no ostensible religious ritual or subsistence-activity training significance, and (3) involving at least two adult individuals. I was interested only in sports which reasonably could be expected to serve as an alternative to war and so distinguished between combative sports and all others.

A combative sport was defined as one played by two opponents (individuals or teams) and fulfilling one or both of the following conditions: (1) There is actual or potential body contact between opponents, either direct or through real or simulated weapons. One of the objectives of the sport appears to be inflicting real or symbolic bodily harm on the opponent or gaining playing field territory from the opponent (which would include placing a disputed object in, or acquiring one from, a guarded location). Wrestling which involves blows or immobilization or subjugation of the opponent (not simply pushing harder than he or causing him to lose his balance and fall) would be considered an example of symbolic bodily harm, as would mock removal of the opponent's head. (2) There is no body contact, harm, or territorial gain but there is patently warlike activity. Such sports, to be classified as combative, must include use of actual or simulated combat weapons against an actual or simulated human being.

Combative sports were considered absent from a society if any ethnographer speaks of the amusements, recreations, and games of the society and does not describe or mention any combative sports or says that the kind of sports which I would classify as combative are missing, and he is not contradicted by any other ethnographer available to me at the time of coding. (As I have mentioned, the society was rejected from the sample unless an ethnographer reported sufficiently on the amusements, recreations, games, and sports of the society to make it seem probable that combative sports would have been mentioned had they been practiced.) Simple tests of strength and so-called wrestling which involves only lifting the opponent or causing him to fall (such as arm- or Indian-wrestling), with no significant subjugation or chance of injury, are *not* considered combative. Contests of skill with hunting tools—such as bow and arrow—by peoples for whom hunting is an important subsis-

TABLE I Correlation Test Results

		Combative Sports		
		Yes	No	
Warlike	Yes	9	1	10
	No	2	8	10
		11	9	20

tence activity at the time of ethnography are *not* classified as combative sports (even though the hunting tool could be used in combat) unless the target is a real or simulated human being. . . .

Analysis of results: Coding results are summarized in Table I. The *phi* value of this distribution is 0.6035. The Fisher Exact Test shows that the probability of getting this, or a less likely distribution in the same direction, by chance alone is less than 0.0028.

The cross-cultural study shows that where we find warlike behavior we typically find combative sports and where war is relatively rare combative sports tend to be absent. This refutes the hypothesis that combative sports are alternatives to war as discharge channels of accumulated aggressive tension in the social frame of reference. It casts strong doubt on the idea that there is such a thing as accumulable aggressive tension, certainly on the social level and perhaps, under most circumstances, even on the individual level. It clearly supports the validity of the Culture Pattern Model and as clearly tends to discredit the Drive Discharge Model. . . .

CONCLUSIONS

Sports and war manifest no functional relationship across time. Cross-culturally, war and combative sports show a direct relationship.

War and combative type sports therefore do not, as often claimed, act as alternative channels for the discharge of accumulable aggressive tensions. Rather than being functional alternatives, war and combative sports activities in a society appear to be components of a broader culture pattern.

However, the Drive Discharge Model is so entrenched in Western science that there should be investigation of other activities which conceivably could act as alternatives to war (and now, as we have seen, to combative sports as well) in the discharge of postulated drive tensions. Likely candidates are suicide, murder, punishment of deviants, drug use, physical assault on family or other community members, gossip, psychogenic illnesses, and malevolent magic. Unless there are definite indications that they serve as alternatives to war and combative sports, we can set aside the Drive Discharge Model with full confidence that it is not applicable to humans.

GENERAL REFERENCES CITED

Andreski, Stanislav
    1968   Military Organization and Society. Berkeley: University of California Press.

Ardrey, Robert
    1966   The Territorial Imperative. New York: Atheneum.
Asch, M. J.
    1952   Social Psychology. Englewood Cliffs: Prentice-Hall.
Atz, J. W.
    1970. The Application of the Idea of Homology to Behavior. *In* Development and Evolution in Human Behavior. Lester R. Aronson, E. Tobach, D. S. Lehrman, and J. S. Rosenblatt, Eds. San Francisco: Freeman, pp. 53–74.
Beals, Ralph L., and Harry Hoijer
    1965   An Introduction to Anthropology. New York: Macmillan.
Becker, Ernest
    1962   The Birth and Death of Meaning. New York: Free Press/Macmillan.
Berkowitz, Leonard
    1962   Aggression: A Social Psychological Analysis. New York: McGraw-Hill.
Bernard, Jessie
    1949   American Community Behavior. New York: Dryden Press.
Bernard, Jessie, T. H. Pear, R. Aron, and R. C. Angell
    1957   The Nature of Conflict. Belgium: UNESCO.
Blanton, S.
    1942   Incoordination and Tension Due to Anxiety. Lancet 62:398–400.
Burton, John
    1964   The Nature of Aggression as Revealed in the Atomic Age. *In* The Natural History of Aggression. J. D. Carthy and F. J. Ebling, Eds. New York: Academic Press. pp. 145–153.
Buss, A. H.
    1961   The Psychology of Aggression. New York: John Wiley and Sons.
Cattell, Raymond B.
    1965   The Scientific Analysis of Personality. Baltimore: Penguin Books.
Chapple, Elliot D.
    1970   Culture and Biological Man: Explorations in Behavioral Anthropology. New York: Holt, Rinehart and Winston.
Clauswitz, Carl von
    1911   On War. Three Volumes. London: K. Paul, Trench, Trubner. (First published in 1832.)
Dollard, J., L. Doob, N. Miller, O. Mowrer, and R. Sears
    1939   Frustration and Aggression. New Haven: Yale University Press.
Durbin, E. F. M., and J. Bowlby
    1939   Personal Aggressiveness and War. New York: Columbia.
Eibl-Eibesfeldt, I.
    1970   Ethnology. New York: Holt, Rinehart and Winston.
Ellis, Florence
    1951   Patterns of Aggression and the War Cult in the Southwestern Pueblos. Southwestern Journal of Anthropology 7(2):177–201.
Fenichel, Otto
    1945   The Psychoanalytic Theory of Neurosis. New York: W. W. Norton.
Flick, G.
    1940   Wille und Sport auf Grund Psychologisher Gutachten von Spitzenkönnern. Soldatentum 7:18–21.
Hallowell, A. I.
    1955   Culture and Experience. Philadelphia: University of Pennsylvania Press.

Hoedemaker, Edward D.
   1968   Distrust and Aggression, an Interpersonal-International Analogy. The
   Journal of Conflict Resolution 12(1):69-81.
Holloway, Ralph L., Jr.
   1968   Human Aggression: The Need for a Species-Specific Framework. In
   War. Morton Fried, Marvin Harris, and Robert Murphy, Eds. Garden City:
   Natural History Press/Doubleday. pp. 29-48.
Jaeger, D.
   1939   Angst und Charakter beim Kampfsport: Eine Untersuchung des
   Durchlebens Angstartige Zustande auf Hinderniskampfbahnen unter den
   Gesichtspunkt des Soldats. Hamburg: Riegel.
Lehrman, Daniel S.
   1953   A Critique of Konrad Lorenz's Theory of Instinctive Behavior. Quar-
   terly Review of Biology 28:337-363.
   1970   Semantic and Conceptual Issues in the Nature-Nurture Problem. In
   Development and Evolution in Human Behavior. Lester R. Aronson, E.
   Tobach, D. S. Lehrman, and J. S. Rosenblatt, Eds. San Francisco: Freeman.
   pp. 17-52.
Lorenz, Konrad
   1966   On Aggression. New York: Harcourt, Brace and World.
Lüschen, Gunther, Ed.
   1970   The Cross-Cultural Analysis of Sport and Games. Champaign: Stipes
   Publishing Co.
McDougall, William
   1964   The Instinct of Pugnacity. In War: Studies from Psychology, Sociology
   and Anthropology. L. Bramson and G. W. Goethals, Eds. New York: Basic
   Books. pp. 33-43. (First published in 1915.)
McNeil, Elton B.
   1961   Personal Hostility and International Aggression. The Journal of Conflict Resolution 5(3):279-290.
Mead, Margaret
   1955   Male and Female. New York: New American Library of World
   Literature. (First published in 1949.)
Montagu, M. F. Ashley, Ed.
   1968   Man and Aggression. New York: Oxford University Press.
Murdock, George P.
   1962-64   Ethnographic Atlas. Ethnology 1:113-134, 2:249-253, 3:199-217.
Murdock, George P., and Douglas White
   1969   Standard Cross-cultural sample. Ethnology 8:329-369.
Murphy, Robert F.
   1960   Headhunter's Heritage. Berkeley: University of California Press.
Murphy, Robert F., and B. H. Quain
   1955   Trumai Indians of Central Brazil. New York: J. J. Augustin.
Otterbein, Keith F.
   1968   Internal War: A Cross-Cultural Study. American Anthropologist
   70(2):277-289.
   1970   The Evolution of War. New Haven: HRAF press.
Perrotti, N.
   1932   La psicologia della sport. Rivista Italiana Psicoanalitica 1:240-247.
Pickford, R. W.
   1940   The Psychology of the History and Organization of Association
   Football. The British Journal of Psychology 31(1):80-93, (2):129-144.

1941   Aspects of the Psychology of Games and Sports. The British Journal of Psychology 31(4):279–293.

Rimland, Bernard
1961   The Relationship of Athletic Ability, Sports Knowledge and Physical Proficiency to Officer Performance and Career Motivation. U.S. Navy Bureau of Naval Personnel Technical Bulletin No. 61-12. Washington.

Roberts, John M., Malcolm J. Arth, and Robert R. Bush
1959   Games in Culture. American Anthropologist 61:597–605.

Roberts, John M., and Brian Sutton-Smith
1962   Child Training and Game Involvement. Ethnology 1:166–185.
1966   Cross-Cultural Correlates of Games of Chance. Behavior Science Notes 4(4):131–145.

Football Brutality

JOHN UNDERWOOD

I.

In 1905, during a football season of unparalleled brutality, President Theodore Roosevelt summoned the leaders of the college game to Washington and demanded that they clean up the sport—change the rules to better protect the players or else. Under such a threat, the rules were quickly and dramatically changed and the game was streamlined. Thus football avoided almost certain self-destruction.

Since a 17-year-old Agoura, Calif. High School football player named Gregory Cole was injured making a head-on tackle and died of a subdural hematoma last November, there has been agitation in that state to make it mandatory that a physician and an ambulance be present at every high school game. On a typical California football weekend there are as many as 1,500 schoolboy games. There are not that many private ambulances in the state.

In June, a lawyer for Gregory Cole's family announced he had filed a suit in which 21 defendants were named.

SOURCE: Excerpts from the three-part series by John Underwood, "An Unfolding Tragedy," *Sports Illustrated* (August 14, 1978), pp. 69–82; (August 21, 1978), pp. 32–56; and (August 28, 1978), pp. 30–41.

In the last four years liability insurance for elementary schools has gone up 345 percent, for high schools 320 percent, for junior colleges 414 percent. "California's public schools face an insurance crisis that could bankrupt them if it remains unchecked," says Wilson Riles, state superintendent of public instruction.

Before he retired eight years ago, Dr. Eric Walker, the president of Penn State, made a plea in the nature of a prediction to football coach Joe Paterno, who is widely respected for his honorable approach to the game. Dr. Walker was one of Paterno's champions, and one of football's. But like Paterno, he was not blind to its failings. He said, "Joe, if football doesn't do something about the injuries, soccer will be our national sport in 10 years."

As soccer, a clean and comparatively injury-free sport, grows in popularity in the U.S., Paterno views Walker's foresight with a growing sense of urgency, as a time bomb ticking. He says he wonders if "enough people realize we have a problem." The injury rate in football cannot be condoned. "It is no longer enough," says Paterno, "to accept it as 'part of the game.'"

Although casualty lists are available in football, no one source ever seems to know exactly how injuries occur or how many there are in a given period for all levels of the game. But indications are that 1977 was a particularly doleful year for the sport which James A. Michener calls "The American Form of Violence" in his exhaustive book, "Sports in America."

Navy Coach George Welsh complained of "more injuries than any time since I've been here," but did not know why. Dr. Donald Cooper, the team physician at Oklahoma State, went onto the field 13 times in one game, "and that never happened before." Texas, No. 1-ranked at the time, was down to its fourth quarterback by midseason. The Detroit Lions lost three quarterbacks and had had 21 knee operations in three seasons. Asked who on his 80-man Maryland team had not missed a game or a practice because of injury, Coach Jerry Claiborne named only one player.

However, no team could match the devastation that was wrought on the football team of LaPorte (Ind.) High School. By mid-October, the Slicers, as they are unfortunately nicknamed, had suffered four broken backs, four broken legs and numerous torn ligaments and cartilages. Fifteen lettermen had major injuries. Coach Lou Famiano told the Michigan City News-Dispatch he had thought of moving practice to the hospital lawn. At the end of one session, Famiano called for a final play. "I shouldn't have," he says. "Our No. 2 punter broke his leg and our No. 1 center suffered a broken hand." In a junior varsity game, as one Slicer lay on the sidelines, awaiting an ambulance with a broken leg, another was hit in the chest. His heart stopped. It took electroshock treatment at the hospital to revive him. Famiano says, "My only explanation is the kids have learned bad habits in the early stages of their career, and that's pure speculation."

The upcoming fall renewal of what is often called "hostilities" on sports pages promises no less grim a harvest. Projecting from recent surveys, it is anticipated that the "part of the game" no one likes to talk about will:

- Injure a million high school players at approximately 20,000 schools.
- Injure 70,000 college players at more than 900 schools.
- Inflict a 100 percent casualty rate (at least one injury for every player) on the National Football League.

The legal profession has found that suing football may result in highly lucrative judgments in several areas, but as of now suits involving the use or misuse of the modern hard-shell football helmet, a device Dr. Cooper calls "the damnedest, meanest tool on the face of the earth," are the most profitable. There is no better way to epitomize the myriad threats to football than to examine the helmet. It is:

- A focal point of coaches' intransigence in teaching dangerous techniques.
- The piece of equipment with which players are most likely to cause the most serious injuries—head and neck injuries are responsible for 80 percent of the game's fatalities.
- The wedge that has opened the sport to the current boom in negligence suits.

Cooper is a onetime 5-foot-1, 105-pound water boy who professes a 35-year love for football that is not diminished by his outspoken desire to straighten it out. As medical consultant to the NCAA Rules Committee for six years (1969–75), he was credited with leading the charge that got college coaches to adopt three important safety measures: Prohibiting the "crackback" block (the legal clip at the line of scrimmage), making mouthpieces mandatory and outlawing below-the-waist blocking on kicks. (The NFL did not get around to legislating against the crackback until two years after the colleges and has not yet taken action on either of the other proposals.)

On the day in 1976 that Cooper railed against the misuse of helmets in a story appearing in the Topeka State Journal, another article in the same paper told of a lawsuit brought by Mrs. Ruth Hayes of San Diego against Riddell, Inc. of Chicago for "unspecified damages equal to one-fourth the total assets of Riddell." Riddell is the nation's largest helmet manufacturer. Mrs. Hayes' 17-year-old son Kip had been paralyzed from the neck down playing football. Mrs. Hayes' lawyer blamed the helmet for Kip's incapacitation.

Six months later, in May of 1977, and a year and a half after his lawyers won a record Dade County (Fla.) judgment of $5.3 million against Riddell, 21-year-old Greg Stead settled out of court for a reported $3 million. The Miami Herald reported Stead's lawyers got $1 million of that. Stead was in a wheelchair, a quadriplegic since the night in 1971 when the face guard of his helmet struck the knee of an opposing high school ballcarrier and sent the back edge of his helmet crashing down on his upper spine. Stead's lawyers charged Riddell with producing a "negligently designed" helmet.

Nationwide, helmet manufacturers now face between $116 million and $150 million in negligence suits. At a minimum, the suits represent five times the annual gross of the industry ($24 million) and 100 times its annual profit. They have caused grave concern. At the time of Stead's suit there were 14 helmet manufacturers in the country. There are now eight.

A helmet has the effect of a bowling ball on impact, says Dr. Cooper. "If a kid isn't seriously hurt by it in a game Saturday, on Sunday he has so many bruises he looks like he's been tattooed with a ball peen hammer. There's nothing wrong with the helmet itself. Doing what it was intended to do—protecting the head—it performs adequately. We seldom see a fractured cheek or skull anymore. What's wrong is the way it is used. Everything that has to do with a meaningful existence runs through that four-inch segment of your body (the neck). Do like the coaches tell you— jam that helmet or face guard into something, force that helmet back and it's worse than a karate chop. The head was not meant to be a battering ram."

One Saturday stands out in Dr. Cooper's memory for its impact on the Big Eight Conference: The star Kansas quarterback, hit by a helmet, had to have knee surgery. The star Oklahoma cornerback, hit by a helmet, had to have shoulder surgery. The star Oklahoma State fullback, hit by a helmet, had to have his left leg put in a cast. Dr. Cooper did the work on the last. He recalls that the year before, the same fullback had his right leg fractured by a helmet. Colorado assistant coach Ron Corradini called the helmet "the worst advancement in football."

In Dallas, Washington Redskin back Bob Brunet, blocking on a running play, smacked headfirst into the knee of a Cowboy defender and was knocked out. The spinal cord compressed as the neck tried to "climb" into his helmet. Brunet had a postgame numbness and tingling pains. It was first feared he had suffered a cervical fracture, but the injury was later diagnosed as a bad bruise and swelling on the spinal cord. Brunet survived, but with his football future in doubt.

After surveying his squad of outpatients last season, then-Redskin

Coach George Allen said, "Coaches are not the reason for injuries. Football is great the way it is. Too many rules changes haven't worked before."

In 1970, the colleges outlawed spearing, which was defined as "the deliberate and malicious use of the head and helmet in an attempt to punish a runner after his momentum has been stopped." Later, the prohibition was broadened to include any deliberate use of the helmet to punish an opponent, whether he had been stopped or not, and to make illegal "striking a runner with the crown or top of the helmet."

The rule is only sporadically enforced. And face-to-numbers blocking and tackling (the front of the helmet or the face guard making initial contact) is still legal, and it is estimated that eight out of 10 coaches teach it. The pros have no rule specifically intended to prevent spearing. Art McNally, the NFL's supervisor of officials, says, "Spearing has never been a problem in the NFL."

Finding the battle lines drawn, equipment manufacturers have pushed for a bill in Congress to provide liability-judgment limitation. Says Howard Bruns, president of the Sporting Goods Manufacturers Association, "The sporting-goods industry itself is under attack. The question is, will football survive?"

"It won't," says Dr. Cooper, echoing a prediction Joe Paterno once heard. "If we don't do something, everybody will be playing soccer."

No, not everybody.

Robert Francis Mudd Jr. will not be playing soccer. He has been paralyzed since making a tackle in a Stockton, Calif., high school scrimmage seven years ago. A $3 million suit was filed on Mudd's behalf by attorneys, one of whom was former San Diego Charger all-pro tackle Ron Mix. The suit alleged that the face-to-numbers technique taught at Lincoln High was inherently unsafe and that coaches and schools were negligent in permitting it.

The trial set a San Joaquin County record for civil jury trials by taking four months to complete. Mudd lost. He has, his parents believe, also lost in life. "You wonder what kind of life he's going to have," says his mother. "Will he meet someone? Will he be able to get married? It's just a catastrophe, there is no other way to put it."

Says the boy, now 21, "You get bored. You don't have any friends. There's really very little you can do."

II.

Ideally, you should be able to play any game without referees or umpires. Players of sport should also be sportsmen. Officials of sport should make rulings, not serve as cops keeping athletes from maiming each other. But that is exactly what is happening in football. It is naive and dangerous to think otherwise. Certain practices of coaching and play have evolved that have increased the likelihood of injury. And the higher the level of play, the more brutal the practices.

Yet, football has not yet become rollerball. Skill, not mayhem, is still its primary attraction. But the game has changed. Skill and technique and teamwork have lost ground to intimidation and wanton aggression.

Ruthless play within the rules has led to unconscionable acts that have contributed to an injury rate that is now unacceptable and to increasing litigation by an increasingly litigious society. Football has become a game in which rule-maneuvering is so much a way of life that the men who coach it, and the men who play it, are often indifferent to the game's aberrations.

"The basic problem of football today," says Davey Nelson, the University of Delaware athletic director and secretary-editor of the NCAA Rules Committee, "is not to see if you can win within the rules, but to see how much you can get away with to help win."

The process by which permissible aggression becomes mayhem is not difficult to trace. Sometimes it can be found simply by listening to the young men who play the game: Dean Payne is a linebacker at Northwestern. He is a sophomore from Chester, Pa. Says Payne, "All the coaches stress gang tackling. You're taught to be there at the ball—once you're there, you're not supposed to stare at it. You're supposed to pile on. It becomes a really violent state of mind—you really get fired up and motivated to get someone. Everyone accepts things like late hits as part of the game."

The college player advances into the pros, where his aggression is marketable and becomes a springboard to affluence. Jean Fugett, from Amherst, now is a tight end for the Washington Redskins. "I never understood the real violence of the game until I played pro ball," Fugett told Charley McKenna of the Milwaukee Sentinel.

"I had to work very hard to be aggressive. I used to have to start making up stuff like, 'This guy raped my mother' to get physical enough to really hit him . . . intimidation is the biggest part of the game. You can't let anyone get away with anything because everything you do is on film. If you let yourself be intimidated, the team you play next week will see it on the films and may try the same thing."

From the twisted logic of "get away with what you can," it is a short hop to malicious mischief, and from there to the deviations that poison a sport. Some of the more recent cases are familiar to fans of televised football:

The Cardinals' Tim Kearney clotheslines Eagle running back Dave

Hampton, crashing a forearm into the side of Hampton's neck. Hampton is unconscious for seven minutes before being carried off the field on a stretcher. Kearney defends the blow as "perfectly legal."

From the hospital, Hampton says, "That's football."

Mel Morgan of the Bengals throws a forearm into the face of Steeler receiver John Stallworth, who has just caught a pass. Morgan gets a penalty and a suspension, Stallworth a concussion. Moments later, Mel Blount of the Steelers kayoes Bengal tight end Bob Trumpy. The score is even.

In retaliation for his late hit on Oakland quarterback Ken Stabler, Cleveland defensive end Joe "Turkey" Jones is speared in the back by Oakland guard Gene Upshaw.

Gene Calhoun, a lawyer who has been refereeing in the Big Ten since 1963, is a voice in the wilderness, crying out for sanity. "If they wanted to clear up all excessive violence in football," says Calhoun, "they could do it with one 30-second bulletin: From now on, no late hits. A guy's down, he's down. We're not going to let you demolish a player anymore. We're going to call 'holding' every time we see it, so don't hold. Don't frustrate players into retaliating. No more hits out of bounds. No more extra hits on quarterbacks. No more piling on. No more gang tackling when a back is clearly in the grasp of a tackler and going down. We're going to put a greater burden on a player to know when to let up, when not to use his body or head as a weapon.

"An official's first responsibility is to the players' safety. He gets a bulletin like that, and he calls a game accordingly. An official can call a game as close as he is asked to. But he wouldn't even try if the coaches aren't going to go along."

Coaches are not monsters. As a group, they are probably as honorable and caring as most. Breaking rules can get them beat or fired. Or both. The great majority think of their calling as a high one, entrusted as they are with the development of young men. But coaches at almost every level, from high school up, are under great pressure to win.

Dan Devine of Notre Dame says, "When a coach starts out, he sees what coaches do and he says, 'I'll do anything to win.' So he cheats. He teaches win at any cost. When he's older, his career is in the balance. He says, 'I'll do anything to stay in.'"

Coaches also have an inherent suspicion of rule changes. The result is that they maintain a death grip on the status quo. Clipping was first taught by Walter Camp in 1908, but it was not outlawed until 1949. The crackback block, murderous on knees and nothing more than a legal clip, was not outlawed until 1971 in the colleges, 1974 in the pros.

According to the Stanford Research Institute's report, 25 percent of lost-time injuries to pro football players involve the knee. It is the part of an athlete's body most susceptible to serious injury, and hardly suited to football.

The Detroit Lions have had 22 knee operations in the last three years. The Miami Dolphins had 11 in 1976. Of the 26 lost-time injuries that ruined a good Maryland team last year, 18 were below the waist. "But I don't know how we could have eliminated them," said Coach Jerry Claiborne.

Knee injuries are death on careers. In his eight years with the St. Louis Cardinals, defensive back Jerry Stovall broke his nose, lost five teeth, fractured his cheekbone, broke a clavicle, ripped his sternum, broke seven ribs, broke a big toe three times and suffered 11 broken fingers. But it was a knee injury that ended his career in 1971.

Yet, says Art McNally, the NFL's supervisor of officials, "it has been shown by studies that only one percent of injuries were on plays that were illegal."

In light of the medical evidence, the growing number of liability suits and the soaring cost of insurance, the following "necessities" should be examined.

- Is it necessary to block any player below the waist on any downfield play? Former coach of the year Ara Parseghian doesn't think so. Parseghian says below-the-waist blocks outside the legal clipping zone four yards on either side of the center, three yards on either side of the line of scrimmage are not necessary at all. "On any play where there's a scramble of 22 men," he says, "blindside hits and unprotected hits on knees occur."

- Is the below-the-waist chop block necessary? No, says Lee Corso. No, says Doug Dickey. No, say Parseghian, Darrell Royal and Washington's Don James. No, no, no.

   The rollup block, in which an offensive lineman "rolls" up the back of a defender's legs, is similar in concept. It also is not necessary.

- Is it necessary for a third, and even a fourth, 260-pound lineman to help two other 260-pounders put away a ballcarrier when he's already trapped or on the way down?

   Norm Evans, the veteran Seattle Seahawk offensive tackle and all-pro, thinks not. Evans is "bugged" by all the piling on he sees in football, the redundant hits on ballcarriers and quarterbacks. He thinks a greater burden should be put on defensive players to make them more aware of the obvious.

   Late, redundant hits go hand in glove with gang tackling, a tactic spawned by Southern college coaches years ago and given widespread respectability under the euphemism "pursuit." Pursuit is an incontrovertible virtue of defense. The trouble with pursuit is that it often translates into vicious finishing-off blows on backs whose momentum has already been stopped.

- Is it necessary for a defensive player to unload on a receiver when it is obvious the ball is overthrown? The colleges now have a rule against this practice, making the defender responsible for knowing where the ball is. The pros don't.
- Is it necessary to tackle players who don't have the ball, just because they might get it?

Lou Holtz of Arkansas can tell you why he doesn't think so, although this is a favored tactic in the college game, where blindside hits on trailbacks in the option play are allowed. Indeed, the accepted defense against the wishbone or veer is to wipe out the quarterback on every play, whether he keeps the ball or not, and blindside the trailback before he gets it.

"It's legal," says Holtz, "but it's not ethical."

- Is any blow to the head necessary? Dubious helmet use in blocking and tackling was covered in part I of this series, but the head is open to other needless attacks. Clubbing, the forearm blow to the neck, has been outlawed in colleges since 1949, but vestiges of it are still around.

Fred Akers, the Texas coach, says he "cringes" when he sees rival teams come on the field "with their arms taped to the elbows. I know it's going to be a long day. You should see some of the forearms (hits) we get on ballcarriers, frame by frame. It makes you want to throw up."

The overall picture is clear: The rules of the game do not protect the players. The rules are not always "fair" to both parties in the more than 2,000 separate one-on-one hits that are made in the course of a normal football game. The rules need revision.

So, it would seem, does the degree of punishment. John Unitas says the easiest way to stop the foul play of the more brutal players is to "throw them out of the game. That would cure it."

Coaches get more safety conscious when it costs them 15 yards. A way to impress them further might be a 20-yard penalty. Would a player think twice before aiming a forearm at someone's neck if he knew it would cost his team 20 yards or even 30? Would a 30-yard penalty make a coach more conscious of his humanity?

Last fall, two separate but similar messages went out to professional and college coaches. One, from Pete Rozelle, warned that playing-field viciousness and misconduct "do not belong in professional football" and would bring "disciplinary action." The other, from Dave Nelson, said that some of the tactics being practiced were "humiliating college football."

Here is a sample of how the brutality in football in 1977 reached quarterbacks. In the first televised college game of the season, Pittsburgh quarterback Matt Cavanaugh, a prime Heisman Trophy candidate, was buried by Notre Dame defensive end Willie Fry just as he released a second-period touchdown pass. Forced backward under Fry's 242 pounds, Cavanaugh put his left hand back to brace his imminent fall and snapped his wrist. Goodby Heisman.

On the first Saturday of play, half the teams in the Big Eight lost their starting quarterbacks. One other Big Eight quarterback was playing hurt with a practice injury. By midseason, eight starting Southeastern Conference quarterbacks had been put out of commission. Texas was down to a fourth stringer as it held desperately to the No. 1 ranking. The Longhorns had lost two quarterbacks in one game in the same quarter.

Georgia, suffering its first losing season in 14 years under Vince Dooley, was down to its fourth quarterback by the time it got to Georgia Tech for the final game. In that one, No. 4 sprained an ankle and No. 5, a freshman, dislocated a fibula. Dooley finished up with another freshman who had been a reserve on the junior varsity.

But that was child's play compared with what the pros were dishing out. On a memorable Sunday in November, Fran Tarkenton of Minnesota, who had never had a serious injury, spun away from a rush on a busted play and was submerged by Cincinnati's Gary Burley. Tarkenton's ankle snapped. On that very same "day at the butcher shop," as one press dispatch called it, James Harris of San Diego was helped off the field with a sprained ankle, Bill Munson of San Diego with a fractured leg, Brian Sipe of Cleveland with a shoulder injury, Lynn Dickey of Green Bay with a broken leg, and Terry Bradshaw with a shoulder injury to go with his dented wrist.

A crackdown on late and redundant hits has been under way in the NFL, according to Art McNally. He instructs his referees to call out when a pass is gone to let charging offenders know the quarterback is no longer fair game. But in 1977 only 47 roughing-the-passer penalties were called in the NFL, compared with 43 in 1976.

By the same token, coaches certainly do not encourage "late hits." A late hit means a 15-yard penalty. Coaches would rather have an abscess than a 15-yard penalty.

Coaches who argue against equal protection under the rule, however, say a quarterback is more likely to run than a punter and is usually better at it and therefore can't be made sacrosanct. Coaches don't want to give quarterbacks license to steal.

If coaches are willing, it is not as difficult to solve the dilemma as some think. However, you must be willing to assume certain things. First, that most defensive players can see. If they can see, they can be made to do things.

Every coach boasts that defensive players are better than ever, bigger, faster, more gifted. That being the case, says Ara Parseghian, and acknowledging the fact that a defender advancing with more caution in the manner of a screening basketball player is less likely to get fooled, a "grab" rule might be put into effect for quarterbacks, at least on a trial basis. If the defender gets there and the quarterback still has the ball, the defender has the same tackling rights as he has in regard to the kicker before the ball is off the ground: No holds barred.

"But if the ball is gone," says Parseghian, "and the defender has got his head up instead of down in that ramming position, he can see enough to hold up and just grab the quarterback. A grab is a lot less likely to break a rib."

It would seem a simple enough equation to work out: Coaches and officials acting together to decide what is "necessary" in football. But the deeper issue is sportsmanship. Bad sportsmanship is always shameful. In a sport that has an inherently high potential for physical damage, it is intolerable. When a coach plots the incapacitation of a player, it is profanity to call him a sportsman. A certain amount of concentrated effort against a star player is acceptable in sport: Guard him relentlessly, double-team him, pitch to him a certain way, shift or zone the defense for him, neutralize him. But "concentrated effort" is not license to indulge in perversions of the rules. The line is crossed with the first deliberate attempt to hurt or weaken an opposing player.

III.

In 1976 a 42-year-old professor of psychiatry at the University of California at San Diego wrote a book about his experience as an unpaid locker room analyst for the San Diego Chargers. In "The Nightmare Season," Dr. Arnold Mandell detailed the shocking use of amphetamines by professional football players desperate to get any edge in a dog-eat-dog battle for dominance and dollars.

The season was 1973. For a while, the nightmare was mainly Dr. Mandell's. His attempts to alert the National Football League to this monstrous situation, and to wean the players under his care from dangerous street "speed" by giving them prescription drugs backfired.

In April of 1974 the NFL made (in Mandell's words) "sacrificial lambs" of the Chargers. At an awkward press conference, the league announced that it had fined and placed on probation the owner of the team (Eugene

V. Klein), its general manager and coach (Harland Svare) and eight players and banned Mandell from further contact with players.

Unfortunately for the NFL, Mandell did not then shut up. Writing in Psychology Today in 1975, he said a "drug agony rages, silently as a plague, through the body of professional football," and that "a clumsy, ham-handed press conference at the end of the season would not solve a problem that is as occupational a disease in pro football as surely as silicosis is in mining."

When the upcoming publication of "The Nightmare Season" was announced in the fall of '76, Mandell says he was warned by Svare that "they"—he didn't say who "they" were—"would sue me or try to get my license."

The book came out.

And in September of 1977 the Los Angeles Times reported that Mandell said, "the football industry persuaded the state of California" to take action against him for prescribing drugs illegally for nonmedicinal purposes. Indeed, the state did take action, for whatever motive. After a 15-day hearing before an administrative officer, Mandell was found guilty of "over-prescribing" drugs. He received a five-year probation but did not lose his license. His right to prescribe drugs was suspended.

When the decision was announced, psychiatrists and physicians across the country rallied around their colleague and launched Concerned Health Professionals for Mandell. A committee was formed to fund his appeal and overturn the ruling (an appeal is forthcoming). The Clinical Psychiatry News wondered if the penalties were "retribution for his fight against drug abuse in professional football."

Despite being put on probation, Mandell continues his crusade. "I haven't done what I set out to do," he says, "which is to get amphetamines out of football." He says they are "the single factor that causes unnecessary violence in pro football today"—not in low doses for fatigue or as appetite depressants, "but in enormous doses, as high as 150 milligrams. Higher than ever.

"People ask (NFL Commissioner) Pete Rozelle why so many quarterbacks went down last season from late and nasty hits. The answer can be found in the nearest pillbox. I'd be interested to see what would happen to the incidence of orthopedic surgery in the NFL if amphetamines were banned and everybody had to take a urine test before games."

The normal "diet" pill or capsule—Benzedrine, Dexedrine, Eskatrol—contains five to 15 milligrams of amphetamine. The prolonged, excited "high" from one pill is familiar not only to fat people but also to long-haul truckers and students cramming for examinations. Imagine what it is like, says Dr. Mandell, to gulp down 30 pills at one time. "The result is a prepsychotic paranoid rage state," he says. "A five-hour temper tantrum that produces the late hits, the fights, the unconscionable assaults on quarterbacks that are ruining pro football. They're at war out there, and the coaches, even if they're not aware (of the drugs' effects), are the generals. Coaches know the game is ideally played in controlled anger. They hang up clippings, and talk vendettas. Players get half crazy anyway, and if 60 percent of them have their heads filled with amphetamines, the injury projection is enormous.

"For the player in this state the negotiation of rules becomes highly complicated, and easily broken if the referee isn't looking. That's when you get the elbows, the hands being stepped on, the knees in the face, the kicking."

Mandell's expertise is in biomedical and pharmacological psychiatry, with 22 years in research, 18,000 hours treating patients. He has written six books and 230 articles in his field. He serves on the editorial board of 11 scientific journals, is past president of the Society of Biological Psychiatry and has received several federal grants, including $500,000 during the last six years for a study of the effects of amphetamines on the brain.

In short, Mandell may be naive but he is no quack, nor is it likely that he is the irresponsible drug dispenser the NFL sought to have him appear. A wiry 5-foot-6, 14-mile-a-day jogger with a Phi Beta Kappa key and a sunburst of curly hair, he has an easy manner that ingratiated him to the Chargers. They called him Arnie and entrusted to him their deepest secrets. He became a close friend of Svare.

Mandell says it took him almost a year to "realize what was going on." He now calls it "The Sunday Syndrome."

"Ordinarily, most football players are warm, loving, decent human beings," Mandell says. "They aren't drug addicts. They have to convert themselves to attain a state of hair-trigger readiness. For a while, I thought it was pure physiology, a group of men who somehow had this capacity. They'd come in on Sunday morning, lighthearted and well dressed. No signs. Gradually they'd begin to change. About 11 o'clock the tension would start to rise. Some would get loud and boisterous, and become more obscene. Others would withdraw, staring. Some would pace in repetitive turns. Those are all signs, together with a wider-based gait, an added clumsiness.

"Amphetamines in large doses produce a paranoid psychosis. That means the guy doing the damage actually thinks the other guy is out to get him. It's Good Guys vs. Bad Guys. The quarterback, as the figurehead of the opposition, is the No. 1 bad guy. It's open season on him. I laugh when NFL players talk about the dangers of synthetic turf and helmets, and all the while they're permitting amphetamine-crazed athletes to go on the

field and assault their quarterbacks. You expect to see the kind of thing
that happened to (Terry) Bradshaw last year. When he got speared in the
back, it almost gave him whiplash."

Analgesics as well as stimulants, amphetamines mask pain—pain
Mandell says would act at least as a partial deterrent to such mayhem.

"The older the player, the more likely his dependence. He gets
desperate. I was trying to get one guy to lower his dosage. He told me,
'It's easy for you to talk, Doc, but I'm making $65,000 a year. If I lose this
job, tomorrow I'm a bartender. I've got three kids, a home . . .'"

The drug subculture that exists in sport has been examined in the past,
with expert testimony from men like Dr. Robert Kerlan, former team
physician of the Los Angeles Dodgers. Professional athletes, reflecting
society as a whole, are well tuned to drug use, to the proposition they
might need help to face extreme pain, or to mask it. Team physicians stuff
them with codeine, pump their knees full of xylocaine, shoot their
inflamed joints with cortisone.

The incidence of drug use in pro football, which is absurd to deny, is
not the question here, however. The injuries it causes is the issue. Other
doctors besides Mandell have spoken out. Dr. Donald Cooper of Oklahoma State has expressed in medical journals his concern over the
"agitated, aggressive, sometimes paranoid behavior" of players high on
amphetamines.

"I've been on the sidelines in pro games where the physician watched
a guy on his team jump offsides two or three times and said to me, 'I know
that guy's problem—he's so high on amphetamines he can't see straight.'

"Sam Huff (the former all-pro linebacker) told me the two times he
tried them he got thrown out of the game for hitting late. He thought he
was playing great."

The recent literature of pro football is laced with drug confessions.
Chip Oliver (Raiders), Dave Meggyesy (Cardinals) and Bernie Parrish
(Browns) gave graphic accounts of amphetamine use. Johnny Sample
(Colts, Redskins and Jets) said "most pro football players eat pep pills like
candy." Meggyesy wrote that "Most NFL trainers do more dealing in
(amphetamines and barbiturates) than the average junky." He said the
"violent and brutal player that television viewers marvel over on Satur-
days and Sundays is often a synthetic product."

The NFL maintains a stiff upper lip through all this. There is no "drug
crisis" in the NFL, says Jack Danahy, director of security for the NFL.
"Alleged drug use in the league has been overstated in the past." NFL
director of information Joe Browne cites the league's "strong drug
preventative program," which has been educating players since 1971, as
well as weekly counts of pills distributed by team physicians and trainers.

Amphetamines? "As far as we can tell," says Browne, "they are not taking amphetamines."

In 1974 the Stanford Research Institute issued a report on injuries in the pros. Although the NFL paid $35,000 for the SRI's recommendations, its response to the report was no response at all. The pros made no appreciable rules changes for 1975 and the high injury rate continued. This year, in a grand show of concern for the game, the NFL made two rules changes: it is now possible for blocking linemen to "hold" a little more convincingly (to extend their arms and open their hands), and second "bumps" on receivers, once they are more than five yards down field, are prohibited.

Injuries did not bring about these changes, however. According to the league's communique, Commissioner Rozelle was "concerned" over the fact that the scoring average in the league was at a 36-year low. The NFL had "to put more offense back in the game."

The SRI report said a lot of things four years ago, but one of its most damning conclusions was something it did not say, in so many words. According to the SRI findings, only 1.3 percent of all injuries in the NFL involved acts that were illegal, that drew penalties. Those in the blood bond who excuse the violence cite this as proof that players are basically rules-abiding fellows and ought to be left alone.

This series has attempted to analyze what is causing all football to suffer an unacceptable injury rate. To ameliorate it, many changes in rules, equipment, playing conditions and coaching philosophies have been proposed—some by coaches, some by physicians, some by officials, some by the author. Perhaps not all of these changes would work. But changes must be made, changes that will once again establish football as the prototypical American sport, a game in which skill is matched by physical commitment. Which is to say a game played within civilized boundaries, for if it is a game, you do not maim.

On that unarguable basis the following rules, some of which were proposed in previous installments, should be instituted. In some cases, they might already be in effect at one level of football or another, but they should be made sportwide:

1. Outlaw all deliberate helmet hits. If the helmet makes the initial contact in blocking or in tackling, it is wrong.
2. Outlaw blocking below the waist on all downfield plays, or on plays outside the legal "clipping" zone. Ban the "chop block" and its relatives at the line of scrimmage.
3. Instruct officials to enforce more stringently the rulings on late, redundant or unnecessary hits, be they on ball carriers, receivers or

quarterbacks. The criterion at its most rudimentary level would be to make tacklers responsible for knowing when a player is stopped, helpless or already going down.

4. Institute a "grab" rule for defensive players tackling quarterbacks in the act of passing, in which only the arms and hands would be used. If this proves inadequate, give the quarterback in the act of passing the same protection the punter is given in the act of punting.
5. Institute a no-hit rule on receivers until they catch the ball.
6. Institute a no-hit rule on tailbacks running the option play. An offensive player without the ball should not be fair game.
7. When it is evident that quarterbacks are being hit on certain types of plays simply as a form of intimidation, warn the coach of the team responsible. If the practice persists, call personal fouls.
8. Crack down on all "momentum" tackles involving out-of-bounds plays and forward progress. A player on offense knows where the boundary lines are. Defensive players should, too.
9. Outlaw all forms of "clubbing" or forearm blows on ball carriers and receivers. Outlaw all head tackles save in interior line play.
10. Penalize all overt forms of bad sportsmanship, including end-zone dances and gestures, and taunting.
11. Increase the penalties for flagrant fouls and unsportsmanlike acts to 20 yards (minimum) or 30 yards. Eject players and coaches who repeatedly dispute officials' calls.

Administratively, do the following:

1. Standardize the rules throughout the game, allowing only for differences dictated by age and physical development (e.g., length of quarters).
2. Make mandatory the representation of physicians and game officials on rules committees.
3. Establish a central registry for injuries, with input on their causes and computer readouts available for high school, college and pro teams. (The NFL can fund this project as a token of its appreciation for having the colleges and high schools as its farm system.)
4. Establish a crew of rules committee members to conduct clinics in which coaches and players would receive instruction on the rules and be warned against injury-causing tactics.
5. Pad the outside surfaces of helmets and shoulder pads. Make mouthpieces mandatory. Study the value of the face guard, and if it is truly a cause of spinal injury, prohibit its use.
6. Make some form of lightweight knee brace mandatory equipment (e.g., the eight-ounce plastic model used at Oklahoma State).
7. Outlaw strong chemical stimulants and institute urine or saliva tests as

is necessary to ensure that players obey the rules against the use of drugs.

8. Monitor practices to make sure the techniques being taught are legal.
   None of these recommendations would affect the esthetic qualities of the game. None would lessen its appeal. They would make life more difficult for coaches, and more costly for administrators, but if they saved half a dozen players from lives spent in wheelchairs, they would be worth it.

Unless there are sweeping changes in the game, a storm of litigation is coming. The thunder is already being heard. Lawyers hang on every broken bone and torn tendon, watching for an opening. The rules and the environment in which the game is played can no longer be left to the whims of coaches and players, because they are at once the cause and the victims of the problem.

Sport and Deviance

D. STANLEY EITZEN

Sport and deviance would appear on the surface to be antithetical terms. After all sport contests are bound by rules; school athletes must meet rigid grade and behavior standards in order to compete; and there is a constant monitoring of athletes' behavior because they are public figures, and because there are officials and organizations whose primary function is to curb their illegal behaviors. Moreover sport is assumed by many to promote those character traits deemed desirable by most in society: fair play, sportsmanship, obedience to authority, hard work, and goal orientation.

In this article I shall argue, to the contrary, that the structure of sport in American society actually promotes deviance. Deviance is defined here as behavior that (1) violates the rules of the game, (2) offends the universal values of sportsmanship and fair play, and (3) illegitimately brings harm

SOURCE: This paper will also appear in *Encyclopedia of Physical Education*, Vol. V, *The Social Science of Sport*, Gunther Luschen and George H. Sage (eds.), (Reading, Massachusetts, Addison-Wesley, forthcoming).

to persons or property (violence). The first meaning is self-explanatory. The rules of a sport create deviance by negatively labeling and punishing rule breakers. A fight among players in a soccer game, for example, is easily defined as rule breaking, and the punishment for such conduct is easily dispensed. The other two meanings are normative ones and require further elaboration. These meanings include as deviance those behaviors that violate ideals that are presumed to have universal acceptance. It is assumed that those activities that give an athlete or team an unfair advantage in a sports event are generally abhorred throughout the world of sport. "Unfair" is meant to connote those means that enhance the chances of victory other than through skill, luck, strategy, and ability. In addition to unfairness, the deliberate harming of people and property is generally decried and defined as deviant behavior.

This paper examines the relationship between sport and deviance, by observing four areas: (1) sport as festival, (2) sport and violence, (3) the interference of outsiders in the outcome of contests, and (4) the corruption of the ideals of sport. The first three sections deal primarily with the mechanisms by which sport promotes deviance among spectators. The last one focuses on the deviant behavior of athletes and coaches in their drive to succeed-at-any costs. Drug abuse, cheating, the corruption of education, and the abuse of the athlete are highlighted in that section.

SPORT AS FESTIVAL

Sporting events share characteristics with such nonsporting events as Mardi Gras and New Years' Eve celebrations, rock concerts, and conventions. The shared characteristics found typically at these seemingly different events, which classify them as festivals, are: music, costuming, ostentatious displays of material possessions, the use of alcohol as a "social lubricant," the buying and selling of memorabilia, and the *existence of "routinized" deviance* (Koval, 1974).

Apparently festivals serve several related escape valve functions for the members of a society: (1) they provide excitement in an otherwise routine world (Elias and Dunning, 1970), (2) they allow adults to react against their oversocialization and retreat at least momentarily to a fantasy world of their youth, and (3) they provide a release from the constraints of the social world. Festivals provide an antidote to normal social life that is bound by pressures to conform in relatively rigid ways. Festivals allow the individual to participate in relatively unstructured and spontaneous behaviors. At sporting events spectators can deviate from society's norms within reasonable limits without penalty. Individuals can drink to excess, shout obscenities, destroy property (e.g., goal posts), act hysterically, and generally make fools of themselves. In other words individuals may behave in ways that would be considered deviant in other social contexts. The game, as a festival, is legitimized by society and its agents of social control as a time to act illegitimately, to be released from the standardized forms of social relationships of the everyday world.

SPORT AND VIOLENCE

Normative violence in sport. The most popular sports in many societies actually encourage player aggression. Not only is the nature of these sports to hit an opponent, but the sport can encourage excessive violence with little or no penalty. For example, a player willfully injuring another player can be reprimanded, fined, removed from the contest, or banished from the sport forever. Hockey is especially well known for its minimal penalities and, in effect, for condoning violence as a crowd-pleasing part of the game. Player fights routinely result in cuts, concussions, and fractures, not only in the professional leagues (Kennedy, 1975), but also in amateur leagues (McMurtry, 1974) and in youth hockey (Smith, 1974). But why do these athletes participate in violence? Smith (1974) has argued that violence in hockey, as in war, is a socially rewarded behavior. The players are convinced that aggression (body checking, intimidation, and the like) is vital to winning. Thus the behavior is approved by fans, coaches, and peers. Younger athletes, of course, idolize the professionals and attempt to emulate their aggressive behaviors at their level of play, thereby perpetuating violence in the sport.

Violence is also an integral part of a sport such as football. Players are expected to be "hitters." They are taught to lower their heads to deliver a blow to the opponent, they are taught to gang tackle—to make the ball carrier "pay the price." The assumption is that physically punishing the other player will increase the probability of the opponent fumbling, losing his concentration and executing poorly the next time, becoming exhausted, or having to be replaced by a less talented substitute. These brutal, win-at-any-cost tactics are almost universally held among coaches, players, and fans in the United States. The unfortunate result is a high injury rate. Data from the 1972 and 1973 National Football League found that each season the 1,040 players suffered an average of 1,101 injuries so severe that they could not return either to that game or to a subsequent game or practice. Moreover each season 136 of the players (13 percent) had to undergo surgery (Surface, 1974).

The high injury rate is a function of playing a violent game. Most important for our purposes is that this violence is considered a normal part of the game. The athletes are expected to behave in ways that in nonsporting, and nonwarlike contexts would be considered deviant.

The function of violent sports for the athletes, spectators, and society.
One can only speculate as to why violent sports thrive in some societies.
Do violent societies need violent sports? Gladiatorial combat on the
athletic field reflects the emphasis, perhaps, of militarized societies. Or is
it possible that violent sports act as a catharsis, ridding the individuals
and, therefore, society of pent-up aggression, thereby lessening the
possibility of war? The rationale for each position follows (Sipes, 1973;
Tandy and Laflin, 1973).

The drive discharge theory begins with the assumption that aggression
by individuals and groups is innate (instinctive). Aggressive tension is
further assumed to accumulate in the individual and society and must be
discharged. War results when these tensions become too great. Warlike
sports will serve to discharge accumulated aggression (catharsis) and
serve as a legitimate alternative to war.

The alternative approach, the culture pattern theory, argues that
aggression is primarily a learned behavior. Therefore, societies will
emphasize activities that promote either competitiveness and aggression
or cooperation and passivity. Warlike sports, then, will be the rule in
aggressive societies. Such sports, rather than providing a catharsis effect,
lead to the enhancement of aggression in the society.

The study by Sipes (1973) was a direct test of these two theories. Two
methods were used. First, twenty tribal societies were randomly selected
to determine whether warlike societies had combative sports or not. This
analysis strongly supported the culture pattern model. Nine of the ten
warlike societies had combative sports while only two of the ten peaceful
societies had combative sports. The second test examined the popularity
of combative sports in the United States from 1920 to 1970 and also
supported the culture pattern model. Sipes found that combative sports
(football, boxing, hockey) increased in popularity in time of war while
the popularity of baseball decreased. His conclusion was that sports are
not alternative channels for the discharge of aggressive tensions. Rather
than lessening aggression, combative sports appear to intensify it. This
conclusion is supported also by the research of others who examined the
effects on spectators of watching violent sports (Goldstein and Arms,
1971; Geen and Berkowitz, 1966; Turner, 1968).

Despite these studies there is no definitive answer as to whether the
existence and popularity of violent sports does or does not drain off
aggressive tendencies in the populace. The existence of violent sports in a
violent society is not proof that one causes the other. Such sports may
indeed perform a safety valve function. Just because there is a high level
of aggression in the United States, for example, does not mean that the
violent sports do not work as safety valves. It may mean that participants
in society are overwhelmed by too many sources of frustration and

aggression. It may mean, in fact, that without violent sports, spectators and players would be all the more aggressive. Clearly, more research is needed before we can answer this interesting speculation with any certainty.

Spectator violence. The word "fan" derives from the word "fanatic." As fanatics supporting a particular athlete or team, spectators engage occasionally in three types of violence: rowdyism, riots, and exuberant celebration.

1. *Rowdyism.* This type of spectator violence refers to interpersonal and property vandalism associated with sports contests. Unlike the other forms of spectator violence, rowdyism or hooliganism, as it is sometimes called, occurs regardless of what happens on the field. It refers to hostile acts aimed at whatever targets are handy. Apparently, sports events provide a locale where angry people can congregate and take out their frustrations individually and collectively.

Connected with soccer matches, such behavior has become a major social problem in England (Taylor, 1972) and is a rising concern in the United States. Even at baseball games (where the game itself is essentially nonviolent), spectators have engaged in such outrageous behavior as setting off firecrackers, interrupting the game by running out on the field of play, throwing objects at players, attacking players as they enter or leave the field, pouring beer on injured players, stealing equipment, damaging the stadium, and the like. Fimrite (1974) has provided several possible reasons for the increased incidence of such offensive behavior: (1) increased drinking at games (one ugly incident by rowdy fans occurred at a Cleveland Indians baseball game in 1974 when the management had a 10 cents-per-beer night, selling some 60,000 ten-ounce cups of beer to the 25,134 fans in attendance); (2) we are living in an age of free expression, and youth, especially, are accustomed to venting their emotions; (3) there is a general contempt for the establishment and authority figures; (4) there has been a trend toward a widening breach between the fans and the professional athletes, as the latter demand ever higher salaries and evidence little loyalty to the fans; (5) many professional teams have shown contempt for the fans by moving to other cities where more money can be made. Fimrite's reasons for rowdyism include both societal factors and sport-related factors. Research is needed to determine whether sport is a source of the frustration or just a convenient outlet for its expression.

2. *Sports riots.* Sports-related riots can be divided into two types, depending on the intent of the participants. One type is a celebration whereby the participants exult in a victory by destroying property. A prime example occurred following the New York Mets' improbable winning of the National League pennant. Their fans literally stripped the

stadium of anything they could carry (signs, bases, turf, lumber, seats). The other type of riot, and the one we will emphasize, is characterized by hostility rather than exuberance.

Since sports riots occur in a social and cultural context, we need to examine the specific social structural strains present in the situation that may lead to these riotous episodes (Smith, 1973; 1975). If there are ethnic, political, economical, class, religious, or other cleavages present in the society, then the potential for intergroup conflict is great. In other words collective violence tends to erupt when the representatives of groups already in conflict meet in a sport contest. The following are some examples:

item: a massive brawl with over 500 injuries occurred in 1962 when a lower class school was defeated by an affluent private school in the Washington, D.C., high school championship football game.

item: in 1971 a major outbreak of violence occurred when the predominantly black Camden High School lost to mostly white Bishop Eustace High School of Pennsanken, New Jersey.

item: In the best two-out-of-three soccer match between Honduras and El Salvador in 1969 for the right to represent the region in the World Cup, much rioting took place resulting finally in the severing of diplomatic and commercial relations and in the attack by the El Salvadorean army on the Honduras border. (The soccer matches that resulted in this war were not responsible for the war because the games took place in an atmosphere of great tension and hostility because of a long-standing dispute between the two countries.)

Another structural strain that may lead to sports-related riots is the unavailability of alternate avenues of protest for grievances. As a general rule the more underdeveloped the society industrially, the fewer the channels for expressing grievances. This may explain the relatively widespread existence of violence associated with soccer matches in Latin America. One soccer riot in Lima, Peru, for instance, ended with 293 fans killed and over 500 injured. A reasonable hypothesis is that where the majority of fans are very poor and there are no outlets for expressing grievances, riots will be relatively commonplace. The poor identify strongly with the players who most often come from similar origins. Defeats in important matches, where the fans have a strong emotional attachment, may be an intolerable deprivation by an already deprived group. A typical result is aggression toward the supporters of the opposing team.

Given these structural conditions, riots emerge when a precipitating event occurs. The spark may be violence by players, the antics of the opponents, individual or small-scale spectator fights, or a disputed judgment by an official. As an example of the latter, in 1950 an official was beaten to death by players and fans following his controversial decision in a Buenos Aires soccer match.

In addition to the riots emerging in an already divisive and, therefore, ripe context, there are sports-related riots that are not related to underlying strains in the society. Lewis calls these "issueless" riots in that they are strictly related to the sports event itself. He lists four hypotheses that specify the variables accounting for this type of sports riot (Lewis, 1975: p. 9):

1. The severity of a sports riot varies directly with the importance in the status of the competition, e.g., playoff game or championship game versus a regular season game.
2. The more important the sporting event in terms of traditional rivalries, the greater the severity of the sports riot.
3. There is a direct relationship between the severity of sports riots and the crowd's perception of an officiating error.
4. There is a direct relationship between the violence of sport *per se* and the severity of a sporting riot.

ILLEGITIMATE ATTEMPTS BY NON-ATHLETES TO INFLUENCE THE OUTCOME OF SPORTS CONTESTS

Spectators at a sports contest essentially have two avenues by which to influence the outcome. The method considered appropriate is to support one's team through organized cheers, music, random shouts of encouragement, and various other displays of loyalty. There are also unsportsmanlike or illegitimate means of affecting a game's outcome. Efforts to distract opponents by unusual noises or through racial or ethnic slurs are unacceptable means of support. Also the excessive booing of an opponent or the cheering of an opponent's injury are considered by most persons to be inappropriate actions. Clearly, a contemptible example of foul tactics by spectators is the attempt to harm an opponent physically by throwing objects or by tripping the athlete.

Another form of deviance generated by sport is the corrupting of athletes by individuals interested in fixing the outcome of games to insure gambling profits. A number of scandals from around the world have shown that gamblers have bribed or attempted to bribe athletes either to lose a contest or to manipulate the point spread. The athletes most vulnerable to these attempts are those who participate in individual sports, e.g., boxing and track, or who play at especially crucial positions in team sports, e.g., goalie, field goal kicker, quarterback, pitcher.

DEVIANCE BY PLAYERS, COACHES, AND ADMINISTRATORS

The *sine qua non* of sport is competition. The goal is winning. In the drive to succeed athletes, coaches, and athletic administrators may use illegal and unfair methods. This section will examine three of these illicit activities: drug abuse, cheating, and the corruption of education to accommodate winning teams.

Drug abuse. Aside from the influence of living in a drug-oriented age, the modern athlete is subject to other pressures to take drugs. If one is a marginal athlete, there will be pressures to take drugs in order to make the team. If one is near the top in the sport, the use of drugs may make the winning difference. Finally, drug use may be strictly an act of self-defense because the athlete assumes that his or her opponents are taking drugs to enhance their performances.

The drugs used by athletes can be roughly divided by their function into two categories: restorative and additive (cf., Gilbert, 1969; Scott, 1971). Restorative drugs are used to restore an injured athlete's skill to what it normally would be. Drugs in this category are painkillers, muscle relaxers, and anti-inflammatants. Ordinarily, these drugs are not controversial unless they are given to allow an athlete to participate when medically he should not.

Additive drugs, e.g., amphetamines and anabolic steroids, are used to enhance an athlete's performance beyond his or her normal capacity. There are two fundamental issues with the use of additive drugs: (1) an ethical one involving the artificial stimulation of performance and (2) the physical and psychological damages that can occur.

The ethical issue is clear (Bueter, 1972). Sport is intended to be a competition between athletes for the joy of participation and to determine supremacy on the basis of ability, strategy, and skill. By introducing drugs that artificially enhance performance beyond normal limits, the question is not whether one athlete is better than another, but which one has the better pharmacist—clearly a perversion of the meaning of sport.

The problem is that additive drugs, especially amphetamines, are used commonly by athletes. Amphetamines are stimulants and are used by runners, cyclists, football, basketball, and soccer players to increase endurance, quickness of reactions, speed, and confidence. Although the exact extent of their usage is unknown, there are numerous examples of its use by athletes. At the 1970 world weight lifting championships, for instance, nine of the first twelve medalists were disqualified when urine tests revealed they had taken amphetamines.

In addition to the ethical problem, the negative side effects from the use of additive drugs should preclude their use in sport. The use of amphetamines is dangerous for several reasons. They can be psychologically addictive. Overdoses or regular usage can cause ulcers, cerebral hemorrhage, paranoia, cardiovascular collapse, nutritional problems, aggressive behavior, and irritability (Scott, 1971). By masking fatigue and overstimulating the heart, death is always a possibility as evidenced by the occasional deaths of cyclists in Europe.

Anabolic steroids are male hormones that increase weight and strength. They are used primarily by football linemen, weight lifters, and weightmen in track. Although researchers are unsure, there is a strong indication that these hormones have dangerous side effects such as cancer of the prostate, testicular atrophy, liver damge, and edema.

The use of drugs in sport is probably to be expected in societies that are already drug-oriented and where winners are demanded. The result is the widespread use of uppers, painkillers, and muscle-builders that harm athletes and subvert the ideal of sport.

Cheating. The goal of winning is so important that many athletes and coaches use illegal means to gain unfair advantage over their opponents (c.f., Luschen, 1976). We have noted elsewhere in this paper three types of cheating: illegal recruiting practices by schools, the use of drugs to enhance performance artificially, and manipulation of the point spread. In this section additional illicit modes will be examined, pointing to the wide range of unfair practices that occur in sport.

Cheating in sport takes many forms. For analytical purposes these can be divided into two types: institutional cheating and deviant cheating. Institutional cheating refers to those illegal acts that are, for the most part, accepted as part of the game. Coaches encourage them or look the other way and the enforcers (referees, league commissioners, and rule making bodies) rarely discourage them, impose minimal penalities, or ignore them altogether. This type of cheating is widespread and more prevalent than deviant cheating. Some examples are:

item: Attempts to put the opponent off-balance psychologically through heckling and "gamesmanship."

item: Pretending to be fouled in basketball in order to receive an undeserved free throw and give the opponent an undeserved foul (cf., Ramsey and Deford, 1963).

item: Wrestlers and boxers who dehydrate themselves just prior to a contest in order to fight at a weight lower than their true weight.

item: Using a loophole in the rules to take unfair advantage of an opponent. For example, in 1973 the University of Alabama was playing the University of California in football and had the ball on the California eleven-yard line. Alabama sent in their field goal kicker with a tee, but a player did not leave the field. California countered by sending in its defensive team against the kick. As the huddle broke, the field goal kicker picked up his tee and dashed off the field, leaving the defense at a distinct disadvantage. Alabama scored on the play and the NCAA Rules Committee later declared such plays illegal (in the future) because a team cannot simulate a substitution designed to confuse an opponent.

item: The practice is common in baseball for the home team to "doctor" its field to suit its strengths and minimize the strengths of a particular opponent. A fast team can be neutralized, for example, by slowing down the basepaths.

item: In baseball the application of a foreign substance to the ball in order to disadvantage the hitter has been a common but illegal occurrence.

item: Basketball players are often coached to bump the lower half of a shooter's body because referees are likely to be watching the ball and the upper half of the shooter's body.

item: Offensive linemen in football are typically coached to use special but illegal techniques to hold or trip the opponent without detection.

These commonplace occurrences in sport are cheating because they take unfair advantage of opponents. But they are coached and acceptable practices, and, therefore, what we might call "routinized deviance" or "institutional deviance."

"Deviant" cheating occurs also in sport but is not accepted and is subject to stern punishment. The use of illegal equipment, drugging a race horse, a golfer improving his lie, accepting a bribe, tampering with an opponent's equipment, throwing lime in an opponent's face are but a few examples of this mode of cheating.

An interesting research question is to determine under what conditions cheating of both types is most likely to occur in a contest. Luschen has hypothesized that the probability of cheating increases as: (1) the level of uncertainty of the outcome increases, (2) the amount of the reward for winning increases, and (3) the proportion of participants with lower class origins increases. The bases for this last hypothesis are that the norms and values of sport are essentially those of the middle class and because the poor realistically assess their chances for upward social mobility as relatively limited (Luschen, 1976).

Because cheating occurs, sport should not be disproportionately reprimanded for at least two reasons. First, where cheating is endemic to society, it will also occur in sport. And second, chances are that cheating in sport probably occurs less than in other institutional areas of society. This is because: (1) sport is more visible, (2) sport is closely monitored by various agents of social control, (3) the rules in sport are usually quite explicit, and (4) the penalities for getting caught may deprive the athlete of further participation. Cheating does occur in sport however, and it is largely ignored by officials and often encouraged by coaches. This raises the important question of whether exposure to sport teaches wholesome character traits as it is so often purported to do.

The corruption of higher education. School sports, especially at the intercollegiate level, have become increasingly dominated by high pressure, commercialism, and a philosophy of winning at any cost. These are manifested in a strong tendency for schools in the "big time" or those striving for that level to use illegal recruiting practices and to abuse athletes, physically and psychologically, for the good of the program. In short intercollegiate athletics has in very fundamental ways corrupted the goals and ideals of higher education.

When the pressure to win becomes too great, the result can be a policy of cheating—offering athletes more than the legal limit to lure them to a school. In a 1929 report the Carnegie Foundation decried the widespread illegal recruiting practices of American colleges and universities (Savage, 1929). Not only has the problem continued, but it has intensified because the economic rewards for winning are now so much greater than fifty years ago. A losing season can mean a considerable loss of alumni contributions as well as gate receipts. When the Ohio State football team went from a 7-2 record in 1965 to 4-5 the next year, alumni contributions dropped by almost $500,000. Conversely, a winning team can dramatically aid a program financially, as evidenced by the contributions in excess of $1 million to North Carolina State's athletic scholarship fund after that school won the 1974 NCAA basketball championship (Denlinger and Shapiro, 1975).

The extent of recruiting irregularities is unknown. A reasonable speculation is that recent scandals involving such schools as Long Beach State, Southwest Louisiana, Minnesota, Oklahoma, and Michigan State are only the visible portion of the iceberg.

A 1974 survey by the National Association of Basketball Coaches said that one of every eight major colleges made illegal offers to prospects, that all the cheaters were offering money, 80 percent were offering cars, and more than half were offering clothing. The survey was conducted among 25 recently graduated college players, 25 current high school standouts, 25 sets of parents, and 25 athletic directors of major college basketball programs. Of the 50 players interviewed, 40 per cent said they had received illegal offers (Denlinger and Shapiro, 1975: p. 42).

In addition to the illegal offering of material things, coaches have also altered transcripts to insure an athlete's eligibility, had substitutes take admissions tests for athletes of marginal educational ability, provided jobs for parents, paid athletes for nonexistent jobs, illegally used government work-studies monies for athletes, and the like. Clearly, such behaviors not only corrupt coaches and athletes alike, but they demean the ideals of higher education.

In such a climate athletes are bound to become cynical about their education. Coaches proclaim that their athletes are students first and only secondarily athletes. This is the typical recruiting speech to prospects and their parents. But in practice the reverse often is true. The athlete has signed a contract and is paid for his athletic services. He is an employee and the relationship between a coach and his athlete is essentially that of employer-employee. Athletes are often counseled to take easy courses whether or not such courses fit their educational needs. Because the demands on athletes' time are so great in the season, they frequently must take a somewhat reduced course load, which means they will not usually graduate in the normal amount of time. Study halls and tutors are frequently available, even required, for college athletes, but their primary function is to insure athletic eligibility, not necessarily the education of the athlete. If the athlete achieves an education in the process, it is incidental to the overriding objective of a winning athletic program.

Some coaches, in their zeal to be successful, are also guilty of behaviors that brutalize and demean their athletes—actions that in other contexts would not be tolerated. The common charge of critics of these practices is that athletes have become tools of the schools. The athlete is dehumanized as he works endless hours to develop machinelike precision. He is dehumanized as coaches demean and belittle him in an effort to increase his performance. The athlete is dehumanized further when he is forced to participate in incredibly rigorous conditioning drills or in drills designed to get marginal players to quit in humiliation and pain (Shaw, 1972; Putnam, 1973).

The athlete is also dehumanized by being treated as a perpetual adolescent, as someone who cannot be trusted. Ironically, this control of the athlete occurs at the very time that the myth is perpetuated by schools and coaches alike that participation in sports teaches one to be self-disciplined, mature, and responsible (Sauer, 1971: pp. 24–27).

The sociological explanation for cheating, hypocrisy, brutality, and authoritarianism by some coaches lies not in their individual psyches but in the intensely competitive system within which they operate. In

American society the success or failure of a team is believed by most persons to rest with the coach. This pressure to win brings some coaches to use illegal inducements to attract athletes to their school, to teach their linemen to hold without getting caught, or to look the other way when athletes (who face the same pressures to succeed) use drugs to enhance their performances. The absolute necessity to win also explains why some coaches drive their players so hard. Thus, what some persons might label brutality has been explained by some coaches as a necessity to get the maximum effort from players (Edwards, 1973: pp. 135–141).

The abuses of athletes have occurred at some of America's most prominent universities. The administrators at these schools have tended to avoid careful scrutiny of their programs because winning and the money and prestige that come in its wake are considered so important. As long as the coaches win games and avoid getting caught in illegal activities, then administrators will not fire or even censure them. The players in such a situation, if they are relatively conscious, must realize that they are just pieces of machinery to be used, abused, and, when worn out or broken, replaced for the good of the school. Clearly, schools that allow such practices to exist have prostituted their ideals for the sake of the prestige and money that accrues from a winning athletic program.

CONCLUSION

Sport is not an island of purity—a privileged sanctuary from real life. That myth must be put aside (Cosell, 1971). Sport is a reflection of society. It has within it the same maladies as the society in which it resides. If the society is beset with problems of poverty, racism, and other cleavages, then sports contests will not be just a means of escape but also will be an occasional battleground. If violence rages in a society, then sport will also be afflicted with it. If politicians and businessmen seek the grail of success via any means, then players and coaches will also succumb to these pressures and use drugs, bribes, and illegal recruiting to insure success.

To stress that sport mirrors society neither excuses sport nor justifies the wrongdoings that are common to it and society. Sport needs reform. School sports need to be put in perspective and promoted for their educational values. The original purpose of sport—the pleasure in the activity—needs to be recaptured. Sportsmanship must be a universal goal. Unfair competition is the enemy of true sport. And while the reform of sport is a laudable goal, it is a futile effort without concomitant efforts to change the other institutions of society.

REFERENCES

"Athletics and Education: Are They Compatible?", the entire issue of *Phi Delta Kappan*, 56 (October 1974).

Bueter, Robert J., "The Use of Drugs in Sports: An Ethical Perspective," *The Christian Century*, 89 (April 5, 1972), pp. 394–398.

Cosell, Howard, "Sports and Good-by to All That," *New York Times* (April 5, 1971), p. 33.

Denlinger, Kenneth, and Leonard Shapiro, *Athletes for Sale: An Investigation into America's Greatest Sports Scandal—Athletic Recruiting*, (New York: Thomas Y. Crowell, 1975).

Edwards, Harry, *Sociology of Sport* (Homewood, Illinois: The Dorsey Press, 1973).

Elias, Norbert, and Eric Dunning, "The Quest for Excitement in Unexciting Societies," *The Cross-Cultural Analysis of Sport and Games*, ed. Gunther Luschen (Champaign, Illinois: Stipes Publishing Company, 1970), pp. 31–51.

Fimrite, Ron, "Take Me Out to the Brawl Game," *Sports Illustrated* (June 17, 1974), pp. 10–13.

Geen, R., and L. Berkowitz, "Name-mediated Aggressive Cue Properties," *Journal of Personality* 34 (1966), pp. 456–465.

Gilbert, Bil, "Drugs in Sport," *Sports Illustrated* (June 23, 1969), pp. 64–72; (June 30, 1969), pp. 30–42; (July 7, 1969), pp. 30–35.

Goldstein, Jeffrey H., and Robert L. Arms, "Effects of Observing Athletic Contests on Hostility," *Sociometry*, 34 (March, 1971), pp. 83–90.

Hanford, George H., *The Need for and Feasibility of a National Study of Intercollegiate Athletics*, (Washington, D.C.: American Council on Education, 1974).

Kennedy, Ray, "Wanted: An End to Mayhem," *Sports Illustrated* (November 17, 1975), pp. 17–21.

Koval, John P., "Football as a Social Festival: A Video-Tape Essay," presented at the Annual Meeting of the Midwest Sociological Society, Omaha, Nebraska (April 1973).

Lewis, Jerry M., "Sports Riots: Some Research Questions," paper presented at the annual meetings of the American Sociological Association, San Francisco, August 1975.

Luschen, Gunther, "Cheating in Sport," *Social Problems in Athletics*, ed. Daniel M. Landers (Urbana: University of Illinois Press, 1976), pp. 67–77.

McMurtry, William R., *Investigation and Inquiry into Violence in Amateur Hockey*, Report to the Ontario Minister of Community and Social Services, Toronto, 1974.

Putnam, Pat, "A Case of Volunteer—or Else," *Sports Illustrated* (July 23, 1973), pp. 22–25.

Ramsey, Frank and Frank Deford, "Smart Moves by a Master of Deception," *Sports Illustrated* (December 9, 1963), pp. 57–63.

Sauer, George, "Interview by Jack Scott with George Sauer on the Reason for Sauer's Retirement from Professional Football While at the Height of His Career," (Hayward, California: California State College, Department of Physical Education, 1971).

Savage, Howard J., *American College Athletics* (New York: The Carnegie Foundation for the Advancement of Teaching, Bulletin 23, 1929).

Scott, Jack, "It's Not How You Play the Game, But What Pill You Take," *The New York Times Magazine* (October 17, 1971), pp. 40-41, 106-109.

Shaw, Gary, *Meat on the Hoof: The Hidden World of Texas Football* (New York: St. Martin's, 1972).

Sipes, Richard, "War, Sports and Aggression: An Empirical Test of Two Rival Theories," *American Anthropologist*, 75 (February 1973), pp. 64-86.

Smith, Michael D., "Hostile Outbursts in Sport," *Sport Sociology Bulletin*, 2 (Spring 1973), pp. 6-10.

Smith, Michael D., "Significant Others' Influence on the Assaultive Behavior of Young Hockey Players," *International Review of Sport Sociology*, 9 (1974), pp. 45-56.

Smith, Michael, D., "Sport and Collective Violence," *Sport and Social Order: Contributions to the Sociology of Sport*, eds. Donald W. Ball and John W. Loy (Reading, Massachusetts: Addison-Wesley, 1975), pp. 281-330.

Surface, Bill, "Pro Football: Is It Getting Too Dirty?" *Reader's Digest* (November, 1974), pp. 151-154.

Tandy, Ruth E. and Joyce Laflin, "Aggression and Sport: Two Theories," *JOHPER* 44 (June 1973), pp. 19-20.

Taylor, Ian, "'Football Mad': A Speculative Sociology of Football Hooliganism," *Sport: Readings from a Sociological Perspective*, Eric Dunning (ed.), (Toronto: University of Toronto Press, 1972), pp. 352-377.

Turner, Edward T., "The Effects of Viewing College Football, Basketball and Wrestling on the Elicited Aggressive Responses of Male Spectators, *Contemporary Psychology of Sport*, Gerald Kenyon (ed.), (Chicago: The Athletic Institute, 1968), pp. 325-328.

■ FOR FURTHER STUDY

Angell, Roger. *The Summer Game*. New York: Viking, 1972.

Angell, Roger. *Five Seasons*. New York: Popular Library, 1978.

Axthelm, Peter. *The City Game*. New York: Harper's Magazine Press, 1970.

Blanchard, Kendall. "Basketball and the Culture-Change Process: The Rimrock Navajo Case." *Council on Anthropology Education Quarterly*, 4 (November 1974), 8-13.

Blanchard, Kendall A. "Team Sports and Social Organization Among the Mississippi Choctaw." *Tennessee Anthropologist* 1 (1975), 63-70.

Boyle, Robert H. *Sport: Mirror of American Life*. Boston: Little, Brown, 1963.

Brailsford, Dennis. *Sport and Society: Elizabeth to Anne*. Toronto: University of Toronto Press, 1969.

Coakley, Jay J. *Sport in Society: Issues and Controversies*. St. Louis: C. V. Mosby, 1978, pp. 15-35, 63-93.

Cozens, Frederick, and Florence Stumpf. *Sports in American Life*. Chicago: University of Chicago Press, 1953.

Durso, Joseph. *The All-American Dollar: The Big Business of Sports*. Boston: Houghton Mifflin, 1971.

Edwards, Harry. *Sociology of Sport*. Homewood, Illinois: Dorsey, 1973, pp. 84-130.

Edwards, Harry, and Van Rackages. "The Dynamics of Violence in American Sport: Some Promising Structural and Social Considerations." *Journal of Sport and Social Issues,* 1 (Summer/Fall 1977) 3–31.

Eitzen, D. Stanley, and George H. Sage. *Sociology of American Sport.* Dubuque, Iowa: Wm. C. Brown, 1978, pp. 14–16.

Felshin, Jan. "Sport Style and Social Modes." JOPER, 46 (March 1975), 31–34.

Fox, J. R. "Pueblo Baseball: A New Use for Old Witchcraft." *Journal of American Folklore* (January 1961), pp. 9–16.

Gilbert, Bil. "Gleanings from a Troubled Time." *Sports Illustrated* (December 25, 1972), pp. 34–46.

Goldstein, Jeffrey H., and Robert L. Arms. "Effects of Observing Athletic Contests on Hostility." *Sociometry,* 34 (March 1971), 83–90.

Guttman, Allen. *From Ritual to Record: The Return of Modern Sports.* New York: Columbia University Press, 1978.

Haerle, Rudolf K., Jr. "Heroes, Success Themes, and Basic Cultural Values in Baseball Autobiographies: 1900–1970." Paper presented at the Third National Meeting of the Popular Culture Association, Indianapolis, 1973.

Hall, Donald. "Baseball Country: A Land of Change and Deja Vu." *New York Times* (October 24, 1976), p. 2S.

Hoch, Paul. *Rip Off the Big Game: The Exploitation of Sports by the Power Elite.* Garden City, New York: Doubleday Anchor, 1972.

Jenkins, Dan. *Saturday's America.* Boston: Little, Brown, 1971.

Kahn, Roger. *The Boys of Summer.* New York: Harper & Row, 1972.

Kanfer, Stefan. "Football: Show Business with a Kick." *Time* (October 8, 1973), pp. 54, 57.

Kenyon, Gerald S. "Sport and Society: At Odds or in Concert." *Athletics in America.* Edited by Arnold Flath. Corvallis, Oregon: Oregon State University Press, pp. 34–41.

Koppett, Leonard. *The Essence of the Game is Deception.* Boston: Little, Brown, 1973.

Kramer, Jerry, ed. *Lombardi: Winning Is the Only Thing.* New York: World, 1970.

Lahr, John. "The Theatre of Sports." *Evergreen Review,* 13 (November 1969), 39–76.

Lever, Janet. "Soccer as a Brazilian Way of Life." *Games, Sport, and Power.* Edited by Gregory Stone. New Brunswick, N.J.: Transaction, 1972.

Lewis, George H. "Prole Sport: The Case of Roller Derby." *Side-Saddle on the Golden Calf: Social Structure and Popular Culture in America.* Edited by George H. Lewis. Pacific Palisades, Calif.: Goodyear, 1972, pp. 42–49.

L'Heureux, W. J. "Sport in Modern Canadian Culture." *JOPER,* 35 (March 1964), 28–29, 61.

Luschen, Gunther. "The Interdependence of Sport and Culture." *International Review of Sport Sociology,* 2 (1967), 27–41.

McIntosh, P. C. *Sport in Society.* London: C. A. Watts, 1963.

McLuhan, Marshall. *Understanding Media: The Extensions of Man.* New York: McGraw-Hill, 1964, pp. 234–245.

Mead, Margaret. "The Pattern of Leisure in Contemporary American Culture." *The Annals of the American Academy of Political and Social Science* (September 1957), pp. 11–15.

Michener, James A. *Sports in America.* New York: Random House, 1976, pp. 420–443.

Morgan, Thomas B. "The American War Game." *Esquire*, 64 (October 1965), 68–72, 141–148.

Morton, H. W. *Soviet Sport*. New York: Collier Books, 1963.

Natan, A. *Sport and Society*. London: Bowes and Bowes, 1958.

Nixon, Howard L. *Sport and Social Organization*. Indianapolis: Bobbs-Merrill, 1976, pp. 9–28.

Norflus, David. "Baseball: A Mirror of Japanese Society." *Arena Newsletter*, 1 (October 1977), 9–12.

Parrish, Bernie. *They Call It a Game*. New York: Dial, 1971.

Ramsey, Frank, with Frank Deford. "Smart Moves by a Master of Deception." *Sports Illustrated* (December 9, 1963), pp. 57–63.

Riesman, David, and Reuel Denney. "Football in America: A Study of Cultural Diffusion." *American Quarterly*, 3 (Winter 1951), 109–319.

Roberts, J. M., M. J. Arth, and R. R. Bush. "Games in Culture." *American Anthropologist*, 61 (August 1959), 597–605.

Roberts, J. M., and Brian Sutton-Smith. "Child Training and Game Involvement." *Ethnology*, 1 (April 1962), 166–185.

Sadler, William A., Jr. "Competition Out of Bounds: Sport in American Life." *Quest*, 19 (January 1973), 124–132.

Sage, George H. "Sport in American Society: Its Pervasiveness and its Study." *Sport and American Society*. 2nd ed. Edited by George H. Sage. Reading, Mass.: Addison-Wesley, 1974, pp. 5–15.

Scotch, N. A. "Magic, Sorcery, and Football Among Urban Zulu: A Case of Reinterpretation Under Acculturation." *Journal of Conflict Resolution* (March 1961), pp. 70–74.

Seppanen, Paavo. "The Role of Competitive Sports in Different Societies." Paper delivered at the Seventh World Congress of Sociology, Varna, Bulgaria, September 14–18, 1970.

Smith, Michael D. "Hockey Violence: Interring Some Myths." *Sport Psychology: An Analysis of Athletic Behavior*. Edited by William F. Straub. Ithaca, N.Y.: Movement Publications, 1978, pp. 141–146.

Stone, Gregory. "Some Meanings of American Sport." *60th Proceedings of the College Physical Education Association*. Washington, D.C.: American Association for Health, Physical Education, and Recreation, 1957, pp. 6–29.

Tandy, Ruth E., and Joyce Laflin. "Aggression and Sport: Two Theories." *JOPER*, 44 (June 1973), 19–20.

Voigt, David O. "Reflections on Diamonds: Baseball and American Culture." *Journal of Sport History*, 1 (Spring 1974), 3–25.

Will, George F. "Is That a Red Dog in the Seam?" *Newsweek* (September 6, 1976), p. 72.

Wolfe, Tom. "Clean Fun at Riverhead." *Side-Saddle on the Golden Calf: Social Structure and Popular Culture in America*. Edited by George H. Lewis. Pacific Palisades, California: Goodyear, 1972, pp. 37–42.

Zimmerman, Paul. *A Thinking Man's Guide to Pro Football*. New York: Dutton, 1971.

Zurcher, Louis A., and Arnold Meadow. "On Bullfights and Baseball: An Example of Interaction of Social Institutions." *International Journal of Comparative Sociology* (March 1967), pp. 99–117.

Three

Sport, Values, and Society

The theme of the last unit—that sport is a microcosm of society— is buttressed further by the articles in this section, which show that a close relationship between American sport and American values exists. But this unit goes beyond the last one by demonstrating how sport is a primary vehicle through which youth are socialized to accept and internalize American values. Thus, sport is viewed as the darling of the conservatives and the culprit of radicals.

Let us begin by defining values and briefly describing the American values related to sport. Americans constantly evaluate other people, ideas, and objects. They consider some to be correct, good, worthy, or moral while others are believed to be wrong, bad, unworthy, or immoral. The culturally prescribed criteria used to make these judgments are values.[1]

The primary American value is success through individual achievement.[2] The self-made person is highly esteemed. So, too, is the competitor who wins. Americans believe that competition is the one quality that has made their society great because it motivates individuals and groups to strive for great accomplishments rather than being content with the status quo. Sport epitomizes the drive to succeed through competitive situations. Only winners are glorified. Some quotes from NFL coaches exemplify this emphasis on winning:

"Winning is not everything. It is the only thing." (Vince Lombardi)

"Every time you win, you're reborn; when you lose, you die a little." (George Allen)

"No one ever learns anything by losing." (Don Shula)

Americans demand winners in school, business, politics, and sports.

90

To lose, regardless of the degree, is failure ("Show me a good loser and I'll show you a loser"). In sport coaches and general managers are fired if they lose, and players are traded, sold, or otherwise eliminated in the search for the winning team. Clearly, winning supersedes humane considerations, a common occurrence in a capitalistic society.

Three values are believed to guarantee success in American society: hard work, continual striving, and deferred gratification. By implication, if one fails, it is because he or she has not worked hard enough, or long enough, or sacrificed enough. By this logic, and it is typical of Americans, the poor are losers because they deserve to be.

In sport, as in the larger society, the goal of individual achievement in competitive situations must be accomplished through continuous hard work and sacrifice. The work ethic translated into the sport ethic is seen in these coaching cliches:

"A hundred percent is not enough."
"Every day you waste you can never make up."
"No one ever drowned in sweat."
"The will to win is the will to work."

Americans also are not content with the present. They strive to improve themselves. They want to conquer nature, improve technology, increase profits, and set new records. The pressure on athletes to constantly improve their performances is tremendous. Athletes, coaches, owners, and schools feel this pressure from the fans, the press, and even from themselves.

Americans also believe that hard work pays off materially. Success can be achieved by outdoing all others, but it is often difficult to know exactly the extent of one's success, so economic barometers (income, wealth, possessions) often become the measures of personal worth. Thus, Americans value material things. Sport provides an excellent example of this emphasis. There is the obvious accent on making money. The contemporary athlete hires a lawyer to negotiate the highest possible bonus and salary arrangements. In 1978 David Thompson signed a new contract with the Denver Nuggets for $800,000 a season, making him the highest paid athlete on a professional team. But this huge amount pales in comparison to the $5.75 million (1977) yearly income of Muhammad Ali. Athletes, like Americans in other occupations, are impressed with high salaries. Money has become more important than loyalty to one's team or the fans of that team, a fact that is lamented by former professional basketball player Tom Meschery:

There was a time, and it was not so long ago, when things such as honor and loyalty were virtues in sport, and not objects of ridicule. It was a time when athletes drew pleasure and satisfaction from the essence of competition, not just from their paychecks. But somehow, with the introduction of big business, the concept of sports in this country has changed. The business psyche has invaded basketball and has made the players nothing but businessmen spurred by the profit motive. In some cases players make more money with their outside financial activities than they do on the court. Their sport becomes a mere showcase to keep them before the public, like an actor's guest appearance on a television talk show. The game no longer has its roots into idealistic bedrock. It's just business: nine to five.[3]

The quest for more money is also evidenced among team owners and colleges who have almost literally sold their souls to television. They allow television to rearrange their schedules and even to dictate time-outs and the like, all for the lucrative contracts. (Each NFL team receives more than $5 million annually in television money, insuring a profit whether fans attend the games or not.)

Fans, too, are enamored by the materialistic side of sport. They like plush stadiums, scoreboards with instant replays, water displays, and fireworks. Their interest in sporting events is also enhanced by the knowledge that the players are playing for high stakes, e.g., the difference between first and second place in a golf tournament may be as much as $30,000.

A final American value that is exemplified in sports is external conformity. As American society has become more urban and bureaucratic, there has been an increased demand for people to conform. To escape anarchy, rules must be followed. This value is found especially in team sports. Coaches tend to be stern disciplinarians, demanding that their athletes conform to their standards, which typically are conservative, and submission of the individual to the team is total.

The two selections in this unit show the reciprocal relationship between sport and values in several ways. The first article, by sociologist Eldon Snyder, shows how coaches explicitly seek to inculcate American values in their athletes by placing sayings, cliches, and proverbs consistent with these values in their locker rooms.

The second essay is by theologian Robert Bueter. It was written when American values were being questioned by the counterculture. It contrasts the Lombardi dictum that "winning is the only thing" with the new values espoused by critics of sport such as Jack Scott and Dave Meggyesy, leaders of the Athletic Revolution. The insight of this essay is that American society and its values are in transition.

NOTES

1. D. Stanley Eitzen, *In Conflict and Order: Understanding Society* (Boston: Allyn and Bacon, 1978), chapter 4.

2. Cf., Robin Williams, Jr., *American Society: A Sociological Interpretation*, 3rd ed. (New York: Alfred A. Knopf, 1970), pp. 438–504; and D. Stanley Eitzen and George H. Sage, *Sociology of American Sport* (Dubuque, Iowa: Wm. C. Brown, 1978), chapter 3.

3. Tom Meschery, "There is a Disease in Sports Now," *Sports Illustrated* (October 2, 1972), p. 56. See also, Bob Briner, "Making Sport of Us All," *Sports Illustrated* (December 10, 1973), pp. 36–42; and Bill Surface, "In Pro Sports, the Dollar is King," *Reader's Digest* (March, 1972), pp. 146–149.

Athletic Dressing Room Slogans as Folklore: A Means of Socialization

ELDON E. SNYDER

Sports and athletic contests are an important social and prestige granting activity within the context of school systems, particularly at the secondary school level (Coleman, 1961, 1965; Snyder, 1969). These activities also represent a potential medium of socialization whereby cultural values become internalized (Helanko, 1957; Cowell, 1960; Kenyon, 1968; Schafter and Armer, 1968; Ulrich, 1968; Snyder, 1970). Roberts and Sutton-Smith (1962, pp. 181–182) view games as "just one part of a cultural participation scale that varies from dreams at one end to full-scale cultural behavior at the other. At the beginning of childhood there are presumably individual dreams and solitary play. As the child develops, these find a matching in such cultural models as songs, dances, folktales, poems, programs, riddles, rhymes, and games". An extension of the Roberts-Sutton-Smith scale would place organized sports at an extreme position beyond games in the degree of cultural participation. Additional studies have considered the interrelationship between sports and the socio-cultural context in which they are embedded (Sutton-Smith, Roberts, and Kozelka, 1963; Lüschen, 1967; Loy and Kenyon, 1969). Implicit in this research is that the general value orientations of the socio-cultural system are distilled in the normative structure of the society and through socialization become internalized by individuals. Agencies and agents of socialization, including sports and athletic coaches, are important in this socialization process.

LeMasters (1970, pp. 221–222) has outlined several models of socialization used in our society and the following model is a modification of the athletic coach model he described:

(1) *Physical Fitness.* The players must be physically fit for the contest. This involves not only vigorous physical activity but also abstention or moderation in smoking, drinking, late hours, and so on.

(2) *Mental Fitness.* The athlete must be psychologically fit—that is, he

---

SOURCE: Eldon E. Snyder, "Athletic Dressing Room Slogans as Folklore: A Means of Socialization," *International Review of Sport Sociology*, 7 (1972), 89–102.

must have confidence in his ability and a feeling that he can compete successfully.

(3) *Knowledge of the Game.* The player must know the rules of the game and the penalty for violating them. At times he may knowingly and deliberately violate the rules—but only after calculating the chances of getting caught and the potential gain if he is not caught.

(4) *Basic Skills and Techniques Must Be Painfully Learned.* There are no "born" star athletes—they may be born with potential but only hard work will permit them to realize that potential. A player that refuses to practice, no matter how gifted, will not be tolerated on the squad.

(5) *The Player Must Have Stamina.* He must not give up or reduce his effort—even when he is tired. As Woody Hayes, coach of the Ohio State football team, once said: "Victory in football means getting up one more time than your opponent does."[1]

(6) *Aggressiveness and Competitive Spirit.* The athlete must desire to compete and to win. There are no "happy losers" among first-rate athletes or their coaches.

(7) *The Player Must Accept Strict Discipline.* Regardless of his status on the team—star or substitute—each player must submit to strict discipline. Violation of basic regulations usually results in suspension or dismissal from the squad.

(8) *Subordination of Self to the Success of the Team.* Each player is expected to put the success of the team ahead of his personal glory. Failure to do this not only brings repercussions from the coach but also from the other players.

The athletic coach model outlines the value orientations that are primary objectives of the socialization process provided by sports. An implied theme of this model is that, while the athletic contest is more specific than "the game of life", it nevertheless contributes to this ultimate objective. Goffman (1969, p. 68) has stated, "that games give the players an opportunity to exhibit attributes valued in the wider social world, such as dexterity, strength, knowledge, intelligence, courage, and self-control". And Loy (1968, p. 11) noted that sports provide an even more formalized instruction than games for the learning of such skills and knowledge as described by Goffman. The value orientations presented by LeMasters were utilized as motifs for classifying the slogans as folklore genres presented in this paper.

I

A fundamental characteristic of the frame of reference for games and sports contests is that the outcome is uncertain. In fact, the fun and excitement associated with games is dependent upon the outcome being problematic (Caillois, 1961, pp. 7-8, 68-69; Loy, 1968 pp. 2-3; Goffman,

1961, pp. 66–69). Coaches frequently remind themselves and their players that they must not become overconfident of winning ("In this league, on any given night, any team can defeat any other team".), and thus, the coaches are admonishing their players to put forth an extreme effort in preparing for, and playing, the game.

While the outcome of sports contests is uncertain, the winning of them is considered by both the coach and players as extremely important. Consistent losses by the team will threaten the coach's self-esteem and perhaps his coaching position, and the players are likely to suffer the loss of status gratification and prestige they receive from family and friends. Furthermore, the coach-player relationship is reciprocal and intense in the sense that players have voluntarily submitted to the coach's control and the coach has, in turn, selected his players.

It is within this context that the practice of coaches putting slogans on the athletic dressing room walls is meaningful. The folklore genres of the slogans represent proverbial phrases, and in some cases, boasts, taunts, and commands. They are used as part of the coach's strategy to affect the players' performance. The slogans define for the players the model of behavior expected of them by the coach with an emphasis on the development of physical, social-psychological, and social attributes that will contribute to winning ball games.

Thus, these genres are instrumental social control mechanisms that use persuasion to bring about cohesion, cooperation, and normative behavior among the players which will presumably improve the team's chances of victory (thus instituting a greater degree of control over the problematic outcome of the game). Additional folklore genres frequently associated with athletic contests include the techniques outlined by Abrahams (1968b) for dealing with problematic situations; these include blessings, curses, prayers, spells, charms, and superstitions. (For example, in the survey of basketball coaches and players from which the slogans presented in the present paper were collected, 61 percent of the coaches and 53 percent of the players indicated that the team always or often had prayer before or during the game.) We would expect that where the socializer and socializee voluntarily participate in the socialization process the participants will be highly motivated and receptive to behavioral changes.

Because athletic teams interact and share experiences together under conditions of close and personal contact for a season, and often for several seasons, traditional in-group expressions in the form of slogans and maxims develop which have the effect of promoting team identification and solidarity (Jansen, 1959). The esoteric-exoteric nature of these slogans will vary from having significance to a specific team situation to a level of generality that includes most males, who have participated in sports (athletic subculture) and in some cases all or most members of the society.

II

In the spring of 1969, with the cooperation of the Ohio Association for Health, Physical Education and Recreation, the author drew a systematic sample of 270 Ohio high schools, one-third of the high schools affiliated with this organization. The sample included a representative cross-section of the schools that participate in basketball in the state. A questionnaire was sent to the basketball coach and two basketball team members from each of the 270 schools; 64.5 percent of the coaches and 50 percent of the players responded to the survey. Responses showed that 70.9 percent of the coaches and 60.9 percent of the players indicated that slogans or statements were put up on the dressing room walls by the coaches. The folklore genres listed below were the slogans and statements provided by the coaches and players to an open-ended item on the survey.

Athletic Dressing Room Slogans Collected from High School Basketball Coaches and Players in Ohio

(Numbers in parentheses indicate the frequency the slogan was listed when listed more than once)

Coaches	Players
1. PHYSICAL FITNESS	1. PHYSICAL FITNESS
	(2) It's easier to stay in shape than to get in shape.
	How well conditioned is the man next to you?
	Good training makes a good athlete.
2. MENTAL FITNESS	2. MENTAL FITNESS
(9) Pride	(5) Pride
(2) Attitude starts with an "A". It comes first.	(3) Dedication
Mental toughness	Mental toughness
Don't be discouraged by your size, champions come in all sizes.	It's all in the state of the mind.
I can do all things through Him who strengtheneth me.	Alertness/hard work = a winner.
	You always become tired mentally before physically.

People are like elevators, they come up after having come down.

It can be done.

Think

It takes a cool head to win a hot game.

Each boy assumes that he has certain limits to his ability; usually this assumed limit is not sufficient to carry out his assignments.

Dedication

Dedication and devotion are keys to success.

You're as good as you want to be

Few games are won in the dressing room.

Think

The guy who complains about the way the ball bounces usually dropped it.

The mark of a true champion is the one who can conquer the fear of making mistakes.

3. KNOWLEDGE OF THE GAME

(2) The team that controls the rebounds controls the game.

Rebound

Defense is fun.

Defense, run, shoot.

Be proud to play defense.

A basket saved is a basket made.

Great players are recognized by their movements, not by their numbers.

Keep on your toes and you won't get caught flatfooted.

Knowledge makes for confidence.

The team that makes the fewest mistakes wins.

Only a fool fouls.

3. KNOWLEDGE OF THE GAME

(5) Defense

(2) Great players are recognized by their movements, not by their numbers.

He who controlleth the backboard controlleth the game.

A basket saved is a basket made.

Beat the boards.

Dribble high for speed and low for control.

Good guys don't win.

A rebound is your chance to score.

Rebound as if you owned the ball.

Position your man.

4. BASIC SKILLS AND TECHNIQUES MUST BE PAINFULLY LEARNED

(4) Valuable things in life don't come free, are you willing to pay the price?

(3) Practice makes perfect.

(3) The will to win is the will to work.

(3) Champions don't just happen.

4. BASIC SKILLS AND TECHNIQUES MUST BE PAINFULLY LEARNED

(4) The harder I work the luckier I get.

(3) Success is 99 percent perspiration and 1 percent inspiration.

(2) Want to be a champion? Then work, practice, practice, practice.

(2) When you're through improving you're through.

(2) To whomever much is given, much is also required.

I believe in luck and the harder I work the luckier I get.

No one ever drowned in sweat.

If what you did yesterday still looks big today then you haven't done much today.

By failing to prepare yourself you are preparing to fail.

Practice like you plan to perform in a game.

Why practice hard and lose?

It takes hard work to be good, and if we are not good, we have no one to blame but ourselves.

Winners are workers.

Where there's a will there's a way.

Are you better than yesterday?

Nothing is successful until accomplished.

Good luck is what happens when preparation meets opportunity.

Good, better, best; never let it rest until your good is better and your better best.

(2) No one ever drowned in sweat.

(2) Practice makes perfect.

(2) Winners are made, not born.

When you're through improving you're through.

If you can't put out, get out.

All you put in a sport is all you get out of it.

If you don't intend to improve tonight, don't come.

The movements perfect in practice will come by reflex in the big game.

The way you practice is the way you play.

There is no substitute for hard work.

Basketball is my business, and if you want to play it, it must be your business, too.

5. THE PLAYERS MUST HAVE STAMINA

(4) Give 100 percent or get out.

(2) It takes courage to excel and excel we must.

We issue everything but guts.

The heart carries the feet.

I feel a player is not tired until he falls to the floor without the strength to catch himself with his hands.

5. THE PLAYERS MUST HAVE STAMINA

(4) We supply everything but guts.

(3) Play your 100 percent.

(2) Never stop trying.

If you have not given 110 percent of yourself get back on the court.

If you come to the end of your rope, tie a knot and

Do your best. Did you do your best?

Anyone can be ordinary but it takes guts to excel.

Desire wins ball games.

Be good or be gone.

Determination, guts, desire, attitude.

Any hag can start but it takes a thoroughbred to finish.

hang on.

They'll be ready, will you?

It's easy to be ordinary but it takes guts to excel and excel we must.

It takes courage to excel and excel we must.

Guts

Always go just a little further.

It's better to wear out than to rust out.

Give all you can.

Make something happen.

Lazy feet cause fouls.

Everyone has a breaking point.

You've won—straight, don't break the streak.

The seniors have given up, how about the juniors?

When the ball goes the wrong way, hustle all the harder and turn on the steam.

A gentleman winning is getting up one more time.

6. AGGRESSIVENESS AND COMPETI-
TIVE SPIRIT

(18) A quitter never wins, a winner never quits.

(16) When the going gets tough, the tough get going.

(6) Desire

(5) Winning isn't everything, it's the only thing.

(3) Winning beats anything that comes in second.

(2) How tall is your hustle?

(2) The will to win will win.

(2) Hustle: you can't survive without it.

(2) Give me five men who hate to lose and I'll give you a winner.

(2) Hustle.

It's not the size of the dog in the fight, but the size of the

6. AGGRESSIVENESS AND COMPETI-
TIVE SPIRIT

(34) A quitter never wins, a winner never quits.

(23) When the going gets tough, the tough get going.

(9) Hustle

(6) Winning isn't everything, it's the only thing.

(3) Winning is everything, but losing is nothing.

(2) Win.

(2) Give me five men who hate to lose and I will have a winner.

(2) Winning is the second step, wanting to is the first step.

(2) You are only as good as you make yourself.

(2) We don't want excuses, we want results.

fight in the dog.

Aim for the stars.

Will the opponent see a lot of you tonight?

Be a winner.

Never be willing to be second best.

Don't be detoured to the top.

Nothing great was ever achieved without enthusiasm.

The team that can't be beaten won't be beaten.

We aim high to achieve goals.

If you miss will you come pretty close anyhow?

You must win to receive recognition.

Nice guys don't win ballgames.

They ask not how you played the game but whether you won or lost.

The greatest aim in life is to succeed.

The determination to succeed is more important than any other single thing.

If you did your best, you won.

Why gripe? Fight.

Be a doer not a tryer.

Don't wait for the breaks, make them.

Man shows what he *is* by what he *does.*

This is bulldog country.

No one likes a loser.

He who tries, doesn't; he who does, does.

Give them nothing.

When they are drowning throw them an anchor.

(2) To explain a triumph, start with the first syllable.

Hustle and desire make a winning team.

We will win.

The difference between winning and losing is hustle.

It's not the size of the dog in the fight, but the size of the fight in the dog.

Aim for the stars and if you don't reach them you'll land pretty high anyway.

Be a champ.

If it doesn't matter if you win or lose, why keep score?

You can have whatever you want.

Nothing great was ever achieved, without enthusiasm.

The team that won't be beaten won't be beaten.

The harder you play the higher we reach.

A moral victory is like kissing your sister.

A hungry dog hunts best.

They ask not how you played the game, but whether you won or lost.

Have you done your best?

To excel is to be excellent.

Fight.

We are number 1.

"When the game is tough and the crowd is yelling, it's great to forget the crowd and go one on one with your opponent to see who is the better man."—Ernie Davis.

Show me a good loser and I'll show you a loser.

Take the fight away from your opponent and keep it.

Win by as many points as possible.

Spirit, drive.

Win is spelled HUSTLE.

Teamwork plus desire = success.

Boys built out of wise and determination are better athletes than the perfect physical speciman who doesn't work.

What good is skill without desire?

Irish plus spirit = victory.

Let's go out and win for.

7. THE PLAYER MUST ACCEPT STRICT DISCIPLINE

(2) The boy who isn't criticized should worry.

(2) Strong men criticize themselves.

Live by the code or get out.

Stay out for sports and stay out of courts.

He who flys with the owls at night can not keep up with the eagles during the day.

The way you live is the way you play.

Anger is a sign of weakness.

8. SUBORDINATION OF SELF TO THE SUCCESS OF THE TEAM

(6) There is no I in team.

(4) Who passed the ball to you when you scored?

(2) Teamwork means success— work together, win together.

The best players help others to be best players.

It's amazing what a team can accomplish when no one cares who gets the credit.

We don't care who scores as long as someone does.

Self-sacrifice.

Talent is God-given, conceit is self-given, be careful.

7. THE PLAYER MUST ACCEPT STRICT DISCIPLINE

(2) The boy who isn't criticized should worry.

(2) Discipline

An athlete is a gentleman who represents his school.

Live by the code or get out.

Act like an athlete and you'll be one.

A true athlete is one all year round.

A mad ball player is a bad ball player.

8. SUBORDINATION OF SELF TO THE SUCCESS OF THE TEAM

(6) There is no I in team.

(2) There is no U in team.

(2) Good players help others to be good players.

Who passed the ball to you when you scored?

Play together, win together.

A player doesn't make the team, the team makes the player.

Cooperate—remember the banana, every time it leaves the bunch, it gets skinned.

United we stand, divided we fall.

Am I doing my job?
Teamwork and spirit, hard
work and success.

An ounce of loyalty is worth
a pound of cleverness.
Ask not what your team can
do for you, but what you
can do for your team.
Teamwork.
No man is greater than the
game he plays.
Basketball requires five strong
men and a strong bench.
Be an Indian, not a chief.
A team is only as good as its
worst player.

9. MISCELLANEOUS

(5) The difference between
champ and chump is U.
Smile and the whole world
smiles with you, cry and you
cry alone.
I complained because I had no
shoes until I met a man who
had no feet.
Garbage tends to collect garbage.
If you get in an urinating
contest with a skunk, you'll
come out smelling like one.
Respect all, fear none.
Are you the answer to our
problems, or are you a part
of it?
Profanity is the ignorant mind
expressing itself.
Don't forget to be polite.
Good behaviour reflects team
behaviour.
Little strokes fell great oaks.
Position for athlete and Christian: knees bent, eyes up.
It's best to remain silent and
to be thought a fool than
to open one's mouth and
remove all doubt.

9. MISCELLANEOUS

(2) The only difference between
champ and chump is U.
(2) Seniors: there is no next
year.
The difference between success
and failure is you.
Three qualities of a winner:
student, gentleman, athlete.
Profanity shows a lack of
vocabulary.
Profane language never made
a man out of a boy.
Send us a boy and we'll return
him a man.
The way you play is the way
you live.
Leave the game the same way
you entered it.
A team is never so good or so
bad as they think.
A player is only as good as
he is compared to his own
best self.

III

The previous discussion focused on the normative, integrative, and cohesive function of some folklore genres surrounding the sport of basketball.[2] The success of athletic teams is primarily determined by their victories. The slogan motifs are normative prescriptions of objectives that are likely to contribute to this primary goal. Groups, such as athletic teams, with specific goals to be achieved cannot tolerate very much deviation in role performance. Each team member has a well-defined role performance and must play his part in relationship to the functioning of the total group.[3] Team integration is maintained by a high degree of consensus, harmony, and esoteric in-group traditions, including the use of slogans. This athletic coach model is probably functional for winning basketball games. However, the assumption that this model is likewise adequate for "playing the game of life" is a partial distortion of what the social universe is like.[4] Conflict theorists have argued that social organization in modern society is not only explained by integrative and associative phenomena but also by conflict, coercion, dissensus, disintegration and competing values. Thus, the perspective developed through socialization for the effective functioning of small groups, such as basketball teams with narrowly defined goals, may not be entirely adequate for macro social systems.

Additional data are needed to fill in the gaps in our knowledge about the eventual functionality of the athletic coach model of socialization within macro social systems. The slogans as folklore do, however, provide empirical data for a better understanding of behavior within the sociocultural milieu of high school basketball.

NOTES

1. Athletic banquet speech reported in the "Milwaukee Journal" (November 14, 1965).
2. Numerous folklorists have stressed the importance of studying the meaning and function of folklore within its socio-cultural content. Bascom (1954, pp. 344-347) has outlined four functions of folklore as: (1) providing a mirror for seeing the culture, (2) justification for the institutions and rituals of the society, (3) a means for transmission of morals, beliefs, and values, and (4) as a means for applying and exercising social control and conformity for the socially acceptable patterns of behavior. Abrahams (1968a, pp. 146-150) has stressed additional functions of folklore as providing for a cohesive and normative force, "answers" and solutions for courses of action, and acceptable modes of expressing aggression.
3. Hans Lenk reports that teams may have internal dissention and still be successful. His research with rowing teams showed that internal conflicts did not reduce performances, providing the members are personally interested in the continuation of the team and its performance (Lenk, 1966, pp. 168-172; also cited in Loy and Kenyon, 1969, pp. 393-397). Additional research is needed to develop knowledge of the type of conflict

and the tolerance for conflict within teams of various sports. The role relationships for a rowing crew requires a synchronization of effort with each crew member performing a similar task. Role relationship for members of a basketball team are more specialized and interrelated.
4. Goffman (1969, pp. 65-66) discusses the manner in which games represent an interaction which is to some extent independent and outside the wider world. In this sense, the internal world of the game is not a mirror of the external social system.

REFERENCES

Abrahams R. D., *Introductory Remarks to a Rhetorical Theory of Folklore*, "Journal of American Folklore" 81 (1968a), pp. 143-158.
Abrahams R. D., *A Rhetoric of Everyday Life: Traditional Conversational Genres*, "Southern Folklore Quarterly" 32 (1968b), pp. 44-59.
Bascom W. R., *Four Functions of Folklore*, "Journal of American Folklore" 67 (1954), pp. 333-349.
Berstein B., *Elaborated and Restricted Codes: Their Social Origins and Some Consequences*, "American Anthropologist" 66 (1964), Part 2, pp. 55-69.
Caillois R., *Man, Play, and Games*, Free Press, Glencoe, Ill., 1961.
Coleman J. S., *The Adolescent Society*, Free Press, Glencoe, Ill., 1961.
Coleman J. S., *Adolescents and the Schools*, Basic Books, New York, 1965.
Cowell C. C., *The Contributions of Physical Activity to Social Development*, "Research Quarterly" 31 (1960), pp. 286-306.
Goffman E., *Encounters*, Bobbs-Merrill, 1961.
Helanko R., *Sports and Socialization*, "Acta Sociologica" 2 (1957), pp. 229-240.
Jansen W. H., *The Esoteric-Exoteric Factor in Folklore*, "Fabula" 2 (1959), pp. 205-211.
Kenyon G. S., *Sociological Considerations*, "Journal of Health, Physical Education and Recreation" 39 (1968), pp. 31-33.
LeMasters E. E., *Parents in Modern America*, Dorsey Press, Homewood, Ill., 1970.
Lenk H., *Maximale Leistung Trotz Innerer Konflickte*, "Kleingruppenforschung und Gruppe im Sport, Kölner Zeitschrift für Soziologie und Sozialpsychologie" 10 (1966), pp. 168-172; also cited in Loy, J. W., Jr. and Kenyon, G. S. (editors), *Sport, Culture, and Society*, MacMillan Company, London, 1969, *Top Performance Despite Internal Conflict: An Antithesis to a Functionalistic Proposition*, translated by D. E. Kenyon, pp. 393-397.
Loy J. W., Jr., *The Nature of Sport: A Definitional Effort.* "Quest", 10 (1968), pp. 1-15.
Loy J. W., Jr., Kenyon G. S., (editors), *Sport, Culture, and Society*, MacMillan Company, London, 1969.
Lüschen G., *The Interdependence of Sport and Culture*, "International Review of Sport Sociology" 2 (1967), pp. 127-141.
Roberts J. M., Sutton-Smith B., *Child Training and Game Involvement*, "Ethnology" 1 (1962), pp. 166-185.
Schafer W. S., Armer J. M., *Athletes Are Not Inferior Students*, "Transaction" 6 (1968), pp. 21-26, 61-62.
Snyder E. E., *A Longitudinal Analysis of the Relationship Between High School Student Values, Social Participation and Educational Occupational Achievement* "Sociology of Education" 42 (1969), pp. 261-270.

Snyder E. E., *Aspects of Socialization in Sports and Physical Education,* "Quest"
14 (1970), pp. 1–7.

Sutton-Smith B., Roberts J. M., Kozelka R. M., *Game Involvement in Adults,* "The
Journal of Social Psychology" 60 (1963), pp. 15–30.

Ulrich C., *The Social Matrix of Physical Education,* Prentice-Hall, Englewood
Cliffs, N.J., 1968.

Sports, Values and Society

ROBERT J. BUETER

From Spiro Agnew's platitudinous status-quo-ism to Charles Reich's
utopian futurism, the various values that Americans live by have been
defended and debunked with much energy and earnestness in recent
years. The value debate has even invaded the realm of sports, which
indeed are a big part of Americans' lives—they preoccupy our children,
pre-empt our television screen and pour huge sums of money into our
economy. The current literature about sports, therefore, may tell us
something about the ideals of man and the visions of society that motivate
both those who praise and those who condemn or poke fun at the
American sports world, and at the same time may help us to understand
our own values. Appropriately—for that is where more and more Americans are spending their time and money—it is on football that most of this
literature centers.

THE WORLD OF VINCE LOMBARDI

In 1970 Jerry Kramer, the All-Pro Green Bay guard whose *Instant Replay*
and *Farewell to Football* took us behind the professional football scene,
edited a book titled *Lombardi: Winning Is the Only Thing*, a memorial to
the late great coach who was the dominant figure in professional football
and in American sports generally during the '60s. In this book 23 men who
knew Vince Lombardi well talk about him and what he represented. One

SOURCE: Robert J. Bueter, "Sports, Values and Society," *The Christian Century*, 89 (April
5, 1972), 389–392.

of them—Frank Gifford, star of the New York football Giants and well known television sportscaster for ABC—laments American youth's indifference to the values Lombardi stood for. "Kids today don't fight like we did," he writes (p. 62). "They can play football and basketball like hell, but they're very gentle . . . They're out playing for fun, and it's not going to interfere with their demonstration for the week or with the things they consider important. If you . . . dropped them under Lombardi, they might say 'What the hell is he talking about?' They wouldn't understand." Another contributor to the book—Bart Starr, the quarterback of Lombardi's greatest teams—agrees that young people are losing the values that made Vince and America great: mental toughness, commitment to excellence, determination to win, pride, loyalty, self-sacrifice, dedication and religion.

That youth becomes the focus of sportsmen's discussion of values seems fitting. Not only is competitive athletics a field primarily reserved for the young, but the shift in America's values is best exemplified in our young people's life style. The values that Gifford, Starr and other contributors to the Lombardi book single out as important are the very values that, they fear, today's youth are repudiating.

This whole set of values is what many describe as "middle class." Let us try to analyze them according to their goal and the means and manner of attaining it.

The goal of middle-class values is success: that is, increasing accumulation of goods leading to higher social status. The means of success is hard work and continual striving on the part of the individual—a means that necessarily fosters elitism and class consciousness. The manner is basically puritanical: disciplined repression of present needs for the sake of future gratification, commitment to law and order accompanied by reliance on authority and tradition, and an optimistic pragmatism whose methods are always open to change.

Now, these are exactly the values that, as his admirers see it, were fundamental in the world of Vince Lombardi. He was a good coach because he was successful; he accumulated a lot of goods for the players who were fortunate enough to be part of his Packer family. He relied on individual hard work and discipline, and instilled in his men the consciousness that they were better and must achieve according to their elite status. His manner was hard and puritanical; he drove his men to their limits, promising them "success" in return. He was strictly authoritarian, yet he was an optimistic pragmatist in his ability to adjust to individuals and situations. But are the values Lombardi represented the ones that young people live by today? Gifford and Starr think not.

Dave Meggyesy doesn't think so either. But in his opinion this is a good thing. Meggyesy, a former All-Pro linebacker with the St. Louis football

Cardinals, says in his book *Out of Their League* that young people are right in rejecting the value system of American society. Indeed, he calls for a revolution in values, for a radical transformation of our society that would make it free, just and humane. And in that society, he says, football would be obsolete—at least football as it now operates. Out of his own experience, Meggyesy cites some of the shameful facts about college and professional football; e.g., the drug usage and the racist policies and practices.

COERCED INTO CONFORMITY

Jack Scott, whose Center for the Study of Sport and Society sponsored Meggyesy's book, repeats these charges in his own book *The Athletic Revolution*. Of the abuses that he says are rampant in college athletics, he mentions particularly the crass and pressurized recruiting, which involves everything from easy sex to junketeering; the lack of concern on the part of coaches for their players' education (many athletes get little time for study; some are given stolen tests or have others take exams for them); the coaches' intrusion into the private lives of the athletes by laying down petty rules governing personal appearance and life style. Summing up, Scott accuses the college "athletic establishment"—administrators, coaches and alumni—of using the athletes to further their own personal and corporate goals.

But these abuses are not Scott's main point. Like Meggyesy, he sees athletics as a symbol of a society whose values are bankrupt. However, Scott asserts that athletics is not only a symbol and a reinforcement of a basically unsound value system, but also one of the principal ways by which young people are socialized into that system. The college athlete, he charges, is not encouraged to develop democratically as a free individual and to set up his own values and goals regardless of society's; instead, he is coerced into conformity with the values, goals and expectations of the people who control the highly authoritarian, militaristic and totalitarian environment. Scott goes so far as to compare American with Russian athletics: Give me a boy, he says, and in Russia I'll give you back a good communist and in America a good capitalist.

A REVOLUTION IN AWARENESS?

Here we are at the heart of the current critique of American middle-class values. It is a widespread critique, deep and serious. Charles Reich, for example, asserts that those values have created a monster, the "corporate state." But he claims that a revolution in human awareness is coming—a revolution that will produce a new man and a new society, endowed with imagination and vitality and a strong sense of selfhood. In short, Reich and a host of others are saying that American society is at a crossroads, on the verge of a revolution in values. For their part, such critics of athletics as Scott and Meggyesy are pointing out that football and organized sports in general are one of the bastions of the evil old order and must be stormed before the revolution can take place.

The values the revolutionists defend can be analyzed under the three headings we applied to middle-class values: their goals, their means and their manner. The goal of the new values is not success—accumulation of goods and all that this entails—but rather the development and cultivation of the person, his growth in awareness and inner peace. The means is not individual striving but rather group participation and cooperation, communal sharing, and mutual engagement with experimental culture forms—all of which lead not to class-consciousness but to increasing openness and acceptance of others. The manner is not puritanical but sensual: gratification is immediate, suppression and discipline give way to free expression, and optimistic pragmatism is replaced by a utopianism that, to be sure, is somewhat pessimistic and nihilistic. Thus the new values repudiate authority and tradition in favor of protest and social change, and they reject technology with its props of elitism and class consciousness.

Obviously, these values are a threat to football and other sports as we know them. (We can't imagine Vince Lombardi saying, "Inner awareness isn't everything, it's the *only* thing.") But they are the values that have driven men like Meggyesy and others out of football and into the radical counter-culture. Jack Scott is one of those who think that the new culture will reform sports as well as all other fields of endeavor. In "Running as a Spiritual Experience," a short essay he appends to his *The Athletic Revolution*, Scott says that sports, besides being a gratifying and immediately enjoyable experience, can foster the group spirit and at the same time develop the individual participant's awareness of himself.

Larry Merchant, a sports columnist for the *New York Post*, takes a lighter view of the criticism of football as a prop of middle-class values. He has said, in effect, "Aw, cut it out, fellas; it's only a game." In his book . . . *and Every Day You Take Another Bite*—the title refers to the inscrutable wisdom of Coach Joe Schmidt of the Detroit Lions, who once summed up his philosophy by stating, "Life is a shit sandwich and every day you take another bite"—Merchant says he has no time for the "sanctimonious people" who exploit football as a gimmick to push their own intellectual wares—whether they defend it as "a game for our times" or decry it as a symbol of a repressive society. "Each of us," he says, "brings our own sensibility and neuroses to the stadium, enabling us to find whatever we want there, from fun and games to hero and scapegoat and even to catharsis and the fount of essential, infinite wisdom" (p. 68).

Merchant makes a good point. Turning such heavy guns on sports in general and football in particular does miss the very important fact that they are still games, played and viewed mostly by people who enjoy them and solely for the pleasure they bring. To say much more tends to be an exercise in intellectual overkill. Even so, Merchant passes over a very real issue. As we have seen, Lombardi's world was part of the world of middle-class values, and the values of the so-called counterculture are in many respects fundamentally opposed to Vince Lombardi's. Meggyesy and Scott have discerned as much. Let us, however, look at their critique a little more closely.

SATURDAY SWINGER, SUNDAY CHARGER

Another young man who plays football—Marty Domres, a quarterback for the San Diego Chargers—takes a far easier view of pro football and American society. His book *Bump and Run* is billed as the story of a "Saturday Swinger and Sunday Charger." The title refers not to the on-the-field maneuver of *bump*ing a pass receiver at the line of scrimmage before *run*ning downfield with him, but to the off-the-field caper of throwing a pass at a girl, scoring in her bed, and getting back to your own in time for curfew check. Slick and saucy stuff, this. But incidentally Domres does talk about the question before us. The authoritarian structure of football and other sports doesn't bother him; it takes a "slave-driver" to keep the athlete in form, he says. In other words, he will use the means necessary to win the goal and will endure the manner. His acceptance of these middle-class values, however, does not blind Domres to the evils of American society. He expresses concern over hunger, poverty, loneliness, war, racism, drugs, and says he wants to do something about them after his lucky days of playing for pay are over. But with that he stops.

Here is the striking contrast between Domres and Meggyesy. Both have been through the same system and have seen the same evils, but have come up with different responses to it. Meggyesy has rejected the system and turned radical. Domres has found personal satisfaction in the system: he is proud of his college and his education, he is grateful to his coaches, and he *likes* playing the violent game that, after all, has rewarded him well.

The contrast between these two young men points up two important facts about current attitudes concerning American values. First, most critics tend to put all young people on one side of the debate and all older people on the other. But the evidence is that the division is not that clear-cut. Not all young people are part of the so-called counterculture, and the many differences among them revolve precisely around values. Second, if Meggyesy and Domres can in the main agree about the evils of American society and of the football system, their basic disagreement must be attributed to their differing value systems. Both see the same situation, but each interprets it in the light of his own views of what is desirable. Hence we conclude, first, that there is no monolithic youth response to America's moral problem; and second, that the nature of values is such that they must be freely chosen and lived by. Values cannot be legislated or forced upon us. Therefore the important thing is that we make a clear choice and stick by it.

CRITICIZING THE NEW PROPHETS

As of now, the contest between the values of the middle class and the counterculture—or between Lombardi's values and Meggyesy's—has not been played out. Meanwhile, both sides have scored some points.

On the one hand, it seems clear that middle-class values are weak in fundamental respects. Two years ago Philip E. Slater asserted—in his article "Cultures in Collision" (*Psychology Today*, July 1970)—that the "core motivational logic" of the old set of values is a logic of "scarcity." The goal, means and manner of the old values will equip an individual, or a society based on them, to get there first with the most, assuming there isn't enough to go around. Such is certainly the situation in sports: there is only one Superbowl, and the winner's share is bigger than the loser's. But in society at large scarcity is not the real problem; there would be enough to go around if it were properly distributed. The basic weakness of the old values is that they overlook this present fact. On the other hand, the "core motivational logic" of the new values is "abundance." If man's external needs were satisfied, he could turn inward, could preoccupy himself not with acquisition but with sharing. Moreover, if you have the goods now, why not enjoy them now? Abundance is certainly a present and growing fact to which some of the new values are an appropriate response. We can conclude then (1) that a shift in values is under way and (2) that this shift is in keeping with our current level of development. But we must also say that the proponents of the new revolution have tried to prove too much and have made statements that are highly suspect.

For example, Peter L. and Brigitte Berger point out (in the *New Republic*) that the critique of "technocracy" by Reich and others has failed to come to grips with the achievement ethic—an ethic that is probably so deeply ingrained in our people that we will work through it rather than go beyond it. Other writers remind us that change in the system will not come without organized effort, and that to be successful such effort will have to rely on some of the values of the achievement ethic. That is, you can't enjoy the fruits of the revolution until you have denied yourself in fighting its battles; and these battles will take organization and bureaucracy along with technology's tools. On another tack, Michael Novak, writing in *Commonweal*, calls the new prophets dupes of the illusion of human perfectibility. And Walter Goodman, writing in *Commentary*, says that those prophets have a "one-to-midnight" mentality, nor do the facts support their claim that ours is a basically repressive society, for in spite of our problems freedom is more widespread in America today than ever before. Finally, many critics insist that opponents of the system present a very idealistic picture of their own values while ignoring the fact that the old values have brought some realistic goods.

EVOLUTION RATHER THAN REVOLUTION

In the face of all this intellectual charge and countercharge, one is inclined to conclude that neither side will win. The new values surely offer much that is needed in America, but the old values just as surely do the same. If Gifford and Starr seem ready to pay too dearly to preserve the values they recognize as their own, Meggyesy and Scott seem too grim and too sweeping in their assessment of the deficiencies of American value structures. Again, though we might find it embarrassing to climb into bed with a swinger like Domres, we cannot but recognize that there is a lot of rationality and good sense in his middle-of-the-road position.

In the end, this debate about America's values as it surfaces in discussions of football and sports should help us see ourselves for what we are: a society in transition. The older values are neither as bankrupt as the prophets of revolution pretend nor as adequate to our current situation as defenders of the Puritan ethic assert. And the new values, while they are a response to new needs, are not a complete answer to what man should or will be. There will be change in our society. But this observer for one does not see a revolution in the offing, but rather a continuing evolution based on the free choice of the values that are necessary for man's ongoing development.

■ FOR FURTHER STUDY

Allen, George, with Joe Marshall. "A Hundred Percent Is Not Enough." *Sports Illustrated* (July 9, 1973), pp. 74–84.

Bain, Linda. "Play and Intrinsic Values in Education." *Quest*, 26 (Summer 1976), 75–80.

Ball, Donald W. "Failure in Sport." *American Sociological Review*, 41 (August, 1976), 726–739.

Boyle, Robert H. *Sport—Mirror of American Life*. Boston: Little, Brown, 1963.

Coakley, Jay J. *Sport in Society: Issues and Controversies*. St. Louis: C. V. Mosby, 1978, pp. 15–23.

Durso, Joseph. *The All-American Dollar: The Big Business of Sports*. Boston: Houghton Mifflin, 1971.

Edwards, Harry. *Sociology of Sport*. Homewood, Illinois: Dorsey, 1973, pp. 71–130, 317–364.

Eldridge, Larry. "Why Must They Win?" *Christian Science Monitor* (August 7, 1978), pps. 14–15.

Etzioni, Amitai. "After Watergate—What?: A Social Science Perspective." *Human Behavior*, 2 (November 1973), 7.

Ford, Gerald R., with John Underwood. "In Defense of the Competitive Urge." *Sports Illustrated* (July 8, 1974), pp. 16–23.

Harris, Donald S., and D. Stanley Eitzen. "The Consequences of Failure in Sport." *Urban Life*, 7 (July 1978), 177–188.

Helanko, R. "Sports and Socialization." *Personality and Social Systems*. Edited by Neil Smelser and William Smelser. New York: Wiley, 1963, pp. 238–247.

Higgins, R. J. "American Athletic Mentality: Identities and Conflict." *Sport Sociology Bulletin*, 5 (Fall 1976), 14–24.

Hoch, Paul. *Rip Off the Big Game*. Garden City, New York: Doubleday Anchor, 1972.

Jeansonne, John. "Loser, A Word to Lose," *The Basketball Bulletin* (Fall 1976), pp. 88–90.

Kempton, Murray. "Jock-Sniffing." *New York Review of Books*, 16 (February 11, 1971).

Kenyon, Gerald S. "Sport Involvement: A Conceptual Go and Some Consequences Thereof." *Aspects of Contemporary Sport Society*. Edited by Gerald S. Kenyon. Chicago: The Athletic Institute, 1969, pp. 77–84.

Leonard, George B. "Winning Isn't Everything: It's Nothing." *Intellectual Digest*, 4 (October, 1973), 45.

Leonard, George B. *The Ultimate Athlete: Re-Visioning Sports, Physical Education, and the Body*. New York: Viking Press, 1975.

Leonard, George B. "Overemphasis on Winning Makes Us a Nation of Losers." *The National Observer* (April 12, 1975), p. 16.

Lowe, Benjamin, and Mark H. Payne. "To Be a Red-Blooded American Boy." *Journal of Popular Culture*, 8 (Fall 1974), 383–391.

Loy, John W., Barry D. McPherson, and Gerald Kenyon. *Sport and Social Systems*. Reading, Mass.: Addison-Wesley, 1978, pp. 379–425.

Matza, David. "Sports and Athletes." *Handbook of Modern Sociology*. Edited by Robert E. L. Faris. Chicago: Rand McNally, 1964, pp. 203–207.

Mears, Ray. "Staff Organization." *The Basketball Bulletin* (Fall 1976), pp. 38–39.

Montague, Susan P., and Robert Morais. "Football Games and Rock Concerts: The Ritual Enactment of American Success Models." *The American Dimension: Cultural Myths and Realities.* Edited by William Arens and Susan P. Montague. Port Washington, New York: Alfred, 1976, pp. 33–52.

Nelson, Linden L. and Spencer Kagan, "Competition, The Star-Spangled Scramble." *Psychology Today,* 6 (September, 1972), 53–56, 90–91.

Nixon, Howard L. *Sport and Social Organization.* Indianapolis: Bobbs-Merrill, 1976, pp. 9–28.

Nixon, Howard L. "Sport, Socialization, and Youth: Some Proposed Research Directions." *Review of Sport and Leisure,* 1 (Fall 1976), pp. 45–61.

Ogilvie, Bruce, and Thomas Tutko. *Problem Athletes and How to Handle Them.* London: Pelham, 1966, chapter 5.

Sadler, W. A. "Competition Out of Bounds: Sport in American Life." *Quest,* 19 (January 1973), 124–132.

Sage, George H. "Humanistic Theory, the Counterculture, and Sport: Implications for Action and Research." *Sport and American Society: Selected Readings.* Edited by George H. Sage. Reading, Mass.: Addison-Wesley, 1974, pp. 415–429.

Sage, George H. "Sports, Culture, and Society." Paper presented at the Basic Science of Sport Medicine Conference, Philadelphia (July 14–16, 1974).

Schafer, Walter E. "Sport and Youth Counterculture: Contrasting Socialization Themes." *Social Problems in Athletics: Essays in the Sociology of Sport.* Edited by Daniel M. Landers. Urbana: University of Illinois Press, 1976, pp. 183–200.

Scott, Jack. *The Athletic Revolution.* New York: The Free Press, 1971.

Snyder, Eldon E., and Elmer Spreitzer. *Social Aspects of Sport.* Englewood Cliffs, N.J., Prentice-Hall, 1978, chapter 3.

Spreitzer, Elmer, and Eldon E. Snyder. "Socialization Into Sport: An Exploratory Analysis." *Research Quarterly,* 47 (May, 1976), 238–245.

Thio, A. "American Success Ideology and Coerced Conformity: Toward Clarifying a Theoretical Controversy." *International Journal of Contemporary Sociology,* 11 (1974), 12–22.

Tutko, Thomas. "Winning Isn't Everything It's Cracked Up To Be." *The Basketball Bulletin* (Fall 1976), p. 88.

Tutko, Thomas, and William Bruns. *Winning Is Everything and Other American Myths.* New York: Macmillan, 1976.

Four

Sports for Children

Children play in all societies. The way that play is structured by adults is an interesting clue about that society. To what extent are children allowed to be spontaneous in their play? What equipment is provided the children? What games are part of the culture—are they aggressive, ritualistic, imaginative? Do adults minimally supervise or absolutely control the activities?

The involvement of boys, and increasingly girls, in adult-supervised sport is characteristic of contemporary American society. About two million boys, aged 8–14, play Little League baseball or its community equivalent; about one million boys play in organized tackle football leagues outside of school; some 5,200 hockey teams exist for youngsters aged 9–12; and organized golf and bowling involve 1.2 million juniors. This wide participation in adult-sponsored sports activities is a phenomenon of the past twenty-five or thirty years. There are at least two reasons for this recent surge in organized children's sports. Foremost is the belief held by most adults that sports participation has positive consequences for youth.[1] Three quotes support this point:

Objectives . . . to promote, develop, supervise, and voluntarily assist in all lawful ways the interest of boys who will participate in Little League Baseball. To help and voluntarily assist boys in developing qualities of citizenship, sportsmanship, and manhood. Using the disciplines of the native American game of baseball, to teach spirit and competitive will to win, physical fitness through individual sacrifice, the values to team play and wholesome well-being through healthful and social association with other youngsters under proper leadership. (From the certificate of Federal charter granted to Little League Baseball, Incorporated, under enactment by the Congress of the United States of America, Public Law 88–378, 88th Congress, H.R. 9234, July 16, 1964.)[2]

We are a competitive people, and it is the spirit of competition which has made our economic system the envy of the world. It's the competitive spirit among the young that causes excellence in adult life. (From a speech at the National Pop Warner Football banquet by Spiro Agnew.)[3]

Organized sports are not democratic nor should they be. They teach respect for authority, discipline, and the individual's role in a group activity. The manager's job is to make the decisions, and he does not poll an electorate. (From former major league player Al Rosen's book, *Baseball and Your Boy*.)[4]

The trend toward adult-sponsored youth sports has coincided with another trend—urbanization. The urban setting provides more leisure time for children and adults than did life in rural environments. Adult community service organizations, YMCA's, and boys' clubs began to sponsor children's sports in order to provide what they considered wholesome leisure time activities and to keep them out of trouble.

But while the youth sports programs have merit idealistically, their actual practice has led to a number of serious charges. Some of these are:

1. Too much pressure is placed on children too early, thus providing great potential for psychological damage.
2. Overzealous parents take the games too seriously.
3. Overstructured activities stifle spontaneity.
4. Until recently, the programs have denied girls from participation; only court action has broken these barriers.
5. The programs have tended to be elitist, developing the skills of only the most talented youngsters and discouraging others.
6. Regimentation has taken the fun out of the activities.
7. There is the danger of physical injuries to youth who pitch too hard (or throw curves too early) or tackle or block opponents.
8. Youth sports encourages the myth that the real value of sport lies in learning to be a winner, that people can be divided arbitrarily into winners and losers, and that sport is a way to make sure that you or your children will end up in the winners' category.
9. The zeal to win leads to excesses such as cheating, taking drugs, dehumanizing drills by coaches, aggressive acts, and the like.

The papers in this section accomplish three things: (1) they describe youth sports and compare them with the spontaneous games more characteristic of previous generations, (2) they document the abuses found in youth sports, and (3) they suggest structural changes to eliminate the abuses and maximize the positive benefits of participation.

NOTES

1. We will explore the arguments, pro and con, for this belief in Chapter 6.
2. Quoted in *This is Little League Baseball: Official Rules* (Williamsport, Pennsylvania: Little League Baseball, Inc., 1973), p. 2.
3. Quoted in James A. Michener, *Sports in America* (New York: Random House, 1976), p. 100.
4. Quoted in *ibid.*, p. 102.

Play Group Versus Organized Competitive Team: A Comparison

JAY J. COAKLEY

One way to begin to grasp the nature and extent of the impact of participation in sport is to try to understand the sport group as a context for the behavior and the relationships of youngsters. In a 1968 symposium on the sociology of sport, Gunther Luschen from the University of Illinois delivered a paper entitled "Small Group Research and the Group in Sport." While discussing the variety of different group contexts in which sport activities occur, he contrasted the spontaneously formed casual play group with the organized competitive team. He was primarily interested in the social organization and the amount of structural differentiation existing in sport groups in general, but some of his ideas give us a basis for comparing the characteristics of the spontaneous play group and the organized competitive Little League team in terms of their implications for youngsters. In general, any group engaging in competitive physical activity can be described in terms of the extent and complexity of its formal organization. Simply put, we can employ a continuum along which such groups could be located depending on how formally organized they are. Figure 1 illustrates this idea.

The spontaneous play group is an example of a context for competitive physical activities in which formal organization is absent. Its polar opposite is the sponsored competitive team in an organized league. It follows that the amount of formal organization has implications for the actions of group members, for their relationships with one another, and for the nature of their experiences. Table 1 outlines the characteristics of

Amount of formal organization

| None
(for example, a spontaneous
play group) | Extensive
(for example, a sponsored
competitive team) |

FIGURE 1. A formal organization continuum for groups in competitive physical activities.

SOURCE: Jay J. Coakley, *Sport in Society: Issues and Controversies* (St. Louis: C. V. Mosby, 1978), pp. 96–103.

118

TABLE 1 Comparison of two groups*

The spontaneous play group: no formal organization	The sponsored competitive team: high formal organization
Action is an outgrowth of the interpersonal relationships and of the decision-making processes of participating members.	Action is an outgrowth of a predesignated system of role relationships and of the role-learning abilities of group members.
Rewards are primarily intrinsic and are a function of the experience and the extent of the interpersonal skills of the group members.	Rewards are primarily extrinsic and are a function of the combined technical skills of group members.
Meanings attached to actions and situations are emergent and are subject to changes over time.	Meanings are predominantly predefined and are relatively static from one situation to the next.
Group integration is based on the process of exchange between group members.	Group integration is based on an awareness of and conformity to a formalized set of norms.
Norms governing action are emergent, and interpretation is variable.	Norms are highly formalized and specific, with variability resulting from official judgments.
Social control is internally generated among members and is dependent on commitment.	Social control is administered by an external agent and is dependent on obedience.
Sanctions are informal and are directly related to the maintenance of action in the situation.	Sanctions are formal and are related to the preservation of values as well as order.
Individual freedom is high, with variability a function of the group's status structure.	Individual freedom is limited to the flexibility tolerated within role expectations.
Group is generally characterized by structural instability.	Group is generally characterized by structural stability.

*A study of the game-playing behavior of elementary school children done by Sylvia Polgar (1976) provides empirical support for the comparison made in this table.

the two groups that would most closely approximate the polar extremes on the continuum.

Before going any further, I should point out that the two descriptions in Table 1 represent "ideal type" groups. In other words, the respective sets of characteristics represent hypothetical concepts that emphasize each group's most identifiable and important elements. Ideal types are necessarily extreme or exaggerated examples of the phenomenon under investigation and as such are to be used for purposes of comparison rather than as depictions of reality. Our concern here is to look at an actual group in which youngsters participate and to compare the actual group with the ideal types in order to make an assessment of what the real group might be like as a context for experience. Of course, the real group will not be an exact replica of either of the ideal types, but will more or less resemble one or the other.

GETTING THE GAME STARTED

The characteristics of each group suggest that the differences between the spontaneous play group and the organized competitive team would be quite apparent as soon as initial contact between the participants occurs. In the spontaneous play group, we might expect that the majority of time would be spent on dealing with organizational problems such as establishing goals, defining means to those goals, and developing expectations of both a general and a specific nature for each of the participants. Being a member of a *completely* spontaneous play group would probably be similar to being involved in the initial organizational meeting of a group of unacquainted college freshmen who are supposed to come up with a class project. Both would involve a combination of some fun, a good deal of confusion, much talking, and little action. For the context of the organized competitive team, we might imagine a supervisor (coach) blowing a whistle that brings a group of preselected youngsters of similar ages and abilities running to fall into a routine formation to await an already known command. This would resemble a "brave new world" of sport where there would be some action, a good deal of listening to instructions, much routinization, and little fun. Fortunately, most group contexts for youngsters' sport participation fall somewhere between these two extremes. The trick is, of course, to find which points on the continuum would have a maximization of both fun and action along with the other characteristics seen as most beneficial to the young participants' development.

From my observations of youngsters in backyards, gyms, parks, and playgrounds, I have concluded that, for the most part, they are quite efficient in organizing their sport activities. The primary organizational details are often partially worked out by physical setting, available equipment, and time of the year, all of which influence the choice of activity and the form the activity will take. To the extent that the participants know one another and have played with each other before, there will be a minimum amount of time devoted to the formation of norms—rules from previous games can be used. But despite the ability of most youngsters to get a competitive physical activity going, there seems to be a tendency for adults to become impatient with some of the "childish" disagreements of the young participants. Adults often become impatient because they do not understand the youngsters' "distortions" of the games—games the adults know are supposed to be played another way. Adults who want to teach youngsters to play the game the *right way* and to help young players avoid disagreements and discussions in order to build up more action time seem to be everywhere. These adults see a very clear need for organization, that is, establishing regular practice times, scheduling contests, and giving positive rewards and encouragement to those whose performances are seen as deserving. Although their motives may be commendable, these adults usually fail to consider all of the differences between the informally organized group and the formally organized team.

Most importantly, the game in the park is in the control of the youngsters themselves, whereas the organized competitive team is supervised and controlled by adults (Polgar, 1976). In the play group, getting the game under way depends on the group members being able to communicate well enough to make organizational decisions and to evoke enough cooperation so that a sufficient amount of the group's behavior is conducive to the achievement of the goals of the game, however they have been defined. In this situation, interpersonal skills are crucial, and youngsters will probably be quick to realize that playing the game depends on being able to develop and maintain positive relationships or, at least, learning to cope with interpersonal problems in a way that will permit cooperative action. This constitutes a valuable set of experiences that become less available to participants as the amount of the group's formal organization increases. It is a rare adult coach who allows youngsters to make many decisions on how the game should be organized and played. In fact, most decisions have even been made for the coach; the availability of the practice field has been decided, the roles defined, the rules made, the sanctions outlined, the team colors picked, the games scheduled, etc. Occasionally the players are allowed to vote on their team name, but that happens only if the team is new and does not already have one. In all, *the emphasis in the organized setting is on the development of sport skills, not on the development of interpersonal skills.*

PLAY OF THE GAME

Differences between the two groups do not disappear once the game begins. For the spontaneous play group, the game experience is likely to be defined as an end itself, whereas for the organized team, the game is a means to an end. In the play group, the game is unlikely to have implications beyond the setting in which it occurs, and the participants are primarily concerned with managing the situation so that *action* can be preserved for as long as possible. To this end, it is quite common for the participating youngsters to develop sets of norms accompanied by rather complex sets of qualifications and to establish handicaps for certain participants. These tactics serve to compensate for skill differences and to ensure that the game can proceed with scores close enough so that excitement and satisfaction can be maximized for as many of the players as possible. For example, if one of the pitchers in an informal baseball game were bigger or stronger than the rest of the youngsters, he/she would be required to pitch the ball with "an arch on it" to minimize the ball's speed and to allow all the batters a chance to hit it. Exceptionally good batters might be required to bat left-handed (if they were right-handed) to minimize the chances of hitting a home run every time they came to bat. A youngster having a hard time hitting the ball might be given more than three strikes, and the pitcher might make a special effort to "put the ball over the plate" so that the batter would have a good chance of hitting the ball rather than striking out. Since a strikeout is a relatively unexciting event in a game where the primary goal is the involvement of all players, one of the most frequently made comments directed to the pitcher by his/her teammates in the field is "C'mon, let'em hit it!"

Similar examples of norm qualifications and handicap systems can be found in other sport groups characterized by a low degree of formal organization. Sometimes these little adaptations can be very clever, and, of course, some participants have to be warned if they seem to be taking unfair advantage of them. This may occur in cases where a young player tends to call time-outs whenever the opposition has his team at a disadvantage or when someone begins to overuse an interference or a "do-over" call to nullify a mistake or a failure to make a play. Although the system of qualifications and handicaps may serve to allow the participants to have another chance when they make mistakes and to avoid the embarrassment associated with a relative lack of skills, the major function of such systems seems to be to equalize not only the players, but also the teams competing against one another. Through such techniques, scores will remain close enough that neither team will give up and destroy the game by quitting. In a sense, the players make an attempt to control the competition so that the fun of all will be safeguarded. Adults do the same thing when given the chance. None of us enjoys being overwhelmed by an opponent or overcoming an opponent so weak that we never had to make an effort.

For the formally organized competitive team, however, the play of the game may be considerably different. The goal of victory or the promotion of the team's place in the league standings replaces the goal of maximizing individual participant satisfaction. The meanings and rewards attached to the game are largely a function of how the experience is related to a desired outcome—either victory or "a good show." Players may even be told that a good personal performance is almost always nullified by a team defeat and that to feel satisfied with yourself without a team victory is selfish (as they say in the locker room, "There is no 'u' in team" or "Defeat is worse than death because you have to live with defeat").

Since victories are a consequence of the combined skills of the team members, such skills are to be practiced and improved and then utilized in ways that maximize the chances for team success. Granting the other team a handicap is quite rare unless any chance for victory is out of their grasp. If this is the case, the weaker players may be substituted in the lineup of the stronger team *unless*, of course, a one-sided score will serve the purpose of increasing the team's prestige or intimidating future opponents.

Also, if one player's skill level far exceeds that of the other participants, that player will often be used where he can be most effective. In the Little League game, it is frequently the bigger youngster with the strongest arm who is made the pitcher. This may help to ensure a team's chance for victory, but it also serves to nearly eliminate the rest of the team's chances for making fielding plays and for being involved in the defensive play of the game. In a 6-inning game, the fact that a large number of the 18 total outs for the opponents come as strikeouts means that a number of fielders may never have a chance to even touch the ball while they are out in the field. A similar thing happens in football. The yough-league team often puts its biggest and strongest players in the backfield rather than in the line. The game then consists of giving those youngsters the ball on nearly every play. For the smaller players on the defensive team, the primary task may be getting out of the way of the runner to avoid being stepped on. Thus on the organized team, intimidation may become a part of playing strategy. Unfortunately, intimidation increases apprehension and inhibits some of the action in the game as well as the involvement of some of the players. Generally, it seems that on the organized team the tendency to employ the skills of the players to win games takes precedence over devising handicaps to ensure fun and widespread participation.

One way to become aware of some of the differences between the informal play group and the formally organized competitive team is to ask the participants in each group the scores of their games. In the formally organized setting, the scores are often one-sided with members of the winning team even boasting about how they won their last football game 77 to 6, their last baseball game 23 to 1, or their last soccer game 14 to 0. Such scores lead me to question the amount of fun had by the players. In the case of the losers, it would be rare to find players who would be able to maintain an interest in a game when they are so completely beaten. If the winners say they enjoyed themselves, the lesson they may be learning through·such an experience should be seriously questioned. It may be that the major lesson is if your opponents happen to be weak, take advantage of that weakness so totally that they will never be able to make a comeback. Such experiences, instead of instilling positive relationships and a sincere interest in sport activities, are apt to encourage distorted assessments of self-worth and to turn youngsters off to activities that, in modified forms, could provide them with years of enjoyment.

In addition to the differences in how the game is organized and how the action is initiated, there are also differences in how action for the two groups is maintained. In the informally organized group, the members are held together through the operation of some elementary processes of exchange that, in a sense, serve as the basis for the participants obtaining what they think they deserve out of the experience (Polgar, 1976). When the range of abilities is great, the older, bigger, more talented participants have to compromise some of their abilities so that the younger, smaller, and less talented will have a chance to gain the rewards necessary to continue playing. The play of the game depends on maintaining a necessary level of commitment among all participants. This commitment then serves as a basis for social control during the action. Although there are some exceptions, those in the group with the highest combined skill and social prestige levels act as leaders and serve as models of normal behavior. For these individuals to deviate from the norms in any consistent manner would most likely earn them the reputation of being cheaters or bad sports. In fact, consistent deviation from the group norms by any of the participants is likely to be defined by the others as disruptive, and the violator will be reminded of his/her infraction through some type of warning or through a threat of future exclusion from group activities. When sanctions are employed in the informal play group, they usually serve an instrumental function—they bring behavior in line so that the game can continue. Sanctions are usually not intended to reinforce status distinctions, to preserve an established social structure, or to safeguard values and principles. Interestingly, self-enforcement of norms in the play group is usually quite effective. Deviation is not totally eliminated, but it is kept within the limits necessary to preserve action in the game. The emphasis is not so much on keeping norms sacred, but on making sure that the norms serve to maintain the goal of action. In fact, norms may change or be reinterpreted for specific individuals or in specific situations so that the level of action in the play activities can be maximized. The importance of maintaining a certain level of action is demonstrated by the informal sanctions directed at a participant who might always be insisting on too rigid an enforcement of norms. This is the person who continually cries "foul" or who always spots a penalty. To be persistent in such a hard-nosed approach to norm enforcement will probably earn the player the nonendearing reputation of being a baby, a crier, or a complainer.

In the informally organized play group, the most disruptive kind of deviant is the one who does not care about the game. It is interesting that the group will usually tolerate any number of different performance styles, forms, and individual innovations as long as they do not destroy action. Batting left-handed when one is right-handed is okay if the batter is at least likely to hit the ball, thus keeping the action going. Throwing behind-the-back passes and trying a crazy shot in basketball or running an unplanned pass pattern in football are all considered part of the game in the play group *if action is not destroyed*. Joking around will frequently be tolerated and sometimes even encouraged *if action can continue*. But if such behavior moves beyond the level of seriousness required to maintain satisfying action for all of the participants, commitment decreases, and the group is likely to dissolve. In line with this, usually those participants with the highest amount of skill are allowed the greatest amount of freedom to play "as the spirit moves them." Although such behavior may seem to indicate a lack of seriousness to the outsider, the skill of the player is developed enough to avoid a "disruptive" amount of mistakes. At the same time, such freedom gives high-ability participants a means through which their interest level can be maintained. Similar freewheeling behavior by a low-ability participant would be viewed with disfavor, since the behavior would frequently bring the action level below what would be defined as acceptable by the rest of the group.

In contrast to the play group, the maintenance of action on the formally organized team depends on an initial commitment to playing as a part of the team. This commitment then serves as a basis for learning and conforming to a preestablished set of norms.[1] The norms apply equally to everyone, and control is administered through the coach-supervisor. Regardless of how priorities are set with respect to goals, goal achievement rests primarily on obedience to the coach's directives rather than on the generation of personal interests based on mutually satisfying social exchange processes. Within the structure of the organized competitive team, deviation from the norms is defined as serious not only when it disrupts action, but also when it *could* have 'been disruptive or when it somehow challenges the organized structure through which action occurs. Thus sanctions take on a value-supportive function as well as an instrumental function. This is demonstrated by the coaches who constantly worry about their own authority, that is, whether they command the respect of their players.

In the interest of developing technical skills, the norms for the formally organized competitive team restrict not only the range of a player's action, but also the form of such actions. Unique batting, throwing, running, shooting, or kicking styles must be abandoned in the face of what the coach considers to be correct form. Joking around on the part of any team member is usually not tolerated regardless of the player's abilities, and the demonstration of skills is usually limited to the fundamentals of the game.

If commitment cannot be maintained under these circumstances, players are often not allowed to quit. They may be told by the coach that "We all have to take our bumps to be part of a team" or "Quitters never win and winners never quit." Parents may also point out that "Once you join a team, it is your duty to stick it out for the whole season" or "We paid our money for you to play the whole season; don't waste what we've given you." With this kind of feedback, even a total absence of personal commitment to the sport activity may not lead to withdrawal from participation. What keeps youngsters going is a commitment to personal honor and integrity or obedience to a few significant people in their lives.

WHEN THE GAME IS OVER: MEANING AND CONSEQUENCES

The implications of the game after completion are different for the members of the informal play group than they are for the members of the formally organized competitive team. For the latter, the game goes on record as a win or a loss. If the score was close, both winners and losers may initially qualify the outcome in terms of that closeness.[2] But, as other games are played, all losses and wins are grouped respectively regardless of the closeness of scores. In the informal play group, the score of a game may be discussed while walking home; however, it is usually forgotten quickly and considered insignificant in light of the actions of individual players. Any feelings of elation that accompany victory or of let-down that accompany defeat are shortlived in the play group—you always begin again on the next day, in the next game, or with the next activity. For the organized competitive team, such feelings are less transitory and are often renewed at some future date when there is a chance to avenge a previous loss or to show that a past victory was not just a fluke. Related to this is the fact that the organized team is usually geared to winning, with the coaches and players always reminding themselves, in the Norman Vincent Peale tradition, that "We can win . . . if we only play like we can." This may lead to defining victories as the expected outcomes of games and losses as those outcomes that occur when you do not perform as you are able. When this happens, the elation and satisfaction associated with winning can be buried by the determination to win the next one, the next one, and so on. Losses, however, are not so quickly put away. They tend to follow you as a reminder of past failures to accomplish what you could have if you had executed your collective skills properly. The element of fun in such a setting is of only minor importance and may be eliminated by the seriousness and determination associated with the activity.

The final difference between the two groups is related to the stability of each. The informal play group is characteristically unstable, whereas the opposite is true of the organized team. If minimal levels of commitment cannot be maintained among some members of the play group, the group may simply dissolve. Dissolution may also result from outside forces. For example, since parents are not involved in the organization of the play group, they may not go out of their way to plan for their youngsters' participation by delaying or arranging family activities around the time of the group's existence. When a parent calls a youngster home, the entire group may be in serious jeopardy. Other problems that contribute to instability are being told that you cannot play in the street, that someone's yard is off limits, that park space is inaccessible, or that necessary equipment is broken or unavailable. These problems usually do not exist for the organized team. Consent by parents almost guarantees the presence of a player at a scheduled practice or game, space and equipment are reserved in advance, and substitute players are available when something happens to a regular team member. Because the team is built around a structure of roles rather than a series of interacting persons, players can be replaced without serious disruption, and the action can continue.

NOTES

1. In some cases, "commitment" may not be totally voluntary on the part of the player. Parents may sign up a son or daughter without the youngster's full consent or may along with peers, subtly coerce the youngster to play.
2. Such qualifications are, of course, used for different effects. Winners use them to show that their challengers were able or that victory came under pressure. Losers use them to show how close they came to victory.

The Myths of Early Competition

THOMAS TUTKO AND WILLIAM BRUNS

> *Charlie Brown, talking to Linus in the* Peanuts *comic strip: "Life is just too much for me. I've been confused from the day I was born. I think the whole trouble is that we're thrown into life too fast. We're not really prepared."*
>
> *Linus: "What did you want . . . a chance to warm up first?"*

If left to their own devices, most youngsters take up a sport just to be with their friends and to have fun. They don't start out putting the emphasis on winning that their parents and coaches do. Their greatest achievement, in fact, is simply to belong, to be a member of a team or a club. The second biggest thing in their life is to make a contribution—to play, not to sit on the bench. Belonging and contributing are normal needs, which can be fulfilled by all of us. But they are being subverted at the childhood level by a gilt-edged emphasis on winning and competition.

I feel that competition is a learned phenomenon, that people are not *born* with a motivation to win or to be competitive. We inherit a potential for a degree of activity, and we all have the instinct to survive. But the will to win comes through training and the influences of one's family and environment. As the song in *South Pacific* says, "you've got to be carefully taught." The song is talking about prejudice, but it's the same thing. From a very early age we are bombarded by direct, indirect, subtle, behavioral, and verbal messages to the effect that the important thing in life is to be a winner—and the earlier the better. If you want to be a successful high school athlete you must specialize, and specialize early.

In view of these influences, parents should question their own particular attitude towards athletics. Some parents, for instance, believe that the most important reason for sports participation is to have youngsters learn to compete. When the father vows, "My boy is going to learn to become a competitor!" his assumption is that the child will learn to set goals, to test his limits, to acquire more self-discipline, and to deal with the emotional ups and downs that are a reflection of real life. But as we have seen, the

---

SOURCE: Thomas Tutko and William Bruns, *Winning Is Everything and Other American Myths* (New York: Macmillan, 1976), pp. 53-63.

idea that sports help build a competitor is a common misperception. Sports may, in fact, be burning the competitive spirit and turning youngsters off athletics. Dr. Muzafer Sherif, a social psychologist at Penn State, points out in *The Physician and Sportsmedicine* that even though competition is normal doesn't mean it's healthy and in the best interest of the child. "We cannot assume that just because the child is competing it's a good catharsis, a healthy release," he says. "It can lead to hostility or good sportsmanship, the results depending on how the competition is organized." He favors a situation where the competition is set up in a cooperative way, as opposed to having winning as the all-important goal.

Other parents strongly believe that "winning is the name of the game," without actually stopping to think what winning really means. For instance, a Queens, New York, Little League official argues, "This is not an instructional league. We're here to win. There's nothing wrong with winning." But why can't the two—instruction and winning—coexist? A win-or-else attitude overlooks the large number of sports-loving youngsters who are weeded out along the way because they lack talent; the youngsters who must ride the bench ("This is a big game—we can't afford to lose"); the players who are made to feel miserable because they lost or contributed directly to a defeat; and the small number of winners there really are in sports. The problem, I think, is that many parents don't know any measurement for success except "Who won?"

It's interesting to note that children often have a different perspective of what sports are about. When they play tennis, for example, and adults aren't around to ask "Who's winning?" the idea is to keep the ball going back and forth, even if it bounces two or three times or goes off the court. That's the thrill; not to slam the ball down the opponent's throat. Unfortunately, the adults soon come along and start insisting that the youngsters "play by the rules"; that is, play to win.

"How can they have fun," we reason, "if they don't play to win? If there's not a situation created where one side wins and the other loses?" At a Little League meeting one night, an obviously uptight father interpreted what I was saying as "Let's not have the kids compete." Was that my philosophy? Because his feeling was that "Competition is life."

I agreed that learning to compete obviously has merit, since one finds himself competing most of his life, either with others or within himself. But I pointed out that adults share a common misconception: that children will not compete unless adults are around to take over and show them how. But children are competing all the time—in school, at home, among their friends, on the playground. Given free time, they love to get into some kind of activity; they do it naturally. If a group of adults were to take eighteen youngsters who liked to play baseball out on the field, and were to hang around just to answer questions about technique, the youngsters would soon choose up teams and they sure as hell would compete. They would work out a balance in the teams and adjust to any imbalance naturally. They wouldn't have uniforms and nobody would be keeping statistics, but everybody would play the entire game and they would all have fun. What's equally import, it would be a growth experience; they would be doing it themselves rather than having the adults run the show.

I realize those days are past, except in small towns and on inner-city streets and playgrounds, when youngsters would organize their own games on dusty sandlots, rock-strewn fields, and frozen ponds. Much as I lament the passing of the old tradition, I know that such a system is impractical if one of our purposes is—and should be—to open up sports to as many children as possible, no matter what their skill or native ability. We need parents and other interested adults to be involved in youth leagues in order to help things run smoothly, and to offer technical advice so that youngsters will improve their skills. The problem is that adults feel they have to organize and run *everything*, from determining the starting line-ups to calling the plays in football, and eventually they can strangle much of the fun by imposing all their rules, traditions, and grandstand pressures. Instead, when the game begins they should think about withdrawing as coaches and overzealous spectators and let the kids learn to run their own affairs, with their own self-imposed pressure to play well.

As I said earlier, I'm not against competition. Everybody *likes* to win. But there's a vast difference between competing for the fun of competing, and regimenting everything with only one goal in mind—to produce a league champion.

Most children in this country, when they reach the age of five or six, can generally find an organized sport waiting for them at the nearest playground, recreation center, gym, skating rink, or swimming pool. This American compulsion to organize everything for our young athletes reflects a growing belief by many parents that the earlier you learn a sport—the earlier you learn to *compete*—the better your chances are of becoming a professional or an Olympic hero. If, that is, you haven't been burned out, injured, or eliminated along the way. Once again we have applied an adult model to a growing child. We continue to raise our expectations of children while lowering the age at which they can compete. We fail to make the critical distinction between learning a sport in a fun, low-key situation and having to compete to win in that sport at a very early age. It's not *when* you start your child in sports that counts; it's what your goals are. If you are starting your five-year-old in ice hockey because you dream that he'll one day play for the Montreal Canadiens (even if you don't admit it to anybody), then your behavior is destructive. On the other hand, early involvement in sports can be a healthy outlet for the child who has sensitive, patient parents and coaches. Vermont ski coach Mickey Cochran, for example, put all four of his children on skis before they were four, not to develop champions but a love for the sport. As he explained:

> Kids progress very rapidly when they learn that young. But at first you have to literally babysit for them. And be extremely patient. My wife and I made up our minds not to get angry or to criticize them for any reason, which took some real tongue-biting at times. We would just about have their skis on and they would say, "I have to go to the bathroom" or "I want a drink of water." All we wanted was for them to have fun. It should be that way with any kids in sports. It may be that they don't have a hankering to be Jean Claude Killy or a Henry Aaron.

Still, all four Cochrans made the U.S. ski team, and daughter Barbara Ann won the slalom gold medal at the 1972 Sapporo Olympics.

Vic Braden, the innovative tennis coach who is director of the Vic Braden Tennis College in Southern California, likes to start youngsters at age three or four. But he stresses that any coach who works with youngsters this young must analyze his motives:

> If the coach is trying to develop champions, then he has to get out of the field because we don't need that approach. In tennis, his goals should be to introduce kids to a terrific hand-eye coordination game and let them have fun, get exercise, play in the sun. Let the kid hit thousands of balls. Let him laugh his guts out and run all over the court. He may only hit one out of five over the net but he'll think he's sensational. The problem comes when the parents start shouting, "You can do it, Johnny! . . . Oh, God, you missed it again."

If the coach is secure in his ability to teach tennis and has analyzed why he's starting youngsters so young, then there will be a positive relationship in teaching sports to infants, Braden feels. He is currently researching his contention that tennis develops "a particular kind of hand-eye coordination that will be related to reading readiness, and that reading is going to improve through sports." Braden believes that an early start in sports—on a low-key basis—is important for another reason:

> Kids who start out young, in a non-pressure situation, usually remember how much fun a game like tennis was. They might lay off for a year or two, get wrapped up in something else, but they always remember how much fun they had, and eventually they want to come back. But youngsters who don't pick up

a game like tennis until high school, for instance, are now looking around to see who's watching. They can't afford to lose face and if they can't play very well you hear them mumbling, "This is a stupid, sissy game." Many of them never play again until they're secure enough on the inside to come back and try. They only remember how much humiliation there was to the game.

Cochran, Braden, and other enlightened coaches maintain that the following guidelines should serve for those parents and coaches who are dealing with very young, beginning athletes: (1) keep it fun, for the child as well as the adults; (2) be agonizingly patient; (3) reward effort, not performance, unless the performance deserves it; and (4) remember that the aim is simply to introduce the child to a sport in a noncompetitive environment where he can learn the fundamentals without the pressure of executing them in front of a critical audience.

Fierce competition should be the last step in the development of young athletes. They should first learn the skills of the sport, the give-and-take of participation, the enjoyment of being active. Children are naturally inquisitive; they want to know how to play a game and how to improve. As they gain confidence they will seek out competition at their own level.

Alas, the reverse is true for many youngsters. They are thrown into competitive sports before they have sufficient confidence and a proper grasp of the fundamentals. Adults are so anxious to test the skills of young athletes, and so worried that children will grow bored with sports unless they "play for keeps," that they try to build the roof of the house before they have the foundation. They put Fenwick in a situation where he must learn to perform a skill under pressure before he is comfortable with the sport. He may still be overcoming his fears of getting hit by a baseball, making a head-on tackle, or falling on the ice at full speed, when suddenly he also has to win. His coach wants to win. His parents want to see their boy win. The child who just wants to learn how to pick up a ground ball and throw it correctly to first base is confounded by the fact that he has to throw out the runner and kill a rally. Not only that, he stands to be accused of not listening or not trying if he goofs up. If he continues to fail, he may be relegated to the bench.

Anyone who has ever taken up a sport knows the frustration—almost impossibility—of trying to pick up a skill while being under pressure to perform that skill. But we expect this of our children all the time. The average person might feel very differently if he himself were once thrust into a pressure situation while being evaluated by his peers and his superiors. For example, how would a mechanic feel if he were suddenly shown a totally new type of engine, given a box of tools, and told to repair the engine while a gallery consisting of his neighbors, friends, and opponents from a competing garage cheered or booed, depending on how he fared with the engine?

The assumption in childhood sports seems to be that if children don't learn to compete early, they're not going to be able to compete later in life. Defenders of this ethic argue that man is competing from the day he is born, and that the rewards in society—good grades, a good job, even finding the right mate—go to the competitor, the person who knows how to win. Where better to learn to compete than in the gym or on the athletic field? A clinching argument, these people feel, is that there is just as much pressure on a youngster when he is taking a math test as when he's up at bat. "What's the difference?" they ask.

My rebuttal is that the athletic pressures are far more severe. When a youngster fails the math test, he's all alone; the teacher may be the only one who knows his real score. Nobody really gives a damn about his test, except maybe his parents. And they don't say, "Boy, on question four, you really understood your math!" But place this youngster on the basketball court and let him miss two free throws with the score tied late in the game: he knows it, his opponents know it, his coach knows it, his teammates know it, and the spectators know it. The poor youngster has nowhere to turn for support.

What if we could take television cameras into Mrs. Magoo's kitchen and show the country how she fixed bacon and eggs? And have people hanging from the rafters staring at the eggs being fried? We would probably see a lot of burned bacon and broken eggs. Perhaps we could even organize a Neighborhood Breakfast League and announce that we were going to pick the number one mother on the block and that everybody was in competition. All the husbands and children would be spectators, and the results and standings would be posted on large scoreboards in all the supermarkets.

Competition like this would cause all sorts of women to fall apart. They certainly would have a different attitude concerning breakfast; in fact, most of them wouldn't even want to get out of bed in the morning. Their husbands would have to be Designated Cooks.

Instead of a situation like this, however, we have some poor little ten-year-old who comes to the plate with the bases loaded in the last inning. The bat's heavier than he is, he's afraid he'll get hurt by the ball, he doesn't even know if he'll hit it—he's just praying for a walk. Yet everybody is evaluating him. Not only that, we tell him this is for his own good; it is building character! No wonder he has a distorted perception of sports—and adults.

I strongly believe that when we force competition prior to the child's capability of handling the pressures involved—and without the proper support and encouragement—the long-term detriments will outweigh any supposed benefits. The years between eight and twelve are a vital identifying period, a time when children are trying to find themselves, in a psychological sense. They are trying to determine their capabilities and their limitations; they want to learn to deal with certain problems and to handle them effectively; they are in the process of trying to relate to other people and trying to discover their own worth, to be of value; it's a period of building confidence and taking on an attitude about themselves.

Children use play during this period as one way of growing up, of "trying out" life, on their own level, at their own pace, among their peers. Play is necessary for their development and should have a serious place in society. Instead, adults have taken over children's play, as if to say that unstructured, unorganized, sandlot games are no longer possible or important in today's society, especially in the suburbs and small cities. If we continue to plunge children too quickly into a grown-up world and cheat them out of the opportunity to prepare for life in a low-key, low-pressure fashion, we can expect a generation of adults to emerge who are totally alienated from competitive sports.

Gale E. Mikles, chairman of Michigan State University's athletic education department, is among those who feel that America is going overboard in the push for competitive sports, especially with six- and seven-year-olds. A former college wrestling coach, Mikles says, "The competitive spirit comes too soon now for most children to handle, tearing down basic values taught at home and destroying valuable young friendships. What organized sport really does with kids is to break down their own individuality and train them to fit into a system. It does not help to develop their own personality." Bill Harper, a philosophy professor and director of intramural sports at Emporia State, Kansas, contends that competitive sports thwart playfulness. "What do coaches from the Little League up say when they want to praise a player?" he asks. "They say he is a hard worker. Any time you have games in which the participants have less control than the organizers about how they play, who they play, when they play, then it is not really play. Kids get started in sports because they are playful, but they get caught in a system where they are playing for other rewards."

By imposing a competitive ethic fashioned by adults, we may be damaging the child's growing-up process. We interfere with a positive development by telling the child that he's not any good in a particular area and by placing great emphasis on that lack of ability. If he continues to be criticized, or rides the bench every season, or always plays on a losing team with a coach who stresses that winning is the most important thing, he may start to take on the identity of a loser—"Ah, I'm no good."

If children can't learn to enjoy themselves outside the confines of winning, if they are led to believe they are failures if they don't succeed, then what values are sports imparting?

Let's take the example of a youngster participating in Little League. He's led to believe that this artifically induced area has some value in the real world, perhaps that it is even a very vital part of life. If he doesn't do particularly well or his team doesn't win or he has a difficult time learning the skills, he may develop a sense that he's a failure. If he continues to try his best in a sport but continues to lose—in an environment where the stress is on winning—he may even begin to feel rejected by his coaches and parents. They may try to hide their disappointment, but you don't fool too many children. This feeling of rejection may begin to interfere with other areas of life, such as social interaction and schoolwork. Instead of athletics helping him develop in other areas, they can actually destroy areas that might be more vital in later life.

By introducing competition too early, by having screening devices, by picking All-Star teams, by handing out trophies and keeping league standings, by emphasizing batting averages and touchdown passes—by many subtle means—we remind the young athlete of whether or not he's a "winner." The trouble with placing an overriding importance on league championships and trophies is that these are unrealistic goals for all but a handful of people. When you start giving out trophies, you differentiate children; unless you give everyone the same kind of trophy, you're telling the loser, "You're different from the winner." But children know who the better ball players are. They're aware of where they stand and how good they are in comparison with their peers. To give out trophies simply accentuates this difference. It makes the youngster who doesn't have talent feel even less capable, and it gives a distorted perspective to the youngster who gets the higher trophy—not to mention his parents, who can display it on the mantel as evidence that they are raising a hell of an athlete, and must therefore be a hell of a set of parents.

How to Win the Soap Box Derby: in which craftsmanship abets the passion for success to produce a tale of moral confusion

RICHARD WOODLEY

The All-American Soap Box Derby will once again be run in Akron, Ohio, in August. But it will be a smaller, cheaper, surely more honest shadow of its former self. The thirty-seven-year-old Derby lost its virginity in a sinful caper last year and almost fell apart.

It will be remembered that last year's winner, fourteen-year-old Jimmy Gronen, was disqualified when an electromagnet was discovered in his racer. The magnet, mounted in the nose, drew the nose against the metal starting gate and caused the car to be yanked ahead when the gate flopped down to start the race.

That incident, and subsequent evidence of rampant skullduggery over the years, caused the Akron Chamber of Commerce to withdraw its sponsorship, asserting that the Derby had become a victim of "cheating, fraud, and hoax."

The befouling of the venerable Derby was not, to be sure, the idea of the children who aspired to its crown, but of the adults who guided the innocents in the childhood game of coasting downhill in a homemade wagon. The proclaimed villain in this case was Jimmy Gronen's guardian uncle, Robert B. Lange, Sr., who was earlier known for his development of the admired plastic-shell ski boot bearing his name. For violating the sanctity of the Derby ("It's like discovering that your Ivory Snow girl has made a blue movie," commented a prosecutor), Lange, forty-eight, of Boulder, Colorado, was ordered by a Colorado court in a "nonjudicial" bargain to pay $2,000 to a boys' club. The judge said Lange owed an apology to the youth of the nation.

But Lange admits only a "serious mistake in judgment," and avers that

SOURCE: Richard Woodley, "How to Win the Soap Box Derby," *Harper's Magazine* (August 1974), pp. 62–69.

cheating has been so rife that all he did was to even his nephew's odds in a dirty system. In fact, when I talked to him not long ago, he was inclined to sue those responsible for disqualifying his nephew without banishing others who had cheated in the same race.

If mores may be defined as the accepted mode of behavior which does not threaten the stability of the community, it is more important to define the community than the mores. The withdrawal of the Chamber of Commerce, combined with information from many others involved with the Derby for many years, confirms that Lange, however wrong in his actions, is right in his assessments. The sponsor of the first thirty-five championships was Chevrolet, which deftly and without substantive explanation withdrew its sponsorship before the 1973 race. It is widely inferred that Chevrolet, while probably not condoning the growing wickedness in the competition, at least turned a deaf ear and blind eye to the problem.

And so the scandal blew, with its fallout, and the Derby, for which children aged eleven to fifteen supposedly build their own $75 racers that supposedly conform to construction rules and supposedly coast unaided down the 954-foot macadam track called Derby Downs, fell prey to what seemed to be a national malaise: winning, being everything, is worth doing anything to achieve. The Derby, like the Presidency, will likely survive, because enough people want it to. At the last minute, the Akron Jaycees picked up the interim sponsorship, and the Derby is scheduled to run in Akron on August 17, with a new rule book and tighter controls. The intention is to return the Derby—which had become sophisticated and expensive, with fiberglass racers, adult engineering, and meddling old grads—to the kids. Such a retreat to morality is publicly welcomed by all; whether such a basic Derby might be too mundane to attract sustaining interest remains to be seen.

A FAMILY EVENT

Lange's son, Bobby, Jr., won the race in 1972, the same year that Jimmy Gronen, because of the lengthy hospitalization of his widowed mother, joined the Lange family. Jimmy won the 1973 race in a car almost identical to Bobby's. Bobby's car disappeared mysteriously from the Lange basement shortly after the scandal about Jimmy's magnet broke. Lange figures that somebody must have just swiped it but insists that it contained no magnet. He admits, however, that it was an illegal car in other ways, as was Jimmy's.

No scandal was hinted at prior to Jimmy's championship race. The pre-race week had gone smoothly; the 138 local race winners—including

19 girls, and entrants from Venezuela, West Germany, and Canada, were greeted with customary hoopla by Akron. There was a police escort into town, welcoming kisses, and ritualistic donning of Derby T-shirts and beanies. The contestants were then deposited at the YMCA's Camp Y-Noah for four days of fun before the championships. Their racers had been impounded for safekeeping at Derby Downs.

Akron was a good host, as it has been for the American Golf Classic, the Firestone-PBA Tournament of Champions for bowlers, big-time spelling bees, and other events which have made the "Rubber Capital of the World" (Firestone, General Tire, B. F. Goodrich, Goodyear Tire) a hub of all-American activities, of which the All-American Soap Box Derby—the "World's Gravity Grand Prix"—was just about the grandest family event of the year. There was a giant parade with bands and Marines and celebrities.

Prior to and during the race heats, contestants milled nervously around their racers in the paddock area. The cars were nothing like what the children's parents had made in earlier years. They were smooth racers, so slender and streamlined that drivers who had grown a bit between their local races in June and July and these finals in August had to wedge themselves in slowly. Many of the models were designed in "layback" style: the drivers were almost lying down, their eyes just visible over the cockpit.

There were differences in design—such as between the high-tailed layback and the "sit-up" models—and they were painted all manner of colors, with the sponsors' names professionally lettered on the sides, along with the drivers' names and car numbers. But beyond that, there was an enforced similarity. Their overall length could not exceed 80 inches, their height no more than 28 inches, their width no more than 34¾ inches, and the wheelbase could not be less than 48 inches. Total weight of car and

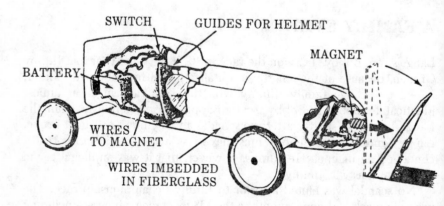

driver could not exceed 250 pounds. Any metal in the car was to be a functional part of the construction; no welded parts were permitted.

All entrants had been issued a brand-new set of computer-matched official gold Soap Box Derby championship wheels to replace the red ones on which they had won in their local towns. They were to be placed on official Soap Box Derby axles, and neither wheels nor axles were to be tampered with in any way.

The rule book stated the whole reason for the Derby to the contestants: "The Soap Box Derby is for YOU. You must build your own car. You must not let adults or anyone else work on your car. You may accept advice and counsel from adults in the design and construction of your car. . . ."

James H. Gronen first raced in the forty-sixth two-car heat. (The official records: "Fourteen-year-old Jim, who is called 'Big Jim' by his friends, is 4-feet, 11-inches tall and weighs 68 pounds. He lost in the first round of the double-elimination Boulder race when a broken steering cable caused him to hit a curb. The damage was repaired and he raced on to victory. He likes skiing, sailing, and motorcycles.") His green fiberglass layback number 12 was carefully walked down the hill to the starting line and set in position in Lane 2 beside the entry from Nashville. The noses of both cars, angled downhill, rested against the spring-loaded steel flaps which rose out of the shimmering macadam.

On signal, the starting flaps dropped forward and the cars rolled, gathering speed to between thirty and thirty-five miles per hour by the time they crossed the finish line. Jimmy Gronen won in a time of 27.48 seconds. On subsequent heats through the afternoon, Jimmy beat cars from Lancaster, Ohio; Appleton, Wisconsin; Columbus, Georgia; and Winston-Salem, North Carolina. In the semifinal, Jimmy beat the Ossining, New York, car with a 27.63 time. In the final, he beat Bret Allen Yarborough of Elk Grove, California, though with his slowest time yet, 27.68.

When Jimmy was presented the trophy, his long, wispy blond hair tossing beneath his helmet edge in the breeze, the braces on his teeth sparkling in the sun, he said simply with a smile, "I was hoping that I'd win." He was also given a gold ring and a $7,500 college scholarship.

When Jimmy received his trophy, there was, amid the cheering, a solidly audible round of boos. Spectators were curious about why Jimmy's times had strangely worsened with each heat. People were showing the officials pictures they had taken of the starts, claiming they showed the Gronen car leaping ahead. And during the heats, it was said, officials had caught Jimmy cheating by buffing his tires on the pavement, and had made him substitute a new set. They had drilled in his car to remove excess weight. And what was this about some cars having been disqualified before the race, and then somehow reinstated? People wondered whether Jimmy's car was in fact Bobby's car from the year before. It was rumored that the Lange cars had cost over $20,000 to build, they they were constructed by experts at the Lange ski factory and were tested in a wind tunnel.

Derby officials began looking over the Gronen car. An inspector found a small button in the headrest, drilled through the headrest, and found wires and a battery. The car was taken to Goodyear Aerospace, near Derby Downs, and X-rayed. That was how the hunk of metal, the magnet, was discovered in the nose. To activate it, Jimmy would have leaned his helmet back against the switch in the headrest. Officials later found a second switch, formed by two supports under the cowling which covered the steering wheel, turned on by Jimmy pulling them together with his thumbs.

On Monday, Chamber of Commerce officials called in the press and announced news of the magnet and Jimmy's disqualification. Bret Yarborough was declared the new champion, and each of the following eight finishers was moved up a notch. The press leaped on the story, spreading the scandal across the nation in a mix of chuckles and pronouncements. In Putnam County, New York, Derby Director Ronald Mills, whose daughter, Diane, had been moved up to second place, said, "It's just unbelievable that anyone would want that ego trip that bad." Andy Noyes, father of now-third-place winner Chris, said, "Let's give the Derby back to the kids, where it belongs."

CHARGES OF CORRUPTION

Gronen's car was immediately locked in a bank storage room (as evidence, should there be lawsuits or criminal charges), and the Chamber of Commerce clammed up. Prosecutors in Akron and Boulder quickly began hearing from people from all over, some anonymously, who described other cheating. Akron Prosecutor Stephan Gabalac said, "If the Chamber doesn't come out swinging now, even the golfers won't want to come here. The whole town is besmirched."

And then Lange issued a statement admitting responsibility for sanctioning the magnet, which Jimmy had installed. He asserted that both Jimmy and Bobby had built their own cars and that no significant expense went into them except in the permissible "area of advice and counsel." He admitted that Bobby's car had been tested in a wind tunnel, which, he said, was neither uncommon nor illegal.

Then he leveled his charges: "Anyone participating in Derby races with eyes and ears open would soon learn, as I did, that . . . the Derby rules have been consistently and notoriously violated by some participants without censure or disqualification." He said it was "common knowledge" that eleven-year-olds cannot build winning racers, and that "it is all that some mechanically inclined and dexterous fourteen- or fifteen-year-old boy can do to carry out the superfine mechanical construction and machine work required." That was why, he said, there were adult professional builders who "build cars for sale to participants or race the cars themselves with young, lightweight drivers, who are known as chauffeurs. Early in my experience one of the professional builders offered to build a car for my son for $2,500, which I promptly refused because I felt the true value of the Derby would come from my son's own efforts."

"After seeing my nephew work hundreds of hours to build his own car," Lange said, "knowing that he would be competing in Akron against professionally built cars, and against cars that would be in violation of the official rules, and having heard and believing that some fast cars in Akron would be equipped with a magnetic nose, I determined that he should build and install a magnetic nose so as to be competitive. I knew that this was a violation of the official Derby rules and consider it now to be a serious mistake in judgment."

As prosecutors continued to receive information of violations, at year's end the Chamber abandoned the race with its "cheating, fraud, and hoax" statement. Later on, I went to see Lange in Boulder.

Lange is a convivial, hospitable man with a smooth manner and modish style, with a moustache, and hair down over his ears. He still carries athletic leanness (he was a swimmer at Harvard, and skis and surfs often now). His wife, Vidie, a graphic artist, is similarly lean and friendly and modish, with long blond hair. We sat in the living room of their spacious, ranch-style house, where we could look out through the glass wall upon the sparsely grassed, yellow foothills of the Rockies. From time to time, their son Bobby, grown tall and gangly, and their nephew Jimmy Gronen, shorter and stockier, stopped by for bits of chat. But at Lange's request, to protect the boys from any further involvement, they were not included in the general Derby discussion.

Lange's ski and ski-boot company was bought in 1972 by the Garcia Corporation. Last summer Lange became inactive as president of his division, though he remains a consultant and draws a $90,000 salary. The Lange factory is in nearby Broomfield, and it is there and in a machine shop in Boulder, as well as in the Lange garage, that the boys built their racers.

"I'm sure that not one Derby official in Akron believes for a second that they built their cars," Lange said, "but they did. Most people violate that rule, but I think the most important thing of all, the most exciting thing for the boys, was the thrill of building their cars and running them down the hill."

Lange's involvement with the Derby, aside from a brief try as a boy, goes back to 1970, with Bobby. "He built a car and lost right here in Boulder. He worked hard on it, but we didn't know anything, and he didn't have a chance." But Bobby wanted to try again, and Lange set about to learn how the Derby worked.

He went to Akron to visit that year's championship, and then to Detroit, where Chevrolet had the winning cars on display. Through casual conversations and careful examination and measurement and photography of the cars, he began to learn about the technology, aerodynamics, and mechanics. Good alignment, he decided, was it. Also, it seemed to him that wooden cars, such as Bobby's first, built in the dry climate of Boulder, would be slowed by absorbing moisture in the dampness of Akron. At a special Soap Box rally in Detroit, he also began to learn of the dark side of the Derby.

"A bunch of us got together and just got to talking, and I began to realize that a lot of these cars just weren't built by kids. These men were building them. One guy said, 'Well, there are drivers and there are builders.' I learned about souping up wheels. They use all kinds of solvents to expand the tires, then when they come back down they're faster. I don't know the full technology about the tires, but they have to be resilient, so that when you go over a tiny bump, the tire kind of pushes back. The flex on the wheels sets up vibrations, and if the car vibrates properly, it goes a lot faster. And there are ways of working on bearings. I also learned that most people do not win with official Derby axles. One guy, a production-line worker, was building axles in his spare time and selling them all over the country. He was bragging about it."

"Were these guys telling you how to cheat?" I asked.

"They were telling me how to *win*," Lange said. "They were just doing me a favor. They don't feel it's cheating; it's so common it's just part of the game. These are ordinary guys, lots of engineers, not rich or anything. It's their life. They just live and die Derby. They probably thought, 'We'll give Lange a little bit of help, but he's never going to be any real problem.' Because I was coming out of nowhere, you know. They knew I wasn't a builder."

DESIGNED TO WIN

Lange's first step along the trail toward scandal occurred four years ago in Detroit, when he paid about $20 for a set of illegal axles for Bobby's second car. That car was made of fiberglass, which wouldn't absorb moisture, and had a metal T strip down the mid-bottom to which the axles could be bolted for sure and precise alignment. Lange made a "female" fiberglass mold from which the fiberglass top and bottom halves, which were identical, could be shaped. "But we didn't work on vibrations that year," Lange said. "We didn't realize how important that was." The second car was a great improvement, but it was beaten in Boulder.

Now, however, Derby was deep in Lange's blood; his competitive nerves were alive. He took Bobby to Anderson, Indiana, where one of the biggest wildcats is held annually after Akron, and Bobby's car was second fastest of about 130 cars. At first he thought they might just make some minor alterations for the coming season, but they actually needed a whole new car for the 1972 Derby, which would be Bobby's third try.

"I didn't work on constructing Bobby's car, but I spent a lot of time designing. Bobby was too far back in that car. Having your weight where you want it is probably one of the most important things in the race. Live weight is high in the center of gravity, whereas dead weight you can put where you want it, which is in the back. Since the car is running at a tilt most of the way, weight in the rear has more drop, so you have more energy in your car. The whole principle is to add dead weight back up the hill, and to balance that you slide the boy forward. Ideally, from an energy standpoint, you would put all your weight over the rear wheels. But that advantage would be overcome by friction when you get down on the flat, friction on the tires and the bearings that takes the resiliency out. So you have to have a balance. I have four slide scales, like doctors' scales, and you put one wheel on each scale so you get it just right."

Also, the car was not aerodynamically correct. "A friend of mine who works at Cal Tech said that what we had was fine in water but was not fine in air doing under fifty miles an hour. The nose has to be rounded, like a tear drop. So when we got the car ready, we shipped it out to California, and my friend put it in the Cal Tech wind tunnel. You mount it up on pins and put fine pieces of thread all over the sides so you can see the airflow, what the laminar flow is and so forth. Computers measure the drag. Aerodynamics is only a small percentage in importance, but at the finish line you're looking for inches."

Lange also applied his ski knowledge. "I had come up with a new theory of the vibration in the car that really made it go fast, just like a downhill ski. If it gets too much oscillation up and down, it goes slow. Even a smooth surface has very slight undulations. Get a ski tip that's too stiff, and it doesn't undulate right. In the suspension of a Derby car, the rear is solid, but if the front gets too solid, or too floppy, it goes slow. The oscillations load and unload the bearings as it goes downhill. You want that action in there, but it has to be just right. We worked on the vibrations by moving the attachment points back and forth, so that all of a sudden we had the right oscillations, and the car just kind of took off.

"And, of course, I was a super-expert in fiberglass, and a super-expert in machining things so they stay in line. I designed a jig just like an engine-block jig, to hold the car while you work on it, where you can lock it in and spin it all around, where the spindles of the axles are kept absolutely square and parallel all the time, and you don't knock it out of line in assembly."

Bobby milled a square end on the T alignment bar, pushed an axle against it, drilled and tapped, and put the dowel pins in. Then he slid the T into the length of the body and assembled the car in the jig, then took it out and balanced it on the scales, making it about ten pounds heavier in the rear. Following the guidance from the wind tunnel, he worked out subtleties in the shape with automobile-body putty.

"The molding was done here in our garage," Lange said, "but all the metalwork and assembly were done in the factory, right out in front of everybody, by Bobby. He learned to run all the machines, and somebody there would just check the setups. Bobby would go down there at 3:30 and work till 10:00 almost every night for three straight months. He loved it."

In order to accommodate the added dead weight without exceeding the 250-pound limit, Bobby was dieting and exercising. "He trained down from 123 to 106," Lange said. "I had him running three miles a day."

With everything honed, shaped, balanced, squared, light, firm, and quick, Bobby won the 1972 Boulder race easily ("There isn't much derby knowledge here, compared with some places where it's really hot and heavy. If you can't win the Boulder race easily, you won't do anything in Akron"), and went on to Akron.

In the course of watching Bobby win the championship, Lange lost whatever faith he had in the honesty of the Derby. "I still didn't know all the things that were really going on until Bobby got into the zoo. I learned right away that a kid can't leave his car for a minute, because of the sabotage there. You don't have to do much—just put a little linseed oil in a guy's bearings, and he's out of the race. And then Bobby had all these stories about guys not building their cars. Guys had illegal welded parts, double-drilled axles, they were juicing wheels—just putting some kind of stuff on their hands, like a spitball pitcher, to rub 'quickies' on their tires.

"And the big talk about the magnets was around. There was supposed to be a car in that race with a magnet, faster than Bobby's, but he cracked up. The whole thing made me sick. After Bobby won, Vidie and I were both glad we were through with that mess."

When Chevrolet dropped its sponsorship, a special Organizational

Board of the Derby was set up, to seek a sponsor and perhaps develop new rules. Lange served on it. "I was through, but I wanted to see the place cleaned up, an entirely different kind of race. But I think in everybody's mind at that point was not to rock the boat, not to do something that would cause the whole race to collapse."

Then the Akron Chamber of Commerce took over, and there were no rule changes for 1973.

That same summer, Jimmy Gronen moved from his home in Dubuque, Iowa, to live with the Langes. Jimmy had never built a racer, and through the following fall and winter showed no interest. "Then in March," Lange said, "Jimmy suddenly asked if he could build a car. I was absolutely shocked."

It was a time, Mr. and Mrs. Lange agreed, for soul-searching. "I was fighting with myself," Vidie Lange said. "The boys enjoyed it so much, building the cars. It's a terrible turmoil in your house, all this sanding, all this fiberglass everywhere. I wondered whether the race was as bad as I thought it was, or whether I was just angry because of the turmoil."

In the end, it was Vidie who encouraged the building of yet one more racer. "When you introduce another person into your house," she said, "you try very hard to make him a part of your family and do the things for him you're doing for your other children."

"So finally we decided to do it," Bob Lange said. "I think it did a great thing for my relationship with Jimmy. But time was so short—just three months before the local race, and you really need about six. So we said we'll design a car that Jimmy can build, but the only way we could get it done in time was to use Bobby's mold—which was not illegal—and build one that was essentially the same. Even so, it would be nip and tuck. Bobby had had three years' experience working in a machine shop. I told Jimmy he just couldn't be a machinist in such a short time. We had to take shortcuts, everything was simplified. Where Bobby used five bolts, Jimmy used three—stuff like that. There was nothing much new we tried to do, just tried to get in the damn race. The only thing we did, since he was so much smaller than Bobby, was to move him further forward in the car. And where Bobby's car was about ten pounds heavy in the rear, we made Jimmy's about forty. He weighed about ninety pounds, but he was chubby, so he started his diet right away."

They made axles, and for weight in the rear Lange used epoxy mixed with buckshot. "Technically the axles were illegal. I knew they couldn't pass a hardness test. But they had never done anything about that anyway. I don't call the buckshot and epoxy illegal; I designed it so they couldn't call it illegal."

Since the car was virtually the same as Bobby's, there was no wind-tunnel test. They assumed they would get to Arkon with it. As expected, despite an accident in an early heat, Jimmy won the Boulder race as easily as Bobby had. And, as they had done with Bobby's car after the Boulder race, they brought Jimmy's car home to paint and letter it for Akron. (It is technically illegal to bring a car home after winning the local race, but the practice is common. Lange didn't want the car touched by "some yokel" who might somehow jar the car out of alignment.)

Then came the magnet. "We had done everything," Lange said. "I had Jimmy down to weight, the car balanced the way I wanted. I knew we had a fast car. But we also knew what we were up against. I had files on other cars. A guy from Michigan told me he had a car that was a whole car-length faster than Bobby's, for example. And we knew the Elk Grove car was going to be superfast. So we said. 'What else can we do? How can you make a car faster? Have we done everything?' We discussed theory. Jimmy came up with some ideas, Bobby with some."

The idea that recurred, although Lange doesn't recall who brought it up first, was a magnet. "Vidie probably would have shot us if she had known we were kicking that around. The year before at Akron, all the builders I talked with knew all about magnets. It wasn't anything new at all. It certainly wasn't *my* idea. I had heard a story about one guy who had a magnet, and somebody turned it on and left it on so it wore down before the race. I'd heard about an inspector measuring a car with a steel tape measure when, bang! it stuck to the thing. They made the driver remove the magnet, but they let him run. We knew Jimmy would be running against all those chauffeurs in professionally built cars, and maybe other cars that had magnets, so we figured that in order to be competitive we should probably try one. It was the only thing we could think of. I figured even if they detected it they wouldn't throw him out, just make him disconnect it."

NO MORAL CRISIS

Given the situation at Akron, Lange did not consider the immorality of using a magnet. "These boys had sat in on meetings with builders. They knew what was in those cars. Our attitude toward the Akron race was that it was one big wildcat, and we were in it. There was no moral crisis for Jimmy. He had been around all these super-illegal cars and saw the whole business. The scene was there, he didn't create it. Jimmy wanted to win the race."

Moreover, he said, he wasn't even sure it would work. And if it did, it would be no greater advantage than good axles, wheels, balance, and all the rest. "There's a lot of things I'd rather have than a magnet. What's more of an advantage than having a guy that's been building racers for eighteen years? Who's kidding who about advantage? You call a magnet a secret motor? You're putting a secret motor in if you add a pound, because your weight is your motor. I don't go along with the magnet being a different type of thing from the other things that are just commonly being done. Sure, I take full responsibility for it because I'm the one that should say yes or no. But I had never seen a magnet, or how they were designed. The kids designed it, and Jimmy put it in. They learn all that stuff in science class in school. All you need is a little ingenuity."

And so Jimmy put the battery in the tail fin, and ran copper wires on either side along the inside seam, where the top and bottom halves were joined. Using a stick to reach the recesses of the fuselage, he glued strips of fiberglass over the wire. He cut a hole in the nose. He bolted together four small pieces of iron, totaling about three inches in length, wrapped them with the wires, laid them in the hole, filled in around them with fiberglass resin and body putty, sanded the metal head smooth to the nose, and painted it over so that there was no visible seam or metal. The entire inside of the car was coated with black primer, which obscured any view. Lange said his only contribution was to suggest the second fail-safe thumb switch under the cowling to protect against the battery running down if one switch was turned on by accident, say, in shipping.

They tested the magnet once, by putting an I beam across the nose and trying to putt the car forward. "You could feel it," Lange said, "but it wouldn't make the car move. And the battery's got to sit for a month, so there's no point in wearing it down by testing it. It's either going to work, or it's not going to work. Anyway, nothing would substitute for a bad car. Jimmy's was a super car without it. As it turned out, he would have won anyway, but at the time I didn't think he could win without the magnet."

And then they went to Akron, where Jimmy was to win. They were attended by controversy from the beginning. Before the races, several cars, including Jimmy's, were listed for disqualification for having illegally hard axles, but officials backed down and allowed all the cars to run, just as Lange had supposed they would. During the races, officials took Jimmy's first set of wheels away because he had been working on them with his hands, and buffing them. Then they drilled in his car to remove some of the buckshot weight, while Jimmy wept in frustration. "Friends kept running up to me," Lange said, "and saying how much the officials were hassling Jimmy. I said, 'He's all right, he's a big boy, you know.'"

And finally Jimmy won it all, just before losing it all, and he said he didn't even have a chance to turn on the thumb switch for the last championship run.

Lange believes that part of the reason for singling out Jimmy for harsh treatment was jealousy from other builders they beat. Also, the Akron Chamber of Commerce, he felt, "wouldn't have made such a big issue over the thing" if it had been aware of what had been going on for years. "As a matter of fact," Lange said, "since Jimmy won about five guys have called me and said they used magnets."

The swirl of claims, charges, rumors, and denials continues. This year at Akron, the contestants will have to demonstrate their skills by duplicating "selected steps in the construction of their car"; "female" fiberglass molds of the Lange type, which can be reused, are prohibited (next year fiberglass may be banned altogether); the insides of the cars, from nose to tail, must be accessible to permit inspection for such things as magnets.

The case of the Soap Box Derby scandal is closed, more or less. Jimmy has not returned his trophy or accepted his disqualification. Lange says his nephew has been quite philosophical. "Sure, he was upset. He said, 'Here they're calling me a cheater, when these other guys are more cheaters than I am.'" But, he said, Jimmy's friends have been "super," and people in general have been sympathetic because "they know what was going on."

I agreed with Lange that to discuss all this with Jimmy would exacerbate old wounds and expose him to further painful publicity, and I wished not to do that. I came away with a sense of charm and spirit within the Lange household, and warmth in the relationships with their children, and I prefer to trust that sense.

But I cannot shake a certain melancholy. Perhaps Jimmy Gronen did not adapt to cheating as easily as all that. When he sat poised in his racer at the top of Derby Downs, with the knowledge of what he was doing, the fear of detection, the hope of winning, the faith in his guardian uncle, and the memories of the past year, he must have felt at least a transient pang of utter loneliness. And I wonder how often that stab has recurred, and will, at odd times, to different stimuli, with varying intensities, and whether winning was worth so scarred a heritage from the age of fourteen.

Pee Wee Pill Poppers

MICHAEL JAY KAUFMAN AND JOSEPH POPPER

At five-foot, seven-and-one-half inches tall and 122 pounds, 14-year-old Craig Blum could by no means be described as a youngster who should be on a diet. But for more than a week the boy with the shaggy blond hair had been on a crash diet that reduced his weight to 116 pounds. That was still not light enough to qualify him for the Intermediate Division football team of the Bethesda, Md., Boys Club. So for the last three days, Craig had not eaten a thing, taking only liquids into his stomach.

It was September 10th—the night before the Capital Beltway League, in which the Bethesda Boys Club competed, would hold its weigh-in—and Craig had only 12 hours left to lose one more pound to make the intermediate weight. Like most youth football programs, the league has a rigid age-weight classification system; the older a player is, the lighter he must be to play in the lower divisions. If Craig did not get down to 115 pounds, he would have to compete in the league's senior division, which would put him against boys who weighed up to 145 pounds.

That was why, in this last practice before the weigh-in, Craig Blum was running around with a plastic trash bag pulled over his jersey. Neck and arm holes had been cut in the plastic bag, which caused him to sweat profusely. After practice, the fullback-middle linebacker headed for a local sauna with five other youngsters who still had to lose weight. En route they met Gene Bovello, the Bethesda Boys Club athletic director and coach of its 85-pound-limit midget football team.

"The coach gave us 'water pills,'" says Craig, who reports that both Bovello and Jim Guandolo, coach of the intermediate team, saw the boys take the pills, though neither coach suggested that parental permission be sought beforehand.

The pill—which is sold over the counter under the brand name "Aqua Ban" as an aid to bodily water reduction—contains ammonium chloride and caffeine. Some doctors believe the drug is harmless. Others, such as Dr. Leonard Naeger, a professor at the St. Louis College of Pharmacy, warns that if improperly used by a child, the drug could cause intestinal irritation and might pose "something of a risk" to someone with a liver

SOURCE: Michael Jay Kaufman and Joseph Popper, "Pee Wee Pill Poppers," *Sport* 63 (December 1976), 16–25.

disorder. These potential problems would not be apparent to coaches in the Beltway League, which does not require players to undergo physicals.

When Craig Blum arrived home at about ten o'clock on the night of September 10th, he suddenly felt sick. "I went to bed, but I couldn't sleep," he says. "Later, when my parents came home, I told them about the pill."

"We were mad," Craig's father, Alan, said during a recent interview at the family's Potomac, Md., home. "Craig and his mother were up half the night.

"We don't let our children take any pills unless we are around to supervise. One reason I let Craig play football is because I heard the kids who do sports don't get into trouble so much, don't get involved with drugs. When a coach of children, who is supposed to be fighting drug abuse, turns around and gives kids pills, to me that's the beginning of taking drugs."

Alan Blum, a 40-year-old building contractor who looks and talks much like actor Robert Blake, paused, then continued: "I spoke to Guandolo the next morning and I told him I was pulling Craig off the team. He told me I shouldn't be upset, it was nothing. I asked him how he would like it if it had happened to his kid? He said, 'I agree with you. Just don't take Craig off the team.' He promised he would have Bovello or someone else in charge call back. We're still waiting."

After several days Blum phoned Kelly Burke of WRC-TV, the NBC affiliate in the Washington, D.C., area. "I wanted to do something to stop coaches from giving children pills," said Blum. "Guandolo told us that it's been going on for years, that it's no problem. But we called our doctor and he said that if a kid has diabetes or kidney trouble, there could be serious side effects from taking the pills."

Burke took a film crew to a Bethesda club practice that Tuesday night, September 14th, and interviewed the coaches. "Bovello lied to me," Burke recalls. "He denied that any pills were given out. Later he admitted he had used pills in other seasons. He told me he didn't consider over-the-counter pills dangerous." Guandolo, however, admitted that he had given one of the pills to a young player.

WRC broke the story Wednesday night. Max Cunningham, commissioner of the Beltway League, told Burke that at the very least, Bovello and Guandolo would be suspended. The next day reporters from the Washington *Star* and Washington *Post* got on the story, and by Friday it was a sensational bit of news locally. The Beltway League is the largest and most competitive youth league in the Washington, D.C., area, consisting of 88 teams with more than 3,000 players in five age-weight divisions, and 300 coaches. The league's annual "Super Bowl" games are sponsored by the Marriott Corporation and carried live on local television. A recent Super Bowl souvenir program proclaimed: "Life's future battles are won on the playing fields of the Beltway League."

"Popping Pills In Youth Football League?" was a page-one headline in Friday's Washington *Star*. By then Cunningham had expelled Bovello from the league and suspended Guandolo from coaching for one year.

During an interview at his Montgomery Village home, commissioner Cunningham explained why Bovello received harsher punishment. "Mr. Bovello is a paid executive director of the Bethesda Boys Club," said Cunningham, a 57-year-old printer who is in his tenth year as volunteer commissioner of the league. "As such, he selects coaches and is, in effect, over coaches. Bovello, by his own admission, gave pills to Guandolo to give to kids. I'm not going to have any coach give any pill to any kid under any circumstances. If the parents do it, there's nothing I can do about it."

An editorial in the Washington *Star* on Sunday, September 19th, called Bovello "a local symbol of a sad phenomenon: The American habit of ingesting pills and relying on drugs of every sort to remedy problems." The editorial concluded: "If the use of medication is common in youth athletics, parents who are not captive to the notion of winning at any cost had better insert themselves into an appalling situation, with urgency."

Bovello, who claims a lifetime won-lost record of 347–12 as a youth football coach, reacted bitterly to his expulsion. He threatened that if Cunningham's decision was upheld by the Beltway League's board of directors, he would tell "what really goes on" in youth football. "I've been around a long time and I've seen it all," he said. "In twenty-five years I've coached thousands of kids and in all that time, I've never had one complaint. Now all of a sudden there is one and everybody's trying to crucify me.

"Let's face it, it's a competitive world, and football prepares kids for life. Sure, we've given kids spirited talks to get the team up, but it's not to harm anyone. It's really just teaching. We teach them everything that has to do with character building and that helps them grow up strong, both mentally and physically."

A player who admitted he had taken pills more than once to make the weights told a *Star* reporter: "I think it's pretty dumb to make such a big stink about it. It goes on all the time. Sure, I've taken water pills. Once I got sick, but that's because I didn't have anything in my system. The other times I just went to the bathroom a lot."

"We want to prove we can win no matter what," said David Freibaum, 12, who plays on Bovello's 85-pound squad. "In the huddle of our last game, we dedicated all our games to 'Mr. Bo,' and we won, thirty-eight-nothing. We showed everybody we are a great team."

Many members of the Bethesda Boys Club were upset by Bovello's expulsion. "All the parents in our club feel that the punishment was too harsh," said club president James B. Swenson, a certified public accountant in Bethesda. "We believe that both coaches have excellent records and deserve another chance. We think they learned from what happened. We appealed the commissioner's decision to the league's executive committee, but it was upheld.

"But," Swenson added, "we don't condone the actions of the coaches, and we've hopefully put a stop to anything like it. It was a dumb thing for them to do and there's absolutely no excuse for it. We have now adopted a written policy forbidding coaches to give out any form of medication and we are rethinking the whole question of the club's role in weight reduction."

Dr. Gabe Mirkin, a Bethesda physician who teaches a course in sports medicine at the University of Maryland, is now acting as medical adviser to the Bethesda Boys Club. "This particular episode is idiotic!" he declared recently. "It's been blown all out of proportion. Those pills are absolutely harmless. But that's not all there is to the problem. I just met with the board of the Bethesda Boys Club and we drafted a whole bunch of new rules about weight loss.

"The first rule is no drugs, period. There are prescription diuretics which are truly dangerous. We have to eliminate dehydration, laxatives and diuretics as approved methods for weight loss. One safe way to lose weight is by dieting in a proper manner, and I have recommended a program that will have kids losing no more than two pounds per week under supervision.

"Bovello's action reflected ignorance, but the league is to blame," Dr. Mirkin said, "because they never issued any guidelines. Now that the problem has been exposed, they're acting self-righteous. The current weight classifications are stupid and have to be redone. They are based on medical tables created years ago and they apply to a different generation. They don't apply to these fat slobs around here. The divisions should be set up so that all the kids can play.

"I'll tell you this—Jim Guandolo is one hell of a decent guy and I feel terrible about what's happened to him. He just got caught up in the way things are."

James Guandolo is a 37-year-old government employee who lives in Potomac, Md. A former high-school and college football player, he has devoted many years to youth league coaching. "This situation was over-emphasized and over-played by the media," he told SPORT. He said that he regretted the incident and went on to describe what he perceives as some of the deeper problems affecting youth-league competition.

"One of the most hypocritical things about this whole business is that after the official weigh-in the kids are allowed to gain back six pounds during the season. This means they have to get down below their normal weight level to make a division. Every year there is some problem connected with the weigh-in. Something should have been done about this a long time ago.

"The really irrational thing is this: Why won't a kid play at his normal weight level? You know, I even advised Craig Blum to play at a higher level, but he said he didn't want to. Well, kids don't want to because maybe they won't be stars and their parents don't like that. A lot of parents really put the pressure on their kids to stay at the lower levels. And, frankly, it's sometimes a coach who stands to lose a good player.

"Judgment can be distorted by the intensity of the competition in these leagues," Guandolo went on. "The kids are mimicking what they see on the tube, and so are the parents. Enjoyment, to a degree, has been lost. Amateur sports is starting to be equated with professional sports. I remember once when I was coaching another team and we had just lost a close game, one of the fathers ran out on the field and grabbed his kid and began shaking him and hollering at him and cursing at him. The little kid just looked over at me with these big tears in his eyes. Finally, I walked over to the father and told him to get the hell off my field, and I took the kid to the sidelines with me.

"And I've seen coaches who treated even the little nine-year-olds like they were in the NFL. I mean, geez, those little kids can't even keep their helmets on straight. They should be having fun and learning a few things and that's all. Some coaches teach their kids that if they lose a game, they are *really* losers. Well, it's fun to win, but it sure as hell isn't that important."

Dr. Mirkin expressed similar feelings. "It's the goddamn parents who are ruining sports for kids. I know this from personal experience and I learned the hard way—with one of my own kids.

"My son was a great runner. In nineteen seventy and seventy-one, when my son was seven and eight years old, he held five world long-distance running records, and I interrupted my own running career as a marathoner to push him. I drove him to meets, to coaches, to clinics. He's not running at all anymore. And you know why? Because it's not fun, and it's not fun because the whole thing was *my* idea. I gave that kid unnecessary problems."

"That's what this story is all about," says Kelly Burke of WRC, "the excessive pressure placed on children involved in sports." He tells of an interview with a woman who told him she knew of cases where kids had taken laxatives for several days before a football weigh-in. The woman said she had actually seen a mother stick her finger down her son's throat to make him vomit after he had failed to make the weight by one pound.

Beltway League commissioner Cunningham also believes that most of the abuses surrounding the weigh-ins are caused by misguided parents. "I recall one incident where a kid was so weak from dieting that his father *carried* the boy to the scale. I refused to weigh him. Last year I saw one kid slumped on the floor and another who walked around in circles from losing so much weight. They were in too bad shape to be weighed. In both cases the problem was parental. I know of another case where the kid was so weak he contracted pneumonia.

"But," Cunningham adds, "that is not what this league is about. I'm talking about an infinitesimal percentage in a league with three thousand boys."

He admitted, however, that it is "highly possible" that there are other coaches who have been "guilty of the same thing as Bovello and Guandolo."

Despite the bad publicity arising from the pill incident, Cunningham speaks with pride of the Beltway League, saying its two competitive conferences "play the best brand of youth football in the area, if not the country . . ." And he is proud of the racial and social integration which he says has been achieved among all the teams in the league.

He denies that the problems in youth football stem from too much emphasis on winning. "The only people who get upset, really upset, when the team loses, are the parents and, to a lesser extent, the coaches.

"Last year, after our Intermediate championship . . . the parents and coaches of the losing team were moaning and groaning, 'There is no tomorrow.' But the kids were off on an adjacent field, playing touch football with the team that had just beaten them."

The drug episode, Cunningham says, is ultimately going to be very beneficial to the league. He says he has accepted Dr. Mirkin's offer to serve as an adviser to the entire league on weight loss.

James Swenson, president of the Bethesda Boys Club, says he now has second thoughts about the intense competition in the league.

Gene Bovello, who had threatened to tell "what really goes on" in the league, refused to say anything to SPORT after his initial comments.

Jim Guandolo, who plans to coach again next season, says, "The thing I've learned now is to avoid the youth-league coaching syndrome—I want the kids to have fun playing football."

Alan Blum and his wife Phyllis say they have no regrets about having exposed the drug story, but they are troubled by the lack of support they received from other parents. In fact, they have received numerous obscene phone calls since the story broke.

As for their son Craig, he is now playing—at his normal 122 pounds—in an instructional league where virtually every boy who turns out gets in the game. "This league is for the kids who are cut from the Beltway

League," he says. And while he makes it clear that he understands the action his parents took, when he refers to his former team . . . there is no denying the disappointment on his face.

What's Best for Kids?

TERRY ORLICK AND CAL BOTTERILL

What is best for kids? This is an extremely crucial question, but one which you will ultimately have to answer for yourself. In attempting to do so, you should consult the kids themselves. This chapter attempts to provide you with some food for thought, as well as some basis on which you can begin to formulate your answers.

Perhaps we can begin by looking at the construction of the game itself. Children generally express some concern over the quality of their sports if they are given the opportunity to do so. In one community, when eight- and nine-year-old children were asked what they liked least about sports, over 80 percent mentioned some negative experience, some boring experience, or some failure experience (Orlick, 1972a). Many children indicate that they would like sports to be scaled down to their level. Some suggestions the children make toward this end include: make the games easier; cut down the length of the games; increase the actual playing time as opposed to sitting or standing around; cut down on boring repetition such as drills; make the playing areas smaller in fields and rinks; adjust goals to enable more success, like lowering basketball nets; have less practice and more playing; cut down on the roughness; and promote honesty and truthfulness in obeying rules. In general, children express a desire to have more fun and experience more success, as opposed to failure. For example, many children feel that baseball should be changed so that they can be at bat and hit the ball more often and get the ball more often in the field. Some of their specific suggestions for accomplishing this include: making the field smaller, making the bases shorter and the bats

SOURCE: Terry Orlick and Cal Botterill, *Every Kid Can Win* (Chicago: Nelson-Hall, 1975), pp. 38–56.

bigger, allowing more swings at the ball and more outs to retire a side. In hockey, children indicate that they do not like being pushed around, checked, boarded, and "freezing." They would like to learn some skills better, like (skating), to feel they are more part of the game, to get the puck more often, and to do more playing and less sitting around.

By implementing some of the children's suggestions, we could make many positive adjustments in children's sports. Interestingly enough, some countries are already beginning to make adaptations in equipment and playing areas for children. Some examples of this include miniature-sized ping-pong tables, badminton nets and courts, volleyball nets and courts, reduced-sized volleyballs, basketballs, soccer balls, soccer playing areas, soccer goals, basketball standards (e.g., 5 foot, 6 inches), miniature courts, and so on. Some of these adjustments make it possible for nursery school children to have fun and to experience "success" in something like basketball with a few modifications in the rules. Many additional adaptations could be made in an attempt to redesign sport for success, such as developing miniature-sized curling rocks and ice sheets for children.

It is important to make sure that when an adjustment is made in equipment, rules, and the like, it actually results in more success and more fun for the children. In some cases it may be more advantageous to increase the size of an object (e.g., baseball, puck, bat) while keeping its weight constant, or to keep the size constant and reduce the weight in order to enable more success for the young child. At any rate, by scaling down the games and making the necessary adaptations, we will provide children with a greater chance to attain some success and conceivably to have a more rewarding and enjoyable experience in the sport.

In attempting to provide for all types of children, we should remember that some children are not interested in activities of a highly competitive or team nature (i.e., child versus child or team versus team). More individual and/or noncompetitive activities should be provided to meet the needs of these children, and facilities should also be made available for children to "just play" without any adult intervention. It should not be a case of "superorganized or unavailable," as one parent expressed it. For kids to have the opportunity to play on their own without a lot of structure is essential. This provides important learning situations in which children have to be completely self-reliant for organization, rules, officiating, teaching, learning, practicing, creating, and so on. Many children indicate that they would like to take part in more individual and noncompetitive outdoor activities such as camping, hiking, climbing, exploring, cross-country skiing, sledding, swimming, archery and horseback riding (Orlick, 1972a; Glassford et al., 1973).

To give the kids increased responsibility within the organized sport setting is also important. This can be done by such things as asking them for their advice and getting their opinions on different things related to practices, games, or the sport itself; by encouraging them to make up new kinds of practice games or new ways of practicing skills; by encouraging them to call their own fouls and do their own officiating in practice and games; by encouraging them to organize on their own; and by gradually increasing the decisions and responsibilities which are given to them to carry out.

It is important that the coach set up an atmosphere in which a child can feel or develop a sense of self-worth. A child's estimate of his own worth or ability is inferred from the words and gestures of other people. Children tend to anticipate and adjust their behavior to the expectations of others. You behave in terms of what you think you are, and what a child thinks he is depends upon what other people think he is.

In order for a child to feel he is a person of worth, other people must treat him like he is a person of worth. This is why approval, praise, and encouragement are so important to a child—to let him know he is an acceptable and worthy individual. As a social being, every child needs this kind of approval. This is also one reason why approval results not only in better learning, but also in better overall adjustment of the child.

Probably the easiest way to develop a feeling of self-worth in sport is to prove to the child by his actions that he is accomplishing something. Physical activity is one place where a child can see and feel improvement quickly. For example, "Two minutes ago you could not do a seat-drop on the trampoline—now you can!" This is indisputable evidence of accomplishment which can make a child feel proud and worthy. Each accomplishment, however small it may seem, should be recognized and rewarded, particularly in the beginning. This will serve to legitimize the child's feelings, which may be needed at the start. The child will experience countless evidences of self-worth as long as he compares himself (and you compare him) to his own past performance. How you treat the child can have a significant effect on how he sees himself.

Coaches and parents have too often resorted to aversive or negative control when working with children (e.g., criticizing, ridiculing, blaming, humiliating, scolding, yelling, threatening, punishing, withdrawing approval, and so forth). This takes its toll on children as can be attested to by drop-out children and young participants alike. To accept imperfection while a child is learning is important. An overconcern with perfection can make a child feel like a failure, causing him to subsequently lower his feelings of self-worth. You can make a child feel successful by rewarding any improvement or anything good, and by making positive suggestions, or you can make the child feel like a failure by always criticizing and yelling that he did this or that wrong, or that he wasn't as good as so-and-so was. For example, a girl may come in last at a swim-meet and feel happy and successful if you compare her to her own past performance, but sad and unsuccessful if you compare her to the winner of the meet. In terms of overall adjustment, as well as learning, to use the positive approach based on individual improvement is much more beneficial for the child.

If you consistently treat a child like a failure, or if he consistently feels as if he has failed, he will soon see himself as a failure. This will in turn have obvious effects on his feelings of self-worth as well as his performance. It can get to a distressing point, as one mother expressed about her eight-year-old son: "Now he's afraid to try anything because he's afraid to fail."

In his book, *How Children Fail*, John Holt comments: "They [children] are afraid, above all else, of failing, of disappointing or displeasing the many anxious adults around them, whose limitless hopes and expectations for them hang over their heads like a cloud" (1970:16).

Remember to let a child know that he is acceptable even if he doesn't excel. He has to know that it is perfectly acceptable to participate just for fun. The child should not be made to feel acceptable *only* when he performs well. Unfortunately adults sometimes reinforce performance at the expense of the child. An example of a parent resorting to negative tactics in the pursuit of excellence came out in an interview with the father of a ten-year-old hockey player. The father told the child that he would buy him the best new skates available if he made the all-star team. The boy made the team and consequently was given his brand new pair of expensive skates. Shortly after this, his father took the skates back from him because "he didn't play well enough." The father said that the boy "put out from then on."

This boy had a lot more than a pair of skates at stake. His father had essentially told him that unless he made the all-star team, and unless he played well once he made the team, he was unacceptable to his dad. No wonder he put out! (How long can the boy take this kind of adverse control and remain psychologically healthy? And more important—what happens when he can't make it?)

Other forms of negative control include such things as always harping at a child about his mistakes, telling him he didn't play well or he didn't skate well, telling him he missed good chances, and so on. In a recent study, many fathers of young players were found to respond negatively to their sons after they had lost a game (Higgs, 1974). This kind of behavior does not appear to serve any useful purpose. It just produces needless anxiety in the child and makes him feel miserable. Similarly, when a coach singles out a child and chastises him in front of everybody for doing something "wrong" like missing a shot, it is extremely distressing for the child and puts him in a situation in which he is scared to death of making a mistake. The child already knows he's made a mistake or that he's lost—there's no reason for the coach or parent to rub it in. If anything, they should help the child to reduce his anxiety or to adjust to the loss by playing it down. Put yourself in the kid's shoes. What if you made an unintentional mistake or were the cause of something going wrong? Would you want someone making you feel even worse? Wouldn't it be better to help the child look forward with some enthusiasm to the next challenge?

Children tend to operate on their expectancies of reinforcement. For example, if they expect fun, approval, or success from sports, they will be motivated to participate. On the other hand, if they expect disapproval, humiliation, or failure, they will not be motivated to participate. Whether a child actually does participate will be dependent upon the relative strength of these conflicting expectations.

Once in the sports environment, children will tend to behave in the manner expected of them or in the manner which will maximize their rewards. This will be true regardless of whether the behavior is positive or negative; for example, passing to a teammate or fighting. There is evidently an increasing amount of violence not only in society and in professional sports but also in children's sport. For example, when eight- and nine-year-old hockey players were interviewed in eastern Canada, it was found that about 50 percent of them had already been in a fight in hockey, half of them having been in a fight three times or more (Bentley and Hunter, 1973). In one province it became necessary to put cages around the penalty boxes and to eliminate shaking hands after the game to prevent young children from fighting. After kids' games the officials stand guard and/or escort the opposing teams to their locker rooms to prevent fights from breaking out.

You ask yourself, "Why does this occur?" There are probably a variety of reasons, but a major one is that violence is being reinforced, as is clearly pointed out in the following two examples. This first excerpt is taken from an interview with a ten-year-old hockey player.

- Q. What do you like best about playing hockey?
- A. Hitting . . . knocking the guy down . . . I just like hitting.
- Q. What does your coach do when you make a good hit?
- A. The coach gets really excited . . . like in practice when you get a good check . . . he yells "yeah" and slaps his stick on the ice.

The next excerpt is taken from an interview with the proud father of another ten-year-old hockey player.

Jason's aggressive. . . . He's not afraid to get in there and hit. The other day he hip-checked a kid and knocked him right out of the play. . . . He's not afraid to go into the boards after them. My other son Rod just sticks his stick in there but he won't hit. . . . I try to tell him . . . what can you do with someone like that?

Obviously aggressive behavior is being rewarded in sports such as hockey and football. It is beginning to take its toll both on and off the playing field. One study indicated that ten-year-old all-star hockey players were more likely to respond aggressively with pushing, hitting, and so forth in normal social situations than their peers who were not involved in sports (Leith and Orlick, 1973).

A particular behavior will become commonplace or disappear depending on the rewards which are given for engaging in the behavior. A behavior is terminated through the removal of positive rewards or through the introduction of negative consequences for engaging in the behavior.

If you feel that violence is not an admirable kind of behavior for kids to engage in and you wish to extinguish it, under no circumstances should kids be rewarded for engaging in it. It is up to you to see that only positive modes of behavior, and not negative ones, are rewarded.

People (parents, coaches, teachers, and others) are inclined to take good behavior for granted and pay attention only when a child misbehaves.

Most of us pay attention to violations. For example, when a player gets a penalty in hockey, it is announced over the public address system, "Number 8—Johnny Jones—two minutes for roughing." Attention to inappropriate behavior serves to strengthen the very behavior that the attention is intended to diminish (see Madsen, 1971). By paying attention, we may actually unintentionally reward what we do not want to occur. Some kids behave in certain undesirable ways, like unfair play, infringing on the rights of others, and doing what they are not supposed to be doing, just to get attention. If we cease to give them attention for behaving in this way, they in turn will stop doing it.

We tend to dwell on what is wrong rather than looking for what is right even when teaching skills. Pay attention to the good behavior! Play a little game—try to *catch the child being good* and then reward the child by giving attention, praise, or smiling. Watch carefully and when the child begins to behave desirably make a comment such as, "You're doing fine, Cathy, very good." Persistence in catching children being good and giving praise and attention will eventually pay off in better behavior, better performance, and more fun for all.

Certain kinds of behavior seem to be obviously desirable, like sharing, cooperation, honesty, concern for others, respect for others' rights and feelings, self-discipline, self-reliance, and so forth. Other kinds of behavior appear to be obviously undesirable, like violence, fighting, disregarding rules, cheating, unfair play, lack of concern for others, selfishness, and so on. It would be extremely beneficial for children if you (parents, coaches, officials, members of the community league, etc.) were to get together to outline the kinds of behavior you feel are desirable and undesirable for (your) children in sports. If the behavior can be listed in concrete, observable terms, you can then all work together to actively encourage desired kinds of behavior and actively discourage undesired kinds of behavior.

A specific example of desirable behavior relating to cooperation and concern for others may be something like helping another child with a skill during practice or after a competition. In wrestling, after a match, a boy could show his "opponent" how he pinned him and how he could have escaped. In gymnastics, competitors could help one another with skills after a meet. This type of beneficial socializing may help the children realize that the other team is not really "the enemy."

In trying to promote honesty and fair play, encourage a child in any sport to call his own infractions. In volleyball he could be encouraged to raise his hand if he touches the net or if the ball is out-of-bounds. Another example may be if a boy or girl unintentionally knocks someone down, he or she could help the person up and apologize for the infraction.

Some specific examples of undesirable behaviors may be such things as punching, elbowing, tripping, yelling profanities at the referee, and so on. It should be made known to the child that this type of behavior is totally unacceptable.

If you were actually to take up this challenge and act upon it, the potential benefit to the kids could be immense. This could lead not only to the formation of desirable rules and behavior for children in sport in your community, but also to desirable behavior for coaches, parents, and officials involved with kids in sport.

Several innovative children's hockey programs which have recently sprung up independently in different parts of Canada have been direct attempts at doing what's best for kids. After speaking with the innovators of four of these programs (George Kingston, University of Calgary hockey coach; Harvey Scott, University of Alberta sport sociologist and former pro-football player; Hal Hansen, University of Ottawa hockey coach; Al Way, innovative minor league hockey coach, Ottawa, Ontario), we saw clearly that they were doing some pretty impressive things with young kids. What follows is a brief description of some of the unique aspects found to exist in any one or all of these programs.

The emphasis in each of these programs is on learning basic skills and having fun doing it. Any boy (or girl, in two of the programs) who wishes to play hockey has a chance to do so and is given an equal amount of time on the ice. The approach is extremely positive with a lot of praise and encouragement given to the kids. For example, if a child falls down and gets back up, rather than yelling at the kid for falling, the response is something like: "That's it Jimmy, that's the way to get back into the action." In two of the programs no official score is kept. They are trying to insure that the fun aspect remains high and to implement the idea that "success" is not dependent upon the number of goals scored or on the number of assists made.

In all of these programs the emphasis is on self-improvement. For example, the kids may be told to "glide on one skate as far as possible" and then to "try to go a little further than you did last time." The coach watches for individual improvement and when he sees the slightest evidence of it will say something like, "Very good John . . . you turned to your left that time . . . that's the best you've done it." Little fun games are used to learn skills, and shinny (spontaneous pickup games) is played cross-ice. Games are generally played cross-ice (three games going at once on a regular hockey rink), which allows all kids to be active at the same time with no one sitting. One coach has the games go for fifteen minutes straight with everybody playing; then there is a five minute break and then he has another fifteen minutes straight. Each child is also given the opportunity to play each position and all coaches actively discourage roughness and foul play.

They are reportedly having tremendous success with the youngest kids, judging by the way the kids are improving, by the fun they are having, and by some of the comments from the parents. Some of the older kids who have been firmly conditioned in the old way of playing for the score, with undue roughness, are not as receptive. "Deconditioning" will not occur overnight, but in time these older kids will again learn to play for enjoyment and to play fairly.

Hal Hansen, president of the Canadian Hockey Coaches Association and member of the Canadian Amateur Hockey Association (C.A.H.A.) Technical Advisory Committee, is a forward thinking individual who has had a wide range of involvement in Canadian minor hockey. For the child in sport he strongly recommends:

A total de-emphasis on winning games, of becoming league champions, of winning trophies with the emphasis being placed upon individual improvement in the particular skill and the learning of new ways and means to enjoy hockey. . . . An alternative lies in the refocusing of hockey as a sport, an endeavor that provides enjoyment, fitness, and skill improvement. It means a de-emphasis on organization and competition under ten or eleven years of age. It means an emphasis on innovation in practice content, and ice utilization so that sound progressions and learning experiences become evident. . . . We must consider the majority and give them the opportunity to participate fully, to enjoy hockey as a sport, to feel the thrill of learning a new skill, or shooting the puck in a net, or just plain maximum activity in learning situations. (1972)

Hansen is now implementing and conducting research on his innovative "alternative" which should ultimately be to the benefit of thousands of youngsters. Jim Duthie of the University of Windsor Sports Research Institute is also involved in the implementation and assessment of an alternative hockey approach which is a direct attempt to "return the game to the children." Twenty-eight teams in the city of Windsor are participating in a no standings minor hockey league. For their eighteen game season no goals are counted, no points are awarded for games won or lost, and no records are kept of leading scorers. The kids just play the game and seem to have a lot of fun in the process. Initial research observations indicate that kids in this league show "less frustration, anxiety and aggression" than those in more traditional leagues ("No-Win Hockey," 1974).

A progressive young women's high school physical education teacher who switched from a negative to a positive approach has shown that new directions can work even with older kids.

She revealed that she used to always look for what was wrong with what people did, but that over the years she found that the girls responded much better when she looked for what was right. "You can always find something good, no matter how bad a girl's ability is. I try to pick out what's good." Her present approach is one which emphasizes fun for all and a concern for others. When she first started teaching she "followed the book" by doing a lot of drills and then allowing about five minutes to "play" at the end of the period. She soon found out that kids wanted to "play" and not "work" at drills. She now lets them play for nearly the whole period. If they are having problems they will ask for help. For example, one time the girls asked, "How come we never score any baskets?" At that time she asked if they wanted to do some shooting practice, which the girls were now ready and willing to do.

The effect of this teacher's encouragement of a concern for others became evident in a volleyball game. After about two months of encouraging the girls to make the teams even and to help one another, the following incident occurred. One of the poorer girls came up to serve. The girls on the "opposing team" told her to move in closer to the net to serve, because they knew she wasn't very good. She walked halfway up the court and managed to barely lob the ball over for a "successful" serve. "It was a marvelous thing to see and a marvelous feeling for me." Instead of being glad that the girl couldn't serve (an easy point for us!) as they were in the beginning, they now considered this girl's feelings and helped her. Other things also began to happen, like girls switching sides to even things up if too many "good" girls seemed to be on one team. The girls really began to enjoy their gym classes.

A community league director and the father of a boy whose team won the league championship in baseball had the following observations on the positive approach:

> My son just happened to be on the team that won the league championship last year. I'm positive that it was because of the coach. He never yelled at the kids and everytime a kid came off the field he'd have something encouraging to say . . . a little pat on the back and some little positive suggestion . . . no matter how bad the kid was (e.g., that's okay Kelly, you gave it a good effort . . . next time maybe try keeping your bat a little more level on the swing). This same little league coach also had the winning team the following year.

Former pro quarterback and head football coach at the University of Western Ontario, Frank Cosentino, is also a strong advocate and model of the positive approach to coaching. He looks for what is good, he is constructive in his criticism, he provides his players with a lot of encouragement, he is empathetic with his players, and he never screams or chews them out. In short, he is a positive-thinking man who has great rapport with his athletes and is sincerely interested in them as individuals as well as football players. Since he began his coaching career, only four years ago, his teams have consistently either won or have been strong contenders for their league title and have also won the Canadian Intercollegiate Championship.

There are other examples of this type of positive approach in different sports which is beginning to take hold. People like those mentioned, as well as others who have attempted to start positive and innovative programs, should be given a lot of credit for going out on a limb in an attempt to do what's best for kids. They may not have all the answers as of yet, but they are well on their way, and it is only by trying new positive approaches that we will eventually come up with what is really in the best interest of kids.

Evidently there are some people presently doing an excellent job with kids in sport, but there are countless more who could be making a similar contribution. Those who seem to be most effective are the ones who have a genuine "relationship" with the kids. They are nonthreatening, straightforward, and enthusiastic. They set a positive atmosphere which permeates the gym, the field, the rink, or the pool. Games and skills are presented in a fun-filled positive way, instructions are simple and easy to follow, and the difficulty of skills is gradually increased. Praise and encouragement are given often, even for partially correct performance or behavior (e.g., I'm pleased with the way you're moving along; you guys did a great job today, etc.). A child is not subjected to offensive, negative criticism for doing something "wrong." Criticism is constructive and is stated in the form of positive suggestions (e.g., try keeping your head up a little more). The children are included in the decision-making process and really feel that the program is their own. It is truly a program *for the kids!*

As long as we keep in mind that the outcome of the child is infinitely more important than the outcome of the game, we will be well on our way toward doing what's best for kids. When an overemphasis is placed on winning, competition breeds the kind of conflict which is not in the children's best interest. People who encourage winning at all costs, cutting and eliminating poorer athletes, violence and fighting, pressure tactics, the complete disregard of rules, and the like, are having a negative effect on children in sport. These individuals, who are organized *only* to win, do more to promote undesirable behavior and to turn kids off sport than any other known factor. The concepts of having to "be first or forget it" or of having to either "do it well or don't do it at all" do not belong in children's sport.

Our contention is that the proponents of these philosophies should be informed of the errors in their ways, presented with positive suggestions for alteration, and encouraged to try some of these alternative methods. If this is done in a positive, constructive manner (which includes explaining why it is best for the kids), people will generally be receptive. There are cases on record of persons who have changed from a completely negative approach to a positive approach based on this kind of feedback. This resulted in children having a good experience, rather than a poor one, which was previously the case. However, if after your sincere attempts, no positive changes ae made, it seems that there is no other option left except to remove these people (negative influences) from all contact with children in sport. This appears to be the only way to protect the children.

Since the child has relatively little control over the situation which exists in children's sport, it is up to you to implement changes. He can't do much to change things, but you can. If you see undesirable behavior being reinforced, kids having bad experiences, or children being mistreated in sport, it is important that you try to do something about it.

■ FOR FURTHER STUDY

Albinson, J., and G. Andrews, eds. *Child in Sport and Physical Activity*. Baltimore: University Park Press, 1976.

Allman, Fred L., Jr. "Competitive Sports for Boys under Fifteen: Beneficial or Harmful?" *Journal of the Medical Association of Georgia*, 55 (November 1966), 464–468.

Ashe, Arthur. "An Open Letter to Black Parents: Send Your Children to the Libraries." *New York Times* (February 6, 1977), section 5, p. 2.

Ball, Donald W. "Failure in Sport." *American Sociological Review*, 41 (August 1976), 726–739.

Berryman, John. "From the Cradle to the Playing Field: America's Emphasis on Highly Organized Competitive Sports for Preadolescent Boys." *Journal of Sport History*, 21 (1975), 112–131.

Broadus, Catherine, and Loren Broadus. *Laughing and Crying with Little League.* New York: Harper and Row, 1972.

Brosnan, Jim. "Little Leagues Have Big Problems—Their Parents." *The Atlantic Monthly*, 211 (March 1963), 117–120.

Brown, Jonathan J. "Little League Baseballism: Adult Dominance in a 'Child's Game'." Paper presented at the Pacific Sociological Association meetings (Victoria, B.C.: April 1975).

Brower, Jonathan G., ed. "Children in Sport." *Arena Review*, 1 (Winter 1978), entire issue.

Caldwell, F. "Adults Play Big Role in Children's Games." *The Physician and Sportsmedicine*, 5 (1977), 103–108.

Collins, George J. "League Baseball and Our Children." *The Physical Educator*, 11 (May, 1954), 37–39.

Deakin, Michael. *The Children on the Hill.* London: Quartet Books, 1973.

Devereux, Edward C. "Backyard Versus Little League Baseball: The Impoverishment of Children's Games." *Social Problems in Athletics.* Edited by Daniel M. Landers. Urbana: University of Illinois Press, 1976, pp. 37–56.

Dowell, Lewis J., "Environmental Factors of Childhood Competitive Athletics." *The Physical Educator*, 28 (March 1971), 17–21.

Frayne, Trent. "Parents, Pressure, and the Puck." *Quest Magazine* (November 1972), pp. 41–43.

Geoffrey, G. W. "Reward System in Children's Games: The Attraction of Game Interaction in Little League Baseball." *Review of Sport and Leisure*, 1 (Fall 1976), 93–121.

Gerson, R. "Redesigning Athletic Competition for Children," *Motor Skills: Theory Into Practice*, 2 (1977), 3–14.

Gibson, Gwen. "Watergate on Wheels," *Ladies Home Journal* (August 1974), pp. 64–70.

Godshall, R. W. "Junior League Football," *Journal of Sports Medicine*, 3 (1975) 139–144.

Hale, Creighton. "Athletics for Pre-High School Age Children." *JOPER*, 30 (December 1959), 19–21, 43.

Harris, Donald S., and D. Stanley Eitzen. "The Consequences of Failure in Sport." *Urban Life*, 7 (July 1978).

Havemann, Ernest. "Down Will Come Baby, Cycle and All." *Sports Illustrated*, 39 (August 13, 1973), 42–49.

Hein, Fred V. "Competitive Athletics for Children." *Contemporary Philosophies of Physical Education and Athletics.* Edited by Robert A. Cobb and Paul M. Lepley. Columbus, Ohio: Charles E. Merrill, 1973, pp. 60–67.

Herron, R., and Brian Sutton-Smith. *Child's Play.* New York: John Wiley, 1971.

Horn, Jack. "Parent Egos Take the Fun Out of Little League." *Psychology Today* (September 1977), pp. 18, 22.

Hotchkiss, Sandy. "Parents and Kids' Sports." *Human Behavior*, 7 (March 1978), 35.

Jackson, C. O. "Just Boys, Not Little Adults." *The Physical Educator*, 18 (May 1961), 42.

Kirshenbaum, Terry. "They're Pooling Their Talent." *Sports Illustrated* (July 10, 1978), pp. 32–43.

Larson, David, Elmer Spreitzer, and Eldon E. Snyder. "Youth Hockey Programs: A Sociological Perspective." *Sports Sociology Bulletin*, 4 (Fall 1975), 55–63.

Leah, Vince. "The Case for Abolishing Hockey Leagues for Youngsters." *Mc-Leans Magazine* (April, 1964), pp. 62–65.

Lever, Janet. "Sex Differences in The Games Children Play." *Social Problems*, 23 (1976), 479–487.

Lever, Janet. "Sex Differences in the Complexity of Children's Play and Games." *American Sociological Review*, 43 (August 1978), 471–483.

Lowe, Benjamin, and Mark H. Payne, "To Be a Red-Blooded American Boy." *Journal of Popular Culture*, 8 (Fall 1974), 383–391.

Loy, John W., and Alan Ingham. "Play, Games, and Sport in the Psychosociological Development of Children and Youth." *Physical Activity: Human Growth and Development*. Edited by G. L. Rarick. New York: Academic Press, 1973, pp. 257–302.

Maggard, Bob. "Avoiding the Negative: Blue Jeans Baseball." *JOPER*, 49 (March 1978), 47.

Magill, R., et al. *Children and Youth in Sport: A Contemporary Anthology.* Urbana, Illinois: Human Kinetics, 1978.

Mantel, R. C., and Lee Vander Velden. "The Relationship Between the Professionalization of Attitude Toward Play of Pre-Adolescent Boys and Participation in Organized Sport." Paper presented at the Third International Symposium on the Sociology of Sport, Waterloo, Ontario (1971).

Martens, Rainer. "Kid Sports: A Den of Inequity or Land of Promise?" *Proceedings of the National College Physical Education Association for Men.* Chicago: University of Illinois at Chicago Circle, 1976, pp. 102–112.

Martens, Rainer. *Sport Competition Anxiety Test.* Champaign, Illinois: Human Kinetics Publishers, 1977.

Martens, Rainer, ed. *Joy and Sadness in Children's Sports.* Champaign, Illinois: Human Kinetics Publishers, 1978.

Martens, Rainer, and Vern Seafeldt, eds. *Guidelines in Children's Sports.* Washington, D.C.: American Alliance for Health, Physical Education, and Recreation, 1978.

Mehl, Jack, and William W. Davis. "Youth Sports for Fun—and Whose Benefit?" *JOPER*, 49 (March 1978), 48–49.

Michener, James A. *Sports in America.* New York: Random House, 1976, chapter 4.

Nixon II, Howard L. "Sport, Socialization, and Youth: Some Proposed Research Directions." *Review of Sport & Leisure*, 1 (Fall 1976), 45–61.

Opie, Iona, and Peter Opie. *Children's Games in Street and Playground.* London: Oxford University Press, 1964.

Orlock, T. D. "Children's Sport—A Revolution is Coming." *Journal of the Canadian Association for Health, Physical Education, and Recreation* (January/February 1973).

Orlick, Terry, and Cal Botterill. *Every Kid Can Win.* Chicago: Nelson-Hall, 1975.

Ralbovsky, M. *Destiny's Darlings.* New York: Hawthorn Books, 1974.

Ralbovsky, M. *Lords of the Locker Room.* New York: Peter H. Wyden, 1974.

Rosen, Al. *Baseball and Your Boy: A Parent's Guide to Little League Baseball.* New York: Funk and Wagnalls, 1967.

Sage, George H. "Socialization and Sport." *Sport and American Society*, 2nd ed.

Edited by George H. Sage. Reading, Mass.: Addison-Wesley, 1974, pp. 162–172.

Scanlan, T. K. "The Effects of Success-Failure on the Perception of Threat in a Competitive Situation." *Research Quarterly*, 48 (1977), 144–153.

Seefeldt, Vern, and John Haubenstricker. "Competitive Athletics for Children— The Michigan Study." *JOPER*, 49 (March 1978), 38–41.

Smith, Murray F. "Adults in Kids' Sports." Paper presented at the International Symposium on the Art and Science of Coaching, Toronto (October 1971).

Smoll, F., and R. Smith, eds. *Psychological Perspectives in Youth Sport*. Washington, D.C.: Hemisphere, 1978.

Smoll, Frank L., Ronald E. Smith, and Bill Curtis. "Behavioral Guidelines for Youth Sport Coaches," *JOPER*, 49 (March 1978), 44–47.

Smoll, Frank L. and Ronald E. Smith (eds.). *Psychological Perspectives in Youth Sports* (Washington, D.C.: Hemisphere Publishing, 1978).

Snyder, Eldon E., and Elmer Spreitzer. *Social Aspects of Sport*. Englewood Cliffs, New Jersey, Prentice-Hall, 1978, pp. 47–53.

Stone, Gregory P. "The Play of Little Children." *Quest*, 4 (Spring 1965), 23–31.

Sutton-Smith, Brian. "Child's Play: Very Serious Business." *Psychology Today* (December 1971), pp. 66–69, 87.

Thomas, Jerry R. "Is Winning Essential to the Success of Youth Sports Contests?" *JOPER*, 49 (March 1978), 42–43.

Underwood, John. "Taking the Fun Out of the Game." *Sports Illustrated* (November 17, 1975), pp. 86–98.

Voigt, David. *A Little League Journal*. Bowling Green, Ohio: Bowling Green University Popular Press, 1974.

Watson, G. G. "Family Organization and Little League Baseball." *International Review of Sport Sociology*, 9 (1974), 5–31.

Watson, G. G. "Games, Socialization and Parental Values: Social Class Differences in Parental Evaluation of Little League Baseball." *International Review of Sport Sociology*, 12 (1977), 17–47.

Five

Sport in Educational Settings

Interschool sports are found in almost all schools and at all levels. There are many reasons for this universality. Sports unite all segments of a school and the community or neighborhood it represents. School sports remind constituents of the school, which may lead to monetary and other forms of support. School administrators can use sport as a useful tool for social control. But probably the most important explanation for the universality of school sports is the widespread belief that educational goals are accomplished through sport. There is much merit to this view; sports do contribute to physical fitness, to learning the value of hard work and perseverence, and to being goal-oriented. There is some evidence that sports participation leads to better grades, higher academic aspirations, and positive self-concept.[1]

There is a negative side, though, to school sports. They are elitist, since only the gifted participate. Sports often overshadow academic endeavors, (e.g., athletes are disproportionately rewarded and schools devote too much time and money to athletics that could be diverted to academic activities).[2] Where winning is paramount—and where is this not the case?—the pressure becomes intense. This pressure has several important negative consequences. Foremost it cheats the participants out of enjoying sports. The pressure is too great for many youngsters. The game is work. It is a business. Writing about the 1978 Class A (smallest classification) basketball championship teams in Colorado, sportswriter Steve Cameron gave the following description and editorial comment:

> Hey, I thought high school basketball tournaments were supposed to be fun. Thrill of a lifetime and all that.

169

Item: Stratton wins a 65–64 thriller from two-time finalist Sargent Friday night to gain a berth in the Class A state championship games. After the game, Coach Tom Pannell calls his team "sorry," yells at his kids behind locked doors, and leaves them in such a state of shock that the players were nearly silent in the locker room.

Item: Merino's machine rumbles to another in a seemingly endless string of victories, carving up tiny Lone Star 68–55 in another Class A semifinal game. The Rams, who have won this tournament two straight years, display emotion on the floor about as often as does Mr. Spock. Calmly, they rout somebody else and listen while Coach Ron Vlasin tells them that they were flat and listless. "We had a little talk," Vlasin says of another closed-door session. "We just weren't ready to play."

These were the winners.

I can hardly wait to see Merino and Stratton on the same floor Saturday night. Pannell and Vlasin can wind up the players like little toys, and they will run plays, shoot 50 percent or better, and never smile. For heaven's sake, never smile.

Maybe I'm getting my priorities out of order, but I thought that basketball for kids 17 years old and younger was supposed to be a good time.

A trip to the state tournament ought to be a reward, a visit to the bright lights for players who have worked hard all year and should be enjoying the spoils.

To watch the demeanor of the teams at the Class A semifinals, you'd think David Thompson's salary [the highly paid Denver Nugget] was at stake. Oh sure, the parents hollered and the cheerleaders screamed, but the coaches make it look like a business.

Pannell, instead of being ecstatic at winning a down-to-the-wire battle to reach the finals, tongue-lashed his players and maintained that the only celebration he was interested in would be after a state championship.

Where does this leave everything those youngsters from Stratton have accomplished so far? Is it all worthless if they don't upset Merino—which is most unlikely, by the way?[3]

The pressure to win also contributes to abuse by coaches, poor sportsmanship, hatred of opponents, intolerance of losers, and cheating. Most significant, although not usually considered, is that while sport is a success-oriented activity, it is fraught with failure (losing teams, bench warmers, would-be participants cut from teams, the humiliation of letting down your teammates and school, etc.). For every ego enhanced by sport, how many have been bruised?

While this description fits all types of schools, big-time college sports deserve special attention for they have some special problems. Athletes in these settings are athletes first and students second; thus they are robbed of a first-class education. They are robbed by the tremendous demands on their time and energy. This problem is further enhanced by athletes being segregated from the student body (in special classes, housed in athletic dorms); thus they are deprived of a variety of influences that college normally facilitates.

Another problem of college sports is that they tend to be ultra-elitist. The money and facilities go disproportionately to the *male* athletes in the revenue-producing sports rather than to intramurals, minor sports, and club sports. Using the University of Maryland as an illustration, Neil Isaacs has pointed out that the sports program, while financed by students, actually discourages participation.

> Consider the values placed on sports as spectacle and sports as participation at the University of Maryland. Students are charged a $30 annual athletic fee, which provides about three-quarters of a million dollars, or about 35 percent of the intercollegiate program's funds.... The students also are charged a separate $44 yearly recreational facilities fee that is used for many purposes. From this, about $47,000 makes its way back to the men's intramural sports office. In other words, the entire men's intramural program, serving about 13,000 participants last year, costs about as much as the education of four to six football players on scholarships. The athletic fee entitles students to attend home games—if enough seats are available in the student section. On the other hand, the limited availability of intramural facilities clearly discourages extensive use of them by the student body. The result for many students is that they are, in effect, paying twice for the privilege of not participating in sports.[4]

The greatest scandal involving college sports is the illegal and immoral behavior of overzealous coaches, school authorities, and alumni in recruiting athletes. In the quest to bring the best athletes to a school, players have been given monetary inducements, sexual favors, forged transcripts, and surrogates to take their entrance exams. In addition to the illegality of these acts, two fundamental problems exist with these recruiting violations: (1) such behaviors have no place in an educational setting, yet they are done by some educators and condoned by others and (2) these illicit practices by so-called respected authorities transmit two major lessons—that greed is the ultimate value and that the act of winning supersedes how one wins.

Finally, the win-at-any-cost ethic that prevails in many of America's institutions of higher learning puts undue pressure on coaches. They must win to keep their jobs. Hence, some drive their athletes too hard or too brutally. Some demand total control over their players on and off the playing field. Some use illegal tactics to gain advantage (not only in recruiting, but also in breaking the rules regarding the allowed number of practices, ineligible players, and unfair techniques). But coaches are not the problem. They are a symptom of the process by which school sports are big business and where winning is the only avenue to achieve success.

The articles in this unit reflect on these problems. They raise the ultimate question of the value of sport in schools—are school sports, as they are currently organized, compatible with educational goals? If not, what can be done to make sport consonant with educational objectives?

The articles focus on two related topics—the problems of school sports and how coaches in schools cope. The first three papers point to the major problems of sport in schools. The fourth, a selection from a former football player at the University of Texas, provides an excellent example of just how much a big time football program can physically and mentally abuse the athletes. The next selection, by John Massengale, a college football coach, gives insight into the pressures that make coaches behave in characteristic ways. Finally, the essay by Eitzen summarizes school and sport problems and provides some possible solutions.

NOTES

1. For documentation of these findings, see especially: John C. Philips and Walter E. Schafer, "Consequences of Participation in Interscholastic Sports: A Review Prospectus," *Pacific Sociological Review*, 14 (July 1971), 328–338, and Elmer Spreitzer and M. D. Pugh, "Interscholastic Athletics and Educational Expectations," *Sociology of Education*, 46 (Spring 1973), 171–182. For the methodological problems in these kinds of studies and other reasons why they may be suspect, see: Christopher L. Stevenson, "Socialization Effects of Participation in Sport: A Critical Review of the Research," *Research Quarterly*, 46 (October 1975), 287–301.
2. Cf., James S. Coleman, *The Adolescent Society* (New York: Free Press, 1961).
3. Steve Cameron, "Hey! Stratton, Merino Coaches, It should Be Fun," *The Denver Post* (March 11, 1978), p. 25.
4. Neil D. Isaacs, "The Losers in College Sports: Student-Athletes Are Pushed Aside by Hucksterism," *The Washington Post* (October 16, 1977), p. C1.

Athletics and the Modern Industrial State

JOEL SPRING

Athletics constitute an important part of our modern technological culture. Among other things, they are big business, and hence reflect the methods and techniques of other industrial enterprises. But more importantly, they utilize the leisure time of large numbers of the population. Many after-work hours are spent in front of the television or in the stands watching the unfolding drama of an athletic event. In this sense, athletics are the major theater of our culture.

As a form of theater, athletics may fulfill one of the functions early promoters assigned to sports in an industrial society. Athletics were viewed as a means of diffusing the discontent and unrest created by a factory organization which robbed work of meaning and individual satisfaction and subjected the worker to the monotony of the assembly line. The worker, it was hoped, would make up for the lack of job satisfaction through proper use of leisure time. In other words, rather than change the industrial organization to add meaning and enjoyment to work, policy makers hoped that satisfaction could be achieved through the consumption of another cultural product.

The original argument that athletics would solve the basic problems of a modern industrial society is interesting because it provides insight into the possible role of athletics in our present culture—and the role of schools in preparing individuals for that culture.

The original ideological argument made sports a panacea for labor unrest, social discontent, the tedium of modern industrial and urban life, and a faltering democratic spirit. In considering these reasons for the expansion of modern sports one must recognize the distinction between physical training and athletics. Physical training in the form of gymnastics has developed in the public schools in the U.S. since the early nineteenth century. Athletics, however, while associated with student clubs and organizations, was not brought formally into the curriculum of the school until the late nineteenth and early twentieth century. This occurred with the development of the argument that sports or team games have formal

SOURCE: Joel Spring, "Athletics and the Modern Industrial State," *Phi Delta Kappan* (October 1974), pp. 114-115.

173

educational value and that sports have a legitimate educational role in public schools and colleges, as well as an important role in the life of the urban worker.

In brief, the arguments supporting the expansion of school and public athletics emphasized that a modern industrial society could no longer afford a democratic spirit that emphasized the rugged laissez faire individualism of the frontier. The compressed living in urban centers and the specialization and organization of modern industry required an individual who could function in a highly interdependent society and determine his own good in terms of the social whole. One of the roles assigned to athletics was the training of the co-operative, democratic citizen. On the athletic field the individual was to learn to work for the good of the group and to define individualism as specialized effort for the good of the team. This cooperative training was to be transferred from the athletic field to the factory, to politics, and to urban living.

In addition to fostering a cooperative democratic spirit, athletics were to introduce a spirit of adventure to counter the tedium of modern living. The meaninglessness of work in a technological society was among factors which bred restlessness and a search for adventure in labor strikes and industrial turmoil. To the proponents of athletics, the cure was not in industrial reorganization but in providing athletic adventure. Training for athletic participation was to begin in the public schools and was to be continued in public park and recreation leagues. Sports would provide the excitement lost as the technological society engulfed the pioneering spirit of the frontier.

A major flaw in this thinking was that accepting the existing technological structure paved the way for distortion of original intentions. It has already been noted that athletics have become big business, a business dependent on a large body of consumers or spectators. Like any technological enterprise, it depends upon a form of expansion which increases the ratio of spectators to players or consumers to workers. For business to be profitable there must be more spectators in the stands than players on the field. The original goal was mass participation in athletics. What has resulted is mass spectatorship.

Even with the development of mass spectatorship and big-business athletics, the schools have retained a vital role in the promotion of sports. One role has been the training of future players for professional sports. In most cases today one must participate in college football before being considered by a professional football team. As in many other phases of society, college training is becoming a requirement for a money-making career in athletics. Thus public school and college athletics are a form of vocational training. In fact, this vocational training can lead to a very economically rewarding career. It is not hard to imagine that, some time in the future, athletic departments may start receiving federal grants for vocational education and that athletic departments in major universities may be given professional school status comparable to that of medicine and law.

The schools also provide training for consumer-spectators. For most students the monotony of school is broken up by participation in frequent pep rallies and the loyal following of the school team. The excitement of school athletics may actually teach the student that the adventure of schooling is not found in the traditional curriculum but in other cultural aspects of schooling. The student might transfer this learning to later life, accept the inevitable tedium of work, and search for satisfaction and meaning in leisure-time athletic participation and spectatorship.

In this sense athletics as the theater of our culture are a very conservative force, providing a cultural antidote to the frustrations of modern living and distracting from a quest to change the organization of industry so that adventure and meaning can be found directly in work and living.

On the other hand, one can view athletics as the best theater provided by our culture. As humanity continually gains control over nature and rationalizes the social process, adventure is lost. Progress as we know it means greater predictability and control. As this is achieved, the unknown and the unpredictable escape from our lives. Athletics thus become good theater because the script and the ending have not been written. Played within simple rules, athletics might indeed be the last area of a technological culture where no one knows how the game will end.

Even as good entertainment, sports carry the seeds of their own destruction. Commercialization and modern managerial techniques introduce a factorylike air that corrupts the potential escape from technological certainty. The professional football draft that occurs each year is a rationalized plan to establish equality of competition between teams. This provides a planned competitiveness and assures large gate and television receipts. Added to this are market research methods which shift teams from place to place without regard for local loyalty. Athletes have begun to talk like workers in other industries and have organized players associations in an attempt to achieve collective bargaining. Witness the players' strike in the National Football League this past summer. The games themselves are played under scientific management with factorylike specialization and expertise.

The situation grows out of the inherent contradictions in our social system. Each method of relief from its rationalizing process becomes another product that must be rationalized and made profitable. But as it is made more profitable its value as a method of relief diminishes. In the end not only the spectators start to get bored but also the players.

This, of course, is the danger for public school athletics. As professionalism and commercialism descend through the ranks of schooling, athletics begin to resemble other forms of school work. They are pursued not because of joy in the activity but in hope of a future career. This of course destroys their value, both as a conservative social force and as good theater.

Commercialism, Entertainment, and Ethics in College Sports

GEORGE H. HANFORD

Three of the major concerns which prompted the call for this inquiry, and which appeared at the outset to have surfaced quite independently, turned out in the course of the inquiry to be inextricably interrelated. They are that intercollegiate athletics have become too commercialized, that big-time college sports have put higher education improperly in the entertainment business, and that the whole enterprise is infected by unethical practices. The interconnections, obvious in retrospect, are that the commercialism in intercollegiate athletics is a function of being in the entertainment business and that the unethical practices are spawned by competition for the entertainment dollar.

COMMERCIALISM IN INTERCOLLEGIATE ATHLETICS

Concern over commercialism in intercollegiate athletics is nothing new to higher education. It existed before and existed since the 1929 Carnegie report. It was one of the primary reasons set forth in the call for this inquiry. Ironically, the charge is sometimes levelled by representatives of institutions which have instructed their athletic directors to break even.

SOURCE: George H. Hanford, *An Inquiry into the Need for and Feasibility of a National Study of Intercollegiate Athletics* (Washington, D.C.: American Council on Education 1974), pp. 63–82.

Indeed most directors of big-time sports programs do not question the instruction; they have for the most part taken the goal of self-sufficiency for granted. Furthermore, the successful ones don't see what the financial fuss is all about.

The fact remains, however, that legislators, college and university trustees, and presidents, not athletic directors and coaches, are responsible for policy determination, and it is against them, when they establish a policy of financial self-support for a program of inter-collegiate athletics, that the charges should be levelled. Misdirected charges of commercialism by faculty members also have a hollow ring when one realizes that by reason of their very self-sufficiency, where it still exists, athletics are not making demands on limited general funds. (So also, incidentally, do their expressions of concern about the recruiting of athletes. Recruiting of faculty members can be, and frequently is, a vicious process, and unlike intercollegiate athletics, there is not even a code of proper behavior.)

But regardless of where the impetus for commercialism comes from, it does exist and does have serious by-products. It puts the athletic department in business as business, in this case in the sports entertainment business with its peculiar (that is, different from the rest of the entertainment world) emphasis on winning. Seasoned athletic directors point out that success is dependent on many factors, but that chief among them is winning, which is in turn a function of team schedules involving "representative" opponents, good coaches, good athletes, and good weather. Because commercial success, a break-even operation, depends so heavily on better-than-break-even records, it is no wonder that athletic departments seek winning coaches and that they in turn go to such lengths to recruit student athletes.

In short, one finding of the inquiry is that the cries of anguish about the overemphasis on winning, and about the growing commercialism of big-time college sports of which that overemphasis is a function, should be directed not at the athletic establishment but at the legislators, trustees, and administrators who today demand that intercollegiate athletic departments support themselves. A national study should undertake to test the validity of this finding and to make recommendations about ways in which institutions can either abandon or rationalize their break-even policies.

INTERCOLLEGIATE ATHLETICS AS ENTERTAINMENT

Concern about the role of big-time, intercollegiate athletics in the field of entertainment was one of the primary considerations leading to the call for this inquiry. Accordingly, one of the questions raised regularly in the course thereof was "Do colleges and universities have either the need or the responsibility to provide public entertainment through the medium of intercollegiate sports (for instance, the private institution to its alumni or the publicly supported institution to the taxpayers)?" There turns out to be a wide difference of opinion, the implications of which should be the subject of careful scrutiny in a national study.

There is no doubt, however, that big-time college sports programs are in fact in the entertainment business whether they like it or not. Presidents, athletic directors, coaches, and even faculty athletic representatives speak openly about "competing for the entertainment dollar." Their concern about the inability to raise ticket prices to keep pace with rising costs is rooted in the fear that further increases would force the consumer to find other uses for his limited entertainment dollars and to partake of his college football by television if at all.

It is, however, on the issue of whether they should be in the business in the first place that opinions differ. Those who argue against the proposition do so mainly on the philosophical ground that public entertainment is neither traditionally nor properly a function of higher education, period. Those who support the proposition do so on essentially three grounds. First, like it or not, the institutions have assumed a responsibility which they cannot now abdicate. The second ground is economic. Even though college sports may not pay for themselves, they provide a focus for alumni, taxpayer and legislator attention which has an indirect pay-off in general financial support for the institution. The third argument is philosophical and rests on the logic that colleges and universities have traditionally and properly been providing entertainment of many kinds over the years. They see inconsistency in the logic of those who find lectures, concerts, recitals and plays acceptable but disapprove of football. They find intercollegiate sports, big-time and low-profile, less corrupting *on the whole* than some other features of higher education. And they call attention to the desirability of an institution's cultivating a variety of constituencies for economic support and that big-time sports in particular attract such support.

Without attempting to labor all the subtleties here, it nevertheless is obvious that, while low-profile football is much closer than big-time programs to these other fields of entertainment provided to the community at large by colleges and universities, the element of having to win or lose does set athletics apart from other forms of entertainment.

The inquiry found validity in the arguments of both camps and suggests that the issue for consideration in a national study is related not to sports entertainment as entertainment but to sports entertainment as big business.

PROFESSIONAL SPORTS AND THE MEDIA

The commercial success, or lack thereof, of big-time intercollegiate athletics is influenced by the competition from professional sports for the entertainment dollar and by the coverage given to college sports by the media.

Professional Sports. The rapid growth of professional sports since World War II has had a marked effect on intercollegiate athletics. As noted elsewhere, they have siphoned off newspaper interest and concentrated what is left in the big-time, big-college sports of football and basketball. They have created standards of entertainment performance that are different from those at the college level. They have opened up, or at least greatly enlarged, career opportunities. And they have been instrumental in establishing unrealistic success models for many of the nation's minority youth.

Most important in the context of commercialism, however, professional sports have provided an alternative attraction for the sports entertainment dollar and won. Except in Los Angeles, there is not a financially successful big-time intercollegiate football program in a city with a professional football franchise. The two Big Ten programs in the deepest financial trouble are the only ones in head-to-head competition with pro teams. As noted elsewhere, it is believed that professional football could drive college football off the air if it wanted to. But because the colleges provide a training ground for professional players, the pro franchises want to keep what some refer to as their gridiron farm system turning out raw material for their consumption. Recognizing this motivation, some observers of the sports scene are suggesting that ways and means be found for generating professional sport support for college athletics; they see the pro-self-imposed ban on Saturday television as insufficient.

Provision of such support would of course create problems of distribution. Support on a per head basis (for instance, providing to an institution one scholarship for each athlete who makes a regular season squad) would only intensify the recruiting of high school athletes, itself already a process suspected of excess. Conversely, because not all college football programs produce pros, support across the board to all colleges does not appear to make sense either. Exploration of some middle ground, within the context of a broader search for bases of cooperation, seems called for at this time.

Because colleges' and universities' athletic programs were there first, their supporters have tended to perceive professional sports as an intrusion. Certainly their actions in building barriers between professional sports personnel and the collegiate athletic community confirm this attitude. For instance, one of the arguments used in explaining the NCAA rule against allowing colleges and universities to rent their stadium to professional football teams went like this: "We don't allow our players or coaches to associate with the pros. I see no reason why we should deny them the chance and then let the institutions do so." Many in the college sports world act generally as if they are convinced that the pros are out to ruin intercollegiate athletics.

Conversations with individuals from the professional side in the course of the inquiry would, however, seem to suggest just the opposite. They recognize the college ranks as their source of raw player material. What they may not so clearly recognize is the possibility that colleges may be training their future consumer-spectators as well. As Froomkin points out, "The increasing popularity of basketball and football as spectator sports has never been convincingly linked to the fact that a growing number of persons in our population who have attended or graduated from post-secondary institutions have had increased exposure to those two sports. The hypothesis is extremely attractive, however."

For professional sports then, particularly football and basketball, it is important that there be strong intercollegiate programs where potential players can be trained and observed and where consumers can be developed. Given this stake in the success of college sports, professional owners, general managers and coaches appear willing to sit down with athletic and administrative representatives from colleges and universities to work out patterns of cooperation which would lend support to college-level activities. For example, professional franchises oversubscribed for season tickets might give priority to individuals holding season tickets for the local college teams. Sequential showing of college and pro coach television programs could attract attention to the former's teams. Possibilities in terms of financial cooperation (for which read "support") have been noted earlier. In working with the press, professional representatives could help by calling explicit attention to intercollegiate competition. In any event a national study could well serve as the medium for joint exploration by the professional and college-level sports world of these and other ways and means by which the former could help support the latter in a much-needed stabilization of the sports entertainment business.

Television. The advent and growth of television have added new problems and new dimensions to some old ones for the world of intercollegiate athletics. In various ways it exerts very direct control on the conduct of televised athletic events, determining when games shall start and when commercial time-outs will be called. In its choice of days, that is by not televising professional football games on Saturday afternoon and Friday evening and by not showing college games on Friday evening, the medium supports an uneasy truce among interscholastic, intercollegiate and professional football. In this context it is seen also as professional sports' answer to the suggestion that they should contribute dollars to the support of the institutions which screen and train their players. The pros argue that by not competing with the NCAA in the Saturday football market, they are in fact making such a contribution. And they are not only losing the money they could earn from such exposure (experience suggests that in a head-to-head competition with college events the pros would win) but they are also filling the colleges' coffers with those same lost dollars.

But Saturday coverage is a mixed blessing. The televised game may be a more attractive alternative than the hometown college game and, unless that college is one of the few that does not charge for admission, a less expensive one. On the other hand, the televised game does pump welcome dollars into the support of intercollegiate athletics, some of it generally to support of the services provided through the national athletic associations and conferences, some of it to the other members of the conferences of the participating teams, but the largest share of it usually to the teams on the tube, which got there because they are successful. Television thus adds to the pressure on coaches to produce winning teams.

It has less direct and more subtle influences as well. Some sociologists claim that it engenders a passive consumerism which takes people out of participation, a claim being refuted at least among today's college-age population by their growing interest in intramural and club sports. At the same time, television has served to stimulate the growth of professional sports in the United States and, in doing so, has affected intercollegiate athletics in several ways. Because of the national and sometimes international character of the big-time professional leagues, their events are capable of regularly generating a national interest, a phenomenon on which the colleges can capitalize only briefly in their post-season bowl games and championship tournaments. According to some, the televising of certain sports adds a sophistication to spectatorship which makes the public at large less satisfied with performance at the college level and therefore more likely, given a professional alternative, not to spend its entertainment dollar on intercollegiate games. Others would hardly call it sophistication in calling attention to college hockey crowds that try to goad players into fights—like those that they see on the tube.

Television also serves to influence the popularity of sports. Gymnastics, for instance, received a great boost as a result of the televising of the 1972 Olympics. In the same way, however, it serves to generate interest among boys and girls, young men and women, in the more regularly broadcast sports and thus to perpetuate the importance of the big-time sports as opportunities for both viewing and playing. There are those, for instance, who believe that in their televised appearances, professional black football and basketball stars come through as success models to their younger brethren and thereby help to set unrealistic career goals for a great many of them. And, of course, television has served to focus the attention of the press on professional sports, the collegiate winners, the bowl games, and championship tournaments and to divert it from intercollegiate athletics broadly perceived.

The Press. The effect or influence of the nation's press is variously perceived as negative toward, disinterested in, uninformed about, captive of, and irresponsible toward intercollegiate athletics.

The charges of disinterest and lack of information are made in the light of the emphasis of the major city newspapers on professional sports. Coaches and athletic directors complain that public interest in college sports is dulled and attendance at intercollegiate events diminished because most space on most sports pages is devoted to professional teams. Women complain that what minimal coverage is given to their sports is replete with evidence of male chauvinism. The press responds of course that it is only giving the public what it wants. These charges are a far cry from those which characterized the 1929 Carnegie report which decried the overemphasis given to the importance of intercollegiate athletics by the nation's press. The fact is that today's press concentrates its attention to college sports on the "top ten."

The charge that the press eats out of the hand that feeds it is leveled against sportswriters in smaller cities which are the homes of the successful big-time university programs. The arguments here are that close association with an athletic department leads inevitably to familiarity and then to prejudice and that unless the local sportswriter caters to the winning coach, the latter will freeze him out of inside dope. This charge is similar to that mounted against members of the big city press assigned to cover professional teams.

The charge of irresponsibility is made by newspaper people who are not sportswriters and by others. It is based on the certainty that sportswriters are aware of the dirty tricks that are being played in the recruitment and subsidy of athletes and on the judgement that those writers are abdicating their responsibility to expose. That they fail to do so is attributed to the belief that they would expose a scandal of such major proportions that it would put big-time intercollegiate athletics *and* them out of business.

Ironically the charge of negativism is lodged against a growing cadre of mostly younger writers who have taken it upon themselves in the press and in the literature to comment upon intercollegiate athletics, not simply to report them. Spawned in the era of campus protest, they have called many of the excesses in intercollegiate athletics to public attention but generated little in the way of public response.

The fact remains, however, that press coverage, its lack thereof or its nature, does have an influence on intercollegiate athletics. (And the fact also remains that this section was written before *The New York Times* series on recruiting in intercollegiate athletics was initiated on March 10, 1974. The contents as well as the fall-out will be interesting to observe.)

Radio. Radio today plays an important though less prominent part than television and the press on the intercollegiate athletics scene. In its news coverage, it is taking the same tack and having the same effect as the press in concentrating national interest on the top teams in the big-time sports. However, in its events coverage it is much more catholic and much less concentrated in its coverage. Because of its relatively low cost as compared with television, it provides an opportunity for local or college stations to broadcast away games back to the home campus and community. At the state level in instances where there are more than one state university, state-wide radio coverage of football and basketball is a prize sought by institutions vieing for public interest and support (for which read "funds"). It is a force not to be overlooked in any study of intercollegiate sports.

COMPETITIVE EXCESSES

External competition from professional sports, selective treatment by the media, pressure from alumni and the public have all combined to put big-time collegiate athletic programs into competition with each other not only on the playing field but in the market for entertainers/performers/athletes. The need to win on the field has thus led to those ethical problems in the recruiting, financial subsidy, and on-campus care-and-feeding of college athletes which formed one of the basic sets of consideration leading to the call for this inquiry. In the course of the inquiry no one has been found who disputes the existence of such problems; what is at issue is their volume.

To reduce what could easily become a polemic to a partial listing, violations which come to the attention of the inquiry team include, but are by no means confined to, the following:

- altering high school academic transcripts
- threatening to bomb the home of a high school principal who refused to alter transcripts
- changing admissions test scores

- having substitutes, including assistant coaches, take admissions tests
- offering jobs to parents or other relatives of a prospect
- promising one package of financial aid and delivering another
- firing from a state job the father of a prospect who enrolled at other than that state's university
- "tipping" or otherwise paying athletes who perform particularly well on a given occasion—and then on subsequent ones
- providing a community college basketball star with a private apartment and a car
- providing a quarterback with a new car every year, his favorite end with a "tip," and the interior lineman with nothing
- getting grades for athletes in courses they never attended
- enrolling university big-time athletes in junior colleges out-of-season and getting them grades there for courses they never attended
- using federal work-study funds to pay athletes for questionable or non-existent jobs
- getting a portion of work-study funds paid to athletes "kicked back" into the athletic department kitty
- forcing injured players to "get back in the game"

The fact that violations played the same role in generating the studies leading to the 1929 Carnegie report and the 1952 ACE effort and yet persist in more virulent form today suggests a formidable challenge to the national study that must be mounted in order, at least in part, to deal with them.

The existence of such violations is admitted by those involved in intercollegiate sports and documented in press reports and the files of the several national associations and athletic conferences. The admissions, however, never relate to the campus or conference or region of the admittee. It is always another coach, another president's institution, another conference, or another region that is guilty. Conceivably, the alumni or booster club could be doing something unethical but no one in authority "on our campus" is aware of them.

Financial Aid in Intercollegiate Athletics. Perhaps the saddest self-commentary by the athletic establishment about the state of its own morality appears in the controversy surrounding the award of financial aid to athletes. At the 1973 NCAA convention a proposal was presented calling for the abolition of full-ride grants-in-aid and the adoption of a policy calling for the award of financial aid to student athletes on the basis of need. Two reasons among others, were advanced in support of the proposal. One, it is standard practice with respect to virtually all other students. This argument makes good sense, particularly to those who decry special treatment of athletes. In fact, most people in the educational community but outside the athletic establishment are all for it and can't understand why it is not standard practice in the first place. Two, it saves money. This potential result is attractive to some inside the establishment.

One large, big-time, independent institution visited in the course of the inquiry suggested an experience roughly as follows: Under NCAA regulations it could award $600,000 in athletic grants-in-aid. Because it, like most private institutions, has much higher tuition than its public counterparts, it needs considerably more scholarship money to support a given athlete. By not awarding all the grants-in-aid that it was entitled to and by making some of the awards it did make partial instead of full ones, the institution got by with $400,000. If it had used the formula of the College Scholarship Service for computing need and made its awards on that basis, it would have cost only $200,000.

With two such compelling arguments on its side, why was the proposal rejected? It was turned down in 1973 and again in 1974 because the big-time intercollegiate athletic establishment on balance doesn't trust itself. The argument was that such a policy would generate even more under-the-table payments than now exist. Note not only the admission that they now exist but also the opinions that the pressure to win is so great that coaches would exceed the need formula and that athletes would accept such awards. (The qualification relating to "big-time" in the second sentence above is an important one. At the 1974 NCAA convention, the Division III colleges at least voted to go with an aid-according-to-need policy.)

In any event the issue of grants-in-aid versus aid-based-on-need promises to remain a controversial one and one to which the attention of the proposed national study Commission on Intercollegiate Sports might profitably be given.

Medical Concerns. Although problems related to the medical aspects of intercollegiate athletics represented a major concern in the study underlying the 1929 report in the sense that injuries reflected an unethical exploitation of athletes, the topic neither appeared as part of the rationale for the mounting of this inquiry nor surfaced without prompting as a matter of moment during the course thereof. In 1929 the focus was on football injuries. Subsequent advances in medical knowledge, training methods, and protective equipment have tended generally to allay concerns on that score. Meanwhile, a review of the literature and the solicitation of opinion during the course of the inquiry suggest that a new generation of problems has appeared. They include the following charges: That the pressure to win has prompted some athletic staffs to employ newly developed short-term medical treatment (in order to get players back in the game) at the risk of long-term disability. That the use of artificial turf has introduced a set of medically related problems (injuries, burns, infections) which, while different from those incurred on grass, are in the aggregate more severe. That an improper and excessive use of drugs has developed—particularly of new drugs to build up strength or to add weight.

In the matter of sports-related injuries, prevailing opinion appears, as already noted, to be that advances in medicine, training, and equipment have served to diminish the incidence of those serious and disabling injuries with which the 1929 report was concerned. Despite the improvements, however, research and experimentation designed to find ways for reducing still further the number and severity of such injuries is continuously in progress.

In the matter of opportunistic use of short-term medical treatment, the charges have most often been initiated by former athletes. They are seldom made or confirmed by the athletic establishment, and then only in the most general terms about someone else's institution. The fact remains, however, that in soliciting opinion with regard to serious problems facing college sports, discussion of this particular subject was not initiated either by institutional staff members or by athletes, past or present. Furthermore, it did not emerge without prompting as one of the factors involved in the exploitation of athletes. . . .

In the matter of medical problems related to the use of artificial turf, there seems to be wide divergence of opinion. Those opposing its use argue that considerations relating to finances (it costs less to maintain) and aesthetics (it looks better on television) have been allowed to override those related to the physical well-being of the athletes. Those favoring its use admit that artificial turf has created its own new brand of injuries but opine that they are on balance less severe than those, particularly knee injuries, suffered on natural turf. And they generally feel that, while its maintenance costs have turned out to be higher than those associated with grass, the fact that the surface can be used 24 hours a day (while grass must be protected) makes the new surfaces a wise investment.

In the matter of the use of drugs in college sports, the results of the inquiry suggest that, as is happening in the society-at-large, the "drug problem" is on the decline. Those within the athletic establishment generally agree that there was a period of extensive experimentation with certain new drugs a few years back, but believe that that period has to all intents and purposes ended. Nevertheless, it has been recognized as a matter worthy of special continuing consideration by the NCAA and is under study at this time.

In summary, while the medically related problems of intercollegiate athletics are not generally perceived as constituting a matter of major concern at this time, they nevertheless appear as a result of this inquiry to be of sufficient importance to warrant specific attention in a national study.

The Incidence of Competitive Excesses. But to return to the main theme of this section, the volume, or more properly the volumetric nature (the numbers, the kinds, and the number of each kind) of unethical practices is subject to wide difference of opinion. The NCAA officials concerned with enforcement report, for instance, that most of the violations reported to them have to do with recruiting (because that is where institutions can keep an eye on each other) but that probably the greater number and certainly the more serious occur in the academic and financial care and feeding of athletes once they are enrolled (and out from under scrutiny by other institutions). Conference and national association officials point to their files for volumetric data. These sources suggest that the number is relatively small but the investigators admit that there are undoubtedly more violations than are reported to them for review, particularly again of the on-campus variety.

College and university presidents tend to fall into three groups: those who avoid the subject, those who talk about it but are not concerned about the situation, and those who are alarmed. The degree of the latter's alarm is evident in some of the solutions that are proposed, from a dramatically enlarged NCAA investigatory force to the abolition of intercollegiate football, basketball, and hockey. Athletic directors and coaches normally generalize in admitting that unethical practices do exist, but the great majority of those reached in this inquiry indicated that they believe that the number of violations is relatively small. Secondary school personnel echo this same belief.

On the other hand, virtually without exception, the recent college graduates who were interviewed in the course of the inquiry as recent participants in big-time football and basketball charged that violations are flagrant and widespread. They name people, places, and events. They agree with the NCAA observation that more violations probably take place in the care and feeding than in the recruiting of athletes. And they indicate that alumni, boosters, and friends are responsible for most of them. But while they believe that athletic directors and coaches may not know specifically who is doing what for whom, they are strongly of the opinion that the staff has at the very least to have a general idea of what is going on and was probably responsible for generating the "what" in the first place.

In response to these charges by athletes, coaches and athletic directors point out that their experience suggests that the players, past and present, tend to exaggerate. For instance, when returning former athletes are asked about the incidence of violations that occurred when they were participating they will frequently first make general accusations of a sweeping nature but then back down when questioned about specifics.

While the findings made in the course of this inquiry are obviously not conclusive, there appears to be sufficient evidence to suggest that the ethical problems relating to the recruiting, subsidy, and on-campus care and feeding of participants in big-time college sports are serious enough, both in kind and in number, to warrant the mounting of a national study of intercollegiate athletics—and so to warrant on their own account and without regard to the financial and other problems besetting the field. The principal inquirer believes, however, that those problems cannot be dealt with in isolation—in isolation either from the commercial, entertainment-related influences which have exacerbated them and which are dealt with above or from the economic and educational considerations which are treated below.

The Collegiate Dilemma of Sport and Leisure: a sociological perspective

GEORGE H. SAGE

Listen carefully and see if you can identify the source of this statement:

Athletics are taken seriously in most American colleges . . . There is not much fun or freedom in the life of the candidate for the . . . team . . . intense rivalry smothers the spirit of fair play and leaves the game short of one of its greatest attractions . . . The newspapers make capital of this in exaggerated paragraphs, and football [games] assume the appearance of a gladiatorial show . . . The money making value of the game is dragging sports down from its true place as a recreation, and, together with the rivalry before alluded to must tell against

SOURCE: George H. Sage, "The Collegiate Dilemma of Sport and Leisure: A Sociological Perspective," NCPEAM Annual, 1976 (Proceedings of the 79th meetings of the National College Physical Education Association for Men, Hot Springs, Arkansas, January 1976).

its best interests. But the evil does not stop here, for smaller colleges, like small boys, try to imitate their big brothers, and so offer distinguished players large salaries to coach their football teams that they may compete with some hope of success; and thus many of the men who become noted in college athletics have professionalism thrust upon them.

Have you identified the author? Jack Scott? Dave Meggyesy? Roger Wiley? You are not even close. This is not a speech that was made last week or last year. It is not something that was written by some sport radical. It was made, though, by a professional physical educator, but not a contemporary one. It was made by R. Tate McKenzie (1893) to the American Association for the Advancement of Physical Education in 1893!

Let's try another one:

When [intercollegiate] athletics are conducted for education the aims are: 1) to develop all the students and faculty physically and to maintain health; 2) to promote moderate recreation, in the spirit of joy, as a preparation for study; and 3) to form habits and inculcate ideals of right living. When athletics are conducted for business, the aims are 1) to win games—to defeat another person or group being the chief end; 2) to make money—as it is impossible otherwise to carry on athletics as business; 3) to attain individual or group fame and notoriety. These three—which are the controlling aims of intercollegiate athletics—are also the aims of horse-racing, prize-fighting, and professional baseball.

It may not surprise you at this point to learn that the statement comes from a 1915 issue of the *Atlantic Monthly*, authored by William T. Foster (1915).

I think these two excerpts make quite clear that we are dealing with a dilemma in higher education that has been with us for a long time. It is, nevertheless, a phenomenon that needs thoughtful analysis, and one hopes, action toward resolving the dilemma.

Snyder and Spreitzer have very eloquently contrasted the relationships of the athletic and the leisure-recreation sub-systems within universities, and, in general, I agree with their analysis. But I shall eschew academic-like weighing of the pros and cons of their paper and will instead use it as a basis to make a more direct approach to the dilemma; let the chips fall where they may: What in the hell is a commercial entertainment enterprise doing on a university campus. Bigtime intercollegiate sports is a business enterprise that is part of a cartel, a form of corporate organization for which there are a number of federal laws prohibiting such structure, but, as James V. Koch (1973) writing in *Law and Contemporary Problems*, says: "Despite the claims of the National

Collegiate Athletic Association (NCAA) that it is a champion of amateur athletics and physical fitness in colleges and universities, the NCAA is in fact a business cartel composed of university-firms which have varying desires to restrict competition and maximize profits in the area of intercollegiate athletics."

Any serious notion that the NCAA is dealing with amateur athletics is quickly dispelled in its own *Manual* (1974). On page 6 of the current edition the following statement appears: "An amateur student-athlete shall not be eligible for participation in an intercollegiate sport if: 1) He takes pay, or has accepted the promise of pay, in any form, for participation in that sport. . . ." But, incredible as it may sound, two pages later, the *Manual* contains a section on *financial aid* to intercollegiate athletes! It reads: "Financial aid, including a grant-in-aid . . . may be awarded for any term . . . during which a student-athlete is in regular attendance. . . . Financial aid awarded by an institution to a student-athlete shall conform to the rules and regulations of the awarding institution. . . ." So much for amateur athletics! And so much for the notion that intercollegiate athletics is primarily an educational function of the universities.

Not only are big-time intercollegiate athletic programs a commercial business enterprise, functioning as part of a cartel, and employing athletes, but the programs are operated with employees (athletes) who are being paid slave wages. Whereas, professional football players earn an average of around $50,000 per year, the average collegiate football player earns around $5,000 for doing essentially the same job— entertaining spectators. Even granting that collegiate football teams play only half the number of games as the pros, the collegiate players are vastly underpaid. A university that reports that its athletic program showed a million dollar profit need not be too proud; it was accomplished at the expense of exploiting its employees.

Now, I realize that there are several forms of intercollegiate athletic programs, each having somewhat unique characteristics, so what is true of one form is not necessarily true of another. I group the types of programs into three categories: the amateur-educational, the big time professional, and the semiprofessional. The first comes close to serving a truly educational function on the campus. Athletes are not given financial aid *just* because they are athletes; and they do not receive special favors. Many colleges operate programs of this type. They should be commended. There is no intercollegiate athletic dilemma at these institutions.

Everybody knows who the big time-professionals are: They are grouped into conferences such as the Big Eight, Big Ten, Pac-8, etc. The group which I call the semi-professionals is made up mostly of middle-sized universities who are trying to emulate the big timers. They are schools without much academic stature who are trying to get visibility through sports. In many cases they offer the full-ride scholarship, but some offer only partial athletic scholarships, even if they have to take it out of OEO federal money or out of the general student's pockets. Since nationwide attention is devoted to the big time-professional programs, and it is here where the greatest dilemma exists, as far as I am concerned, my remarks will be directed towards them.

Snyder and Spreitzer are right, of course, the contemporary university is a many-splintered thing; but, as they note, we certainly might suppose that its main goals are the transmission of knowledge, the discovery of new knowledge, and the pursuit of truth. What does big time sports contribute to the goal attainment function? I suspect that they contribute very little; as I pointed out earlier, a big time program is a business—the business of making money through sports contests. As one pro coach (Bridges, 1969) said: "In pro football, it's obvious that you must win. In college football there's sometimes talk of other goals, but when you get right down to it, that's what really matters there, too." The Heisman Trophy winner, Steve Owens (1969) said, while he was at Oklahoma: "In high school the game was almost entirely fun. Here it's a business. We're supposed to fill the stadium with 60,000 fans and win . . . I still love the game, but there's so much pressure, sometimes it makes me wonder." Andre McCarter (1974), a UCLA basketball player, recently noted: "There's no rah-rah stuff about the game. . . . We look at it like a business, a job. . . . It's like the pros, except you don't have any income." Finally, Sonny Randle (1975), the University of Virginia football coach, said this fall: "We've stopped recruiting young men who want to come here to be students first and athletes second."

The notion that a big time intercollegiate athletic program has anything to do with the educational goals of a university is absolutely bizarre when you consider the fact that some of the most esteemed universities in the world do not have intercollegiate sports: Oxford, Cambridge, University of Heidelberg, etc. Even in the United States, some of the most prestigious universities have an amateur-educational program: University of Chicago, MIT, Cal Tech, and some others.

This is not to say that there may not be some indirect impact on the academic programs because of successes in sports. As Snyder and Spreitzer say: "The favor resulting from such a program does promote political and economic support." Presidents at state universities feel that a successful athletic program yields greater support from the legislature, and several universities have documented that alumni contributions fluctuate with the successes and failures of the teams.

Frankly, I have several reactions to this state of affairs. First, it should not be too surprising that legislators and alumni judge the success of a university by its athletic teams. After all, the public relations milieu of the universities is devoted to projecting the athletic teams as the symbols of the quality of the university. Offices of sports information directors and their staff of assistants make a persistent and consistent effort to get the public to identify with the teams. If the athletic teams falter, what can one expect in the way of financial support. It's easy to see how the thinking of legislators and alumni could go: "The university is failing; let it know you don't like it—withhold funds." The way to resolve this problem is to turn the sports information offices into academic information offices and promote the ongoing scholarly activities on the campuses. Who knows, perhaps the several publics who financially support a university could be persuaded to evaluate the institution by its contributions to education. As one University of Nebraska professor noted: "If we were able to make our presentations [to the state legislature] without the distraction of football ratings, we could fare well with the legislators. Reason usually prevails" (Budig, 1972).

Another reaction I have to using sports to generate funds for academic purposes is related to the exploitation of student-athletes. I question the morality of using student-athletes to hustle money for the university—the university profits from the sweat of the athletes. At least the student-athlete should be paid a decent wage by the employers, if one of his functions is to produce capital, either directly or indirectly.

Another reaction: At what cost to the athlete, not in financial terms but in academic terms, do these big time programs squeeze money out of the alumni, legislators, and spectators? Some of the best collegiate athletes have been involved in sad endings to their collegiate careers—not athletically, but academically. Allen Brenner (1969), a recent captain of Michigan State's football team said: "Playing college football is becoming a delusion. It takes too much of your time. There are fall meetings, fall practice, spring practice, weight programs. The plight of the player-student is almost impossible. He doesn't have enough time to study."

At what cost to the athlete in psychological terms is the university treasury supplemented? Gary Shaw (1972), a former Texas football player, says: "What they do to those kids is nothing short of criminal. When a boy doesn't measure up, they put him out there 'head knocking' until he quits. They've left cripples all over the state of Texas." A couple of years ago at Florida State, the football coaches conducted illegal practices during the winter in which they placed athletes in a room with a false ceiling of chicken wire about 4 to 5 feet high and made them fight and wrestle until they collapsed. The next time you hear that a winning football or basketball team has been responsible for favorable legislation or increased alumni giving, consider at what cost in human terms this was achieved.

Moving away from the relationship between the educational goals and big time sports, another favorite claim of apologists for intercollegiate athletics is that they serve a social integrative function—that athletics develops a loyalty and identification with the institution on the part of students, faculty, and alumni. Indeed, Snyder and Spreitzer make this point. They state: "It is clear that the realization of community on campus is facilitated through athletic contests and their associated pageantry." The editor of the Notre Dame student newspaper made the case for the integrative nature of intercollegiate football this past January (Grasser, 1975). He wrote: "What is the value of the fiction of football? . . . Perhaps most importantly, football at Notre Dame is a ritualistic event that more than any other single activity helps to unite all the people that have been, are, and will be connected with Notre Dame."

Well, how can anyone doubt the argument that universities need big time sports to keep everyone loyal and identifying with the institution. It is, of course, very difficult because we have all been so thoroughly indoctrinated by the sports establishment who have hammered this theme so persistently, using the "big lie" technique, that we have all internalized this as truth. The big lie technique was eloquently articulated by Adolf Hitler, to wit: "The great masses of people . . . will more easily fall victims to a big lie than to a small one."

The idea that universities need big time programs for loyalty and identification maintenance is easily exposed for the hoax that it is, if we can pull ourselves away from the propaganda to which we have been exposed. Many of the great universities do not have big time programs, but they do not seem to suffer from an integration problem. Indeed, their pride and loyalty seems to be directed to the academic programs. The student editor at Notre Dame says that, ". . . football . . . more than any other single activity helps to unite all the people that [are] connected with Notre Dame." Unite them for what? Is there an enemy out there preparing to attack Notre Dame? It makes one wonder about the academic climate of a university which must depend upon a game for its unity. It is curious that an institution of higher education cannot find support, nourishment, intellectual stimulation, and even unity, if that is necessary, from its scholars—its students and faculty.

But, of course, the whole idea that a major university must depend upon its athletic teams for social integration is absolute nonsense when one gives the idea a few moments of objective thought. It is true, of course, that for some students their identification with their institution comes from the athletic teams, but most students at a major university have little direct or indirect association with the athletic program, so it can hardly be said to bind them to the organization.

Let's look briefly at one final supposed function of big time intercollegiate programs—the entertainment function. It is often contended that athletic contests provide wholesome entertainment for students, but at the most there are five home football games and 12 to 14 basketball games per year, and these are typically the sports that provide the most spectator interest. Seventeen to 20 days of entertainment in a normal 200 day collegiate academic year hardly constitutes a major form of entertainment, especially when the costs to the students, state, alumni, etc., are considered.

As to entertaining the public, we do not insist that banks, factories, department stores, and other businesses provide entertainment for their employees, clientele, customers, present or past, or the general public. Universities are institutions of equal importance to society, insofar as they attend to their main purposes. There is no compelling reason why universities should be in the professional sports industry. Lord knows we have enough of these—120 businesses that may be called major-league professional teams.

Well, I must wrap up my presentation quickly. The intercollegiate dilemma, in essence, is how can we reconcile commercial athletic enterprises on collegiate campuses? I believe we can't, and we ought to take steps to remove these operations from our campuses. Time prohibits me from enumerating the various ways that this might be accomplished, but I will say one thing—this Association ought to formulate a clear and unequivocal statement against professional collegiate athletics and support for educational-based athletics in colleges. The leisure-recreation programs . . . are the educational programs which we have on campus, and these might include an intercollegiate program, providing that it is conducted for the students' welfare. The cards are only "stacked toward the extrinsic world of athletics and against the intrinsic shape of leisure," . . . because of the past and present dealers. There is no reason why the cards cannot be removed from one dealer's hand and placed in another's. This could very well result in a re-stacking, in favor of educational recreation and sport.

REFERENCES

Brenner, A., Quoted in "Scorecard," *Sports Illustrated*, March 24, 1969, pp. 16–17.

Bridges, J., Quoted in "Scorecard," *Sports Illustrated*, January 6, 1969, p. 8.

Budig, G. A., "Grid Stock Up—Academic Stock Down," *Phi Delta Kappan*, LIV (September): 56, 1972.

Foster, W. T., "An Indictment of Intercollegiate Athletics," *The Atlantic Monthly*, 116 (November): 577–587, 1915.

Grasser, J., *Scholastic*, (Notre Dame, Indiana: Notre Dame University) vol. 116, No. 8, January 24, 1975, p. 50.

Koch, J. V., "A Troubled Cartel: The NCAA," *Law and Contemporary Problems*, 38 (Winter–Spring): 135–150, 1973.

McCarter, A., In Barry McDermott, "After 88 Comes Zero," *Sports Illustrated*, January 28, 1974.

McKenzie, R. T., "The Regulation of Athletic Sports in Colleges," *Department Congress of Physical Education, Proceedings and Reports*, American Association for the Advancement of Physical Education, July, 1893.

NCAA Manual 1974–75, NCAA, Shawnee Mission, Kansas, 1974.

Owens, S., "Intercollegiate Athletics," *Sport*, November, 1969, p. 94.

Randle, S., Quoted in "Scorecard," *Sports Illustrated*, September 1, 1975, p. 12.

Shaw, G., *Meat on the Hoof*, New York: St. Martin's Press, 1972.

Snyder, E. and E. Spreitzer, "The Collegiate Dilemma of Sport and Leisure," *NCPEAM Annual*, 1976.

Meat on the Hoof

GARY SHAW

"What's happened to yesterday's high school football hero? Is he a hoss of the highest degree in the Southwest Conference today?

"Maybe, but don't make any wagers that he is. If you insist on a bet, come to us. We will pull the money out of your hand after flashing a few facts before your eyes.

"At great expense (five cups of coffee during the research period) we offer the following note: Of 432 high school players recruited by SWC schools in 1963 only 131 will touch a football field this fall. Even with our C-minus background in arithmetic that comes out as a sixty-two percent dropout figure (For Texas 75 percent dropout rate).

"You can't say though that sixty-two percent of the recruits were duds. Some of the youngsters who signed letters in 1963 never made it to their chosen SWC schools. A few decided to go elsewhere at the last moment. Maybe they were injured and couldn't play. Maybe they struck out with the books. Maybe some saw they didn't have a chance to play and decided to just concentrate on their studies. And maybe, just maybe, a few took some well-placed hints and departed."[1]

An integral part of spring training was "shit drills." These drills were

---

SOURCE: Gary Shaw, *Meat on the Hoof: The Hidden World of Texas Football* (New York: St. Martin's Press, 1972), pp. 122–134.

for the purpose of running guys off—making them quit. However, they were not just to force some of us to give up football; they were designed to be part of an experience so devastating that we would be "persuaded" to sign away our scholarships. Now Coach Royal and his assistants weren't crude enough to be doing this simply for the sadistic pleasure in it. There was a practical reason. The conference rule was that at any one time a school could have only the money equivalent of a hundred full scholarships. This, in effect, meant that no more than one hundred boys could be on a full football scholarship at one time. The limit could be exceeded by a couple, but anywhere close to ten percent over the conference was to take action.

Here's an example of how this worked. If one of us dropped out of school or otherwise gave up his scholarship after three months, then that player would have gotten money for only three months—and that three months would be all that was counted against Royal's scholarship allotment. In other words, this would be only about a third of a scholarship based on nine months. So the limit that couldn't be exceeded was the total money allotment which was equal to one hundred boys being on full scholarship. Technically each one of us could keep our scholarships and not even show up for the first workout, and this would still count as a full scholarship and would take one-hundredth of all the total money.

From 1961 to 1964, Texas gave two hundred and seven full scholarships.[2] Since Royal could legally have only a hundred on scholarships, over half this two hundred plus had to give up their scholarships for Royal to stay inside the conference limit. Yet according to the official handbook of the Southwest Athletic Conference, "An athletic scholarship or other aid may not be cancelled or modified during the period of its award: (a) on the basis of a student-athlete's prowess or his contribution to a team's success; (b) because of an injury which prevents the recipient from participation in athletics; or (c) for any other athletic reason, except such scholarship or aid may be cancelled or modified if the recipient (1) voluntarily renders himself ineligible for intercollegiate competition, or (2) fraudulently misrepresents any information on his application, letter of intent or tender, or engages in serious misconduct warranting substantial disciplinary penalty." "Serious misconduct" means conduct of sufficient gravity that if comparable conduct occurred in other departments of the institution, a similar substantial disciplinary penalty could properly be imposed. And, an "athletic scholarship, during the period of its award, may not be reduced or cancelled for disciplinary reasons, except by the committee of the institution appointed to handle disciplinary problems for all students."

Thus, it was nearly impossible for Coach Royal to simply take away our scholarships. But the more boys he had to pick from the more likely he was to have a winner. So the big problem for Royal was to get enough of us to give up our scholarships—"voluntarily" render ourselves ineligible. But how do you convince over a hundred boys to give up several thousand dollars of education that they'd been promised? And add to this the fact that the basic building block of your program is "never to quit." Obviously, some drastic action was needed. It was supplied.

An SWC Rule change in 1966 eliminated the 100 full scholarships limit. Instead a yearly limit of 50 was imposed which meant it was legal to have up to 200 players on scholarship at any one time. The need for "shit drills" was greatly reduced and the retention rate of the next year's (1967) SWC recruits almost doubled the 1963 and 1964 rate. Some 60.5 per cent of the 1967 stayed for four years (63 per cent at Texas).[3]

However, recently the SWC reinstituted a full scholarship limit—this time at 130. It will be interesting to see if the retention rates suddenly begin dropping again.

After four or five days of spring training, our freshman year, approximately forty-five players were instructed to follow Pat Culpepper to the northeast corner of the practice field—an area within a few yards of the creek. These shit drillers were farther away from the rest of us than other drills; but more importantly they were surrounded by a psychological wall that separated them from the rest of us. These forty-five were all scholarship players who happened to be below the fourth team. There was no division according to interior linemen, ends or backs, and for these forty-five, there was only one coach—Culpepper. While the rest of us went from one area of the field to another with different drills and coaches, these forty-five stayed in their one corner repeating the same few drills over and over.

To the untrained eye some of these drills might seem of no different nature from any other. And of course, the coaches would publicly claim that they were simply for the purpose of practicing fundamentals. But we all knew the difference—especially the players participating in them. Part of the differences were physical, part psychological. There were only a few of these drills, so I'll diagram them. They began with this drill:

Two players lined up ten yards apart, facing each other between two blocking dummies. One was to be the ballcarrier, the other the tackler. They were to run to point X, turn ninety degrees up the field, and then go full speed toward one another. It doesn't sound so bad until you consider a few of the unique factors in this drill. For one, there was no discrimination as to who carried the ball. Linemen carried it just as often as backs. Apparently, one of the fundamentals the coaches were interested in developing was the ball-carrying ability of the guards and tackles. And as any running back knows, it is an acquired knowledge to learn to protect yourself while carrying the ball. Another unusual characteristic of this

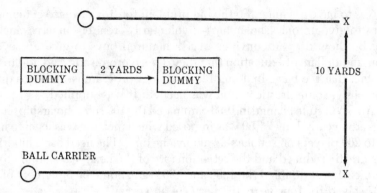

drill was that there was no tackling; the two were to meet full speed ahead—helmet to helmet—two bulls butting heads. Also in this drill, as in the others, it seemed that the boys just never could quite do anything right, and there was, shall we say, a frequent amount of immediate repetition.

In another drill five players were able to participate at the same time. The one in the middle held a football and was called the ball carrier. Four men surrounded him, each at a distance of fifteen yards. Each of these four was given a number, one through four. Culpepper would call out one of the numbers and whoever had that number was to head with "reckless abandon" at the ball carrier who could not move except in a stationary jog. The "numbered" player was to tackle the ball carrier.

But again there were a few original added attractions. One was that Culpepper would quite frequently become a bit confused in his timing and call out two, three, even four numbers consecutively, without a pause. This meant that one of the four would still be several yards from the ball carrier when another tackler's number was called. This second

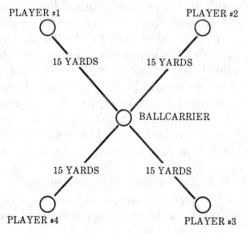

tackler was not to wait for the ball carrier and first tackler to get off the ground. He was to drill directly into them, and if a third or fourth was right behind, they were all to meet in this mass centered on the ball carrier. Naturally, the ballcarrier was usually tackled again while still on the ground. Worse yet, he would be about halfway up in getting to his feet when cracked from behind, or neatly sandwiched by two players arriving simultaneously. This drill did not serve to just toughen the ball carrier, it also worked for the tacklers. This was due to the fact that their bodies often traveled to the center at the same time, which made for quite a tangle of bodies. This drill was rather cynically referred to by Culpepper as "broken-field running."

The third drill was the fifteen-yard sideline drill, and was first developed for Tommy Cade and Chachie Owens, who were proving somewhat resistant to getting their fundamentals down.

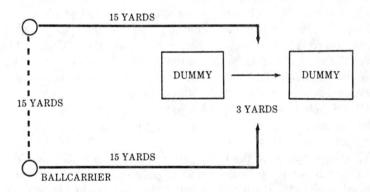

Here there were two players fifteen yards apart, one with the ball and one without. They were to run fifteen yards and then turn upfield, and while running as fast as they could, meet between the dummies with their heads. Now heading full speed straight at someone from fifteen yards apart rarely happens in a football game, and when it does, as perhaps on a kickoff, someone is often shaken up or hurt. As anyone connected with football will tell you, if you do this enough times, someone will get hurt. This is especially true if a player has gone repeatedly when his body is aching and tired. Under these circumstances it is much more difficult for him to be able to protect himself. These head-on collisions at such distance are most likely to occur on kickoffs, which is why they have special teams in pro football called "suicide squads." And even on those kickoffs, the ball carrier and tackler are usually not both going full speed at the point of the tackle. Even if they are, the tackle is generally made at some kind of angle, not head-on. In addition, the men involved in those kickoffs are usually fresh and rested, making it less likely they'll get hurt.

Besides, the pros realize the great risk factor in this type of collision, and don't even practice kickoff tackling during the week. But these drills went on for two and a half hours a day. And as Chachie, who was one of the forty-five, said, "Most were literally killed off. They would pit us in a way to most quickly eliminate people. For a long time I went against John Jolly who was five feet six and 210 pounds. I killed Jolly off, but Jolly killed off lots of others. Our punishment was injuries."

Coordinated with all the physical abuse were the psychological factors. The rest of us could hear Culpepper all over the field: "You guys are the sorriest excuses for football players I've seen." Here is an example which I observed and was typical. The chief assistant coach for Orange Hill School—Chachie's high school—came to workouts to see Chachie. He was introduced to the coaches and was brought over to the "shit drills." When Chachie's next turn came, Culpepper said, "All right, Charles O-w-e-n-s"—dragging his last name out for emphasis—"let's see you hit someone for a change." After contact was made, Culpepper went into an animated rage. "We're going to make a football player out of you or run you off. Do it again." And after the second time: "Charles Owens, you're the sorriest excuse for a football player I've ever seen. Get out of my sight—go back to the end of the line." The entire time Chachie's high school coach was not more than fifteen feet away.

"The whole time Culpepper knew I was injured and hadn't been able to hit anyone for three days, and that I'd be embarrassed in front of my old coach."

Chachie's injuries at the time were one badly separated shoulder and one that was severely bruised and slightly separated. But he was not allowed to go to the doctor since it was Medina who decided if the injury was serious enough to see a physician. After spring training Chachie went to a hometown doctor who verified these injuries.

In a fourth drill there were again two players approximately fifteen to twenty yards apart. Both were to run full tilt toward point X twenty yards away. Culpepper was standing twenty yards from point X and had a football. Just before they both reached this point, he would throw the football to the one marked runner.

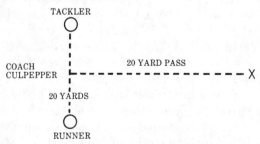

The idea was that just as the runner was reaching up to catch the football the tackler would hit him. Of course, reaching up for the pass would leave the runner unprotected. If a pass receiver gets hurt it's usually on this type of contact, they dread it more than any other kind of contact. And again, part of the fundamentals the coaches seemed interested in developing was having guards and tackles learning how to catch a pass while being tackled.

What effect did these drills have on their participants?

"The psychological impact was knowing that you were big enough to kill off these guys, but also realizing that daily you were coming apart physically so that one day soon you would be so weakened that you would get yours. It was knowing that there was no chance of survival, yet your pride wouldn't let you quit. We soon realized that there was no interest in our athletic ability, and we stopped killing each other off and began to 'brother-in-law.' We were determined to best them [coaches] at their own game if we accomplished nothing else. This led them to devise the all-against-one drill."[4]

Most of these drills, at least superficially, could be explained possibly by Coach Royal in a way to convince one that they were simply for the development of fundamentals. But one drill—the all-against-one or euphemistically called "the Sideline Drill" by Culpepper—would give even Royal's persuasive powers extreme difficulty.

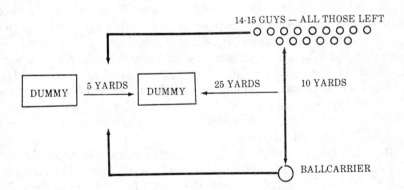

At this point there were only fifteen of the original forty-five left, and these fifteen had obviously learned to beat the coaches at their own game, to be still surviving. So for them it was going to take something a little cruder. This drill was it. One ball carrier stood ten yards away from all the rest. To make sure everyone got up enough momentum, they were to run twenty-five yards before turning upfield. All were to meet (at the same time) between the two dummies which were five yards apart. Fifteen en masse on one side, a lone ball carrier on the other. Chachie Owens told me what happened to him the first time he was this lone ball carrier.

"Five guys got there first and tackled me, the other ten ran over me. Someone's cleats ripped my calf open. I didn't get up fast and Culpepper came screaming for me to get up. He took one look at my open leg and gagged, then called the trainers, who slowly walked over. The doctor and I walked a block and a half to his truck, and he drove me to the health center. There it took about a hundred stitches to close my calf."

At this point one of his shoulders was already separated, the other hurt.

"Getting my leg injured saved my career at Texas. I couldn't have taken four weeks of it—no one could have."

This statement about no one being able to take four weeks of these drills is not a statement based on just his particular situation. Those drills started out with forty-five guys and ended after three weeks with just five guys left, and they weren't part of the original forty-five.

Every time I looked over at those drills, someone else was down on the ground, hurt. It was a constant reminder to put out and not fall below the fourth team.

The rest of us were very wary about being around these shit drillers—especially when it seemed they were getting close to quitting. I remember Rusty telling me I'd better start avoiding Chachie because he had overheard Chachie wondering aloud if it was all worth it. Rusty liked Chachie but genuinely felt his suggestion of avoiding him was in my own interest. He said that I had a bright future ahead as a Longhorn and that being around Chachie might get me thinking in the wrong way. Soon I sensed that Chachie did want to quit, so I began to make up excuses why I couldn't see him . . . and tightened my resolve to survive. "X-ing" out my friend when he was a shit driller, depressed, and close to quitting was part of being a winner. And while we might have been sympathetic, we were sympathetic at a safe distance.

Still I used to worry about my associating with some of the shit drillers—I didn't want Coach Royal to think they influenced me. Because there was the general belief among the rest of us that most of these shit drillers were lacking something. So if any coaches were around I'd pretend to ignore Chachie and the rest. Yet I never remember seeing Coach Royal watch "shit drills." In fact, no coach besides Culpepper would get near them.

Of course, the main way of getting out of these drills was to be injured seriously enough. But with the policy of Medina determining who saw a doctor, the injury had to be of sufficient gravity and flagrantly obvious. Yet many, like Chachie, were seriously enough injured anyway, so how did the coaches keep pressure on those not physically able to work out?

Here Royal was not lacking in imagination. He had all injured players (if below the first few teams) wear a jersey with a big red cross stenciled on both sides. And if at all able to walk, the injured were to continually jog around the practice field the complete workout. The red crosses were to be signs of humiliation. And throughout the spring, Royal would refer to the guys that would do anything to get out of workout and "couldn't take it." It may sound silly, but it was really an embarrassing stigma to be standing out there on the practice field with a big red cross on your jersey. I only missed eight spring training workouts the entire four years—all coming that first spring. But those eight I missed, I wore the jersey and red cross. Any time a player on one of the first two teams came near me, I would suddenly be occupied—ducking my head and hoping that they wouldn't notice. It was never explained to us why only those injured below a certain team were "fake injuries." There were always several members on the first few teams who were injured, yet they wore only solid jerseys.

So why didn't the players on lower teams just quit? "Every coach likes to impress on his squad that defeat is something that comes from within. Defeat must be admitted before it is a reality," Royal has said.

And if you're like most, you think you can hold out—and maybe you can for a year, even two; but that's a lot of days, a lot of Medinas, a lot of running the stands, and a lot of "shit drills." And how long do you really think you can spend all your time around people who think you're shit?

NOTES

1. Bob Galt, Dallas *Times Herald*, August, 1966.
2. Compiled from 1961–1964 issues of *Texas Football*.
3. Figures from an article by Bob Galt, Dallas *Times Herald*, Summer 1970.
4. Chachie Owens recounting the effects he felt.

Coaching as an Occupational Subculture

JOHN D. MASSENGALE

Coaches have been called many things—particularly by rival coaches—but rarely something as erudite, or as apt, as an occupational subculture. Yet the unique position occupied by coaches in the academic bureaucracy has isolated them from their peers and created for them a game with decidedly nonacademic rules.

A subculture displays distinctive ways of thinking, feeling, and acting that separate it from the larger culture.[1] Although coaches participate in a larger group—the total educational organization—and share most of its culture, they remain in an occupational subculture. This subculture, perpetuated apart from subject matter teaching responsibilities—in many cases even apart from the teaching of physical education—is characterized by a particular set of behaviors, values, language, and life-style.

The teacher-coach usually perceives his main—and occasionally his only—responsibilities as coaching and winning.[2] Coaches count on support from fellow coaches who function under similar pressures far different from the standard academic pressure (at the college level) to publish or perish.

RECRUITMENT, SOCIALIZATION, PROMOTION

The members of a subculture are recruited from a larger group, socialized and/or educated, and then often promoted for their success within the subculture. Coaching is no exception to this process. Coaches are a product of the American athletic system.

Athletes entering the field of coaching are so thoroughly socialized that they bring with them certain personality traits characteristic of athletes and coaches and distinct from other members of the faculty.[3] Coaches as a group are aggressive and highly organized, seldom paying

SOURCE: John D. Massengale, "Coaching as an Occupational Subculture," *Phi Delta Kappan*, 56 (October 1974), 140-142.

attention to what others say. They display unusually high psychological endurance, persistence, and inflexibility. Coaches appear to dislike change and tend to be very conservative politically, socially, and attitudinally.

In addition to the apparent socialization resulting from athletic participation, coaches are often formally educated in the field of physical education. Physical education majors tend to have little in common with other students in the field of education.[4] They have a more traditional philosophy of education and a slightly lower social class background. They tend to be more dogmatic and appear to have different social values from other prospective teachers.

Absorption of coaching's unique values and behaviors begins within the teacher preparation program. Aspiring coaches are themselves coached by representatives of the subculture, learning what is expected and accepted within their chosen occupation. Social sanctions, such as preferential grading, may be applied to prospective coaches when expected behaviors, values, and lifestyles are not followed. These sanctions become very evident in the closed, preferential hiring practices associated with coaching positions. Young coaches soon discover that good coaching positions are seldom gained through placement bureaus, and that an open, competitive hiring situation is rare. The more prestigious coaching jobs may be gained with the support of other members of the occupational subculture. That support is earned by conforming to the expected values and behaviors of the subculture, both during the formal educational process and the early years of coaching and teaching. The subculture can become a referral system to vested interest groups such as alumni organizations or athletic booster clubs, or it can become an acceptable sponsor and offer unsolicited firsthand personal recommendations. Members of the subculture can also use a "favored models" concept, emphasizing an applicant's similarities to successful coaches favored by subculture members. Thus many schools have attempted to hire proteges or assistants of Oklahoma's Bud Wilkinson, hoping that some of his winning ways will have been communicated to those well versed in his coaching techniques. That same "nothing succeeds like success" frame of mind has created a ready market for coaches in the identifiable style of a Bear Bryant or a Duffy Daugherty.

The all-important values and behaviors are taught by placing the student teacher-coach in practicum, internship, or practice teaching roles. One of his supervisory teachers will usually be an experienced teacher-coach and a member of the occupational subculture. Student teacher-coaches must learn to emulate these subculture representatives, or they may never make it professionally. The power of the academic letter grade, and the power of the professional recommendation, however subjective, become significant tools of social control within the subculture.

Allegiance to the subculture's values is reinforced by professional coaching organizations and coaching journals. Most teacher-coaches, regardless of their teaching field, tend to ignore teaching journals and become devoted readers of coaching journals. They also tend to ignore educational conferences, but regularly attend coaching conventions, clinics, and workshops.

SUBCULTURE MAINTENANCE

Open opposition from the academic community strengthens the isolation caused by the uniqueness of coaching. That hostility reinforces the subculture by creating alienation and polarization; the separation is maintained by the complete or partial exclusion of the coach from the academic in-crowd.

The result of this extreme polarization between the coaching and the academic communities is the creation of an in-group/out-group relationship.[5] The two groups identify each other as opponents, and each group regards itself as the guardian of its members' virtues, values, and loyalties. The out-group becomes viewed as a threat to the cherished values of the in-group.

Clearly, such an antagonistic relationship develops solidarity in the coach's occupational subculture and tends to rally the membership around specific beliefs. To have an opponent is very important for subculture maintenance, particularly when the opponent can become a scapegoat.

This occupational isolation allows coaches to assume the role of professionals or "cosmopolitans."[6] They feel very little loyalty or commitment to their school, and become devoted to professional coaching careers that exceed all organizational boundaries. Coaches cannot develop loyalty to an organization when they view their position as temporary. If they are successful, they will attempt to move upward to a better position; if they are unsuccessful, they will expect to be fired.

The stereotypes of coaches often held by other members of the faculty contribute to subculture solidarity. The critics view coaches as dehumanizing, autocratic, and insensitive to the individuality of the athletes they coach.[7] Faculty members often view coach/faculty alienation as a direct result of the unusually stern, authoritarian leadership behavior of coaches, citing examples such as rigid rules and an overemphasis on discipline.

In contrast, coaches maintain that authoritarianism does not cause alienation, but that alienation is caused by the overreaction of an uninformed, anti-athletic faculty. Critics of authoritarian coaching methods often assume that such leadership is bad, forgetting that most coaches are concerned with the good of the team member as well as the good of the team.[8]

At the root of the problem of authoritarianism in coaching is the traditional role of the coach as father figure. Coaches are expected to fulfill many of the functions of the archetypal father: to be strong, virile, and tough.[9] Although fast disappearing from the home, firm discipline is still demanded in athletics. Coaches such as the late Vince Lombardi of the Green Bay Packers and Washington Redskins derive much of their authority and power from presenting the image of an extremely tough father-figure. Lombardi ran his phenomenally successful teams like the overlord of a large family; his players played to their limits for his approval. The father role is seldom initiated by, or expected of, other members of the faculty; it is a must for the coach. However, coaches seldom receive extra credit merely for fulfilling this role; they must win to receive credit. Coaches view their authority as a prerequisite for molding a winning team. Any real or imagined attempt to strip them of their authority greatly increases the coach/faculty alienation.

The academic community often views the coach's authoritarian control of the athlete as a violation of individual rights and freedoms, an unnecessary restraint on the athlete's total educational development. Coaches seldom question their right of infringement, for they consider themselves faculty experts in coaching and assume the ultimate responsibility for the total performance of the team. They demand dedication, obedience, and loyalty, for they, not the team members, are held responsible for losing.

Coaches are seldom fired for their academic reputation. Winning often substitutes for academic inadequacies, if inadequacies exist. However, academic excellence and teaching expertise will seldom substitute for losing. Faculty outside the coaching subculture do not face this dilemma, and seldom understand the problem. This dilemma, as well as the failure of the academic community to appreciate the complexity of the coach's role as decision-making executive, adds to the problem of alienation, often creates polarization, and results in the formation of a very homogeneous group of coaches, both locally and nationally.

Further coach/faculty alienation may be caused by the decision-making powers of the coach. An important aspect of coaching decisions is the method and manner in which they are made. Coaching decisions are characteristically practical, rational, and expedient; often they are made in the shortest possible time. This type of rapid-fire decision making comes easy to the coach, since it is the type he is forced to use in day-today and game-to-game situations. An example would be the instructions all coaches issue to their players during a time-out situation near the end of a game. The decision upon which victory may rest must come from one person—the coach. Continued success with this type of pressure decision making leads to its repeated, and increasingly sophisticated, use at critical times.

Success with instant decision making may also be the main reason that coaches constantly criticize the time-consuming decision-making process of the faculty and the administration. Most coaches' criticisms of faculty and administration decision making cite delay tactics and dependence on theory rather than down-to-earth reality. Coaches tend to view indecision as no decision at all, and usually maintain that even a bad decision is better than indecision. Many coaches view indecision as weakness, and weakness is seldom acceptable to coaches, since it is a trait that is not allowed in their occupation. Prominent coaches have condemned administrators for lack of knowledge and understanding of the coach/player relationship, fear or decision making, weakness under pressure, inability to understand coaching responsibilities, and various forms of gutlessness.[10] Such polarization aids in the creation and maintenance of the coaching subculture.

Coaches have attempted to use athletic governing bodies and professional organizations to bolster what they view as a diminishing authority structure within their occupation. While this trend increases coaching autonomy and subculture solidarity, it also increases coach/faculty alienation, especially when public policy statements are issued that attempt to reinforce the coach's position.

Coaches continually attempt to gain more control of their position, although they realize that complete control is impossible. The more control gained, the stronger their position. They willingly accept total responsibility for team performance, but also insist on no outside interference. Coaches ask for, and completely accept, responsibility for positions filled with uncertainty, in order to eliminate as much uncertainty as possible. Much of coaching's authoritarianism and inflexibility may be caused by the institutional demand that coaches assume total accountability for extremely uncertain situations.[11] When coaches are held accountable for the total performance of a team, they demand complete authority to make any decisions necessary for team success.

FAILURE, DEMOTION, AND DISMISSAL

Subculture support is very important to coaches, since they realize they may be fired at the end of any losing season, even though the losing record may not have been their fault. An example of a built-in occupational coaching hazard would be a coach's position at West Point. There the coach has little control over the prowess of his raw material, but must instead hope that the Academy will attract suitable candidates. Occasionally, such as during the 1973 football season, those hopes are in vain. Through the subculture, coaches learn how they, as well as the school organization, are expected to manage failure, demotion, and dismissal. The situation causes organizational strain; management of that strain becomes a necessity.

The organization can manage the strain by making rather obscure demotions. Coaches can be demoted by placing them in assistant coaching positions, or by making them head coaches of what the organization has designated as less important sports. In some cases the school administration chooses to manage the strain by complete dismissal, making replacements as soon as possible.

Management of the strain may also take the form of promotion. Coaches can be promoted to positions with lesser responsibilities such as assistant athletic director, attendance counselor, or executive coordinator of something that does not need executive coordination. In a sense, they can be promoted out of the way, as explained so aptly by Laurence Peter in *The Peter Principle*. They can be assigned to a lower job status, then receive a raise in salary, or at least keep their same salary, which in many cases is higher than that of other faculty members.

Coaches must learn to manage failure, even though their own view and that of the subculture may be that they have not failed. Coaching failure is seldom determined by peer-group evaluation. It is usually determined by those who have no expertise for making such decisions; therefore, the decision is often ignored by the membership of the subculture. Coaches often depend on, and receive, the support of their subculture when they feel they have been unfairly evaluated.

Losing becomes the only measure of failure and the source of stigma. That stigma creates a process of downward mobility, with a corresponding loss of social prominence in the community.

In the end, coaches can personally manage failure by accepting one of three options. They can change jobs, which amounts to changing sports or changing specific responsibilities in the same sport; change careers, either within or outside their present organization; or change organizations and start all over again.

NOTES

1. James W. Vander Zanden, *Sociology: A Systematic Approach* (New York: Ronald Press, 1970).
2. Harry Edwards, *Sociology of Sport* (Homewood, Ill.: Dorsey Press, 1973).

3. Bruce C. Ogilvie and Thomas A. Tutko, "Sport: If You Want To Build Character, Try Something Else," *Psychology Today*, October 1971, pp. 61–63.
4. Gerald S. Kenyon, "Certain Psychosocial and Cultural Characteristics Unique to Prospective Teachers of Physical Education," *Research Quarterly*, March, 1965, pp. 105–12.
5. Herbert Blumer, "Social Movements," in Alfred M. Lee, ed., *Principles of Sociology* (New York: Barnes & Noble, 1965).
6. Alvin W. Gouldner, "Cosmopolitans and Locals," in Barney G. Glaser, ed., *Organizational Careers* (Chicago: Aldine, 1968).
7. Jack Scott, *The Athletic Revolution* (New York: Free Press, 1970).
8. George H. Sage, "The Coach as Management: Organizational Leadership in American Sport," *Quest*, January, 1973, pp. 35–40.
9. Arnold Beisser, *The Madness in Sports* (New York: Appleton-Century-Crofts, 1966).
10. John Underwood, "The Desperate Coach," *Sports Illustrated*, September, 1969, pp. 68–70.
11. Edwards, op. cit.

School Sports and Educational Goals

D. STANLEY EITZEN

Can you imagine an American junior or senior high school without an interschool sports program for students? Probably not, because virtually every school has such a program. The universality of sports in educational settings implies that sport must accomplish educational objectives. That, however, is the ideal. Rather, the pressure to win is foremost and when taken to its extreme, runs counter to the stated goal of athletics—to foster the optimum physical, mental, emotional, social, and moral growth of the participants. Schools demand that their athletic teams win but there is something fundamentally wrong with such a demand. It means, for example, that the livelihood of coaches and their families depends exclusively on whether their teams win. Thus, many coaches drive their players too hard, bend the rules, teach unfair tactics, and demand the total control of their players. These reactions to the win ethic are understandable but they are wrong because they are antithetical to the stated purposes of educational institutions.

SOURCE: This article was written for this volume.

The assumption is often made that "sports build character." But do they? Those responsible for educational programs must continually monitor the athletic program to assess whether educational objectives are being met. Some questions these monitors might ask are:

- Are educational goals being met when coaches are selected primarily for their win-loss record?
- Are educational goals being met when practice sessions are run like a marine boot camp?
- Are educational goals being met when coaches physically or verbally assault their athletes?
- Are educational goals being met when players are denied the rights and freedoms guaranteed by the Constitution (e.g., freedom of speech)?
- Are educational goals being met when athletes, coaches, and fans taunt and intimidate their opponents?
- Are educational goals being met when all decisions are made for the young athletes by adults?
- Are educational goals being met when players are treated as interchangeable parts?
- Are educational goals being met when athletes are encouraged to use certain drugs to enhance their performance artificially?
- Are educational goals being met when athletes are taught to cheat (how to hold in football without getting caught or how to feign a foul to receive an undeserved free throw in basketball)?
- Are educational goals being met when the athletic program is reserved for the elite few?
- Are educational goals being met when administrators and coaches resist giving equal importance to women's athletics? *q¬FOD CORRUPTION*

These queries call into question many existing practices allowed in educational settings from junior high school to our most prestigious universities. They suggest that sports programs tend to be win-oriented rather than player-oriented. Educators must ask is this the way it should be, or is there a better way?

The pressures on school personnel to win in sports are enormous and unrelenting. But to give in to these pressures is the easy way out. The leaders of schools (school board members, administrators, coaches) must have integrity and be sincerely interested principally in the development of youth. This means that educational goals must always remain paramount and not be sacrificed for a "win-at-any-costs" philosophy. Neither individual coaches nor administrators can accomplish this, however, without the support of their counterparts in other schools. Otherwise the demand to win will result in their dismissal. This problem can be countered by State High School Athletic Associations or leagues adopting rules that maximize the probability that educational goals remain central for all member schools. Here are some possible rule changes that would help bring this about:

- Eliminate all play-offs and championships to reduce pressure and to allow more individuals and teams to experience success. Tom Meschery, former professional basketball player, has said that school sports "should be directed toward lessening tension, not creating it. There is no need for high school state basketball tournaments. This may seem drastic, but at that age it seems counterproductive to arrive at an ultimate winner when we could have half a dozen winners. It is good for the young to argue the never-to-be-settled championship."

- Establish rules and demand proper equipment to insure the maximum safety of the athletes. There is strong evidence that playing football on artificial turf, for example, is much more dangerous than natural turf. How can school administrators allow their teams to play in situations where the probability of injury is higher than is absolutely necessary?

- Establish leagues for all levels of playing ability and size. This would allow maximum participation for students.

- Make it mandatory that all players participate in every game. For example, in baseball players could be required to play at least one full inning, once substituted for a player could return to the game, and all players (starters and substitutes) could constitute the batting rotation. In basketball starters could play the first and fourth quarters but not be allowed to play in the middle two quarters.

- Allow teams to practice and/or play games but only three times a week, leaving the remaining two days for participation in other extracurricular activities. This would open the facilities for use by others and allow athletes to broaden their interests and skills.

These suggestions, if implemented, would work to accomplish educational goals within the leagues organized to achieve them. Competition would remain keen but coaches, players, and teams would be organized to be player-oriented rather than exclusively win-oriented. Within each school, the goal of promoting educational objectives would be enhanced further by hiring coaches who are absolutely honest. Second, schools should insist that these coaches emphasize sport as an enjoyable activity. Third, coaches should be encouraged to promote democracy by allowing athletes to make their own training rules, make decisions during the game, select their own captains, and have a voice in starting lineups. As it is, the norm is for an athletic team to be a dictatorship. Is that organizational form an appropriate setting to learn how to participate effectively in a democracy? Moreover, coaches should allow their charges to express grievances without reprisal and to express their individuality in clothing and hair styles. Coaches have no business requiring conformity to their or the community's standards if they are unrelated to athletic training or performance. What is the educational value of controlling athletes on and off the field? It would appear that a system which denies personal autonomy fosters dependence and immaturity, rather than the presumed virtues of participation—leadership, independence, and self-motivation.

Finally, the aim of every athletic program should be maximum participation. If being on a team promotes physical health as well as teamwork and discipline, then that privilege should be open to all students not just the gifted. This has at least three implications for school policy. First, the programs for boys *and* girls should be given equal priority. Second, if there are too few teams to accommodate the persons who want to take part, then more coaches should be hired and teams added. The typical response, however, is to cut players from the teams, which most likely means removing those persons who could most benefit from the experience. Last, each participant should be considered a vital part of his or her team and be given equal coaching during practice sessions and approximately equal playing time for games.

This essay has raised some serious doubts about the educational value of sports as they are presently organized in America's schools. The "win-at-any-costs" philosophy, taken to its extreme led to such events as Watergate and the bombing of neutral Cambodia. And it is this very philosophy, so common in our schools, that has been tolerated, even encouraged, by those in authority. While winning is a worthy goal, is a natural high, and promotes unity, we should not lose sight of its negative effects. An over-zealous drive to win may promote dishonest practices, make fun work, and lead to failure for so many. If, on the other hand, participation for fun were stressed, if democracy superseded autocracy, and if the personal growth of persons were more important than winning, then school sports would deserve the disproportionate amounts of time and money that are now spent on them.

■ FOR FURTHER STUDY

Amdur, Neil. *The Fifth Down: Democracy and the Football Revolution.* New York: Delta, 1972.

Benagh, Jim. *Making It to #1: How College Football and Basketball Teams Get There.* New York: Dodd, Mead, 1976.

Bend, Emil. *The Impact of Athletic Participation on Academic and Career Aspiration and Achievement.* New Brunswick, N.J.: National Football Foundation and Hall of Fame, 1971.

Berger, Bennett M. *Looking for America.* Englewood Cliffs, N.J.: Prentice-Hall, 1971, pp. 44–53.

Birrell, S. "An Analysis of the Inter-Relationships among Achievement Motivation, Athletic Participation, Academic Achievement, and Educational Aspirations." *International Journal of Sport Psychology,* 8 (1978).

Buchanan, Hugh Troy, Joe Blankenbaker and Doyice Cotten. "Academic and Athletic Ability as Popularity Factors in Elementary School Children." *Research Quarterly,* 47 (October 1976), 320–325.

Buhrmann, H. "Scholarship and Athletics in Junior High School." *International Review of Sport Sociology,* 7 (1972), 119–131.

Carey, Henry. "Recruiting: Tricky Deals Used on Black Athletes." *Black Sports,* 2 (March 1973), 24–27, 48, 53.

Coakley, Jay J. *Sport in Society: Issues and Controversies.* St. Louis: C. V. Mosby, 1978, chapters 6 and 7.

Coleman, James S. "Athletics in High School." *Annals of the American Academy of Political and Social Science,* 338 (November, 1961), 33–43.

Coleman, James S. *Adolescents and the Schools.* New York: Basic Books, 1965, chapter 3.

Corbin, Charles B. *The Athletic Snowball.* Champaign, Illinois: Human Kinetics Publishers, 1977.

Cousins, Norman. "Football and the College." *Saturday Review* (September 28, 1963), p. 36.

Denlinger, Kenneth, and Leonard Shapiro. *Athletes for Sale: An Investigation into America's Greatest Sports Scandal—Athletic Recruiting.* New York: T. Y. Crowell, 1975.

Divoky, Diane, and Peter Schrag. "Football and Cheers." *Saturday Review* (November 11, 1972), pp. 59–65.

Durso, Joseph. *The Sports Factory: An Investigation into College Sports.* Boston: Houghton Mifflin, 1975.

Eidsmore, R. M. "High School Athletes Are Brighter." *School Activities,* 35 (November 1963), 75–77.

Eitzen, D. Stanley. "Athletics in the Status System of Male Adolescents: A Replication of Coleman's 'The Adolescent Society'." *Adolescence,* 10 (Summer 1975), 267–276.

Eitzen, D. Stanley. "Sport and Social Status in American Public Secondary Education." *Review of Sport and Leisure,* 1 (Fall 1976), 139–155.

Eitzen, D. Stanley, and George H. Sage, *Sociology of American Sport.* Dubuque, Iowa: Wm. C. Brown, 1978, chapter 4.

Feltz, Deborah L. "Athletics in the Status System of Female Adolescents." *Review of Sport & Leisure,* 3 (Fall 1978), 98–108.

Friedenberg, Edgar Z. *Coming of Age in America: Growth and Acquiescence.* New York: Vintage, 1967.

Friesen, D. "Academic-Athletic-Popularity Syndrome in a Canadian High School Society." *Adolescence,* 3 (Spring 1968), 39–51.

Gilbert, Bil. "Imagine Going to School to Play." *Sports Illustrated* (October 13, 1975), pp. 89–98.

Haerle, Rudolph K., Jr. "Education, Athletic Scholarships, and the Occupational Career of the Professional Athlete." *Sociology of Work and Occupations,* 2 (November 1975), 373–403.

Hanks, Michael P., and Bruce K. Eckland, "Athletics and Social Participation in the Educational Attainment Process." *Sociology of Education*, 49 (October 1976), 271–294.

Hansen, William J., and Floyd B. Lueptow. "Participation in Athletics and Academic Achievement." *Sociological Quarterly*, 19 (Spring 1978), 304–309.

Isaacs, Neil D. *Jock Culture U.S.A.* New York: W. W. Norton, 1978, chapter 8.

Johnson, William. "The Greatest Athlete in Yates Center, Kansas." *Sports Illustrated* (August 9, 1971), pp. 27–31.

Jones, Frank B. "Intercollegiate and Interscholastic Athletic Programs in the 1970's." *Sportscope* (June 1970), pp. 1–20.

Jordan, Pat. "The Man Who Was Cut Out for the Job." *Sports Illustrated* (October 11, 1971), pp. 90–102.

Kay, R. D., et al. "Sports Interests and Abilities as Contributors to Self-Concept in Junior High School Boys." *Research Quarterly*, 43 (1972), 208–215.

Klein, Frederick C. "Hoopster Hoopla: High School Basketball is a Serious Matter in a Small Illinois Town." *Wall Street Journal* (March 1, 1970).

Kennedy, Ray. "427: A Case in Point." *Sports Illustrated* (June 10, 1974), pp. 87–100, and (June 17, 1974), pp. 24–30.

Loy, John W., Barry D. McPherson, and Gerald Kenyon. *Sport and Social Systems*. Reading, Mass.: Addison-Wesley, 1978, pp. 226–234.

Lueptow, L. B., and B. D. Kayser. "Athletic Involvement: Academic Achievement and Aspirations." *Sociological Focus*, 7 (Winter 1973–74), 24–36.

Markus, Robert. "Athletics Have Helped Kent State Overcome Tragedy." *NCAA NEWS* (February 1, 1973).

Michener, James A. *Sports in America*. New York: Random House, 1976, chapter 7.

Naison, Mark, and Jim Ford. "College Sports—Out of Control." *Left Field*, 1 (June 1978), 1, 7.

Otto, Luther B., and Duane F. Alvin. "Athletics, Aspirations, and Attainments." *Sociology of Education*, 42 (April 1977), 102–113.

Putnam, Path. "A Case of Volunteer—or Else." *Sports Illustrated* (July 23, 1973), pp. 22–25.

Rehberg, Richard A. "Behavioral and Attitudinal Consequences of High School Interscholastic Sports: A Speculative Consideration." *Adolescence*, 4 (Spring 1969), 69–88.

Rehberg, Richard A., and Walter E. Schafer. "Participation in Interscholastic Athletics and College Expectations." *American Journal of Sociology*, 73 (May 1968), 732–740.

Rehberg, Richard A., and Michael Cohen. "Athletes and Scholars: An Analysis of the Compositional Characteristics and Damage of These Two Youth Culture Categories." *International Review of Sport Sociology*, 10 (1975), 91–107.

Ricke, Tom. "Town Where Boys are Kings and the Court Business Is Basketball." *Detroit Free Press* (March 14, 1971).

Sabock, Ralph. *The Coach*. Philadelphia: W. B. Saunders, 1973.

Sage, George H. "Occupational Socialization and Value Orientation of Athletic Coaches." *Research Quarterly*, 44 (October 1973), 269–277.

Sage, George H. "An Occupational Analysis of the College Coach." *Sport and the Social Order*. Edited by Donald W. Ball and John Loy. Reading, Mass.: Addison-Wesley, 1975, pp. 395–455.

Schafer, Walter E. "Some Sources and Consequences of Interscholastic Athletics: The Case of Participation and Delinquency." *International Review of Sport Sociology*, 4 (1969), 63–79.

Schafer, W. E., and J. M. Armer. "Athletes are not Inferior Students." *Transaction*, 5 (November 1968), 21–26.

Schendel, Jack. "Psychological Differences Between Athletes and Non-participants in Athletics at Three Educational Levels." *Research Quarterly*, 36 (March 1965), 52–67.

Scott, Jack. *The Athletic Revolution.* New York: Free Press, 1971.

Shultz, Fredrick D. "Broadening the Athletic Experience," *JOPER*, 43 (April 1972), 45–47.

Simpson, George. "College Football's B.M.O.C. Crisis: Battered and Maimed on Campus." *Sport*, 63 (November 1976), 26.

Snyder, Eldon. "High School Athletes and Their Coaches: Educational Plans and Advice." *Sociology of Education*, 45 (Summer 1972), 313–325.

Snyder, Eldon E. "Aspects of Social and Political Values of High School Coaches." *International Review of Sport Sociology*, 8 (1973), 73–87.

Snyder, Eldon E. "Athletic Team Involvement, Educational Plans, and the Coach-Player Relationship." *Adolescence*, 10 (Summer 1975), 192–200.

Snyder, Eldon, and Elmer Spreitzer. "Correlates of Sport Participation among Adolescent Girls." *Research Quarterly*, 47 (December 1976), 804–809.

Snyder, Eldon, and Elmer Spreitzer. "Participation in Sport as Related to Educational Expectations among High School Girls." *Sociology of Education*, 50 (January 1977), 47–55.

Snyder, Eldon E., and Elmer Spreitzer. "Sport and Education." *Encyclopedia of Physical Education*, vol. 5. Edited by Gunther Luschen and George H. Sage. Reading, Mass.: Addison-Wesley, 1979.

Spady, W. G. "Lament for the Letterman: Effect of Peer Status and Extracurricular Activities on Goals and Achievement." *American Journal of Sociology*, 75 (January 1970), 680–702.

Stern, Barry E. "The Cultural Crisis in American Sports," *JOPER*, 43 (April 1972), 42–44.

Talamini, John T. "School Athletics: Public Policy Versus Practice." *Sport and Society*. Edited by John T. Talamini and Charles H. Page. Boston: Little, Brown, 1973, pp. 163–182.

Tannenbaum, Abraham J. "Adolescents' Attitudes Toward Academic Brilliance." Doctoral Dissertation, New York University, 1960.

Underwood, John. "The Desperate Coach." *Sports Illustrated* (August 25, September 1, and September 8, 1969).

Underwood, John. "Beating Their Brains Out." *Sports Illustrated* (May 26, 1975), pp. 84–96.

UNESCO. *The Place of Sport in Education: A Comparative Study.* Educational Studies and Documents, No. 21 (Paris, UNESCO, 1956).

Wall, William L. "Time to Clean Up Basketball." *Sports Illustrated* (February 14, 1972), pp. 20–21.

Waller, Willard. *The Sociology of Teaching.* New York: John Wiley, 1965.

Six

Sports Participation as a Builder of Character

There is a persistent belief held by most persons that sports participation has positive benefits for those involved. The following quotation from *Time* summarizes this assumption:

> Sport has always been one of the primary means of civilizing the human animal, of inculcating the character traits a society desires. Wellington in his famous aphorism insisted that the Battle of Waterloo had been won on the playing fields of Eton. The lessons learned on the playing field are among the most basic: the setting of goals and joining with others to achieve them; an understanding of and respect for rules; the persistence to hone ability into skill, prowess into perfection. In games, children learn that success is possible and that failure can be overcome. Championships may be won; when lost, wait until next year. In practicing such skills as fielding a grounder and hitting a tennis ball, young athletes develop work patterns and attitudes that carry over into college, the marketplace and all of life.[1]

It is no wonder, given the universality of this belief, that parents, schools, and communities push sports programs for youth so vigorously. Mostly forgotten or ignored, however, is the negative side of sports participation, a position that is summarized by Charles Banham:

> It [the conventional argument that sport builds character] is not sound because it assumes that everyone will benefit from sport in the complacently prescribed manner. A minority do so benefit. A few have the temperament that responds healthily to all the demands. These are the only ones able to develop an

attractively active character. Sport can put fresh air in the mind, if it's the right mind; it can give muscle to the personality, if it's the right personality. But for the rest, it encourages selfishness, envy, conceit, hostility, and bad temper. Far from ventilating the mind, it stifles it. Good sportsmanship may be a product of sport, but so is bad sportsmanship.[2]

The problem is that sports produce positive and negative outcomes. This dualistic quality of sport is summarized by Terry Orlick:

For every positive psychological or social outcome in sports, there are possible negative outcomes. For example, sports can offer a child group membership or group exclusion, acceptance or rejection, positive feedback or negative feedback, a sense of accomplishment or a sense of failure, evidence of self-worth or a lack of evidence of self-worth. Likewise, sports can develop cooperation and a concern for others, but they can also develop intense rivalry and a complete lack of concern for others.[3]

The selections in this section summarize what we know about the ability of sports participation to build character. The first essay, by Charles Kniker, a professor of education, reviews the research and concludes that neither the proponents nor the critics of athletics can offer substantial evidence to prove that sports per se are either beneficial or harmful.

Tutko and Bruns also look carefully at this issue, but they conclude that sport does not build positive character for all participants. This conclusion should not be taken lightly because Tutko, along with his colleague in sport psychology, Bruce Ogilvie, have studied the effects of competition on personality more comprehensively than any other research team.[4] In over twenty years of research, for example, they have studied approximately 60,000 athletes, including more than 15,000 who have taken a test that measures eleven traits common to athletes. Tutko's conclusions, then, are not based on his particular ideological bent but on hard data.

The final selection, by Glenn Dickey, examines the effects of sports participation on one character trait—self-discipline. He argues that, contrary to the commonly accepted belief, sport produces followers, not leaders.

NOTES

1. "Comes the Revolution: Joining the Game at Last, Women are Transforming American Athletics," *Time* (June 26, 1978), p. 55.
2. Charles Banham, "Man at Play," *Contemporary Review*, 207 (August 1965), 62.

3. T. D. Orlick, "The Sports Environment: A Capacity to Enhance—A Capacity to Destroy," paper presented at the Canadian Symposium of Psycho-Motor Learning and Sports Psychology (1974), p. 2.
4. Bruce C. Ogilvie and Thomas A. Tutko, "Sport: If You Want To Build Character, Try Something Else," *Psychology Today*, 5 (October 1971), 61–63.

The Values of Athletics in Schools: a continuing debate

CHARLES R. KNIKER

As school yearbooks, athletic association reports, and television rating polls redundantly confirm, Americans are deeply interested in and committed to athletic programs. At the high school level almost four million boys and slightly over 800,000 girls participate in interscholastic programs. During the 1971–72 academic year 172,000 males and 31,000 females were members of collegiate teams at National Collegiate Athletic Association-affiliated institutions. An estimated 100 million spectators attend high school basketball games annually.[1]

The intense interest in athletic programs is further revealed in the ingenious ways schools and colleges have maintained their activities in the wake of the energy crisis. Last winter, for example, two California colleges conducted their scheduled swim meet despite a gasoline shortage that prevented travel. Each team swam in its own pool. Telephone lines were used to hook up an amplifying system at the schools, and an electric starting apparatus was wired in to synchronize timing clocks.

Though this swim meet was held, some athletic events in other places—holiday basketball tournaments, for example—have been canceled. It is a fitting time, then, to raise questions about the priorities of our personal and community activities, including athletics.

The purpose of this article is to review current popular opinion and research findings which attempt to answer such questions as: How valuable are athletic and sports programs? What values are gained from participation in athletics?

The current literature on values in athletics and at least one of several recent conferences on the role of sport in American life concur that the most commonly advocated values to be gained from athletic participation include control, competition, social security, physical well-being, and spirit.[2] Before discussing these values, however, we should define the terms "athletics" and "values."

Athletics involve a competitive activity whose purpose is "victory." This activity is characterized by a spirit of dedication, sacrifice, and

---

SOURCE: Charles R. Kniker, "The Values of Athletics in Schools: A Continuing Debate," *Phi Delta Kappan*, 56 (October 1974), 116–120.

intensity.[3] School athletics are organized by the school authorities and are placed under the supervision of a coach. Although this definition logically includes intramural programs, we shall deal here primarily with interscholastic and intercollegiate athletics. It seems that intramural programs are closer to the concept of sport, which can be defined as a diversion primarily intended for fun, permeated by a spirit of moderation.

Values are those attitudes which determine action or deliberate nonactivity. This concept is similar to that of Raths, Harmin, and Simon, who say that values must include choosing, prizing, and acting.[4] Values, then, are something more than the feelings which athletic competition provides its participants and the society at large. Values, in other words, incorporate both attitudes and actions that may prove beneficial or detrimental to the individual, the school, or the community.

THE CONTROL VALUE

Most discussion today appears to revolve around what might best be labeled the value of control. Control is an umbrella term, encompassing both personal and social dimensions. These two dimensions include such specifics as the individual's self-discipline, the coach's control over the athlete, the community's pressure on athletic behavior, and the growing debate over who should control athletic policy.

Participation in athletics, it is asserted, will aid the individual in gaining control of his or her aggressive habits, in developing poise under pressure, in using leisure time more efficiently, and in building character. Through the rigors of training, such qualities as courage, endurance, and patience come to the athletic participant.

Most critics of athletic programs, ranging from the former pro football player Dave Meggyesy to philosopher Paul Weiss,[5] emphasize the loss of individual control. The word "dehumanization" is frequently used. Some coaches offer numerous reasons why training rules and grooming codes promote self-discipline.[6]

Can athletics build character, as the traditional argument goes? Many say yes. Others may conclude with sportscaster Heywood Hale Broun that sports do not build character, but reveal it. And Weiss would add, with some wit, that athletics in many ways are based on deceiving people. Consider the basketball "fake," football's "trick play," and boxing's "feint."[7] Do such skills nurture good character?

Some believe that society as well as the individual benefits from athletics. These regulated events can channel aggressive behavior and may lower crime rates. "Keep kids off the streets" and "give them something to keep them busy" are common expressions of this sentiment.

Historically, pioneers in physical education, such as Luther Gullick, a YMCA founder, claimed that athletics could control "mass emotions."[8] Some critics would grant the entertainment value of athletics but counter that our society has now been diverted from more important matters. Meggyesy calls football America's "national theater," often portraying symbolically the struggles in our society: youth against an "over-the-hill" gang, the corporation's desire to win new territory, or the glory of one region over another.[9]

The most serious issue of the future may be who will control athletic policies, including the eligibility of players. It is obvious that the control of secondary interscholastic programs increasingly involves state departments of instruction and statewide athletic associations. At the college level, critics have focused on the warped priorities which result in expansive athletic facilities being built before basic academic buildings are constructed and on recruiting scandals which show universities obtained good players but poor scholars.[10]

One issue of major significance yet to be settled is discrimination in athletic programs. It is an issue which has many ramifications for control of athletics if federal intervention comes. Title IX of the Educational Amendments Act of 1972 prohibited discrimination at educational institutions; it includes provisions to cut off federal funds in cases of noncompliance. If it is applied to college athletics, it is likely that separate departments for men and women in physical education will merge, "equal" scholarships (in total number and dollar amount) will be given, and integrated intercollegiate teams would be formed. Needless to say, the development has caused grave concern among such bodies as the NCAA.[11]

What evidence, positive or negative, is there to support the belief that athletic participation promotes control? Lowell Cooper has surveyed studies of athletic personalities and has concluded that most studies paint a picture of persons who are outgoing, socially confident, socially aggressive (have leadership tendencies); are less compulsive and less impulsive than the average person; and have greater than average tolerance for physical pain. Cooper added, however, that much of the research seemed to be an attempt to justify participation in athletics and physical education.[12]

Typical of the supporting research is Max Shifrer's thesis, which reports on 74 "former country town high school athletes" who were asked to reflect on the value of their sports experiences. More than 80% believed that their participation in high school athletics had helped them develop "calmness and poise under pressure" (88%); 84% indicated they had gained "courage and self-confidence."[13] More recently, a study of junior high boys noted a positive relationship between their reported interest in sports and their reported self-concept; the researchers concluded that interest in sports is correlated with physical ability.[14] In 1967, using the *California Test of Personality* and the *Pictorial Study of Values*, Richard Davidson compared high school student athletes with nonathletes, male and female. He found the groups to be significantly different, but was careful to avoid stating that athletics was the cause for the personality differences.[15]

Bruce Ogilvie and Thomas Tutko made a similar judgment after their studies of 15,000 athletes. Although they have received much publicity for their announced verdict that sports do not build character, they have also stated that they do believe athletes display more positive qualities than the nonparticipants in athletics.[16] Their reasoning is that the "ruthless selection process" rather than any molding process of athletics determines why certain personality characteristics are common among athletes.

Some studies, however, do seem to indicate that negative effects may accrue from athletic participation. A three-year study by Jack Schendel compared the changes which ninth-graders, athletes and nonathletes, underwent as they completed schooling. As a group, the nonathletes experienced more positive changes in their sense of self-worth and confidence than did the athletic group. In reviewing the study, Donald Hellison urged caution in interpreting this to mean that athletics are harmful. The athletes may have been more mature than the nonathletes in ninth grade, he said, and hence had a smaller range of change.[17] The most recent of several studies on sportsmanship states that when high school students (categorized as athletic participants, spectators, or nonspectators) were studied, "the athletic participants and spectator groups displayed the least desirable sportsmanship values."[18]

The literature, then, reveals some evidence on each side. Yet even the researchers whose studies appear to support athletics urge caution in affirming that athletics cause changes in behavior. Because of the control issue, it was hoped that some reports or studies on club sports might be found. None was.

THE COMPETITION VALUE

If Hellison is correct in his assumption that the overriding value orientation in American life is toward achievement and success, and if success in competition is highly rewarded, then it follows that the value of experiencing competition in athletics is also prized. A standard cliché is that life is competitive, hence athletics prepare one for playing the game of life.

A number of the critics join proponents in agreeing that under certain conditions competition is healthy. The sheer joy of finding out how far one can extend his or her body, the thrill of breaking a personal barrier, such as a time for running a race, is hard to describe. To compete against onself has many merits, it is argued. There are times when a group competes against another group to weigh its performance; again, critics do not fault all these comparative efforts.

Unhealthy competition is often identified as the result of a "win at all costs" philosophy that encourages manipulation of athletes, unethical practices in recruiting, and the use of drugs to gain unfair advantage over opponents.

Jack Scott, the former athletic director of Oberlin College and a founder of the Institute for the Study of Sport and Society, contends that competition often does not heighten individual efforts, but rather promotes conformity. A contest forces the participants to perform quite similarly, each wearing the same type of uniform. Differences in outcome may be measured in fractions of a second. Weiss would add that most athletic games have elaborate rules structures, or handicap systems, which attempt to standardize play.[19] Are there as many rules in life to force competitors into similar molds?

Are athletic competitors more successful in life than noncompetitors? If so, does the success derive from competitive skills transferred from athletics? Few studies attempt to answer these questions. Ogilvie's observations of girl swimmers throughout preadolescence and adolescence led him to conclude that with success in competition the girls became more outgoing, less reserved, and did increase their "toughmindedness."[20] Other studies report that athletes tend to exhibit a high need to achieve, especially in their particular specialties, but also point out that nonparticipants are probably just as inclined to be achievement-oriented, though in other areas.[21]

Surprisingly few studies have been done on the topic of the pressure to win. Hellison has shown that, unsurprisingly, coaches have a greater desire to succeed than do their players.[22] Preliminary findings from a dissertation in progress suggest that pressure on high school coaches to win has been less than is commonly assumed.[23]

The fact that research studies are rare in this area does not mean that abuses do not exist, of course. For example, Big Eight Commissioner Charles Neinas recently indicated that four members of the conference have either been placed on probation or sanctions by the conference. There are many stories about drug abuse by athletes, but documentation has not appeared in the research journals.[24]

THE SOCIAL SECURITY VALUE

A review of reasons why athletics should be considered valuable has usually included some references to such things as the social status athletes gain; the increased chances for economic advancement, especially for the ghetto student; and possible advancement in social class standing. Less often mentioned is the prosperity a good athletic program brings to the local business community. There is much debate building over the socioeconomic values of athletics, and the term "social security" crystallizes these issues.

Supporters of collegiate athletics increasingly emphasize that athletic scholarships ensure some students the opportunity to study as well as play. Of course not every student will study or attempt to gain training for a career. Coaches may speak of higher graduation rates of athletes than for the general student population. The critics are not convinced, however. Harry Edwards, the black sociologist, debunks the concept that social mobility for the ghetto poor is a valid reason for maintaining athletic programs, and he suggests that the evidence does not bear out the claim.[25]

The charges of professionalism in college sports, recruiting violations at the high school level, and the rising costs of athletic programs are additional factors which prompt a closer look at the evidence supporting or denying the value of social security.

There are few studies which challenge the findings of James Coleman and others verifying that athletes do indeed enjoy greater social status among their peers than do scholar-students, and that academic performance and school attendance (i.e., not dropping out) probably benefit from athletic participation.[26]

Data on the costs of athletic programs are much more controversial. Several recent studies attempt to show criteria by which the cost of athletic programs may be weighed.[27] A study issued by the NCAA in 1970 underscored the problems created by financing athletic programs, and indicated some plans its member schools had for curtailing some programs. However, it concluded that athletic financing and costs were still manageable.[28] Joel Spring, a historian, has suggested that colleges have made rather poor use of studies of athletic costs. For example, a Carnegie Foundation study made in 1927 showed that major sports programs were generally losing money, but evidently the universities ignored the findings.[29]

Another dimension of social security is being examined more closely in the literature now. It has been estimated that approximately 90% of the student body at the high school level does not participate in interscholastic programs. Such programs, it is argued, cater to the "athletically gifted." These students, predominantly male, have a disproportionate share of the physical education and athletic staffs to guide their progress. Likewise, a disproportionate amount of the athletic facilities is used for interscholastic events. Critics argue that the narrow numerical boundaries of athletic participation weaken the point that athletics can provide social mobility for any significant number of students. It should be added that those who seek greater athletic participation by females are not merely seeking a duplication of male programs, but also hope to bring qualitative changes to all athletics.[30]

Because of the legal questions mentioned above, and because of the moral issues which some observers raise, the value of social security is likely to receive more attention in the future. The need for more research on the socioeconomic benefits of athletics, actual participation rates, and the costs of athletic programs should be obvious.

THE PHYSICAL WELL-BEING VALUE

Although improvement in one's total physical well-being would appear to be a major benefit from participation on athletic teams, current literature does not list this as the primary value of athletics.

Physical well-being can be interpreted in several ways. In physical education circles today, athletics are promoted for their value in building cardio-vascular fitness. Interestingly, some researchers are stressing the benefits athletic participation may bring in nonchemical "highs." Both the feelings of elation and the phenomenon of vertigo which follow intense periods of physical activity are under investigation.[31] In this article physical well-being refers to the total response, physical and emotional, which results from intense athletic involvement.

To ask if athletes are in better physical condition than nonathletes is not the most pertinent question, as Vanderzwaag points out.[32] We should first ask what we want from athletics: conditioning or interaction? Jogging may be the most beneficial exercise. Allowances must also be made for specific sports differences in such areas as agility, flexibility, and strength. As an Ohio State University study has demonstrated, athletes skilled in one sport, such as baseball, frequently perform less well than nonathletes in another physical activity (e.g., riding a stabilometer).[33] Another study concluded that the physical well-being of interscholastic athletes was not significantly different from that of intramural athletes.[34]

If there is any debate over physical well-being today, it centers on the physical injuries which may occur when young athletes are not physically ready for participation. Newspapers frequently refer to football injuries. Yet the literature reviewed revealed little in the way of injury research in this country. By contrast, German sports scientists have studied sports injuries extensively and have found that 10% of all hospitalized accident cases in Germany were due to sports accidents.[35]

In conclusion, this area appears to be the least controversial of the five value areas. Even here, however, there are many assumptions about the value of physical well-being which need to be examined more thoroughly, with results disseminated more widely.

THE SPIRIT VALUE

The claim that athletics promote cooperation, teamwork, and school spirit still receives considerable endorsement, even from the critics. As Scott suggests, relatively few school activities foster working together for a common goal. Athletics also promote community spirit. This is as true for the neighborhood of Brooklyn's Power Boys' High School as it is for the town of Montezuma, Iowa, and its girls' basketball team.

Further, an athletic contest is something from the school world that most parents can understand. How does one explain daughter Mary's accomplishments in her open-spaced school or son Joey's achievement on the computer terminal to a visiting relative? The objectives of the game and the accountability of players and coach are much easier to comprehend.

Few would contradict the concept that alumni identify with their alma mater through athletic contests. One study found that 94% of the alumni surveyed had returned to campus because of an athletic event. The editor of University of Illinois alumni publications came under fire recently when he suggested downplaying athletics at that institution.[26]

Those who believe that the value of spirit has become overemphasized offer arguments similar to those used against control. First, the individual is often sacrificed for the good of the team. Coaches cite the value of teamwork as a way to gain an inordinate amount of authority over the players.[37] Second, overzealous fans have produced situations at both the high school and college levels which have resulted in the barring of spectators and the deploying of large security forces.[38]

Once again, few studies are available which either confirm or deny these opinions about the value of spirit. One dissertation which measured student values and their relationship to an intercollegiate athletic program found few academic or social differences between those who approved of the program and those who saw little benefit in it.[39]

THE CONTINUING DEBATE

A review of literature and the Institute of National Affairs Conference at Iowa State University left this observer with certain general impressions:
   1. Substantially the same arguments are being used today to promote

athletics as were being used 50 years ago, although there has been a shift in the language used, as well as a new ranking of the arguments.

2. The literature in physical education journals and conference reports suggests that athletic coaches and physical educators are two distinct groups with varying philosophies and goals.

3. The research done in the area of values and athletics has been sparse, typically involving little more than Likert scales asking for degrees of agreement, or for one's opinion about some aspect of athletics.

4. Neither the proponents nor the critics of athletics were able to offer substantial evidence to prove that athletics is either beneficial or harmful.

No doubt the values of athletic programs will continue to be the subject of debate. There are those who would argue that it is futile to try to measure the values mentioned above. Because athletics are such a major social phenomenon, it could, and I believe should, be argued that more research needs to be done. Here are some suggestions concerning future directions which may prove profitable for measuring values in athletics and developing techniques to improve the way athletics are conducted.

Thomas Sheehan and William Alsop hypothesize that athletic participation can be a vehicle for what they term value transfer. Values can be transferred through a precise sequence. To date, few studies have tried what may be a promising technique.[40]

The Pflaum/Standard Company has published a values clarification kit for the secondary level which contains a unit of sentence completion strategies on competition. Such instruments are difficult to score, but may prove to be a good way to gain new insights.[41]

Vanderzwaag concludes that many of the values society wishes students to gain from athletic competition are socialization values. If that is so, what better way to find out if a student is socialized than through the use of peer evaluation instruments?[42]

Anyone exploring values and athletics cannot overlook the extensive work of Ogilvie and Tutko. For an introduction to their work and their instrument, the Athletic Motivation Inventory (AMI), read Tutko and Richards, *Psychology of Coaching*, previously cited.

Merely improving techniques for measuring values in athletics today, some would argue, is not sufficient. The structure of athletics (coach/player relationships, rules, financing) can be improved, also. Some of the ideas which have emerged include the development of club sports; deemphasizing state and national tournaments, so there would be more regional winners and less emphasis on being "number one"; increasing the power of accrediting agencies to certify that all student-athletes at a college fit the profile of typical students at that school; and introducing new games which stress physical well-being and undercut the need to win.[43]

Let the debate, and the research, continue.

NOTES

1. Sources included *1973 Sports Participation Survey*, issued by the National Federation of State High School Associations, 400 Leslie St., Box 98, Elgin, Ill. 60120. In it NCAA statistics were obtained through a telephone interview in February, 1974. From these sources it was learned that at the interscholastic level 27 different sports are available for males, 20 for females. At the collegiate level males compete in 24 areas and females in 19. Basketball attendance figures cited are from Keith W. Jennison, *The Concise Encyclopedia of Sports* (New York: Watts, 1970), pp. 20–22.
2. During the week of January 18–22, 1973, a conference on "Sport in American Life" was held at Iowa State University. Many speakers graciously consented to be interviewed and granted permission for the author to cite their speeches. References from this conference, whether a speech or an interview, will be identified as INA (Institute of National Affairs).
3. Harold Vanderzwaag, *Toward a Philosophy of Sport* (Reading, Mass.: Addison-Wesley Publishing Co., 1972), pp. 19, 34, 35.
4. Louis Raths, Merrill Harmin, and Sidney Simon, *Values and Teaching* (Columbus, O.: Charles E. Merrill, 1966), pp. 27–30.
5. Dave Meggyesy, *Out of Their League* (New York: Simon and Schuster, 1970, 1971); Paul Weiss, *Sport, A Philosophical Inquiry* (Carbondale, Ill.: Southern Illinois University Press, 1969).
6. Tony Simpson, "Real Men, Short Hair," *Intellectual Digest*, November, 1973, pp. 76, 78 (a condensation of an article in *Texas Coach*, May, 1973). Simpson, a junior high coach, believes that there are several valid reasons, including biblical doctrine, which make it necessary to have hair codes.
7. Paul Weiss, "The Mystique of Sport," INA, January 18, 1974; Haywood Hale Broun, INA, January 15, 1974.
8. Joel Spring, "Sports, Militarism, and American Public Education," INA, January 16, 1974.
9. Dave Meggyesy, "The Football Myth," INA, January 13, 1974.
10. The American Council on Education has been studying collegiate athletic programs, as indicated by the *New York Times*, March 10, 1974.
11. NCAA memorandum, February 21, 1974, to chief executive officers of NCAA member institutions. The American Alliance for Health, Physical Education, and Recreation has also been concerned with this issue. See their monthly *Update* magazine for comments.
12. Lowell Cooper, "Athletics, Activity, and Personality: A Review of the Literature," *Research Quarterly*, March, 1969, pp. 19ff. The best summary of recent research in this area is Robert N. Singer, *Coaching, Athletics and Psychology* (New York: McGraw-Hill, 1972).
13. Max F. Shifrer, "What Happened to 74 Former Country Town Athletes and What Did They Think of Their High School Athletic Experience" (master's thesis, Brigham Young University, 1956).
14. Richard S. Kay, Donald Felker, and Ray O. Varoz, "Sports Interests and Abilities as Contributors to Self-Concept in Junior High Boys," *Research Quarterly*, May, 1972, pp. 208–15.
15. Richard A. Davidson, "A Study of Personality Traits and Value Systems of High School Athletes and Nonathletes" (doctoral dissertation, University of Kentucky, 1967). See also Jearald R. Gregg, "A Philosophical Analysis of the Sports Experience and the Role of Athletics in the Schools" (doctoral dissertation, University of Southern California,

1971), who supports the position that athletic programs can provide heightened awareness of self.

16. Bruce C. Ogilvie and Thomas A. Tutko, "Sport: If You Want To Build Character, Try Something Else," *Psychology Today*, October, 1971, pp. 61-63. See also Thomas A. Tutko and Jack W. Richards, *Psychology of Coaching* (Boston: Allyn and Bacon, 1971), p. 42.

17. Jack Schendel, "The Psychological Characteristics of High School Athletes and Nonparticipants in Athletics: A Three-Year Longitudinal Study," in *Contemporary Psychology of Sport*, cited by Donald R. Hellison, *Humanistic Physical Education* (Englewood Cliffs, N.J.: Prentice-Hall, 1973), p. 21.

18. Michael Feldman, "Some Relationships Between Specified Values of Student Groups and Interscholastic Athletics in Selected High Schools" (doctoral dissertation, University of Massachusetts, 1969). See also Harry Webb, "Professionalization of Attitudes Toward Play," in Gerald S. Kenyon (ed.), *Aspects of Contemporary Sport Sociology* (Chicago: Athletic Institute, 1969), pp. 161-78. Webb's study of students in five different elementary grades indicated that the older the child the lower the rating of playing the game fairly. As Singer notes in *Coaching*, p. 74 (see fn. 12), studies of college students consistently show that varsity lettermen and subsidized athletes score lower on sportsmanship measurements than do nonparticipants.

19. Jack Scott, "The Athletic Revolution," INA, January 14, 1974. Weiss and Spring, INA addresses previously cited. National Collegiate Athletic Association, *Preliminary Report by the Committee on Financial Aid*, booklet published by the NCAA, 1970, pp. 14, 15.

20. Singer, op. cit., p. 73.

21. Ibid., p. 72.

22. Hellison, op. cit., p. 45.

23. Ted E. Runyan, "Assessment of the Pressures on Coaches Toward Having a Winning Season in High School Athletics" (doctoral dissertation, Iowa State University, in progress, 1974). Runyan surveyed coaches in football, basketball, and wrestling to learn how they perceived the pressure to win in their communities. He used an "echo" technique to find out how others in the community saw the pressures, sending similar questionnaires to superintendents, school board members, student-athletes, and parents of student-athletes.

24. Charles Neinas, "Intercollegiate Athletics in American Society," INA, January 18, 1974. Reference here is to the high school and college levels. Most "exposé" books describe drug use at the professional or Olympic levels. In the *NCAA Proceedings*, January 11-13, 1971, p. 64, Frederick M. Garfield stated, "I know of no survey specifically directed to nonmedical drug use among athletes."

25. Harry Edwards, *Revolt of the Black Athlete* (New York: Macmillan, copyright by the Free Press, 1969). See also Harry Edwards, *Sociology of Sport* (Homewood, Ill.: The Dorsey Press, 1973).

26. James Coleman, "Sports and Studies as Paths to Success," in John Loy and Gerald Kenyon, *Sport, Culture and Society* (New York: Macmillan, 1969), pp. 287-305. See also Singer, op. cit., p. 124, citing the study of Shafer and Armer (1968).

27. James M. Luetjen, "Per-Pupil Cost and Relative Contribution of the Athletic Program and Specific Academic Areas among Public Secondary Schools in Missouri" (doctoral dissertation, University of Missouri, 1971). Jerome A. Wray, "Costs of Secondary Schools Athletic Programs," *School Management*, November, 1972, pp. 26-28.

28. Mitchell H. Raiborn, *Financial Analysis of Intercollegiate Athletics* (Kansas City, Mo.: National Collegiate Athletic Association, 1970).

29. Spring, INA, as cited.

30. Katherine Ley, "Women in the World of Sport—Where Do We Go from Here, Boys?" INA, January 14, 1974; Marie Hart, "Woman as Elite Athlete—Explosion in Social Roles," INA, January 17, 1974. M. Marie Hart, "On Being Female in Sport," in M. Marie Hart (ed.), *Sport in the Socio-Cultural Process* (Dubuque, Ia.: Wm. C. Brown, 1972), pp. 291-302.

31. Charles O. Dotson and W. J. Stanley, "Values of Physical Activity Perceived by Male

University Students," *Research Quarterly*, May, 1972, pp. 148–56. Gerald S. Kenyon, "A Conceptual Model for Characterizing Physical Activity," in Loy and Kenyon, op. cit., pp. 71–81.

32. Vanderzwaag, op. cit., pp. 151ff.
33. Singer, op. cit., pp. 19, 20.
34. Eugene P. Powers, "A Study of the Effects of Interschool Athletics on the Physical Well-Being, Mental Health, and Social Acceptance of Boys in Grades Four, Five, and Six" (doctoral dissertation, Temple University, 1955).
35. Helmut Baitsch, et al., *The Scientific View of Sport* (Berlin: Springer-Verlag, 1972), p. 262, citing Hans Groh, "Sport Injuries and Damage to the Locomotor System" (1962). The NCAA committee on injuries is headed by Carl Blyth, Department of Physical Education, University of North Carolina, Chapel Hill, N.C. 27514.
36. Neinas, INA, as cited. *Illinois Alumni News*, March, 1974, p. 2.
37. David Martin, "Are Competitive Athletics Wasting Money and Ruining Kids?" *American School Board Journal*, August, 1972, pp. 16–20. Martin cites a Florida study which reported that 93% of the coaches who had 20 or more years experience claimed the right to prescribe hair and dress codes. Sixty-six percent of those coaching less than five years agreed with that position.
38. The last few years has seen the emergence of manuals such as the AAHPER's *Crowd Control for High School Athletics* (1970), prepared by the National Council of Secondary School Athletic Directors.
39. John P. Williams, Jr., "Sports on Campus: A Study of the Relationship between Students' Values and Their Attitudes Toward Intercollegiate Athletics" (doctoral dissertation, Iowa State University, 1973).
40. Thomas J. Sheehan and William L. Alsop, "Educational Sport," *Journal of Health, Physical Education and Recreation*, May, 1972, pp. 41–45.
41. The Center for Learning, *Search for Values* (Dayton, O.: Pflaum/Standard, 1972).
42. Vanderzwaag, op. cit., p. 208.
43. Club sports is here interpreted as a group of players organized on an informal basis, without school funds, who usually select their own coach. In some colleges the club may move toward a more formal position which includes representing the school. They may then interview and select the coach on behalf of the college, along with representatives of the college. Tom Meschery, Jack Scott, and Paul Weiss made some of these suggestions at the INA conference.

Sports Don't Build Character— They Build Characters

THOMAS TUTKO AND WILLIAM BRUNS

Perhaps the most enduring rationale for participating in athletics is the belief that sports build character. As far back as the 1920s, this myth that competition leads to desirable personality traits was in the national consciousness. John R. Tunis, a sportswriter who was forty years ahead of most of his cohorts in questioning the intrinsic value of sports, wrote:

> The Great Sports Myth ... is a fiction sustained and built up by ... the news-gatherers [and other] professional sports uplifters ... who tell us that competitive sport is health-giving, character-building, brain-making, and so forth. ... They imply more or less directly that its exponents are heroes, possessed of none but the highest of moral qualities; tempered and steeled in the great white heat of competition; purified and made holy by their devotion to ... sport. Thanks to [coaches and sportswriters], there has grown up in the public mind an exaggerated and sentimental notion of the moral value of great, competitive sport spectacles. ... Why not stop talking about the noble purposes which sports fulfill and take them for what they are? ... In short let us cease the elevation of [sport] to the level of a religion.

The years since Tunis, in fact, have produced little documentation to support the character-building theory of sports. In his book *Sociology of Sport*, Dr. Harry Edwards compiled a list of characteristics that are ascribed to athletic participation: character development, loyalty, altruism, discipline, fortitude, preparation for life, opportunities for advancement, physical fitness, mental alertness, educational achievement, religiosity, and nationalism. Based on exhaustive research, Edwards found that in all cases the evidence for such claims was inconclusive, unsubstantiated, or nonexistent. "The claims made on behalf of sport do not have a sufficient basis in current knowledge to justify the dogmatic certainty with which they are expressed," he concluded.

The evidence appears to be that the athlete who reaches the top (or who fails) would have done so despite his surface personality traits. In 1971, Dr. Bruce Ogilvie and I wrote in *Psychology Today*: "For the past

SOURCE: Thomas Tutko and William Bruns, *Winning is Everything and Other American Myths* (New York: Macmillan, 1976), pp. 38–45.

eight years we have been studying the effects of competition on personality. Our research began with the counseling of problem athletes, but it soon expanded to include athletes from every sport, at every level from the high school gym to the professional arena. On the evidence gathered in this study . . . we found no empirical support for the tradition that sport builds character. Indeed, there is evidence that athletic competition limits growth in some areas. It seems that the personality of the ideal athlete is not the result of any molding process, but comes out of the ruthless selection process that occurs at all levels of sport. Athletic competition has no more beneficial effects than intense endeavor in any other field. . . . Sport is like most other activities—those who survive tend to have stronger personalities."

One athlete who feels that sports is failing to build "sound minds in sound bodies" is George Sauer, the former All-Pro receiver for the New York Jets. Sauer has said:

It's interesting to go back and listen to the people on the high school level talk about sport programs and how they develop a kid's self-discipline and responsibility. I think the giveaway that most of this stuff being preached on the lower level is a lie is that when you get to the college and professional levels, the coaches still treat you as an adolescent. They know damn well that you were never given a chance to become responsible or self-disciplined. Even in the pros you are told when to go to bed, when to turn your lights off, when to wake up, when to eat, and what to eat. You even have to live and eat together like you were in a boys' camp.

Another skeptical athlete is former San Francisco quarterback John Brodie, who was quoted in *Psychology Today* as saying, "Sport is one of the few activities in which many Americans spend a great deal of time developing their potentialities. It influences character, I think, as much as our schools and churches do. But, even so, it falls far below what it could be. It leaves out so much. I would love to see a sports team developed with a more fulfilling purpose." In Brodie's view, "sport is so important in creating values in America" that it should be "more than winning at any cost, more than beating people up and making money and getting ahead over somebody else's dead body."

While some personality traits do become modified and developed as a result of the social experiences and pressures inherent in competitive athletics, all too often we endow our athletes with virtues that have nothing to do with how fast they run or how well they shoot the ball. The "halo effect" often protects the athlete from a censure he may deserve and helps to provide him with attributes he may not necessarily possess. For instance, many fans assume that a person in sports who wins and reaches the top has all the desirable traits. He is, in fact, given credit for having traits that have nothing to do with winning. He is seen as a nice guy, modest, sincere, and considerate of others. Conversely, the loser is often judged by the fan to be weak and lacking in character.

Basketball great Bill Russell, a man of refreshing candor, once said: "This business about an athlete being so great is a fiction. It is a fiction written by nonathletes who may be acting out their own fantasies. One who writes about athletes sometimes gets to admire them so much, he doesn't accept the real person; or if he sees flaws in his hero, he ignores them." It has been a great shock for some people in recent years to find that their sports heroes are really human and that they have a great many undesirable traits. Witness the hostile reaction by many disillusioned football fans during the 1974 strike, as they listened to the vitriolic language and self-serving arguments that passed back and forth between players and owners.

After observing months of what he termed "nasty behavior, distasteful words and disgusting actions on both sides," San Francisco columnist Wells Twombly concluded: "This is tribal warfare, pure and brutal. . . . It all speaks so well of character building and all that. If a single boy-child in this nation actually feels uplifted by all this, then somebody ought to get his name. The reaction has been quite the opposite."

Where did we get the notion that sports makes such an important contribution to man and mankind? First, we have testimonies by famous people who tie their success to previous athletic participation. Second, we hear from those within the profession who seek to justify what they're doing. And third, we have national leaders and banquet speakers telling us so. A few examples will illustrate the point.

Gen. Douglas MacArthur: "[Sport] is a vital character builder. It molds the youth of our country for their roles as custodians of the republic. It teaches them to be strong enough to know they are weak, and brave enough to face themselves when they are afraid. It teaches them to be proud and unbending in honest defeat, but humble and gentle in victory. . . . It gives them a predominance of courage over timidity, of appetite for adventure over loss of ease. Fathers and mothers who would make their sons into men should have them participate in [sports]."

Jess Hill, then the athletic director of the University of Southern California: "Athletics develop a dedication and a desire to excel in competition, a realization that success requires hard work and that life must be lived according to rules. A youngster can learn a sense of loyalty and a respect for discipline, both of which are lacking in this country today. . . ."

Sociologist David Riesman: "The road to the board room leads through the locker room."

The Little League motto: "From the ranks of boys who stand now on the morning side of the hill will come the leaders, the future strength and character of the nation."

Gerald Ford: "Broadly speaking, outside of a national character and an educated society, there are few things more important to a country's growth and well-being than competitive athletics. If it is a cliché to say athletics build character as well as muscle, then I subscribe to the cliché."

Those who believe in all-out competition and the verities of sports will invariably point to some glaring success story, such as Supreme Court Justice Byron "Whizzer" White, the former football All-American, or President Ford himself, a standout for Michigan in the early 1930s. The message is, "See what football did for these men." Yet to attribute their ultimate success to sports is misleading. They had successful personality styles to begin with, and sports just happened to be one of the things they took up; even if they hadn't participated, they would have been a success in other fields.

Similarly, every season we read about the youngster who fought his way out of the ghetto by playing basketball, or the truck driver's son who signed a football contract for $250,000. Thousands of other examples abound where sports have helped give a sense of direction to youngsters who lacked ambition or direction or responsibility, or who stuck it out in high school simply because they wanted to be on the football team.

This is fine. But what I object to is having these examples brought out to supposedly justify all the youngsters who are damaged by sports, physically or psychologically. We have verification only by highly successful people. We don't have failures say, "Look, I also didn't make it when I was playing football. I just sat on the bench and caused a lot of trouble." Nor do we have people suggesting that sports may be instrumental in destroying character. We never seem to hear the story of Fenwick, a nice kid who got along with his friends, had good grades, and liked his parents. Then he went out for high school football. As a result, he had three teeth knocked out, he dislocated his shoulder, he was too tired after practice to study and his grades fell apart, he hated his coach, and one day he took a tire iron to a kid he didn't like.

I had a friend whose son had just finished his second year of Little League. The boy had bad marks in school and problems with deportment, but he was a great Little League ball player. He was even named the team's most valuable player. However, two weeks later he was picked up for stealing. What moral fiber was sports helping to build in this youngster? They took Little League away, and he didn't have anything.

It could even be argued that many of President Nixon's problems could be traced back to his old football days as a bench warmer at Whittier College. Nixon told a pro football Hall of Fame gathering in

1971: "Chief Newman, my coach, an American Indian, produced some very fine teams at that small, little college at Whittier. . . . There were no excuses for failure. He didn't feel sorry for you when you got knocked down."

Writer Robert Lipsyte later noted in the *New York Times Magazine*: "Sports is a human process shaped by a society, and Nixon was nourished by the specific values of sport—team loyalty, discipline, perseverance, physical courage, respectful fear and hatred of the opposition, winning as the only criterion for success."

When we talk about "building character," my criteria are not that an athlete receive a college scholarship, sign a pro contract, and make a lot of money. The goal of those in sports should be to develop more mature, contented people who are emotionally and physically healthy.

We should all admire the coach who is trying to achieve this in his players, the coach who can say, "Harvey's become a hard worker and he's getting better grades now" because of his involvement in sports. I would respect any coach—regardless of his won-lost record—who told me, "Okay, if you don't believe me, here's what I've done. For the last ten years, I've kept track of each one of my players. They all have a job today, they've been promoted, they're active in community work, they're good family men, and they're happy." Tennessee basketball coach Ray Mears has made an effort to do this, and he has one of the most successful records in college history. He's clearly concerned about his players and he follows their progress after they graduate. It is also important that a coach keep track of all of his athletes, not just the successful ones. If he takes credit for the successes, he should also take responsibility for the failures.

I think one only has to look at reality—if you will, the daily sports page—to realize that while sports may indeed be building character in certain athletes, it is also building characters. The way the sports establishment handles these "characters" is an example of the fallacy that athletic competition automatically produces a "good" person. Deviant personalities—"troublemakers"—are screened out at every stage of the way through youth, scholastic, and collegiate sports. Those who do survive into the pros certainly don't receive sensitive handling. If the player is a questioning, doubting, independent, and outspoken soul, he's usually branded as a bad egg, an unfortunate draft choice, or a trade that went sour. Unless this athlete has a bright, perceptive, patient coach, he'll be cut or traded or allowed to waste away his talent by feuding with those who say he has a "bad attitude." Instead of trying to help the athlete work out his problem, instead of trying to act in a humanistic fashion, the club says, "Trade him, we don't need that kind of trouble." Which is a lousy way to run a franchise that might be worth $15 million.

If sports were really building character, most of these athletes would be able to resolve their problems. I do not mean to imply, however, that the problems are *all* with the coaches or owners. There are athletes who have deep-seated problems and who will continue to make trouble wherever they go. Athletics should be an area where these problems are more easily detected; what is even more important, it should be an area where there is at least a start in helping athletes with their problems.

Athletes And The Self-Discipline Myth

GLENN DICKEY

It always amuses me when coaches, particularly football coaches, talk of the need for self-discipline and the way sports produces leaders. That has been one of the rationales for sports since God knows when—the old argument went that the battle of Waterloo was won on the playing fields at Eton—but if there was ever any validity to that argument, it has long since been lost.

In fact, sport produces followers, not leaders. I still remember when the original student demonstrations started at the University of California and football coach Ray Willsey bragged that none of his players were involved, possibly because he had nothing else to brag about at the time, Cal's football fortunes being at an all-time low. He should have been ashamed of that, because it proved there were no leaders on the football team, nor even any players who were thinking for themselves. The Cal student body, whether in favor of the demonstrations or opposed to them, was fervently aroused over the issue, but on the football team, passivity reigned. That was no surprise, because the system encourages reliance on others, usually coaches, for ideas and the very patterns of life. Conformity is the desired goal, and conformists are not leaders.

Teamwork is important in sports, more so in some sports than others. Obviously, a football team cannot win if one lineman decides he wants to

---

SOURCE: Glenn Dickey, *The Jock Empire* (Radnor, Penn.: Chilton Book Company, 1974), pp. 156–166.

block in one direction and another lineman in another, and the team concept is legitimate in that context. Unfortunately, many coaches carry it much further.

Hank Stram of Kansas City, for instance, has always attributed much of his success to the fact that his team projects an image of togetherness; on the road, they wear team blazers. ("They look like a bunch of mechanical men," scoffs Oakland Raider tackle Art Thoms.) But other teams have been successful without this kind of regimentation. The Raiders, for instance, have all sorts of hair styles and dress. Billy Cannon used to wear dirty blue jeans on road trips, and Thoms has been known to wear a T-shirt advertising "Acapulco Gold" on the front. None of this has seemed to hurt their play on the field.

The concept of team unity is generally ridiculous, anyway, whether it's in appearance or reality. The Oakland A's won a world championship in 1972 while fighting with each other, their manager and their owner. Even in their great moments, they were unhappy. After Vida Blue saved their championship win with four innings of relief, he and starter John Odom almost fought in the dressing room because Odom thought Blue had made the "choke" sign in talking to him. It wasn't any better in 1973. Joe Rudi complained because he was benched—apparently at Charlie Finley's order—and Reggie Jackson sounded off when he was given a day of rest he didn't want. Significantly, these complaints came as the A's were making a run at the American League West lead.

Baseball is such an individualistic sport that team unity is seldom a factor, but even on a football team unity is a much overrated virtue. Daryle Lamonica is such a loner that virtually the only friend he had with the Raiders after he was traded there in 1967 was another quarterback, Cotton Davidson. There was, in fact, so much antipathy between Lamonica and the rest of the team in those years that a story made the rounds that Lamonica and Cannon had had a fight, variously reported as happening in the locker room or an airplane. The story had no basis in fact, but Lamonica never pretended that he wanted any friends on the team. "I want respect, not friends," he said on many occasions. "I might have to kick some ass in the huddle, and I don't want to have to worry about friends." And thus, in the first three years Lamonica was with the Raiders, the team was 13-1, 12-2 and 12-1-1.

Later, as Lamonica started to suffer injuries more and more, George Blanda got his chance to shine, particularly in the miracle year of 1970. That galled Lamonica, who muttered to friends that Blanda was simply taking advantage of the situation. "The teams are geared to stop me, and George has a different style. That throws them off." It was a valid point.

Blanda tried to downplay the rivalry, but he obviously enjoyed his late-career success and was more popular with his teammates, though he often relieved them of money in the card games on airplane trips. But whatever quarterback was at the helm, the Raiders continued to win.

By 1972, a third quarterback—Ken Stabler—had entered the already chaotic quarterback situation. Obviously at Al Davis' request, Stabler started the season opener in Pittsburgh. When he was ineffective—and unlucky—Blanda came in, but could do no better. Finally, Lamonica was sent in for the fourth quarter and got the Raiders three touchdowns in a gallant, though insufficient, comeback. From that point, Lamonica was back as the starting quarterback, while Stabler seethed on the bench and debate continued in the press and among the Raiders themselves as to which quarterback should be starting. The result of all this dissension? The Raiders were 10–3–1 and won their division for the fifth time in six years. Stabler became the starter in the fourth game of the '73 season, once more forcing the unhappy Lamonica back to the bench, and the Raiders again won their division.

You would think examples like this would at least make coaches wonder if team unity is all that important, but it doesn't. Most coaches even decide what players should eat and wear, and how close they should cut their hair and when they should go to bed. The idea of a curfew should be repugnant to any athlete; unfortunately, there are only a few who truly rebel. Those who violate it usually do it as a little boy would break a rule his parent has made, just to see if he can get away with it.

Can you imagine what would happen if a bank decided that its employees must go to bed at 11 P.M. every night and sent a boss around to check? That bank would have to close its doors in a minute. But virtually every football team, from the high school through the pro level, does that. Even a team as relaxed about other aspects of discipline as the Raiders insists on a curfew.

The idea is that if the coaches don't check on the players, the players will be out drinking and screwing all night long, without being conscious of the effect they'll have on the team the next morning. And, undoubtedly, some would be, because they've been treated as children all their lives. If somebody else makes decisions for you for many years, you don't start making your own overnight.

The system is, or should be, humiliating for coaches, too. My wife was appalled when she made a trip to San Diego a few years back and talked to Diane Spencer, wife of offensive lineman coach Ollie Spencer of the Raiders. Diane could not even sleep in the same hotel as her husband, and she had to wait until he was through tucking players in at 11 P.M. before they could go out to dinner. It may or may not be a coincidence that the Spencers' marriage broke up a couple of years later.

It seems to me that the curfew system is self-defeating. Because athletes are not forced to exert self-discipline off the field, they do not develop it on the field, either. In tight spots, they look for help from the sidelines. Undoubtedly if the curfew were abolished, there would be some who would take advantage of that and ultimately hurt their game performances. But those types of athletes are hardly the ones you want to rely on in a game, anyway, and it might be best to weed them out beforehand. That would leave those who had the emotional maturity to take care of themselves, which would seem to be preferable.

Tommy Prothro tried to bring some sense to this whole system when he was hired to coach the Los Angeles Rams in 1971. Practically his first act was to abolish the curfew in training camp, which horrified other coaches. Unfortunately, Prothro failed to win a divisional title in two years, though not because he had abolished the curfew, and he was fired. It will be a brave coach indeed who tries abolishing the curfew again because, in pro football's mind, the linkage has been firmly made: no curfew, no title. By now, everybody has conveniently forgotten that the one big problem with the '72 Rams was a quarterback, Roman Gabriel, who could throw effectively only about every third game. The lack of curfew had no effect on Gabriel.

Prothro's problem illustrates another facet of the football business. An intelligent and well-rounded man, Prothro tried to approach coaching a pro football team with the same maturity he approached other problems. Unfortunately, he extended this thought of maturity to his players, who didn't deserve it. Specifically, he thought to tell them the truth: when they played San Francisco, he told them they were playing a good team and had to play their best to win, which they did. When they played Denver, he told them they were playing a weak team. The players took that to mean they didn't have to play well against teams like Denver, and so they lost several games they should have won. It seems incredible that a professional athlete, whose livelihood depends on playing well, has to be encouraged to do so, but as we have seen, athletes are not accustomed to making any important deductions for themselves.

But even if a coach is justified in assuming that he has to make all the on-field decisions, it remains incredible that he thinks he should have the power to decide how short a player should wear his hair. And yet, the majority of coaches feel that way.

Certainly, there is no reason to think that hair has any effect on an athlete's performance. There have been some quite good teams whose players have had short hair, and some quite bad ones with the same attribute. Hank Stram's teams at Kansas City have all been short-haired, but when Ed Khayat tried the same approach at Philadelphia, the Eagles continued to be the losers they've always been. Sparky Anderson guided a team of short hairs to the '72 National League pennant, but he lost the World Series to the A's, who looked like a throwback to the old House of David teams.

Playing ability is more important than hair length. And yet, the idea persists among coaches that short hair has a significance far beyond appearance. There was an article in May 1973, in "Texas Coach," by Tony Simpson, head football coach at a junior high in the suburbs of Houston, which delineated some of the worst aspects of the hair code business in sports. Simpson's article contended that long hair on boys and men is the sign of a "sissy" and should be banned from American athletic fields: "It is time that American coaches stopped allowing themselves to be personally represented by male athletic teams and individuals that look like females." He continued:

Only in the animal world is the male designed to be most attractive or the prettiest—for example, the male lion has the mane, the male peacock has the feathers. This is normal in the animal world only. However, a male with long hair is cute, he is pretty and he is sweet. If the coaches of America would grow long hair like their athletes, we might be able to scare the Russian and Chinese Communists to death with our lack of masculinity.

It should be pointed out here that the only reason males are free to look like females and their coaches are free to permit this is because we had real men that were not cute, not sweet and not pretty with courage and sense enough to kill our enemies on battlefields all over the globe.

If common sense indicates that long hair on a man is a disgrace, let's stop compromising our common sense by allowing it. A good hair code will get the abnormals out of athletics before they become coaches and bring their 'loser' standards into the coaching profession.

Simpson said keeping his hair short is a sign of male discipline. "Without self-discipline and respect for authority, you have an uncontrollable problem among the youth with drug abuse, crime and sexual perversion. And this describes the U.S. in 1973."

He said a woman who wants a man with long hair is not a "real woman in her soul."

But the American male youth—and many not so young—wear their hair long simply because they know the female will like it. These so-called males are in submission to the warped norms and standards of the females who like to set the dress and grooming standards for their mousy husbands, their pantywaist boyfriends and feminine sons.

It is hard to know where to start with this nonsense except to point out that a lot of men who have accomplished some good in this world have had long hair, starting with the obvious example of Jesus of Nazareth.

Sports has been the backwater of society in the hair issue, and it is enough to make us all despair. The story is hardly new; on every level from Little League to the majors, it keeps popping up. Eventually, I think reason will prevail—Simpson "resigned" as coach shortly after this article appeared—but it's ridiculous that all hair codes haven't disappeared long before this.

Usually, the hair and dress issue is only a symbol for a larger issue beneath. When coaches and officials try to enforce their outmoded hair and dress codes on younger athletes, they are really worried that long hair and flamboyant dress are symbols of revolt, that an athlete who could decide to wear his hair long might think he could make other decisions for himself. This is abhorrent to most coaches; like the colonial rulers in underdeveloped countries, they want to retain the status quo.

The point on which the hair-dress conscious coaches all founder is their inability to detect the difference between reasonable rules and those based only on personal prejudices. Hair styles have nothing to do with performance; it is all a matter of styles in society, and nothing more. Coaches wear short hair because that was the norm as they were reaching adulthood, but Jesus Christ had long hair, George Washington wore a powdered wig and Abe Lincoln had a beard. No doubt, Simpson would not have any of them playing on his team. Short hair has become such a fetish with some that it has been observed that anybody with short hair who wears a Brooks Brothers suit can get away with almost anything, which may be why it took so long to uncover the Watergate gang.

Along with this idea of short hair goes the curious notion that "masculinity" is synonymous with force. Simpson gives himself away with his talk of "sissies," which is his obvious code for homosexuals. We have all known coaches and physical education teachers like this, who are determined to promote their idea of masculinity at the expense of their charges. Long hair means softness, i.e., femininity, and thus must be discouraged; it is a sexual fantasyland.

In truth, it is at least as important for a boy to learn tenderness as toughness. I submit that masculinity has nothing to do with learning how to beat up on somebody but has everything to do with learning to be gentle and considerate with a woman, with being loving to a child and even with learning to cry at great moments of sadness or joy. Simpson and his kind would never understand that. His obsession with masculinity makes me wonder. A man who is secure in his masculinity does not feel the need to talk about it.

Even in relatively nonviolent sports, toughness is sought after among coaches and managers. Billy Martin, manager of the Detroit Tigers, often tries to provoke a fight with the other team to get his team stirred up, and woe to the player who does not come off the Tiger bench to get in on the fight. Conformity reigns again. In spring training, 1973, Giants manager Charlie Fox let it be known that any player who did not participate in a team brawl would be fined. Team unity again.

Football coaches seem especially prone to this kind of talk becuase football, with its armor plate and simulated war conditions, is so often treated as a proving ground for men and boys. Supposedly, a football player proves his courage by going out on the field and hitting other players. Yet, this actually has nothing to do with courage; it is simply a personal attribute. Some men like body contact and some do not, and the ones who like it are the ones who gravitate to football. If blocking and tackling are signs of courage, how do you explain the terror with which football players usually watch the approach of a hypodermic needle?

Football players are courageous when they play with injuries, but in many cases, they are pulled along by a combination of their teammates' enthusiasm, the excitement which acts almost as an anesthetic, and the unmentionable—drugs. When football coaches talk about the necessity for courage and self-discipline, they are talking errant nonsense. True courage and self-discipline would enable players to buck the conformist thinking of their coaches; I know no coach who wants that.

On the college level, the philosophy of toughness is probably best exemplified by Woody Hayes of Ohio State, who makes a point of coaching in shirt sleeves on the sidelines in cold weather, as if to say the weather can't affect him. It is no coincidence that Hayes' players are generally like robots, discouraged from any personal initiative or self-discipline.

Hayes and his pupil, Bo Schembechler of Michigan, are fanatics on the subject: football to them is a game of infantry, of foot soldiers, and they carry it to the extreme. It is no wonder that Hayes admires Gen. George S. Patton; he thinks the same way. Players are mere pawns in his grand strategy. (Parenthetically, it should be noted that the one chink in his strategic armor is passing. Like many another infantry general, he has never believed in air war, and his teams neither throw well nor defend well against the pass. If everything else is relatively equal, always bet on a good passing team against one of Woody's.)

Hayes' and Schembechler's approach to the game is best shown by their trips to the Rose Bowl. In the belief that winning justifies everything, both virtually locked up their players. Schembechler even took his players to Bakersfield to practice for one Rose Bowl, and Jack Tatum once told me what it was like in the last Rose Bowl he played in, for an Ohio State team that was regarded as perhaps the best in collegiate history—until it lost to Stanford.

"I wasn't terribly upset because I felt I played well," he remembered, "and I didn't think we were going to have a great game. There were a lot of players who were very unhappy with the coaching staff, and they couldn't forget that and go out and play the way they would have otherwise. There were a lot of things that disturbed us. For one, we came out a day early because we were told that would give us more time to relax, but we just got off the plane and went right out onto the practice field. We had a predominantly senior team, but the curfew was 10 o'clock every night. We asked them to make it 12 o'clock for at least a couple of nights, but they wouldn't do it."

Fortunately, as Simpson noted in another context, the times are changing. Even Hayes modified his approach before the '74 Rose Bowl; he gave his players some freedom, and they won. Coaches with different ideas are getting into the profession and are inevitably changing it. One such is Mike White. As an assistant at Stanford, White was responsible for much of John Ralston's success because he persuaded Ralston that short hair, dress codes and unreasonable curfews had no place in college football. Stanford, a marked underdog both times, beat the tight Ohio State and Michigan teams in back-to-back Rose Bowls.

Ralston went on to coach the Denver Broncos and White, who had his choice of either Ralston's old job or the one opening up at Cal, opted for Cal, his alma mater. In addition to the problems any new coach faces of changing the system (old coach Ray Willsey was very conservative; White believes in a pass-oriented system) White has had additional problems because Cal has been on NCAA probation.

As a result, White had a very disappointing first season, winning only three games although his team finished strong with a dramatic win over Stanford in the closing seconds of the Big Game. White has not been a miracle worker at Cal, but I think he will ultimately be a winner, and, more importantly, he is bringing a breath of fresh air to the college game. He has ideas whose time has come.

Mike has imagination, and he also has a verve and enthusiasm he is able to transmit to the athletes. More important, he has moved with the times. He is from the awful, passive, crew-cut era of college sports, graduating in 1958 when athletes—and students—did as they were told, no questions asked, but he understands that today's athlete is much different.

"Today's athlete will play just as hard for you as a guy 20 years ago," says White, "but you can't get him to play by coaching the same way they did in 1910. The Knute Rockne stuff doesn't go any more."

White does it by treating players as individuals, being aware of their problems and their needs, not hassling them about dress and haircuts and seeing that they get their diplomas. One of the first things he did when the Bears convened for practice before their opening game in September, 1972, was to abolish the curfew. He let the players regulate their own conduct, and he had no problems.

White does not downgrade the importance of collegiate football— "We're the one thing that can pull the entire university student body together"—but he has not lost his perspective. "We should be an integral part of the University," he says. "I'm a teacher, and I want to show our faculty that there is a place for sports in the college curriculum, that we do have a contribution to make."

I think White is a forerunner of a movement that will eventually wash such as Simpson and Hayes out to sea, never to be mourned by a thinking man. And eventually, coaches may be able to talk of self-discipline for athletes and really mean it.

■ FOR FURTHER STUDY

Bend, Emil. "Some Potential Dysfunctional Effects of Sport Upon Socialization." Paper presented at the Third International Symposium on the Sociology of Sport, Waterloo, Canada (August 1971).

Berger, Richard A., and Donald H. Littlefield. "Comparison Between Football Athletes and Nonathletes on Personality." *Research Quarterly*, 40 (December 1969), 663–665.

Berkowitz, L. "Sports, Competition, and Aggression." in *Proceedings*: 4th Canadian Psycho-Motor Learning and Sport Symposium (Ottawa, 1972).

Coakley, Jay J. *Sport in Society: Issues and Controversies*. St. Louis: C. V. Mosby, 1978, pp. 106–112.

Cooper, Lowell. "Athletics, Activity, and Personality: A Review of the Literature." *Research Quarterly*, 40 (March 1969), 17–22.

Kay, R. S., D. W. Felker, and R. O. Varoz. "Sports Interests and Abilities as Contributors to Self-Concept in Junior High School Boys," *Research Quarterly*, 43 (1972), 209–215.

Kennedy, Ray. "Wanted: An End to Mayhem." *Sports Illustrated* (November 17, 1975), pp. 17–21.

Layman, E. M. "The Role of Play and Sport in Healthy Emotional Development: A Reappraisal." *Contemporary Psychology of Sport*. Edited by Gerald Kenyon. North Palm Beach, Florida: The Athletic Institute, 1968.

Malmisur, M. C. "Social Adjustment Differences Between Student Athletes and Student Non-Athletes as Measured by Ego Development." *Sport Sociology Bulletin*, 4 (1975), 2–12.

Merriman, J. Burton. "Relationship of Personality Traits to Motor Ability." *Research Quarterly*, 31 (May 1960), 163–173.

Orlick, Terry, and Cal Botterill. *Every Kid Can Win*. Chicago: Nelson-Hall, 1975.

Phillips, J. C., and Walter E. Schafer. "The Athletic Subculture." Paper presented at the American Sociological Association meetings, Washington, D.C. (1970).

Phillips, John C., and Walter E. Schafer, "Consequences of Participation in Interscholastic Sports: A Review and Prospectus." *Pacific Sociological Review*, 14 (July 1971), 328–338.

Rehberg, R. A. "Behavioral and Attitudinal Consequences of High School Interscholastic Sports: A Speculative Consideration." *Adolescence*, 4 (Spring 1969), 69–88.

Richardson, D. "Ethical Conduct in Sport Situations." *66th Proceedings* of the

National College Physical Education Association for Men (Washington, D.C.: National College Physical Education Association for Men, 1962).

Schafer, Walter E. "Participation in Interscholastic Athletics and Delinquency: A Preliminary Study." *Social Problems*, 17 (Summer 1969), 40–47.

Schendel, Jack. "Psychological Differences Between Athletes and Nonparticipants at Three Educational Levels." *Research Quarterly*, 36 (March 1965), 52–67.

Seymour, E. W. "Comparative Study of Certain Behavior Characteristics of Participant and Nonparticipant Boys in Little League Baseball." *Research Quarterly*, 27 (1956), 338–346.

Singer, Robert N. *Myths and Truths in Sports Psychology.* New York: Harper and Row, 1975, pp. 89–105.

Snyder, Eldon. "Aspects of Socialization in Sports and Physical Education." *Quest*, 14 (June 1970), 1–7.

Snyder, Eldon E., and Elmer Spreitzer. "Basic Assumptions in the World of Sports." *Quest*, 24 (Summer 1975), 3–9.

Stevenson, Christopher. "Socialization Effects of Participation in Sport: A Critical Review of the Research." *Research Quarterly*, 46 (October, 1975), 287–301.

Seven

Sport and Politics

When most of the African nations boycotted the 1976 Olympic Games, many observers decried the action because they felt that sport and politics should be separate. The thesis of this unit is not only that sport and politics are related in a number of ways, but that they are inevitably intertwined. There are several fundamental reasons for this strong association.[1]

First, athletes typically represent some social organization (e.g., school, community, or nation), and they are pitted against the representatives of some other similar type of organization. Each side uses ritual to reaffirm symbolically fidelity to their organization. Victory or defeat for the athletic team reflects on the worth of the organization that team represents. This is easily seen at international competitions where the outcomes are often interpreted politically as winning nations construe victory as a reaffirmation of their nation's superior culture, economic system, and military might.

A second basis for the strong correspondence between sport and politics is inherent in the process of social organization itself. As the interest in sport has grown, teams, leagues, players' associations, and ruling bodies have been created. Power relationships exist among these social organizations: some have authority over others, and some attempt to destroy the credibility of others. An interesting sociological observation is that these organizations, once created, eventually become more interested in maintaining or increasing their power than in securing the goals for which the organizations were originally created. Isaacs has put it this way:

Success in sports means attaining status in the status quo. Arising from the imposition of rules, structures, and orderly procedures, sports are nurtured in the rigid maintenance of things as they are and have always been. Elaborate bureaucratic superstructures are erected to define, codify, regulate, legislate, and chronicle those things and to keep things that way. In time, the function of the bureaucracy becomes as always, to maintain itself, which is seen as the way to maintain the game.[2]

The third linkage between sport and politics occurs as governments impose their wills through laws, regulations, and political acts that encourage or discourage international competition. Congress decides which sports body has the authority to determine the composition of our Olympic team. Congress provides sports with certain exemptions to laws. Congress decides whether or not games can or cannot be blacked out on local television. The courts decide whether sport is exempt from antitrust laws. The State Department decides whether American teams should or should not travel to certain countries.

Sports events and political situations have reciprocal effects on each other and provide another basis for the close relationship between sports and politics. A soccer match between El Salvador and Honduras started a war, for example. Sport also decreases the tension between countries as previously hostile countries may cautiously allow athletes from the two countries to interact as a prelude, if all goes right, to open relations. This occurred recently when American ping-pong players were the first to travel in Red China, and American basketball players competed in Cuba as a prelude to easing cold relations.

Political events, of course, also can have an impact on sports. Some recent examples of this are the ways that apartheid policies of South Africa have caused the boycotting of sports events involving that country; how Canada, under pressure from Red China, an important source of exports, refused to allow Taiwan athletes to participate in the 1976 Olympics; and the cancellation of occasional sports events because the relations between the two countries involved have become tense.

A final source of the strong relationship between sport and politics stems from the institutional character of sport itself. As Eitzen and Sage have said:

Sport, as with the institutions of the polity and religion, is conservative; it serves as a preserver and legitimator of the existing order. The patriotic pageants that accompany sporting events reinforce the political system. Moreover, sport perpetuates many myths, such as, anyone with talent regardless of race or social station has an equal chance to succeed. Sport also legitimizes ideas such as "winning is not everything, it is the only thing." Sport is a model of law and order.[3]

The initial selection, by sociologist Jay Coakley, examines the possibility that sport is an opiate of the masses.

The next selection is from a speech by Spiro Agnew when he was vice-president of the United States. In this speech Agnew examines sport in a clearly political way. First, he attacks the critics of sport as being unAmerican. Second, he argues that sport promotes the very values that have made and continue to make America and Americans great. And, third, Agnew feels that sports provide the vital function of helping to hold society together.

The final selection is from the introduction to Richard D. Mandell's analysis of the Olympic Games of 1936—the highly political Nazi Olympics that Hitler used as a stage to demonstrate the glory that had returned to Germany.

NOTES

1. D. Stanley Eitzen and George H. Sage, *Sociology of American Sport* (Dubuque, Iowa: Wm. C. Brown, 1978), pp. 143–144.
2. Neil D. Isaacs, *Jock Culture U.S.A.* (New York: W. W. Norton, 1978), p. 88.
3. Eitzen and Sage, *Sociology of American Sport*, p. 144.

Sport as an Opiate

JAY J. COAKLEY

Thus sport, which began originally, perhaps, as a spontaneous reaction against the machine, has become one of the mass duties of the machine age. It is a part of that universal regimentation of life—for the sake of private profits or nationalistic exploit—from which its excitement provides a temporary and only a superficial release. Sport has turned out, in short, to be one of the least effective reactions against the machine. There is only one other reaction less effective in its final result: the most ambitious as well as the most disastrous. I mean war. (Mumford, 1934).[1]

In this 1934 statement, Lewis Mumford pinpoints what he believed to be one of the more significant paradoxes of our technological world. Contemporary sport as seen by Mumford was devoid of any of the characteristics of play out of which it emerged. Instead, sport had become a self-defeating spectacle that served only as a stabilizer of the existing social order by providing a temporary distraction from a highly structured, standardized, machine-dominated world. More recently, Paul Hoch (1972) has taken this general idea and, after combining it with a Marxist orientation, has concluded that the culprit is not our machine civilization, but rather the monopolistic capitalist organization of the production process. In other words, contemporary sport in much of the Western world has emerged not as an antidote to the existence of machines, but as an aid to the maintenance of a capitalist system, "which robs people of their power to make decisions and their creativity, and sets them in search of opiates in consumption and entertainment" (1972). In Hoch's analysis, sport in a capitalist society or for that matter, sport in any society that is not "humane and creative" will inevitably serve as a mass narcotic, an object for consumption, and a perpetuator of militarism. *In other words, sport is an opiate.*

To make this position more understandable, we need some definitions and explanations. According to Hoch (1972), an opiate is "anything that tends to frustrate the solution of social problems by providing individuals with either (1) a temporary high ... which takes their minds off the problem for a while but does nothing to deal with it; or (2) a distorted

SOURCE: Jay J. Coakley, *Sport in Society: Issues and Controversies* (St. Louis: C. V. Mosby, 1978), pp. 26–30.

frame of reference or identification which encourages them to look for salvation through patently false channels." Marx, of course, described religion in such terms. Religion focuses attention on the supernatural, provides individuals with a spiritual as well as a psychological lift, and tends to emphasize improvement through a change of the self rather than of the social order. This was taken by Marx as an indication that religion deadens awareness of the "here and now" and promotes the maintenance of the status quo by giving priority to the goal of spiritual salvation. He further concluded that a religious belief system could be exploited by those in positions of power. If the vast majority of the members of a society believed that enduring pain and experiencing self-denial or accepting one's status in this world would open the door to everlasting happiness in the afterlife, those in power could be reasonably sure that those under their control would be hard working, docile, or both. If those in power went so far as to manifest their own commitment to such beliefs, their hold over the people could be strengthened even further. Such a manifestation would, after all, show that they had something in common with the masses.

In an advanced capitalist society where people are usually not very likely to look to the supernatural for explanations of events and for answers to questions, religion may be supplemented by the addition of other activities with similar narcotic effects. Hoch points out that along with religion, the contemporary opiates in a capitalist society include "sport spectacles, whiskey, and repressively sublimated sex." These combined with the opiates of nationalism, racism, and sexism serve to distort people's perspectives and encourage self-defeating behavior (1972).[2] Although all of these can be effective and mutually reinforcing as opiates, sport stands out as especially significant. Unlike other forms of entertainment, sport spectatorship is often accompanied by an extremely intense identification with players, teams, and the values perceived to be at the basis for success in athletics. According to Hoch, this identification brings sport further into the lives of the spectators and captures their attention on a long-term basis. When the game ends, fan involvement usually does not cease, but carries on between games and into the off season.

The extent to which fan involvement occurs and has an impact on behavior has been illustrated by Lever in her discussion of soccer in Brazil. She cites a study done in Sao Paulo indicating that when the most popular team in the city wins its weekly game, the production output of the city increases 12.3% during the following week. During the week following a loss, the number of work-related accidents increases by 15.3% (Lever, 1969). These data could be used by those who define sport as an opiate as supportive of their position, but in presenting their argument, they would also have to point out that sport involvement need not lead to production increases to contribute to the maintenance of the status quo; it must only give the workers something on which to focus their attention so that their minds can be diverted from thinking about how tedious and alienating their jobs are. As long as the workers are thinking about and discussing with their co-workers the fate of their local team (whether it wins or loses), they are less likely to be devoting time to criticizing their jobs and seeing the futility of their work careers.

Beyond occupying people's time and distracting their attention and energy, sport functions in other ways to help maintain the position of the power elite. According to Hoch, some of our most popular sport activities such as football, hockey, and boxing are set up in a way that fosters a justification for officialized, rule-governed violence and that perpetuates a distorted definition of masculinity in our society. These as well as other less violent sport activities also serve to encourage people to develop the idea that hard work is both a necessary and sufficient cause for success in our system. In other words, Hoch argues that sport influences our values in ways that lock us further into a social system based on coercion and the exploitive use of power. Thus the more we witness violent sport, the more we are apt to condone the use of violence in other settings—even when it is directed at ourselves. The Kent State shootings have been used as an example of this. Additionally, Hoch makes the case that our involvement in violent sport tends to focus our attention on strength and the lack of emotion and feeling as traits necessary for success. The athlete who is the embodiment of brute strength and speed is held by many as the model epitomizing manhood. This was noted at the turn of the century by the sociologist-economist Thorstein Veblen. In *The Theory of the Leisure Class* (1934), he makes the case that sport was not only an occasional diversion, but also a mechanism through which the power elite perpetuated the predatory characteristics of ferocity and cunning. These, according to Veblen, were the personality characteristics that encouraged the use of force and fraud in the affairs of everyday life.

According to Hoch's analysis, one of the most important ways sport serves the interests of the power elite is by generating the belief that success is solely the result of hard work and that hard work, including dedication and discipline, is always necessary for success. Such an ideology of success encourages the masses to look up to the power elite in society as being paragons of virtue and to look down on those who have experienced no success as deserving of their position. When teams win consistently, success is attributed to hard work, discipline, and team solidarity ("You make your own breaks"); when teams lose consistently, there are references to a failure to "put out," bad attitudes, and teamwork problems, and the fans call for changes in personnel—not a restructuring of the game or its administration ("If you lost, you have nobody to blame but yourself"). Hoch points out that this way of looking at things blinds people to a consideration of the problems inherent in the social and economic structure and engenders the notion that success depends only on attitude and personal perseverance. It also leads to the belief that failure is to be blamed on the individual alone and is to be accepted as an indication of personal inadequacies and of a need to work harder in the future.

In a capitalist society, sport not only serves as an opiate and a perpetuator of establishment values, but also becomes defined as an object to be consumed; it changes from an activity to a product and is promoted and marketed accordingly. Sport leagues along with individual teams try to generate large pools of fans as well as sponsors for media coverage. Youngsters are lured into the spectator role by trading cards, Miami Dolphin pajamas, Boston Red Sox baseball caps, National Basketball Association tennis shoes, and a multitude of other products designed to create an interest in sport and sport teams that will grow into an adulthood desire to become a season ticket holder. The tendency for youngsters to identify with athlete-entertainers is exploited in an effort not only to generate interest, but also to sell the many products the athletes endorse. With the help of a little imagination, a helmet, a jersey with the proper number on it, an autographed glove, and so on, the role of athlete, unlike most other adult roles, is both highly visible and relatively easy to emulate. Thus attachments to sport heroes can serve as the basis for the creation of an interest in sport along with a "need" for consumer goods.

Youngsters are not the only ones taken in by the promotional efforts of capitalists in the world of sport. Despite the oftentimes exorbitant admission prices, fan interest continues strong; people will pay to watch their teams perform. Additionally, an increasing number of middle- and upper-income individuals and families are joining athletic clubs where they are paying to participate or paying for the chance to learn how to participate, which costs even more. Sporting goods manufacturers are finding that effective advertising efforts can lead to more and more equipment defined as absolutely necessary for successful involvement and participation. Of course, if fellow participants are to be given the impression that you are sufficiently knowledgeable about the "tools of the trade," the top-of-the-line equipment is what you should purchase and display. It has gotten to the point where participants can prove themselves through their ability to consume the appropriate equipment as well as through a demonstration of their talent. Materialism and overproduction have combined to lead people to deal with one another in terms of images in sport rather than in terms of human qualities.

Although the business of sport has been quite effective in selling its wide range of products from admission tickets to fluorescent tennis balls, it receives plenty of free advertising through media coverage. Hoch discusses the mutually supportive relationship between newspapers and sport and points out that, since the turn of the century, the demand for sport coverage sells papers and the papers sell sport. The genesis of this alliance is rather easy to explain. It has been estimated by people from the press that 30% of those who purchase newspapers do so to keep informed about sport and sporting events (Hoch, 1972). Sport reporters are very aware of the fact that their job security and success depend on providing their readers with the kinds of information they desire. However, the reporter's access to such information is frequently controlled by the coaches and the management of the teams being covered. If material is written that is critical of sport or the local sport establishment, access will quickly be denied to that information needed for the paper to retain its readers and for the reporter to retain his/her job. If, on the other hand, the reporter does an effective job of selling sport and intensifying long-term fan interest, he/she is usually rewarded with increased access to information along with other benefits. Of course, this situation leads to some very slanted press coverage of the world of sport, but it serves to sell both papers and admission tickets (Edwards, 1973a).

In all, Hoch sees sport as a dehumanizing escape for the masses and a tool of coercion and exploitation for the powerful. Athletes are often pawns (gladiators) bought off by the controllers of the sport establishment with material rewards, publicity, or both. In the long run, no one benefits from sport except the power elite, and it continues to be in their interest to maintain things exactly the way they are for the present. As negative as this description of sport sounds, Hoch (1972) emphasizes that he does not intend his analysis as an indictment of sport, but only as a disclosure of how sport has been perverted "by forces less interested in sport than in their own continued wealth and power."

NOTES

1. Mumford, L. 1934. Technics and civilization. Harcourt Brace Jovanovich, New York.
2. For some reason, Hoch does not include chemical drugs other than alcohol in his list of opiates. It may be that some revolutionaries use various types of drugs without feeling they have deadened their awareness of significant social problems.

In Defense of Sport

SPIRO T. AGNEW

In recent years strident voices have been raised to reorder the priority that competitive sport enjoys in American life. Among the most publicized of these critics is a small number of individuals who have opted to reject sports competition for their own reasons, not the least of which was the lucrative publication of books on their experiences. In fact, one reviewer has characterized this phenomenon as a whole new literary movement: the "I was a Vampire for the Chicago Bears" school of biography.

To be sure, we have always had our Dave Meggyesys in sports, just as there have been "drop outs" in every profession. However, the singular difference between this and past eras is that in former years such "drop outs" weren't exalted by professional malcontents in what David Brinkley calls the "Academic-Political-Intellectual-Journalistic" complex and by commercial promoters of the so-called "counter-culture."

Inevitably, since our system of competitive sports is so much a part of American life, it has become a prime target of these perma-critics who come before the American people under various banners and behind often-times impressive-sounding, if misleading, facades.

Take, for example, one Jack Scott . . . who operates something called The Institute for the Study of Sport and Society out of Oakland, California. Mr. Scott, in case you haven't heard, was Dave Meggyesy's ideological mentor, and is described by sportswriter "Red" Smith as the "spiritual leader" of a movement that holds coaches to be—to quote Mr. Smith—"crewcut, and often bigoted, authoritarians. . . ." In addition to his Institute directorship, Mr. Scott is also esteemed by his followers as the former Berkeley instructor who once taught a course called the "Socio-Psychological Evaluation of Intercollegiate Athletics and Higher Education." For those insensitive souls who might seek some slight enlightenment as to the nature of such a course, let me simply note that the instructor's tenure was highlighted by his role in instigating a petition among his students calling for "unilateral withdrawal of all United States forces in Southeast Asia." According to Mr. Scott, and, we may presume, those who subsidize his Institute, sports in America today is, "one of the

SOURCE: Spiro T. Agnew, address by the Vice President of the United States to the Touchdown Club of Birmingham honoring University of Alabama football coach Paul "Bear" Bryant (January 18, 1972).

255

most reactionary enterprises in our society." What is needed, he says, is a reordering of priorities which would "abolish the authoritarian, racist, militaristic nature of contemporary college athletics."

But wait, there's more: Mr. Scott has—guess what?—written a book. It's titled *The Athletic Revolution*. Now, if the title doesn't tell you something about the book, the fact that it has an opening inscription by Bernadette Devlin should. And if that isn't enough, this audience will be especially interested in the fact that the author holds a rather low socio-psychological opinion of our trophy recipient ["Bear" Bryant].

I, for one, am *pleased* to note that Mr. Scott doesn't think much of the University of Alabama's athletic director and head football coach. The reason I'm pleased is that he doesn't think much of me either, and it's a source of encouragement to know that I share some detractors with Americans like Paul Bryant.

But for the record, let me quote what our guru from Berkeley had to say about Coach Bryant and one of his colleagues: "Given their years of unquestioned authoritarian rule," wrote Mr. Scott, "coaches like Paul 'Bear' Bryant and Ben Schwartzwalder are about as likely to begin behaving democratically as is General Franco."

Coach Bryant, as a longtime student and target of this kind of radical rhetoric, I can inform you that, despite the fact that General Franco's government, friendly to our own, is much less rigid than it used to be, the author of that sentence did *not* mean it as a compliment.

On the contrary, had the author meant to be complimentary, he might have compared you and Coach Schwartzwalder to someone the New Left considers a *genuine* democratic leader—like Fidel Castro. Or, if a New Left critic wanted to go out of his way to be flattering, he might have ranked your organizing abilities along with those of some truly inspirational leader of the young—for example, Che Guevara or Rennie Davis.

My point is that while the utopian leftist critics of our institutions decry the alleged "hypocrisy" of American society, they themselves operate from a hypocritical double-standard. Ostensibly, these self-declared revolutionaries want to correct the imperfections in our social machinery. Or, to borrow two of their favorite cliches, they seek only to make sports more "meaningful" and "relevant" to our society as a whole and to young people in particular. But through their words and deeds, they reveal within themselves an unremitting contempt, indeed a detestation of the values which the overwhelming majority of Americans hold dear.

Not the least of these values is the American competitive ethic which motivates young Americans like Pat Sullivan and John Musso to strive toward excellence in everything they undertake. For such young Americans—whether on the athletic field, in the classroom, or on the job—the importance of our competitive ethic lies in the fact that it is only by trial of their abilities—by testing and challenging—can they discover their strengths and, yes, their weaknesses.

Out of this process of self-discovery, painful though it may be at times, those young Americans who compete to excel learn to cope with whatever challenges lie ahead in life. And having given their best, they also emerge from the competitive test with greater ability to determine for themselves where their individual talents lie.

Life is a great competition. In my judgment it will remain so despite the efforts of the social architects to make it a bland experience, controlled by their providing what they think is best for us. Success is sweet, but it entails always the risk of failure. It is very, very important to learn how to lose a contest without being destroyed by the experience.

For a man who has not known failure cannot fully appreciate success. A person cannot know pleasure to any greater degree than he has known pain. And from defeat, from failure, from hardship, something builds within a person. If a person can throw off disappointment and come back and try again, he develops a personal cohesiveness that holds him together as a man throughout his life—and that gives him the durability to convert temporary defeat into ultimate victory.

The same is true of a nation. It might be said that the seeds of the American ethic were sown as much in the ordeal of Valley Forge as in the victory at Yorktown.

And so, to me, that is the message of competitive sports: not simply trying to win, and to achieve, but learning how to cope with a failure—and to come back.

In this regard, let me say something about my personal philosophy concerning the meaning of success and failure in sports for young Americans. First, I believe that sports—all sports—is one of the few bits of glue that holds society together, one of the few activities in which young people can proceed along avenues where objectives are clear and the desire to win is not only permissible but encouraged.

Opponents of the free-enterprise system tell our young people that to try for material success and personal status is bad; that the only thing worthwhile is to find something to wring your hands about; that the ultimate accomplishment is to make everybody feel better.

I, for one, would not want to live in a society that did not include winning in its philosophy; that would have us live our lives as identical lemmings, never trying to best anybody at anything, all headed in the same direction, departing not from the appointed route, striving not for individual excellence. In short, I would rather be a failure in the competitive society which is our inheritance than to live in a waveless sea of nonachievers.

To those who dispute the value of the American competitive ethic, my response is simply to point to the record. Through two centuries—centuries of struggle and challenge, often in the face of formidable obstacles—the American people have built their country into the greatest force for individual freedom and social progress the world has ever known.

No, ours is not a "perfect" system. But let me submit that an imperfect *free* society, which provides each citizen an opportunity to achieve his individual potential, is preferable to any ideologically "pure" system based on the premise that the best in life can be attained by the psychological retreat of a person—or a nation—into a cocoon of false security and self-satisfied mediocrity.

The late Vince Lombardi, who like his coaching colleagues in this audience was a devout believer in the American competitive ethic, had as his guiding motto a thought from Corinthians. On the eve of a championship game, Coach Lombardi once quoted this line: "Know ye not that they which run in a race run all, but one receiveth the prize? So run, that ye may obtain."

Today, more than at any time in our country's history, there is a prize to be realized by Americans everywhere, of every region, every race and every creed; if not in one field of endeavor, then in another; if not on first effort, then on renewed effort. As individuals, ours is the challenge of excellence. As a nation, we shoulder the responsibility of greatness.

"Revolutionary" critics to the contrary, I do not believe that young Americans intend to forsake their individuality and "drop out" of the race. Doomsday critics notwithstanding, I know that we, as a nation, are not going to shirk the challenge of greatness.

So long as there is an America—so long as there are Americans—we are going to stay in the competitive race. And we are going to run *to win*.

The Nazi Olympics

RICHARD D. MANDELL

As the XIth Olympiad of the modern era opened, the masters of National Socialist Germany were tense. They had told the German people that their athletes were going to win the 1936 Olympics. Now everyone knew that German athletes as a group had never done well in international competition. Since the first modern Olympiad, in 1896, Americans had dominated the Games.

After the first day of the Berlin Olympics, American track and field athletes, many of the best of whom were Negroes, made a haul of medals. The Nazi leaders were fiercely embarrassed. They scrambled to devise some sort of scoring system that could hide the size of the American lead. One candidate would have disregarded all medals won by Negroes, whom the Nazis considered subhumans. Then, as the days went on, Germans, in events ranging from gymnastics to marksmanship and yachting won more gold, silver, and bronze medals than the athletes from any other nation, thus emerging victorious (though the ideologues of the Olympic movement forbade such rankings). German athletes, then, capped a festivity that at the time was a vessel without fissure, a seamless garment of happiness for the Nazis.

The Olympic Games of 1936 were an important episode in the establishment of an evil political regime. Giving some of the story away early, I shall claim that much of the success of the 1936 Olympics was due to the pursuit by the National Socialists of supremacy in mass pageantry. Hitler's success as a whole is inconceivable without the application of the contrived festivity that enveloped Nazism from beginning to end.

Festivity may be a societal need. We know, for example, that the success of early Christianity was in part due to its transformation of venerable pagan rites into the holidays of Christmas, Easter, and the innumerable saints' days. In a Mexican province I saw a large church whose great cross at the altar was entwined by a huge, gilded serpent, the persistent symbol of a pre-Columbian cult. Perhaps an aggravation of modern man's *ennui* and *Angst* has been the obliteration of any sort of mythological calendar that could reinforce communal solidarity and would guarantee, by its periodicity, the frequent expression, forced or

SOURCE: Richard D. Mandell, *The Nazi Olympics* (New York: Macmillan, 1971), pp. ix–xv.

otherwise, of joy. None of the bourgeois participants in the rites of the Masons or Elks believes in the efficacy of their silly ceremonies, yet the lodges live on—perhaps largely because it is fun to go through staged, unapologetically bogus festivals. To admit that modern man may welcome, indeed may need, this kind of synthetic recreation is to admit that he has bad taste as well as a gap in his rational facilities. The German festivals were, to be sure, purposefully contrived and could appear vulgar to cynical outside observers, but they were effective techniques for channeling the vigor of a skilled people. Comparisons of national susceptibilities to festivity are hazardous because modern competitors of the Nazis as festival makers just have not existed. The National Socialists were pragmatic and had a uniquely enthusiastic view of the didactic and civic uses of pageantry. Furthermore, it is much too simple to ascribe to the pageant masters of the Third Reich a desire for political power only. They actually sought to maximize the happiness of the German *Volk*. The millions of participants enjoyed themselves immensely.

As an example of Nazi festivity, the XIth Olympiad was exceptional because its intended beneficiaries were foreigners as well as Germans. The hundreds of foreign journalists, businessmen, and diplomats invited to the 1936 Games had their judgment skewed (a predictable consequence of festivity) by what they experienced there. Even as the thousands of athletes struggled before hundreds of thousands of onlookers and happy millions more reveled in the massed parades, flapping banners, and staged solemnities, there was ample evidence that the masters of Germany had charted that nation on a collision course. In August of 1936 Hitler was meddling purposefully in the Spanish revolution and becoming more ambitious in his plans for Austria and Czechoslovakia. The generous congratulations he and his lieutenants received for their Olympic successes were both emboldening to them and deceiving to their opponents. So, besides being a success, the 1936 Olympics were also a vast razzle-dazzle that blurred the outlines of a growing threat to Western civilization. I must state quickly, however, that it will be a point of this narrative to make clear that the results of the Nazi Olympics— immediately happy, though tragic in the end—were only partly due to such pageant masters as Hitler, Dr. Carl Diem, the chief of the organizing committee, Avery Brundage, and Leni Riefenstahl, the maker of the Olympics film. The artistic and falsifying aspects of festivity were in the modern Olympics from the beginning. Indeed, festivity was part of the seductive charm of the ancient Olympics as well.

The descriptions in Chapter 1 of sport in classical Greece are intended to introduce several themes. The Nazis viewed their sporting program as an integral part of their cultural renaissance and proclaimed themselves rivals of the classical Greeks as leaders of a golden age. I also wish to show (as almost no other writer on the subject has) that the connection between the ancient Games and modern ones is as tenuous as the temporal abyss might suggest. The individual most responsible for the foundation of the modern series of international sporting meets called the Olympic Games was Baron Pierre de Coubertin (1863–1937). Coubertin, in spite of the cant of peaceful idealism that now is his halo, originally hoped his international meets would reinvigorate French youth by shaming them and inspiring them with the spectacle of performances of superior athletes from other lands. Coubertin's skilled planning for periodic international meets included the use of decorative symbolism. And his festivals succeeded in seducing persons for whom the private joy (or indeed the supremacy) of agonistic effort was inconceivable. He also sought to convince ruling elites that sport for the masses (i.e., physical education) had paramilitary value. That the supreme levels of athletic excellence as manifested in the Olympics might have little relevance to democratic physical education (which in turn may have almost no relevance to the skills demanded for modern warfare) was not considered by Coubertin or by the Nazis or, in fact, by the military strategists of the 1970's. But these matters will remain largely outside the rubric of this book.

It is ironic that the anathema of Coubertin's youth, the nation that in the 1930's patriotically prepared its people to destroy peace, was the host for the Olympiad that reached an artistic and festive zenith. Ironically, too, the inspirational élan of superpatriotism appears (no other explanation is at hand) to have provided an extra boost for a few dozen German athletes who won all those medals.

My object in narrating the course of the actual athletic events of the 1936 Olympiad is merely to relate the facts. Therefore, I shall discuss most of the events as though they were parts of ordinary meets. A separate chapter will discuss the roles of three athletic heroes. But implicit in all the sports stories is my belief that all the athletes who competed at Garmisch-Partenkirchen and at Berlin were made to feel that they were the corporeal manifestations of intellectual and political forces let loose to compete in other spheres later in that troubled decade.

The world drew lessons from the Berlin Olympics. The effectiveness of the festive arrangements proved to many skeptics who had been incredulous in 1933 that the group of wild men in charge of Germany was administratively capable and would stay that way. The ranking of athletic victors by nationality was also instructive. Athletes from totalitarian nations performed strikingly well—and the most totalitarian performed best of all. The reinvigorated Germans were the winners and everyone knew it. The only democratic nation whose athletes ranked high was the United States, but we should note that the American team was larger than any previous one and that, in spite of this, the Germans put them in second place. Germany's enemies (and in 1936 the fateful lineup was already taking form), France and Great Britain (or rather their athletes—I use the rhetoric of 1936), did badly—thus indicating to many the wave of the future. Depending upon what side you were on, many immediate lessons of the 1936 Olympics, even at the time, were grim.

Other lessons might have been learned from the 1936 Olympics. The superior performances of American Negro athletes, particularly those of Jesse Owens, a hero even to the Germans, were a flat refutation of certain of the National Socialist race theories. Why did the Germans not learn from this? The athletes harmonized at the Olympic Village, as planned. The great numbers of polyglot spectators fraternized without friction. Why was this peaceful intermixing not continued? The Reich could arrest Jew-baiting for the Olympics, apparently without suffering therefrom. Why was this ghastly campaign not permanently reversed? The technicians of the new Germany had demonstrated that they could manage the German people extremely well. Why did they not rest there? As a whole, the sporting festivals of 1936 offered to a troubled era a political rest and colossal, sensuous theater. The 1936 Games, then, were an amalgam of the potentially good and the potentially bad. But the end result was tragic, because the new Germans were almost universally viewed as not only powerful and stable, but respectable as well.

The impression dominant among us as to what took place at the 1936 Games has been largely due to Leni Riefenstahl's film, *Olympia*, which was released in 1938 and which has gained status as a popular classic in the last decade or so. In her film, this great director almost invented the sport film as art. I have tried to cast Leni as a priestess of art at the 1936 Olympics.

Many individuals who played important roles at the Berlin Olympics are still alive. The reader will notice that I have avoided recent personal recollections of many of the actors there. Leni Riefenstahl is a case in point. She has granted many interviews since 1945. Her stories of the Nazi years are inconsistent and at odds with statements she made before the war. The repeated yarns that Jesse Owens pulls forth for historically oriented journalists become more sweetly nostalgic as time goes on. I have avoided Owens for I feel no need to embellish a tale that is splendid enough when based on sources from the time when he was a young Olympic victor. I must also confess my distaste for an aging gentleman who uses his glory as a youth to huckster beer as Jesse Owens did in the revolting commercials that interrupted the television viewing of the 1968 Olympics for the American public. I met and spoke with Avery Brundage, but we were both in transit and were unable to arrange a lengthy interview.

As I worked on this book, I tried to determine whether the 1936 Games as an episode and the modern Olympics as a movement have been forces for peace—as Coubertin's admirers loyally claim. I have already stated my belief that the festivities of 1936 disguised the extent to which the diabolical aspects of National Socialist ideology were being used against an unfortunate people. I claim that the Olympics were an obscuring layer of shimmering froth on a noxious wave of destiny.

It is absurd to think that an amalgam of competing patriotisms will result in peaceful idealism; yet the ideologues of Olympism treasure this belief. Inevitably, journalists feed "incidents" to the yellow and not-so-yellow press whose readers are too torpid to experience kinesthetic empathy with sport's great individuals and who are impatient with the formal drama of contests between teams. The patriotic pressure for the prestige that winners bring has made victims of the physically endowed citizens of many nations. Patriotic sports czars have consciously deformed youths to make them the kept monsters of ambitious political regimes. One reads of Hungarian and Polish coaches feeding male hormones to female teenagers in order to give them the sinews for victory in the international arenas of sport. The girls' lives are, of course, ruined. Already in the modern Olympics the figure of the loser is often a focus of national disgrace rather than merely a poignant case of individual disappointment.

Ought the Olympics to go on? There is no question that—barring military calamity—they shall. The moguls of television reap harvests from sports broadcasting and the public appetite for it. The International Olympic Committee is now financially dependent upon the quadrennial sale of world-wide television rights at the Games. Still I grasp this opportunity to urge international sportsmen to labor to remove some of the patriotic rites from the modern Olympics. We could start by eliminating the victory ceremonies with their inappropriate clanging of national anthems. Anthems, flags, point systems, ranked victory platforms, medals (and especially national totals of them) have played roles that are more dangerous than they are irrelevant. The world would be better off— certainly the world of sport would be better off—if the Olympics centered on the athletes and the sporting contests rather than on collectives that have only the weakest ties with sport's outstanding personages and teams.

◾ FOR FURTHER STUDY

Agnew, Spiro T., with John Underwood. "Not Infected with the Conceit of Infallibility." *Sports Illustrated* (June 21, 1971), pp. 60–75.
Balbus, Ike. "Politics As Sports: The Political Ascendency of the Sports Metaphor in America." *Monthly Review*, 26 (March 1975) 26–39.
Baley, James A. "Suggestions for Removing Politics from the Olympic Games." *JOPER*, 39 (March 1978), 73.

Ball, Donald W. "Olympic Games Competition: Structural Correlates of National Success." *International Journal of Comparative Sociology*, 13 (September/December 1972), 186–200.

Ball, Donald W. "A Politicized Social Psychology of Sport: Some Assumptions and Evidence from International Figure Skating Competition." *International Review of Sport Sociology*, 8 (1973), 63–71.

Davenport, Joanne. "The Women's Movement into the Olympic Games." *JOPER*, 39 (March 1978), 58–60.

Deford, Frank. "The Once and Future Diplomat." *Sports Illustrated* (March 1, 1971), pp. 63–75.

Douglas, S. "Uses of Sport in Domestic Politics." Paper presented at the Fifth Popular Culture Association Meeting (St. Louis, March 1975).

Edwards, Harry. *The Revolt of the Black Athlete*. New York: Free Press, 1969.

Eitzen, D. Stanley, and George H. Sage. *Sociology of American Sport*. Dubuque, Iowa: Wm. C. Brown, 1978, chapter 6.

Ford, Gerald R., with John Underwood. "In Defense of the Competitive Urge." *Sports Illustrated* (July 8, 1974), pp. 16–23.

Gilbert, Bil. "Gleanings From a Troubled Time." *Sports Illustrated* (December 25, 1972), pp. 34–46.

Goodhart, Phillip, and Christopher Chataway. *War Without Weapons*. London: W. H. Allen, 1968.

Heinila, K. "Notes on the Inter-Group Conflicts in International Sport." *The Cross-Cultural Analysis of Sport and Games*. Edited by G. Luschen. Champaign, Illinois: Stipes, 1970, pp. 174–182.

Herman, Robin. "The Soviet Union Views Sports Strength as a Power Tool." *New York Times* (July 11, 1976), p. 158.

Hoberman, John. "Sport and Political Ideology." *Journal of Sport and Social Issues*, 1 (Summer/Fall 1977), 80–114.

Hoch, Paul. "The World of Playtime, USA." *Daily World* (April 27, 1972), p. 12.

Hoch, Paul. *Rip Off the Big Game: The Exploitation of Sports by the Power Elite*. Garden City, N.Y.: Doubleday Anchor Books, 1972.

Hogan, John C. "Sports in the Courts." *Phi Delta Kappa*, 56 (October 1974), 132–135.

Isenberg, Jerry. *How Many Miles to Camelot?* New York: Pocket Books, 1971.

Johnson, William. "Sport in China." *Sports Illustrated* (September 24 and October 1, 1973).

Kimball, George. "Scott Attacked by Agnew." *The Phoenix* (February 2, 1972), p. 8.

Kirschenbaum, Kerry. "Assembly Line for Champions." *Sports Illustrated* (July 12, 1976), pp. 56–65.

Kolatch, Jonathan. *Sport, Politics and Ideology in China*. Middle Village, New York: Jonathan David, 1972.

Lapchick, Richard E. "Apartheid Sport: South Africa's Use of Sport in its Foreign Policy." *Journal of Sport and Social Issues*, 1 (1976), 52–79.

Lapchick, Richard E. *The Politics of Race and International Sport: The Case of South Africa*. Westport, Conn.: Greenwood Press, 1975.

Lapchick, Richard E. "A Political History of the Modern Olympic Games." *Journal of Sport and Social Issues*, 2 (Spring/Summer 1978), 1–12.

Lever, Janet. "Soccer: Opium of the Brazilian People." *Trans-action*, 7 (December 1969), 36–43.

Lipsky, Richard. "Toward a Political Theory of American Sports Symbolism." *American Behavioral Scientist*, 21 (January/February 1978), 345–360.

Loy, John W., Barry D. McPherson, and Gerald Kenyon. *Sport and Social Systems*. Reading, Mass.: Addison-Wesley, 1978, pp. 287-290.

Matthews, Vince, and Neil Amdur. *My Race Be Won*. New York: Charterhouse, 1974.

Meggyesy, Dave. *Out of Their League*. New York: Paperback Library, 1971.

Melnick, M. J. "Footballs and Flower Power." *JOPER*, 40 (October 1969), 32-33.

Michener, James A. *Sports in America*, New York: Random House, 1976, chapter 12.

Natan, Alex. "Sport and Politics." *Sport, Culture, and Society*. Edited by John W. Loy and Gerald S. Kenyon. New York: Macmillan, 1969, pp. 203-210.

"Diplomacy Through Sports," *Newsweek* (September 4, 1972), p. 42.

Norton, Derrick J. "A Comparison of Political Attitudes and Political Participation of Athletes and Non-Athletes." Master's thesis, University of Oregon, 1971.

Novak, Michael. "War Games: Facts and Coverage." *National Review* (September 3, 1976), pp. 953-954.

Padwe, Sandy. "Sports and Politics Must be Separate—At Least Some Politics, That Is." *Philadelphia Inquirer* (December 14, 1971), p. 35.

Petrie, Brian M. "Sport and Politics." *Sport and Social Order*. Edited by Donald W. Ball and John W. Loy. Reading, Mass.: Addison-Wesley, 1975, pp. 185-237.

Petrie, Brian M., and Elizabeth L. Reid. "The Political Attitudes of Canadian Athletes." *Proceedings of the Fourth Canadian Psycho-Motor Learning and Sports Psychology Symposium*. Waterloo, Canada: University of Waterloo, 1972, pp. 514-530.

Reed, J. D. "Gallantly Screaming." *Sports Illustrated* (January 3, 1977), pp. 52-60.

Rehberg, Richard, and Michael Cohen. "Political Attitudes and Participation in Extracurricular Activities." *Social Problems in Athletics*. Edited by Daniel Landers. Urbana: University of Illinois Press, 1976, pp. 201-216.

Reston, James. "Sports and Politics." *New York Times* (November 26, 1971).

Sage, George H. "Occupational Socialization and Value Orientation of Athletic Coaches." *Research Quarterly*, 44 (October 1973), 269-277.

Sanders, Thomas G. "The Social Functions of Futbol." *American Universities Field Staff Reports*. East Coast South America Series, vol. 14, no. 2 (July 1970).

Sauer, George, and Jack Scott. "Interview by Jack Scott with George Sauer on the Reasons for Sauer's Retirement from Professional Football While at the Height of His Career." Research paper, Department of Physical Education, California State College, Hayward, California, 1971).

Scott, Jack. *The Athletic Revolution*. New York: Free Press, 1971.

Scott, Jack, and Harry Edwards. "After the Olympics: Buying Off Protest." *Ramparts* (November 1969), pp. 16-21.

Snyder, Eldon E. "Aspects of Social and Political Values of High School Coaches." *International Review of Sport Sociology*, 8 (1973), 73-87.

Strenk, Andrew. "Sport as an International Political and Diplomatic Tool." *Arena Newsletter*, 1 (August 1977), 3-9.

Thirer, Joel. "The Olympic Games as a Medium of Black Activism and Protest." *Review of Sport & Leisure*, 1 (Fall 1976), 15-31.

Viller, Don. "Survey '71." *The Athletic Journal* (October 1971), p. 58.

Washburn, John N. "Sport as a Soviet Tool." *Foreign Affairs*, 34 (April 1956), 490-499.

Wicker, Tom. "Patriotism for the Wrong Ends." *New York Times* (January 19, 1973).

Eight

The Economics of Sport

Roger Kahn said, "Sport is too much a game to be a business and too much a business to be a game."[1] That dilemma characterizes contemporary professional sport and much of what is called amateur sport in America. The evidence of the strong relationship between sport and money is overwhelming. The following are a few examples:

item: The Brooklyn Dodgers, although operating at a profit, moved to Los Angeles in 1958, where the potential profits were very much greater.

item: Colgate-Palmolive spent $7 million in 1978 for prizes and promotions of sports events.

item: *Runners World,* a magazine devoted to serious running, started as a newsletter in 1966 by Bob Anderson, grew to a $10 million operation by 1978 through the sale of magazines, advertising, mail order products, and the sponsoring of other sports publications (*Nordic World, Soccer World,* and *Bike World*).[2]

item: During 1977 "Broncomania" swept the Rocky Mountain region as the success of the Denver Broncos resulted in the sale of approximately $4.5 million for T-shirts, beer mugs, decals, pennants, and other memorabilia. The Denver defensive team was known as the Organge Crush, and their success sold $3 million in Orange Crush T-shirts and increased the sales of Orange Crush soft drinks by 100 percent.

item: Bruce Jenner, the decathalon winner at the 1976 Olympics translated his success as an amateur into great commercial success. His income from endorsements, speeches, and appearances for 1977 was estimated to be $500,000.[3]

item: The State of Louisiana built the Superdome at a cost of $163.5 million as a multipurpose sports arena. Although two professional teams play their home games in that arena, the Superdome functions at an annual deficit of between $6 and $8 million.

item: The U.S. Open golf tournament was played at Denver's Cherry Hills in 1978. That event brought an estimated $7 million to Denver, benefiting mostly restaurants, hotels, and cab companies.[5]

item: In 1976 the yearly income for the players of the Philadelphia 76ers was: Julius Erving, $600,000; George McGinnis, $500,000; Caldwell Jones, $250,000; Darryl Dawkins, $250,000; Steve Mix, $75,000; and the other four players combined earned about $250,000—a total of $2,325,000.

item: David Thompson, the Denver Nugget, signed a five-year contract beginning with the 1978–79 season for $800,000 annually, which breaks down to $4.25 a second, $204 a minute, and $9,756 for each game.

item: Beginning in 1978, the management of each NFL team received $5.5 million annually in television revenue alone.

item: In 1976 there were more than 250 cheerleader clinics, which trained more than 100,000 schoolgirls, and grossed $7 million.

item: Before the AAU would sanction a 1973 United States tour by the Russian gymnastics team, they insisted on a contract ensuring that Olga Korbut would perform at each performance on the tour (thereby guaranteeing that all seats would be sold).

item: In 1977 Muhammad Ali grossed $5.75 million.

item: O. J. Simpson has parlayed his football ability into an annual income exceeding $1.5 million. This money comes from his football contract ($733,358), movies ($200,000 per movie), and advertising for Hertz, Shindana Toys, Dingo Boots, Wilson Sporting Goods, Tree Sweet orange juice, and Hyde Spot-Bilt Athletic shoes ("Juicemobiles").

item: Bjorn Borg, the tennis great, is covered from head to toe with endorsements. Taking it from the top in 1977, he received $50,000 a year to wear a headband advertising Tuborg, a Danish beer. The Scandinavian Airlines System patch on Borg's left shoulder was good for $25,000. He got $200,000 for donning Fila shorts, socks and warmup suits, $100,000 for using Bancroft rackets—plus $2,000 for having them strung with VS gut—and $50,000 for wearing Tretorn tennis shoes. By also lending his name to cars, cereals, games, comic books, statues, bed linen, jeans and towels, Borg earned from $1.5 million to $2 million.[6]

item: It is estimated that $50 billion is gambled annually on sports in the United States.

item: A 60-second commercial during the telecast of the 1978 Super Bowl cost $325,000.

item: By the age of 26 Michael Trope had negotiated more than 120 contracts for athletes at a total value of $30 million. For these efforts he pocketed $2.4 million.[7]

item: Chris Evert won $503,134 in 1977 and almost $1.5 million in prize money over a five-year span.

item: Following the 1976 Olympics, gold medal winners in track were typically paid $1,500 per meet illegally by the meet promoters.[8]

Although these examples are diverse, there is a common thread— money. Money is the motivator of athletes. Players and owners give their primary allegiance to money rather than to play. Playing for high monetary stakes is exciting for fans, too. Television money dictates schedules, the timing of time-outs, and even controls what sportscasters say.[9] Superathletes can become millionaires. Modern sport, whether professional or big-time college is "corporate sport." The original purpose of sport—pleasure in the activity—has been lost in the process. Sport has become work. Sport has become the product of publicity agents using super-hype methods. Money has superseded the content as the ultimate goal. Illicit tactics are commonplace. In short American sport is a microcosm of the values of American society. Roger Angell has said of baseball what is applicable to all forms of corporate sport:

> Professional sports now form a noisy and substantial, if irrelevant and distracting, part of the world, and it seems as if baseball games taken entirely—off the field as well as on it, in the courts and in the front offices as well as down on the diamonds—may now tell us more about ourselves than they ever did before.[10]

The papers selected to illustrate the problems and issues involving sport and economics focus on sport at the professional level. They involve a variety of issues related to the general question: is professional sport a business or not? The first selection is from a study by the House Select Committee on Professional Sports. It outlines the history of the law pertaining to the professional sport level. The laws in two domains are especially important for our consideration: (1) the antitrust exemption enjoyed historically by professional sport; and (2) the right of team owners to own their players. These are important issues as recent court judgments in these areas have shown vividly.

The next statement is by Edward Garvey, Executive Director of the NFL Players Association. It provides the players' interpretation of how the system (antitrust exemption and contract regulations) has worked to their detriment.

The players' view is countered by the statement of Pete Rozelle, Commissioner of the National Football League and representative of the owners. Rozelle argues that (1) football is nothing more than a form of entertainment; (2) the better the entertainment, the better the profits, which also result in better player benefits; and (3) to ensure the most benefits to all (owners and players) and produce the best entertainment level (benefiting the fans), the league needs to be a monopoly.

The next two selections cite several fundamental reasons that professional sport is foremost a business. Excerpts from the excellent series by *Sports Illustrated* on the impact of money on sports are included to show (1) how the professional sports industry operates as a monopoly, and the economic advantages that accrue from this advantageous situation; (2) the tax advantages of professional team ownership; and (3) how the taxpayers subsidize professional teams. Finally, the selection by Eitzen argues that team owners are primarily motivated by profit, not philanthropy. Evidence for this is found in capital gains sales, maximization of television revenues, the moving of franchises to more lucrative markets, and by pricing tickets according to demand.

NOTES

1. Quoted in CBS Reports, "The Baseball Business," television documentary, narrated by Bill Moyers (1977).
2. "Off to a Running Start," *Dollars and Sense*, No. 35 (March, 1978), pp. 8–9.
3. Barry McDermott, "Back to Bruce in a Moment. First, This Commercial," *Sports Illustrated* (September 26, 1977), pp. 42–48.
4. Testimony of William J. Connich, Secretary-Treasurer of the Louisiana Superdome Authority, Hearings before the House Select Committee on Professional Sports, *Inquiry into Professional Sports*, Part I (Washington, D.C.: U.S. Government Printing Office, August 4, 1976), p. 499.
5. "$7 Million Golf Spending Seen in Denver Area," *Rocky Mountain News* (June 11, 1978), p. 6.
6. Ray Kennedy and Nancy Williamson, "For the Athlete, How Much Is Too Much?" *Sports Illustrated* (July 24, 1978), p. 49.
7. John Pananek, "Scorecard," *Sports Illustrated* (July 24, 1978), p. 12.
8. Harry Stein, "The Gold and the Money," *Sport* (June 1977), pp. 33–41.
9. Peter Gruenstein, "Is the TV Sports Fan Being Cheated?" *Left Field* 1 (June 1978), 1, 4–5.
10. Roger Angell, "The Sporting Scene: In the Counting House," *The New Yorker* (May 10, 1976), p. 107.

Professional Sports and the Law

SELECT COMMITTEE ON PROFESSIONAL SPORTS

The past decade has seen a radical change in the public face of professional sports. Once the traditional sports page preoccupation was with the hopes engendered by the opening of training camps, or box scores and statistics, or the rise of new heroes and the fall of old reliables, or harmless gossip and mythmaking. Now the American sports fan is presented with an almost daily barrage of socio-legal crises which threaten to, and at times succeed in, over-shadowing the efforts and accomplishments of the athletes on their respective fields of play.

The establishment of the Select Committee on Professional Sports on May 18, 1976[1] was stimulated by a period that appeared to mark an unparalleled level of convulsive activity in the sports world. Within the space of a short few weeks the sports pages of the nation's papers were filled with news of threatened franchise movements, franchise failures, impending league mergers, threatened legal action, settlements of law suits, reports on testimony offered in several on-going trials, findings of unfair labor practices by the Labor Board, threats of player strikes, the avoidance of disruption of an All-Star game, and, finally, a near frantic series of player trades and sales, subsequent nullification of the sales, and the filing of a multi-million-dollar legal action to contest the nullifications. It is rare that the formation of a special investigation committee receives such instant justification for its existence.

The mandate of the Select Committee is to investigate the situation currently prevailing in the four major professional sports, i.e., baseball, basketball, football and hockey, and to assess the need for any recommended changes in the law. However, in view of the substantial involvement and impact court adjudications have had on the manner and form of operations of professional sports leagues, the Committee has requested the preparation of a study of the development and present status of the law of professional sports. A background paper of this nature was felt necessary in order to provide the Committee with a base point from which to commence its inquiry into the root causes of the apparent present instability in the sports world and to pinpoint the targets of any

SOURCE: *Professional Sports and the Law*, a study by the Select Committee on Professional Sports, House of Representatives, 94th Congress, Second Session (Washington, D. C. U.S. Government Printing Office, 1976).

potential legislative action. Consonant with that request, this paper will proceed as follows. Section I will outline the major points of contact the professional sports industry has with the Federal government. Section II briefly describes the key characteristics of the operation and organization of professional sports leagues. Section III traces the development to date of the significant lines of legal precedent in each of the four major professional sports. Finally, the concluding section will attempt to summarize the most recent events and highlight their potential legal significance.

I. THE FEDERAL INTEREST

Professional sports activities touch upon, directly or indirectly, numerous points of major Federal concern. Most prominent of late is Federal anti-trust policy. This comes about as a result of the nature of the organization of professional sports leagues. In the most simple terms, a sports league is composed of independent competing businesses which agree to act collectively to produce a saleable entertainment. Such collective action by all competing businesses in an industry is also known as a cartel and violates Federal law when its exclusive power is improperly used to someone's detriment.[2] In the past, Congress has granted limited exemptions from anti-trust liability to enable the merger of competing sports leagues[3] and to allow sports leagues to enter into television pooling agreements with broadcasters.[4] In one instance the Supreme Court accorded an anti-trust exemption to baseball,[5] a privilege it has since refused to bestow on any other professional sport.[6] Also, since 1951, Congress on numerous occasions has considered proposals that have ranged from granting blanket immunity from the anti-trust laws to all sports to subjecting all aspects of all sports to those laws.[7] Most recently Congress refused to sanction the merger of American Basketball Association (ABA) with the National Basketball Association (NBA).[8]

Successful utilization of the tax laws has been pointed to as a key factor in the economic viability of major league clubs and as a significant impetus to league expansions and franchise sales and movements.[9] Among the tax provisions most beneficial to owners are those allowing depreciation of player contracts,[10] capital gains,[11] carryover losses,[12] and the formation of Subchapter S corporations.[13] Players too have benefitted from favorable tax treatment of deferred income,[14] capital gains,[15] and through income averaging,[16] income splitting,[17] and other tax saving devices.

The rapid development of trade unionism in major league sports has been in no small measure aided by the Federal labor laws. All four major sports have active player associations which have utilized the National

Labor Relations Board to obtain certifications as the exclusive bargaining representative of their players[18] or for redress of unfair labor practices,[19] and the Federal Mediation and Conciliation Service during breakdowns in collective bargaining negotiations.[20] Labor relations strife in the sports world has seen two strikes take place in recent years, one lasting 42 days, and the expiration of collective bargaining agreements without renewal.[21] The failure to negotiate new agreements, in addition to placing in limbo useful arrangements for peaceful resolution of disputes such as contractual grievance and arbitration procedures, places in jeopardy players pension funds which are funded exclusively by employer contributions.[22]

Immigration policy has become a more prominent point of concern with regard to the annual influx of some 743 Canadian and European hockey players to staff National Hockey League (NHL) teams and their minor league affiliates and over 300 baseball players from Carribean and Latin-American countries to play in the major and minor leagues. Under 8 U.S.C. 1182(a)(14) the Secretary of Labor issues entrance certificates to the players.[23] The situation is particularly acute in hockey where although only 3 of the 18 NHL teams are based in Canadian cities, over 90% of the players are foreign citizens.

Another point of significant Federal contact with sports involves the national communications policy. Revenue from television and radio contracts accounts for approximately 25 percent of baseball's annual income and 35 percent of that of football.[24] It may be expected that the National Basketball Association's revenue figures are comparable to that of football. On the other hand, the failure of the World Football League and the American Basketball Association to procure comparable television agreements may be speculated to be a significant factor in the failure of those leagues. As indicated earlier, the leagues' ability to enter into such lucrative television arrangements is the direct result of Congress' action in exempting such pooling agreements from the anti-trust laws in 1961.[25]

Recent Congresses have shown a renewed interest in the regulation of sports broadcasting policy. In 1973 Congress enacted Public Law 93-107 which prohibited local blackouts of network games which were sold out 72 hours in advance. Although the legislation expired on December 31, 1975, a revised version has been passed by both Houses and is now in conference. The major differences in the bills[26] involve the question whether the extension should be permanent or for 3 years, and whether the blackout area should be limited. Also before Congress are important issues involving the importation of distant sports signals by cable television systems and the development of pay T.V.[27]

Finally, sports broadcasting is, of course, subject to the regulations and policies of the Federal Communications Commission.[28]

From the aspect of simply sheer size professional sports (in all its related facets) is a billion dollar-plus industry. Baseball and football alone generate annual revenues in excess of $150 and $171 million respectively.[29] The economic impact on interstate commerce and on the national economy as a whole is therefore not insignificant.

But perhaps the most far-reaching Federal concern is the fan interest in competitive sports. Chairman Sisk expressed this concern in his opening statement to the Committee:[30]

> But perhaps more important is the long-range deleterious effect this distorted picture of athletic endeavors will have on the perspective of the American sports fan, and I want to emphasize the sports fan because I think that is primarily the area in which this Committee should confine its interests and concern.
>
> I do not think we can minimize the importance of sports, and particularly professional sports, in the fabric of American life. The healthy competitive spirit, the sense of hard but fair play, and the enthusiastic involvement in team play that we wish to nurture in our youth can only be diminished by an incessant diet of reports which breed cynicism towards athletic life. Nor can we play down the effect of such reports on the pure entertainment value of sporting events for the individual spectator.
>
> I do not mean to say that I would, if it were at all possible, blind the public to the reality that the participants in professional sports are not immune from the profit motive. But I believe if some action is not taken soon to restore a semblance of balance and stability in the world of professional sports, we stand the possibility of losing much of the meaning and value intrinsic in athletic competition.

In a similar vein, one commentator familiar with the sports scene has described the potentially destructive effect of a continuing flow of news which is intrusive on a sports fan's normal psychological expectations as follows:

> Things are radically different today. Not a week goes by without producing a major law story on the nation's sports pages. No decision is made by any sports authority without prior advice of counsel. A major item of operating expense is legal fees.
>
> The new situation has met with considerable hostility on all sides. To begin with, all but the lawyers (and even some of the lawyers) are thoroughly bewildered, and that is never a pleasant feeling. Then there are two deep psychological conflicts at work. To fans (and to the journalists who are their extension), sports is appealing precisely because they are fun-and-games, essentially escapist entertainment in which good guys and bad guys are gloriously identifiable, and win-lose decisions satisfyingly clear cut. When real life questions of equity, compromise, search-for-justice, logical reasoning and legal status impinge on these fundamentally emotional entertainment, the fun is

spoiled. A fan knows (or is convinced he knows) everything significant about the sport and the people he follows; when they veer off into legal areas his sense of certainty is lost, and he resents it. Koppett, Sports and the Law: An Overview, 18 New York Law Forum 815, 816 (1973).

The importance of the identification process for the sports spectator is described by one eminent psychologist in the following manner:

> [The] mechanism of identification is expanded . . . to include a wide variety of situations and persons and enables the individual to experience vicarious achievements, feelings of adequacy, and other satisfactions through his various identifications. . . .
> Such identifications, particularly in the form of "hero worship," may play an important role in shaping [one's] personality. . . .
> Most people identify themselves with the hero or winner and this achieves increased feeling of adequacy or worth. However, sometimes identification backfires as when we identify ourselves with a group that does not accept us or when our football team continues to lose games and is scoffed at by sports writers and friends. In such cases our identification leads to self-devaluation rather than self-enhancement.

J. Coleman, Abnormal Psychology and Modern Life 103 (3d ed. 1964); see also, Hart, Sports in the Socio-Cultural Process (1972). For similar reasons, the psychological impact on a community of the movement of a franchise while perhaps unquantifiable, would appear to be a matter of no small moment.

A further, though more material potential Federal concern is the rapid acceleration of the cost of attending professional sports events (and in some instances even access to tickets) which is making attendance by the average fan close to prohibitive.

There is no organized "fan" lobby today. If there is a fan interest that is protectable and that interest faces danger, it would appear the Federal government may be able to contribute toward affording effective protection for it.

II. THE ORGANIZATION AND OPERATION OF PROFESSIONAL SPORTS LEAGUES

The nature of the product sold by professional team sports has effectively determined the characteristics of their sales organization. The product is an entertainment consisting of competing teams of relatively evenly matched aggregates of players in which the outcome of any particular contest is in reasonable doubt. In organizing leagues of such teams a method of player allocation is usually devised so as to maintain a relative competitive equality between the teams, the unpredictability of the outcome of the games, and the unquestioned integrity of the contests. The organization of a league is designed also to insure the attraction of investment capital necessary to finance its operations. Based upon these apparent requirements professional sports leagues have developed a common pattern of organization and operation characterized by a restriction of competition and division of markets among the business entities composing the leagues.

There are two main categories of restriction. The first deals with the limitation of, and until the very recent past the absolute prohibition against, competitive bidding among teams for the services of players. This has been accomplished by reserve and option clauses in player contracts, agreements not to compete for players among club owners, and the development of draft systems for the entry of new players. The second category of restriction concerns the limitations on the marketing rights of the component business units of the league. This would include restrictions on the territorial rights of franchise holdings, the right to relocate a franchise, the admission of new franchises, the right to market radio and television broadcasts, and the right to share in home team gate receipts.

Before turning to the specifics of the above-outlined characteristics, it is well to note immediately that the fact that leagues are cartels is of no determinative significance by itself. In *Northern Pacific Railway Co.* v. *United States*,[31] the Supreme Court acknowledged that, though the Sherman Anti-Trust Act's prohibition "is literally all encompassing, the courts have construed it as precluding only those contracts or combinations which 'unreasonably' restrain competition."[32] With specific regard to professional sports, a district court in an anti-trust case involving the National Football League noted the uniqueness of the professional sports business as follows:

Professional football is a unique type of business. Like other professional sports which are organized on a league basis it has problems which no other business has. The ordinary business makes every effort to sell as much of its product or services as it can. In the course of doing this it may and often does put many of its competitors out of business. The ordinary businessman is not troubled by the knowledge that he is doing so well that his competitors are being driven out of business.

Professional teams in a league, however, must not compete too well with each other in a business way. On the playing field, of course, they must compete as hard as they can at all times. But it is not necessary and indeed it is unwise for all the teams to compete as hard as they can against each other in a business way. If all the teams should compete as hard as they can in a business way, the stronger teams would be likely to drive the weaker ones into financial failure. If this should happen not only would the weaker teams fail, but eventually the whole league, both the weaker and the stronger teams, would fail, because without a league no team can operate profitably.[33]

The conflict between the Sherman Act's hostility to private restraints on free competition and the apparent practicality of joint action to achieve balanced, sustained and geographically dispersed professional athletic competition has been primarily fought in the courts although, as indicated earlier, certain legislative measures have been invoked to remedy particular problems. The remainder of this section will attempt to define the particular subject matter that has become the object of that litigation and legislation.

Player Allocation System

In order to equalize the playing strength of teams, professional sports leagues control the distribution of player talent within the league. In the past this control has been achieved either by a tightly restrictive "reserve clause" in baseball and hockey, or by variants of somewhat less restrictive "option clauses" in the other major sports. The clauses[34] are normally coupled with league rules restricting interteam competition and rules regulating the entry of new players into the league ("draft" rules). Since we are at the moment concerned only with the definition of terms and fundamental principles, we will temporarily ignore the significant events that have occurred in the courts and at the bargaining tables since December 1975, deferring discussion and analysis of the specific changes brought about by those events until the theoretical and legal framework necessary for understanding them is established. It must be emphasized, however, that although some of the mechanics of the player allocation system have been altered, its basic principles and objects remain intact.

The reserve clause.—The most familiar aspect of the player allocation system is the so-called reserve clause; that is, a clause (and associated rules) in a player contract that assigns to a particular team the exclusive right to deal with an athlete for his entire playing life. Technically, only baseball and hockey actually had reserve clauses. In those sports a player could change teams only if the team holding his contract released him from the obligation of that contract or granted another team the right to deal with the player.

The option clause.—The option clause theoretically binds an athlete to his club for only one year beyond the expiration of the term of his contract. When the athlete elects to play out his option he may receive only 90 percent of his salary for the prior year. After the expiration of the one year period he is relieved of the obligations of his contract (in the parlance of sports he becomes a "free agent") and may negotiate with any other team. Thus under an option system a team has the right to the services of a player for one year beyond the term of his contract whereas under a reserve system the player is bound perpetually.

Option systems have had one further aspect, however, which in actual practice has made them almost as restrictive as the reserve system. This is the so-called "Rozelle rule" which provides that if another team signs an athlete who has played out his option, that team must either come to a mutual agreement over compensating the team losing the player, or submit the question of indemnity to the league commissioner who may require the assignment of players or future draft choices or both to the athletes former club. The Rozelle-type option rule, which has been in effect in football and basketball, has served as a disincentive for teams to sign players who have played out their options.[35]

No tampering agreements.—The key to an effective player allocation system is an agreement among the teams in a league not to compete for players. Each sports league has rules governing the relations between teams, including prohibitions against negotiating with players whose rights are held by other teams. A team that contacts a player to determine if he might be interested in changing teams is guilty of tampering and can be severely punished by the league.[36] Tampering rules, while effectively negating interteam competition for players, also arguably aid in maintaining the image of game integrity. For example, if it was known a player was negotiating with a rival club, a lapse in playing skill could be attributed (by fans) to that situation.

The draft system.—All professional sports leagues have selection procedures which, together with reserve or option systems, permit the control over the entry and distribution of new player talent. The "draft" system has operated generally as follows. The order of selection is roughly inversely related to the quality of the team, which is normally determined by how the team finished in the league standings at the end of the previous season. Once a team drafts a player, it acquires exclusive rights to bargain with him. In basketball, football and hockey such rights were perpetual. That is, the player had to strike a bargain with the club holding draft rights to him or refuse to play. In baseball, exclusive rights to negotiate with a player lapsed after six months, after which time the players name was again placed in the player pool. The original team could not select him again without his permission.

The effectiveness of the draft system again depends on an agreement between the teams of a league to respect each others exclusive rights. Such agreements are most severely tested during periods of interleague warfare when the competition for scarce new talent may produce desperate tactics.[37]

Limitations on Marketing Rights

The unique economics of professional sports has given rise to unusual decision making practices and market allocation procedures. Although franchise owners have the apparent power to make independent decisions, they actually wield little real power by themselves. Decisions of any magnitude are generally interdependent, involving league functions. Thus the league is the focus of decision-making.

Agreement at the league level as to the geographic division of market areas is a prominent characteristic of league organization. Thus, all professional sports leagues have complex sets of rules and practices that limit competition in selling the product of the industry. In particular, they deal with the most valuable resources of the leagues: rights in franchises, admissions revenues, and broadcasting revenues.[38]

Franchises:—Each league has rules governing the location of teams in the league. Although rules vary between leagues, they generally prohibit a member team from locating in a city which already has a league team unless that team gives its permission. Often the prohibition will extend to a specified geographic area. Within the alloted franchise territory a team has the exclusive right to sell admissions to its games.

Leagues also control the movement of existing franchises to cities without teams. A team wishing to relocate must gain the approval of a substantial majority of the other teams.[39] Further, the entrance of new franchises is controlled by the established teams which require substantial entrance fees and dictate the location of the new team. If a new team infringes on the territorial rights of an established franchise it may be required to pay it an indemnity fee.[40] As with the player allocation system, the exclusivity of franchise rights is threatened only by the emergence of interleague competition.

Admissions revenues.—Admissions receipts constitute one of the major sources of revenues for teams. Attendance potential differs from franchise to franchise and appears to be a factor in the divergent financial health between teams in any one league.[41] Although revenue sharing in order to equalize the disparities between teams with large and small attendance potentials has been suggested as a possible solution, no uniform pattern of gate sharing has emerged amongst the leagues. Gate sharing practices vary widely from sport to sport ranging from no split with the visiting teams in basketball and hockey, to an 80/20 and about 90/10 split in the American and National baseball leagues, respectively, to a 60/40 sharing by National Football League teams. The effect of the varying gate sharing policies on franchise viability and team performance has been the subject of considerable study and debate.[42]

Broadcasting.—Competition over television and radio broadcasting of professional sports contests is limited in two ways. First, the rights to national broadcasts of games in each sport are controlled by the league. This comes as a result of the exemption from the antitrust laws granted by Congress in 1961 which allowed leagues to enter into pooling arrangements with networks to sell broadcast rights to their games.[43] The revenues from these arrangements are shared equally among all teams in the league. Second, each team has exclusive rights to broadcast all home games that are not part of the league's national broadcasting package and to prevent the broadcast in its home territory of any game not in the package. This is true for all sports except football where the team can sell radio rights for all games and television rights for exhibition games. Since all teams either have local monopolies or compete with only one other team in its sport, these rules create a local monopoly in broadcasting that can be more important to a team than league arrangements for national telecasts.

III. SPORTS IN THE COURTS

The law governing sports activities has been in large measure shaped by litigation and in particular by litigation over aspects of player allocation systems and restrictive marketing practices. This survey will start by tracing the development of the law as it has been applied to baseball. This would appear to be a useful approach not only because case law reports of baseball litigation appear as early as 1890, but also because early rulings caused other professional sports to model the baseball structure, a circumstance some say is at the root of much of the sports world's present problems.

Baseball.—The first reserve system was established by secret agreement in 1879 among National League club owners who agreed that each would reserve a certain number of players for his own team which the others would not hire.[44] A reserve clause first appeared in player contracts in 1887. It gave the teams the right to reserve fourteen players for the following season providing their salaries were not cut. The clause was almost immediately the object of litigation by a team attempting to prevent a player under contract from moving to another league. It failed to hold up. In *Metropolitan Exhibition Co.* v. *Ward*[45] the court held that the clause was too uncertain and indefinite to enforce, or if it was certain, it was perpetual, and thus too unfair to enforce. Similar clauses were later struck down for the same reasons.[46]

The tide turned in favor of baseball, however, in 1922 in a case that had nothing to do with the reserve clause. *Federal Baseball Club* v. *National League*[47] involved the claim of the holder of the Baltimore franchise in the defunct Federal League that the American and National Leagues had conspired to drive their competitor, the Federal League, out of business in violation of the Federal antitrust laws. Specifically, Baltimore claimed that the defendants had caused its rival to collapse by deliberate efforts to buy out its other members. The Supreme Court rejected the contention and in an opinion by Justice Holmes it held that the anti-trust laws did not apply since "the business is giving exhibitions of baseball, which are purely state affairs"[48] and thus not within the federal jurisdiction over interstate commerce. The movement of players across state lines was viewed as "a mere incident, not the essential thing."[49] This removal of baseball from antitrust coverage was quite in harmony with the Courts' conservative definition of commerce at that time. In 15 years the Court was to abandon its narrow view of commerce.[50] But by that time baseball and its imitators were irreversibly committed to the type of system fostered and encouraged by *Federal Baseball*.[51]

A re-examination of *Federal Baseball* was aborted by the settlement of the litigation in 1949 in *Gardella* v. *Chandler*.[52] In that case the Second Circuit reversed a district court ruling that barred hearing plaintiff's antitrust claims when the reserve clause was invoked to bar his return to organized baseball after spending a season playing professionally in Mexico. The court majority gave every indication that it was inclined to reverse *Federal Baseball* in anticipation of a Supreme Court reversal.

The opportunity for reversal came quite soon but to the suprise of many the Court in 1953 stood firm in *Toolson* v. *New York Yankees*.[53] Toolson was a minor league player who was ordered by the Yankees to report to Binghamton from its Newark farm team but refused. The Binghamton club placed Toolson on the "ineligible" list which thereby barred him from playing professional baseball. The Supreme Court acknowledged that there was no inherent logic in making baseball exempt from the antitrust laws and that it disagreed with the Holmes view in *Federal Baseball*.[54] But it reasoned that baseball had been allowed to develop for 30 years with the explicit understanding that it was free from antitrust consideration. Much money had been invested on that premise, and an elaborate structure had been built on it. To reverse the original ruling might open the floodgates of litigation and require judgments about specific practices which a court could not properly weigh. It was up to Congress, the Court said, to decide, by specific legislation, whether or not it intended baseball to be subject to the antitrust laws because it could weigh the issues involved in hearings and also because there would then be no problem of retroactivity.[55]

Congress did not act to resolve the issue in the ensuing years and in 1970 another attack was mounted, this time under the auspices of the baseball players association. *Flood* v. *Kuhn*[56] arose as a result of a trade between the St. Louis and Philadelphia National League clubs. One traded player, Curt Flood, refused to accept the trade and sign a contract with his new employers, and instead challenged the reserve clause. Baseball defended not only on the ground of *stare decisis*, but also contended that when the players association was formed as the bargaining agent for all major league players, the reserve system became part of the collective bargaining agreement and was therefore exempt under the labor antitrust exemption[57] and that Flood's sole recourse was to the National Labor Relations Board.

The case reached the Supreme Court in 1972 and again the Court reaffirmed *Federal Baseball*, which was characterized by the majority as:

> [A]n aberration that has been with us now for half a century, one heretofore deemed fully entitled to the benefit of *stare decisis*, and one that has survived the Court's expanding concept of interstate commerce. It rests on a recognition and an acceptance of baseball's unique characteristics and needs.[58]

Reiterating the logic of the *Toolson* ruling, the Court stressed again that it was the responsibility of Congress, not the judiciary, to change this long-standing anomaly. The Court therefore never addressed the important secondary issue of whether there are limits to the antitrust violations to which labor and management can agree.

Flood in retrospect was the highwater mark in terms of the ability of baseball owners to control the players they employ. The seeds of revolutionary change were planted the next year in the form of the arbitration clause of the 1973 collective bargaining agreement between baseball management and the players association.

The arbitration mechanism had been utilized with dramatic results in the 1974 case of Catfish Hunter who was declared a free agent by baseball Arbitrator Peter Seitz because his team, the Oakland A's, had failed to provide all of the compensation, in the form in which he wished to receive it, as required by his contract, and thus was in breach of contract. Hunter subsequently signed a multi-million dollar contract with the New York Yankees. The precedential value of the *Hunter* case was limited by its facts. The subsequent case of Andy Messersmith, however, was not so limited.

Messersmith signed a one year $90,000 contract in 1974 with the Los Angeles Dodgers. As a result of a dispute over the terms of his 1975 contract, he played the entire season without signing a contract. The Dodgers renewed the contract in accordance with paragraph 10(a) of the Uniform Players Contract, which contains a renewal clause and was an integral part of baseball's reserve system.[59] At the end of the season Messersmith and the players association took the position that he was a free agent, and when baseball disagreed the association filed a grievance contending he was free to sign with any other club. Baseball countered by contending that the alleged claims did not come within the ambit of the grievance procedure of the collective bargaining agreement and therefore the arbitration panel had no jurisdiction over the matter. The owners then applied to a Federal district court in Kansas City to enjoin the proceedings. At the behest of the judge, the parties stipulated to go ahead with the arbitration hearing and agreed that the court would hear and determine the jurisdictional question afterward.

Seitz, after a complex analysis of the provisions of the agreement and its history, held that the panel had jurisdiction to arbitrate disputes over the proper interpretation and application of the reserve system. Then, on the merits, Seitz held that the renewal clause was for only one year (not perpetual) and that after that year there was no contractual bond between player and club. Further, he held that since the only players who could be reserved under Major League Rule 4-A are players who are under contract, no player who had played out the renewal year could thereafter be reserved. Finally, since the no tampering rule, Rule 3(g), prohibits negotiations or dealings only with players who are under contract to or reserved by other teams, Seitz concluded that players who had played out their renewal year were free to negotiate with any team in the Major Leagues. Therefore Messersmith was declared a free agent. And Seitz was fired.

The owners appealed the decision to the Kansas City district court. On the critical issue of whether the arbitration panel had jurisdiction to hear and consider the grievances, the court found that it did.[60] The Court of Appeals for the Eighth Circuit affirmed.[61]

The practical effect of *Messersmith* was to allow all players currently under contract to play out their option year and become free agents. The consequence of the decision is described in section IV.

Hockey.—The very creation of the World Hockey Association (WHA) in 1971 assured that there would be a substantial volume of litigation. This was so because of the organization of that sport. First, there was no substantial pool of uncommitted hockey players from which to make up 12 full team rosters. All minor, semi-professional and amateur leagues were then affiliated with the rival National Hockey League. Moreover, all NHL and minor league contracts contained perpetual reserve clauses, and the remaining semi-professional and amateur leagues had agreed to deal only with the NHL.[62]

When WHA started its first season of play in 1972 it had 345 players, over 200 of whom were subject to reserve clauses of contracts they signed the previous season. NHL teams of course brought legal action to enjoin the jumping athletes from performing. Of four actions that came to decision in 1972 the WHA won three and arguably gained greater benefit from the fourth which the NHL technically "won."

Boston Professional Hockey Association v. *Cheevers*[63] turned on the perpetual nature of the NHL reserve clause. After reviewing the clause, the agreement between the NHL and the minor leagues, and the NHL By-Laws, the court ruled, ". . . there is a probability this tangled web of legal instruments will . . . be found to restrain trade in professional hockey."[64] The jumping players were therefore allowed to play in the WHA. Similarly, the court in *Nassau Sports* v. *Hampson*[65] denied a preliminary injunction to the New York Islanders, noting that the NHL's perpetual reserve clause ". . . seems, plausibly, one aspect of a contractual scheme constituting a violation of sections 1 and 2 of the Sherman Antitrust Act . . ."[66]

In *Philadelphia World Hockey Club* v. *Philadelphia Hockey Club*,[67] the WHA was on the offensive seeking to enjoin the NHL from attempting to enforce its reserve clause. The court granted the injunction, finding that through the use of the reserve clause and agreements with minor, semi-professional and amateur leagues, ". . . the NHL overwhelmingly controls the supply of players who are capable and available for play in a new league . . .",[68] which control the court held to be proscribed by section 2 of the Sherman Act.

The one "defeat" in this period occurred in *Nassau Sports* v. *Peters*[69] where the court enjoined Gary Peters from playing for the WHA for one year. The NHL had contended, however, that the reserve clause renewed itself each year and that the injunction should have been for three years, to coincide at least with the term of the NHL players association collective bargaining agreement. Indeed, the NHL in this case appeared to be abandoning any argument that its reserve clause was perpetual. It would seem that at best the victory for the NHL in this case was for a one year option.

In any event, in November 1973 the NHL abandoned its perpetual reserve clause and adopted a one year option clause coupled with a compensation arrangement involving "equalization" arbitration.[70]

Basketball.—In an early case involving a player attempting to switch leagues, the question was raised whether a player in his option year had to actually play out that year or may he sit it out. In *Lemat Corp.* v. *Barry*[71] the court held that actual playing was not necessary. The decision is in apparent conflict with *Dallas Cowboys* v. *Harris*[72] which seems to stand for the proposition that NFL players will have to play out their option in order to become free agents.

Another interesting early ruling is the 1961 decision in *Central New York-Baseball, Inc.* v. *Barnett*.[73] There the Syracuse Nationals of the NBA sought to enjoin Dick Barnett from playing with the Cleveland team of the American Basketball League. At issue was basketball's reserve clause which at that time was identical to baseball's. Barnett argued that the clause was perpetual and therefore unreasonable; Syracuse argued that it only provided for a one year renewal. The court adopted the team's construction of the clause as "reasonable, rational, practical, just and in accordance with [contract construction] principles".[74] The decision therefore foreshadowed *Messersmith* and was in fact relied on by Arbitrator Seitz in his landmark baseball opinion.

But the most important decision concerning the operation of basketball is the 1975 ruling in *Robertson v. National Basketball Association*.[75] There the court had before it a motion for summary judgment by the NBA seeking dismissal of the suit brought by NBA players in 1970. The NBA players sought to enjoin the then proposed merger of the NBA and ABA on the grounds that the merger would create a monopoly in violation of the Sherman Act, and to bar the continued use of the player draft and basketball's option system on the ground they were in restraint of trade in violation of the Sherman Act.

The court denied the motion and in the process discussed the possibility that the antitrust "per se" doctrine might apply to basketball's draft and option compensation system. There was also some suggestion in the opinion that even application of the "rule of reason" might not save those rules.[76]

The question of which antitrust standard of proof will be applicable may be critical to a determination of the legality of player allocation rules, as will be evidenced by the two important football decisions to be discussed below. As was previously mentioned, the antitrust laws do not proscribe all restraints of trade, only those which are unreasonable. The "rule of reason" test,[77] simply stated, is that courts will consider the effect of the agreement upon the entire industry in question in light of prevailing conditions, and if found unduly restrictive, or if the dominant purpose of the agreement is the restraint of trade, the agreement will be held violative of the Sherman Act. Conversely, if the industry can show an overriding justification for the restrictive agreement in rule of reason cases, such agreement will generally be held legal. In short, the legalities of agreements in this type of situation is determined on a case-by-case basis.

But some activities have been determined to be so clearly contrary to public policy as to be held illegal per se under the Sherman Act. Examples of such activities are horizontal price-fixing agreements,[78] division of markets,[79] tying arrangements,[80] and secondary boycotts.[81] The per se rule, where applicable, renders immaterial such considerations as the degree of market dominance and commercial necessities, and thus obviates the need for inquiry into the nature and historical development of the industry in question.

It should be clear, then, that those anxious to overturn aspects of player allocation systems seek to analogize them to arrangements in other industries that have been held per se violations since no further burden of proof would then be required. Thus the *Robertson* opinion is important because of its strong hint that the per se rule might be applicable.

Football.—The Supreme Court held nearly 20 years ago that football was subject to antitrust laws in *Radovitch* v. *National Football League*.[82] Five years after *Radovitch*, R. C. Owens played out his option with the San Francisco 49ers and began negotiating and ultimately signed with the Baltimore Colts. In response, the NFL replaced its reserve clause with the so-called Rozelle rule which, as indicated above, allows a player to become a free agent after playing out his option but requires a new team signing him to compensate his prior team. The Rozelle rule was first tested in *Kapp* v. *National Football League*.[83] In that case Kapp, a successful quarterback, decided to play out his option year with the Minnesota Vikings because of a dispute over pay. During that year (1970) he was traded to the New England Patriots and came to an oral agreement to play for them for three years for a total of $600,000. At the beginning of the 1971 season Kapp reported to spring training camp and was asked to sign a Standard Player Contract. He refused, was expelled from the camp, and then brought suit against the NFL charging, inter alia, violation of the antitrust laws. In a motion for partial summary judgment, Kapp argued that the NFL's option, tampering and compensation rules, as well as its rule requiring signing of the standard contract, constituted a combination among defendants to refuse to deal with players and that such refusal amounted to a boycott which was illegal per se under the antitrust laws, without regard to whether reasonable purposes might exist for them. He also contended that the rules were unreasonable in any event.

The NFL denied that their rules constituted a per se violation of the antitrust laws, arguing that the professional sports business is unique because although teams compete on the field, they cannot be competitors in business since the very purpose of professional sports is to provide reasonably matched teams for field competition in order to attract and sustain the interest and trust of fans. If there was free competition better financed or otherwise better advantaged clubs would be able to accumulate the better players which would destroy the possibility of balanced competition and might even drive some clubs out of business.

The court ruled that the reasonableness test should apply[84] and then found the Rozelle rule patently illegal because its effect "would be to perpetually restrain a player from pursuing his occupation. . . ."[85] The rule was therefore held to be illegal, the court stating:

> We conclude that such a rule imposing restraint virtually unlimited in time and extent, goes far beyond any possible need for fair protection of the interests of the club-employers or the purposes of the NFL and that it imposes upon the player-employees such undue hardship as to be an unreasonable restraint and such a rule is not susceptible of different inferences concerning its reasonableness; it is unreasonable under any legal tests . . .[86]

In a recent trial for assessment of damages as a result of the violation a jury found he had not been damaged and awarded him nothing. Kapp is appealing the verdict.

The most recent (December 29, 1975) district court ruling on the Rozelle rule, *Mackey* v. *National Football League*,[87] follows *Kapp* in finding that rule invalid. The *Mackey* court, however, went even further than *Kapp*, finding not only that it was violative under the rule of reason standard, but that it was also a per se violation of the antitrust laws because it was a concerted refusal to deal, a group boycott, and contrary to public policy.[88] The court rejected virtually the same uniqueness argument the League presented in *Kapp*.

Mackey is also significant for the court's ruling with regard to the NFL's claimed labor exemption. In this regard the court held that "[t]he Rozelle Rule is a nonmandatory, illegal subject of bargaining", and further since it was "a per se violation of the antitrust laws and otherwise violative of the antitrust laws under the Rule of Reason standard, [it] cannot constitute a mandatory subject of bargaining as that phrase is used in labor law."

Litigation has not been nearly as extensive with regard to the restrictive marketing practices of professional sports leagues. No decisions have been reported, for example, concerning the terms and conditions on which franchises are granted or by a thwarted franchise seeker.[89] In one reported decision the American Football League lost an antitrust suit against the National Football League claiming that the NFL's expansion practices sought to exclude the AFL from key cities. But despite the coincidence of NFL expansion with the launching of the new league, the court found that the "relevant market" for major league football was a national one, not local or regional, so that the NFL did not have the requisite degree of market power to exclude another league from competition.[90]

Sale of broadcasts rights has seen some significant litigation. In *United States* v. *National Football League*,[91] the Justice Department succeeded in attacking a provision of football law which prohibited telecasts of competing professional games in home territories of other teams as being a territorial restriction unlawful under section 1 of the Sherman Act and in striking down the football commissioners powers to control all television and radio broadcasts. The decision plainly inhibited the ability of the commissioner to maximize radio and television revenue. In 1961 the League entered into a contract with CBS in which the television rights of all league teams were pooled and the revenues from the contract were divided equally among the teams. The league sought approval of the arrangement from the same court since it was still under that court's 1953 injunction. The court disapproved the contract on the ground that it gave the network the sole discretion on where games were to be televised and was thus a restriction on the rights of the individual clubs.[92] That same year the league sought and obtained congressional approval for such pooling arrangements.[93]

IV. RECENT DEVELOPMENTS

With the foregoing as background, the fast-breaking developments in the sports world since December 1975 may be placed in their proper perspective. They may be seen not as a haphazard series of events, but rather as part of the natural successor phase to a 4-year period which has seen a restrictive player allocation system fall before the intense pressure placed upon it by labor union activity in the courts and at the bargaining tables. It may be speculated that we are now entering a period in which the players associations will seek to consolidate their gains and management will seek an accommodation with the reality that labor possesses real strength and that a working rather than antagonistic relation will ultimately profit all parties. The history of labor relations in America has taught that the process of labor-management accommodation is often uneven and fitful. But the most recent events give hope that the process may be starting in the professional sports industry.

Baseball.—Even before the *Messersmith* decision collective bargaining negotiations were in progress. Eight days after Arbitrator Seitz handed down his ruling, the old agreement expired. Although negotiations continued, they were apparently unsuccessful, for on February 23 the team owners refused to open the spring training camps until an agreement was reached, a situation which prevailed until March 18 and seemed to threaten the entire baseball season. Ultimately, the Commissioner ordered the camps opened and negotiations resumed.

At the same time the pressures of the *Messersmith* decision were building. Approximately 50 players were playing out their option year.

Then at almost the last hour before the tolling of baseball's June 15 trading deadline, Charles Finley, owner of the Oakland A's, consummated a sale of three of his star players, Joe Rudi, Rollie Fingers, and Vida Blue.[94] Rudi and Fingers were sold to the Boston Red Sox for $1 million each and Blue to the New York Yankees for $1.5 million. All three were playing out their options. It may be recalled that under the *Messersmith* ruling the players would have become free agents at the season's end and able to sign with any other major league club and the signing club would not have had to compensate the A's.[95] Also, it should be noted that under baseball law no player contracts may be assigned to another club after June 15 without offering that player to all other major league clubs for the waiver price of $20,000.[96]

On June 16 the Commissioner of baseball ordered a hearing to be held on the player assignments. On June 18, following the hearing,[97] the Commissioner refused to approve the assignments on the ground that they were "inconsistent with the best interests of baseball, the integrity of the game and the maintenance of the public confidence in it."[98] The Commissioner cited the Major League Agreement and Major League Rule 12 as authority for his action.[99] He ordered the three players returned to the active roster of the A's.

In response, Mr. Finley filed a civil action in the Federal district court in Chicago[100] against the Commissioner, both leagues, the Major League Council, and the Yankees and Red Sox, alleging, inter alia, that the Commissioner had acted in excess of the authority of his office; that the disapproval action of the Commissioner was part of a conspiracy with other baseball owners to restrain, restrict and limit access by Finley to the exclusive market for the purchase and sale of major league ballplayers in violation of the Federal antitrust laws; and that the action of the Commissioner deprived Finley of valuable property rights in violation of his rights to due process under the Fifth and Fourteenth Amendments. As a remedy, Mr. Finley seeks an order forcing completion of the sales, or, alternatively, money damages. A hearing is scheduled to be held in early September on baseballs motion to dismiss the case.

The final and most important recent baseball event was the announcement July 12 that the baseball owners and players' represesentatives had reached agreement on a four-year collective agreement. The key provisions of the agreement were reported to be the following:[101]

A player will have the right to demand to be traded after having played in the major leagues for 5 years. He will have a veto right over six clubs. If he is not traded he will become a free agent. After six years he may opt to become a free agent.

Players who become free agents, including those who now are governed by the *Messersmith* decision, will be able to negotiate with a maximum of 12 teams starting with the inverse order of the previous seasons standings. Each club will be limited in the number of free agents it may sign, being permitted a maximum of one if the free agent pool totals 1 to 14 players. However, a club will be able to sign as many free agents as it might lose in a season.

The only compensation for a lost player will be a draft choice. If one of the 12 lowest teams signs a free agent it will lose a second round draft choice. If one of the top 12 teams signs a player, it forfeits its No. 1 draft choice.

Salary arbitration is reinstituted. But if a player is eligible to be a free agent, his dispute can go to arbitration only by mutual consent of the player and club.

The minimum salary is to be raised from $16,000 to $21,000 by 1979.

The owners agreed to add $1.85 million to the players pension fund.

The agreement now must be ratified by the votes of the individual owners and the players.

Basketball.—On April 29 representatives of the National Basketball Association owners and the players association announced that they had reached a settlement of the *Robertson* case and had agreed to a new collective bargaining agreement. The settlement presaged the merger of the NBA with the rival American Basketball Association which was announced shortly thereafter.

The *Robertson* suit, it will be recalled, was instituted in 1970 and contended that the NBA's common draft, its option clause with the equivalent of football's Rozelle rule, and the then proposed merger with the ABA violated the antitrust laws. The settlement agreement and collective bargaining agreement, which may be treated as one package, provide essentially as follows with regard to the key issues:

A team which drafts a player has one year to sign him. If the player is not signed he may be drafted a second time and that team has 1 year to sign him. If he does not sign after a year he becomes a free agent and may be signed by any team without compensation or penalty.

Except in certain instances for rookies or where specifically agreed to by a veteran, option clauses are eliminated. Hereafter until the end of the 1980–1981 playing season a player who completes the term of his contract may negotiate with any other club in the league. The club that signs the free agent must compensate the old team. If an agreement on compensation is not reached, the Commissioner may award the prior team players and/or draft picks and/or cash.

After the 1980–1981 season and until the end of the 1986–1987 playing season the compensation rule is abolished. Instead, during that period a veteran free agent may negotiate with any club. However, his prior club has the opportunity to substantially match the new offer (right of first refusal) and if it does, the player remains with the old club. Disputes over equivalency of offers will be taken to arbitration.

The NBA agrees to pay an indemnity of $4.3 million to the players that brought the suit plus attorneys fees and costs totalling in excess of $900,000.

In addition, the collective bargaining agreement provides: the minimum wage is raised to $30,000 per year; the playoff pool will be increased from $1 million to $1.15 million by 1979 (or $1.25 million if 12 teams participate); a minimum of 11 players must be kept on the active list; and for the hiring of Peter Seitz as Impartial Arbitrator.

The proposed merger agreement has not been finalized as of this date but details revealed in the press give its outlines as follows: Four ABA teams (New York, Denver, Indiana and San Antonio) will be added to the NBA. The two remaining ABA teams, Kentucky and Salt Lake City, will be dissolved and their players will be subject to draft by all the remaining teams. The dissolved teams will be compensated for not being included in the merger. The entering teams will pay an entrance fee.[102] In addition, the New York Nets will indemnify the New York Knicks for "infringement" of their territorial rights.[103] The former ABA teams will not share in television revenues for five years nor will they vote on gate sharing proposals for two years.

Football.—Football appears to have made the least progress in settling its labor-management difficulties of any of the four major professional sports. Indeed, it might be more accurate to say it has made no progress at all. There has been no collective bargaining agreement in effect since January 31, 1974. Current negotiations are at an apparent standstill. Free agents are being signed by most clubs but there seems to be no wholesale movement to glamor or more affluent teams.[104]

Litigation remains the vehicle of first resort. The Yazoo Smith trial ended in June and a ruling by the court is awaited. And on June 30, National Labor Relations Board Chief Administrative Law Judge Charles W. Schneider announced his rulings on a series of unfair labor practice allegations filed against the NFL Management Council and the NFL clubs by the players association.[105] In brief summary ALJ Schneider found that the NFL and/or certain clubs had:

> Violated the statutory duty to bargain in good faith by failing and refusing to provide the players association with information necessary to fulfill its collective bargaining function including copies of all standard players contracts, raw data pertaining to player inquiries, copies of stadium lease agreements, and a copy of the Commissioner's employment contract;
> Violated the duty to bargain by unilaterally adopting or putting into effect increased pre-season wage scales;
> Discriminatorily traded, waived or released four players because of their participation in union or concerted activities on behalf of the players association; and

Interfered, restrained or coerced players by demanding the return of bonuses, threatening to put players on waivers, and by threatening reprisals for attendance at association meetings.

The ALJ issued a cease and desist order against repetition of such conduct and also ordered the four players reinstated with back pay.

Judge Schneider dismissed as unproved allegations that the NFL and/or its clubs unlawfully refused to supply the union with information about fines and denied insurance claims, unlawfully adopted the sudden death rule and changed the punt rules without bargaining first, discriminatorily traded Ken Reaves because of his pro-union activities, and that players were kept under surveillance to discourage their union activities.

The ALJ's decision is subject to appeal to the National Labor Relations Board and thereafter to a federal court of appeals and possibly the United States Supreme Court.

Hockey.—The hockey scene has been relatively quiet. Both leagues have collective bargaining agreements in effect. Free agents are moving between clubs but not in great numbers or with great notoriety except for the case of Bobby Orr's transfer from Boston to Chicago of the NHL.

The movement of several weak franchises appears to be the most significant recent development. In this regard the NHL has given approval for its California Golden Seals to move from Oakland to Cleveland and approval for the Kansas City Scouts to be sold and moved to Denver is imminent. Previously, the WHA Cleveland franchise moved to St. Paul, Minnesota, and the Toronto Toros were transferred to Birmingham, Alabama.

There is no indication of any movement toward merger by the two leagues.

Another issue that continues to plague the sport is the apparent high level of violence on the ice. On June 30, a Toronto jury acquitted Dan Maloney of the Detroit Red Wings (NHL) of assault on an opposing player on November 5, 1975. The jury stated "these actions in hockey are in no way condoned by us." This criminal proceeding is the latest in a series, all of which have resulted in acquittals. Another case, involving Rick Johzio of the Calgary Cowboys (WHA) is scheduled to be heard August 30 in Quebec. In response to these occurrences the NHL has adopted several new rules designed to limit violence through monetary and playing penalties.

The developments briefly outlined above, as indicated at the outset of this section, seem to represent a generally healthy change with regard to the way labor and management now view each other in three of the four major sports. This should not be taken to mean there are no serious issues remaining, even in the labor relations area. For example, the *Mackey* case raises the question whether any variant of the Rozelle rule could ever be a valid subject of bargaining. The issue still remains as to how far the labor anti-trust exemption may be used to insulate anti-competitive activity. Also the NBA-ABA merger may be subjected to further antitrust scrutiny. Many other matters remain ripe for investigation. The public policy issues raised by the movement of franchises from one locality to another has never been seriously addressed by Congress. Similarly, the question of the continued efficacy of self-regulation by professional sports leagues is raised by some of the events discussed above. The issue of violence in the contact sports merits perusal also. It may be expected that the hearings soon to be held will shed light on those issues mentioned as well as some others.

NOTES

1. House Resolution ₁18o. The resolution and its legislative history are set forth in Appendix A.
2. 15 U.S.C. 1, 2 (1970).
3. 15 U.S.C. 1291 (1970).
4. Public Law 87-331, 75 Stat. 732 (1961), as amended 15 U.S.C. 1291-95 (1970).
5. *Federal Baseball Club* v.ₚ*National League*, 259 U.S. 200 (1922).
6. *United States* v. *International Boxing Club*, 348 U.S. 236 (1955) (boxing); *Radovich* v. *National Football League*, 352 U.S. 445 (1957) (football); *Deeson* v. *Professional Golfers Association of America*, 358 F. 2d 165 (9th Cir.), cert. denied, 385 U.S. 846 (1966) (golf); *Blalock* v. *Ladies Professional Golf Association*, 359 F. Supp. 1260 (N.D. Ga. 1973) (golf); *Haywood* v. *National Basketball Association*, 401 U.S. 1204 (Douglas, Circuit Justice, 1971) (basketball); *Nassau Sports* v. *Peters*, 352 F. Supp. 870 (E.D.N.Y. 1972) (hockey); *Washington State Bowling Proprietors Association* v. *Pacific Lanes, Inc.*, 356 F.2d 371 (9th Cir. 1966), cert. denied 384 U.S. 963 (1966) (bowling).
7. *Flood* v. *Kuhn*, 407 U.S. 258, 281 n. 17 (1972), the Court catalogued numerous examples of inconclusive legislative deliberations. There are two bills presently before the House which would affect professional sports. One, H.R. 11382, would amend the antitrust laws to specifically cover all professional sports, including baseball. The other H.R. 2355, would prohibit such practices as the Rozelle rule, the reserve clause and other facets of the player allocation system used by professional sports leagues.
8. S. 2373, reported out of the Senate Subcommittee on Antitrust and Monopoly on Sept., 18, 1972, following hearings held throughout 1971 and 1972.
9. See, e.g., Koppett, Sports and the Law: An Overview, 18 N.Y.U. Law Forum 815, 826 (1973).
10. Internal Revenue Code, sec. 1967(a).
11. Internal Revenue Code, secs. 1201, 1202.
12. Internal Revenue Code, secs. 1211, 1212.
13. Internal Revenue Code, secs. 1371-1379.
14. Internal Revenue Code, secs. 404, 1348(b)(1), 83(c)(1).
15. Internal Revenue Code, secs. 1201(b), 1348(b), 56(a).
16. Internal Revenue Code, sec. 1301 et seq.
17. Hundley, Jr., 48 TC 339 (1958).
18. Only the National Football League Players Association has N.L.R.B. certification. Jurisdiction over baseball was established in a case involving umpires, American League of Professional Baseball Clubs and Association of National Baseball League Players, 180 N.L.R.B. No. 30 (1969).

19. See, e.g., National Football League Management Council and National Football League Players Association, Case No. 2–CA–13379, decided June 30, 1976, per Schneider, Chief Administrative Law Judge.
20. W. J. Usery, Jr., former Director of the Federal Mediation and Conciliation Service, attempted to mediate the September 1975 impasse in football negotiations. Oversight Hearings on National Football League Labor-Management Dispute, Subcommittee on Labor-Management Relations, House Committee on Education and Labor, 94th Cong., 1st sess., pp. 36–37 (1975).
21. The strikes were in baseball and football. Football has been without a collective bargaining agreement since Jan. 31, 1974. Baseball recently concluded an agreement after an almost seven month hiatus. Basketball and hockey entered into agreements after protracted negotiations in April and May 1976, respectively.
22. A threat to disrupt the 1976 baseball All-Star game was settled by the owners agreement to make its annual contribution to the players pension fund.
23. For ten years prior to the 1975 playing seasons the Department of Labor had issued blanket certifications to baseball and hockey. It was discovered about that time that certain personnel peripheral to the players were gaining entrance under the blanket policy. As a result the Labor Department now issues certificates on an individual basis. This has allegedly caused processing delays. In addition, the Department had questioned in the case of hockey the necessity (in the face of claimed inadequate United States citizen counterparts) of foreign officials, coaches and trainers.
24. Statement of Bowie K. Kuhn, Commissioner of Baseball, Before the Senate Finance Committee, Mar. 24, 1976, Table III.
25. 15 U.S.C. 1291 (1970).
26. H.R. 11070 and S. 2554.
27. For an exhaustive review of sports broadcasting legislation see Hochberg, Congress Tackles Sports and Broadcasting, 3 Western State Univ. L.R. 223 (1976).
28. 47 U.S.C. 151 (1970).
29. Proceedings, Conference on the Economics of Professional Sports (Burman, ed. 1974), p. 1: Statement of Bowie K. Kuhn, supra, note 24.
30. The entire text of Chairman Sisk's statement is set forth at Appendix B.
31. 356 U.S. 1 (1958).
32. 356 U.S. 1, 5.
33. *United States* v. *National Football League*, 116 F. Supp. 319, 323 (E.D. Pa. 1953).
34. In actuality, the reserve system is normally made up of clauses in the player contract and league rules and not simply one clause in a contract. In baseball it was comprised of paragraph 10(a) of the Uniform Player Contract, which allowed the club to renew the contract for one year periods, and Major League Rules 4–A and 3(g) which authorized clubs to reserve 40 players and which prohibit tampering with other players, respectively. The Major League rules are incorporated in the Uniform Players Contract by paragraph 9(a).
35. *Kapp* v. *National Football League*, 391 F. Supp. 73, 82 (N.D. Calif., 1974); Government and the Sports Business (Noll, ed. 1974), pp. 3–4 (hereafter, Noll); Morris, In the Wake of Flood. 38 Law and Contemporary Problems 85, 87–88 (1973).
36. See, e.g., Major League Rule 3(g).
37. A recent example occurred during the A.B.A.–N.B.A. war. George McGuiness was drafted by the NBA Philadelphia club but chose to play with Indiana of the A.B.A. Thereafter he played out his contract and signed with the New York Knicks of the NBA. Philadelphia protested on the basis of its prior draft right. The NBA Commissioner awarded McGuiness to Philadelphia and fined New York and deprived it of a future draft choice.
38. A fourth source of revenue is concessions and parking. Generally this is a matter solely in the hands of the franchise and not subject to league-wide rules.
39. In baseball, for example, a ³/₄'s vote in each league is required.
40. Under the proposed N.B.A.–A.B.A. merger agreement the New York Nets will be required to pay the New York Knicks for "infringing" on their territory.
41. Noll, supra, note 35, at pp. 15–16.

42. Id. at pp. 38, 57-58, 100-101, 131, 134, 155, 356-357.
43. 15 U.S.C. 1291 (1970).
44. H.R. Rep. No. 2002, 82d Cong., 2d sess., 34 (1952).
45. 24 Abb. N. Cas. 393, 9 N.Y.S. 779 (S. Ct. 1890).
46. *Brooklyn Baseball Club* v. *McGuire*, 116 F. 782 (E.D. Pa. 1902); *Cincinnati Exhibition Club* v. *Johnson*, 190 Ill. App. 630 (1914).
47. 259 U.S. 200 (1922). The full text of the decision may be found in Appendix E.
48. Id. at 206. Contrary to popular myth, Holmes never said that "baseball is a sport, not a business" or words to that effect.
49. Id. at 208-209.
50. *N.L.R.B.* v. *Jones & Laughlin Steel*, 301 U.S. 1 (1937).
51. "It is widely believed (but not widely admitted) in the sports world today that perfectly feasible league structures could have been built on a firmer base than the 1922 decision that set the course of baseball and of its imitators. It is almost universally believed by sports promoters and their lawyers that various specific monopolistic aspects of sports structure can be defended, and could have been so defended, step by step, over the years. But because of the 1922 decision, its continuing applicability to baseball and its nonapplicability to everything else, players and club owners are only now trying to work out accommodations in contract areas that have a 50-year crust of intransigence. What might have developed gradually must now be dealt with as an indigestible lump." Koppett, Sports and the Law: An Overview, 18 N.Y.U. Law Forum 815, 825 (1973).
52. 172 F.2d 402 (2d Cir. 1949).
53. 346 U.S. 356 (1953).
54. Id. at 357.
55. Id. at 357.
56. 407 U.S. 258 (1972).
57. See, e.g., *Amalgamated Meat Cutters etc.* v. *Jewel Tea Co.*, 381 U.S. 676 (1965).
58. 407 U.S. at 282.
59. For elements of baseball's reserve system, see note 34, supra.
60. *Kansas City Royals Baseball Corp.* v. *Major League Baseball Players Association*, Civil No. 75-712-W-1 (W.D. Mo., Feb. 3, 1976). The court also had before it the question whether the award should be enforced on its merits. It sustained the award, following the general rule in arbitration cases that awards will be upheld if it can be said to be within the "scope of the arbitrator's authority" or to be an award which "draws its essence from the collective bargaining agreement" in effect at the time of the grievance. *United Steelworkers of America* v. *Enterprise Wheel & Car Corp.*, 363 U.S. 593, 597 (1960); *Bell Aerospace Co.* v. *Local 516, UAW*, 500 F.2d 921 (2d Cir. 1974); *Crigger* v. *Allied Chemical Co*, 500 F.2d 1218 (4th Cir. 1974).
61. *Kansas City Royals Baseball Corp.* v. *Major League Baseball Players Association*, 532 F.2d 615 (8th Cir. 1976). In addition to affirming the lower court's disposition of the jurisdiction and merits issues, the court rejected a contention that the relief fashioned by the district court was inappropriate.
62. Sobel, The Emancipation of Professional Athletes, 3 Western State University L.R. 185, 194 (1976).
63. 348 F. Supp. 261 (D. Mass.), remanded 472 F.2d 127 (1st Cir. 1972).
64. 348 F. Supp. at 267.
65. 355 F. Supp. 733 (D. Minn. 1972).
66. Id. at 735.
67. 351 F. Supp. 462 (E.D. Pa. 1972).
68. Id. at 509.
69. 352 F. Supp. 870 (E.D.N.Y. 1972).
70. National Hockey League By-Laws, sec. 9A.
71. 275 Cal. App. 2d 671, 80 Cal. Reptr. 240 (1969).
72. 348 S.W. 2d 37 (Tex. Civ. App. 1961).
73. 190 Ohio 2d 130, 181 N.E. 2d 506 (1961).
74. 181 N.E. 2d at 510.
75. 389 F. Supp. 867 (S.D.N.Y. 1975).

76. Id. at 892–893. For details of the *Robertson* settlement, see Section IV, infra.
77. The test was first enunciated in *Standard Oil Co. of New Jersey* v. *United States*, 221 U.S. 1 (1911), and governs the majroity of antitrust decisions to this day. See, e.g. *United States* v. *Arnold, Schwinn & Co.*, 388 U.S. 365 (1967).
78. I.e., price fixing agreements between parties within the same competitive level, such as retail merchants. *United States* v. *Socony-Vacuum Oil Co.*, 310 U.S. 150 (1940).
79. *Timken Roller Bearing Co.* v. *United States*, 341 U.S. 593 (1951).
80. *International Salt Co.* v. *United States*, 332 U.S. 392 (1947).
81. *Klor's, Inc.* v. *Broadway-Hale Stores, Inc.*, 359 U.S. 207 (1959). A secondary boycott consists of the application of coercive pressure on a third party to refrain from dealing with a competitor of the party applying the pressure.
82. 352 U.S. 445 (1957).
83. 390 F. Supp. 73 (N.D. Calif. 1974).
84. Id. at 83.
85. Id.
86. Id.
87. 5 Trade Reg. Rep. (1975-2 Trade Cas.) sec. 60, 647 (D. Minn., Dec. 30, 1975).
88. Id. at 67,816. The trial lasted 55 days and resulted in 12,000 pages of testimony transcript.
89. The City of Seattle dismissed its suit over baseball's abandonment of it after only one season when the American League awarded it a new franchise which is to commence operations in 1977.
90. *American Football League* v. *National Football League*, 205 F. Supp. 60 (D. Md. 1962), aff'd 323 F.2d 124 (5th Cir. 1963).
91. 116 F. Supp. 319 (E.D. Pa. 1953).
92. 196 F. Supp. 445 (E.D. Pa. 1961).
93. Act of Sept. 30, 1961, Public Law 87-331, as amended, 15 U.S.C. 1291-1295 (1970).
94. Technically of course it was the sale and assignment of the individual player contracts.
95. The complaint in *Finley* v. *Kuhn* alleges in paragraph 18(d) that in anticipation of the sale of Blue, Finley signed Blue to a three year, no-cut contract. Thus the A's apparently will not lose Blue at the end of the season. But the complaint also alleges that the A's would not have signed Blue for the amount of the contract ($690,000) if it had known it could not be assigned.
96. Major League Rule 10.
97. The hearing was attended by Finely, representatives of the Boston Red Sox, New York Yankees and the Baseball Players Association.
98. The full text of Commissioner Kuhn's decision may be found at Appendix C.
99. Copies of the Major League Agreement and Rule 12 may be found in Appendix D.
100. No. 76 C 2358, N.D. Ill. E.D., filed June 25, 1976.
101. New York Times, July 12, 1976, p. 1, col. 1.
102. The entrance fee is reported to be $3.2 million each.
103. The exact amount has not been revealed.
104. Washington Post, July 7, 1976, sec. D, p. 1, col. 1.
105. Case No. 2-CA-13379.

The Reserve Clause from the Players' Perspective

EDWARD R. GARVEY

Mr. Chairman, and members of the Monopolies and Commercial Law Subcommittee, I am Ed Garvey. I have held the position of Executive Director of the National Football League Players Association since May of 1971. The NFL Players Association is a certified union, having received NLRB certification in January of 1971. Our offices are located at 1300 Connecticut Avenue, N.W., Washington, D.C.

We appear here this morning in support of legislation that would establish the freedom of the professional athlete, in order that he may be treated like other workers in our society.

Let me say at the outset that we understand that there are problems confronting this Subcommittee that demand a much higher priority than the fate of the professional athlete. Despite a very short career, athletes are well paid compared with most other people in our society. Most will go on to another career. Many in society would gladly change places with Billy Kilmer or Roy Jefferson. The athletes' problems do not compare with those of migrant workers or with those locked into the ghettos of our cities. The reserve clause cannot compete with the important of school integration, a national energy policy, or unemployment in our country.

But, let me also say that no member of Congress can, in good conscience, allow this system to continue. No member can focus on the lack of freedom of the athlete and simply write it off as being a necessity for a "sport".

No one can look Kermit Alexander in the eye and say that he should be bought, sold, traded or forced to stay with a particular club and say that it is the right thing to do. And we state unequivocally that no one can come before this Committee and justify the reserve clause in any sport on the basis of anything other than opinion testimony by those who have a vested interest in maintaining the system as it currently exists. There have been no studies that support the owners' contention that the reserve clause

SOURCE: Testimony of Edward R. Garvey, Executive Director of the National Football League Players Association, before the Subcommittee on Monopolies and Commercial Law of the Committee on the Judiciary, House of Representatives, *Rights of Professional Athletes*, Serial No. 59 (Washington, D.C.: U.S. Government Printing Office, 1975).

is necessary to maintain competitive balance. There has been no definition of that hollow phrase "competitive balance" by any representative of the member clubs of the National Football League. Every objective source that has considered the Rozelle Rule, the reserve clause and other restrictive practices has concluded that they bear absolutely no relationship to competitive balance. They do find that these practices allow club owners to control both on-field and off-field conduct of the employees in their industry. They allow a coach to indiscriminately fine, allow a team to restrict the right of free expression and deprive the individual of the right to employment of his choice.

The professional athlete is not the typical citizen. He is a gifted athlete who was an outstanding performer in high school, an All-American in college and one of only 200 who make it in a given year in the National Football League. He is one of a gifted few.

HOW THE SYSTEM WORKS

After four years of high school football and four years of college football, the athlete who is good enough to make it in professional football finds that he has been "drafted" by one of twenty-six teams. He is contacted by the team which has drafted him and informed that they would like him to come to that team city to "negotiate" a contract. When he arrives he finds that he cannot *negotiate* a contract because if he wishes to play in the National Football League he must sign the contract offered to him. If he is the first or second player chosen by the club he will likely receive a high contract and a reasonable signing bonus. If he is taken on a higher round he will find that the contract offered is much lower than his expectations.

If he decides not to accept the offer, he has the choice of playing in Canada or not playing professional football. For a brief moment he had the choice of going to the World Football League, but because of many factors, including the exclusive lease arrangements between various stadiums and NFL teams, the World Football League is no longer a viable alternative.

Typically, he will be forced to sign a three-year contract with a one year option. He will not sign one document, but rather three, and he does not understand why. If he makes the team and is an outstanding performer, then he will be obligated to play under those contracts for the next three years. If, on the other hand, the team wishes to cut him at any time, then the contracts are cancelled unilaterally by the team.

If he is too injured to play the second year, he is "in breach of his contract" because he failed to report in "excellent physical condition" for the second or third contract. Thus, what is known as the long-term contract protects the *club* from renegotiation by the player but offers the player no protection whatsoever.

The player then finds that he can be traded or sold to another team and he has nothing to say about that. He learns that if he has a dispute with his team over compensation or any other matter, it will be decided by the commissioner of the National Football League. The commissioner, he learns, is selected and paid by the owners, chairs their meetings, initiates changes in the Constitution and By-laws. If he prefers to go to court instead of having the commissioner decide his dispute, he will find that the league will quickly move to have the matter submitted to arbitration by the commissioner since he had signed a contract giving the commissioner complete authority over any dispute that he might have with his team and that the commissioner's decision will be "final, binding, unappealable and conclusive."

He has learned through the press that if at the end of his contract he wishes to play for another team all he has to do is play out "his" option. He will soon find out, however, that if he does play out the option that he will take a pay cut and, at the end of the rainbow, will find that no other teams will sign him to a contract because of what is known as the "Rozelle Rule".

Only the fortunate survive the first four or five years, since the average career is 4.62 years. In any event, if he escapes a career-ending injury, his chances of moving to another team are almost non-existent unless that club wishes to trade him or unless the club has fired him. That is the life of the professional athlete under the system created by the twenty-six owners of the National Football League. The union has never had input into any of these rules, practices or restrictions. While at one time the union agreed that the commissioner would be the arbitrator, it made no difference since if they failed to reach agreement on that subject, the commissioner is the arbitrator under the Standard Player Contract.

Who signs the Standard Player Contract? The answer is that everyone who wants to play in the National Football League *must* sign a Standard Player Contract. If he does not, the commissioner of the National Football League will not allow the player to perform in the league and if the player doubts that, he is referred to Joe Kapp who was denied access to the National Football League because of his refusal to sign a printed standard-form contract. That contract gives all power and authority to the club and the league, while guaranteeing the player almost nothing.

HISTORY OF THE RESERVE CLAUSE

On July 24, 1957, the Antitrust Subcommittee of the Committee on the Judiciary, met to consider the relationship of the antitrust laws to organized professional football. The catalyst was the Supreme Court decision, *Radovich* v. *NFL*, which had been handed down on February 25th of that same year. In that case the court held that football was subject to federal antitrust laws as distinguished from baseball which, as you know, is exempt under court decisions. Immediately after *Radovich*, while the case was still on remand to the District Court in the Northern District of California, the club owners sought congressional relief from the *Radovich* decision.

Chairman Celler, in his opening statement, said:

"Unlike baseball, however, where the reserve clause applies throughout the playing life of the performer, the reserve clause in football is *limited to two years*." (Emphasis added.)

What the owners sought was exemption for the football reserve clause, common draft, the powers of the commissioner, as well as territorial restrictions. Fortunately, Congress refused to exempt those matters.

Since that hearing some eighteen years ago, much has happened. The football "reserve clause" has been unilaterally changed by the owners to make it nearly indistinguishable from the baseball reserve clause in practice. Congress exempted the NFL from antitrust laws for the pooling of television rights and exempted the merger of the American Football League and the National Football League. The popularity of the game, as well as the economic power of the owners, have grown tremendously since those hearings in 1957. In a real sense, football as discussed in 1957 was a different industry from that which we discuss here this morning.

ROZELLE RULE

Three years after those hearings were held in 1957, the National Football League had a bigger problem than *Radovich* to contend with. The American Football League was born. For the first time in over a decade, there was limited competition for player services. The competition was limited to two teams—one from the AFL and one from the NFL since both leagues drafted players and thus restricted competition for any one player to one team per league. Thus, Kermit Alexander was drafted by both the Denver Broncos of the American Football League and San Francisco of the National Football League, but he could not ask the Los Angeles Rams to bid for his services, nor could he ask the Kansas City Chiefs to bid for his services, since all recognized the exclusive rights of the Broncos and the 49ers to his services.

Despite the fact that a player could play out the team's option and become a "free agent" in both the AFL and the NFL, there was a *gentlemen's agreement* in both leagues to not sign another team's "free agent". Thus, the only time in a player's career that he could play one bid off against another was at the start of that career. When he is most vulnerable, when he is most naive about negotiating contracts and when he is simply glad to have been selected.

In addition to the other restrictions, it was clear that the National Football League would boycott players who signed with AFL teams and that AFL teams would not sign players who were currently under contract to NFL teams.

There was no "raiding" by either the NFL of the AFL for the first several years of the AFL's life. In 1963 the NFL announced that any vested player who signed with an AFL team would lose his pension rights if the commissioner so decided. Thus, there was great pressure on players to remain within the "NFL family", and no way to get in for a player who first signed with the AFL.

From the point of view of National Football League owners, a terrible thing happened in 1963. Carroll Rosenbloom, Baltimore Colt owner, broke the gentlemen's agreement and signed R. C. Owens to a contract to play for the Baltimore Colts. Owens had played out the San Francisco 49ers' option the previous year, and he was thus a "free agent". Rosenbloom signed him to a contract and panic broke out. Now a veteran player could actually sell his services to another team *within* the National Football League. NFL public relations releases stating that the option clause was "better for the player than the reserve clause in baseball" were, heaven forbid, coming true. I am certain that had hearings been held at that time, club owners or their commissioner, would have explained that "free agent" doesn't really mean "free agent". They had simply forgotten to mention the gentlemen's agreement during the 1957 testimony. They forgot to ask the Committee to "exempt our gentlemen's agreement not to sign free agents" along with the draft and the option clause.

How to deal with the Rosenbloom problem was the question plaguing NFL owners. There was no concern about player rights, no one suggested meeeting with the NFL Players Association, no one came to Congress to seek exemption for a new reserve clause. They quietly adopted a new provision now called the Rozelle Rule.

The Rozelle Rule states:

"Any player, whose contract with a League club has expired, shall thereupon become a free agent and shall no longer be considered a member of the team of that club following the expiration date of such contract. Whenever a player, becoming a free agent in such manner, thereafter signed a contract with a different club in the League, then, unless mutually satisfactory arrangements have been concluded between the two League clubs, the Commissioner may name and then award to the former club one or more players, from the Active, Reserve, or Selection List (including future selection choices) of the acquiring club as the Commissioner in his sole discretion deems fair and equitable; and such decision by the Commissioner shall be final and conclusive."

Because of the success of the AFL, salaries for all players were increasing and no one seemed to even notice the adoption of the Rule. No one outside of the "club" understood the ramifications of the Rule until after Congress had exempted the NFL–AFL merger.

It is interesting to examine the reasons for the merger. In our view, the merger occurred because of a decision by the American Football League to negotiate contracts with established NFL players—primarily quarterbacks. This decision, similar to the Rosenbloom signing of R. C. Owens, means that there would be true competition for veteran players. This thought was startling to the National Football League owners. When Wellington Mara signed Pete Gogolak, a Buffalo Bill "free agent," real competition was just around the corner for veteran players as well as rookies. This drove all concerned to decide that it was time to merge, reassert the league's control of players, implement the option clause-Rozelle Rule, have a common draft, and once again rob players of all freedom for all time. The rest is obvious to this Committee since the Committee was attempting to continue hearings on the matter when Congress exempted the merger from the antitrust laws.

OPERATION OF ROZELLE RULE

David Parks was an outstanding wide receiver with the San Francisco 49ers. In 1966 he played out the club's option and as of May 1, 1967, became a "free agent". New Orleans, the newest franchise, offered a contract to Dave Parks that called for less money than that offered by the 49ers, but he signed it and everyone was happy with the exception of the 49ers.

Kevin Hardy was an outstanding lineman at Notre Dame in 1966. He was voted as the outstanding college lineman and was the first player selected by New Orleans in the common draft. He moved to New Orleans and helped to promote the sale of season tickets, found an off-season job, and looked forward to working for the New Orleans Saints as well as living in the city. One morning in training camp he was informed that Pete Rozelle had sent him to San Francisco as compensation for David Parks. While he threatened legal action, he eventually went to San Francisco. Pete Rozelle also named the first draft pick of New Orleans in 1968 as additional compensation for Parks.

The word was now out. Stay away from "free agents". Now that the merger was completed, Congress had exempted it from the antitrust laws, the gentlemen's agreement could be strictly enforced. The NFL cannot tolerate competition for veteran players—after all, wasn't that the reason for the merger?

Since the Parks-Hardy decision, Rozelle has had to act in only a few cases. The reason is obvious to us—clubs are afraid to sign players because of the unknown compensation to be named by Rozelle. The same year as Parks, the Redskins signed Pat Fischer and Rozelle named two draft choices. In 1972, no team would sign Dick Gordon, all-pro wide receiver from the Chicago Bears; and thus Rozelle named a first round draft choice in 1974 as compensation and immediately the Rams signed Gordon to a contract. In 1975, Carroll Rosenbloom signed Ron Jessie who had played out the Detroit option, and Rozelle named Cullen Bryant, a veteran running back, as compensation for Jessie. Bryant and his attorneys applied for a temporary restraining order and Judge Warren Ferguson granted that TRO and stated that the Rozelle Rule appears to violate Section 1 of the Sherman Act. Rozelle backed down and named a draft choice as well as future considerations to Detroit, instead of Cullen Bryant.

Since it then seemed clear that veteran players could not be named as compensation, George Allen signed Dave Butz and Al Davis of Oakland signed Ted Hendricks to contracts. The "gentlemen's agreement" was again in jeopardy.

NEW EXEMPTION

The owners were unsuccessful in 1957 and 1958 in obtaining antitrust immunity from Congress for the reserve clause. Thus far the federal courts have ruled that the Rule violates the antitrust laws. They have now turned to the players' union for antitrust immunity denied them by Congress and the courts. Since labor has an exemption from the antitrust laws, the owners now demand that the union approve the Rozelle Rule, agree to defend it in court, eliminate the right of players in our collective bargaining unit to test the rule in federal court, and thus give to the owners the long-denied antitrust immunity for their restrictive practices.

We respectfully decline. Nevertheless, unless Congress reaches out to redress the balance that it has upset through the granting of two exemptions to the owners, sooner or later the National Football League will force the union to accept the Rozelle Rule. The NFL takes pride in the fact that there has been only one fully litigated case involving football's reserve clause. The reason is obvious to us. Twenty-six millionaire owners divide equally the costs of litigation. No player can personally afford to take on the economic strength of the NFL owners. Economic strength granted to them by the Congress of the United States. Economic strength that gives them the power to engage in group boycotts of players without any fear of retaliation. Economic strength to crush the players' union.

We believe that the Congress must move to undo the damage that has been done by the merger of the two leagues. By adoption of this legislation, it will at least give the player an opportunity, *at one point in his career*, to negotiate a contract openly and honestly with other employers. It will not destroy the league. It will allow players to have freedom of choice and will take from the club owners that incredible power that they now exercise over the rights of their employees. If it raises salaries, so be it. The Congress of the United States cannot continue to allow the employers in professional sports to continue depriving people of their liberty based on hollow arguments of "competitive balance" without any proof that any of the restrictive measures has anything to do with the success or failure of franchises in the National Football League.

The history of professional sports is a sad chapter in American history. The National Football League recently has offered a $5,000 scholarship to the student who can best explain the contribution of the National Football League in American history. This is part of the Bicentennial celebration. If we were to write that essay we would say that the NFL's contribution to American history is to demonstrate that unbridled economic power can be used to crush a union, deprive people of their liberty, eliminate their rights of free speech and justify group boycotts. The reserve system in professional sports is plain and simply an outrage.

THE SUPERSTARS

The NFLPA would have to be crazy to sponsor litigation or legislation to aid only the superstars. It has been charged that elimination of the Rozelle Rule will help only the superstar and will actually hurt the journeyman players. We say nonsense. The only people who can take advantage of the reserve system *now* are the superstars, such as Joe Namath or Kareem Jabbar. They can threaten not to play. The journeyman threatens retirement and the next thing you know he is retired!

Elimination of the rule is designed to help the journeyman—not the superstar.

We wish to thank you, Mr. Chairman, for this opportunity to express our views on this important topic.

Professional Sports:
the view of the owners

PETE ROZELLE

Now, what are these so-called player restraint issues in the NFL? The NFL players' union has an understandable tendency to think of the structure of football as oriented to the owners' interests and against the interests of the players. But this, in my opinion, is simply not so. Football is nothing more than a form of entertainment. If the entertainment level is kept high, everybody benefits. The spectacular rise in player salaries and in player employment benefits and opportunities over the last decade or more is directly related to the entertainment value of the game—the money paid for TV rights, the number of fans willing to purchase tickets, the levels of ticket prices. As the total package has grown, player benefits have not only grown with it, players are getting an even larger share of the total pie.

That is what all the player controls in professional football are all about—to bring about a dispersion of the more talented players among all of the teams, so that on any given Sunday, the outcome of each contest is in doubt.

When small boys get together for sandlot baseball or football, they choose captains and then let the captains choose alternatively among the players. If they did not do this, the stronger players would all end up on the same team. The game would be of little interest to even the players, and certainly not to spectators. All the player controls in the NFL, and an even larger number of NFL rules having nothing to do with players—are designed to produce this balancing effect; the squad limits, the player selection system, the waiver system—the latter two principles giving the least successful teams the first choice of available talent—the no-tampering rules, the contract controls, and the compensation rule for option playouts.

The objective is not, as the league's critics so often suggest, to deprive players of bargaining opportunities or to require players to play out their

---

SOURCE: An excerpt from the testimony of Pete Rozelle, Commissioner of the National Football League, before the Subcommittee on Monopolies and Commercial Law of the Committee on the Judiciary, House of Representatives, *Rights of Professional Athletes*, Serial No. 59 (Washington, D.C.: U.S. Government Printing Office, 1975).

careers with losing teams. The purpose is to bring about a league where there are no Siberias; where all teams have a roughly equal run at the championship, roughly equal payrolls, and roughly equal employment opportunities.

An unqualified free market for players would destroy all of this; playing field equality, fan interest, TV values, and even the league as we know it. Under such conditions, the league would be down to 10 or so teams in a matter of years.

The players' reaction to these rules is not unnatural. But this reaction has elements of contradiction. What many players desire is freedom from these rules for themselves as individuals, with considerably less thought being given to the fact that this privilege would necessarily have to be accorded to all other players as well. Moreover, they want the lucrative salaries, the national attention, and the extraordinary fringe benefits which the present system of football affords. But they do not like the necessity of having to bear personally any of the results of this structure.

Another factor influencing player views comes from the fact that professional football players are basically transients. Few players view themselves as permanently identified with football in an employment sense. But the league's present rules have brought the game to where it is today, and current players are the beneficiaries of the league's past methods of operation. Still, most current players have not been through the process of the league's development, and do not necessarily appreciate how the league arrived at its present position.

The basic objective of the league rules is to reverse the process by which the weak clubs get weaker and the strong clubs get stronger; that is, to transform losers into winners over the cycle. The league cannot legislate good management, but it can legislate operating principles where each club has at least the opportunity to succeed. A San Diego or a Green Bay club may be down today, but such clubs have at least the prospect of getting up tomorrow under the existing rules.

No realist can really question pro football's need for some sort of device, such as the NFL player selection system, for spreading available talent throughout the league in some sort of rough balance. If one accepts this, all of the other rules of professional football follow as a matter of course.

If you turned everything loose, the number of future players who could find employment in professional football would be drastically reduced. Overall player income would go down. Unsuccessful clubs would have no sources of income to maintain their player payrolls at their present levels, and after payment of some liquidation dividends, only a few players would be benefited.

It is not at all unreasonable to suggest that in a totally free market, those players who complain the most about the league rules would actually be earning less money in professional football, or no money at all. I am personally convinced, for example, that many current player critics would never have been able to obtain employment in the NFL if it had not been for the NFL's equalization rules.

Professional football's rules, which give a player relief from the no-tampering rules and the opportunity to make his own deal by playing out his option, have long been the least restrictive rules in professional sports. A district judge in New York noted a few years back that professional football's rules are considerably more liberal than those of baseball. A district judge in Philadelphia recently spoke of the picture of relative openness and availability of players in professional football. Other leagues have recently moved in the direction of the more relaxed rules long effective in the NFL, at least one with the full approval of its players association.

NFL clubs compete with each other bitterly—on the playing field, and within the confines of the established rules. Indeed, clubs are experts at finding loopholes in the established rules which they can exploit to their own competitive advantage. From time to time, it has been necessary for clubs as a group to close out these loopholes, in the interest of a balanced league and equality of playing field competition. For example, the practice of certain stronger clubs such as Green Bay in drafting red shirts during the 1960's enabled them to stockpile future players in the circumstance where weaker clubs were not in a position to do so. As a result, the league banned the drafting of red-shirted college players until they had actually completed their college football careers.

The league has also taken action to ban similar abuses in the area of unlimited taxi squads and minor league affiliations, practices which in the past had enabled certain NFL clubs to maintain control over a significant number of nonactive players through minor league contracts or through unlimited numbers of future contracts.

You cannot isolate these rules one from another. They all tie to the same theme. In order for the player selection system to have the desired equalization effect, there must be league operating principles which at least accord the club which drafted him some roughly equivalent player rights in return. Similarly, squad limits prevent stockpiling. The waiver rules give first choice rights to the down clubs, and the option playout rules seek to preserve the balancing effects which the player selection system makes effective.

The entire history of professional football supports the importance of these rules. Leagues do not come and go, and one sport does not gain on another, because of the superiority of their stronger teams. Favorable results are the product of the degree to which each league can stabilize itself through its own competitive balance, and league-wide club income potential.

The World Football League has illustrated what can happen when a football league ignores these principles. So, also, did the experience of the All-American Conference, which collapsed primarily because the Cleveland Browns dominated that league to such a degree that fan interest was destroyed. By the end of that cycle, fans were not even attending Brown games.

And what kind of a league have the NFL player rules and other team equalization rules managed to produce? We now have a league which has staged nine Super Bowl Games. Those nine Super Bowl games have produced seven different winning teams, only one of which—the New York Jets—was from a really major U.S. city.

We have a league which, during the last 20 years, has produced shifting cycles of glamour teams, teams which college and veteran players are anxious and eager to affiliate with. These have included the Cleveland Browns in the 1950's, the Baltimore Colts of the late 1950's and early 1960's, the Green Bay Packers of the mid-1960's, the Miami Dolphins of the early 1970's, and now the Pittsburgh Steelers.

The way things are going, Buffalo, which openly accepts the fact that it would never have survived as a football franchise if it had not been for the 1966 single league plan and congressional assistance, may well turn out to be the league's next glamour team. They are right now 4 and 0.

We also have a league where, during the 1974 season, exactly one-half of all the regular season games, played in 26 different cities throughout 14 weekends, were decided by 7 points or less. We have a league where coaches and general managers commonly accept the fact that no team in the league is more than three or four players from developing a team headed for the playoffs.

We have a league where the networks are willing to give equal television coverage to the games of each team of the league, and guarantee the home team fans of each team the away games of the home club. And these regional network patterns, the only ones in sports, now cost the networks approximately $100,000 in production and line costs for each game presented, which is a heck of a cost when it is applied to each of 12 Sunday telecasts.

And we offer an entertainment medium which can compete with All In The Family on Monday night telecasts, with the network which purchases this NFL program not even having the contract right to determine which NFL games are presented.

And what has this meant to NFL players? In 1959, the NFL operated with 12 teams. In 1976, the NFL will operate with 28 teams. As recently as 1957, the NFL player squad limit was 32. Today, the NFL squad limit is

43, with these squad limits spread over more than double the number of teams.

Thus, the number of player employees within the NFL has more than tripled within the last 15 years. In 1946—and you showed some interest in finances; I will touch on some—in 1946, the annual total of regular season salaries for the Pittsburgh Steelers team was $100,000. During the heyday of the championship Browns teams of the 1950's, they had a total payroll of $250,000. In 1974, the Steelers' payroll for regular season salaries alone for one season was over $2 million.

Lamar Hunt testified in the Minneapolis litigation that the player payroll of the Kansas City Chiefs in 1974 was twice what it was in 1969, just 5 years earlier. This was right during the merger period before the evolution of the World Football League, or its impact on the Kansas City Chiefs in any event—double the payroll during the year when the Chiefs won the Super Bowl.

Lou Groza was one of professional football's all-time greats. He had a salary of $5,000 in 1946. By 1960, his 15th year in professional football, his base salary had risen to $15,000. In 1974, another NFL tackle—who, incidentally, was not also a placekicker, as Mr. Groza was—before he negotiated upward his most recent contract, had a contract salary of $120,000 a year.

Don Shula was a veteran starting defensive back for an NFL championship team in 1957. His contract salary for that year, which included the preseason, was $9,700. Today, marginal players in the NFL receive salaries which bear no relation to these figures. I know of one uninjured NFL player who received more than $60,000 for exactly one reception during an entire regular season.

In 1953, Chuck Noll, presently coach of the world champion Pittsburgh Steelers, as a player in the NFL's only playoff game, received $700. In the following year, when his team won the NFL championship, he received $1,500. Today, the NFL member clubs have offered to guarantee the members of the team which wins the Super Bowl in future years a minimum of at least $31,500 for their three-game postseason participation.

In 1960, the NFL had no player pension plan. Today, it functions with a noncontributory pension plan, providing extraordinary benefits. Under the management council's most recent proposal, a 10-year player would receive, at age 65, and on a guaranteed basis, annual pension compensation of $37,421. In 1964, during the period of intense competition between the NFL and the AFL, AFL clubs averaged total player costs of $710,000 a year. NFL clubs averaged somewhat higher. In 1974, the NFL club average player costs—which included all of the former AFL clubs, and two additional franchises—roughly quadrupled, to a $2,933,000 average per club.

In 1964, total average NFL club player cost was 36.9 percent of total average NFL club gross income. This figure rose to 45.4 percent in 1974—and incidentally, as well as testifying before you today, a congressional committee, with these figures, these figures have also been given in Federal court in Minneapolis.

Meanwhile, average NFL club profits, expressed as a percentage of average club total income, have declined markedly since 1966, the last year of the NFL-AFL competitive warfare.

These dramatic increases in job opportunities offered by the NFL, and the equally dramatic rise in player compensation levels during the last decade, are overwhelmingly attributable to one thing; the hold which NFL football managed to acquire on the American public—not on Pete Rozelle, not on Ed Garvey, not on any individual player—but collectively, the hold which this sport was able to establish with the American public. That hold was not found. It was created by some 50 years of trial and error and league experimentation, directed at improving the entertainment qualities of NFL football games.

The present employment market for the professional football player is entirely a product of those circumstances. In the late 1920's, Babe Ruth, operating under the lifetime contract holds provided in baseball, obtained a salary of $85,000, which was somewhat more than that paid the President of the United States. During that same period, a professional football player was doing well to earn $50 a game.

Today, we have professional football players earning more than the President of the United States. The American soccer or lacrosse professional today, regardless of his talents, cannot even aspire to the NFL salary minimums. The differences are simply the levels of fan interest. The NFL must have been doing something right with respect to its game, and with respect to its players, since those early days, to produce the six-figure salary levels which are becoming increasingly common in professional football.

What I am suggesting is that those who would liberate the professional league athlete from his so-called bondage ought to consider whether, in doing so, they are also liberating him from his present employment potential and job opportunities. No Federal law can guarantee the survival of the dozen or so NFL franchises which could not survive open market conditions within the NFL. No Federal law can guarantee the league's continued operation with 43-man squads, or the continued network willingness to pay large sums annually for NFL games, or the present levels of ticket-buying interest in 26 cities.

The professional athlete's interests are thus just as much identified with the entertainment aspects of his business as are the interests of his employers. Players may say that interests other than money will determine their choice of team in a wholly unqualified free market. That may be true today, where the league functions with 26 teams having roughly comparable payrolls, a chance for a successful season, an adequate supporting cast, and roughly equal employment opportunities at each franchise location. But eliminate the league's equalization rules, and no realistic choice would actually exist.

The difference? The difference would be the difference between Shreveport and Los Angeles, and between guaranteed salary payments and exposure to contract claims in bankruptcy proceedings.

One other circumstance is of major importance. The immediate response of the antitrust mind is in the direction of a series of assumptions derived from experience in other business fields; that is, that the NFL member clubs stand in the relation of horizontal business competitors to one another, that the league office is the equivalent of a businessman's trade association, that all limitations on player freedom of movement were conceived for the purpose of depressing player salaries, that such limitations are preserved solely as cost-saving devices, and that player interests are wholly unrelated to such limitations.

In fact, none of this is so, in my opinion. The NFL is nothing more than a joint venture operation among its member clubs, directed at the presentation of a form of popular entertainment. Because it is entertainment, methods have to be achieved for insuring that it is successful entertainment; and the only method of producing that form of entertainment is on a joint venture basis.

NFL franchises are neither conceived of, nor intended to be, business competitors of one another. The Dallas Cowboys and the Washington Redskins have no business interest in defeating each other in a business sense. It is just as much in the Cowboys' interest, or the Cardinals' interest, to have the Redskins as one of the teams they regularly play, home and away, functioning as a successful business operation, as it is for its own team to do so, because the television revenues of games between them are shared equally by all teams of the league, and because road-game receipts are of almost equal importance to an NFL team's income picture.

Even the Redskins' ability to draw fans at the Cowboys' home games is a matter of business importance to the Cowboys. In fact, if the Dallas Cowboys should be unable to meet their player payroll, or if that team experienced bankruptcy—an unlikely event, in light of Mr. Murchison's ownership—the Redskins would be routinely expected to contribute to the Cowboys' payroll payments. I cite this, Mr. Seiberling, as an example of Goodrich and Goodyear. I do not think if Goodyear had problems that Goodrich would help Goodyear with their player payroll. Again, just one distinction that we are talking about here today in professional sports, as against the normal business entity.

And, if the Redskins' team should be decimated by a plane accident, the league's rules would require the Cowboys, along with the other NFL teams, to assign to the Redskins a sufficient number of their own player contracts to enable the Redskins to continue to field a representative team. This is simply not the relationship which exists between Macy's and Gimbel's, or between two Washington law firms, or between Esso and Gulf. NFL teams are partners, not business competitors.

The business context in which the NFL player rules operate is therefore quite unusual. The NFL maintains a team in Washington and a team in Baltimore, and two teams in New York and in the Bay area, on one assumption; that the teams do not, in fact, compete with one another in a business sense. If it were established that damaging competitive effects are produced by these situations, it would not be in the interest of either of the teams, or of the league itself, to maintain these situations.

These partnership aspects of NFL functioning touch every phase of each NFL club's operations, and represent the principal business of the league itself. The league is designed to permit NFL franchises to compete with one another, but on two planes only; on the playing field, where the fans' primary interest lies, and in the exercise of management skills within the league's equalization rules, for the purpose of fielding the most successful team.

The NFL believes that the fans are involved in this latter form of competition as well, as the hanging of coaches in effigy occasionally suggests. But there are neither fan interests, league interests, city interests, or franchise interests in simple, pocket-book competition for successful football teams. The very business context in which these NFL player rules operate, therefore, needs to be basically rethought. There is nothing whatever to suggest that the NFL clubs would be willing to continue to act as partners on all other phases of their operations while they are compelled to eat their young in one of their most significant areas of operation.

Of the three fundamental interests involved in professional sports—the interests of the fans, the players, and the clubs—none can be permitted to have full sway. The owners have their investments to protect. The players have their collective bargaining and contract interests to pursue. But it is the American public which ultimately determines the levels of rewards to all concerned.

The bottom-line premise of all antitrust law is that some ultimate public benefit can be expected to flow from the open, competitive process imposed on American business generally, either in reduced consumer prices or improved consumer service. But the proposal before this committee would have exactly the opposite effect. Public disadvantage, and even player disadvantage, can be routinely expected in terms of franchises lost to various NFL cities, reduced operations nationally, smaller team squads, lost municipal stadium tenants, declining TV and fan interest, lost job opportunities, and higher ticket prices at least until the declines set in.

In short, I do not view the present bill as designed to serve the public interest, but as one to disadvantage it.

The Economic Benefits of Professional Team Ownership: monopoly and subsidy

RAY KENNEDY AND NANCY WILLIAMSON

FACT: The professional sports industry is a self-regulating monopoly.

Monopoly. Antitrust. Restraint of trade. For years those loaded words have been lobbed like mortar rounds at the oak-paneled bunkers of sports management. Monopolistic control is the cornerstone on which the sports industry has been built and from which all of its benefits, both financial and competitive, are derived. Moreover, it is the only self-regulated monopoly in America. Unlike the broadcasting and airline industries, whose monopolistic practices are regulated by the Federal Communications Commission and the Federal Aviation Administration, respectively, the sports business has been left to referee itself.

To understand how and why this comfy arrangement has come about takes some hacking through legal and political thickets, but the trip is worth it. Suffice it to say that this Fact is so crucial to Moneyball that the fan should forget the boom-a-lackas and concentrate on a new mantra: *mo-nop-o-ly, mo-nop-o-ly.*

SOURCE: Three excerpts from Part I of a three-part series by Ray Kennedy and Nancy Williamson, "Money: The Monster Threatening Sports," *Sports Illustrated* (July 17, 1978), pp. 35–38; 54–57; and 71–72.

Many owners, even protective of their Boardwalks and Park Places, strive mightily to convince the public that they are playing some other game. They have their own chants. Jerry Hoffberger does whole oratorios, equating his needy Orioles with the Baltimore City Orchestra as a community cultural asset. In Gene Klein's rhapsody, his San Diego Chargers are not engaged in anything so crass as turning a buck; they are, he says, celebrating an "art form." Usually, though, the monopolists fall back on a classic all-purpose fudge that was first used in baseball: "It is too much of a sport to be a business and too much of a business to be a sport."

The sports industry is indeed schizoid. While, financially speaking, General Motors does not care one toot if it drives Ford into the emergency lane, the Montreal Canadiens have a lot to lose by overwhelming the Washington Capitals on the ledger books as well as on the ice. Rivals in combat, they are also partners in a group venture called the NHL.

Just as you cannot be a bully if there is no one to pick on, a team obviously cannot flourish if it drives all or most of its rivals out of business. So the big guys theoretically have to pull their punches; they slap the little guys around just enough to keep them in their places, but no so hard as to put them away for good. Unless, of course, some pip-squeak rival league tries to invade the big guys' turf. Then, watch out, because that's when the heavyweights in the established league go for the clubs and tire chains.

Thus the owners are tugged in two directions at once. To keep their cross-purposes from clashing requires a pliancy and objectivity that few of them possess. To protect themselves from one another, therefore, the owners operate as a cartel, an economic entity in which a group of firms (teams) within the same industry (league) make agreements on matters of mutual interest (rules, expansion, promotion, schedules, etc.). Such agreements are illegal in most other U.S. businesses, because they tend to lead to nasty things like collusion, price-fixing and restraint of trade.

Unregulated as they are, owners ask that the public accept their actions as being in good faith. Critics like Ohio Congressman John Seiberling are unwilling to grant that acceptance. An antitrust lawyer and one of the many federal legislators who have introduced bills that would put an end to the owners' monopolistic privileges, Seiberling says, "Whenever artificial barriers are created to the normal forces of the marketplace and free enterprise, the American people end up paying a higher price and getting less of the commodity."

All of which gives rise to the big question about the sports industry: is it a sport and, therefore, something so unique that its survival requires special hands-off treatment under the law; or is it a business and, therefore, something so commercial that it should be subject to the same restraints imposed on other profit-making enterprises? Asked that very question during a congressional hearing, Bowie Kuhn, scrambling like a runner caught between third and home, concluded, "We are a sports business."

Baseball has good reason for wanting to have it both ways. By a venerable decree of the United States Supreme Court, it is the only professional sport that is exempted from antitrust laws. Because the reasons for this singular honor have long confounded the nation's legislators and the Justice Department's lawyers, pro football, basketball and hockey have also benefited, by default, from the same exemption. Explains Congressman Frank Horton of New York, a member of the 1976 House Select Committee on Professional Sports, "Basically, all four sports enjoy an immunity—baseball because it is immune by judicial decision, and the others because the executive branch and the Justice Department just have not really followed up and tried to enforce the antitrust laws. . . ."

Not that government officials agree that sports deserve controversial privileges. Hear the testimony of U.S. Deputy Assistant Attorney General Joe Sims, an antitrust specialist, before the 1976 House Select Committee on Professional Sports: "I know of no economic or other data which supports in any way the conclusion that professional sports should be exempted from the antitrust laws. . . . In the absence of such evidence, our belief is that the exemption should be terminated; and indeed should never have been started and wouldn't have been except for a misinterpretation of the commerce clause."

How this "misinterpretation" shaped the future of the nation's professional pastimes is one of the more bizarre chapters in American jurisprudence. It dates back to a 1922 U.S. Supreme Court decision on a suit brought against organized baseball by one of the teams in the short-lived Federal League. The suit charged that the National and American Leagues had conspired to kill off the new rival by buying out its teams and monopolizing the player market. The opinion, written by Justice Oliver Wendell Holmes, said that the business of baseball was not interstate commerce but rather the giving of local exhibitions. Thus the sport was immune to the antitrust laws. "Not one of Mr. Justice Holmes' happiest days," a fellow member of the Supreme Court later remarked. Although the antitrust laws were subsequently broadened to include all manner of exhibitions, ranging from ballet to boxing; although baseball has grown and prospered to the point where its commerce is not only interstate but also international; and although Holmes' decision has been retested five times in the Supreme Court, the original decision has held firm.

The Court's reluctance to reverse itself stems from its thinking that, however unsound the 1922 ruling, a sudden change now might be a greater injustice to an industry that for decades has been allowed to develop on the basis of that decision. Indeed, several owners have testified that the antitrust exemption was one of the major reasons they bought into baseball. And for baseball's proprietors it has conveniently happened that Congress, the other branch of the government that might have worked to rectify the big misinterpretation, has been reluctant to enact remedial legislation.

Which is not to say that Congress has not busied itself pondering the antitrust question; it's just that lobbyists for the sports industry have been even busier. The congressional debate on curtailing pro sports' exemption has been droning on for more than half a century. And though there have been 11 hearings, more than 70 bills and enough hot air to levitate a zeppelin in the past two decades alone, the net result is zero. Or more precisely, minus two. The only sports antitrust laws ever enacted by Congress, the 1961 Sports Broadcast Act, which enriched the teams by allowing them to bargain for TV money as a group, and the 1966 Football Merger Act, which ended the salary war between the NFL and AFL by permitting the two leagues to merge, granted the sports industry further exemptions not enjoyed by most other businesses.

Nevertheless, Congress figures to go on making threatening noises for three reasons. First, while politicians' utterances on most other issues get little or no play in the media, their comments on sports are all but guaranteed to receive publicity that is instant, wide and generally favorable. Second, according to one congressional assistant, some of the pols are genuinely concerned "whether the fans are getting screwed, and if there is anybody protecting their interests." And, third, many Congressmen are just plain angry that Washington no longer has a major league baseball team.

Still, Congress figures to keep its long record of indecisiveness on the antitrust issue intact, because, compared to inflation and the threat of war in the Middle East, alleged transgressions in the sports business are not exactly issues of burning congressional concern, and because there is no great public outcry for reform.

In sum, says Professor Lionel Sobel, author of *Professional Sports and the Law*, the mishandling of the big misinterpretation has been an "embarrassing comedy of errors involving the Congress and Supreme Court, and some shrewd tactics on the part of major league executives."

So what does all this have to do with the guy munching on a cold hot dog in the far reaches of Section K? Everything. Under the structure that has evolved from the big misinterpretation, the owners not only have the power to make, change and, through the office of a commissioner whom they hire and fire, enforce the rules of Moneyball, but they also control the time, place, number, quality and price of the games that the Section K fan pays to see. These unique monopolistic rights have left it to the owners to determine whether their pursuit of private gain is also for the public good.

These rights are also the target of forces that have lately been zeroing in on three major areas in which management has established restrictions on competition. They are: (1) the distribution of franchises, (2) the sale of broadcast rights and (3) the movement of players. In fact, the current big money war in sports is the result of several recent direct hits by the players' unions on the barriers that restrain player movement. However, the other two restricted zones have so far proved largely impervious to attack.

And management aims to keep them that way, arguing that restrictions on the business side are necessary to maintain free-wheeling competition on the playing field. Critics like Ed Garvey, executive director of the football players' union, call that the old "best-interest-of-the game" dodge. "When the owners say that," Garvey says, "the 'game' means the business, and the business means the 'best interest' of those who own those teams." Garvey protests too loudly, according to economist Roger Noll, because the only way the owners can afford to pay higher salaries is by protecting the monopoly rights that insure greater income. Noll says, "In most cases, the interests of the players coincide with the interests of the owners, and both tend to benefit from the restrictive practices that are costly to fans."

Territorial rights, Noll adds, are "perhaps the most egregious wrong of all the monopolistic practices in professional sports. . . . The number of franchises can be controlled by owners, who can dole them out, just as any other monopolist would, creating a contrived scarcity. Many more cities could support teams if the supply were not limited. In recent years, as sports have become more popular, the response of the monopolist has been predictable—ticket prices go up and up and up. In a competitive industry, higher ticket prices induce new firms to compete, but the monopolist simply takes in higher revenues. Now the owners share in the take with the players and the union. The financing looks good, but the fan is being ripped off."

Remember, *mo-nop-o-ly, mo-nop-o-ly.*

FACT: Pro teams are lucrative tax havens.

"It is almost impossible not to make money on a baseball club when you are buying it new because, unless you become inordinately successful, you pay no income tax," Bill Veeck confessed in *The Hustler's Handbook*, published in 1965. "It is, in fact, quite possible for a big league club to go on forever without *ever* paying any income tax.

"Look, we play *The Star-Spangled Banner* before every game. You want us to pay income taxes, too?"

Veeck should know. Early in his career, while studying accounting at night and dreaming up new ways to promote baseball by day, he hit on a wild idea. No, not the midget batter, but a gimmick of far greater consequence. Traditionally when an investor bought a team the players were considered part of the inventory, an existing asset like the shipping crates full of finished products in a widget company's warehouse.

Veeck's brainstorm was to buy the players' contracts in separate transactions and thereby make them a depreciable asset. The idea, which others later refined into an arcane science, was to arrange it so that the buyer could *depreciate* the cost of the players under the same tax laws and in the same manner that a farmer writes off his breeding cattle. After all, the theory goes, players depreciate in value—or get "used up"—just as aging bulls or creaky machines do.

When word of the Veeck variation swept through the offices of pro sports in the early 1960s, it was as if one of his exploding scoreboards had gone off in the accounting department. Some measure of the eventual impact of his idea can be gained from the fact that since 1959 football, baseball, basketball and hockey franchises have swelled from 42 to 101. A big reason for the increase was the desire of rich investors to take advantage of this sports tax shelter; no other industry in the land assigns a value to its employees and then writes them off as depreciable assets.

When an investor buys a team, he acquires two basic assets, player contracts and a bundle of monopoly rights called the franchise. The franchise is an intangible, non-depreciable asset; not only is its useful life span indeterminate but also its value, as we have seen, tends to accelerate. While that is another inspiring reason to leap into the sports business, the buyer cannot write off the non-depreciable cost of the franchise to reduce or "shelter" the income from his other businesses. For tax purposes, then, it is to the buyer's advantage to ascribe as small a portion of the purchase price as possible to the cost of the franchise. On many teams' books it is carried at a value of $50,000.

That done, the only things left for the buyer to do are to allocate the rest of the purchase price to the cost of the players and to decide how fast he wants to write that amount off—the span usually ranges from three to seven years. Until a recent revision in the tax laws set down more realistic but still generous guidelines, the buyer was encouraged to use his imagination. Example:

If an owner—let's call him Harry Hypothetical—bought his team for $10 million, allocated 75%, or $7.5 million, of the purchase price to the cost of the players and decided to depreciate them over the customary five years, he would have had a write-off of $1.5 million a year. If Harry was so inept or neglectful (he had other businesses to tend to, mind you, his *real* businesses) that the club showed an operating loss of $500,000 for its first season, for tax purposes the team's total loss would have been $2 million—the $500,000 operating loss plus the $1.5 million in player depreciation. If the team had been incorporated in a certain way (a tax device called a subchapter S corporation is favored) and if Harry, who was making a bundle in his other businesses, was in the 50% tax bracket, then he would have enjoyed a savings of $1 million—50% of the $2 million loss—on his income tax.

And so, after subtracting the out-of-pocket operating loss of $500,000 from the $1 million windfall resulting from player depreciation, there was Harry, decrying the perils of the sports business while palming a half-million-dollar profit. Even if the team had managed to earn an operating profit of $500,000, it still would have shown a book loss of $1 million. And Harry, though $1 million richer, would have been able to plead that, according to his tax records, the team was losing a bundle.

Harry's only problem was that he was being too cautious in assigning a mere 75% to player depreciation. In practice the percentages have been much higher. In 1966, when a group purchased the Milwaukee Braves for about $6.2 million and moved them to Atlanta, they wrote off 99%, which the IRS later brutally slashed to 91.7%.

Then there was the group that bought an NBA expansion franchise for $3 million and, moving in for a quick kill, wrote off 83% of the price on a fast-break schedule of just 18 months. As computed by Benjamin Okner, a government tax expert, this rapid depreciation of players, plus some modest tax advantages accrued from deferred player salaries and some non-cash team expenses, allowed the team to show a book loss of $1.6 million in its first season, while actually earning a $300,000 cash-flow profit. Okner concludes, "If the tax benefit to the owners from the $1.6 million book loss is calculated at a modest 50% tax rate, the $1.6 million loss is converted into a $1.1 million profit!"

And the player depreciation gambit is just for openers. When it came time for Harry Hypothetical to sell—and there was every inducement for him to do so once the depreciation cycle had expired—he could have cashed in on another tax break. As seller, Harry could have reversed the process, allocating 75% of the selling price to the franchise on the grounds that his astute managerial skills had enriched the team and caused its good-will value to soar. This maneuver would have allowed him to write off 75% of the profit from the sale as long-term capital gains, which would be taxed at a rate of about 30%. Meanwhile, the remainder, the suddenly diminished player contracts, would have been subject to something called depreciation recapture, meaning that it would have been taxed at ordinary income rates, which in Harry's case is 50%.

All told, Harry figured to have earned a return on investment that, depending on the sport, ranged from respectable to wow! If he had bought his team in the early boom period of 1962 and sold it in 1967, for example, economist James Quirk has estimated that Harry's rate of return would have been: baseball, 10.4%; basketball, 30.2%; football, 51.0%.

Following a study of pro basketball, economists Okner and Noll warned in 1972 of the "socially undesirable incentives for team owners. Except for a very few teams, the maximum profit a team could hope to earn is a few hundred thousand dollars. This is dwarfed by the tax avoidance made possible by depreciation. The gains to a rich individual or a corporation from owning a team depend very little on the quality of the team or its operations. In fact, among the most profitable teams are the lowly NBA expansion franchises. They field poor teams and do poorly at the gate, but the fast write-off of the expansion fee saves the owners half a million to a million dollars a year in income taxes. According to our conception of the public interest, society would be better served if the profitability of a team depended upon its ability to please the fans, not the tax accountant."

The obvious question about the sports tax shelter is: should public funds contribute to private profit? It is agreed that tax privileges are necessary to preserve pastimes that are of social benefit to a wide spectrum of citizens. Tax shelters are intended to encourage investments in high-risk ventures, the success of which is rewarding to the plungers and public alike. But how special should the tax treatment be—if special at all? When does encouragement to take a leap become license to hit and run?

Evidence indicates that minimizing financial risk maximizes another danger, that of attracting investors who are less interested in contributing to the development of their sport than they are in sheltering their income for a short while and then escaping with a profit. Indeed, the tax advantages tend to add to the value of franchises, thereby increasing the incentive for owners to get in early and get out quick. In fact, franchise values have soared so resolutely in the face of reported book losses that some cynics claim that they can foretell the day when an owner will decide to sell on the basis of his player-depreciation schedule and no other factor.

Dealings have reached that point in some basketball transactions. The 11 teams in the ABA experienced 27 changes of ownership in the league's 10-year history. Even the more established NBA has felt the impact of tax sheltering; between 1963 and 1975, the league had a turnover of 44 owners and principals. In many instances the owners seemed to be getting "used up" faster than the players they were depreciating. While old reliable John Havlicek pumped away like a well-oiled punch press through 16 seasons, eight different sets of Boston Celtic owners were writing him off for a total of more than $1 million in tax savings.

However, if some of the owners' maneuvers seem excessive, so too does the implication that vast numbers of teams have been snapped up in some kind of mad tax-haven boom. For one thing, the number of franchises with long-standing ownership militates against any easy generalizations about fast-buck artists. For another, many teams, particularly in the NFL, are too profitable in and of themselves to be subject to the whims of a quick-turnover market.

Still, the tax-shelter motive is there. It is strong and it has had a big impact on the course of the sports business. But critical to the shelter's future are reforms that evolved from a landmark tax case involving the Atlanta Falcons. When the Falcons joined the NFL in 1966, the owners allotted 91% of the $8.5-million entry fee to player costs. The IRS reduced that portion to 12%, thereby turning a book loss of more than a million dollars into a $1.2 million profit for the Falcons' first two seasons. Appealed and reappealed, the case was not resolved until early this year, when the Supreme Court upheld a ruling that had set the portion allowable for player costs at 38.8%.

Meanwhile, Congress passed the 1976 Tax Reform Act, which tightened the loophole with two half hitches. The act stipulates that the portion of the purchase price that the buyer allocates to player costs cannot exceed the portion allocated by the seller; there can be no more of what the IRS calls "whip-sawing." And it sets a limit on the allowance for player costs at 50%. Beyond that, the burden of proof is on the taxpayer.

While some owners fret that the tax reform might reduce franchise values by as much as one-third, that seems unlikely. There is still considerable room to maneuver under the new shelter—and in Congress, where the professional-sports lobby has been known to rush for a few first downs. Eagle President Jim Murray says, with a note of expectation, "The tax laws change more often than the standings."

But for now, Uncle Sam is only a half partner in the teams.

FACT: Pro teams are subsidized by taxpayers.

In ancient Rome, stadiums were financed by taxes levied on brothels. It was not that the feed bills for the lions were too high—Christians being a glut on the market—nor a question of whether celebrity gladiators would draw all that well. No, stadiums had to be subsidized because they were so inherently unprofitable that no private investors would touch them, least of all the sports promoters. Their money was tied up in superstars like Diocles, a free-agent charioteer who switched stables for a cool 31 million sesterces ($1.8 million). "Decent men groan," wrote some

Roman Ring Lardner, "to see this former slave earn an income that is 100 times that of the entire Roman Senate."

Nothing has changed except that today every taxpayer, be he panderer or prude, foots the bill for his local Colosseum. Stadiums still lose money and decent men still groan, some of them on the floor of the United States Senate.

Four months ago, Senator William Proxmire denounced as a "knuckle-headed ripoff" a deal allowing the Yankees to pay only $170,681 in rent to New York City last year, on a gross of $13.4 million. What the Wisconsin Senator neglected to mention is that his state's major league baseball team, the Brewers, pays only $1 in rent on the first million admissions to Milwaukee County Stadium and only 5% of its gross on the next half million. Last season, with an attendance of 1,114,938 and an average ticket price of $3.68, the Brewers paid the county a mere $21,149, which is perhaps the lowest rent in professional sports. Fact is, all but a few of the teams that perform in public facilities enjoy sweetheart leases that would make Shylock blush.

It is estimated that by charging low rents, forgoing property taxes and paying the stadiums' operating losses, local governments subsidize teams by more than $25 million annually. While some leases involve tricky sliding scales, the average team pays slightly less than 10% of its home gate receipts. Here is a rundown on the rents some teams pay:

NHL HOCKEY

Vancouver Canucks	$508,000
Pittsburgh Penguins	250,000

FOOTBALL

Kansas City Chiefs	$557,633
San Diego Chargers	300,054

BASKETBALL

Golden State Warriors	$300,000
Detroit Pistons	82,000

BASEBALL

Philadelphia Phillies	$1,014,068
Milwaukee Brewers	21,149

In some cases the disparities are offset by other compensations. For example, the Chiefs retained a small percentage of the proceeds from concessions, parking and souvenirs, while the Pistons, who in 1977–78 were in the last year of a contract at Cobo Arena that required them to pay only $2,000 a game, received no income from concessions or parking.

Regardless of the details of the deals between the teams and the landlords, this fact holds true: 70% of the stadiums and arenas used by pro franchises have been built with public funds, and they are piling up an indebtedness that will cost taxpayers some $6 billion through the turn of the 21st century.

Nevertheless, even while construction costs have kept soaring, so, too, has the mania for more grandiose playgrounds. In 1965, Atlanta-Fulton County Stadium was completed at a price of $314 a seat; in 1970, Pittsburgh's Three Rivers Stadium came in at $700 a seat; and in 1975, New Orleans' Superdome cost $2,333 a seat. Operating losses have risen accordingly, and only one public facility, Anaheim Stadium, home of the Angels, claimed a profit ($758) last year. That occurred only because of the income from rock concerts.

There is a rationale for the profligacy. When future archeologists dig along the banks of the San Antonio River, they may unearth the remains of the Convention Center Arena and some of the 6,000 seats that are being added at a cost of $3.7 million. "Aha!" one of the diggers will exlaim, "this was a big league city!" That, at least, seems to be the hope of San Antonio Mayor Lila Cockrell, who is typical of stadium boosters all over the country. In agreeing to a lease that required the Spurs to pay only $500 a game last season—a figure that will gradually increase to $2,400 in 1986— her honor admitted that it was a partial subsidy, but added, "We have a great opportunity in this city through the gaining of national stature on the sports scene. This will help attract industry and assist our economy."

Yes, ma'am. And that's why the Houston Chamber of Commerce has said, "We know of almost no case in which the Astrodome was a factor in a business moving to Houston."

Which is not to say that athletic facilities have no positive impact. Like any industrious society, 20th-century America is bent on erecting monuments to itself. The great railway stations of the 19th century have been superseded by stadiums that look like steel-belted radials lying on their sides. As an extra, some even come complete with hubcaps. Though hardly works of art, they are nonetheless imposing symbols of civic pride and the old can-do spirit. And the Age of the Stadium does contribute to the sporting and economic vitality of a community. As the late Hubert Humphrey once said, without the action at Metropolitan Stadium, the Twin Cities would be a "cold Omaha."

Recent surveys estimate that the Blue Jays' first season at Exhibition Stadium pumped $66 million into the Toronto economy, while the Pirates and their Three Rivers digs generate $21 million annually. "A stadium has to be thought of in more terms than whether it is self-financing," says Expo President Charles Bronfman. "It has to be thought of in terms of what tourist dollars and additional revenue it brings into a city. And in those terms some taxpayer subsidy is warranted, because it does return money and jobs to people."

That's what the former executive director of the Superdome, Bernard Levy, kept saying, even while his stadium showed immense losses. The Superdome had a whopping $11 million deficit in fiscal 1977. Following the Super Bowl bash in the city, Levy exclaimed, "We estimate conservatively that the impact of the Super Bowl on our economy was $25 million to $35 million."

Louisiana voters can be forgiven if they are wary of the numbers game. After all, the modest $35-million, "self-supporting" football stadium that they approved in 1966 turned out to be the "world's largest indoor people-gathering place" with a price tag of more than $300 million, including $130 million in interest charges. Though extravagant in the extreme, the Superdome epitomizes a pattern that has evolved in other cities seeking the big league imprimatur. Understated price. Overstated revenues. Glowing promises. Political maneuvering. Charges of irregularities. Legal roadblocks. Cost overruns. Work stoppages. Delays and more delays.

The citizenry's edifice complex can easily be exploited by teams, and Buffalo, New York and Baltimore are exhibits A, B and C.

The Bills set the pace in 1964 when they threatened to leave town if Civic Stadium was not enlarged. The city complied. In 1970 the NHL Sabres took up residence, but only after the city agreed to add a $12-million balcony to Memorial Auditorium. In addition, the Sabres were granted a generous lease, half the concessions income and free use of the arena's offices. In return they agreed to pay their own telephone bills.

In 1971 the Bills announced that they had "no alternative to moving" unless a new stadium was built. Lest there be any doubt about the seriousness of the team's intentions, it was also made known that owner Ralph Wilson was threatening to go to Seattle and negotiate a transfer. The Erie County legislature gave in, and while Buffalo was still paying for the enlargement of Civic Stadium, the Bills moved into the new $23.5-million Rich Stadium. Says Leslie Foschio, the city's corporation counsel, a "host of serious problems," such as garbage disposal and law enforcement, "were put on the back burner so a major league stadium could be built. The psychological pressure leaves municipalities at a team owner's mercy and with one choice—pay the owner's price for a stadium or get whipsawed."

The Yankees used their cutting edge to good advantage in 1971 by threatening to follow the NFL Giants to New Jersey. They got the city to remodel Yankee Stadium, a job that was supposed to cost $24 million but exceeded $100 million when it was all done.

When George Steinbrenner bought the Yankees from CBS in 1973, the deal included a freshly drawn lease with a humdinger of a clause that allows the team to deduct stadium maintenance costs from its rent. In

1976, when the Yankees grossed $11.9 million in gate receipts and concessions, they theoretically should have paid the city $854,504 in rent. Instead, after maintenance was deducted, the city ended up *owing* the Yankees $10,000. Mayor Ed Koch recently made an appeal on the grounds of "decency," saying that in view of the city's financial plight, "it would be nice if Steinbrenner said, 'We made some and we're going to give some back.'" Steinbrenner replied, "A lease is a lease."

Except in Baltimore, where the Colts, who are opposed to renegotiating players' contracts, nevertheless demanded in 1976 that their Memorial Stadium lease be rewritten. The city not only went along, but also approved a unique two-for-one contract in which the Colts and Orioles pay the same rent. Previously each team had paid a flat 7% of its ticket sales; now the Colts and Orioles figure their rents, and whichever is the lower is the amount that each team pays. As applied retroactively in 1975, the formula allowed the Colts to ante up only $53,000, instead of the $217,000 they would have owed under the old rental deal.

And the beat goes on. In Minneapolis the Vikings and the Twins are pressing for a new $55-million dome, and in Boston Mayor Kevin White is backing a proposed $35-million arena that "would pay for itself." In Seattle, boosters drumming for the construction of the Kingdome brought in luminaries such as Mickey Mantle to back up their claims that the stadium would be a civic asset that would host the "world's most famous entertainers, Presidents of the United States and the great religious leaders of our time." Last week King County won a breach of contract suit against the company that originally signed up to build the Kingdome. The $12.3 million award from that action will cut the stadium's price to about $47 million—a mere $7 million more than the original estimate.

The Business of Team Ownership

D. STANLEY EITZEN

There are a number of reasons that the rich choose to own a professional sports team. Some of the possibilities are fun, excitement, ego fulfillment, power, visibility, personal satisfaction from knowing athletes ("jocksniffing"), vicarious identification as an athlete, another goal to conquer, and community service. These psychic gratifications are typically superseded, however, by financial considerations.[1]

Contemporary professional sport is foremost a business, despite the rhetoric to the contrary. Professional team owners and their spokespersons continually argue before the courts and Congress and in the media that their activity is a sport and should receive special treatment such as exemption from antitrust laws, special tax benefits, and subsidized arenas. The truth is that sports teams are profit-seeking and profit-maximizing organizations whose contribution to the community is only incidental, (albeit necessary), to their primary goal.

Several important characteristics of contemporary sport tend to make owning professional sports teams profitable investments. First, the value of sports franchises has consistently increased, allowing for capital gains when sold (only 40 percent of the capital gains are subject to income tax under the current laws). For example, Carroll Rosenbloom purchased a majority interest in the Baltimore Colts for $13,000 in 1953. He later bought out his partners for $1 million, paid for by the Colts' revenues. In 1972 he traded the Colts for full ownership of the Los Angeles Rams, a franchise valued at $19 million.[2] While Rosenbloom's enormously successful investment is an extreme example of the potential profits to be made by team ownership, one should note that the purchasing of sports teams has consistently been a good investment. For example, the Boston Celtics franchise increased in value from $2.8 million in 1965 to $6.2 million in just four years. The Philadelphia Eagles cost but $250,000 in 1949 and were estimated to be worth $25 million in 1978.

The value of sports franchises has increased even more rapidly recently as television revenues have skyrocketed. Television income for

---

SOURCE: This essay was written expressly for this volume.

the established professional sports is very lucrative indeed. Starting with the 1978 season, each National Football League franchise received $5.5 million annually making it virtually impossible for any team to suffer a loss (broadcast revenues alone, by the way, under this arrangement exceed the total player costs by an average of $1.75 million for each club).

> For example, for a franchise with average costs to lose money next year [1978], its income from ticket sales would have to be less than $1.22 million. Even if the team did not draw a single fan into its stadium during home preseason and regular season games, its 40 percent share of the gate at away games should amount to almost that figure.[3]

Similarly, in professional baseball, the television money paid to each team pays all payroll and pension plan expenses with something left over—and this is in an era of very high salaries.[4]

Owners have continually sought to expand television revenues at the cost of giving up control of the contests themselves. Television has intruded into the various sports by changing schedules, calling timeouts (the lucrative TV deal for football beginning in 1978 included the increase of one-minute commercial breaks per game from 20 to 22), and violating the privacy of locker rooms and the sidelines—at the inconvenience of the players and the spectators.

Another aspect of professional sports that make them profitable ventures is the tax loophole that allows for the depreciation of players. This is a unique privilege to professional sport, since no other business can write off its employees. This procedure allows teams to appear less profitable than they really are. For example, a team that ends the year with $1 million in actual profit but shows a loss of $700,000 by declaring that the value of their players has depreciated by $1.7 million.[5] This serves the owner in three ways: (1) gain appears as a loss for the public, thereby giving the team owners the appearance of being civic-minded rather than profit-minded; (2) ever higher ticket prices are justified as is the need for extremely low rents in the already subsidized arenas; and (3) the wealthy owners can offset their paper losses by subtracting them from their nonsport investments.

Another tax subsidy to owners is less direct but profitable nevertheless. Various businesses buy season tickets to sports events and are allowed to write this off as a business expense for tax purposes. This loophole costs the federal treasury about $150 million annually. It benefits team owners by guaranteeing the sale of season tickets. In baseball this is a substantial amount, as 80 percent of the average major league teams season tickets are purchased by businesses.[6] This price bargain to businesses (i.e., the cost of season tickets is reduced substantially by tax refunds) also makes raising ticket prices easier.[7]

Publicly financed arenas are a financial bonanza to professional team owners. In the National Football League, for example, 26 of the 28 teams play in taxpayer-financed stadiums built at a total public cost of $833 million. Although privately owned, the teams are typically viewed as community assets. Thus taxpayers and/or city councils seem willing to subsidize arenas paying huge sums ($100 million to renovate Yankee Stadium and $163 million to build the Superdome in New Orleans). Not only do publicly built arenas save owners the great cost of constructing the stadiums, but they also save the cost of property taxes.[8] As an illustration of how lucrative the municipal subsidies are to team owners, the owners of the Denver Broncos gave Mile High Stadium to the city of Denver in 1968. On the surface this would appear to express the ultimate in civic-mindedness. But this move was one that made very good sense financially to the owners. By no longer owning the stadium, the Bronco management was no longer responsible for property taxes or for renovation expenses. The city then paid $265,000 to install more lights so that the stadium would qualify for Monday Night Football telecasts; they later spent $25 million to enlarge the stadium by 20,000 seats, which added $222,400 in income for each home game at current ticket prices—all at a nominal rental fee.[9]

That the structure of professional team sports tends to be lucrative is established, but what about the primary motivations of the owners for their involvement? Are they profit-oriented entrepreneurs or wealthy persons willing to take financial risks to provide a service to their respective communities? This is an important question, because its answer should dictate whether professional sport is a sport or a business. In other words, if it is a business, then special tax concessions, antitrust exemptions, and arena subsidies are inappropriate. If, on the other hand, professional team owners deserve these advantages because they are providing a community service, then their profits should be scaled down, with the benefits accruing to the players and the fans.

Perhaps the best test of the owners primary motivation involves their policies regarding ticket prices. The test is simple—if the owner is basically civic-minded, then the better the attendance during the season, the lower the prices. A study using data from 1970 and earlier showed the opposite, namely, that prices tended to be positively correlated with attendance.[10] Does this finding still hold as television revenues have guaranteed a profit? Let's examine the data for 1976–1978.

Professional football

In 1978 the average NFL team averaged gross profits of $3.93 million, not counting tax breaks that probably added another $1 million.[11] This high profit was virtually guaranteed by the new television contract. What was the impact on ticket prices? Current data are not available, but recent ticket price information would lead to the prediction that prices will *not* decrease. In 1976, for example, the record showed that teams with the better records, and hence, increased demand for seats, tended to charge the high ticket prices.[12] The Denver Broncos in 1976 were consistently sold out at the third highest average ticket prices in the NFL—$11.12. When the city of Denver added about 20,000 seats for the next season (for $25 million), the new seats were quickly seized by new season ticket holders guaranteeing a sellout for every 1977 game. Demand for tickets was not satiated as the waiting list for tickets reached 10,000. With the increased profits to the owners (television money plus the additional 20,000 fans at each game), were the ticket prices reduced? No! Technically, they were not even increased for 1978, but season ticket holders were forced to pay for two preseason games at the same high regular season rate.[13]

Professional hockey

In the 1977-78 season the average ticket price for an NHL game was $7.87. Again, the generalization holds that the greater the demand for tickets, the higher the prices tend to be.[14] Most instructive of the tendency to price according to the principle of supply and demand is the case of the Montreal Canadiens, the most successful hockey team in recent years and perennially sold out at home games. Winners of the Stanley Cup for two straight years (and destined to win again in 1978), the Canadiens' management had the highest average ticket prices in 1978 ($11), a full $2 higher than the next most expensive team.

Professional basketball

The average 1977 ticket price for NBA teams was $6.76.[15] The positive relationship between demand and price is present in professional basketball as it is in the other sports, but it is not as strong. The Denver Nuggets provide an illustration, though, of how one team tends to gouge fans when the product being sold is popular. Denver had the highest attendance in the league for two years running, yet their ticket prices were the third highest in the league. A better example of this principle is furnished by the ticket policy of the San Antonio Spurs. The lowest priced seat for one of their home games is $4 yet when all the seats are sold, they sell standing room tickets for $5.

Professional baseball

The average cost of a baseball ticket to a major league game in 1978 was $3.98.[16] The relationship between average ticket price and total attendance is stronger in baseball than in any of the other major team sports. For instance, of the 16 teams that raised ticket prices for 1978, 12 (75 percent) were already above the median in ticket cost—again substantiating the claim that the goal of sports team ownership is ultimately to obtain as much profit as possible. This is perhaps best exemplified by the decision of the Cincinnati Reds to raise prices for the 1978 season by 50 cents (the second price hike in three years, to an average price of $4.33 (second highest in the National League). This increase raised an additional $1.25 million above the 1977 profits of $6 million for the ownership. Such prices and profits, in the words of Jim Ford, "epitomize the monopoly-gouging approach characteristic of many major professional sports teams."[17]

CONCLUSION

The public has been led to believe that professional team owners are basically civic-minded persons interested more in providing the public a product than in profit. The rationale usually accompanying ticket increases is that costs are skyrocketing, especially the high salaries of superstars. Thus, fans typically vent their anger at the well-paid athletes rather than at the owners. This anger is misplaced, as the fans do not recognize that greed motivates owners as well as players. Owners profit, and usually handsomely, at public expense. This is, of course, the basic rule of capitalism. Still, the owners cannot have it both ways. If they are capitalists, then let the subsidies stop. Their monopoly should not be supported by the Congress and the courts. Tax breaks should be eliminated. And if public arenas are provided teams, then the rent must be fair to both the owner and the citizens of the city.

NOTES

1. Cf., Jonathan Brower, "Professional Sports Team Ownership: Fun, Profit, and Ideology of the Power Elite," *Journal of Sport and Social Issues*, 1 (1976), 16–51; and Dan Kowet, *The Rich Who Own Sports* (New York: Random House, 1977).
2. Bob Oates, "Meet Mr. Rosenbloom, New Owner of the Rams," *Los Angeles Times* (July 14, 1972), part 3, pp. 1, 4.
3. Peter Gruenstein and Jim Ford, "NFL Profits Soar," *Left Field*, 1 (January 1978), p. 1.
4. CBS Reports, "The Baseball Business," television documentary, narrated by Bill Moyers (1977).
5. Cf., D. Stanley Eitzen and George H. Sage, *Sociology of American Sport* (Dubuque, Iowa: Wm. C. Brown, 1978), pp. 180–183; William Johnson, "Yankee Rx is Group Therapy," *Sports Illustrated* (February 12, 1973), pp. 46–49; and Ron Scherer, "How Costly Baseball Players Save Owners Taxes," *The Christian Science Monitor* (August 11, 1976), p. 11.
6. "Baseball Average Ticket Prices and Business Purchases," *Left Field* 1 (April 1978), 4.

7. Peter Gruenstein, "The Case for Financial Disclosure," *Left Field*, 1 (March 1978), 4.
8. Benjamin A. Okner, "Subsidies of Stadiums and Arenas," *Government and the Sports Business*, Roger G. Noll, ed. (Washington, D.C.: The Brookings Institution, 1974), pp. 325–347.
9. "Robbing Peter to Pay Paul—with the Taxpayers as Peter," *Rocky Mountain News* (March 25, 1976), p. 54.
10. Roger G. Noll, "Attendance and Price Setting," *Government and the Sports Business*, Roger G. Noll, ed., (Washington, D.C.: The Brookings Institution, 1974), pp. 115–157.
11. Gruenstein and Ford, "NFL Profits Soar."
12. David Meyer, "The Prices You Pay," *Left Field*, 1 (November 1977), 1, 3.
13. Cf., Woodrow Paige, Jr., "Ticket-Tack-Toe," *Rocky Mountain News* (February 26, 1978), p. 54.
14. Jim Ford, "NHL Tickets Average $7.87," *Left Field*, 1 (February 1978), 1, 4.
15. David Meyer, "NBA Tickets Average $6.76," *Left Field*, 1 (December 1977), 1, 4.
16. Tim Fedele, "Baseball Tickets Average $3.98," *Left Field*, 1 (April 1978), 1, 5.
17. Jim Ford, "F. A. N. S.' Analysis: Reds = $$$," *Left Field*, 1 (May 1978), 1.

■ FOR FURTHER STUDY

Angell, Roger. "The Sporting Scene: In the Counting House." *The New Yorker* (May 10, 1976).

Angell, Roger. "The Sporting Scene—The Long Green." *The New Yorker* (April 25, 1977), pp. 103–129.

Barry, Rick, and W. Libby. *Confessions of a Basketball Gypsy.* Englewood Cliffs, N.J.: Prentice-Hall, 1972.

Blount, Roy, Jr. "Greed, Here's What It's Done . . ." *Sport*, 64 (June 19-7), 19–20.

Briner, Bob. "Making Sport of Us All." *Sports Illustrated* (December 10, 1973), pp. 36–42.

Burck, Charles G. "Why the Sports Business Ain't What It Used to Be." *Fortune*, 95 (May, 1977), 295–308.

Chandler, Jean M. "TV and Sports." *Psychology Today*, 10 (April 1977), 64–76.

Cicarelli, J., and D. Kowarsky. "The Economics of the Olympic Games." *Business and Economic Dimensions*, 9 (1973), 1–5.

Coakley, Jay J. *Sport in Society: Issues and Controversies.* St. Louis: C. V. Mosby, 1978, chapter 8.

Daymont, Thomas N. "The Effects of Monopsonistic Procedures on Equality of Competition in Professional Sport Leagues." *International Review of Sport Sociology*, 10 (1975), 83–99.

Department of Labor. "Careers in Professional Sports." *Occupational Outlook Quarterly*, 17 (Summer 1973), 2–5.

Dollars & Sense. "Depreciating the National Pastime." *Dollars & Sense*, 27 (May–June 1977), 4–5.

Durso, Joseph. *The All-American Dollar: The Big Business of Sports.* Boston: Houghton-Mifflin, 1971.

Eitzen, D. Stanley, and George H. Sage. *Sociology of American Sport.* Dubuque, Iowa: Wm. C. Brown, 1978), chapter 7.

Eldridge, Larry. "Playing for the Big Money," *Christian Science Monitor* (August 9, 1978), pp. 12–13.

Embry, Wayne. An interview with John Devaney, "The Owners are Destroying the Game." *Sport*, 64 (June 1977), pp. 23–31.

Flood, Curt. *The Way It Is*. New York: Trident Press, 1970.

Gilbert, Bil. "Sis-Boom-Bah for Amalgamated Sponge." *Sports Illustrated* (January 25, 1965).

Gilbert, Bil. "Gleanings from a Troubled Time." *Sports Illustrated* (December 25, 1972), pp. 34–46.

Hearings before the Subcommittee on Antitrust and Monopoly of the Committee of the Judiciary. U.S. Senate, 92nd Congress, 1st Session (1971).

Horvitz, J., and T. Hoffman. "New Tax Developments in the Syndication of Sports Franchises." *Taxes—the Tax Magazine* (March 1976), pp. 175–186.

Johnson, Arthur T. ed. "Political Economy of Sport." *American Behavioral Scientist*, 21 (January/February 1978), entire issue.

Kahn, Roger. "Money, Muscles—and Myths." *Nation*, 185 (1957), 9–11.

Kahn, Roger. "Can Sports Survive Money?" *Esquire*, 84 (October 1975), 105–109.

Keith, Larry. "After the Free-for-all Was Over." *Sports Illustrated* (December 13, 1976), pp. 29–34.

Kennedy, Ray, and Nancy Williamson. "Money: The Monster Threatening Sports." *Sports Illustrated* (July 17, July 24, and July 31, 1978).

Kirshenbaum, Jerry. "On Your Mark, Get Set, Sell." *Sports Illustrated* (May 14, 1973).

Koch, James V. "The Economics of 'Big-Time' Intercollegiate Athletics." *Social Science Quarterly*, 52 (September 1971), 248–260.

Koch, James V. "A Troubled Cartel: The NCAA." *Law and Contemporary Problems*, 38 (Winter-Spring 1973), 135–150.

Kowet, D. *The Rich Who Own Sports*. New York: Random House, 1977.

Lipsyte, Robert, *Sportsworld: An American Dreamland*. New York: Quadrangle/New York Times, 1975.

Looney, Douglas S. "The Salesmen Run a Costly Race at Indy." *The National Observer* (May 25, 1974), p. 18.

Loy, John W., Barry D. McPherson, and Gerald Kenyon. *Sport and Social Systems*. Reading, Mass.: Addison-Wesley, 1978, pp. 256–283.

McPherson, Barry D. "Sport Consumption and the Economics of Consumerism." *Sport and Social Order*. Edited by Donald W. Ball and John W. Loy. Reading, Mass: Addison-Wesley, 1975, pp. 243–275.

Maur, M. Auf der. *The Billion-Dollar Game: Jean Drapeau and the 1976 Olympics*. Toronto: James Lorimer, 1976.

Merchant, Larry. *The National Football Lottery*. New York: Holt, Rinehart and Winston, 1973.

Meschery, Tom. "'There is a Disease in Sports Now...'" *Sports Illustrated* (October 2, 1972), pp. 56–63.

Michener, James A. *Sports in America*. New York: Random House, 1976, chapter 11.

Neale, Walter C. "The Peculiar Economics of Professional Sports." *The Quarterly Journal of Economics*, 78 (February 1964).

Noll, Roger G., ed. *Government and the Sports Business*. Washington, D.C.: The Brookings Institution, 1974.

Parrish, Bernie. *They Call It a Game*. New York: Dial Press, 1971.

Preston, Frederick W. "Hucksters at the Circus." *Urban Life*, 7 (July 1978), 205–212.

Quirk, J. "An Economic Analysis of Team Movements in Professional Sports." *Law and Contemporary Problems*, 38 (1973), 42–66.

Ross, G. "The Determination of Bonuses in Professional Sport." *The American Economist*, 19 (Fall 1975), 24–34.

Sack, A. L. "Yale 29—Harvard 4: the Professionalization of College Football." *Quest,* 19 (Winter 1973), 24-34.

Sack, A. L. "Big Time College Football: Whose Free Ride?" *Quest,* 27 (Winter 1977), 87-97.

Scully, G. W. "Economic Discrimination in Professional Sports." *Law and Contemporary Problems,* 38 (1973), 67-84.

Scully, Gerald. "Pay and Performance in Major League Baseball." *American Economic Review,* 64 (December 1974), 915-930.

Shrake, Edwin. "The Juice on a Juicy Road." *Sports Illustrated* (August 19, 1974), pp. 36-40.

Snyder, Eldon E., and Elmer Spreitzer. *Social Aspects of Sport.* Englewood Cliffs, N.J.: Prentice-Hall, 1978, chapter 10.

Stein, Harry. "The Gold and the Money." *Sport,* 64 (June 1977), 33-41.

Surface, Bill. "In Pro Sports, the Dollar is King." *Reader's Digest* (March 1972), pp. 146-149.

"The Affluent Activists." *Forbes* (August 1, 1976), pp. 22-25.

"The Boom in Leisure: Where Americans Spend 100 Billions." *U.S. News and World Report* (May 23, 1977), pp. 62-63.

Wright, George. "The Political Economy of the Montreal Olympic Games." *Journal of Sport and Social Issues,* 2 (Spring/Summer 1978), 13-18.

Nine

Sport and Religion

There are several facets to the relationship between sport and religion. The first is the strong possibility that sport is the functional equivalent of religion. Some striking similarities exist between the two phenomena that may allow individuals to receive the benefits from sport that are usually associated with religion. Some of these parallels include idols, proverbs, shrines, pilgrimages, fanatic believers, rituals, testimony, miracles, rules, judgment, and mysticism. Let us briefly consider two of these.

Ritual is basic to religion. Through the repetition of particular symbolic acts, worshippers are reminded of the supernatural and unified in a common belief with others sharing in the ceremony. Ritual is also very important to sport. Prior to, during, and after games, the faithful sing songs and recite chants that pledge fidelity to the team and implore the athletes to greater achievements. The national anthem is also part of every athletic event. For the athletes there are rituals such as the interlacing of hands with the coach to express team unity. There are also rituals common to particular sports, such as in baseball's "seventh inning stretch," or in boxing, where the combatants touch gloves at the beginning of the first and last rounds.

Common to all religions is the element of mysticism. Belief in the mystical is to have faith in supernatural forces (powers that transcend normal human experience). The mystical is also found in sport. There is the belief that the individual with the greatest "heart" or "spirit" will win. There is also the intangible quality of team spirit, considered such an important ingredient of success. As a final example of the supernatural forces in sport, there is that elusive factor in a game known as momentum.

Although the parallels between religion and sport should not be overdrawn, the similarities are interesting and provide insight about the similar functions of these two institutions of society. The first selection in this section, by philosopher/theologian Michael Novak, addresses this issue directly.

Sport and religion are also related because each uses the other for its own ends. Sport uses religion to legitimize itself through the use of invocations during the pregame rituals. Religion is also used in sport to maximize the performance of athletes. Religion has always been used to calm persons who face stressful situations and to get individuals to reach beyond themselves for superhuman effort. Thus, chapel services, the availability of team chaplains, and team prayers before a game may all help to ease the tension and to prepare the athletes to perform at their highest levels.

Religion also exploits sport for its own purposes. In this century the churches have found sport as a way to gain converts. By providing teams, leagues, and gymnasiums, churches have enticed people to become associated with them. Religious leaders have also found sports heroes helpful in reaching persons beyond the church. Of relatively recent origin are religious organizations designed specifically for athletes. Organizations such as Athletes in Action and the Fellowship of Christian Athletes have grown rapidly and are used to proselytize other athletes to Christianity. The second selection in this unit, by sportswriter Frank Deford, shows how these groups use sports to win converts. He also shows why this brand of conservative, evangelical religion appeals to many athletes. Most significant is Deford's observation that these sport-oriented religious groups are content to exploit sport, but make no effort to solve the problems of contemporary sport such as racism, cheating, and dirty play.

Superstition is a form of magic whereby the individual believes that he or she can control the supernatural forces that affect performance. Athletes are particularly vulnerable to the appeal of superstitious behaviors, because so much of what happens in sport is subject to luck. In the last essay of this unit, George Gmelch, a former minor league baseball player and presently an anthropologist, examines the superstitious behavior of baseball players using the explanatory framework of the famous anthropologist Bronislaw Malinowski.

The Natural Religion

MICHAEL NOVAK

A sport is not a religion in the same way that Methodism, Presbyterianism, or Catholicism is a religion. But these are not the only kinds of religion. There are secular religions, civil religions. The United States of America has sacred documents to guide and to inspire it: The Constitution, the Declaration of Independence, Washington's Farewell Address, Lincoln's Gettysburg Address, and other solemn presidential documents. The President of the United States is spoken to with respect, is expected to exert "moral leadership"; and when he walks among crowds, hands reach out to touch his garments. Citizens are expected to die for the nation, and our flag symbolizes vivid memories, from Fort Sumter to Iwo Jima, from the Indian Wars to Normandy: memories that moved hardhats in New York to break up a march that was "desecrating" the flag. Citizens regard the American way of life as though it were somehow chosen by God, special, uniquely important to the history of the human race. "Love it or leave it," the guardians of orthodoxy say. Those on the left, who do not like the old-time patriotism, have a new kind: they evince unusual outrage when this nation is less than fully just, free, compassionate, or good—in short, when it is like all the other nations of human history. America should be *better*. Why?

The institutions of the state generate a civil religion; so do the institutions of sport. The ancient Olympic games used to be both festivals in honor of the gods and festivals in honor of the state—and that has been the classical position of sports ever since. The ceremonies of sports overlap those of the state on one side, and those of the churches on the other. At the Super Bowl in 1970, clouds of military jets flew in formation, American flags and patriotic bunting flapped in the wind, ceremonies honored prisoners of war, clergymen solemnly prayed, thousands sang the national anthem. Going to a stadium is half like going to a political rally, half like going to church. Even today, the Olympics are constructed around high ceremonies, rituals, and symbols. The Olympics are not barebones athletic events, but religion and politics as well.

Most men and women don't separate the sections of their mind. They

---

SOURCE: Michael Novak, *The Joy of Sports: End Zones, Bases, Baskets, Balls, and the Consecration of the American Spirit* (New York: Basic Books, 1976), pp. 18-21, 27-32.

honor their country, go to church, and also enjoy sports. All parts of their lives meld together.

Nor am I indulging in metaphor when I say that nearly every writer about sports lapses into watery religious metaphor. So do writers on politics and sex. Larry Merchant says television treated the Super Bowl "as though it were a solemn high mass." Words like *sacred, devotion, faith, ritual, immortality,* and *love* figure often in the language of sports. Cries like "You gotta believe!" and "life and death" and "sacrifice" are frequently heard.

But that is not what I mean. I am arguing a considerably stronger point. I am saying that sports flow outward into action from a deep natural impulse that is radically religious: an impulse of freedom, respect for ritual limits, a zest for symbolic meaning, and a longing for perfection. The athlete may of course be pagan, but sports are, as it were, natural religions. There are many ways to express this radical impulse: by the asceticism and dedication of preparation; by a sense of respect for the mysteries of one's own body and soul, and for powers not in one's own control; by a sense of awe for the place and time of competition; by a sense of fate; by a felt sense of comradeship and destiny; by a sense of participation in the rhythms and tides of nature itself.

Sports, in the second place, are organized and dramatized in a religious way. Not only do the origins of sports, like the origins of drama, lie in religious celebrations; not only are the rituals, vestments, and tremor of anticipation involved in sports events like those of religions. Even in our own secular age and for quite sophisticated and agnostic persons, the rituals of sports really work. They do serve a religious function: they feed a deep human hunger, place humans in touch with certain dimly perceived features of human life within this cosmos, and provide an experience of at least a pagan sense of godliness.

Among the godward signs in contemporary life, sports may be the single most powerful manifestation. I don't mean that participation in sports, as athlete or fan, makes one a believer in "God," under whatever concept, image, experience, or drive to which one attaches the name. Rather, sports drive one in some dark and generic sense "godward." In the language of Paul Tillich, sports are manifestations of concern, of will and intellect and passion. In fidelity to that concern, one submits onself to great bodily dangers, even to the danger of death. Symbolically, too, to lose is a kind of death.

Sports are not the highest form of religion. They do not exclude other forms. Jews, Christians, and others will want to put sports in second place, within a scheme of greater ultimacy. It is quite natural and normal to envisage human life and responsibilities as falling within schedules of ultimacy. Each "world" can be ultimate of its own kind, yet subsumed within a larger circle. The family is a good in itself, not derivative from the state. It is "ultimate" in its responsibilities. Yet the individual has claims against the family. So does the common good. A sport, like the family, can be in its own sphere an ultimate concern and a good in itself, while yet being subject to other and greater claims on the part of individuals and the common good.

For some, it may require a kind of conversion to grasp the religiousness at the heart of sports. Our society has become secular, and personal advancement obliges us to become pragmatic, glib, superficial, and cynical. Our spirits often wither. Eyes cannot see; ears cannot hear. The soil of our culture is not always fertile for religious life. Americans must read religious messages in foreign languages. And so many will, at first, be tempted to read what I am saying as mere familiar metaphor. A change of perspective, and of heart, may be necessary.

Sports are religious in the sense that they are organized institutions, disciplines, and liturgies; and also in the sense that they teach religious qualities of heart and soul. In particular, they recreate symbols of cosmic struggle, in which human survival and moral courage are not assured. To this extent, they are not mere games, diversions, pastimes. Their power to exhilarate or depress is far greater than that. To say "It was only a game" is the psyche's best defense against the cosmic symbolic meaning of sports events. And it is partly true. For a game is a symbol; it is not precisely identified with what it symbolizes. To lose symbolizes death, and it certainly feels like dying; but it is not death. The same is true of religious symbols like Baptism or the Eucharist; in both, the communicants experience death, symbolically, and are reborn, symbolically. If you give your heart to the ritual, its effects upon your inner life can be far-reaching. Of course, in all religions many merely go through the motions. Yet even they, unaware, are suprised by grace. A Hunter pursues us everywhere, in churches and stadia alike, in the pews and bleachers, and occasionally in the pulpit and the press box. . . .

The hunger for perfection in sports cleaves closely to the driving core of the human spirit. It is the experience of this driving force that has perennially led human beings to break forth in religious language. This force is in us, it is ours. Yet we did not will its existence, nor do we command it, nor is it under our power. It is there unbidden. It is greater than we, driving us beyond our present selves. "Be ye perfect," Jesus said, "as your heavenly Father is perfect." The root of human dissatisfaction and restlessness goes as deep into the spirit as any human drive—deeper than any other drive. It *is* the human spirit. Nothing stills it. Nothing fulfills it. It is not a need like a hunger, a thirst, or an itch, for such needs are easily satisfied. It is a need even greater than sex; orgasmic satisfaction does not quiet it. "Desire" is the word by which coaches call it. A drivenness. Distorted, the drive for perfection can propel an ugly and considerably less than perfect human development. True, straight, and well targeted, it soars like an arrow toward the proper beauty of humanity. Sports nourish this drive as well as any other institution in our society. If this drive is often distorted, as it is, even its distortions testify to its power, as liars mark out the boundaries of truth.

Sports, in a word, are a form of godliness. That is why the corruptions of sports in our day, by corporations and television and glib journalism and cheap public relations, are so hateful. If sports were entertainment, why should we care? They are far more than that. So when we see them abused, our natural response is the rise of vomit in the throat.

It may be useful to list some of the elements of religions, to see how they are imitated in the world of sports.

If our anthropologists discovered in some other culture the elements they can plainly see in our own world of sports, they would be obliged to write monographs on the religions of the tribes they were studying. Two experiments in thought may make this plain.

Imagine that you are walking near your home and come upon a colony of ants. They move in extraordinary busy lines, a trail of brown bodies across the whitish soil like a highway underneath the blades of grass. The lanes of ants abut on a constructed mudbank oval; there the ants gather, 100,000 strong, sitting in a circle. Down below, in a small open place, eleven ants on one side and eleven on the other contest bitterly between two lines. From time to time a buzz arises from the 100,000 ants gathered in their sacred oval. When the game is over, the long lines of ants begin their traffic-dense return to their colonies. In one observation, you didn't have time to discover the rules of their ritual. Or who made them up, or when. Or what they mean to the ants. Is the gathering mere "escape"? Does it mirror other facets in the life of ants? Do all ants everywhere take part? Do the ants "understand" what they are doing, or do they only do it by rote, one of the things that ants do on a lovely afternoon? Do ants practice, and stay in shape, and perfect their arts?

Or suppose you are an anthropologist from Mars. You come suddenly upon some wild, adolescent tribes living in territories called the "United States of America." You try to understand their way of life, but their society does not make sense to you. Flying over the land in a rocket, you notice great ovals near every city. You descend and observe. You learn that an oval is called a "stadium." It is used, roughly, once a week in certain seasons. Weekly, regularly, millions of citizens stream into these concrete doughnuts, pay handsomely, are alternately hushed and awed and outraged and screaming mad. (They demand from time to time that certain sacrificial personages be "killed.") You see that the figures in the rituals have trained themselves superbly for their performances. The combatants are dedicated. So are the dancers and musicians in tribal dress who occupy the arena before, during, and after the combat. You note that, in millions of homes, at corner shrines in every household's sacred room, other citizens are bound by invisible attraction to the same events. At critical moments, the most intense worshipers demand of the less attentive silence. Virtually an entire nation is united in a central public rite. Afterward, you note exultation or depression among hundreds of thousands, and animation almost everywhere.

Some of the elements of a religion may be enumerated. A religion, first of all, is organized and structured. Culture is built on cult. Accordingly, a religion begins with ceremonies. At these ceremonies, a few surrogates perform for all. They need not even believe what they are doing. As professionals, they may perform so often that they have lost all religious instinct; they may have less faith than any of the participants. In the official ceremonies, sacred vestments are employed and rituals are prescribed. Customs develop. Actions are highly formalized. Right ways and wrong ways are plainly marked out; illicit behaviors are distinguished from licit ones. Professional watchdogs supervise formal correctness. Moments of silence are observed. Concentration and intensity are indispensable. To attain them, drugs or special disciplines of spirit might be employed; ordinary humans, in the ordinary ups and downs of daily experience, cannot be expected to perform routinely at the highest levels of awareness.

Religions are built upon *ascesis*, a word that derives from the disciplines Greek athletes imposed upon themselves to give their wills and instincts command of their bodies; the word was borrowed by Christian monks and hermits. It signifies the development of character, through patterns of self-denial, repetition, and experiment. The type of character celebrated in the central rituals, more likely than not, reveals the unconscious needs of the civilization—extols the very qualities that more highly conscious formulations are likely to deny. Thus, the cults have a revelatory quality; they dramatize what otherwise goes unspoken.

Religions also channel the feeling most humans have of danger, contingency, and chance—in a word, Fate. Human plans involve ironies. Our choices are made with so little insight into their eventual effects that what we desire is often not the path to what we want. The decisions we make with little attention turn out to be major turning points. What we prepare for with exquisite detail never happens. Religions place us in the presence of powers greater than ourselves, and seek to reconcile us to them. The rituals of religion give these powers almost human shape, forms that give these powers visibility and tangible effect. Sports events in baseball, basketball, and football are structured so that "the breaks" may intervene and become central components in the action.

Religions make explicit the almost nameless dreads of daily human life: aging, dying, failure under pressure, cowardice, betrayal, guilt. Competitive sports embody these in every combat.

Religions, howsoever universal in imperative, do not treat rootedness, particularity, and local belonging as unworthy. On the contrary, they normally begin by blessing the local turf, the local tribe, and the local instinct of belonging—and use these as paradigms for the development of larger loyalties. "Charity begins at home." "Whoever says that he loves God, whom he does not see, but hates his neighbor, whom he does see, is a liar and the truth is not in him."

Religions consecrate certain days and hours. Sacred time is a block of time lifted out of everyday normal routines, a time that is different, in which different laws apply, a time within which one forgets ordinary time. Sacred time is intended to suggest an "eternal return," a fundamental repetition like the circulation of the human blood, or the eternal turning of the seasons, or the wheeling of the stars and planets in their cycles: the sense that things repeat themselves, over and over, and yet are always a little different. Sacred time is more like eternity than like history, more like cycles of recurrence than like progress, more like a celebration of repetition than like a celebration of novelty. Yet, sacred time is full of exhilaration, excitement, and peace, as though it were more real and more joyous than the activities of everyday life—as though it were *really living* to be in sacred time (wrapped up in a close game during the last two minutes), and comparatively boring to suffer the daily jading of work, progress, history.

To have a religion, you need to have heroic forms to try to live up to: patterns of excellence so high that human beings live up to them only rarely, even when they strive to do so; and images of perfection so beautiful that, living up to them or seeing someone else live up to them, produces a kind of "*ah!*"

You need to have a pattern of symbols and myths that a person can grow old with, with a kind of resignation, wisdom, and illumination. Do what we will, the human body ages. Moves we once could make our minds will but our bodies cannot implement; disciplines we once endured with suppressed animal desire are no longer worth the effort; heroes that once seemed to us immortal now age, become enfeebled, die, just as we do. The "boys of summer" become the aging men of winter. A religion celebrates the passing of all things: youth, skill, grace, heroic deeds.

To have a religion, you need to have a way to exhilarate the human body, and desire, and will, and the sense of beauty, and a sense of oneness with the universe and other humans. You need chants and songs, the rhythm of bodies in unison, the indescribable feeling of many who together "will one thing" as if they were each members of a single body.

All these things you have in sports.

Sports are not Christianity, or Judaism, or Islam, or Buddhism, or any other of the world religions. Sports are not the civil religion of the United States of America, or Great Britain, or Germany, or the Union of Soviet Socialist Republics, or Ghana, or any other nation.

But sports are a form of religion. This aspect of sports has seldom been discussed. Consequently, we find it hard to express just what it is that gives sports their spirit and their power.

Athletes are not merely entertainers. Their role is far more powerful than that. People identify with them in a much more priestly way. Athletes exemplify something of deep meaning—frightening meaning, even. Once they become superstars, they do not quite belong to themselves. Great passions are invested in them. They are no longer treated as ordinary humans or even as mere celebrities. Their exploits and their failures have great power to exult—or to depress. When people talk about athletes' performances, it is almost as though they are talking about a secret part of themselves. As if the stars had some secret bonding, some Siamese intertwining with their own psyches. . . .

Religion in Sport

FRANK DEFORD

. . . religion itself has increasingly become a handmaiden to sport. Clergymen are standing in line to cater to the spiritual needs of the deprived athletic elite, and the use of athletes as amateur evangelists is so widespread that it might be fairly described as a growth industry. "Jocks for Jesus" is what *The Wittenburg Door*, an acerbic contemporary religious magazine, derisively calls the movement. "Who gives these people authority but the pagan world in which we live?" asks the magazine, its cover adorned with an athletic supporter festooned with a cross. But Jocks for Jesus is booming. It is almost as if a new denomination had been created: Sportianity. While Christian churches struggle with

SOURCE: Excerpted from Frank Deford, "Religion in Sport," *Sports Illustrated* (April 19, 1976), 92, 95–96, 98–99.

problems of declining attendance, falling contributions and now even reduction in membership, Sportianity appears to be taking off.

Today every major league baseball and football team—all 50 of them—holds Sunday chapel services, home and away. . . . Sunday services are also held in sports as varied as stock-car racing and golf. In many cases, week-night Bible classes have been started up so that wives may participate.

Athletes In Action has 250 full-time staff men (domestic missionaries, really). Eight are assigned to large cities where their only job is to minister to the pro athletes. Athletes In Action deploys two proselyting basketball teams, two wrestling teams, plus squads in gymnastics, track and weight lifting. With the AIA teams, the major thrust is toward the colleges. Says Greg Hicks, a 1974 national AAU wrestling champion and an AIA assistant athletic director, "We believe in a real soft sell. As an athlete, I can get into a fraternity, a locker room, where nobody else would be permitted."

Sports Ambassadors is an overseas equivalent of the AIA. Since 1952, "in a world gone berserk with sports," it has sent basketball and baseball teams into more than 40 countries in Europe, the Orient, Africa and Central and South America, playing and preaching under the organization's name or Venture For Victory. A newcomer in the field is the basketball team known as News Release, which carries its pray-for-play ministry to Europe, even behind the Iron Curtain.

The Fellowship of Christian Athletes, which is the patriarch of Sportianity, does not subsidize teams, but uses older athletes to bring younger ones to Christ, mainly at summer sports camps ($110 a week) and in high school group sessions known as "Huddles." The FCA's annual budget is $2.2 million, and its president, John Erickson, refers to it as a "para-church."

For years, some coaches who are not members have complained that the Fellowship—which bills itself as the "muscle and action" of Christianity—operates as a powerful lobby when one of its member coaches is up against an outsider for a job. As a result, there are coaches who feel that they have to protect themselves by signing on as FCA members. "It's like getting a union card," says one. "If you don't join, some coaches in the Fellowship will badmouth you with kids they're recruiting, tell 'em you're a drunk or your marriage is breaking up. I know, because kids I've recruited told me."

Another substantial organization, Pro Athletes Outreach, was founded largely as an intramural peace-keeping force because the giants of Sportianity, AIA and FCA, were squabbling so indecorously over enlisting the best missionary athletes. It was an outgrowth of Sports World Chaplaincy, Inc. but is now a thriving operation with an annual budget of

$250,000, and it sends phalanxes of pros off on what it calls "speaking blitzes" of the U.S. The PAO stars also entertain with flag football games, tugs-of-war, wrist-wrestling and other fun games.

The movement has grown so that it has even spawned a think tank, the Institute for Athletic Perfection, which formulates dogma for athletic religion. Moreover, the presses of Sportianity are flooding the market with pamphlets, books, newsletters, magazines, even comic books and films (*A Man & His Men*, featuring Tom Landry. . . . "The thrill of victory, the agony of defeat, the impact of a Christian life"). Athletes In Action sends out taped vignettes and interviews that have been played on more than 150 radio stations. It established a national television network for its top basketball team this past season, with John Wooden mike-side.

Sport and religion were not total strangers before all this began. Billy Sunday, the turn-of-the-century evangelist, was a reformed weak-hitting major league outfielder. Dr. James Naismith was a seminarian before he invented basketball at the YMCA. C. T. Studd, a millionaire British missionary, was the progenitor of groups like Athletes In Action. Studd was a great cricket player who agreed to make a tour of army garrisons in India if he could preach after his innings. And remember Deacon Dan Towler? The Vaulting Vicar, Bob Richards? The House of David baseball team? Other athletes went on to the ministry when their playing days were done: Albie Pearson, Donn Moomaw, Henry Carr. Bill Glass, the former All-Pro end, is now one of the nation's top evangelists. Jerry Lucas, whose previous enterprises included fast food and magic, has opened up Memory Ministries, a nonprofit organization that will instruct the nimble-minded, for a $20 fee, in memorizing all 89 chapters of the four Gospels. Lucas' new book, *Remember The Word*, has sold almost 60,000 copies. . . .

That religion should suddenly be a factor in sport while its influence elsewhere is declining is not the paradox it seems. Certain members of the religious community have quite openly set out to mine athletics. The belief in these ecclesiastical pockets is that athletes need special spiritual assistance, that they are especially vulnerable to preaching and, finally and most important, they they are ideal instruments to be used in bringing others into the fold. Addressing the Cincinnati Reds at chapel at Fenway Park during the World Series last October, the Rev. Billy Zeoli, the biggest individual star in Sportianity, told the players, "I hope you have a concept of how much you affect people, how they look up to you. Let me remind you that your national influence on youth is greater than that of any single pastor, priest or rabbi."

Arlis Priest, the head of Pro Athletes Outreach, is convinced that athletes can strongly influence moral and religious life in the United States. . . . He explains how athletes are crucial to saving America:

"We're losing. We've lost our perspective, turning to drugs, free sex—and did you know there are now 26,000 suicides a year? And here we are, more blessed than any nation in the history of the world. Do we really think we're that much smarter that we can turn away from God? Well, professional athletes can reach the people who want to find God, who want to be Christians, but don't know how to. Particularly the young people—they'll listen to athletes. Pros have the right background. Why, they're probably the most disciplined group of people left in this country. They're dedicated, they're taught to play as part of a team, and they're willing to pay the price. This is what we need in America.

"Two years from now I expect to have half the professional athletes as Christians. Yes, half. I will be disappointed if we don't have half. And then, as Romans 1:16 says, the power is in the Gospel, and it is the athletes in our society who can best carry that message."

Like Priest, virtually all the leaders in the Christian athletic movement are fundamentalist. Organizations such as the Fellowship of Christian Athletes and Athletes In Action are studiously nondenominational, and even the individual stalwarts, ministers like Zeoli and Tom Skinner (who is associated with the Washington Redskins), avoid mentioning their particular church affiliation. Evangelistic Catholicism has been under steam for almost a decade, and this has helped bring Roman Catholic recruits from that wing of the church into Sportianity—Mike McCoy of the Green Bay Packers is one Catholic invariably cited. But the sense and thrust of the movement still comes from the Bible Belt.

The Bible is to be taken literally. The message is simple, all or nothing; there is no truck with intellectualizing, the appeal is gut. It does not seem surprising that football—authoritarian, even militaristic—is the sport at the heart of the movement. The pregame football chapel services are important not so much because they take place on the Sabbath, but because they take place on a game day, when the players are sky high and emotionally exposed. A pro star who once was active in Sportianity but left in disgust says, "Why do you think this simplistic type of religion appeals to athletes? Because you're talking to people who operate primarily with their bodies, not their minds. . . ."

Being essentially fundamentalist, the movement draws its strength from the South and the rural areas of the nation where that type of theology has thrived. Despite its growth and clout, the Fellowship of Christian Athletes has failed to make inroads into the more sophisticated areas of the nation. There are now 1,600 high school Huddles in the U.S., but only a dozen of these—.8% of the total—are located in the Northeast, where 15% of the population resides. The FCA is hardly more successful in California. The bulk of the Huddles are found in the South, Southwest and Midwest, and most of the stars who participate in the program were brought up in those areas, in white, middle-class environs. . . .

Sportians, humorless and persevering, appear to be attracted to sport as an evangelical device that can be used baldly and also because, as an institution, sport is going to hell just like the rest of the country. All the talk in sport is cynical—of money, money, money, drugs and camp followers, dissension and dissatisfaction. Sin! Today's best-known white athlete is Joe Namath, whose womanizing and drinking are broadly publicized. It is said that his celebrated example provided some of the impetus for the Sportian movement.

Sportians are out to save sport by saving athletes. Once they are converted, they are cast as neo-crusaders. The field is to be an altar, the game a sacrifice. Paul Neumann, a Sports Ambassadors official who was a first-rate NBA player for several years, says, "A Christian is always keyed up before a game because he knows he is playing for his *real* coach." Alvin Dark goes further, suggesting everything he does is for the glory of Jesus Christ. In the sermon in which he revealed Charlie Finley's fiery future, Dark also said, "The more we read the Bible, the more we begin to turn our lives over to the Lord. For example, I gave the Lord my golf game. When I dedicated my life . . . one of the first things I did was turn my golf game over to the Lord."

Jesus has been transformed, emerging anew as a holler guy, a hustler, a give-it-100-percenter. While students of the new religion glumly acknowledge that his only known athletic performance was throwing the moneychangers out of the temple, Jesus' sad, desperate last hours have become a kind of Super Bowl. Wes Neal, previously with AIA, left that organization to set up the Institute for Athletic Perfection in Prescott, Ariz. He has become an accepted theoretician for the movement; the pamphlets published by the institute are handed out by many Sportian groups.

The new image of Jesus, the blue-chipper, is set forth in a Neal tract entitled *Total Release Performance*, which refers to the brand of ball that Jesus played on the cross: "It was another situation that would reveal his WINNING character. . . . At any point Jesus could have turned back from His mission, but He was a WINNER!" To prove that Jesus had guts, the physical effects of being crucified are described in gory detail. Apparently, this is to shame athletes into competing more intently, whatever their injuries, their limitations or frame of mind. The crucifixion becomes an athletic sacrament, and athletes are asked to be martyrs. Without equivocation, the Institute lists as "SIN" such things as "failure to reach maximum athletic potential" and "fear of an opponent."

Clearly, the trickiest thing in mixing religion with sport is the matter of asking God for victory. It is a no-no to do so, but, unfortunately, it is quite common for athletes to get carried away and to pray precisely for that. "He's just an overly enthusiastic baby Christian," Billy Zeoli, the inspirational chapel speaker, said after a pro football player came flat out in pregame prayers and asked Jesus to give his team a win. "Please don't get on him." Zeoli, however, felt it was unnecessary to discuss the impropriety of a victory prayer with the player. The line can be a fine one. When Kermit Zarley, one of the outspoken Christians on the PGA tour, won the Canadian Open a few years ago, he credited his success to God for having found him a new driver. Now, if that was not quite like saying that God hit tee shots for Kermit Zarley, the implication was clear that Zarley won the Canadian Open because God hung around pro shops with him when he was hunting for new clubs. Regrettably, whatever Sportianity is trying to project, the public often has another impression. Most viewers believe that teams assembling for a televised prayer after a victory are Pharisees, thanking God, paying Him off for getting them another big one in the W column. A poll of young Christian athletes, teenagers who have been specifically instructed by the movement, asked, "What does it mean to be a Christian athlete?" The response most often received was, "To have God on my side." Jesus, it seems, is coming across as the next best thing to a homecourt advantage.

At the same time, no one in the movement advises athletes to pray for victory. On the contrary, the try ethic, epitomized by Christ's Total Release Performance at Gethsemane on Maundy Thursday, is almost universally taught. The message is virtually the same all over: try your hardest, and then, win or lose, you will not be in conflict with Christian tenets. The favorite scripture comes from Paul, who is heard so regularly that he has become rather like the Curt Gowdy of Sportianity—and not only because both tend to get windy. The essence of Paul's endorsement of competition and Total Release Performance is found in 1 Corinthians 9:24, which quotes him thus in a modern paraphrase text of the New Testament: "Surely you know that in a race all the runners take part in it, but only one of them wins the prize. Run, then, in such a way as to win the prize." Also cited regularly are Paul's familiar words from 2 Timothy 4:7: "I have fought a good fight, I have finished my course, I have kept the faith." Unfortunately, Paul's most direct statement about athletics (1 Timothy 4:7-8) does not fit in Sportianity, so it is never quoted: ". . . exercise thyself rather unto godliness. For bodily exercise profiteth little.". . .

"The trouble with these people is that they worship sport as much as they do Jesus. They are so thrilled to be working with hotshot stars that they can see nothing wrong with athletics. They don't want to. I'm afraid that it is not religion that has come into sport, but athletic groupies."

More than a decade ago a deeply religious pitcher named Allan Worthington protested that he would quit the Chicago White Sox unless the club stopped stealing opponents' signals by illegal means. Since that time players in all leagues have struck righteously for more money, more benefits, more power. But not until five months ago, when Bobby Hull refused to suit up for a hockey game in protest against the violence in his sport and in fear that someone might be killed, has a single player dared put himself publicly on the line against something he considered ethically remiss.

Sportianity casts stones at players like Joe Namath for personal behavior. Dave Hannah of Athletes In Action is still angry that Lance Rentzel was doing work in Sportianity at a time when he was having deep psychological disturbances; Hannah thinks that Rentzel was inconsiderate in bringing such bad sexual publicity to the movement. But no one in the movement—much less any organization—speaks out against the cheating in sport, against dirty play; no one attacks the evils of recruiting, racism or any of the many other well-known excesses and abuses. Sport owns Sunday now, and religion is content to lease a few minutes before the big games. Religion seems to have become a support force for athletics, like broadcasters, trainers, cheerleaders and ticket-sellers. John Morley, a British statesman, wrote, "Where it is a duty to worship the sun, it is pretty sure to be a crime to examine the laws of heat." As long as it can work the territory, Sportianity seems prepared to accept athletics as is, more devoted to exploiting sport than to serving it.

Baseball Magic

GEORGE GMELCH

> We find magic wherever the elements of chance and accident, and the emotional play between hope and fear have a wide and extensive range. We do not find magic wherever the pursuit is certain, reliable, and well under the control of rational methods.
>
> Bronislaw Malinowski

Professional baseball is a nearly perfect arena in which to test Malinowski's hypothesis about magic. The great anthropologist was not, of course, talking about sleight of hand but of rituals, taboos and fetishes that men

SOURCE: George Gmelch, "Baseball Magic," *Transaction*, 8 (June 1971), 39–41, 54.

resort to when they want to ensure that things go their own way. Baseball is rife with this sort of magic, but, as we shall see, the players use it in some aspects of the game far more than in others.

Everyone knows that there are three essentials of baseball—hitting, pitching and fielding. The point is, however, that the first two, hitting and pitching, involve a high degree of chance. The pitcher is the player least able to control the outcome of his own efforts. His best pitch may be hit for a bloop single while his worst pitch may be hit directly to one of his fielders for an out. He may limit the opposition to a single hit and lose, or he may give up a dozen hits and win. It is not uncommon for pitchers to perform well and lose, and vice versa; one has only to look at the frequency with which pitchers end a season with poor won-lost percentages but low earned run averages (number of runs given up per game). The opposite is equally true: some pitchers play poorly, giving up many runs, yet win many games. In brief, the pitcher, regardless of how well he performs, is dependent upon the proficiency of his teammates, the inefficiency of the opposition and the supernatural (luck).

But luck, as we all know, comes in two forms, and many fans assume that the pitcher's tough losses (close games in which he gave up very few runs) are eventually balanced out by his "lucky" wins. This is untrue, as a comparison of pitchers' lifetime earned run averages to their overall won-lost records shows. If the player could apply a law of averages to individual performance, there would be much less concern about chance and uncertainty in baseball. Unfortunately, he cannot and does not.

Hitting, too, is a chancy affair. Obviously, skill is required in hitting the ball hard and on a line. Once the ball is hit, however, chance plays a large role in determining where it will go, into a waiting glove or whistling past a falling stab.

With respect to fielding, the player has almost complete control over the outcome. The average fielding percentage or success rate of .975, compared to a .245 success rate for hitters (the average batting average), reflects the degree of certainty in fielding. Next to the pitcher or hitter, the fielder has little to worry about when he knows that better than 9.7 times in ten he will execute his task flawlessly.

If Malinowski's hypothesis is correct, we should find magic associated with hitting and pitching, but none with fielding. Let us take the evidence by category—ritual, taboo and fetish.

RITUALS

After each pitch, ex-major leaguer Lou Skeins used to reach into his back pocket to touch a crucifix, straighten his cap and clutch his genitals. Detroit Tiger infielder Tim Maring wore the same clothes and put them on exactly in the same order each day during a batting streak. Baseball rituals are almost infinitely various. After all, the ballplayer can ritualize any activity he considers necessary for a successful performance, from the type of cereal he eats in the morning to the streets he drives home on.

Usually, rituals grow out of exceptionally good performances. When the player does well he cannot really attribute his success to skill alone. He plays with the same amount of skill one night when he gets four hits as the next night when he goes hitless. Through magic, such as ritual, the player seeks greater control over his performance, actual control over the elements of chance. The player, knowing that his ability is fairly constant, attributes the inconsistencies in his performance to some form of behavior or a particular food that he ate. When a player gets four hits in a game, especially "cheap" hits, he often believes that there must have been something he did, in addition to his ability, that shifted luck to his side. If he can attribute his good fortune to the glass of iced tea he drank before the game or the new shirt he wore to the ballpark, then by repeating the same behavior the following day he can hope to achieve similar results. (One expression of this belief is the myth that eating certain foods will give the ball "eyes," that is, a ball that seeks the gaps between fielders.) In hopes of maintaining a batting streak, I once ate fried chicken every day at 4:00 P.M., kept my eyes closed during the national anthem and changed sweat shirts at the end of the fourth inning each night for seven consecutive nights until the streak ended.

Fred Caviglia, Kansas City minor league pitcher, explained why he eats certain foods before each game: "Everything you do is important to winning. I never forget what I eat the day of a game or what I wear. If I pitch well and win I'll do it all exactly the same the next day I pitch. You'd be crazy not to. You just can't ever tell what's going to make the difference between winning and losing."

Rituals associated with hitting vary considerably in complexity from one player to the next, but they have several components in common. One of the most popular is tagging a particular base when leaving and returning to the dugout each inning. Tagging second base on the way to the outfield is habitual with some players. One informant reported that during a successful month of the season he stepped on third base on his way to the dugout after the third, sixth and ninth innings of each game. Asked if he ever purposely failed to step on the bag he replied, "Never! I wouldn't dare, it would destroy my confidence to hit." It is not uncommon for a hitter who is playing poorly to try different combinations of tagging and not tagging particular bases in an attempt to find a successful combination. Other components of a hitter's ritual may include tapping the plate with his bat a precise number of times or taking a precise number of warm-up swings with the leaded bat.

One informant described a variation of this in which he gambled for a certain hit by tapping the plate a fixed number of times. He touched the plate once with his bat for each base desired: one tap for a single, two for a double and so on. He even built in odds that prevented him from asking for a home run each time. The odds of hitting a single with one tap were one in three, while the chances of hitting a home run with four taps were one in 12.

Clothing is often considered crucial to both hitters and pitchers. They may have several athletic supporters and a number of sweat shirts with ritual significance. Nearly all players wear the same uniform and undergarments each day when playing well, and some even wear the same street clothes. In 1954, the New York Giants, during a 16-game winning streak, wore the same clothes in each game and refused to let them be cleaned for fear that their good fortune might be washed away with the dirt. The route taken to and from the stadium can also have significance; some players drive the same streets to the ballpark during a hitting streak and try different routes during slumps.

Because pitchers only play once every four days, the rituals they practice are often more complex than the hitters', and most of it, such as tugging the cap between pitches, touching the rosin bag after each bad pitch or smoothing the dirt on the mound before each new batter, takes place on the field. Many baseball fans have observed this behavior never realizing that it may be as important to the pitcher as throwing the ball.

Dennis Grossini, former Detroit farmhand, practiced the following ritual on each pitching day for the first three months of a winning season. First, he arose from bed at exactly 10:00 A.M. and not a minute earlier or later. At 1:00 P.M. he went to the nearest restaurant for two glasses of iced tea and a tuna fish sandwich. Although the afternoon was free, he observed a number of taboos such as no movies, no reading and no candy. In the clubhouse he changed into the sweat shirt and jock he wore during his last winning game, and one hour before the game he chewed a wad of Beechnut chewing tobacco. During the game he touched his letters (the team name on his uniform) after each pitch and straightened his cap after each ball. Before the start of each inning he replaced the pitcher's rosin bag next to the spot where it was the inning before. And after every inning in which he gave up a run he went to the clubhouse to wash his hands. I asked him which part of the ritual was most important. He responded: "You can't really tell what's most important so it all becomes important. I'd be afraid to change anything. As long as I'm winning I do everything the same. Even when I can't wash my hands [this would occur when he must bat] it scares me going back to the mound. . . . I don't feel quite right."

One ritual, unlike those already mentioned, is practiced to improve the power of the baseball bat. It involves sanding the bat until all the varnish is removed, a process requiring several hours of labor, then rubbing rosin into the grain of the bat before finally heating it over a flame. This ritual treatment supposedly increases the distance the ball travels after being struck. Although some North Americans prepare their bats in this fashion it is more popular among Latin Americans. One informant admitted that he was not certain of the effectiveness of the treatment. But, he added, "There may not be a God, but I go to church just the same."

Despite the wide assortment of rituals associated with pitching and hitting, I never observed any ritual related to fielding. In all my 20 interviews only one player, a shortstop with acute fielding problems, reported any ritual even remotely connected to fielding.

TABOOS

Mentioning that a no-hitter is in progress and crossing baseball bats are the two most widely observed taboos. It is believed that if the pitcher hears the words "no-hitter" his spell will be broken and the no-hitter lost. As for the crossing of bats, that is sure to bring bad luck; batters are therefore extremely careful not to drop their bats on top of another. Some players elaborate this taboo even further. On one occasion a teammate became quite upset when another player tossed a bat from the batting cage and it came to rest on top of his. Later he explained that the top bat would steal hits from the lower one. For him, then, bats contain a finite number of hits, a kind of baseball "image of limited good." Honus Wagner, a member of baseball's Hall of Fame, believed that each bat was good for only 100 hits and no more. Regardless of the quality of the bat he would discard it after its 100th hit.

Besides observing the traditional taboos just mentioned, players also observe certain personal prohibitions. Personal taboos grow out of exceptionally poor performances, which a player often attributes to some particular behavior or food. During my first season of professional baseball I once ate pancakes before a game in which I struck out four times. Several weeks later I had a repeat performance, again after eating pancakes. The result was a pancake taboo in which from that day on I never ate pancakes during the season. Another personal taboo, born out of similar circumstances, was against holding a baseball during the national anthem.

Taboos are also of many kinds. One athlete was careful never to step on the chalk foul lines or the chalk lines of the batter's box. Another would never put on his cap until the game started and would not wear it at all on the days he did not pitch. Another had a movie taboo in which he refused to watch a movie the day of a game. Often certain uniform numbers become taboo. If a player has a poor spring training or a bad year, he may refuse to wear the same uniform number again. I would not wear double numbers, especially 44 and 22. On several occasions, teammates who were playing poorly requested a change of uniform during the middle of the season. Some players consider it so important that they will wear the wrong size uniform just to avoid a certain number or to obtain a good number.

Again, with respect to fielding, I never saw or heard of any taboos being observed, though of course there were some taboos, like the uniform numbers, that were concerned with overall performance and so included fielding.

FETISHES

These are standard equipment for many baseball players. They include a wide assortment of objects: horsehide covers of old baseballs, coins, bobby pins, protective cups, crucifixes and old bats. Ordinary objects are given this power in a fashion similar to the formation of taboos and rituals. The player during an exceptionally hot batting or pitching streak, especially one in which he has "gotten all the breaks," credits some unusual object, often a new possession, for his good fortune. For example, a player in a slump might find a coin or an odd stone just before he begins a hitting streak. Attributing the improvement in his performance to the new object, it becomes a fetish, embodied with supernatural power. While playing for Spokane, Dodger pitcher Alan Foster forgot his baseball shoes on a road trip and borrowed a pair from a teammate to pitch. That night he pitched a no-hitter and later, needless to say, bought the shoes from his teammate. They became his most prized possession.

Fetishes are taken so seriously by some players that their teammates will not touch them out of fear of offending the owner. I once saw a fight caused by the desecration of a fetish. Before the game, one player stole the fetish, a horsehide baseball cover, out of a teammate's back pocket. The prankster did not return the fetish until after the game, in which the owner of the fetish went hitless, breaking a batting streak. The owner, blaming his inability to hit on the loss of the fetish, lashed out at the thief when the latter tried to return it.

Rube Waddel, an old-time Philadelphia Athletic pitching great, had a hairpin fetish. However, the hairpin he possessed was only powerful as long as he won. Once he lost a game he would look for another hairpin, which had to be found on the street, and he would not pitch until he found another.

The use of fetishes follows the same pattern as ritual and taboo in that they are connected only with hitting or pitching. In nearly all cases the player expressed a specific purpose for carrying a fetish, but never did a player perceive his fetish as having any effect on his fielding.

I have said enough, I think, to show that many of the beliefs and practices of professional baseball players are magical. Any empirical connection between the ritual, taboo and fetish and the desired event is quite absent. Indeed, in several instances the relationship between the cause and effect, such as eating tuna fish sandwiches to win a ball game, is even more remote than is characteristic of primitive magic. Note, however, that unlike many forms of primitive magic, baseball magic is usually performed to achieve one's own end and not to block someone else's. Hitters do not tap their bats on the plate to hex the pitcher, but to improve their own performance.

Finally, it should be plain that nearly all the magical practices that I participated in, observed or elicited, support Malinowski's hypothesis that magic appears in situations of chance and uncertainty. The large amount of uncertainty in pitching and hitting best explains the elaborate magical practices used for these activities. Conversely, the high success rate in fielding, .975, involving much less uncertainty, offers the best explanation for the absence of magic in this realm.

■ FOR FURTHER STUDY

"Are Sports Good for the Soul?" *Newsweek* (January 11, 1976), pp. 51–52.

Becker, Judy. "Superstition in Sport." *International Journal of Sports Psychology*, 6 (1975), 148–152.

Bianchi, E. "Pigskin Piety." *Christianity and Crisis*, 32 (1972) 31–34.

Boyle, Robert H. "Oral Roberts: Small BUT OH, MY." *Sports Illustrated* (November 1970).

Brasch, Rudolph. *How Did Sports Begin?* New York: David McKay, 1970.

Brownridge, David. "Karate and Christianity: Parallels on Different Planes." *Sport Sociology Bulletin*, 4 (Spring 1975), 56–59.

Cox, Harvey. *The Feast of Fools: A Theological Essay on Festivity and Fantasy.* Cambridge, Mass.: Harvard University Press, 1969.

Deford, Frank. "Religion in Sport." *Sports Illustrated* (April 19, April 26, May 3, 1976).

Desmonde, W. "The Bullfight as a Religious Festival." *American Imago*, 9 (1952), 173–195.

Dirkson, Jay. "The Place of Athletics in the Life of the Christian." *Sport Sociology Bulletin*, 4 (Spring 1975), 48–55.

Eitzen, D. Stanley, and George H. Sage. *Sociology of American Sport*. Dubuque, Iowa: Wm. C. Brown, 1978, chapter 5.

Elias, Jacob W. "Games Christians Watch." *The Mennonite*, 88 (November 20, 1973), 666-668.

Eskenazi, Gerald. "Superstition Wields Power Over Athletes." *Chicago Tribune* (November 29, November 30, 1976).

Fagin, Ralph, and Paul Brynteson, "The Cohesive Function of Religion and Sport at a Sectarian University." *Sport Sociology Bulletin*, 4 (Spring 1975), 33-47.

Falls, Joe. "More and More Athletes Turn to Religion." *Parade* (April 23, 1978), pp. 6-7.

Fellowship of Christian Athletes. *The Christian Athlete* (any issue).

Fox, J. "Pueblo Baseball: A New Use for Old Witchcraft." *Journal of American Folklore*, 74 (1961), 9-16.

"Golfing for God," *Newsweek* (July 31, 1972), pp. 60-61.

Gregory, C. Jane, and Brian M. Petrie. "Superstitions of Canadian Intercollegiate Athletes: An Inter-Sport Comparison." *International Review of Sport Sociology*, 10 (1975).

Gutkind, Lee. "Striking a Blow for Christ." *Sports Illustrated* (July 30, 1973), pp. 32-34.

Herald, Childe. "Freud and Football." *Reader in Comparative Religion*. 2nd ed. Edited by William A. Lessa and Evon Z. Vogt. New York: Harper & Row, 1965, pp. 250-252.

Hesburgh, Theodore M. "The True Meaning of the Game." *Sports Illustrated* (December 12, 1966), pp. 56-57.

Hogan, William R., "Sin and Sports." *Motivations in Play, Games, and Sports*. Edited by Ralph Slovenko and James A. Knight. Springfield, Ill.: Charles C. Thomas, 1967.

Huskel, E. "Should Christians Play on Sunday?" *Literary Digest*, 88 (1926), 27-28.

Jable, J. Thomas. "The English Puritans—Suppressors of Sport and Amusement?" *Canadian Journal of the History of Sport and Physical Education*, 7 (May 1976), p. 33-40.

Jable, J. Thomas. "Sunday Sport Comes to Pennsylvania: Professional Baseball and Football Triumph Over the Commonwealth's Archaic Blue Laws, 1919-1933." *Research Quarterly*, 47 (October 1976), 357-365.

Jares, Joe. "Hallelujah, What a Team!" *Sports Illustrated* (February 1977).

Katz, Fred, ed. *The Glory of Notre Dame*. Hong Kong: Bartholomew House, 1971.

Kirshenbaum, Jerry. "Reincarnation and 13 Pairs of Socks." *Sports Illustrated* (March 28, 1977), pp. 30-33.

Koppett, Leonard. "Athletes in Action Spread Gospel Efficiently." *New York Times* (March 15, 1977), p. 50.

Kucharsky, David. "It's Time to Think Seriously About Sports." *Christianity Today*, 20 (November 7, 1975), 18-20.

Lewis, Guy. "The Muscular Christianity Movement." *JOPER*, 37 (May 1966).

Louis, Arthur M. "Should You Buy Biorhythms?" *Psychology Today*, 11 (April, 1978), 93-96.

Lyon, Bill. "Athletes Ardent Believers in Omens, Hexes." *The Sporting News* (May 14, 1977), pp. 45, 52.

MacAloon, J. "Religious Themes and Structures in the Olympic Movement and the Olympic Games." Paper presented at the International Congress of the Physical Activity Sciences, Quebec City (July, 1976).

Malinowski, Bronislaw. *Magic, Science and Religion*. Garden City, New York: Doubleday, 1948.

Marbeto, Joseph A., Jr. "The Incidence of Prayer in Athletics as Indicated by Selected California Collegiate Athletes and Coaches." Master's thesis, University of California, Santa Barbara, 1967.

Miller, David L. *Gods and Games: Toward a Theology of Play*. Cleveland: World, 1969.

Milton, B. "Sports as a Functional Equivalent of Religion." Master's thesis, University of Wisconsin, Madison, 1972.

Real, M. "Superbowl: Mythic Spectacle." *Journal of Communication*, 25 (Winter 1975), 31–43.

Roberts, Oral. "A Witness to 40 Million Sports-Conscious Men . . . By Going Into Their World." *Abundant Life*, 25 (February 1971), 10.

Rogers, Cornish. "Sports, Religion and Politics: The Renewal of an Alliance." *The Christian Century*, 89 (April 5, 1972), 392–394.

Rudin, A. James. "America's New Religion." *The Christian Century*, 89 (April 5, 1972), 384.

Schloz, R., et al. "Sport and Religions of the World." *Sport and the Modern World*. Edited by O. Grupe et al. New York: Springer-Verlag, 1973.

Scotch, N. A. "Magic, Sorcery, and Football Among Urban Zulu." *The Journal of Conflict Resolution*, 5 (1961), 70–74.

Simonson, T., ed. *The Goal and The Glory—America's Athletes Speak Their Faith*. Westwood, N.J.: Revell, 1962.

Slusher, Howard S. *Man, Sport and Existence: A Critical Analysis*. Philadelphia: Lea and Febiger, 1967.

Wallace, Francis. *Notre Dame from Rockne to Parseghian*. New York: David McKay, 1966.

Weiss, Paul. *Sport: A Philosophic Inquiry*. Carbondale: Southern Illinois University Press, 1969.

Wenkert, Simon. "The Meaning of Sports for Contemporary Man." *Journal of Existential Psychiatry* (Spring 1963), pp. 397–404.

Ten

Racism in Sport

By definition a minority group is one that is: (1) relatively powerless compared to the majority group; (2) possesses similar traits that make them stand apart from others; (3) systematically condemned by negative stereotyped beliefs; and (4) singled out for differential and unfair treatment (discrimination). Unquestionably, blacks constitute a minority group in American society.[1] But although the members of this minority have been the objects of discriminatory treatment throughout American history, there is the widespread and persistent belief that contemporary sport is an island free of racial animosities and tensions. After all, the argument goes, blacks are disproportionately represented in sport, constituting approximately two-thirds of all professional basketball players, two-fifths of all professional football players, and one-fifth of all professional baseball players while they are but 11 percent of the population. Moreover, blacks are among the highest paid athletes. And, perhaps most important, sport is one area of American life where performance is all that counts (and since it is accurately measured, skin color is irrelevant).

The papers selected for this unit make the opposite case. The thesis is that sport is a microcosm of society, reflecting the biases present in all of society. The first paper, by sports columnist Terry Bledsoe, addresses the question of why blacks appear to dominate in sports. He argues that, because of the restricted opportunities for blacks in American society, disproportionately large numbers channel their energies and talents into sport.

The second selection, by economist Gerald Scully, examines racial discrimination in baseball. Of special interest historically is the attitude of the powerful in baseball at the time of Jackie Robinson's breaking of the racial barrier in 1946–1947. The bulk of Scully's paper, however, presents contemporary empirical data on the prejudice among fans, discriminatory hiring practices, performance differentials by race, entry barriers, and stacking by position.

The final selection, by sociologists Eitzen and Yetman, is similar to Scully's but broader in scope. It summarizes the known data on discrimination in football, basketball, and baseball in three basic areas: stacking by position, rewards and authority, and unequal opportunity for equal ability.

The data presented in this paper and the others in this section overwhelmingly negate the commonly held assumption that sport is free of racial discrimination.

NOTES

1. The discussion in this unit is limited to blacks because they are the most prominent minority in American sports.

Black Dominance of Sports: Strictly from Hunger

TERRY BLEDSOE

There they stand, the 1973 San Francisco Golden State Warriors of the National Basketball Association (NBA), sterling proof that racial discrimination in sports is a bygone thing. Look at this team, one of the finest in all basketball, and reflect on the evidence it offers that success in the NBA is open to anyone, regardless of race, creed, or color. Don't look at the black coach on the bench. Look at the four white guys on the starting team. *That's* the surprise.

It is a measure, too, of how swiftly black athletes have moved to dominate professional basketball. No area of athletics has been visited so heavily by black excellence, and, hearteningly, no area of athletics has responded so promptly to black involvement in management. But basketball is merely the most natural channel of a black tide that has been flooding professional sports with some of the most remarkable achievers in a hierarchy of achievers.

Professional football probably tapped black sources first and kept at it with the greatest diligence; professional baseball has been in the business of including blacks only since 1947; professional basketball has but recently achieved the national impact that made it a fair measuring ground for black achievement.

Consider, in 1972–1973, the results of black effort in American professional sports:

- The five top hitters in baseball's National League, and three of the five top hitters in the American League, are black.
- Blacks occupy three of the five places on the NBA's first all-league team, and seven of the ten places on the first two teams.
- Blacks hold nine of the twenty-two places on the National Football League's all-pro team.

It is a black man, Hank Aaron, who is baseball's super hero, breathing hot on the heels of the game's most hidebound record of its most

SOURCE: Terry Bledsoe, "Black Dominance of Sports: Strictly from Hunger," *The Progressive*, 37 (June 1973), 16–19.

hidebound immortal, the 714 home runs of Babe Ruth. It is a black man, Larry Brown, who is the National Football League's reigning most valuable player. It is a black man—Wilt Chamberlain? Kareem Abdul-Jabbar?—who is the dominant force in professional basketball.

Black dominance of any pursuit would merit study, given the fact that only eleven per cent of the nation's population is black. For example, black dominance of the carpenter's trade would raise eyebrows, the disproportionately high percentage of blacks on casualty lists from Vietnam became a national curiosity—although never quite the national concern it should have been.

But black dominance of sports has become a highly visible sociological phenomenon. After all, the President of the United States, who displays camaraderie with football luminaries, does not tend to call carpenters to the telephone.

Professional athletes are the dream stuff of a nation, and black dominance of sports is reshaping the hero symbols of a society. The phenomenon is easier to discern than the reasons for it. It is hardly stylish to lean upon the weary crutch of the Step 'n Fetchit days of black prominence: "You people certainly have got rhythm." That fiction provided solace to generations of white Americans attuned to the boxing grace of the Henry Armstrongs and the Joe Louises, and all the way back to the Jack Johnsons and the Peter Jacksons.

There has to be more to it than that. There must have been more to it than that all along. Perhaps, had Americans faced up to the fact in the years before bigotry had to go underground, a truer cliche could have been devised: "You people certainly have got hunger." For that may be the key to all of it, a way out of the jungle of black poverty and often the only way out.

James Baldwin, the noted black writer, provided an insight without mentioning sports. He once wrote: "Every Negro boy realizes, at once, profoundly, because he wants to live, that he stands in great peril and must find, with speed, a 'thing,' a gimmick, to lift him out, to start him on his way. And it does not matter what the gimmick is."

For many black youths, the gimmick has been sports. Pursued with the single minded dedication of desperation, sports have opened a route upward, out of the ghetto, for dozens, hundreds, even thousands of black young men. Obversely, sports have been a siren song of tragedy for hundreds and thousands of other blacks, who staked their adolescence on the hope of achieving rare excellence in a sport, fell short, and had nothing else to fall back on.

Jack Olsen, a senior editor of *Sports Illustrated*, once quoted Will Robinson, a noted black coach, on the subject: "The white boy has other things he would rather do. People keep reminding me that there is a difference in physical ability between the races, but I think there isn't. The Negro boy just practices longer and harder. The Negro has the keener desire to excel in sports because it is more mandatory for his future opportunities than it is for a white boy. There are nine thousand different jobs available to a person if he is white."

The relative unavailability of those 9,000 jobs has been a source of bitterness and frustration to blacks, as surely as to any arbitrarily excluded minority throughout history. But while that anger has been in large measure unanswered in American society as a whole, it has served to concentrate black effort on the few areas that have opened up. Sports, for the generations of blacks who have matured since the end of World War II, have provided a gateway, and blacks have poured through the narrow opening into Establishment life.

The power of that tide has been remarkable, but it is not new. Novelist Budd Schulberg, who found in the brutal simplicity of professional boxing a poetry of the underprivileged, described it as rather a noble succession of the downtrodden:

"For if racing is the sport of kings," he wrote in *The Harder They Fall*, "boxing is the vocation of the slum dwellers who must fight to exist. When were the sons of Erin monopolizing the titles and glory: the Ryans, Sullivans, Donovans, Kilbanes, and O'Briens? When waves of Irish immigration were breaking over America. Gradually, as the Irish settled down to being politicians, policemen, judges, the Shamrock had to make room for the Star of David, to the Leonards, Tendlers, and Blooms. And then came the Italians: Genaro, La Barba, Indrissano, Canzoneri. Now the Negroes press forward, hungry for the money, prestige, and opportunity denied them at almost every door. . . ."

Schulberg wrote that in 1947, but the truth of his observation has not faded. For athletics have come to mean a gateway to sophistication, for whites and blacks alike. The rise of the athletic scholarship and the abuses thereof have become twin opportunities for advancement, licit and illicit. A college education today is a way station on the road to Schulberg's "money, prestige, and opportunity," and if too often the athlete finds himself cruelly and unfairly channeled into snap courses, it is certainly valid to wonder if a half-hearted education is not preferable to no education at all.

It is pointed out (by whites) that black progress in the last two decades of American history has been greater than in all of American history before that, and it is pointed out (by blacks) that that does not disguise the fact that outrageous discrimination still exists and must be eradicated. Both sides are right, of course, and both sides must know the historical truth that any improvement in a bad situation can only increase impatience for further improvement.

But those in the business of sports, and sports fans, have shown improvement in their racial attitudes; a fair analysis must conclude that the sports world has been quicker to react to wrongs than other segments of society. It should be hastily added, however, that good for goodness' sake has been no more frequent a virtue in professional sports than in, say, the huckstering of soap. Professional sports have responded to the demands of black athletes because black athletes were simply too good to be ignored—especially after Branch Rickey demonstrated in 1947 that if your favorite baseball team didn't want Jackie Robinson, his Brooklyn Dodgers did.

In the middle 1960s, when Vince Lombardi quietly changed the training camp rooming assignments of his Green Bay Packers to a strict alphabetical system, he was responding to a personal code of ethics that demanded he strike down the black and black, and white and white, sets of roommates. But Lombardi was too much of a pragmatist not to realize that by acting against segregation he also was removing a potential source of difficulty on a football team dependent on black men. In that case, good moral practice and good business took parallel paths, and Lombardi set up a system that is now widely followed.

In an earlier time, so moderate a step forward was regarded as an advancement of significance—and in an earlier time, perhaps it was. But discrimination takes many forms, and the National Football League still has its share. Not entirely—not perhaps even mainly—through the NFL's own fault. But in recent years "stacking" has come to be a swear word among blacks in the League, and what happens in the NFL is often a direct result of what happens at the college level. Because pro football, unlike pro baseball, uses the colleges as a direct source of largely finished products, the position a man plays in college is far more often than not the position he will play as a pro. There are exceptions, of course, but they remain just that.

"Stacking" can be loosely defined as the practice of channeling black athletes into relatively few positions, and declaring other positions off limits to them. Coaches scoff at the charge, citing the reasonable argument that only a fool would deprive himself of a needed talent on racial grounds.

Yet stacking continues, in statistically provable amounts. It is widely assumed that the football position least available to black men is quarterback—not coincidentally, the highest paid of all pro football jobs, coach included. However, that isn't quite true. An assistant professor of sociology at the Fullerton branch of the University of California, Jonathan J. Brower, took on the mind-boggling task of surveying NFL rosters for a dozen years. He uncovered four black quarterbacks and one (albeit brief) starter, James Harris of the Buffalo Bills.

Brower also found that in the twelve years there had never been a black center. Now, it is possible, considering the limited appeal of taking the special beating pro football centers absorb, that this merely illustrates the superior intelligence of black men. But Brower concluded that the position was regarded as one demanding considerable intelligence—it does—and was an example of a place where the Jim Crow signs still hung out.

Brower delineated what he called "constellations" of positions. He reported that in the twelve years, seven per cent of the quarterbacks, centers, and linebackers were black. (Presumably, the grouping was topheavy with linebackers, since the two other positions had already been shown to be whiter than a Klansman's sheet.) Only one per cent of the kickers and punters was black. Thirteen per cent of the guards, offensive tackles, and tight ends were black, as were eighteen per cent of defensive ends and tackles. Of running backs, wide receivers, defensive backs, and kick returners, Brower reported, a full sixty-two per cent were black.

Brower sometimes strained to find an explanation consistent with his thesis. For instance, he concluded that the dearth of kickers and punters was due to the coaches' insistence on "ability to stand pressure and make decisions under the gun." He ignored the fact that a kick returner faces greater pressure than a kicker, makes more decisions, and runs the risk of getting his block knocked off besides.

But all this aside, the fact of stacking was obvious in Brower's study. Indeed, sometimes stacking is the result of black initiative, for intelligent athletes are likely to conclude that they would rather switch jobs than fight the system.

Gene Washington of the San Francisco 49ers may be the premier wide receiver in professional football today; at the least he is an all-pro. But few people remember that as a sophomore at Stanford University in 1966 he was the starting quarterback. By his own choice, while still at Stanford, he switched to wide receiver, because he discerned a greater chance to be another black pass catcher than the only black quarterback.

"It was strictly a matter of economics," Washington said. "I knew a black quarterback would have little chance in pro ball unless he was absolutely superb. What usually happens is that a pro team tells you there's no place for you at quarterback, but they can use you as a defensive back or flanker. And then they tell you they can't give you as much money because you'd be learning a new position. So I decided to beat them to it."

In the final analysis, though, stacking must be regarded as the result of conclusions by coaches—high school, college, and pro—that blacks are best suited for specified positions. That may well be true, and it does not necessarily connote a plantation owner's mentality, for it carries with it the corollary that white players also are best suited for certain positions. Thus, if blacks are more apt to be wide receivers than centers, then whites must be less apt to be wide receivers. Perhaps it is no accident that the football positions most filled by blacks—wide receiver and defensive back—are also the football positions that come closest to demanding the free, flowing physical grace of basketball players.

Pete Axthelm, in his excellent book, *The City Game*, prowled the playgrounds in New York in search of basketball's bedrock, and he found it most often on the cracked asphalt of Harlem playgrounds. He saw in the game a test of manhood—a step closer to the essence than The Way Out—and almost without trying he found himself chronicling the tribal rite of Black America.

Al McGuire, whose consistent success as basketball coach at Marquette University has rested largely on his ability to attract and communicate with black youngsters, has a simple explanation for black dominance of basketball. "It's the brothers' game," he said. "The white kid can be as good, but first he has to be as serious about it."

But McGuire sees another side to the coin, too: "Maybe you can't play as many blacks at the same time," he said. "That's a hard thing to talk about, but maybe it's the answer. Black players don't have the discipline most white players do. They spend their summers on the playgrounds, playing free lance ball, and coming back to college ball probably is more difficult for them." Yet it is that very willingness to dedicate a summer to achieving excellence—the perfection of a jump shot, for example—that has propelled the black athlete to the fore of basketball and baseball and football competition. But, with infrequent exception, similar black willingness has not provided similar achievement in more esoteric sports.

Arthur Ashe is a world class tennis player; Lee Elder is following the path cleared by Charlie Sifford in professional golf. But they are all but alone; black awareness has not triggered corresponding assaults on those sports. Part of the reason may be that in good golf and good tennis, private clubs often provide the lifeblood of these more elite sports. Also, careful and meticulous tutoring is necessary for good golf and good tennis; a boy can, with proper physical tools, teach himself the nuances of a jump shot, but he can swing a golf club from now until Shrove Tuesday and fail to hit anything unless someone informs him about the interlocking grip.

At any rate, the impressive success of black men in the three major spectator sports can be counted upon to draw black youngsters to those sports. "It's a thing that works its way down," McGuire said. "If Kareem wears one red shoe and one white one, in seven years some grade school kid will be wearing one red shoe and one white one, too."

The financial rewards are fantastically high for the black athlete—just as high, in all probability, as for the white athlete of similar status. The two stars of the Milwaukee Bucks of the NBA are both black; Kareem Abdul-Jabbar makes $400,000 a season, Oscar Robertson $233,000. Baseball's Atlanta Braves pay Hank Aaron $200,000 a year.

Yet, with the exception of pro basketball, blacks have been denied the next logical step, that of progressing from an outstanding playing career to the management level. It is a galling omission. Frank Robinson of the California Angels, long recognized as one of baseball's finest players, wants badly to become Big League baseball's first black manager and has been waiting five years for the chance. Pro football, which shows exemplary progress in most other matters, has a mere sprinkling of black assistant coaches and not even a particularly likely candidate for a head job.

The National Football League commissioner, Pete Rozelle, is aware of the problem, and has talked of attacking it in a dramatic and startling way. "We're going to have to face the problem of minority ownership," he said. "Forty per cent of the players in the League are black. Yet we have almost no blacks in front office positions. We will have to consider that seriously when we determine our expansion plans. It could, in effect, wind up as discrimination in reverse."

A statement like that, of course, can be counted upon to work wonders. At the moment, the only potential site for a new pro football team with a black man near the top is Orlando-Jacksonville, which lists a former NFL linebacker named Rommie Loudd as its managing general partner. But other potential as well as present franchises may be counted upon to respond quickly to the hint—which, very possibly, was precisely what Rozelle had in mind.

Basketball is different. The Golden State Warriors, with their beguiling reverse English, have the unusually high number of four white starters and one of the NBA's two black coaches, Al Attles. Wayne Embry is the Bucks' general manager, and as such he is the highest ranking black in any sports organization. Simon Gourdine is an assistant commissioner of the NBA.

Part of the reason for the remaining reticence about blacks in the other sports is undoubtedly a lingering fear on the part of the front office—it exists to some extent in basketball, too, for that matter—that what white American ticket buyers really want to see is a white American athlete, the second generation descendant of the "white hope" they kept trotting out to meet Joe Louis.

It is an unarticulated fear, and at bottom probably less a fear than an excuse. It is difficult to sustain the thesis that three black starters on a five man basketball team are all right, but four are not; that four are acceptable, but five are not; that five might be all right as long as the coach is white. The permutations are so varied that the entire thesis collapses in the face of an example such as the Bucks, who have had five black starters for two years and have posted the NBA's fourth best attendance in its smallest arena.

If history offers a lesson, though, it is that the black tide in athletics will slacken, once society gets around to opening alternate avenues to prosperity and recognition. One day, perhaps, other oppressed people will elbow their way through the door. But in the meantime the white man's games are the black man's salvation.

Discrimination: the case of baseball

GERALD W. SCULLY

Major-league baseball is America's oldest and most venerable professional sport, billed from the beginning as the national pastime. It has cultivated an ethos of "fair play" in an effort to protect its privilege of self-regulation and to secure immunity from the standards by which others are judged. The motives of men in baseball are rarely questioned, and their actions tend to be rationalized as being in the interest of the "integrity of the game."

Major-league baseball is more than a business and a sport. It has long been regarded as a symbol of the American meritocracy. Ethnic minorities have sought through sports, which requires only particular athletic skills, what they could not attain elsewhere because of educational and language difficulties. On the field, it was and is asserted, all men compete equally. For Germans, Irish, Italians, and, now, Negroes, baseball has been the symbolic exit from the ghetto.

Despite the image of sports as a symbol of opportunity, those seeking

SOURCE: Gerald W. Scully, "Discrimination: The Case of Baseball," *Government and the Sports Business*, Roger G. Noll (ed.), (Washington, D.C.: The Brookings Institution, 1974), pp. 221-247.

to better their circumstances through baseball and other sports may incur great disappointment.

At the most, sports has led a few thousand Negroes into a better life while substituting a meaningless dream for hundreds of thousands of other Negroes. . . . For every Willie Mays or Bob Hayes there are countless Negroes who obviously had abundant will and determination to succeed, but who dedicated their childhoods and their energies to baseball gloves and shoulder pads. If there were other ways out and up, they were blinded to them by the success of a few sports celebrities. . . . This has been the major effect of sports on the Negro, and it overrides all others.[1]

It is a commonly held belief that baseball, unlike the greater society at large, has afforded Negroes equal status and equal opportunity. Nevertheless, "Negro athletes do not agree. . . . [They] say they are underpaid [and] shunted into certain stereotyped positions."[2] Surely, evidence cannot be found to sustain such a charge against major-league baseball! After all, the Negroes who have made it in the sport are successful by any standard. Nearly 25 percent of all major-league players are black, and many earn $100,000 or more annually. Yet, there is in fact evidence of racial discrimination in baseball: Negro ballplayers face markedly stiffer entrance requirements and earn significantly less for equivalent performance than whites do. This chapter explores the history and present status of these findings.

THE ROOTS OF DISCRIMINATION

The signing of Jackie Robinson, on October 23, 1945, to play with the Dodger organization at Montreal was widely touted as the beginning of a new phase in race relations in the United States. But the monumental efforts required of the civil rights movement during the fifties and sixties belie the wider importance of the Robinson event, although the signing was certainly an important breakthrough for both baseball and society as a whole. In any event, the signing of Robinson at least made public declarations of racist attitudes in baseball unfashionable. Personalities in baseball, both black and white, became silent on the race issue. It is significant that not one word concerning race discrimination was uttered either in testimony before the Celler committee in 1951[3] or in the Senate hearings conducted by Senator Estes Kefauver in 1958.[4] This silence created the illusion that baseball had adjusted to the presence of blacks in its ranks. Even Jackie Robinson, who was later to speak of the opprobrium that had been heaped on him,[5] was silent on the problem of the Negro ballplayer in his testimony before the Senate.[6] Thus, the period from 1947 until about 1970, when some black athletes began to speak critically about their position in professional sports, was characterized by a sense of euphoria about the state of race relations in sports. The large number of Negro major leaguers and the high salaries of the black superstars have contributed to the illusion that racial inequalities do not exist in baseball. This section establishes that with the signing of Robinson discrimination was not eliminated, but simply became more subtle in form.

Discrimination During the Early Period, 1845—98

Baseball originated in the urban areas of the North before the Civil War. The first professional baseball team, the Knickerbocker Club of New York City, was founded in September 1845. The institution of baseball quickly came to be regarded as a perfect manifestation of American democratic principles. Though dating from the First World War, the remarks of John K. Tener, president of the National League and former governor of Pennsylvania, accurately reflect the feelings of men in baseball throughout its history: "I tell you that baseball is the very watchword of democracy. There is no other sport or business or anything under heaven which exerts the leveling influence that baseball does. Neither the public school nor the church can approach it. Baseball is unique. England is a democratic country, but it lacks the finishing touch of baseball."[7] Indeed, in many respects, baseball was ahead of its time in measuring men by ability and not by ethnic origin. Throughout the post–Civil War period, minority groups, especially those of Irish and German descent, represented the majority of professional ballplayers.[8]

The opportunities available for Negroes were always limited. As early as 1867, Negro players and clubs were formally banned from playing with white teams. The National Association of Baseball Players (NABBP), at its national convention in Philadelphia in 1867, approved the proposal of its nominating committee to exclude Negroes from baseball. It was accurately reported that the purpose of the ban was "to keep out of the Convention the discussion of any subject having political bearing. . . ."[9] This motivation is borne out by the official records of the convention.[10]

The NABBP ban was effective for a while. Although the National Association of Professional Baseball Players (NAPBBP), formed in 1871 to replace the NABBP, did not incorporate a formal ban on Negro players, they were effectively excluded for a time by a "gentleman's agreement." But the ban against Negroes was never totally effective after the establishment of the NAPBBP. John W. (Bud) Fowler, who was the first paid Negro ballplayer, was on a white team in New Castle, Pennsylvania, in 1872.[11] It is also believed that there were "one or two other Negro players on white teams during the late 1870s and early 1880s."[12]

Opportunities for blacks in the early period reached their height in 1884–88; some have judged that this was a period when baseball was actually integrated.[13] But even in the peak year of 1887, the number of Negro players on white teams or in white leagues was minuscule. The period was initiated by the signing of Moses Fleetwood Walker with Toledo in 1883. The following year, Toledo entered the old American Association, making Walker the first Negro major leaguer. Later in the 1884 season his younger brother Weldy W. Walker played in six games when Toledo was shorthanded, thus becoming the second Negro major leaguer. At the end of the 1884 season, Fleet Walker was released by Toledo after several disabling accidents, and Negroes were not to play in the majors again until 1947. In 1885, only Fleet Walker and Bud Fowler were in the organized white leagues.[14] In 1886, with the addition of George W. Stovey and Frank Grant, four Negroes played on white minor-league teams.[15] By 1887, the number of Negro players had grown to about eight.[16] More importantly, in the same year the League of Colored Base Ball Clubs obtained recognition as a legitimate minor league; however, it collapsed almost immediately owing to the precarious financial position of its teams.

Despite these gains, there was every indication that the integration of Negroes into organized baseball would be only temporary. The fielding of Fleet Walker by Toledo caused several players and teams to declare that they would refuse to play if Walker were in the lineup. For example, in 1887, Adrian ("Cap") Anson refused to allow the Chicago White Stockings to play in an exhibition game against Newark until Stovey and Walker were removed. In the same year, the entire St. Louis Browns team, except Charlie Comiskey and Ed Knouff, signed a letter protesting a scheduled exhibition game with the Cuban Giants, the first Negro professional team.[17] Syracuse and Buffalo also had protests from their white players because of the signing of Robert Higgins and Frank Grant.[18] Douglas Crothers and Henry Simon, two white players at Syracuse, refused to have their picture taken with Higgins in an incident that was obviously racial in origin.[19]

To counteract the growing prejudice against Negroes, blacks and whites inside baseball adopted the ploy of advertising Negroes as Cubans or Spaniards. In 1886, when Frank Grant moved from Meriden, Connecticut, of the Eastern League, to Buffalo, of the International Association, the Buffalo *Express* reported that Grant was a Spaniard.[20] The first Negro professional team called itself the Cuban Giants and spoke in faked Spanish on the field.[21] Of the same genre was the attempt of John J. McGraw in 1901 to field the great Negro second baseman Charles Grant by advertising Grant as an Indian named Charlie Tokohama.[22]

By 1887, player pressure was building to formally exclude Negroes from the minor leagues. At the meeting in Buffalo of the International League clubs on July 14, 1887, "several representatives declared that many of the best players in the League were anxious to leave on account of the colored element, and the board finally directed Secretary White to approve of no more contracts with colored men."[23] The International League "liberalized" its racial ban the following year in a meeting in Toronto: it agreed to a policy of one Negro per team.

In 1888, John Montgomery Ward attempted to sign George Stovey, who had won thirty-five games for Newark during the previous season, for his New York Giants. Cap Anson, who emerged as a powerful figure in baseball during this period as the head of the Chicago White Stockings, succeeded in blocking the deal.[24] After the 1888 season, a few Negro players continued in organized baseball, but clearly the death knell had been sounded for the participation of Negroes in white baseball. The last Negro team to play white teams was the Acme Colored Giants, who played in the Iron and Oil League until mid-July 1898.[25]

From 1898 to 1946, Negroes were barred from organized baseball by an unwritten rule. They continued to play the game, but were confined to their own leagues. On a few occasions, teams attempted to add colored players to their rosters, but failed. The extent of racial discrimination is indicated by the attempt of Walter McCredie, the manager of Portland in the Pacific Coast League, to add Lang Akena, a player of Chinese-Hawaiian origin, to his roster. Akena was released because of "strenuous objections from prospective team mates."[26]

Racial Attitudes, 1933—45

With few exceptions, little of importance concerning the Negro in organized baseball appears to have occurred from 1898 until the 1930s. In the thirties, agitation began for the admission of Negroes into baseball's ranks. Influential sportswriters, such as Heywood Broun, Jimmy Powers, and Shirley Povich, spoke out against the ban. Their main theme was that a great wealth of Negro playing talent was going untapped. They argued that the skill of such outstanding athletes as Leroy (Satchel) Paige, James ("Cool Papa") Bell, Walter (Buck) Leonard, Slim Jones, and Josh Gibson would benefit baseball as much as it would the "Negro cause." Baseball's spokesmen were divided on how to respond to the pressure, and many of the statements of the baseball leadership on this issue during the thirties and forties were self-contradictory or conflicted with one another.

One defense was to deny that a ban against Negroes existed. In 1933, the president of the National League, John A. Heydler, stated: "I do not recall one instance where baseball has allowed either race, creed or color to enter into the question of the selection of its players."[27] In response to a charge by Leo Durocher that the commissioner of baseball was blocking the signing of Negroes, Judge Kenesaw Mountain Landis replied: "Negroes are not barred from organized baseball by the commissioner and never have been during the 21 years I have served as commissioner." [28]

In 1942, the *Pittsburgh Courier* contacted twenty-six owners and managers concerning the color ban, six of whom replied. Two said nothing. Three agreed with Landis, but had no suggestions on how to introduce Negroes into the structure of baseball. Clark Griffith of the Washington Senators offered this solution: "My idea is that the Negro leagues should be developed to the place where they will also assume a commanding place in the baseball world . . . Someday the top teams could play our top clubs for the world championship and thus have a chance to really prove their calibre." [29]

Shortly thereafter, baseball's unofficial voice, *Sporting News*, finally spoke out on the color ban:

> There is no law against Negroes playing with white teams, nor whites with colored clubs, but neither has invited the other for the obvious reason they prefer to draw their talent from their own ranks and because the leaders of both groups know their crowd psychology and do not care to run the risk of damaging their own game. Other sports had their Joe Louis, Jesse Owens, Fritz Pollard, and like notables, respected and honored by all races, but they competed under different circumstances from those dominating in baseball. [30]

The editorial went on to make three further points: (1) fan-player and interplayer relationships would probably take on racial overtones, which would be damaging to the game; (2) Negro players were doing well in the Negro leagues, and competition by the white teams for Negro players would decimate the Negro leagues financially; and (3) Negro agitators pressing for integration of organized baseball had the interests of neither the sport nor their race at heart.

In the early 1940s, several attempts were made to arrange tryouts for Negro players. In the spring of 1943, tryouts were promised by two Pacific Coast League executives, Clarence Rowland, president of the Los Angeles Angels, and Vince DeVencenzi, owner of the Oakland club, but in both cases the offers were withdrawn. [31] In the same year, Bill Veeck announced plans to purchase the Philadelphia Phillies and resuscitate the team with Negro players for the 1944 season. According to Veeck, although an agreement had been reached and financing arranged, Landis blocked the deal. [32] Finally, in 1945, Negro players were given tryouts by the Dodgers, the Red Sox, and the Braves. None resulted in signings, although one of the players who tried out for the Red Sox was Jackie Robinson, who later charged that the Red Sox had not been serious. [33]

Baseball's Adjustment to Integration, 1946

Robinson and baseball were not to be denied. Within six months, Branch Rickey announced that Jackie Robinson had been signed to play in the Dodger organization at Montreal. Baseball's official response to the agitation for racial integration and to the signing of Robinson was to create a steering committee "to consider and test all matters of major league interest."[34] Uppermost in the minds of the owners were the Mexican league, the growing attacks on the reserve clause, attempts at the unionization of players, and the player demands for a pension fund. But also to be considered was how baseball should respond to the pressure for racial integration. The report of the committee was the last official racist statement from organized baseball. Considering that Robinson was already playing for Montreal, the tone of the report is surprising. A few passages will indicate the depth of the anti-integration sentiment within the baseball hierarchy. Among the arguments made were the following:

(1) *Integrationists are no good*

Certain groups in this country, including political and social-minded drum-beaters, are conducting pressure campaigns in an attempt to force major league clubs to sign Negro players. Members of these groups are not primarily interested in professional baseball. They are not campaigning to provide better opportunity for thousands of Negro boys who want to play baseball. They are not even particularly interested in improving the lot of Negro players who are already employed. They know little about baseball—and nothing about the business end of its operation. They single out professional baseball for attack because it offers a good publicity medium.

(2) *Black fans will ruin the game*

The employment of a Negro on one AAA League club in 1946 resulted in a tremendous increase in Negro attendance at all games in which the player appeared. The percentage of Negro attendance at some games at Newark and Baltimore was in excess of 50 percent. The situation might be presented, if Negroes participate in major-league games, in which the preponderance of Negro attendance in parks such as the Yankee Stadium, the Polo Grounds, and Comiskey Park could conceivably threaten the value of the major league franchises owned by these clubs.

(3) *Negroes cannot play baseball as well as whites*

Comparatively few good young Negro players are being developed. This is the reason that there are not more players who meet major-league standards in the big Negro leagues. Sam Lacey, sports editor of the Afro-American newspapers, says, "I am reluctant to say that we haven't a single man in the ranks of colored baseball who could step into the major-league uniform and disport himself after the fashion of a big leaguer . . . There are those among our league players who might possibly excel in the matter of hitting or fielding or base running. But for the most part, the fellows who could hold their own in more than one of these phases of the game are few and far between—perhaps nil." Mr. Lacey's opinions are shared by almost everyone, Negro or white, competent to appraise the qualifications of Negro players.

(4) *Separate but equal status benefits blacks*

[The] Negro leagues cannot exist without good players. If they cannot field good teams, they will not continue to attract the fans who click the turnstiles. Continued prosperity depends upon improving standards of play. If the major leagues and the big minors of professional baseball raid these leagues and take their best players—the Negro leagues will eventually fold up—the investments of their club owners will be wiped out—and a lot of professional Negro players will lose their jobs.

(5) *Segregation is good business*

The Negro leagues rent their parks in many cities from clubs in organized baseball. Many major and minor league clubs derive substantial revenue from these rentals. (The Yankee organization, for instance, nets nearly $100,000 a year from rentals and concessions in connection with Negro league games at the Yankee Stadium in New York—and in Newark, Kansas City, and Norfolk.)[35]

Fear of economic loss weighed heavily on the minds of the club owners. It was believed that the introduction of black players would, by raising Negro attendance, drive away white fans. Another concern was the loss of frequently lucrative stadium rentals to teams in the Negro leagues. The solicitude expressed for the financial status of the Negro leagues was gratuitous, and the charge that few black players were of major-league caliber, spurious.

While baseball management was less than enthusiastic about the prospect of Negroes playing in the majors, some of the players felt strongly enough actually to attempt to block Robinson's appearance. Rickey was alleged to have asked each player, when he signed, if he had any objections to the transfer of Robinson from Montreal.[36] During spring training in 1947, there was a near mutiny of the Dodgers players,[37] but Rickey was able to quell the player revolt before it became effectively organized. Early in the season, the Phillies, Cubs, Cardinals, and possibly the Pirates threatened strikes. Some Phillies players showered Robinson with such scurrilous abuse that National League President Ford Frick and Commissioner Albert ("Happy") Chandler had to warn them against further racial baiting.[38] The threatened Cardinals player strike was the most serious, although baseball has never officially acknowledged that such a strike had been planned. Ford Frick prevented the disaster by threatening to suspend all strikers.

RACIAL ATTITUDES TODAY

The existence and depth of racial prejudice in baseball can be documented only before 1947. Since then, sports commentators, owners, managers, and both black and white players appear for the most part to have entered into a conspiracy of silence concerning racial tension and discrimination in the sport.

Prejudice among Fans

Baseball management was concerned that attendance would decline with the introduction of Negro players. In 1946, attendance was 18.5 million for both leagues; in 1970, it was 28.7 million. Measured in terms of average attendance per team, however, this growth was insignificant.[39] Although the popularity of baseball may not have actually declined, this does not necessarily mean that the introduction of Negro players into the game did not adversely affect attendance. Fans are attracted to ball parks by the quality of team performance, among other things, and may or may not consider the race of the players in their decision to attend. It is difficult to separate variations in attendance that are due to team performance from those that are due to the presence of Negro players if the team is used as the unit of measurement.

The following test, which uses the player as the unit of measurement, attempts to determine if racial prejudice is a characteristic of the American baseball fan. The only position in which players are rotated on a regular basis is pitcher. Moreover, starting pitchers are announced in the press before the game. The variation in pitchers and the advance knowledge of who will start offers the discriminatory fan the opportunity of deciding whether to attend on the basis of the race of the pitcher.

The average home attendance of fifty-seven National League starting pitchers was calculated for the entire 1967 season.[40] It was hypothesized that the average home attendance would vary by the pitcher's team and by the mix of games pitched (that is, the percent of games pitched after July 1 and the percent of night games, double-headers, and weekend games. . .).

The most important feature of the regression results is the sign of the race variable, which suggests that an average of 1,969 fewer fans attend games pitched by blacks than those pitched by whites.[41] The variable does not measure racial differences in pitching performance, since black pitchers have significantly better pitching records than whites.[42] For example, in the 1967 season, black pitchers won an average of 2.7 more games than white pitchers. Thus, it appears that fans do alter their attendance on the basis of the race of the pitchers.

Discrimination in Hiring Players

That racial entry barriers continue to exist in baseball today is a view that is not widely shared. In 1972, blacks occupied every position except that of manager, and very often their presence was disproportionately large. If a comparison is drawn between the proportion of blacks in baseball and in the population at large, a convincing case can be made that baseball is free of racial bias in its hiring and promotion practices. By 1957–58, the percentage of blacks in baseball was about the same as in the U.S. population, but before 1953 (and for some teams even today), "tokenism" would accurately describe the racial hiring practices of most baseball teams.

The period 1947–53 was one of slow expansion in the number of black players fielded. The National League averaged three additional black players every two years, and the American League about one every two years. After 1953, black players were added more rapidly. From 1953 to 1960, the percentage of black players rose by 2.2 points per year in the National League and by 0.6 points per year in the American League. The slow response of the American League in hiring Negroes created an everwidening interleague differential, but in 1960, the American League began to accelerate its hiring of blacks, while the increase in Negro players in the National League slowed. From 1960 to 1971, the American League added blacks at a rate that increased their share of the total available positions by 1.4 percentage points annually, in comparison to 0.6 points in the National League. In 1964, the interleague differential nearly vanished, but accelerated hiring of blacks in the National League thereafter kept it ahead of the American League in the number of black players.

Substantial differences exist in the number of black ballplayers per team. Pittsburgh, with the most black players, averaged about 35 percent black from 1960 to 1971 (see Table 1), and in 1967, over half of the Pittsburgh team was black. On September 1, 1971, the Pirates fielded an all-black team in a game against the Phillies.[43] Second-ranked San Francisco and third-ranked St. Louis fall considerably short of Pittsburgh in percentage of blacks. Los Angeles, which pioneered the use of black players, has recently ranked toward the bottom of the league in percent black. In the American League, the average spread between the first- and second-ranked teams is substantially less than in the National League. Cleveland, the first American League team to integrate in 1947, has remained among the leaders in hiring blacks: in 1968, 40 percent of the team was black. Only one other American League team could approach such a record for any year. Even so, only two National League teams (except the new franchise at Montreal)—Chicago and New York—have averaged fewer blacks than Cleveland over the entire period. The least integrated teams in the American League are Boston, which was the last team to integrate when it hired Elijah ("Pumpsie") Green in 1959, California, and Baltimore (which, however, has recently increased its number of blacks).

Interteam differences in the percent of black players, like the inter-league differential, have remained fairly constant. The trend in intra-league inequality can be determined from the coefficients of variation presented in Table 2. In the American League, the coefficients of variation show no definite trend, with the values fluctuating around an average of 30.3 percent. In the National League, there is evidence of growing inequality among the teams.[44]

The Economics of Hiring Black Players

Increased hiring of black players, particularly in the National League from 1953 to 1960, may be explained in part by changes in the cost differential in acquiring blacks and whites of comparable talent. Pascal and Rapping concluded that other clubs followed Brooklyn's lead for solid economic reasons: the period of unlimited free-agent bonus compe-tition raised the relative price of white ballplayers and compelled teams to substitute lower-cost black players of comparable quality.[45] The increase in black players did coincide with an increase in bonus pay-ments, which were becoming more and more of a drain on team resources (see Table 3). The bonus costs to teams in the major leagues from 1958 to 1969 were $63.2 million. In 1961, the year of the first American League expansion and a peak year in bonus payments, major-league teams spent about $8.5 million acquiring potential talent, with an average of about $470,000 per team. Since average team salaries per player were about $17,350 in 1961,[46] bonus costs actually exceeded player salaries for the twenty-five-man roster.

The data further show that a greater proportion of white ballplayers (over one-third) received bonus payments in excess of $20,000 in the period 1959–61 than in 1958 or earlier,[47] yet there were only three black players receiving such bonuses in the period. It seems reasonable to infer that the unlimited free-agent bonus competition, which began in 1947 as a response to rising postwar attendance and the maldistribution of talented ballplayers and as a by-product of Branch Rickey's development of the farm system,[48] pressured teams to search for a supply of talented but less expensive players. A pool of qualified blacks willing to join teams for smaller, or no, bonus payments provided the answer.

In 1961, the leagues attempted to restrain bonus competition by requiring the clubs "to keep bonus rookies on the major league roster for

TABLE 1. Percentage of Black Players on Major-League Baseball Teams, 1960-71

Team	Average, 1960-71	1971	1970	1969	1968	1967	1966	1965	1964	1963	1962	1961	1960
National League													
Atlanta[a]	27	40	40	32	28	28	24	32	16	24	20	16	24
Chicago	19	12	20	20	24	24	28	16	20	16	20	16	16
Cincinnati	25	32	28	36	28	32	24	24	16	20	20	20	20
Houston[b]	24	36	36	32	28	28	32	16	12	12	12	—	—
Los Angeles	22	24	24	16	20	12	32	24	20	24	20	24	20
New York[b]	18	16	16	20	16	12	16	24	16	20	20	—	—
Philadelphia	26	20	24	28	24	28	20	32	20	20	24	32	28
Pittsburgh	35	48	44	36	44	56	44	32	28	32	28	16	16
San Francisco	28	24	20	28	32	32	32	32	32	28	28	20	28
St. Louis	28	32	44	36	36	40	24	24	16	24	20	16	24
Montreal[c]	20	8	20	32	—	—	—	—	—	—	—	—	—
San Diego[c]	24	16	24	32	—	—	—	—	—	—	—	—	—
Average	25	26	28	29	28	29	28	26	20	22	21	20	22

American League

Baltimore	17	36	36	36	24	12	12	8	12	8	8	4	12
Boston	14	12	12	12	24	24	24	12	12	12	8	8	4
California[b]	17	24	20	20	16	16	20	24	16	16	8	8	—
Chicago	18	28	20	24	16	20	20	20	20	12	12	20	8
Cleveland	21	20	16	24	40	32	20	16	16	28	12	20	12
Detroit	18	16	20	28	16	20	24	20	20	16	20	16	4
Minnesota[d]	22	24	32	24	24	32	24	24	16	16	16	12	16
New York	17	20	20	28	20	20	20	24	20	12	12	12	8
Oakland[e]	21	24	28	24	12	24	24	24	16	24	24	20	8
Washington[b]	17	28	24	16	24	16	16	16	12	16	8	16	—
Kansas City[e]	24	16	28	28	—	—	—	—	—	—	—	—	—
Milwaukee[c,f]	19	20	12	24	—	—	—	—	—	—	—	—	—
Average	18	22	22	22	22	22	20	17	17	16	12	12	9

SOURCE: Calculated on the basis of data on black major leaguers available in *Ebony*, June issues, 1960–71. Figures are rounded.

a. Franchise located in Milwaukee until 1966.
b. Expansion team in the American League in 1961 and the National League in 1962.
c. Expansion team in 1969.
d. Franchise located in Washington, D.C., until 1961.
e. Franchise located in Kansas City until 1968.
f. Milwaukee franchise formerly located in Seattle.

TABLE 2. Intraleague Variations in the Percentage of Black Major-League Baseball Players, 1962-71

	Coefficients of variation	
Year	National League[a]	American League[b]
1962	21.7	38.7
1963	25.8	37.5
1964	31.1	22.1
1965	24.6	31.5
1966	28.6	19.6
1967	43.8	30.5
1968	28.6	38.5
1969	26.1	28.4
1970	35.6	32.0
1971	39.5	24.4
Average, 1962-71	30.5	30.3

SOURCE: Calculated from Table 1.
a. Excludes Montreal and San Diego.
b. Excludes Kansas City and Milwaukee.

two years before playing them."[49] This action, coupled with other measures, reduced bonus payments significantly in 1962 and 1963,[50] simultaneously, the percentage of black players in the National League leveled off. In fact, between 1962 and 1964, the number of black players in the National League declined. By checking bonus competition, baseball had altered the relative price of black and white players and thus reduced the economic incentive of teams to hire blacks. The adoption of the free-agent draft in 1965 seemed to have no appreciable effect on average bonus costs per team or the average bonus payment per player. While average payments have never returned to the 1961 high, they rose steadily through 1968. Negro players were still relatively more attractive financially to the teams, which probably contributed to the renewed increase in their employment.

Racial Performance Differentials and Equality of Opportunity

Comparison of the percentage of blacks in baseball with their proportion in the population may give a misleading picture of the racial situation in the major leagues. Rosenblatt suggests that numbers do not necessarily imply equality of opportunity.[51] Superior performance appears to be a requirement for the entry and retention of blacks in the game. Rosenblatt

TABLE 3. Bonus Payments to Players Signing Their First Major-League Baseball Contracts, 1958–69

Year	Number of players	Total bonus payments[a] (thousands of dollars)	Average bonus payments per team[b] (thousands of dollars)	Average bonus per player signed (dollars)	Percent of players drafted[c]	Average bonus of drafted players (dollars)	Average bonus of nondrafted players (dollars)
1958	1,473	6,456	404	4,383	—	—	—
1959	1,144	4,880	305	4,266	—	—	—
1960	1,277	5,352	335	4,191	—	—	—
1961	1,486	8,460	470	5,693	—	—	—
1962	1,113	3,863	193	3,471	—	—	—
1963	1,083	3,479	174	3,212	—	—	—
1964	1,117	5,134	257	4,596	—	—	—
1965	1,084	4,610	231	4,253	38.8	8,059	1,837
1966	1,149	4,985	249	4,339	48.8	7,756	1,077
1967	1,173	5,216	261	4,447	57.8	6,786	1,243
1968	1,109	5,249	262	4,733	58.5	7,249	1,182
1969	1,340	5,549	231	4,141	54.7	6,605	1,166
Total	14,498	63,233	—	—	—	—	—
Average	1,208	5,269	281	4,361	51.7	7,291	1,301

SOURCE: *Curtis C. Flood v. Bowie K. Kuhn et al.*, 316 F. Supp. 271 (S.D.N.Y. 1970), trial transcript.

a. Does not include salaries or college scholarship commitments.
b. From 1958 to 1960, there were sixteen teams; in 1961, eighteen teams; from 1962 to 1968, twenty teams; and in 1969, twenty-four teams.
c. The free-agent draft was introduced in 1965.

379

uses lifetime batting average as a measure of ability for nonpitchers,[52] and shows that during the period 1953–65 a racial differential of about twenty points existed.[53] In 1965, 36 percent of the black players hit 0.270 or better and well over 50 percent hit 0.250 or above. Although the black superstar may not be affected, "more places are available in the majors for the substar white player than for the comparably able Negro."[54] Moreover, there is no evidence that the differential is narrowing. On the contrary, the average rate of change in the batting average differential from 1957 (the year when the percentage of blacks in baseball approximated that in society) to 1965 was +0.8 percentage points per year. If anything, the performance criterion for blacks is becoming stiffer.

Two rationalizations, other than discriminatory hiring and promotion practices, for the racial performance differential have been advanced: (1) the existence of racial differences (in the means or in the variances) in the distribution of baseball playing talent; (2) the existence of "endemic societal wage discrimination in most callings and lesser discrimination in baseball [that] may result in a systematic difference in the ability distributions of black and white baseball players through the process of occupational choice."[55]

The belief that blacks are genetically endowed with more athletic skills than whites is widespread and not without some basis in fact. It is known, for example, that Negro and Caucasian skeletons have somewhat different properties. At birth, holding prenatal environment constant, Negroes and whites differ in body weight.[56] Furthermore, Negro motor skill development proceeds more quickly during the early period of childhood.[57] But, for the genetic argument to be given serious consideration requires more than isolated and tenuously connected associations. It requires that particular baseball skills be isolated, that the differences in the amount of these skills within any group be shown to be due to genetic factors, and that the amount of these particular skills be demonstrated to vary by race. Until such an investigation is undertaken, arguments based on genetic differences must be viewed as speculative.

The second hypothesis is based on the argument that if there is discrimination in nonbaseball occupations, the incomes of blacks will be higher in the sport than outside. However, if the initial distribution of playing skills is racially invariant, there is no reason to expect that the black players attracted to the sport for economic reasons will have *higher* average ability.

Pascal and Rapping[58] argue that, while baseball would attract a higher percentage of above-average blacks, mediocre black players would also be attracted by the wage differential, so that the net effect on racial ability distributions would be unclear. The existence of racial income differentials does not ensure a uniform impact on supply. The supply of players of both races at any given ability level is determined by the elasticity *at that level*. In any range of ability, the supply of black players will be more elastic than that of whites, so that the fraction of players who are black should exceed the fraction of blacks in the total population. However, the income differential between sports and other occupations widens at higher ability levels, until it is finally so large as to make the "stars" of both races perfectly inelastic with respect to salary. If ability distributions are assumed to be invariant by race, the proportion of "stars" that are of a particular race should equal the proportion of that race in the total population.

Racial Entry Barriers by Position

It is possible that racial differences in ability (as measured by lifetime batting averages) could be accounted for by other factors, such as the racial distribution of players by position. For example, since outfielders have higher mean batting averages than infielders, a higher proportion of black outfielders could be the source of the performance differential. Table 4 shows that, in 1969, blacks occupied 24.1 percent of all of the available playing positions, but that their representation by position was not uniform. Specifically, relatively more blacks were in the outfield (49.6 percent) and relatively fewer in pitching (11.0 percent). Moreover, if Latin American blacks are removed from the sample, the proportion of North American blacks in the outfield becomes nearly three times (40.0 percent) that of their representation in all positions (15.8 percent). Furthermore, North American blacks are found in significantly smaller numbers in both infield (10.0 percent) and pitching (8.1 percent) posi-

TABLE 4. Percent of Available Positions[a] Filled by Blacks, and by Blacks Born in North America, Major-League Baseball, 1969

Position	Filled by blacks	Filled by blacks born in North America
All playing positions	24.1	15.8
Outfielder	49.6	40.0
Infielder	23.1	10.0
Pitcher	11.0	8.1
Nonplaying positions	3.4	3.4
Coach	4.2	4.2
Manager	0	0

SOURCES: *Ebony*, Vol. 24 (June 1969), pp. 138ff.; *New York Times*, April 6, 1969; *Sporting News*, Vol. 167 (April 26, 1969).
a. Available positions obtained from the 1969 opening day rosters.

tions. The absence of blacks from coaching and managerial positions is well known: in 1969, only 4.2 percent of the coaches and none of the managers were black.

The distribution of black players by position is relatively stable, as shown in Table 5. In 1960, the ratio of black infielders to black pitchers was about 2.6. In the period 1967–70, this ratio varied from about 2.4 to 2.7, but in 1971 it fell to 2.2. The real gain for black players was in the outfield. Where there were 5.6 times as many black outfielders as pitchers in 1960, by 1971 there were over 6.7 times as many. Since 1960, of a net increase in black players of eighty-four, forty-eight were outfielders. During the same period, blacks increased their share of the available outfield positions at the average annual rate of 2.4 percentage points. Meanwhile, blacks, mostly Latin American blacks, increased their share of the infield positions at the average annual rate of only 0.34 percentage points. Most of the increase in black infielders occurred after 1965. In 1969, a peak year, twenty-seven blacks (seven of them Latin American) held one of the approximately two hundred forty pitching slots. From 1960 to 1971, the average annual increase in the share of pitching slots going to blacks was 0.26 percentage points.

The performance differential apparent in the aggregate also persists at a more disaggregated level. Furthermore, the magnitude of the performance differential is related systematically to the proportion of black

TABLE 5. Percent of Available Playing Positions[a] Filled by Blacks in Major-League Baseball, 1960–71

| Year | Position | | |
	Outfield	Infield	Pitcher
1960	33.3	16.0	6.0
1961	34.0	16.5	5.0
1962	37.0	15.0	8.5
1963	44.0	16.0	9.5
1964	47.0	15.0	7.5
1965	50.0	16.3	9.0
1966	58.0	22.0	9.5
1967	57.0	25.0	10.0
1968	60.0	22.5	9.5
1969	56.7	26.7	11.3
1970	59.2	24.6	9.2
1971	61.7	20.0	9.2

SOURCE: *Ebony*, June issues, 1960–71.
a. Available playing positions per team were assumed to be five positions for outfield, ten for infield, and ten for pitchers, to form a twenty-five man roster. This division is quite close to the actual average divisions by positions in recent years.

ballplayers. From a sample of 453 veteran ballplayers, Pascal and Rapping have calculated racial performance differentials by position. For non-pitchers they followed Rosenblatt and used cumulative lifetime batting averages. For pitchers, they measured performance by the number of games won in the 1967 season. Their calculated performance differentials are shown in Table 6. All differences in the means are significant at the 5 percent level, except for the second baseman and shortstop category. The existence of performance differentials that favor blacks is consistent with the view that baseball has racial entry barriers. Moreover, these barriers are higher for certain positions than for others. Generally, where there is less exclusion of blacks, the performance differential is narrower than in the high exclusion positions of catcher and pitcher.[59]

Another possible explanation for the racial difference in the distribution of positions may lie in the different early environment of black and white players. Opportunities for supervised amateur and semiprofessional baseball are probably more available to young whites than to young blacks. In the South, school and societal segregation may have caused young black players to play on poorer fields without instruction. And in northern cities, opportunities for recreation off of the streets are limited. Under those circumstances, defensive skills would probably become relatively less developed among blacks than among more intensively supervised whites. Hitting ability probably develops more fully without supervision and independently of the quality of the playing field. Consequently, the poorer environment in which blacks learned the game may be responsible for their superior hitting records.

While this explanation accounts for the relatively high proportion of

TABLE 6. Performance Differentials by Race and Position, Major-League Baseball, as of 1967

Position	Percent black	Performance differential [a]	Black-white performance ratio
Outfielder	56.6	0.120	1.047
Catcher	8.6	0.320	1.141
First and third base	33.3	0.190	1.075
Second base and shortstop	29.5	0.010	1.004
Pitcher	10.9	2.7	1.360

SOURCE: Anthony H. Pascal and Leonard A. Rapping, "The Economics of Racial Discrimination in Organized Baseball," in Anthony H. Pascal (ed.), *Racial Discrimination in Economic Life* (Heath, 1972), pp. 138–39.

a. Except for pitchers, where the measure is games won during the 1967 season, the performance measure is the arithmetic averages of individual lifetime major-league batting averages through 1967.

Negroes in the outfield, it is inconsistent with their superior pitching and fielding performance. Negro players are among the top ten lifetime fielding leaders in nearly every playing category,[60] and as pitchers they win more often than whites. While early environment may well have been unfavorable to the development of black catchers, pitchers, and infielders, racial entry barriers appear to be the primary cause for the lower representation of Negroes in these positions. Perhaps the intensive coaching, in both the minor and major leagues, that white coaches would be required to devote to black infielders and pitchers leads to racial bias in the selection of players by position. Perhaps, since team leadership cannot easily be exercised except in the infield, it is an unwillingness to assign leadership responsibilities to blacks.

Or, perhaps it is because the real drama of baseball takes place in the infield. It is true that outfielders more frequently are the superstars, but they are not the featured actors in the game. To the stadium fan, his proximity to the outfielder is inversely related to the price of his seat; the inexpensive seats are closer to the outfield than to home plate. The television fan sees the outfielder only when he bats and fields, except momentarily during a break in the action or at the end of the inning as he trots off the field. If the pitching is at all effective, this exposure is only a fraction of the viewing time devoted to the battery (the catcher and pitcher). The greater frequency of fielding plays in the infield and the occasional conference of infielders at the pitcher's mound means that the exposure of infielders is between that of the battery and the outfielders. Skin color and un-Caucasian-like facial features, rather than race per se, may thus be the prime factor in blacks being all but excluded from battery positions and having lower representation in the infield than in the outfield.

The possibility that skin color was associated with the distribution of blacks by position was tested, using the pictures of all black major leaguers published annually by *Ebony* magazine (see Table 7). The 159

TABLE 7. Skin Color and Position Assignment of Black Baseball Players, 1969

Skin color	Percentage of nonoutfielders
Very light	80.0[a]
Light brown	67.9[a]
Medium brown	56.8
Dark brown	53.5
Very dark	25.0[a]
All black players	54.8

SOURCE: Calculated from the sample of 159 black ballplayers in *Ebony*, Vol. 24 (June 1969), pp. 138–46.
a. Significant at the 1 percent level.

TABLE 8. Characteristics of Major-League Baseball Managers, 1947–67

Characteristic	Percent of total
Background	
Former player	93.5
Outfield	17.6
Infield	67.6
First base	12.1
Catcher	19.4
Other	36.1
Pitcher	8.3
Nonplayer	6.5
Region of birth	
Non-South	66.7
Northeast	22.2
Midwest	32.4
West	12.0
South	33.3

SOURCE: Calculated from data in *The Baseball Encyclopedia* (Macmillan, 1969), pp. 356–453, 501–1688, 2206–37. Figures are rounded.

players were identified only by code, and grouped by skin color using five color classifications that largely followed those of G. Franklin Edwards.[61] It was hypothesized that the proportion of nonoutfielders in each skin color category would be the same as their proportion among all black ballplayers. This hypothesis had to be rejected in three cases: very light and light brown players had significantly higher representation in the infield, catching, and pitching positions than predicted, while very dark brown players had significantly lower representation.

Major-league baseball has no black managers and only a few black coaches. In part, this may reflect the relatively small supply of former black players with the necessary skills and experience for these jobs. But the exclusion of blacks from coaching and managerial positions can also be related to certain characteristics of managers—their regional origin and former playing position. From 1947 to 1967, there were one hundred eight individuals who managed major-league teams (some, of course, managing more than one team). The regional origin of managers (see Table 8) conforms closely to the regional origin of ballplayers. About two-thirds of the managers came from nonsouthern states, while 74 percent of the 9,659 known U.S.-born players and managers in the major leagues from 1871 to 1968 were born outside of the South.[62] On the other hand, about 63 percent of the North American blacks in the 1969 sample used in Table 7 were southern born.[63] Even more striking is the fact that 67.6 percent of all managers were former infielders,[64] but only 26.3

percent of the available infield slots were filled by North American blacks in 1969.

Most managers have had some previous coaching experience. The majority of a team's coaching staff devotes itself to the infielders, catchers, and pitchers, so it is reasonable that coaches are selected predominantly from these positions. Of the four black coaches in 1969, all had been infielders. That former infielders, rather than pitchers, tend to become managers probably stems from the fact that infielders have leadership responsibilities. (Most team captains are infielders.) Pitchers, on the other hand, play, at most, 20 percent of the time and are segregated from the rest of the team during the game. Furthermore, they are relatively passive in team decision making on the field, as are outfielders.

The exclusion of blacks from managerial and coaching positions thus appears to be intimately linked to the underrepresentation of blacks in the infield. This underrepresentation certainly is not connected with poorer performance on their part; their performance is, in fact, superior to that of whites. The evidence points to the conclusion that racial prejudice is responsible for this pattern.

NOTES

1. Jack Olsen, "The Cruel Deception," *Sports Illustrated*, Vol. 29 (July 1, 1968), p. 16.
2. Ibid., p. 15.
3. *Study of Monopoly Power*, Pt. 6, *Organized Baseball*, Hearings before the Subcommittee on Study of Monopoly Power of the House Committee on the Judiciary, 82 Cong. 1 sess. (1952).
4. *Organized Professional Team Sports*, Hearings before the Subcommittee on Antitrust and Monopoly of the Senate Committee on the Judiciary, 85 Cong. 2 sess. (1958).
5. Carl T. Rowan with Jackie Robinson, *Wait Till Next Year: The Life Story of Jackie Robinson* (New York: Random House, 1960).
6. "Statement of Jackie Robinson, Formerly with the Brooklyn Dodgers," in *Organized Professional Team Sports*, Senate Hearings, pp. 294–302.
7. Harold Seymour, *Baseball: The Early Years* (New York: Oxford University Press, 1960), p. 83.
8. Seymour (ibid., p. 334) notes that "so many Irish were in the game that some thought they had a special talent for ball playing. Fans liked to argue the relative merits of players of Irish as against those of German extraction."
9. *Beadle's Dime Base-Ball Player* (New York: Beadle and Co., 1868), p. 55.
10. Seymour, *Baseball*, p. 42.
11. A. S. ("Doc") Young, *Negro Firsts in Sports* (Johnson, 1963), p. 16.
12. Robert Peterson, *Only the Ball Was White* (Prentice-Hall, 1970), p. 21. This is a good account of the history of the Negro leagues.
13. Young, *Negro Firsts*, p. 56.
14. Peterson, *Only the Ball Was White*, p. 24.
15. Ibid., p. 25.
16. Ibid., p. 26. Lee Allen, *100 Years of Baseball: The Intimate and Dramatic Story of Modern Baseball from the Game's Beginnings up to the Present Day* (Bartholomew House, 1950), p. 282, claims that there were about twenty Negro players on white teams in 1887, but this estimate seems high.

17. *Sporting Life*, Vol. 9 (Sept. 21, 1887), p. 3.
18. Ibid.
19. *Sporting Life*, Vol. 9 (June 11, 1887), p. 1.
20. *Express* (Buffalo), July 13, 1886.
21. Interview with Sol White, reported in Alvin F. Harlow, "Unrecognized Stars," *Esquire*, Vol. 10 (September 1938), p. 75.
22. Lee Allen, *The American League Story* (Hill and Wang, 1962), pp. 20-22.
23. *Sporting Life*, Vol. 9 (July 20, 1887), p. 1.
24. Young, *Negro Firsts*, p. 56, and Allen, *100 Years*, pp. 282-83.
25. Peterson, *Only the Ball Was White*, pp. 50-51.
26. *Chicago Daily Defender*, Jan. 16, 1916.
27. *Pittsburgh Courier*, Feb. 25, 1933.
28. Ibid., July 25, 1942.
29. Ibid.
30. *Sporting News*, Vol. 113 (Aug. 6, 1942), p. 4.
31. *Pittsburgh Courier*, May 15, 1943.
32. Bill Veeck with Ed Linn, *Veeck—As in Wreck: The Autobiography of Bill Veeck* (Putnam, 1962), pp. 171-72.
33. Rowan, *Wait Till Next Year*, pp. 99-100.
34. *Organized Baseball*, House Hearings, p. 474.
35. "Report of Major League Steering Committee for Submission to the National and American Leagues at Their Meetings in Chicago," in *Organized Baseball*, House Hearings, pp. 483-84.
36. Arthur W. Mann, *Branch Rickey: American in Action* (Houghton Mifflin, 1957), pp. 256-57.
37. Rowan, *Wait Till Next Year*, pp. 175-76.
38. *Sporting News*, Vol. 123 (May 21, 1947), p. 4; Rowan, *Wait Till Next Year*, p. 183.
39. In 1946, there were sixteen teams, with an average attendance of 1.2 million per team. In 1970, there were twenty-four teams, also with an average of 1.2 million. Barry R. Chiswick has pointed out that constant average attendance per team implies a decline in attendance per game, since the number of games per year increased. This is not surprising, given the growth of competing sports (football, golf, basketball), the development and decreasing cost of television, and the rise in the opportunity cost of time (attending a game requires more time than observing it at home, and the value of time increases as earning capacity rises). However, the impact of television may be somewhat softened by the fact that baseball is probably the game that is least adaptable to television coverage because of the size of the viewing area required for full appreciation of the play.
40. Source: *New York Times*, issues during the 1967 baseball season.
41. On a one-tail test, the coefficient is significant at the 5 percent level.
42. See Table 6.
43. *Sports Illustrated*, Vol. 35 (Sept. 13, 1971), p. 14.
44. Anthony H. Pascal and Leonard A. Rapping, "The Economics of Racial Discrimination in Organized Baseball," in Anthony H. Pascal (ed.), *Racial Discrimination in Economic Life* (Heath, 1972), pp. 146-47, suggest that competitive pressures within the league would bring about an equalization of the proportion of black players among the teams. That is, in view of the superior playing ability of the black players, no team that wanted to win could afford to have its percentage of black players fall too far below that of its competitors. The data in Table 2 do not support this hypothesis.
45. Ibid., pp. 134-35.
46. Calculated on the basis of: (1) average player salaries for 1956, estimated at $13,800 from data available in *Organized Professional Team Sports*, Senate Hearings, pp. 794-99; and (2) player salaries for 1965, averaged at $19,500 (from Arthur D. Little, Inc., "Economic Analyses of Certain Aspects of Organized Baseball" [n.d.; processed], p. 3).
47. Pascal and Rapping, "Economics of Racial Discrimination," p. 136.
48. Ralph Andreano, *No Joy in Mudville: The Dilemma of Major League Baseball* (Schenkman, 1965), p. 120.

49. Ibid., p. 121.
50. See Table 3.
51. Aaron Rosenblatt, "Negroes in Baseball: The Failure of Success," *Transaction*, Vol. 4 (September 1967), pp. 51–53.
52. Batting average is, of course, only one component of performance. Performance measures are discussed below.
53. Pascal and Rapping found this still to be true in 1967.
54. Rosenblatt, "Negroes in Baseball," p. 52.
55. Pascal and Rapping, "Economics of Racial Discrimination," p. 141.
56. Arthur R. Jensen, "How Much Can We Boost IQ and Scholastic Achievement?" *Harvard Educational Review*, Vol. 39 (Winter 1969), p. 87.
57. Ibid., pp. 86–87.
58. Pascal and Rapping, "Economics of Racial Discrimination," pp. 141–42.
59. Although it may not be strictly proper to compare the performance differentials for positions that required a different measure of performance.
60. *The Baseball Encyclopedia* (Macmillan, 1969), p. 71.
61. *The Negro Professional Class* (Free Press, 1959). Edwards found that black lawyers, physicians, and teachers had significantly lighter skin than blacks as a group.
62. *The Baseball Encyclopedia*, p. 30.
63. Calculated from the sample of 159 black ballplayers in *Ebony*, Vol. 24 (June 1969), and data on place of birth from *The Official Encyclopedia of Baseball*.
64. Infielders constitute about 40 percent of a team roster.

Immune From Racism?

D. STANLEY EITZEN AND NORMAN R. YETMAN

No other aspect of sport in America has generated more sociological interest than race relations. The research interest in race undoubtedly has been influenced by the turmoil of the late fifties and sixties that generated increased academic and critical attention to all phases of black life in America. At the same time the American sports world became increasingly open to black participation during the civil rights era.

Since the early 1960s the percentage of black competitors in each of the major professional team sports (football, basketball, and baseball) has exceeded blacks' proportion (11 percent) of the total U.S. population. In baseball, for example, the 1957–58 season was the year that blacks achieved a proportion equivalent to their percentage in the U.S. popula-

SOURCE: D. Stanley Eitzen and Norman R. Yetman, "Immune from Racism? Blacks Still Suffer from Discrimination in Sports," *Civil Rights Digest*, 9 (Winter 1977), 3–13.

tion. The watershed year in professional football was 1960 (see Table 1); in professional basketball it was 1958 (see Table 3).

By 1975, blacks comprised better than 60 percent of all professional basketball players, 42 percent of all professional football players, and 21 percent of major league baseball players. An additional 11 percent of major league baseball players were Latin Americans.

The large proportion of blacks and the prominence of black superstars such as Kareem Abdul-Jabbar, Hank Aaron, and O. J. Simpson have led many Americans—black and white—to infer that collegiate and professional athletics have provided an avenue of mobility for blacks unavailable elsewhere in American society. Sports, thus, seems to have "done something for" black Americans. Many commentators—social scientists, journalists, and black athletes themselves—have argued, however, that black visibility in collegiate and professional sports has merely served to mask the racism that pervades the entire sports establishment. According

TABLE 1 The Distribution of White and Black Players by Position in Major League Football, 1960 and 1975 (in percentages)

Playing Position	1960* % of all Whites	% of all Blacks	Percent Black by Position**	1975 % of Whites	% of Blacks	Percent Black by Position
Kicker/Punter	1.2	0	0	9.0	.2	1.3
Quarterback	6.3	0	0	9.7	.5	3.5
Center	5.3	0	0	6.7	.5	4.9
Linebacker	11.5	3.6	4.2	17.4	8.6	26.0
Off. guard	8.0	1.8	3.0	8.7	4.5	26.9
Off. tackle	8.3	23.2	28.3	8.6	5.7	31.8
Def. front four	11.0	14.3	15.4	12.3	15.7	47.6
End/flanker	22.6	7.1	4.6	11.6	20.2	55.3
Running back	16.5	25.0	17.5	8.1	21.1	65.2
Def. back	9.3	25.0	27.5	8.1	23.2	67.3
	100.0	100.0		100.2	100.2	
Total number	(199½)	(27)	12.3	(870)	(620)	41.6

*The 1960 data were compiled by Jonathan Brower, who obtained them from the media guides published annually by each team. Whenever a player was listed at two positions, Brower credited him as one-half at each position. 1975 data are taken from 1975 *Football Register* published annually by *The Sporting News*. Since both the media guides and the *Football Register* are published before each season, they include only information on veterans. The total N for 1960 is smaller than one would expect, presumably because Brower was unable to obtain media guides for all teams.

**Since blacks were 12.3 percent of the player population in 1960, those playing positions with a black percentage less than 12.3 were underrepresented. In 1975 those positions less than 41.6 percent black were underrepresented.

to these critics, the existence of racism in collegiate and professional sports is especially insidious because sports promoters and commentators have projected an image of athletics as the single institution in America relatively immune from racism.

In a previous article (*Civil Rights Digest*, August 1972) we examined racial discrimination in American sports—in particular, college basketball. This article examines three aspects of the athletic world alleged to be racially biased—the assignment of playing positions, reward and authority structures, and performance differentials. The analysis will focus primarily on the three major professional team sports (baseball, basketball, and football) where blacks are found most prominently, and therefore slights the obvious dearth of blacks in other sports (e.g., hockey, tennis, golf, and swimming).

STACKING TEAM POSITIONS

One of the best documented forms of discrimination in both college and professional ranks is popularly known as stacking. The term refers to situations in which minority-group members are relegated to specific team positions and excluded from competing for others. The result is often that intrateam competition for starting positions is between members of the same race (e.g., those competing for running back slots are black, while those competing for quarterback slots are white). For example, Aaron Rosenblatt noted in *Transaction* magazine that while there are twice as many pitchers on a baseball team as outfielders, in 1965 there were three times as many black outfielders as pitchers.

Examination of the stacking phenomenon was first undertaken by John Loy and Joseph McElvogue in 1970, who argued that racial segregation in sports is a function of "centrality" in a team sports unit. To explain racial segregation by team position in sports, they combined organizational principles advanced by Hubert M. Blalock and Oscar Grusky.

Blalock argued that:

1. The lower the degree of purely social interaction on the job . . . , the lower the degree of [racial] discrimination.
2. To the extent that performance level is relatively independent of skill in interpersonal relations, the lower the degree of [racial] discrimination.

Grusky's notions about the formal structure of organizations are similar:

All else being equal, the more central one's . . . location: (1) the greater the likelihood dependent . . . tasks will be performed, and (2) the greater the rate of interaction with the occupants of other positions. Also, the performance of dependent tasks is positively related to frequency of interaction.

Combining these propositions, Loy and McElvogue hypothesized that "racial segregation in professional team sports is positively related to centrality." Their analysis of football (where the central positions are quarterback, center, offensive guard, and linebacker) and baseball (where the central positions are the infield, catcher, and pitcher) demonstrated that the central positions were indeed overwhelmingly manned by whites, while blacks were overrepresented in noncentral positions.

Examining the data for baseball in 1967, they found that 83 percent of those listed as infielders were white, while 49 percent of the outfielders were black. The proportion of whites was greatest in the positions of catcher (96 percent) and pitcher (94 percent), the most central positions in baseball.

Our analysis of data from the 1975 major league baseball season showed little change from the situation described by Loy and McElvogue in 1967. By 1975 the percentage of infielders who were white had declined slightly to 76 percent, but the outfield was still disproportionately manned by blacks (49 percent). Moreover, pitcher (96 percent) and catcher (95 percent) remained overwhelmingly white positions.

Table 1 compares the racial composition of positions in football for the 1960 and 1975 seasons. The conclusions to be drawn from these data are clear. While the proportion of blacks has increased dramatically during this 15-year period, central positions continue to be disproportionately white. One difference between 1960 and 1975 is that blacks have increasingly supplanted whites at noncentral positions.

On the other hand, blacks appear to have made some inroads in the central offensive positions—for example, a shift from 97 percent white to 87 percent white from 1960 to 1975. But when length of time in the league is held constant, the overwhelming proportion of whites in these positions remains. Among those players in the league 1 to 3 years, 79 percent were white in 1975; 4 to 6 years, 80 percent white; 7 to 9 years, 80 percent white; and 10 or more years, 96 percent white. (The latter may be a consequence of the league's having a small proportion of black players in the past.)

The effects of stacking in noncentral positions are far reaching. In 17 of the 26 pro football teams surveyed, approximately three-fourths of all 1971 advertising slots (radio, television, and newspapers) were alloted to players in central positions.

Second, noncentral positions in football depend primarily on speed and quickness, which means in effect that playing careers are shortened for persons in those positions. For example, in 1975 only 4.1 percent of the players listed in the *Football Register* in the three predominantly black positions—defensive back, running back, and wide receiver (65 percent of all black players)—had been in the pros for 10 or more years, while 14.8 percent of players listed in the three predominantly white positions— quarterback, center, and offensive guard—remained that long. The shortened careers for noncentral players have two additional deleterious consequences—less lifetime earnings and limited benefits from the players' pension fund, which provides support on the basis of longevity.

ASSIGNMENT BY STEREOTYPE

The Loy and McElvogue interpretation of these data rested primarily upon a position's spatial location in a team unit. However, Harry Edwards argues that the actual spatial location of a playing position is an incidental factor in the explanation of stacking. The crucial variable involved in position segregation is the degree of leadership responsibility found in each position. For example, quarterbacks have greater team authority and ability to affect the outcome of the game than do individuals who occupy noncentral positions.

Thus, the key is not the interaction potential of the playing position but the leadership and degree of responsibility for the game's outcome built into the position that account for the paucity of blacks at the so-called central positions. This is consistent with the stereotype hypothesis advanced by Jonathan Brower (specifically for football, but one that applies to other sports as well):

> The combined function of . . . responsibility and interaction provides a frame for exclusion of blacks and constitutes a definition of the situation for coaches and management. People in the world of professional football believe that various football positions require specific types of physically- and intellectually-endowed athletes. When these beliefs are combined with the stereotypes of blacks and whites, blacks are excluded from certain positions. Normal organizational processses when interlaced with racist conceptions of the world spell out an important consequence, namely, the racial basis of the division of labor in professional football.

In this view, then, it is the racial stereotypes of blacks' abilities that lead to the view that they are more ideally suited for those positions labelled "noncentral." For example, Brower compared the requirements for the central and noncentral positions in football and found that the former require leadership, thinking ability, highly refined techniques, stability under pressure, and responsibility for the outcome of the games. Noncentral positions, on the other hand, require athletes with speed, quickness, aggressiveness, "good hands," and "instinct."

Evidence for the racial stereotype explanation for stacking is found in the paucity of blacks at the most important positions for outcome control in football (quarterback, kicker, and placekick holder). The data for 1975 show that of the 87 quarterbacks in the league only three were black; of the 70 punters and placekickers mentioned in the *Football Register*, only one was black; and of the 26 placekick holders, not one was black.

It is inconceivable that blacks lack the ability to play these positions at the professional level. Placekick holders must, for example, have "good hands," an important quality for pass receivers, two-thirds of whom were black, but no black was selected for the former role. Kicking requires a strong leg and the development of accuracy. Are blacks unable to develop strong legs or master the necessary technique?

The conclusion seems inescapable: blacks are precluded from occupying leadership positions (quarterback, defensive signal caller) because subtle but widely held stereotypes of black intellectual and leadership abilities still persist in the sports world. As a consequence, blacks are relegated to those positions where the requisite skills are speed, strength, and quick reactions, not thinking or leadership ability.

Another explanation for stacking has been advanced by Barry D. McPherson, who has argued that black youths may segregate themselves in particular positions because they wish to emulate black stars. Contrary to the belief that stacking can be attributed to discriminatory acts by members of the majority group, this interpretation holds that the playing roles to which black youths aspire are those in which blacks have previously attained a high level of achievement. Since the first positions to be occupied by blacks in professional football were in the offensive and defensive backfield and the defensive linemen, subsequent imitation of their techniques by black youths has resulted in blacks being overrepresented in these positions today.

Although his small sample makes his findings tentative, Brower has provided some support for this hypothesis. He asked a sample of 23 white and 20 black high school football players what athletes they admired most and what position they would most like to play if they had the ability and opportunity. The overwhelming majority of blacks (70 percent) had only black heroes (role models) whereas whites chose heroes from both races. More important for our consideration is the finding that black high school athletes preferred to play at the "noncentral" positions now manned disproportionately by blacks in the pros.

Brower concluded that "Since the young blacks desire to perform at the 'standard' black positions, these findings make plain the impact and consequences of the present football position structure on succeeding generations of professional football players." Although the role model orientation does not explain the initial discrimination, it helps to explain why, once established, the pattern of discrimination by player position tends to be maintained.

Since McPherson produced no empirical support of his explanation, others sought to determine whether black athletes changed positions from central to noncentral more frequently than whites as they moved from high school to college to professional competition. Data from a sample of 387 professional football players indicated a statistically significant shift by blacks from central positions to noncentral ones.

That blacks in high school and college occupied positions held primarily by whites in professional football casts doubt on McPherson's model. Athletic role models or heroes will most likely have greater attraction for younger individuals in high school and college than for older athletes in professional sports, but professional players were found distributed at all positions during their high school playing days.

The socialization model also assumes a high degree of irrationality on the part of the player—it assumes that as he becomes older and enters more keenly competitive playing conditions, he will be more likely to seek a position because of his identification with a black star rather than because of a rational assessment of his own athletic skills.

It is conceivable, however, that socialization does contribute to racial stacking in baseball and football, but in a negative sense. That is to say, given discrimination in the allocation of playing positions (or at least the belief in its existence), young blacks will consciously avoid those positions for which opportunities are or appear to be low (pitcher, quarterback), and will select instead those positions where they are most likely to succeed (the outfield, running and defensive backs).

Gene Washington, all-pro wide receiver of the San Francisco Forty-Niners, was a college quarterback at Stanford through his sophomore year, then switched to flanker. Washington requested the change himself. "It was strictly a matter of economics. I knew a black quarterback would have little chance in pro ball unless he was absolutely superb. . . ."

STACKING IN BASKETBALL

Although social scientists have examined the stacking phenomenon in football and baseball, they have neglected basketball. They have tended to assume that it does not occur because, as Edwards has put it:

. . . in basketball there is no positional centrality as is the case in football and baseball, because there are no fixed zones of role responsibility attached to specific positions. . . . Nevertheless, one does find evidence of discrimination against black athletes on integrated basketball teams. Rather than stacking black athletes in positions involving relatively less control, since this is a logistical impossibility, the number of black athletes directly involved in the action at any one time is simply limited.

However, two researchers reasoned that positions in basketball do vary in responsibility, leadership, mental qualities of good judgment, decision making, recognition of opponents' tactics, and outcome control. To confirm this judgment, they undertook a content analysis of instructional books by prominent American basketball coaches to determine whether there were specific responsibilities or qualities attributed to the three playing positions—guard, forward, and center—in basketball.

They discovered surprising unanimity among the authors on the attributes and responsibilities of the different positions. The guard was viewed as the team quarterback, its "floor general," and the most desired attributes for this position were judgment, leadership, and dependability. The center was pictured as having the greatest amount of outcome control because that position is nearest the basket and because the offense revolves around it; the center was literally the pivot of the team's offense.

Unlike the traits for other positions, the desired traits mentioned for forwards stressed physical attributes—speed, quickness, physical strength, and rebounding—even to the point of labeling the forward the "animal."

Given this widespread agreement that varied zones of responsibility and different qualities are expected of guards, forwards, and centers, the researchers hypothesized that blacks would be overrepresented—stacked—at the forward position, where the essential traits required are physical rather than mental, and underrepresented at the guard and center positions, the most crucial positions for leadership and outcome control. Using data from a sample of 274 NCAA basketball teams from the 1970–71 season, they found that blacks were, in fact, substantially overrepresented as forwards and underrepresented at the guard and center positions. Whereas 32 percent of the total sample of players were black, 41 percent of forwards were black; only 26 percent of guards and 25 percent of centers were black. This pattern held regardless of whether the players were starters or second-stringers, for college or university division teams. Thus racial stacking is present in college basketball.

But in professional basketball in 1972, which was two-thirds black, this pattern was not present. It would be interesting to see whether such a pattern may have occurred earlier in the history of professional basketball, since during the 1974–75 collegiate season, the races were relatively evenly distributed by position. The pattern of stacking detected in 1970–71 had not persisted. Thus, although stacking has remained in football and baseball, the situation in basketball (most heavily black in racial composition of the three major sports) would appear to have undergone substantial change during the first half of the 1970s.

REWARDS AND AUTHORITY

Discrimination in professional sports is explicit in the discrepancy between the salaries of white and black players. At first glance such a charge appears to be unwarranted. Black players rank among the highest paid in professional baseball (seven of 10 superstars being paid more than $100,000 in 1970 were black), and the mean salaries of black outfielders, infielders, and pitchers exceed those of whites. However, it was reported that substantial salary discrimination against blacks exists when performance levels were held constant. Blacks earned less than whites for equivalent performance. In addition, the central positions in football are those where the salaries are the greatest.

An obvious case of monetary discrimination becomes apparent if one considers the total incomes of athletes (salary, endorsements, and off-season earnings). The Equal Employment Opportunity Commission report of 1968 revealed that in the fall of 1966 black athletes appeared in only 5 percent of the 351 commercials associated with New York sports events. Our own analysis of the advertising and media program slots featuring starting members of one professional football team in 1971 revealed that 8 in 11 whites had such opportunities, while only 2 of 13 blacks did.

Blacks do not have the same opportunities as whites when their playing careers are finished. This is reflected in radio and television sportscasting where no black person has had any job other than providing the "color."

Officiating is another area that is disproportionately white. Major league baseball has had only two black umpires in its history. Professional basketball has only recently broken the color line, and in football, blacks are typically head linesmen.

Although the percentage of black players in each of the three most prominent American professional sports greatly exceeds their percentage of the total population, there is ample evidence that few managerial opportunities are available to blacks. (Black ownership, of course, is nil.) Data from 1976 sources (*The Baseball Register, Football Register,* and *National Basketball Association Guide*) show that of the 24 major league baseball managers and 26 National Football League head coaches, only one was black. Five of the 17 head coaches (29 percent) in the National Basketball Association (NBA) were black.

Assistant coaches and coaches or managers of minor league baseball teams also are conspicuously white. In 1973, there were but two black managers among more than 100 minor league teams. During the same year in the National Football League, which had a black player composition of 36 percent, there were only 12 blacks, or 6.7 percent, among the 180 assistant coaches.

Finally, despite the disproportionate representation of blacks in major league baseball, only three coaches (less than 3 percent) were black. Moreover, black coaches were relegated to the less responsible coaching jobs. Baseball superstar Frank Robinson, who was appointed the first black major league field general after the conclusion of the regular 1974 season, has pointed out that blacks are excluded from the most important roles. "You hardly see any black third-base or pitching coaches. And those are the most important coaching jobs. The only place you see blacks coaching is at first base, where most anybody can do the job."

Robinson's appointment, coming more than 27 years after the entrance of another Robinson—Jackie—into major league baseball, was the exception that proves the rule. So historic was the occasion that it drew news headlines throughout the nation and a congratulatory telegram from President Ford.

The dearth of black coaches in professional sports is paralleled at the college and high school levels. Although many predominantly white colleges and universities have, in response to pressures from angry black athletes, recently made frantic efforts to hire black coaches, they have been hired almost exclusively as assistant coaches, and seldom has a coaching staff included more than one black. As of this writing (1976), not a single major college has a black head football coach, and only a handful of major colleges (Arizona, Georgetown, Harvard, Illinois State, E. Michigan, and Washington State) have head basketball or track coaches who are black.

Blacks, however, are increasingly found on the coaching staffs of college basketball teams. Researchers have reported that the number of black head coaches increased from two in 1970 to 21 in 1973. However, their data are misleading since they included both major (NCAA Division I) and smaller schools. Nevertheless, an appreciable change did occur between 1970 and 1975, when the percentage of black head basketball coaches at major colleges increased from 0.64 percent to 5.1 percent, while the percentage of major colleges with black members on their coaching staffs increased from 20 percent in 1971 to 45 percent in 1975.

The pattern of exclusion of blacks from integrated coaching situations also has characterized American high schools. Blacks, historically, have found coaching jobs only in predominantly black high schools. And, although the precise figures are unavailable, it would appear that the movement toward integration of schools in the South during the 1960s has had the effect of eliminating blacks from coaching positions, as it has eliminated black principals and black teachers in general. So anomalous is a black head coach at a predominantly white high school in the South, that when, in 1970, this barrier was broken, it was heralded by feature stories in the *New York Times* and *Sports Illustrated*. And the situation appears to be little different outside the South, where head coaches are almost exclusively white.

The paucity of black coaches and managers could be the result of two forms of discrimination. Overt discrimination occurs when owners ignore competent blacks because of their prejudice or because they fear the negative reaction of fans to blacks in leadership positions.

The other form of discrimination is more subtle, however. Blacks are not considered for coaching positions because they did not, during their playing days, occupy positions requiring leadership and decision making. For example, in baseball, 68 percent of all the managers from 1871 to 1968 were former infielders. Since blacks have tended to be "stacked" in the outfield, they do not possess the requisite infield experience that traditionally has provided access to the position of manager.

Blacks are also excluded from executive positions in organizations that govern both amateur and professional sports. In 1976, only one major NCAA college had a black athletic director. On the professional level, there was no black representation in the principal ownership of a major league franchise. No black held a high executive capacity in any of baseball's 24 teams, although there was one black assistant to Baseball Commissioner Bowie Kuhn. Nor have there been any black general managers in pro football. Professional basketball's management structure is most progressive in this regard, although ownership remains white. Two of 17 NBA clubs had black general managers in 1973. However, it was a noteworthy event, when in 1970, former NBA star Wayne Embry was named general manager of the NBA Milwaukee Bucks, thereby becoming the first black to occupy such a position in professional sports.

ABILITY AND OPPORTUNITY

Another form of discrimination in sport is unequal opportunity for equal ability. This means that entrance requirements to the major leagues are more rigorous for blacks. Black players, therefore, must be better than white players to succeed in the sports world. Aaron Rosenblatt was one of the first to demonstrate this mode of discrimination. He found that in the period from 1953 to 1957 the mean batting average for blacks in the major leagues was 20.6 points above the average for whites. In the 1958-to-1961 time period the difference was 20.1 points, while from 1962 to 1965 it was 21.2 points. In 1967, he concluded that:

... discriminatory hiring practices are still in effect in the major leagues. The superior Negro is not subject to discrimination because he is more likely to help win games than fair to poor players. Discrimination is aimed, whether by design or not, against the substar Negro ball player. The findings clearly indicate that the undistinguished Negro player is less likely to play regularly in the major leagues than the generally undistinguished white player.

Since Rosenblatt's analysis was through 1965, we extended it to include the years 1966–70. The main difference between blacks and whites persisted; for that 5-year period blacks batted an average of 20.8 points higher than whites. Updating this analysis, we found that in 1975 the gap between black and white averages was virtually identical (21 points) to what it had been previously.

The existence of racial entry barriers in major league baseball was further supported by Anthony H. Pascal and Leonard A. Rapping, who extended Rosenblatt's research by including additional years and by examining the performance of blacks and whites in each separate position, including pitchers. They found, for instance, that the 19 black pitchers in 1967 who appeared in at least 10 games won a mean number of 10.2 games, while white pitchers won an average of 7.5. This, coupled with the findings that blacks were superior to whites in all other playing positions, led to the conclusion that: "... on the average a black player must be better than a white player if he is to have an equal chance of transiting from the minor leagues to the major."

Moreover, Gerald Scully's elaborate analysis of baseball performance data has led him to conclude that, "... not only do blacks have to outperform whites to get into baseball, but they must consistently outperform them over their playing careers in order to stay in baseball." Similarly, another analysis of professional basketball in 1973 revealed that black marginal players are less likely to continue to play after 5 years than are white marginal players.

Jonathan Brower found that the situation in professional football paralleled that in baseball and basketball. First, the most dramatic increases in the numbers of black professional football players occurred during the middle sixties and early seventies. Table 2 shows the increasing percentages of blacks in professional football; basketball data is in Table 3.

Moreover, Brower found that, as in baseball and basketball, "Black ... players must be superior in athletic performance to their white counterparts if they are to be accepted into professional football." His

TABLE 2   Percentage of Blacks in Professional Football

Year	Percentage of Black Players
1950	0
1954	5
1958	9
1962	16
1966	26
1970	34
1975	42

data revealed statistically significant differences in the percentages of black and white starters and nonstarters. Blacks were found disproportionately as starters, while second-string status was more readily accorded to whites. Whereas 63 percent of black players were starters in 1970, 51 percent of white players were. Conversely, 49 percent of white players, but only 37 percent of black players, were not starters in that year. These findings led Brower to conclude that "mediocrity is a white luxury."

INEQUALITY ON THE BENCH

Our earlier research investigated whether black athletes were disproportionately overrepresented in the "star" category and underrepresented in the average, or journeyman, category on college and professional basketball teams. Our investigation showed that the black predominance in basketball is a relatively recent phenomenon, and that basketball, like

TABLE 3   Racial Composition of College and Professional Basketball Teams 1948–1975

Year	% of Teams with Blacks	College Black Players as % of Total	Average # of Blacks on Integrated Squads	Professional Black Players as % of Total
1948	9.8	1.4	1.4	none
1954	28.3	4.5	1.6	4.6
1958	44.3	9.1	2.0	11.8
1962	45.2	10.1	2.2	30.4
1966	58.3	16.2	2.8	50.9
1970	79.8	27.1	3.4	55.6
1975	92.3	33.4	5.0	63.3

football and baseball, was largely segregated until the late 1950s and early 1960s.

There are records of black basketball players on teams from predominantly white colleges as far back as 1908, but such instances were rare during the first half of the century. In professional sports, the National Basketball Association remained an all-white institution until 1950, 3 years after Jackie Robinson had broken the color line in baseball and 4 years after blacks reentered major league football after having been totally excluded since the early 1930s.

Table 3 documents the striking changes in racial composition of basketball since 1954. From the immediate post-World War II situation (1948), when less than 10 percent of collegiate squads were integrated, to 1975, when over 90 percent contained members of both races, substantial and impressive progress was made toward integration. Not only were more schools recruiting blacks, but the number of black players being recruited at each school increased dramatically. The most substantial increase among collegiate teams was during the period between 1966 and 1975, which can be partly attributed to the breakdown in previously segregated teams throughout the South.

Although blacks comprise approximately one-tenth (11 percent) of the total U.S. population, by 1975 they accounted for more than one-third (33.4 percent) of the nation's collegiate basketball players. The percentage of black players on college basketball teams is even more striking when one considers that in 1975 blacks comprised only 9 percent of undergraduate students, and nearly half (44 percent) attended predominantly black institutions.

The change in the professional game is even more marked, for blacks have clearly come to dominate the game—numerically and, as we shall note more fully below, statistically as well. As contrasted to the situation two decades ago, organized basketball—on both the collegiate and professional levels—has eliminated many of the barriers that once excluded blacks from participation. The changes in professional baseball and football, while not so dramatic, occurred primarily during the middle sixties.

Having determined that black players are disproportionately overrepresented on collegiate and professional basketball teams relative to their distribution within the general population, we systematically examined the roles they played. Specifically, we wanted to determine whether blacks have been found disproportionately as starters and whether the average number of points they score has been higher than that of whites. In order to determine whether starting patterns had changed significantly in the years during which the percentage of black players had increased so dramatically, it was necessary to examine the distribution of blacks by scoring rank over time (see Table 4).

TABLE 4 % of Blacks Among the Top Five Scorers

1958	69
1962	76
1966	72
1971	66
1975	61

Defining the top players as those with high offensive productivity as measured by their scoring average, we discovered the same situation of unequal opportunity for equal ability in basketball that others found in professional baseball. Using data from 1958, 1962, 1966, and 1970 professional and collegiate records, we found that the higher the scoring rank, the greater the likelihood that it would be occupied by a black player.

While black players comprised no more than 29 percent of all the members of integrated teams during the years 1958–70, in each of these years nearly half—and in some years, more than half—of the leading scorers were black. Conversely, blacks were disproportionately under-represented in the lowest scoring position. Moreover, our data revealed that between 1958 and 1970, no less than two-thirds—and in some years as high as three-fourths—of all black players were starters.

RECENT PROGRESS

Data from the 1975 season, however, indicates that although blacks continue to be overrepresented in starting positions, a steady and substantial decline has occurred between 1962, when 76 percent of all black college basketball players were starters, and 1975, when the percentage had dropped to 61.

These changes are shown above. In other words, black basketball recruits are no longer only those likely to be starters. Thus, unlike professional baseball and football, which show little change during the past two decades, college basketball appears increasingly to provide equal opportunity for equal ability. Moreover, these changes parallel the decline in positional stacking and the increase of black coaches in college basketball previously noted.

In professional basketball, where they have come to dominate the game, blacks were slightly overrepresented in starting roles until 1970, when equal numbers of blacks were starters and nonstarters. Following Rosenblatt's approach in comparing white and black batting averages, we compared the scoring averages of black and white basketball players for 5 years (1957–58, 1961–62, 1965–66, 1969–70, 1974–75).

Although scoring averages were identical for both races in 1957–58, blacks outscored whites in the remaining years by an average of 5.2, 3.3, 2.9, and 1.5 points, respectively. While a slight gap remains between the scoring averages of whites and blacks, the magnitude of the difference has declined as the percentage of black players in the league has increased. This is in contrast to the situation in professional baseball, where the mean batting average for blacks has remained 20 points greater than the average for whites for nearly two decades.

BLACK PARTICIPATION

The data presented here suggest both continuity and change in traditional patterns of race relations. Perhaps the most striking fact is that black participation in intercollegiate and professional sports continues to increase—especially in football and basketball. Several possible explanations for this phenomenon—the genetic, the structural, and the cultural—have been advanced.

First, it has been suggested that blacks are naturally better athletes and their predominance in American professional sports can be attributed to their innate athletic and/or physical superiority. As sociologists, we are inclined to reject interpretations of black athletic superiority as genetically or physiologically based, especially since racial categories in any society, but particularly in the United States, are socially and not scientifically defined. At best, given the paucity of data to support such a position, our stance can be no better than an agnostic one.

Another explanation that has been advanced to explain the disproportionate number of blacks in professional and collegiate sports resides in the structural limitations to which black children and adults are subjected. Since opportunities for vertical mobility by blacks in American society are circumscribed, athletics may become perceived as one of the few means by which a black can succeed in a highly competitive American society; a black male's primary role models during childhood and adolescence are much more likely to be athletic heroes than are the role models of white males. And the determination and motivation devoted to the pursuit of an athletic career may therefore be more intense for blacks than for whites whose career options are greater.

Jack Olsen, in *The Black Athlete*, quotes a prominent coach:

People keep reminding me that there is a difference in physical ability between the races, but I think there isn't. The Negro boy practices longer and harder. The Negro has a keener desire to excel in sports because it is more mandatory for his future opportunities than it is for a white boy. There are nine thousand different jobs available to a person if he is white.

A final explanation of the disproportionate black prowess in major sports emphasizes the extent to which the cultural milieu of young blacks positively rewards athletic performance. James Green has questioned whether the lure of a professional career completely explains the strong emphasis on athletics among blacks. He argues that the explanation that a black manifests a "keener desire to excel . . . because it is mandatory for his future . . ." simply reflects the commentator's own future orientation.

An alternative explanation of strong black motivation, according to Green, is the positive emphasis in black subculture that is placed on the importance of physical (and verbal) skill and dexterity. Athletic prowess in men is highly valued by both women and men. The athletically capable male is in the comparable position of the hustler or the blues singer; he is something of a folk hero. He achieves a level of status and recognition among his peers whether he is a publicly applauded sports hero or not.

Nearly as dramatic as the proportion of blacks in player roles is the dearth of blacks in administrative, managerial, and officiating positions. Although significant advances have occurred for black athletes in the past quarter of a century, there has been no comparable access of blacks to decision-making positions. With the exception of professional basketball, the corporate and decision-making structure of professional sports is virtually as white as it was when Jackie Robinson entered major league baseball in 1947. The distribution of blacks in the sports world is therefore not unlike that in the larger society, where blacks are admitted to lower-level occupations but virtually excluded from positions of authority and power.

The fact that black participation in the three major professional team sports continues to increase has led many observers to conclude incorrectly that sports participation is free of racial discrimination. As our analysis has demonstrated, stacking in football and baseball remains pronounced. Blacks are disproportionately found in those positions requiring physical rather than cognitive or leadership abilities.

Moreover, the data indicate that although the patterns have been substantially altered in collegiate and professional basketball, black athletes in the two other major team sports have been and continue to be found disproportionately in starting roles and absent from journeymen positions. The three interpretations previously considered—the genetic, the structural, and the cultural—appear inadequate to explain these patterns.

A genetic interpretation cannot explain the prevalence of blacks in starting roles or their relegation to playing positions that do not require qualities of leadership or outcome control. Even if blacks possessed genetically based athletic superiority, they should not be systematically overrepresented in starting positions or "stacked" in "black" positions, but should still be randomly distributed throughout the entire team.

As Jim Bouton (a former major league baseball player who has challenged the racial composition of major league baseball teams) has written, "If 19 of the top 30 hitters are black, then almost two-thirds of all hitters should be black. Obviously it is not that way." Similarly, explanations emphasizing the narrow range of opportunities available to blacks or the emphasis upon athletic skills in black subculture fail to explain adequately the distribution of blacks by position and performance.

SPORT AS EXAMPLE

Despite some indications of change, discrimination against black athletes continues in American team sports; sport is not a meritocratic realm where race is ignored. Equality of opportunity is not the rule where the race is a variable. These conclusions have implications that extend beyond the sports world. If discrimination occurs in so public an arena, one so generally acknowledged to be discrimination free, and one where a premium is placed on individual achievement rather than race, how much more subtly pervasive must discrimination be in other areas of American life, where personal interaction is crucial and where the actions of power wielders are not subjected to public scrutiny.

■ FOR FURTHER STUDY

Aikens, Charles. "The Struggle of Curt Flood." *The Black Scholar*, 3 (November 1971), 10-15.

Ashe, Arthur. "An Open Letter to Black Parents: Send Your Children to the Libraries." *New York Times* (February 6, 1977), section 5, p. 2.

Axthelm, Pete. *The City Game*. New York: Simon and Schuster Pocketbooks, 1971.

Behee, John. *Hail to the Victors: Black Athletes at the University of Michigan*. Ann Arbor, Mich.: Ulrich's Books, 1974.

Bennett, Bruce. "Bibliography on the Negro in Sports." *JOPER*, 41 (January 1970), 77-78; and (September 1970), 71.

"Black Dominance." *Time* (May 9, 1977), pp. 57-60.

Boyle, Robert H. "A Minority Group—The Negro Baseball Player." *Sport—Mirror of American Life*, Edited by Robert H. Boyle. Boston: Little, Brown, 1963, pp. 100-134.

Brower, Jonathan J. "The Racial Basis of the Division of Labor Among Players in the National Football League as a Function of Stereotypes." Paper presented at the meetings of the Pacific Sociological Association. Portland, 1972.

Brower, Johathan J. "The Quota System: The White Gatekeeper's Regulation of Professional Football's Black Community." Paper presented at the meetings of the American Sociological Association. New York, August 1973.

Brown, Roscoe C., Jr. "A Commentary on Racial Myths and the Black Athlete." *Social Problems in Athletics.* Edited by Daniel M. Landers. Urbana: University of Illinois Press, 1976, 168–173.

Brown, Roscoe C., Jr. "The Jock-Trap—How the Black Athlete Gets Caught!" *Sport Psychology: An Analysis of Athlete Behavior.* Edited by William F Straub. Ithaca, N.Y.: Movement Publications, 1978, pp. 195–198.

Chalk, Ocania. *Pioneers of Black Sport.* New York: Dodd, Mead, 1975.

Coakley, Jay J. *Sport in Society: Issues and Controversies.* St. Louis: C. V. Mosby 1978, chapter 11.

Davis, John P. "The Negro in Professional Football." *The American Negro Reference Book.* Englewood Cliffs, N.J.: Prentice-Hall, 1966.

Dickey, Glenn. *The Jock Empire.* Radnor, Penn: Chilton, 1974, chapter 19.

Dodson, D. "The Integration of Negroes in Baseball." *Journal of Educationa. Sociology,* 28 (October 1954), pp. 73–82.

Dommisse, John. "The Psychology of Apartheid Sport." *Journal of Sport and Social Issues,* 1 (Summer/Fall 1977), 32–53.

Edwards, Harry. "The Myth of the Racially Superior Athlete." *Intellectual Digest,* 2 (March 1972), 58–60.

Edwards, Harry. "The Black Athlete on the College Campus." *Sport and Society.* Edited by John Talamin and Charles Page. Boston: Little, Brown, 1973, pp. 202–219.

Edwards, Harry. *The Revolt of the Black Athlete.* New York: Free Press, 1969.

Edwards, Harry. *Sociology of Sport.* Homewood, Illinois: Dorsey, 1973.

Eitzen, D. Stanley, and George H. Sage. *Sociology of American Sport.* Dubuque, Iowa: Wm. C. Brown, 1978, chapter 9.

Eitzen, D. Stanley, and David C. Sanford. "The Segregation of Blacks by Playing Position in Football: Accident or Design?" *Social Science Quarterly,* 55 (March 1977), 948–959.

Eitzen, D. Stanley, and Irl Tessendorf. "Racial Segregation by Position in Sports: The Special Case of Basketball." *Review of Sport and Leisure* (June 1978).

Gaillard, Frye. "Crumbling Segregation in the Southeastern Conference." *The Black Athlete—1970.* Race Relations Information Center, August 1970, pp. 19–40.

Govan, Michael. "The Emergence of the Black Athlete in America." *The Black Scholar,* 3 (November 1971), 16–28.

Gutkind, Lee. "'I Want to Carry My Load.'" *Sports Illustrated* (June 30, 1975), pp. 32–43.

Hare, Nathan. "A Study of the Black Fighter." *The Black Scholar,* 3 (November 1971), 2–8.

Henderson, E. B. *The Black Athlete—Emergence and Arrival.* New York: Publishers Company, 1968.

Henderson, E. B. *The Negro in Sports.* Washington, D.C.: Associated Publishers, 1969.

Henry, C. D. "The Black High School Coach—Will He Become Extinct?" *The Physical Educator,* 30 (1973), 152–153.

Henry, Grant G. "A Bibliography Concerning Negroes in Physical Education, Athletics, and Related Fields." *JOPER,* 44 (May 1973), 65–66.

Johnson, Norris R. and David P. Marple. "Racial Discrimination in Professional Basketball." *Sociological Focus,* 6 (Fall 1973), 6–18.

Jordan, James. "Physiological and Anthropometrical Comparisons of Negroes and Whites." *JOPER,* 40 (November/December 1969), 93–99.

Kane, Martin. "An Assessment of 'Black is Best'." *Sports Illustrated* (January 18, 1971), pp. 72–83.

Lapchick, R. E. '*The Politics of Race and International Sport: The Case of South Africa.* Westport, Conn.: Greenwood Press, 1975.

Leonard, Wilbert M., "Spatial Separation and Performance Differentials of White, Black and Latin Pro Baseball Players." Paper presented at the meetings of the American Sociological Association, Chicago, 1977.

Leonard, Wilbert M., and Susan Schmidt. "Observations on the Changing Social Organization of Collegiate and Professional Basketball." *Sport Sociology Bulletin*, 4 (Fall 1975), 13–35.

Loy, John W., and Joseph F. McElvogue. "Racial Segregation in American Sport." *International Review of Sport Sociology*, 5 (1970), 5–24.

Madison, Donna R., and Daniel M. Landers. "Racial Discrimination in Football: A Test of the 'Stacking' of Playing Positions Hypothesis." *Social Problems in Athletics.* Edited by Daniel M. Landers. Urbana: University of Illinois Press, 1976, pp. 151–156.

McClendon, McKee, and D. Stanley Eitzen. "Interracial Contact on Collegiate Basketball Teams." *Social Science Quarterly*, 55 (March 1975), 926–938.

McPherson, Barry D. "Minority Group Involvement in Sport: The Black Athlete." *Exercise and Sport Sciences Review*, 2 (1974), 71–101.

McPherson, Barry D. "The Segregation by Playing Position Hypothesis in Sport: An Alternative Hypothesis." *Social Science Quarterly*, 55 (March 1975), 960–966.

McPherson, Barry D. "The Black Athlete: An Overview and Analysis." *Social Problems in Athletics.* Edited by Daniel M. Landers. Urbana: University of Illinois Press, 1976, pp. 122–150.

Michener, James A. *Sports in America.* New York: Random House, 1976, chapter 6.

Olsen, Jack. *The Black Athlete.* New York: Time-Life Books, 1968.

Pascal, Anthony M., and Leonard A. Rapping. *Racial Discrimination in Organized Baseball.* Santa Monica, California: The Rand Corporation, 1970.

Peterson, Robert. *Only the Ball was White.* Englewood Cliffs, N.J.: Prentice-Hall, 1970.

Phillips, John C. "Toward an Explanation of Racial Variations in Top-Level Sports Participation." *International Review of Sport Sociology* (1976), pp. 39–55.

Putnam, Pat. "The Z Bombs." *Sports Illustrated* (December 6, 1976), pp. 49–56.

Rainville, Raymond E., and Edward McCormick. "Extent of Covert Racial Prejudice in Pro Football Announcers' Speech." *Journalism Quarterly*, 54 (Spring 1977), 20–26.

Robinson, Frank, with Roy Blount, Jr. "I'll Always Be Outspoken." *Sports Illustrated* (October 21, 1974), pp. 31–38.

Rosenblatt, Aaron. "Negroes in Baseball: The Failure of Success." *Transaction*, 4 (September, 1977), 51–53.

Russell, William F. "Success Is a Journey." *Sports Illustrated* (June 8, 1970), pp. 81–93.

Rust, Art, Jr. *Get That Nigger Off the Field!* New York: Delacorte Press, 1976.

Smith, Marshall. "Giving the Olympics an Anthropological Once-Over." *Life* (October 23, 1964), pp. 81–84.

Snyder, Eldon E., and Elmer Spreitzer. *Social Aspects of Sport.* Englewood Cliffs, N.J.: Prentice-Hall, 1978, pp. 123–128.

Spirey, Donald, and Thomas A. Jones. "Intercollegiate Athletic Servitude: A Case Study of the Black Illini Student-Athletes, 1931–1967." *Social Science Quarterly*, 55 (March, 1975), 939–947.

Stuart, Reginald. "All-Black Sports World Changing." *Race Relations Reporter*, 2 (April 19, 1971), 8–10.

Thirer, Joel. "The Olympic Games as a Medium for Black Activism and Protest." *Review of Sport & Leisure*, 1 (Fall 1976), 15–31.

Van Dyne, Larry. "The South's Black Colleges Lose a Football Monopoly." *The Chronicle of Higher Education* (November 15, 1976), p. 1, 8.

Wolf, David. *Foul! The Connie Hawkins Story.* New York: Warner Books, 1972.

Yetman, Norman R., and D. Stanley Eitzen. "Black Athletes on Intercollegiate Basketball Teams: An Empirical Test of Discrimination." *Majority and Minority.* Edited by Norman R. Yetman and C. Hoy Steele. Boston: Allyn and Bacon, 1971, pp. 509–517.

Yetman, Norman R., and D. Stanley Eitzen. "Black Americans in Sports: Unequal Opportunity for Equal Ability." *Civil Rights Digest*, 5 (August 1972), 20–34.

Eleven

Sexism in Sport

Traditionally, sex role expectations have encouraged females to be passive, gentle, delicate, and submissive. These cultural expectations clashed with those traits often associated with sport, such as assertiveness, competitiveness, physical endurance, ruggedness, and dominance. Thus, females past puberty were encouraged to bypass sports unless the sport retained the femininity of the participants. These "allowable" sports had three characteristics: (1) they were aesthetically pleasing, e.g., ice skating, diving, and gymnastics; (2) they did not involve bodily contact with opponents, e.g., bowling, archery, badminton, volleyball, tennis, golf, swimming, and running; and (3) the action was controlled to protect the athletes from overexertion, e.g., running short races, basketball where the offense and defense did not cross half-court.

In effect these traditional expectations for the sexes denied women equal access to opportunities, not only to sports participation but also to college, and to various occupations. Obviously, females were discriminated against in schools by woefully inadequate facilities—compare the "girls gym" with the "boys gym" in any school—and in budgets. As late as 1973-74, the typical high school budget for boys' athletics was five times greater than for the girls, and at the college level it was thirty times greater. The consequences of sexual discrimination in sport were that: (1) the femininity of those females who defied the cultural expectations was often questioned giving them marginal status; (2) approximately one-half of the population was denied the benefits of sports participation; (3) females learned their "proper" societal role, i.e., to be on the sidelines supporting men who do the actual achieving; and (4) women were denied a major source of college scholarships.

Presently, quite rapid changes are occurring. Unquestionably, the greatest change in contemporary sport is the dramatic increase in and general acceptance of sports participation by females. Evidence of the transformation that sport is undergoing is found in the following examples and in the article by Candace Hogan:

item: In 1970 only 294,000 high school girls participated in interscholastic sports, while in 1976–77, the number was 1.6 million—almost a 600 percent increase.

item: In 1972 the first all-women minimarathon in New York drew 78 entries, whereas the same event in 1978 drew 4,360 competitors.

item: At North Carolina State the budget for women has risen from $20,000 to $300,000 in four years, with scholarships increasing from none to 49.

These swift changes have occurred for several related reasons. Most prominent was the societal-wide women's movement which has gained increasing momentum since the mid-1960s. Because of the consciousness-raising resulting from this movement and the organized efforts to break down the cultural tyranny of sex rules, court cases were initiated to break down sexual discrimination in a number of areas. In athletics legal suits were successfully brought against various school districts, universities, and even the Little League (see the article by Jan Felshin).

In 1972 Congress passed Title IX of the Education Amendment Act. The essence of this law, which has had the greatest single impact on the move toward sexual equality in all aspects of schools, is:

No person in the United States shall, on the basis of sex, be excluded from taking part in, be denied the benefits of, or be subjected to discrimination in any educational program or activity receiving federal financial assistance.

Since most schools receive federal monies (in 1978 colleges and universities received $12.2 billion while public schools were the recipients of $4.9 billion), the threat of its loss caused schools to change their practices whether or not they were willing to show progress in overcoming sexual bias by the target date of July 1978.

But although women's sport programs have indeed come a long way in a short time, there is plenty of evidence of continuing discrimination.

item: At the University of Michigan the 1978 budget called for thirty scholarships for women at a cost of $100,000 compared to 190 for men worth $700,000.

item: At U.C.L.A. the 1978 budget for women's athletics was $527,000 versus $3.7 million for men.

item: At Colorado State the 1976 women's budget was increased 50 percent for the next year, but the new total amount ($151,500) was only 9.8 percent of the budget for men's athletics for that year.

These examples, when added to those provided in Hogan's article, show that while women have made rapid gains, they continue to be substantially behind men's programs—in scholarships, facilities, number of coaches, remuneration of coaches, and travel monies. The fundamental question is whether women will continue to progress toward equality. The major roadblock at the college level is that currently the major men's athletic programs—football and basketball—are financially successful, and, therefore, subsidize the other athletic programs. Should the football program be curtailed in order to equalize budgets for both sexes? This is a major question, and the guidelines for Title IX are unclear as to how it should be handled. The article in this unit by George La Noue proposes some practical solutions to this and related problems.

Despite still lagging behind the men's programs, women's programs are beginning to have the resources to make fundamental changes in their policies. This raises the question as to their ultimate goal. Do the women want to emulate the men's programs? The concluding paper in this section, by physical educator George Sage, addresses this question. Women can choose between moving toward corporate sport by copying the mistakes and problems of men's programs and thereby losing the educational values of sport and the original reason for sport (enjoyment in the activity) or they can seek another direction that maximizes the self-actualizing potential of sport. The dilemma is that the former is the more glamorous and financial successful avenue, so that if the choice moves in another direction, the charge of unequal programs in sports is again justified. The current trend, however, is that this will likely not be a problem, because women's athletic programs in the large universities at least are moving swiftly toward corporate sport.

The Status of Women and Sport

JAN FELSHIN

One of the concerns of status is the legal character or condition. This becomes a central aspect when people actively pursue social change through legal means. The whole concept of an activist approach as part of the equality revolution in the United States has been tied to legal frameworks. Even the sound and fury of protest and civil disobedience revolved around legal inequities or failures, and as these faded with the end of the 1960s, legal action has become synonymous with militance.

It is too late to ask whether or not the ancient Greeks had the "right" to bar women from Olympia, it is not too late to insist that a woman has the "right" to enter the press box in the stadium of Yale University, even during a football game. Insistence on rights, however, even when "fairness" or "humanity" is invoked has not proved to be socially effective. Legal recourse has. Interestingly enough, the institution of sport has proved less vulnerable to legal action than any other. The confusion of Supreme Court decisions relative to the application of federal antitrust laws to professional sport is the most obvious testimony to the fact that sport in American society occupies a special place as a social conception.

Somehow, the whole tradition of sport includes a host of quasi-legalistic assumptions and attendant rules and policies that affect not only how contests shall be conducted, but who shall play, and how players shall conduct themselves. The weight of tradition and the idealized social vision of sport have been substantive support for the organized groups that regulate sport. It seems apparent that if Curt Flood could challenge the "reserve clause" in baseball, and Wimbledon could be boycotted as it was by the men's players association in 1973, that times are changing. Men's sport will undoubtedly be modified as a result of legal and political action; women's sport may be revolutionized.

POLITICS AND LAW

The Citizen's Advisory Council on the Status of Women reported that "Unprecedented political, legal, and economic advances made 1972 an

---

SOURCE: Jan Felshin, "The Status of Women and Sport," in Ellen W. Gerber, Jan Felshin, Pearl Berlin, and Waneen Wyrick, *The American Woman in Sport* (Reading, Mass.: Addison-Wesley,1974), pp. 212–221.

412

historic year for women" (May, 1973, p. 1). Cited as evidence were such things as political power; election to public office; passage of the Equal Rights Amendment in the Senate on March 22, 1972 and the ratification process; as well as the passage of other Federal and State legislation improving the legal and economic status of women.

The ERA is the most symbolic legislative act. Writing in *The New York Times Magazine*, Thimmesch presented "three simple sections" and then commented, "If the sentences are simple, they are rich with far-reaching legal and ultimately social implications . . ." (June 24, 1973, p. 9). The ERA has until March 22, 1979 to be ratified. At the time that Thimmesch was reporting, twenty-nine states had voted final ratification, thirteen states had rejected the ERA, it was stopped before it reached the floor of the legislature in six states, and one state, Nebraska, had responded to a growing counter-offensive of public opinion and voted to rescind its ratification. Although Congress may have to decide upon the legality of voting to rescind ratification, the Counsel to the Constitutional Amendments Subcommittee of the U.S. Senate concurred with the Attorney General of Idaho in declaring such action null and void. In addition, six states ratified Equal Rights Amendments to their State Constitutions in November, 1972—Colorado, Hawaii, Maryland, New Mexico, Texas and Washington, thus joining Illinois, Pennsylvania, and Virginia who had done so previously, and Connecticut projected such consideration for 1974 (p. 69). Pat Goltz, international president of the Feminists for Life, commented that even if the ERA is never ratified it has accomplished its purpose (July, 1973, single page).

Amendment 11375 revised Executive Order 11246, which was geared toward affirmative action in employment, to include sex. This Amendment and the Equal Employment Opportunity Act of 1972, giving the Equal Employment Opportunity Commission authority to enforce Title VII of the Civil Rights Act of 1964, affirm a changed social view. Because of Title VII, the EEOC can file complaints in court in relation to discrimination in employment because of race, color, religion, sex, or national origin. On March 31, 1972, the EEOC issued revised guidelines on discrimination because of sex, and established the relationship of Title VII to the Equal Pay Act.

Government has limitations with reference to social change, but in the present society political action is seen as the most viable means to legitimizing both social conditions and ideology. The prevailing status of women (as well as other groups with minority characteristics) became socially intolerable and dissonant with the realities of industrialization and affluence. Because there was, in fact, some consensus in the society that inequities existed, the incipient move toward social revolutions, rebellions, and civil strife as avenues toward change proved defeating. Social change is resisted, most often, because the members of a society have been socialized to accept certain elements that are congruent with the status quo. It is important to remember that socialization implies attitudes, customs, moral sentiments, and even personal feelings. All of these are most strongly affected specially in terms of such a pervasive and personalized aspect of life as one's sex, and generally in terms of the appropriate roles and behaviors of the sexes.

In the present society, then, there seems to be some general agreement that an inequitable and "unfair" situation does exist. The principle of equality of opportunity is an important one in American society, and takes on the proportion of a moral sentiment for most people, so it is fairly well accepted that women should have equal pay for equal work, and should not be denied *all* professional opportunities on the basis of sex alone. Beyond that level, however, a great deal of political effort is required to change either existing perceptions of women and their appropriate status in society or the social mechanisms that would enable change. The focus of political efforts is a dual one and includes demands for: (1) equality as permitted by social structures, but denied by sexist attitudes and practices, and (2) change in both existing attitudes and structures.

Although one of the arguments for maintaing the social *status quo* for women is that they themselves are satisfied, this is obviously not the case. The legal activity on behalf of women as a result of changing legislation has been phenomenal and successful. In a multitude of cases, most of them brought by the EEOC, the courts have ordered employers and unions to stop discriminatory practices and policies, and have enjoined them to set up improved hiring, transfer, classification, and promotion practices and affirmative action programs. Furthermore, in most cases, the large amounts of money involved discourage employers from continuing discrimination. A recent suit against the General Electric Company, for instance, was settled with an agreement that would cost the company $300,000 in back pay and an additional $250,000 annually in higher wages (*The Spokeswoman*, August 15, 1973, p. 2).

POLITICAL ACTION IN SPORT

The legal and political action in sport in society is less impressive than that occurring generally on behalf of women. The Women's Liberation Movement was slow to recognize the importance of sport as a symbolic domain for women's advances. Of course, the infinitely greater visibility of men's sport led to its early recognition as a target for political action, and the Black Power salute at the Mexico City Olympics received worldwide attention. There is also still a vaguely embarrassed attitude on the part of most women toward athletic involvement, so that Nora Ephron's piece in *Esquire* about Bernice Gera, the first woman umpire in professional baseball, is satiric. Ephron commented that "I should say, at this point, that I am utterly baffled as to why any woman would want to get into professional baseball, much less work as an umpire in it" (January, 1973, p. 36).

Bernice Gera's experience provided some insight into the kinds of difficulties inherent in the issue of women in sport and, ultimately, reflected the changing political scene. For whatever reasons, this woman was an avid devotee of baseball. In the early 1960s she sought employment in baseball in any capacity, and met with consistent rejection. In 1967, she filed an application to the Al Summers Baseball Umpires School in Florida, was accepted, and then rejected when Summers discovered she was a woman. Bernice Gera did enroll in the National Sports Academy in West Palm Beach, Florida in June, 1967, and graduated with honors. Lawsuits began in 1968 when Gera could not obtain employment, and in 1969, she was given a contract by the New York-Pennsylvania Class A League. When the president of the National Association of Professional Baseball Leagues invalidated the contract by refusing to sign it, Mario Biaggi, her attorney, filed a complaint with the New York State Human Rights Commission. The Commission ruled in November, 1970 that the National League discriminated not only against women, but against men belonging to short ethnic groups as well (the League had used Gera's height of 5'2" as unacceptable qualification for being an umpire). There was an appeal and further litigation, but the State Court of Appeals upheld the Human Rights Commission ruling and on July 25, 1972, Bernice Gera signed a contract with the New York-Pennsylvania League.

The happy ending, of course, did not occur. In the opener of the New York-Pennsylvania League season in Geneva, New York, Gera was both harassed and not very effective; she announced "I've just resigned from baseball" at the end of the game, and burst into tears. The National Organization for Women was not involved in any of Bernice Gera's efforts, but she was contacted by them afterward. It is fairly clear that this woman was acting in terms of her own motivations and not as a political symbol, but the successful legal maneuvers involved did establish both precedent and encouragement with reference to women in sport. In some ways, then, the case of Bernice Gera is a landmark example, and does, in fact, represent the extent of the time period involved in the use of legal action to change women's roles in sport.

Women jockeys provided the first significant breakthrough in terms of new sport roles for women in professional sport. The triumph of women in horse racing incorporated all the elements of drama, self-assertion, and ultimate vindication of the underdog so dear to American mythology. Although the greatest resistance to women riders came from male jockeys, and many men were generally amused or upset, public sentiment seemed to be with the women. Perhaps because horsemanship has always been considered an appropriate feminine and upper-class activity, the idea of women racing was not quite so upsetting. In fact, it was Kathy Kusner, the Olympic equestrienne, who paved the way by winning a court order forcing the Maryland Racing Commission to license her.

There were several women fighting for the right to ride at the same time, and all of them were attractive and feminine according to prevailing social standards. At the same time, it is possible that the fact that male jockeys are obviously considered somewhat less desirable men because of their size contributed to the view that their objections could be discounted. Both Penny Ann Early and Barbara Jo Rubin were boycotted by male jockeys following their successful campaigns to be licensed by the Racing Commission. The boycotts ended, however, when the Florida State Racing Commission upheld the Tropical Park stewards who had fined thirteen jockeys a hundred dollars each for the part they took in the demonstration against Barbara Jo Rubin. These efforts on the part of women jockeys began in 1968, and in February, 1969, Tuesdee Testa became the first woman rider ever to compete in a regular race at Santa Anita, although she did finish last.

Perhaps, the fact that racing is more a contest between horses than humans also contributed to the acceptance of women jockeys. In any case, despite the social furor, the proliferation of jokes, and other attempts to ridicule them, the woman jockey seems to be a permanent part of the sport. It also became quickly apparent that women had, in fact, been part of the horseracing scene for some time. They had served as hot-walkers, who walk the horses after a race or workout to cool them, pony persons (pony boys), grooms, and exercise persons. The existence of women jockeys served both to legitimize these auxiliary roles and to attract more girls and women to them, and the participation of women in the world of horseracing seems to be established.

Once established, the procedure of bringing suit against discriminatory practices in sport was manifest in diverse ways. Elinor Kaine, the sportswriter who was refused the right to sit in the press box of the Yale Bowl, won an out-of-court settlement when she brought suit. Legal action was threatened by Stephanie Salter, a writer for *Sports Illustrated*, who was refused admission to the annual banquet of the New York chapter of the Baseball Writers Association of America [*The Sportswoman* (Spring, 1972), p. 5]. Debbie Seldon sued the American Motorcycle Association for refusing to license her as a professional and when Kerry Kleid brought similar action, she became the first professional woman rider.

After several suits were initiated on behalf of girls who wanted to play in Little League baseball, and several contradictory rulings, the strongest suit was filed in May, 1973 by Carolyn King, the Ypsilanti American Little League, and the city of Ypsilanti against the National Little Leagues organization over its "no girls allowed" rule. In this case, Carolyn King won her position as a centerfielder on the basis of her ability over a hundred competing boy players. The Ypsilanti City Council ordered the local league either to let her play or lose the use of city facilities, staff, and financial aid, and when they complied, the National Little League office revoked their charter [*The Spokeswoman* (August 15, 1973), p. 2]. On June 20, 1973 Representative Martha W. Griffiths introduced bill H.R. 8854 into the United States House of Representatives to amend the Little League Baseball Federal Charter to include girls as well as boys. On August 25, 1973, the Little League World Series in Williamsport, Pennsylvania was picketed by members of the National Organization for Women. In November, 1973 the New Jersey Civil Rights Division ruled that the league should let girls play, and Sylvia Pressler of the Division said, "The institution of Little League is as American as the hot dog and apple pie. There is no reason why that part of Americana should be withheld from girls." On February 27, 1974, a three-judge panel of the appellate division of Superior Court responded to a request by Little League, Inc. for a stay of the order issued by the State Division on Civil Rights. The League had argued that girls were not physically fit to play, but the judges ordered that girls must be allowed to play in New Jersey and should be allowed to register immediately (*The New York Times*, February 28, 1974).

In addition to legal efforts, other kinds of pressures have served to change women's sport. As Myron Stuart wrote, "Women's lib in golf and tennis has finally come of age. Girls who used to play for silver trophies topped off, perhaps, by a kiss on the cheek from the tournament's chairman, finally are playing for gold—big chunks of it" (June, 1973, p. 44). Earnings and the inequities between what men and women earned, frequently for the same job, were obvious targets in a society where women, in fact, were paid fifty-eight percent of what men were paid. Although sport is a separate case when it comes to the "value" of work or the "worth" of athletes, it was logical that the differentials of money in men's and women's sports would be an issue.

Sports Illustrated reported that although Billie Jean King became the first woman athlete to win $100,000 (the congratulatory phone call from President Nixon let the nation know that even if women's sport wasn't important, money always was) in 1971, Rod Laver's earnings that year were $290,000. When King won $10,000 for winning the U.S. Open at Forest Hills in 1972, her male counterpart, Ilie Nastase, collected $25,000, and while golf's leading woman money winner, Kathy Whitworth, collected $65,063 in 1972, in 29 tournaments, Jack Nicklaus won $320,542 in 19 (May 28, 1973, p. 92).

At the time that Billie Jean King and other women tennis players protested the disparity in purses for men's and women's events in 1970, the ratio in most tournaments approached ten to one. The support of Gladys Heldman, the formation of the Women's International Tennis Federation, the suspension of the dissenting players by the USLTA, and the successful Virginia Slims Tour was an appropriate drama for the women's movement in sport. The drama was heightened by the challenges of Bobby Riggs who billed himself as "the greatest women's tennis player in the world." On September 20, 1973, Billie Jean King, at twenty-nine, and Bobby Riggs, at fifty-five, played a $100,000 winner-take-all singles match on the floor of the Astrodome before a crowd of 30,492 and a national television audience, "that turned the event into a one-of-a-kind 3-million-dollar spectacular filled with circus trimmings" (*The New York Times*, December 23, 1973). Riggs had staged a similar match against Margaret Court the previous Mother's Day and had won that $10,000 event handily. Billie Jean King became an important heroine of the women's movement when she beat Riggs 6–4, 6–3, 6–3. Although the Riggs-King match was less sport than entertainment in its social connotations, the contest itself did ultimately become the drama, and women and tennis were well served by King's victory. A kind of backlash effect was the fury directed toward Rosie Casals who assisted in reporting the event and adopted a fiercely partisan and feminist stance.

Tennis became the symbolic testimony that is exploding the myth that people neither care about women athletes nor will watch them. The United States Open Tennis Championships at Forest Hills in 1973 became the first tournament of any consequence to give men and women financial parity through equal prize monies. The World Team Tennis League is not only sexually integrated, but the player drafts clearly indicated that women stars were the most desirable drawing cards. Prize money for women has continued to increase, and in 1973, Margaret Court became the first woman to exceed earnings of $200,000. In the richest tournaments for women, Rosemary Casals won $30,000 in the Family Circle tournament at Sea Pines, South Carolina, and Chris Evert, who earned $123,000 in 1973, collected $25,000 of it beating Nancy Gunter at Boca Raton, Florida. It seems impossible that between August, 1972 and September, 1973, NBC televised 366 hours of "live" sport with *one hour* of it, the finals at Wimbledon, devoted to women (*Sports Illustrated*, May 28, 1973, p. 96). Surely, that will never happen again.

WOMEN'S STATUS IN SPORT

Both sport and women's status are changed by women serving in prestigious or unique roles in sport. There is, of course, a danger of "tokenism" insofar as a single woman may be permitted to advance or to do something as a way of quieting criticism. In terms of social change, however, it seems more often that even a single woman fulfilling a heretofore "masculine" role becomes a substantial aspect of a changed consciousness as social conception.

When NOW challenged Roone Arledge about the insufficient network treatment of women's sports, he commented that he would "hire any woman as competent as Ellie Riger." She has since been named a full producer for ABC and says, "At ABC sports, we keep working to promote women all the time" (*Ms.*, September, 1973, p. 20). In January, 1974 Ellie Riger produced a Special on Woman Athletes.

New York City named its first woman golf pro in 1971, after more than eighty years of municipal golf. In May, 1973, Bobbie Montgomery of Anderson, South Carolina became the general manager of a baseball team in the Western Carolina League. In February, 1971, a story about Idaho State University rejecting the application of Nila Gilcrest to be an assistant football coach, without pay, was distributed by UPI. In the same week in August, 1973, both *The New York Times* and *Sports Illustrated* reported that Lee Corso, head football coach at Indiana University, was looking for a woman to fill the position of assistant varsity coach in charge of academics and counseling, and had received fifty applications.

In the Colgate-Dinah Shore Winners Circle golf tournament in the spring of 1973, the $139,000 in prizes was impressive, but so was the fact that ninety women were involved in the conduct of the tournament, from caddying to running the press scoreboard.

Jan Magee became Michigan's only registered woman football official in the fall of 1972. Maxine Shields, who became the third woman to hold a professional motorcycle racing license, came in second in the Internationals race in Valley Hermosa in Mexico in 1972; the only woman in flat track racing at the time (*The Sportswoman*, Summer, 1973, p. 22).

In contemporary society, women are prizefighting and running in distance events (as well as in the Boston Marathon, at last). They are playing the same excellent hockey and lacrosse they have throughout the century, as well as taking part in all the traditionally feminine and social activities like swimming, tennis, and golf, but softball, basketball, soccer, and football are popular too. *The Sportswoman* reports professional women's football teams in Los Angeles, Toledo, Dallas, Detroit and "supposedly Cleveland, New York, and Buffalo" (Summer, 1973, p. 19). And international soccer for women is thriving.

There is no end to the contemporary chronicle of change in both the individual participation of women in sport and the collective phenomenon of women's sport, but there is a question as to the real social significance of these examples. It's true that *Sports Illustrated* reported that two women, Donna Buckley and Truda Gilbert, *finished* the AuSable Canoe Marathon, a 240-mile race [(August 27, 1973), p. 36]. And women drag racers and ice hockey players consistently make the news. Women in professional track seem to be doing as well as the men are, but Denise Long, the Iowa basketball superstar who was drafted by the Golden State Warriors in San Francisco, has had to give up her sport in frustration.

Questions about the importance of sport opportunities for women or of the significance of the phenomenon of women's sport simply cannot be answered in contemporary terms. There have been few attempts to study sport in relation to women in social views, and the ones that exist are clearly obsolete. It is apparent that some inroads have been made on the assumption that the word "sport" itself refers only to male behavior, and women in sport are more visible in the media. . . .

Title IX: From Here to Equality

CANDACE LYLE HOGAN

Fueled by an almost chemical interaction of a federal anti-sex-discrimination law, the women's liberation movement, and what is called the temper of the times, women's sports took off like a rocket in 1972. Women's opportunity in school sports was practically nil before, so naturally the initial winnings seem to rank right up there with hitting the number on a roulette wheel.

SOURCE: Candace Lyle Hogan, "Title IX: From Here to Equality," *WomenSports* 4 (September 1977), excerpts from pp. 16–17, 19, 22, 24, 60.

In 1972, when women students were staying up all night in line outside of the gym to make sure they could get a coveted spot in a p.e. class when sign-ups opened in the morning, the University of California at Berkeley was budgeting $5,000 toward women's athletics. The following year the women's budget jumped to $50,000. This fall it will be $448,000, almost 90 times what it was five years ago.

In 1974, two years after Title IX was law, an average of only 2% of the money budgeted by colleges and universities for athletics was earmarked for women. This year, estimates of women's share of athletic funding average anywhere from 4 to 8%. In 1974 about 60 colleges offered athletic scholarships to women; now more than 460 do.

The public consciousness has been raised, as it were, and is manifesting liberal behavior toward women in sports. Organizations from community leagues to state legislatures are beginning to play sugar daddy to women athletes. Backing the notion of "equal pay for equal play" for the first time in 31 years, the Delaware Association of Pushmobile Derby awarded the same prizes to girl winners as to boy winners last month. In a $1.3 million measure for funding nonrevenue-producing collegiate sports, The House Education Committee of the Oregon legislature earmarked a special $986,480 grant for women's intercollegiate athletics in a one-shot deal intended to avoid elimination of minor sports and cutbacks in major sports in the state's university system.

Girls' participation in interscholastic sports has increased 460% in the six-year period between 1971 and 1977. A survey by the National Federation of State High School Associations reports that in the 1970–71

TABLE 1 Growth in College Participation, 1971–76

Sports	Number of Schools				
	'71–72	'72–73	'73–74	'74–75	'75–76
Basketball	215	346	466	600	640
Volleyball	181	285	396	467	594
Tennis	198	300	417	506	560
Softball	120	175	254	303	342
Swimming & Diving	135	213	265	298	327
Track & Field	76	138	180	226	283
Field hockey	165	213	249	284	256
Gymnastics	123	182	238	263	246
Golf	77	132	145	155	165
Badminton	70	98	124	125	117
Total AIAW member schools	301	409	603	739	843

From a December 1976 survey by the Association for Intercollegiate Athletics for Women of the number of its member schools offering intercollegiate competition for women.

school year, 3,666,000 boys and 294,000 girls played sports on an inter-scholastic level. In other words, only 7% of all students participating in high school sports in 1970 were girls. During the 1976–77 school year, 1,645,000 girls played interscholastic sports—29% of the 5,754,000 total.

These sudden and rapid increases, which appear substantial because of the previous dearth of support and participation, constitute the boom in women's school sports. But what assurances are there that this boom will be sustained? Those who care that women achieve equal opportunity in sports know that the present is not just a time for celebration of progress, but a time for vigilance to ensure the continuation of support and to guide its direction.

There are indications that progress is not a sure bet just because you hit the number once on a roulette wheel. According to educated guessers, the factors involved in the initial blast-off in women's sports might get women's budgets from zero to 20% of total budgets. But what are the factors that will move them nearer to equality—from 20% to 50%?

There are already signs of a slowdown in growth rate in high school sports participation. Girls' interscholastic participation increased by 345,000 in the past two years, but this is significantly less growth for girls than the increase of 483,000 between the 1972–73 and the 1974–75 surveys, and the increase of 523,000 between the 1970–71 and the 1972–73 surveys.

The National High School Federation cites "The deteriorating financial situation of school districts in many areas of the country" as the reason for the slowdown in growth. But women students and coaches who feel the rate of growth slowing down could cite discrimination. Many administrators simply are refusing to upgrade women's programs when they think it means changing or cutting back on men's programs. It seems that

TABLE 2   Growth in High School Participation

Sports	1970–71		1972–73		1976–77	
	Schools	Athletes	Schools	Athletes	Schools	Athletes
Track & Field	2,992	62,211	7,292	178,209	12,636	395,271
Basketball	4,856	132,299	8,718	203,207	14,931	387,507
Volleyball	1,550	17,952	6,158	108,298	10,607	245,032
Softball	373	9,813	4,251	81,379	6,496	133,458
Tennis	2,648	26,010	4,219	53,940	6,991	112,166
Swimming & Diving	853	17,229	2,079	41,820	3,285	85,013
Gymnastics	1,006	17,225	2,154	35,224	3,379	79,461
Field hockey	159	4,260	1,572	45,252	1,675	59,944
Golf	116	1,118	1,228	10,106	2,596	32,190
Cross-country	77	1,719	433	4,921	2,631	30,798

From girls' interscholastic sports participation surveys by the National Federation of State High School Associations.

TABLE 3 Seven Big-Ten Budgets, 1976-77

Schools*	Women's Athletics	Men's Athletics	Women's % of Total
Indiana	$218,000	$3,500,000	5.86
Iowa	250,000	2,000,000	11.11
Michigan	180,000	5,000,000	3.47
Michigan State	256,000	4,500,000	5.38
Minnesota	400,000	3,400,000	10.53
Ohio State	300,000	5,700,000	5.00
Wisconsin	209,000	2,217,000	8.62
Average	259,000	3,759,714	7.14

* Figures unavailable for Illinois, Purdue, and Northwestern. Budgets listed may not include the total money spent since some salaries and administrative costs may be reflected in other budgets.

when economics and law meet in the minds of school administrators, money gets tighter and their interpretation of tne law gets looser. Push is coming to shove. . . .

In general, women's athletics are being treated the way men's "minor" sports have always been dealt with, low on the totem pole compared with revenue-producing sports like football, but higher in priority than intramural sports. Yet many women in education do not believe in the practice of allocating funds according to how much a sport brings in at the gate. It is interesting to note that Judy Sweet of the University of California at San Diego—the first female athletic director in the nation in charge of both men's and women's athletics—has instituted a policy to regard all sports there as "major." Her budget for the 30 intercollegiate teams there this past year was $117,000, while $132,000 were spent on intramurals. San Diego offers no athletic scholarships and recruits neither men nor women. Participation-oriented, her program is admired but not yet copied.

In general, though, schools have been trying to fit women's athletics into the established sports structure instead of trying to change the entire structure to accommodate a more participation-oriented philosophy. The result is a potpourri of approaches which tells more about the established system of intercollegiate sports in this country than it does about women's potential place in it.

Nationwide, schools seem to be spending the new money for women on the basics first—equipment, uniforms and travel—and on coaches' pay last. Equalization of practice times and use of facilities are among the most thorny problems, and the solutions range from the sublime to the ridiculous. . . .

It seems that what many schools define as "confusion over what Title IX means" is really frustration over their own useless attempts to avoid the law. Economic problems are real, but they do not exempt schools from obeying Title IX. Title IX doesn't order schools to double their money; it just says that they must split equitably what they have.

It is a formidable law, and schools cannot keep hiding behind economics to avoid it. As Elizabeth LaGrua said after West Morris High School had denied her daughter the opportunity to play soccer, "I have been told that the board has a problem with insufficient funds to set up more girls' programs. Well, income tax is a problem for me, too, but I pay it."

Athletics and Equality: how to comply with title IX without tearing down the stadium

GEORGE R. LA NOUE

"No person in the United States shall, on the basis of sex, be excluded from participation in, be denied the benefits of, or be subjected to discrimination in any education program or activity receiving federal financial assistance. . . ."
—Title IX, Education Amendments of 1972

On May 27, 1975, a former University of Michigan football center, now President of the United States, signed the so-called Title IX guidelines. A few weeks later, the Department of Health, Education, and Welfare issued the "final" Title IX regulations. However, in such a complex area, the law is by no means final and will not be until Congress and the courts speak definitively. Indeed, HEW gave institutions a year for self-evaluation, and serious enforcement may not begin for several years. In the meanwhile, although Title IX is the immediate issue, athletic directors in public institutions must still be concerned about possible

SOURCE: George R. La Noue, "Athletics and Equality: How to Comply with Title IX Without Tearing Down the Stadium," *Change*, 8 (November 1976), 27-30, 63-64.

litigation under the 14th Amendment, various state laws, and eventually the Equal Rights Amendment. What all these laws have in common is the requirement of sexual equality.

A major source of the controversy over Title IX and athletics is the meaning of equality. Equality may be measured in terms of opportunities, procedures, or results. Equality may be defined as treating every group in the same manner, as treating some handicapped groups preferentially, or as enhancing the unique capacities or interests of each group according to need. As if the conceptual problems were not complex enough, Title IX issues have been further exacerbated by the hidden agendas of interest groups in the struggle to formulate guidelines. Some educators have seen Title IX as a tool to cut back on the expenditures and abuses of bigtime intercollegiate sports. Believing that athletic departments and their boosters can not or will not provide matching funds for women's athletics, they see Title IX forcing a reversion to amateurism.

Some of the more militant feminists seem less interested in creating new opportunities for women athletes than in striking a blow against masculine culture as represented by certain athletic traditions. Their adamant opposition to separate but equal teams and physical education classes thus seems motivated less by a concern for equal resources than by a hostility to the type of socialization that takes place on all-male teams. Finally, the opposition to Title IX athletic regulations from some of the major universities and their football and basketball coaches seems to stem mainly from a desire to protect the competitive edge their affluence buys. While voicing a concern for the health of sports in general, they have done very little, until the threat of Title IX and the recent recession, to redistribute sports revenues to women, to intramural programs, to minor sports, or to the "have not" schools on their schedules. Now the National Collegiate Athletic Association (NCAA) has begun to act, but professional sports are generally far ahead in their efforts to equalize competition.

Whatever one's personal views about the appropriate scope and value of intercollegiate athletics (for the record my sympathies are with those who would preserve, reform, and equalize college sports), it is an abuse of federal power to utilize Title IX to achieve any comprehensive change except sexual equality. Congress barely thought about the application of Title IX to athletics when the legislation was passed and since then, although forcefully presented with the issue, has been unable to arrive at a consensus. Moreover, however diligent and conscientious, the HEW staff that drew up the Title IX guidelines is neither representative nor accountable. To the extent that they alter athletics beyond the letter of the law, they create an unreasonable bureaucratic control of education and culture. The problem remains; the law requires equality. What is equality when applied to the payrolls, the facilities, and the leisure-time choices of the men and women in higher education?

In a few sports, coed teams or scores combining the totals of separate male and female teams are possible. Gymnastics, golf, tennis, even track might use this approach, but most of the major sports involve contact, strength, and size. In those sports, in the foreseeable future, women and men will not compete equally in equal numbers.

Some would accept separate but equal teams, but would insist that the total resources spent on women's and men's athletics be the same in a particular institution. HEW insists that its guidelines do not require equal spending. Yet in listing the items used to measure compliance, it is not clear how else equality will be calculated. Just as judicial overturning of severely malapportioned state legislative districts led eventually to court requirements of such mathematically equal districts that computers had to be employed, so many wonder whether HEW will ever find any policy short of absolutely equal spending to meet its interpretation of Title IX.

Yet equal spending might result in very unequal opportunities for males and females according to some definitions of equality. As a generalization, the sports males prefer to play are much more expensive because they require more equipment and facilities than the sports traditionally preferred by females. Thus equal spending imposed now would severely limit the number of male participants or would eliminate entirely some expensive sports like football and ice hockey. Further, since college sports must compete with their professional counterparts for spectators, a severe reduction in the budgets of male spectator sports might undermine the quality of the collegiate spectacle to the point where there would be substantially less money for both male and female athletes. The problem, therefore, is to work out a concept of athletic equality that will improve opportunities for women, be legally defensible, and reflect the multiple purposes of collegiate sports.

It is that last consideration that has been neglected in the Title IX debate. Title IX discussions have generally focused on the relative facilities and funds available to male and female athletes. On this level, the treatment of women athletes by universities was often shabby at best, and Title IX will surely eliminate such abuses. But it is unrealistic to view college athletics wholly from the athlete's viewpoint. While it is not common elsewhere in the world, the athletic spectacles put on by American universities are a significant ritual and diversion for the general population. Title IX need not and should not uproot this traditional form of entertainment. Nor should Title IX deprive universities of the community outreach, publicity, and income sports create.

At the moment the sports that generate this interest at both college and professional levels are male sports. One can foresee a gradual increase in spectator interest in women's sports, but it will not happen overnight and it can not be legislated. Therefore, universities must seek to provide

equality for the woman athlete while maintaining quality in their spectator sports. How can this be accomplished?

I suggest that Title IX compliance needs to be viewed according to the
purpose of the various sports schools play. A typical university's sports
program, for example, may comprise four categories: intramural, intercollegiate developing, intercollegiate participant-oriented, or intercollegiate spectator-oriented. Title IX might have different implications in
each category.

Intramural sports are played primarily for the benefit of the participants. Institutional income and publicity in these sports are nonexistent.
Consequently, programs should be flexible. The number of teams and
sports should depend on interest shown. Intramural sports might be coed
or single sex as the participants prefer. Some objective means of establishing interest should be created. Thus assuming fair sign-up procedures, if
500 men and 250 women choose intramural basketball then it should be
consistent with Title IX to have twice as many male teams. But equipment
and facilities must be equal for teams of both sexes.

Intercollegiate sports may be divided into those sports that are played
principally for the participants' sakes and those that command a traditional spectator interest. In addition, some sports are in a stage of
development and are not yet clearly participant or spectator oriented.
Particular sports will fall into different categories at different institutions.
For example, lacrosse is a spectator sport at Johns Hopkins, while
wrestling is participant oriented. The reverse is true at Lehigh.

Intercollegiate participant-oriented sports, such as cross country or
crew, may be treated for Title IX purposes in the same manner as
intramural sports. They are not quite the same, since the institution will
probably reap some favorable publicity from good participant-oriented
teams even if very few people want to watch the event. In these sports the
number of teams would depend on student interest. No athletic grants
should be awarded participants, and the sports should be funded according to intrinsic costs. As with intramural sports, compliance with Title IX
should depend on an institution's response to student interest. If males
want crew and women do not, that choice would not violate Title IX; if
both sexes want crew, then equipment, facilities, and schedules should be
comparable.

The traditional spectator-oriented sports present more complex issues.
For one thing, how should institutional expenditures be measured? If it
takes $1 million to field a big-time football team but gate receipts total
$1.1 million, has football really cost the university anything? Given those
figures, in Title IX terms, what does equality for women's sports mean?
Suppose gate receipts dropped to $900,000 the next year. Does the Title
IX requirement change? Indeed even in this case, has the university

actually suffered a loss, given the auxiliary income and publicity a major football program can generate? In addition to the complexity of measuring the costs it is not so clear that even a sport such as football should be considered a male sport for Title IX purposes. Certainly for the foreseeable future all of Saturday's heroes will be males, but many of the spectators in the stadium are female. Do they not derive some benefit from the sport? If not, why are they there? How are they to be figured into the Title IX account?

It seems to me these are not complexities that Title IX was designed to handle. The goal of Title IX should not be to undermine the traditional spectator sports, even if males are the primary participants, but to create flexibility so that women's sports may achieve spectator status if that is desired. The knotty question is what to do with coaching salaries and athletic grants in the spectator sports. Currently, the big-name coaches in the male spectator sports receive salaries considerably higher than coaches (male or female) in other sports. To compete successfully in the male spectator sports, an institution must be prepared to fund more than a hundred athletic grants. Federal law requires equal pay for equal work, and Title IX states that institutions must provide opportunities for each sex to receive grants in proportion to the athletic participation of each sex. HEW's discussions of the athletic grant policy are frustratingly ambiguous. Requirements are stated in one sentence and seem to be taken back in the next. But "reasonable proportionality" must at some point be measured if it is to be enforced. Measurement implies some numerical formula. HEW's denials to the contrary, those formulas will lead to quotas of uncertain flexibility.

A reliance on quotas to solve complex social issues is not an unusual bureaucratic solution, but HEW's position seems to call for equal pay (athletic scholarships) for unequal work or skill. After all, only those male athletes who are on teams that fulfill institutional goals (spectators and publicity) receive athletic scholarships. Further, some male athletes whose teams fulfill those goals do not personally receive aid because of the positions they play or skills they lack. HEW seems to be saying that even if women's teams or athletes are unable or unwilling to foster these institutional goals, they should still share proportionately in athletic grants. Unlike other grants or scholarships, these athletic grants apparently cannot be given on the basis of personal merit or institutional goals if a sexual disproportion results. That is a standard HEW has never applied previously, even in the area of race.

In addition to the questionable practice of requiring quotas only for athletes, a more fundamental objection is that, in the name of equality, the regulations may deny women's sports the flexibility they need at a critical period in their development. Among the leaders of women's athletics there is strong opposition to turning women's sports into an imitation of men's. They do not want to engage in widespread off-campus recruiting. They would prefer to remain teachers instead of becoming win-at-any-cost sports promoters.

When the Board of Regents of the University of Maryland announced that it was reconsidering the university's athletic scholarship policy in light of Title IX, six coaches of women's sports wrote immediately to oppose inclusion of women in the athletic grant program. The women declared: "The practice of athletic scholarships is not consistent with an educational philosophy; the emphasis in such a program shifts from the individual to the desires and pressures of the university." Buttressing their position with the traditional policies of the Association for Intercollegiate Athletics for Women (AIAW), four of the women said they would refuse to coach in a program with athletic grants and have since resigned. With the shift in women's athletics from teaching to recruiting, many female professionals in physical education will be forced out.

Athletic participation for women is affected by discrimination by cultural choice, and by physical characteristics. Public policy should be sensitive to these differences and not equate equality for women with current patterns in male sports. If only one pattern is permitted, then for every university that cuts out athletic scholarships, intense recruiting, and win-at-any-cost coaches because women don't like that approach, there will be ten institutions that will force women's sports into the male mold because men control the decision and because bigtime college sports are so popular. Even attempts at self-regulation by women may prove fruitless. Thus the AIAW's recent policy expanding grant and recruiting practices for women athletes is probably still illegal under Title IX, because the NCAA's policy for male athletes is even more flexible. The ultimate consequences of HEW's rigid interpretation of Title IX may well be to force women athletes to replicate all of the worst features of men's sports.

Finally, while athletic departments might otherwise be induced to support growth in women's athletics since it expands their domain, the HEW quota policy will unnecessarily increase resistance to the development of women's sports. If taken literally, the policy would require a university that had, say, 100 grants for the 300 males on its teams to have 50 grants for female athletes if there were 150 women team participants. The women's grants would be new money that would either have to be raised afresh or taken out of the men's budget. Suppose, in this situation, that 30 women decide they would like to have a field hockey team. The athletic department would not only have to find a coach, equipment, and money for travel, which is only fair, but it would have to fund nearly ten new athletic grants for women to meet the HEW proportions. It is not difficult to imagine what athletic directors will do in this situation. They will inflate the number of male participants as much as possible by setting up feeder teams to the varsity while simultaneously discouraging the creation of new women's teams.

How can Title IX permit men and women to choose different athletic options? For instance, if the men's basketball team has 12 athletic grants, should the women's team automatically have 12? Should the coaches be paid the same? One answer is that it should depend on whether women's basketball is conceived of as a spectator or participant sport; and, if a spectator sport, how successful it is in attracting a following. For example, it may not be unreasonable to pay higher salaries to coaches of spectator sports than to those of participant sports. This is often standard practice, since the former ordinarily work longer hours, have more administrative responsibility, and endure greater pressure. Moreover, a coach of a participant sport may survive a string of losing seasons, but losers in spectator sports have short tenure.

Considering athletic grants, it should be remembered that the justification for them in the first place is the need to recruit and support enough athletes to maintain a level of competition sufficient to attract spectators. Men's basketball at most levels has proven its ability to attract spectators; women's basketball has not, though its popularity is growing. At the moment, then, it seems unfair to require the same number of grants for women playing a participant sport (normally with reduced training, practice, and travel commitments) as for men playing a spectator sport. There is, of course, not even a female equivalent to the most expensive spectator sport—football.

One response to this situation is for the institution to say that all spectator sports teams are open to males and females. The grants would be awarded to those athletes who could jump the highest or hit the hardest, as the sport required. In this situation women would get few athletic grants. A better approach would be to find athletic grants on the basis of team spectator appeal according to formulas established by institutions or conferences. For example, a particular conference might permit one basketball grant-in-aid for every 5,000 in attendance. Both the men's and women's teams would be funded within that formula. If there were a difference in the number of grants for men and women, it would be legally and logically defensible as reflecting both demonstrated spectator interest and benefit to the institution.

There are several objections to a formula approach. One, having nothing to do with Title IX, is that it helps the rich schools, or at least the better located schools, get richer, since their attendance will be directly translated into increased athletic resources. This is the situation that already prevails. Equalization of athletic resources will not come unless the "have" schools are kept from stockpiling athletes. This could be done by limiting the number of athletic grants that can be awarded, and the formula proposed here can be set within such limits.

A more substantial objection will be raised by some advocates of women's sports. While the funding proposal made earlier would provide adequate support for women's intramural and participant sports, it would not allocate much money for women's athletic grants in the near future. Women's basketball may eventually draw as well as men's basketball, but not right away. On the other hand, the formula approach would give women the time to consider whether they want their sports converted to spectator sports with subsidized athletes and coaches who must win. Using a formula approach, Title IX could be interpreted to permit a men's subsidized spectator sport and a women's unsubsidized participant sport to be considered equal if that is the choice of the majority of men and women, and if both sexes were fairly represented in the decision-making body.

The formula approach is not inflexible. Sports might shift from participant to spectator categories or vice versa over time. Since women are potentially half of any sports audience they could, if they wished, demonstrate their preference for women's spectator sports by patronizing those events, though I doubt that sexual polarizations would occur very often. Still it may be objected that the formula approach entrenches the traditional advantage of male spectator sports. The huge following of the Alabama Crimson Tide or the UCLA Bruins, after all, requires a lot of publicity and money. Since women's sports have never received that kind of cultivation, it would be unfair to ask them to compete immediately for spectators.

This argument has considerable merit. The same point may be made for some of the men's sports that are new on some campuses—soccer, hockey, and lacrosse, for example. For that reason, I have suggested a fourth category—developing sports. Such a sport is too new to have reasonably developed a following, and its sponsors may be uncertain about the direction they wish it to take. Definition of a developing sport might be made by conference or institution. Any sport that had played an intercollegiate schedule for less than five years might be classified as developing. A developing sport would be eligible to receive extra funds for facilities, coaching, and athletic grants. Since a higher proportion of women's sports than men's sports would fit in the developing category, this device could be used to stimulate women's sports and spectator interest, thus redressing some of the imbalance caused by the basic formula. A developing sport that did not generate spectator interest after a specified period would become a participant sport with no athletic grants. The developing sport concept should give women's athletics the chance they need.

Any formula, of course, may create undesirable rigidity or have unintended results. But some solution must be found. After more than two years, HEW is still unable to say what Title IX means in college athletics except that equality but not equal expenditure is required. The problem is enormously complex, but HEW's indecision creates the worst of all possible situations. The affluent schools are already spending large sums to achieve dominant positions in women's sports, while at the "have not" schools athletic directors are sitting on their hands or making token gestures because they have no cogent theory or formula by which to act. On the other hand, HEW's acceptance of trial and error as an appropriate administrative enforcement mechanism creates an opportunity for considerable bureaucratic mischief. Dependence on the "reasonableness" of the policemen is an intolerable way to enforce a civil rights law. Clear regulations can create equal opportunity for women athletes consistent with the overall purposes of college sports.

Women in Sport: cooptation or liberation?

GEORGE H. SAGE

Liberation movements have a way of promising more than they deliver. The underlying idealism and optimism produces an aura of excitement and anticipation. People expect that justice is about to prevail and that social oppression is about to be eliminated for another group of people. It turns out, however, that the liberationists were only after a piece of the existing pie rather than striving for truly alternative modes of living for large blocks of humanity. Never mind that the pie has many ingredients that are spoiled, sour, or downright hazardous to health. The important thing is "getting a piece of the action," "getting what's coming to one." The idealism and the potential for "real" change—change that promotes human growth throughout the broad spectrum of human life—gets blunted and diffused as the liberationists get absorbed into the mainstream of the social system; they are co-opted.[1]

SOURCE: George H. Sage, "Women in Sport: Cooptation or Liberation?" *Colorado Journal of Health, Physical Education, and Recreation*, 1 (March 1975).

Granted, the mainstreamers may have to make some accommodations and concessions to the liberationists, but gradually, as the latter begin to obtain the "goodies" of the mainstream, they adopt and internalize most mainstream orientations, thus becoming a "new class" of powerful persons with limited perspectives of equalitarianism and very protective of the power and influence they now hold.

What does this have to do with women's sports? Well, I think that it is obvious that the field of sport has witnessed a liberation movement within the past eight years—women's sports liberation. The women's sports movement has been one of the most significant liberation activities of the century. We really must applaud it. God knows that females need the same opportunities as males to engage in healthful sports. The female sex stereotyping which has discouraged female sports involvement has been an integral part of Western Civilization for over 2,000 years, and the need to break this cultural bondage was long overdue.

What have been its consequences? Well, surely it has opened up unprecedented opportunities for girls and women to engage in sports. While social attitudes do not change overnight, or even in a decade, female achievements in sport have produced new attitudes among both males and females about females' potential as athletes and as human beings. In many ways, it has given females a new respect for themselves.

Like most liberation movements, the women's sports movement has not achieved some of the outcomes that many had hoped and wished for. When it began a few years ago, there was an excitment and an anticipation that women were not only going to move into greater sport involvement but that they were going to develop a new model for interscholastic and intercollegiate sports. A model that would contain the best features of the male programs but that would exclude the worst features, a model that would add new, exciting, humane features.

It was reasoned that for over 50 years women had the opportunity to observe, sometimes with horror, as male high school and collegiate athletics, in the process of fostering healthful, educational sports, entered the field of professional entertainment. For the male coaches, marketplace criteria became virtually the only measure of coaching ability, and "win" became synonymous with success, and "lose" became associated with failure. Prestige in coaching was based upon won–loss records. This system tended to emphasize the treatment of athletes for what they could do for the coach—win—rather than the treatment of athletes based upon what coaches could do for the personal–social growth of athletes as persons.

Surely, many thought, leaders of female inter-school sports programs would, in their wisdom and with their years of observing male sports programs, advance an alternative educational sports model. It is now clear that there is no intention on the part of women physical educators and coaches of doing this at all. The main thrust of the women's sports movement is to mirror the men's programs in virtually every respect in the name of equality of opportunity. The opportunity to observe the strengths and weaknesses of male programs over the past half century and to select the strengths for emulation and reject the weaknesses as unwanted has been sacrificed in the quest to have exactly what the males have, regardless of the consequences (and historians say we learn from history!).

I am being facetious now, but it almost makes one wonder if the women's sports movement has not been a very subtle and clever scheme of male chauvinists. If male chauvinists in sports had intentionally set out to co-opt females into the mainstream orientations of the sport social system they could not have been more successful. Their grand strategy would have gone like this:

Give them (female sports leaders) a piece of the action. Of course, we will have to make some concessions, but basically we will continue to operate as usual. But once the females are in the business, there will be at least two benefits for male sports programs. First, the females will have to stop bellyaching about the enormous sums of money and human resources that are expended in male programs because the females will now be part of the problem—that is, they'll be spending large sums too. Second, in order to protect their own newly won empires, the females will be supportive of male programs because they know that their programs depend on the health of male programs. Neat, the entire effect is to reinforce the existing mainstream school sports system, the one that has serious problems which are acknowledged by coaches such as Joe Paterno and Frank Broyles, football coaches at Penn State and Arkansas, as well as by thoughtful educators throughout the country.

Earlier in this essay, I mentioned that once a liberation group secured its immediate demands and became co-opted by the mainstream of the social system, its members tend to adopt a rather narrow perspective of equalitarianism. Let me use one example of how this notion is related to the women's sports movement. It quickly became evident that when women sports leaders spoke of equality of women's intercollegiate sports with men's collegiate sports they included the granting of athletic scholarships. Oh, there was a brief show by the AIAW denying the desire for athletic scholarships, but few really took this seriously, and many women physical educators and coaches did not agree with this position. Besides, it was clear that this policy would be tested in court rather quickly. And so it was.

Now, the stage was set. If men give athletic scholarships, women could too. But surely a stronger argument than that is needed, and sure enough, it was available; the men have been using it for years. It goes like this: Athletic scholarships can be justified on the basis that they are "talent" scholarships. Athletes have a special talent and one way of rewarding talent is to give some monetary reward—it's the All-American way. Female sports leaders had their justification. Female athletes, like male athletes, possess a talent—a talent that has been developed through years of practice. Why shouldn't colleges award scholarships to these talented athletes—females as well as males?

Fine, but, and here is where we get into the limited perspectives of liberationists' notions, if we are going to award "talent" scholarships to football, field hockey, basketball and track athletes, why not soccer, table tennis, billiards, judo, figure skating and sky diving athletes? Are not skilled performers in these latter sports, and many others, as "talented" as those in the former group? How about modern and contemporary dancers? Are they not skilled? Athletic? Dedicated? Talented? Why are not the dance teachers at collegiate institutions given a specific number of athletic scholarships just as the coaches of football, field hockey, basketball, etc.?

Let's face it, at every college in the country there are many students who possess talents for which they receive no financial remuneration from the institution. Why are they less worthy to receive talent scholarships? My guess is that most coaches would say that their talent is not marketable; that is, it cannot be used to entertain or amuse. Or it might be contended that the scholarship group practices long hours to maintain the award. Thus, athletic scholarships are justified on the moral basis of rewarding the talented, but the exclusive nature of the awards is based upon financial, entertainment, and public relations considerations. I wonder if this is consistent with a real liberation, or equalitarian, perspective? I hope you will give it some thought.

I want to note, in concluding this essay, that I don't want to seem to be overcritical of the emerging women's sports program. Men have lived with a number of serious programs in their inter-school sports programs for the past half century and have made little effort to correct these problems. It may be too much to expect that women will be able to develop an ideal sports model in the first decade of intensive interschool sports involvement. But we can hope for better things because an alternative sports structure which stresses cooperation, participation, expressiveness, fun, intrinsic motivation, and self-actualization would be a refreshing substitute for the current emphasis in interscholastic and intercollegiate programs. What is needed is a better model for these sports programs to make them truly "educational."

NOTES

1. Phillip Selznick defines cooptation as "the process of absorbing new elements into the leadership or policy-determining structure of an organization as a means of averting threats to its stability or existence." (Selznick, P., *TVA and the Grass Roots*, New York: Harper Torchbook, 1966).

■ FOR FURTHER STUDY

Beisser, Arnold. *The Madness in Sports.* New York: Appleton-Century-Crofts, 1967.

Boslooper, Thomas, and Marcia Hayes. *The Femininity Game.* New York: Stein and Day, 1973.

Butt, Dorcas Susan. "New Horizons for Women in Sport." *Sport Psychology: An Analysis of Athletic Behavior.* Edited by William Straub. Ithaca, N.Y.: Mouvement Publications, 1978, pp. 189–194.

Coakley, Jay J. *Sport in Society: Issues and Controversies.* St. Louis: C. V. Mosby, 1978, chapter 10.

"Comes the Revolution: Joining the Game at Last, Women are Transforming American Athletics." *Time* (June 26, 1978), 54–60

Creamer, Robert. "Women's Worth." *Sports Illustrated* (January 17, 1977), p. 6.

Davenport, Joanna. "The Women's Movement into the Olympic Games." *JOPER*, 39 (March 1978), 58–60.

De Beauvoir, Simone. *The Second Sex.* New York: Alfred A. Knopf, 1952.

Dunkle, M. C. "What Constitutes Equality for Women in Sport?" *Newsletter for the Project on the Status and Education of Women*, Association of American Colleges, Washington, D.C., 1974.

Edwards, Harry. "Desegregating Sexist Sport." *Intellectual Digest*, 3 (1972), 82–83.

Fasteau, Brenda Feigen. "Giving Women a Sporting Chance." *Ms.*, 2 (July 1973), 56–58, 103.

Felshin, Jan. "The Triple Option . . . For Women in Sport." *Quest*, 21 (January 1974), 36–40.

Feltz, Deborah L. "Athletics in the Status System of Female Adolescents." *Review of Sport & Leisure*, 3 (Fall 1978), 98–108.

Fields, Cheryl M. "July 31: Title IX Deadline." *The Chronicle of Higher Education* (November 14, 1977), pp. 9–11.

Fields, Cheryl M. "Women's Athletics: Struggling with Success." *The Chronicle of Higher Education* (May 22, 1978), pp. 5–6.

Gerber, E. R., J. Felshin, P. Berlin, and W. Wyrick. *The American Woman in Sport.* Reading, Mass.: Addison-Wesley, 1974.

Gilbert, Bil, and Nancy Williamson. "Women in Sport." *Sports Illustrated* (May 28, 1973, June 4, 1973, and June 11, 1973); and a progress report (July 29, 1974).

Griffith, Patricia S. "What's a Nice Girl Like You Doing in a Profession Like This?" *Quest*, 19 (January 1973), 96–101.

Hannon, Kent. "Too Far, Too Fast." *Sports Illustrated* (March 20, 1978), 34–45.

Harding, Carol, ed. "Women in Sport." Special issue of *Arena Newsletter* (April/June 1977).

Harris, Dorothy V. "The Sportswoman in Our Society." *Women in Sport.* Edited by Dorothy V. Harris. Washington, D.C.: American Association for Health, Physical Education, and Recreation, 1971, 1-4.

Harris, Dorothy V., ed. *Women and Sport: A National Research Conference.* Penn State HPER Series No. 2, The Pennsylvania State University, 1972.

Hart, M. Marie. "Women Sit in the Back of the Bus." *Psychology Today,* 5 (1971), 64-66.

Hart, M. Marie. "On Being a Female in Sport." *Sport in the Socio-Cultural Process.* 2nd ed. Edited by M. Marie Hart. Dubuque, Iowa: Wm. C. Brown, 1976, pp. 438-447.

Huckle, Patricia. "Back to the Starting Line." *American Behavioral Scientist,* 21 (January/February, 1978), 379-392.

Klafs, C. E., and M. J. Lyon. *The Female Athlete.* 2nd ed. St. Louis: C. V. Mosby, 1978.

Ley, Katherine. "Women in Sports: Where Do We Go From Here, Boys?" *Phi Delta Kappan,* 56 (October 1974), 129-131.

Loggia, Morjorie. "On the Playing Fields of History." *Ms.,* 2 (July 1973), 62-64.

Malmisur, Michael C. "Title IX Dilemma: Meritocratic and Egalitarian Tension," *Journal of Sport Behavior,* 1 (August 1978), 130-138.

Metheny, Eleanor. "Symbolic Forms of Movement: The Feminine Image in Sports." *Sport and American Society.* 2nd ed. Edited by George H. Sage. Reading, Mass.: Addison-Wesley, 1974, 289-301.

Michener, James A., *Sports in America.* New York: Random House, 1976, chapter 5.

Novak, Michael. "Football for Feminists." *Commonweal,* 101 (1974), 104, 119.

Roark, Anne C. "Court Rejects NCAA Challenge to Ban on Sex Bias in Sports." *The Chronicle of Higher Education* (January 16, 1978), p. 1.

Schafer, Walter E. "Sport and Male Sex-Role Socialization." *Sport Sociology Bulletin,* 4 (Fall 1975), 47-54.

Scott, Jack. "Making Athletics a Masculinity Rite." *Ramparts,* 10 (January 1973), 64.

Scott, Jack. "The Masculine Obsession in Sports." *Women's Athletics: Coping with Controversy.* Edited by B. J. Hoepner. Washington, D.C.: American Association for Health, Physical Education and Recreation, 1974.

Sherriff, Marie C. "The Status of Female Athletes as Viewed by Selected Peers and Parents in Certain High Schools of Central California." Master's thesis, California State College, Chico, 1969.

Snyder, Eldon E., and Joseph E. Kivlin. "Women Athletes and Aspects of Psychological Well-Being and Body Image." *Research Quarterly,* 46 (May 1975), 191-199.

Snyder, Eldon E., and Joseph E. Kivlin. "Perceptions of the Sex Role Among Female Athletes and Nonathletes." *Adolescence,* 12 (Spring 1977), 23-29.

Snyder, Eldon E., Joseph E. Kivlin, and Elmer Spreitzer. "The Female Athlete: An Analysis of Objective and Subjective Role Conflict." *Psychology of Sport and Motor Behavior.* Edited by Daniel M. Landers. University Park: Pennsylvania State University Press, 1975, 165-180.

Snyder, Eldon E., and Elmer Spreitzer. "Correlates of Sport Participation Among Adolescent Girls." *Research Quarterly,* 47 (December 1976), 804-809.

Snyder, Eldon E., and Elmer Spreitzer. "Participation in Sport as Related to Educational Expectations Among High School Girls." *Sociology of Education*, 50 (January 1977), 47–55.

Snyder, Eldon E., and Elmer Spreitzer. *Social Aspects of Sport.* Englewood Cliffs, N.J.: Prentice-Hall, 1978, chapter 8.

Wilmore, Jack H. "Inferiority of the Female Athlete: Myth or Reality." *Sports Medicine Bulletin*, 10 (April 1975).

Twelve

The Future of American Sport

This collection of articles is intended to show that sport is a microcosm of society. The future shape of sport, then, depends on the society it reflects. The key to its future lies in whether American society will continue on its present course with the emphasis on nationalism, competition, technology, and materialism or whether scarcity, ecological disasters, and lowered affluence will change its values? An equally plausible scenario can be developed for either possibility. If society continues on its present path, then sport will be more and more characterized by its corporate nature. Big business, television, and gambling interests will dominate sport in the future. Technology will change current sport as stadiums change, as fans determine strategy through collective decision making via instantaneous communication, as officials are replaced by electronic sensors, and as athletic performances are heightened by new knowledge and techniques—the ultimate being the creation of super athletes through genetic engineering. Probably, too, governments will use sport increasingly as political tools for nationalistic ends.

If society moves in the opposite direction, and people realize that the traditional values of competition, materialism, and emphasis on progress actually are the sources of many problems, then sport will change dramatically. Participation in sport would likely become more widespread, and therefore, less elitist. It would be less competitive, with more emphasis on participation and creativity. Physical activities such as hiking, scuba diving, rafting, hang gliding, skateboarding, and Frisbee might supersede organized, bureaucratic sports. High schools and colleges might disband their big-time sports for activities at the club sport level, where participation would be for fun and participants from competing teams could share a keg of beer after the game. Other possible scenarios depend on a number of other factors. The future shape of society and sport will be greatly influenced by the composition of the population (size, distribution, proportion of persons in various age groups, and levels of education). The political climate is another extremely important variable. Will the U.S. be increasingly nationalistic or internationally minded? Will domestic power be centralized or decentralized? Will society be democratic or not? The economy, too, is crucial. Will there be equality of opportunity, equality of outcomes, or continued inequality? How will goods and services be distributed? Will race continue to be a salient factor, giving the majority advantages while continuing to disadvantage minorities? Will women achieve an equal place with men in the occupational world?

The articles presented in this concluding unit address four issues involving the future of sport. The first, the oft-quoted essay by sportswriter William O. Johnson, examines the fundamental question of the direction that sport will take in the future. He suggests two quite different alternatives—technosport and ecosport.

The second essay, by newspaperman Tom Ricke, focuses on the impact of science on athletes in the future. He shows how present and future developments in sports medicine, computers, diet, hormone synthesis, and electrical engineering will have great potential for the benefit or the abuse of athletes.

Another sportswriter, Frank Deford, examines two present trends— that the players increasingly are black and that the spectators increasingly are white—and speculates about their impact on the future of sport. He suggests that this increasing racial segregation in sport may mean the eventual demise of the now popular team sports and the rise of "white sports" such as ice hockey, car racing, and soccer. This is a distinct possibility as long as society and its members continue to be racist.

Although sport has been presented as a reflection of society, sport could also be an agent of social change. Through sport the schools and other groups could, for example, teach youngsters to be more cooperative and more creative. One illustration of how sport could be used as a tool to promote societal changes is provided in the last selection by football coach George Davis. Davis argues that sport serves educational goals when it prepares the participants for life. Thus, the experience in sport must train people to be self-reliant, to be decision makers, and to respect rules. The typical coaching philosophy, however, promotes the opposite traits because it relies on regimentation, arbitrarily imposed rules, punishment, and authoritarian control. This is inadequate preparation for life in a democracy. Davis advocates using democracy in football. His players determine and enforce the team rules. More significant, the members of his teams determine their own starting line-ups. Davis's football philosophy is revolutionary. Youngsters exposed to it likely will be quite different from those who experience traditional programs.

Some of Davis's critics have called his way of coaching communistic. Is it? Is Davis's approach the wave of the future? Should it be?

From Here to 2000

WILLIAM O. JOHNSON

It is possible . . . that the very personality of the American population as it develops in the next 25 years will be more active than passive, more involved than inert. For the rest of the 20th century will be dominated by the energetic, hell-raising crowd of activist-skeptics born during the Baby Boom of the early '50s, plus the less obviously dynamic but perhaps equally dubious bunch who came a few years later. Some 80 million Americans were born between 1945 and 1965, a birth rate of 23.3 per thousand (an enormous increase compared to the 18.7 rate of 1935 and the slackening rate of 14.9 in 1973). This great bulge of people will affect American demographics right through the millennium. The average age in the U.S. will rise dramatically—from 28 in 1970 to 35.8 in 2000.

The numerical influence of this crowd will be impressive. The Department of the Interior, for example, predicts that whereas there were 14 million backpackers in 1970, by the year 2000 there will be 43 million. Last year no fewer than 21 national parks required campsite reservations. These large numbers work the other way, too: whereas American professional sports are now riding the crest of the Baby Boom and have the greatest pool of young athletic talent available in the history of the world, within a few more years, perhaps only five, that pool will be drying up and the level of excellence will fall as the lower birth rates of the late '60s begin to affect the number of excellent athletes available.

Beyond its numerical force, this crowd has a further influence. In his book *Sociology of Sport*, Berkeley sociologist Harry Edwards wrote: "Here we have a category of people who have seldom, if ever, known material want, who have for the most part been insulated from the more mundane struggles of day-to-day existence, and many of whom have come to view the sphere of organized sport as crass, vulgar and oppressive. . . . If these definitions of the significance and character of sport persist among members of the youth culture into their adult years, sport as we know it today is likely to decline for want of attention and interest."

David N. Campbell, associate professor of education at the University of Pittsburgh, sees another, more specific shift in that generation's view of sport: "They were a revolutionary generation who rejected competition.

SOURCE: Excerpt from William O. Johnson, "From Here to 2000," *Sports Illustrated* (December 23, 1974), pp. 78–83.

They had endured it to a degree that the rest of us never knew. They were ranked, graded and sorted in every effort they undertook. There were too many people for every possibility, every activity, every job, every class. That put most people into a losing status and now we have a society with a majority of losers. And as for competition, I don't think it's ever going to come back as strong as it used to be. These kids have just had too much of it. There's a myth in this country that's propagated by Ford and Nixon that America was made great by competition. If you read American history, you'll find that pioneers were not competitive people, they were a cooperative people. They wouldn't have survived otherwise, so competition is no more an intrinsic part of the American Way than these new generations see it—and they've rejected it."

Competition or non-competition, the future of American sport probably best fits into two broad scenarios: Technosport, that sport which is the product of machines and technicians, and Ecosport, that sport which springs from the natural relationship between man and his environment. They are opposites, yet they are in no way mutually exclusive for, as a number of tomorrow-experts have said, a dominant characteristic of our future will probably be "pluralism," that which allows nearly everything to exist with nearly everything else.

A Technosport scenario will bring a deluge of complexities. Dr. Edward Lawless of the Midwest Research Institute, a Kansas City think thank, says, "Technological developments are likely to get piled upon one another, which will decrease the role of the human being. There will be more 'technological fixes'; urine tests for athletes will be mandatory because drug stimulants will be so common. Football players will be so padded they will begin to look like grotesque robots."

There is talk today, still theoretical, of "genetic engineering," a kind of technological biology in which men can be specifically designed *before* birth to become nine-foot basketball centers with the hands of concert pianists or 375-pound, eight-foot running backs who do the 100 in eight flat. This kind of *Brave New World* concept fits the Technosport scenario, for fans of these games will be spectators supreme—pathological watchers who worship the specialist, adore the elite athlete.

Although jock-breeding might be desirable to Technosport fanatics, it seems unlikely it will be more than a theory by the year 2000. Says Dr. Laurence E. Karp, an obstetrician who does research in reproductive genetics at the University of Washington School of Medicine, "Breeding super athletes may be possible, but there is really no guarantee that mating an athletically inclined male with a similarly inclined female will produce an athletic offspring. Once the fertilization process begins, the genetic roulette wheel is spun. The two strong mates could produce a Milquetoast."

However, perhaps massive genetic engineering—nature's way—has already begun to give us supermen. Dr. Robert Hamilton, a Chicago orthopedic surgeon who works with several high school teams, says, "We will see 360-pound 7½-foot tackles in football in 15 years. Take a high school roster 15 years ago, examine the heights and weights and you will find a 15% to 20% increase today—in some cases 50%."

Laurence E. Morehouse of the Department of Kinesiology at UCLA agrees. "There is no limit at the present time to the size people we will produce," he says. "Men eight feet tall, weighing 350 pounds, are possible in the future. The reasons are not genetic engineering, but random mating in an increasing population to bring together diversified genes, plus better nutrition and the absence of childhood diseases." Everyone agrees that one mandatory change in both football and basketball of the future will be larger playing areas to contain tomorrow's giants.

Technosport stadiums will be grand monuments—domed, air-conditioned, artifically turfed—vast Sybaritic arenas equipped with everything from push-button vending machines at each seat to individual TV replays that can be punched up at will. Architect Charles Luckman, whose firm designed the new Madison Square Garden, the L.A. Forum and the still incomplete Honolulu Multi-Sport Movable Stadium (which will have mobile sections on air cushions to change the stadium from a baseball to a football arena), predicts the day is not far off when people will be led to their seats by the sound of ocean waves, of wind, of singing birds, of gurgling brooks, a lovely addition to the cold artificial environs of a typical Technosport stadium.

Computers will be important in Technosport, and every dugout, every sideline bench will have one to pop out sheets of probability tables to help call each play, each pitch, each infield shift. Moreover, spectators will be able to punch up computerized odds and bet against management on every kind of trivial possibility.

Technosport spectators will also feel closer to the game. They will be able to listen in to press-box scouts giving advice to the bench, to miked-and-wired conversations at the pitching mound, to quarterback's calls in the huddle, to halftime pep talks.

Lee Walburn of Atlanta's Omni group has a wild, but possibly not too far-out, idea for bringing the fan even closer to the contest. "At least by early in the 21st century," he says, "we will have something called Feel-A-Vision—electronic sensory perceptors so the spectator who may lack the ability to take part in sport himself can experience the pain, the emotion, the physical actions of the athletes. You could go in a theater, sit down, have buttons on your seat which are hooked into a certain player—to his heartbeats, his brain waves, his pulmonary system. And you could get the transmissions from a quarterback when he throws a touchdown pass. You could feel how Ali felt when Foreman was trying to hit him on the ropes. You could even have been wired into Evel Knievel—but, for God's sake, what if he got killed? Think of the thrill you'd get."

Perhaps a more probable addition to Technosport spectating is something that might be called Democracy Football. It is a Monday night in November, 1999, and the Houston Oilers are about to play the Chicago Bears. In this scenario there are 556,191 homes in Houston with television sets, each equipped with a console containing rows of multicolored buttons. Each viewer has a playbook for the Oiler offense, a playbook for the defense. In Chicago there are 817,911 TV homes, each identically equipped, except, of course, the viewers have Bear playbooks. Now the official flips the coin. Heads for Houston. The Houston viewers vote by pushing a button—529,876 to receive, one (idiot!) to kick off. The vote is instantly counted, computerized, flashed into the helmets of the Houston team. The Democracy Football game is under way. A Houston back returns the kickoff to his 38-yard line. All over Houston viewers consult their playbooks (they have one minute) and then they press a combination of buttons to call a play. Instantaneously, the computer totals the Oiler fan-coaches' votes: 307,278 vote for a zig-out pass into the left flat to the tight end; 121,908 for an off-tackle slant to the right with the fullback carrying; 100,689 for a sweep to the right; one man votes for a quick kick (same idiot). Meanwhile, all of Chicago is voting on which defense to use and the plurality—315,924—pushes buttons calling for a four-three-four.

The wishes of the Oiler TV fans are relayed to the Houston quarterback's helmet. He cannot disobey, of course. He calls the pass to the flat. The Oilers move to the line of scrimmage. The Bears go into the defensive formation their fans have called. The Oilers try the prescribed pass to the left flat. It is knocked to the ground by a Bear linebacker. Houston moans, Chicago cheers. It is second and 10. The viewers vote. And so it goes. Houston plays Chicago, *literally* citizen against citizen. Thus would Technosport produce a technological miracle of something which might hitherto have been thought a contradiction in terms: Spectator-Participation.

Now Ecosport. Here we have the other extreme, for technology and artificiality are abhorred, disdained. Ecosport consists of natural play, unstructured, free-blown. Its games are open, flowing, perhaps without boundaries, often without rules, usually without scoreboards, sometimes without end or middle or measurable victory. Everyone participates and the overriding slogan might well be, "If a sport is worth playing, it is worth playing badly."

Many think there will be a massive new enthusiasm for natural sport. Michael Novak, author and philosopher, says, "A convulsion is coming, an attempt to throw off the corporation and professionalization—to shake off the cold hand of the 20th century—and return sports to their primitive vigor." The chairman of the Human Development program at the University of Chicago with the incredible name of Mihaly Csikszentmihalyi, says: "We have moved from spontaneity to point ratings, from individual talent to computerized cards. There are far more statistics than heroics in sports and I think there will be a reaction against all this, a change back to naturalness."

In the era of Ecosport men may not only begin to doubt the famed Vince Lombardi motto, "Winning isn't everything, it's the only thing," they may actually swing around to author George Leonard's proclamation that, "Winning, is not only not everything, winning is not *anything*." As John McMurtry, a philosopher from Canada's University of Guelph, said during a sports symposium last year: "Actually, the pursuit of victory works to reduce the chance for excellence in the true performance of the sport. It tends to distract our attention from excellence of performance by rendering it subservient to emerging victorious. I suspect that our conventional mistake of presuming the opposite—presuming that the contest-for-prize framework and excellence of performance are somehow related as a unique cause and effect—may be the deepest-lying prejudice of civilized thought.... Keeping score in any game—especially team games—is a substantial indication that the activity in question is not interesting enough in itself to those who keep score."

The forms of Ecosport will be enormously varied. Soccer, which may be one of the Big Four in America within a decade, is an offspring of Ecosport, for it is flowing, natural and played by men who are built on a human scale and need no sophisticated equipment. The fine and gentle pastimes will increase, such as orienteering, hiking, non-competitive swimming.

The emphasis in Ecosport is on *un*structured play. Perhaps the ultimate event in such a scenario is something one may call the Never Never Game, since it is a sport invented on the spot for a given afternoon, something that was never, never played before and will never, never be played again. The Never Never Game eliminates all specialists, all statistics. It demands the ordinary all-round person, the average man, since one can never know what skills will be demanded in the game of the day.

The Never Never Game: It is a soft sunny afternoon and on a meadow somewhere in the U. S. about 100 people—men, women, children—have gathered. They separate into two groups, approximately equal, and a man carries a small container filled with beads of half a dozen different colors. Under his arm he has the Never Never Game Book. This book is filled with myriad possibilities for games—one section has different kinds of balls or stones or items to be used, another section has lists of field sizes and shapes, another the rules of play for many games. Each of the different items in each section is identified with a color combination. The man in the center of the meadow reaches into the Never Never bead jar and without looking takes out a handful of beads and throws them on the ground. The colors are two reds, a yellow, four blues, a white, two greens. In the Never Never Book section on "game balls" he finds "a disk the size of a pie plate" next to this color combination. He throws more beads on the ground, finds that the combination in the "field size" section calls for a circular area 300 yards in diameter. More beads: the game will last three hours. More beads: players will hop on one leg. They will use forked sticks to carry the disk to the perimeter of the field. When one player carries the disk through the other team he may hop on either leg but when two players share in carrying the disk with their forked sticks they may both use both legs—etc., etc.

After consultation to arrange tactics and review the rules, the Never Never Game begins. After three hours it is over. The score is inconsequential, no records are kept, and no specialists are discovered or developed. Everyone has played, some better in this Never Never Game than in another. This game will never be played again. The next Never Never Game may involve flocks of butterflies as the "game ball," perhaps a net across the field with which to catch them, perhaps balloons to fend off the other team's butterflies. Who knows? Who cares? The point of Ecosport—as of all sport—is to play, to enjoy, to exist.

Future Jock: scientific witchcraft may conjure up the ideal athlete—or make sports a black-magic nightmare

TOM RICKE

They came for Barbara just after she turned 11. The government car took her away to the special school where she would spend the next five years training to be an Olympic swimmer. For her parents it was an honor and a loss. They would see little of their daughter until she reached her 20s and retired from her active career. At that time, hopefully, she would have chosen a proper husband—a swimmer with all the right measurements, bone structures, strength, and flexibility deserving of their daughter. And their grandchildren—if everything worked out right—might end up breaking their daughter's records.

Only one in hundreds of thousands was picked. The new legislation didn't set up quotas, but it did make it a serious violation of the law not to comply with the Department of Athletic Development when one of your children was chosen.

Barbara's closest adviser during her training would be a computer. It would plan just the right amount of exercise for her each morning before her studies and each afternoon after her school hours. It would prescribe her diet. Steroids would be mixed in with her food at the proper time of her growth. She would also receive special pills to help her recover from the fatigue of her workouts.

They would insert special plastic tubes in her veins so the right amount of blood could be saved before competition and be put back into her system just before the event.

Each week her strength would be tested by a machine connected to her computer. Each month she would perform before the videotape machines that were also connected to her computer. The computer would then instruct her exactly where she might be wasting energy with her

SOURCE: Excerpt from Tom Ricke, "Future Jock," *WomenSports*, 4 (February 1977), 47–50.

body motions—where she could improve her performance by modifying her strokes and kicks.

Her muscle development would be aided by an electronic machine that would exercise the right muscles with electric current. Any muscle's strength could be increased 40 percent in a matter of days. The machine would also help her compete even if she were injured.

Every three months she would undergo muscle fiber tests to see if her white and red twitch fibers were developing in the right ratio for a swimmer. She would also undergo extensive psychological testing, and her computer would let her instructors know exactly what she felt and thought during every waking moment. And if her body composition stayed right and her growth patterns were true to the computer's prediction, Barbara might be among the handful of the 1,000 chosen young women who actually made the team they had trained for. . . .

Wait a minute. This is pure fantasy, you say. Right now, yes. But in the explosive field of sports medicine, everything described in the above fable is technically possible.

The science of sports medicine is as ancient as Hippocrates but, for a variety of reasons, it has exploded in the U.S. in the last five years. In 1973 alone, 17 sports medicine institutes were started here. It seems any university worth its gymnasium has entered the field. Hundreds of specialists are making extensive studies in every possible area. The results, for the most part, are debatable and reported only in academic and scientific journals. In the meantime, new machines for testing and improving performance are popping up all over.

The explosion of interest in the field has been triggered by several factors: the win-at-all-cost philosophy of our professional sports teams; the fear that the Soviets and East Germans have developed scientific magic that will make us look like real losers in Olympic competition; and the growth of computer technology. Computers that cost millions a decade ago are now within the financial range of many more institutions today.

As a nation, we are entering this new era of sports science at a breakneck speed, and at present, there are two areas of concentration: improving performances of professional and Olympic athletes and preventing injuries at all levels of sports, from that of the most highly trained athlete to that of the Friday-night bowler. Possibilities for nightmarish abuse are abundant. But possibilities of preventing millions of unnecessary injuries each year are just as real.

What happens depends on how carefully we use the information and technology that are currently being developed. "We are coming out of the age of witchcraft in sports, and into the age of science," says Dr. Gideon

Ariel, director of research for Computerized Biomechanical Analysis in Amherst, Massachusetts. . . .

With the help of computers, an elaborate videotape and film system, and mathematical formulas developed by Newton in the 17th century, Dr. Ariel is able to scrutinize every motion of an athlete in each fraction of a second. He can tell where the exact center of gravity is at a given second and where it should be. He can spot inefficient and wasted motions. For example, U.S. discus thrower Mac Wilkins showed a 16-foot improvement in his throw soon after Ariel pointed out to him that he was wasting energy overcoming friction between his right foot and the ground. . . .

As the science of sports medicine develops, so do athletes' expectations of what modern science can do for them. Pressured by complaints from American athletes who are afraid they can't compete with Eastern European sports medicine, the United States Olympic Committee has formed a panel of experts to study every aspect of the field. Heading the panel is Dr. Irving Dardik of Tenafly, New Jersey, who was a member of the U.S. Olympic medical staff in Montreal.

One of the first controversies Dr. Dardik will investigate is the effects of anabolic steroids, synthetic male hormones that supposedly increase the body's ability to absorb protein and convert it to muscle. . . .

Dardik will also study blood doping—the controversial new practice of drawing super-oxygenated blood from an athlete when in top physical condition and then pumping it back in to enhance stamina just before an event.

Perhaps the most intriguing piece of sports hardware that Dr. Dardik will study is a machine that uses electric current to make muscles contract very rapidly. Soviet scientists claim that 20 applications of the machine can increase muscle strength by as much as 40 percent. They also claim it can do wonders for sprained ankles and pulled muscles so that athletes, after a few immediate treatments, can be ready for competition within hours of an injury. In the United States, the machine is manufactured by two Texas firms and used by a few major league baseball pitchers. But American doctors say there is no evidence to substantiate the Soviet claims.

In addition to investigating what seem like fads and gimmicks, Dr. Dardik and his panel will do further research into more basic areas like nutrition and training. . . .

What does the future hold? Will these advances be used to prevent injuries and improve health in general? Or will our win-at-all-cost mentality abuse both the science and our athletes?

The Big Game is Over: this way to the exit, bwana

FRANK DEFORD

Frank Robinson bombed on broadway, Toots Shor's went out of business, and Jackie Robinson died with a bitter taste in his mouth. Sports today are no longer sequestered in a fantasy world. They are affected by and reacting to all the change and turmoil in America. As a result, big-time football, baseball, and basketball are changing fast—in popularity and profitability—and the future for all three appears to have about the same prospects as railroads and downtown department stores had a generation ago.

Demographically, professional sports have exhibited the same shift as the rest of society, tilting to the South and West and from the central cities to the suburbs. The Washington Senators did not really move from Washington to Dallas, or even to Dallas-Ft. Worth. Rather, they left a black, Eastern city for a white, Southwestern interstate highway interchange. The original Senators went to Bloomington, Minnesota, a suburb of Minneapolis-St. Paul. The Boston Patriots have relocated in Foxboro, Massachusetts, down near the Rhode Island line, and renamed themselves the New England Patriots. The Los Angeles Angels left the city for Orange County and became the California Angels. The New York Giants baseball team left Manhattan for California, and the New York Giants football team is leaving the Bronx for suburban New Jersey. Ultimately, things go full circle. Washington lost its baseball team to an interchange, but now it is gaining a hockey team and a basketball team because someone is building an arena out in its suburbs at an interchange named Largo, Maryland.

In terms of business, sports have been expansive and diversified, just like the rest of the economy. For years, franchise ownership was in the hands of devoted entrepreneurs: Connie Mack managed the team he owned in Philadelphia; a bookmaker, Tim Mara, passed the football Giants on to his children; and other franchises stayed in the family—the Comiskeys and Wrigleys of Chicago, the Rooneys of Pittsburgh, the Griffiths of Washington. Promoters like Eddie Gottlieb, Ben Kerner, and Danny Biasone took basketball out of the dance halls, carrying the

SOURCE: Frank Deford, "The Big Game Is Over," *Oui* (Spring 1973), pp. 51, 132, 134.

franchises to the big time in their hats. But increasingly, ownership has moved into the chilly, efficient grasp of impersonal corporations. Walter Brown of Boston sold his furniture in the Fifties so his Celtics could stay afloat for one more payday; hardly a decade later, ownership of the team had gotten so enmeshed in corporate high finance that there was, at times, serious confusion over who actually owned the team. Because several teams depend so heavily on TV subsidies for survival, sponsors effectively control them. More and more, sports have become a tax dodge or a stock deal or a vanity item for the businessman who yearns for fame, civic attention, and a fast buck. Finally, sports are threatened with federal controls—an all-sports bill in Congress will, if passed, make athletics even more like other large institutions.

Sports have become increasingly fluid and sensitive to changing tastes and attitudes. Never again will one sport establish itself as our "national pastime" for anything even approaching half a century as baseball did. Certain sports are likely to fall in and out of fashion in the future, like hair styles, comedians, or wars.

Football has definitely succeeded baseball as the nation's most popular game. Automobile racing is suddenly much more popular than horse racing. Hockey is a national game in solid competition with basketball at the pro level. Wrestling has disappeared, and boxing, king at the turn of the century and second to baseball for quite some time, is no longer a sustaining American sport. Instead, it is merely an occasional event, rather like a Bob Hope TV special or a good murder trial that only momentarily diverts the usual prime-time fare or front-page Vietnam coverage. By contrast, golf is a tour, a regular part of sports' landscape, and tennis is beginning to broaden its base of appeal, too. Overall, there is a decided preference for professional sports over amateur ones. In a society where sudden change has become a way of life, it should not be surprising that sporting tastes are changing as well. But principals in athletics are accelerating the process of change to one of rampant disorder. Once teams can jump cities and players can jump teams, willy-nilly, as has become the case, then a climate is created where fans are encouraged to jump whole sports. Allegiance, not competition, has always been the keystone of big-time professional sports, and fans are cheated as much by players and owners who mock team/city loyalty as by those who fix games. Either way, the illusion is badly damaged.

All of this would be threatening enough to the future of the major games, but things are much worse. Football, baseball, and basketball are approaching an identity crisis, the same one that all but destroyed boxing when it ran out of white boxers for the white ticket buyers to identify with. How long will white pride—white racism, if you will—support black athletics?

Contrary to accepted dogma, sports have made no more civil rights progress than is commonly found elsewhere. Blacks have been suffered where their talents are in demand, but until very recently (and then only in basketball), they have been denied promotion to managerial or executive positions. Wayne Embry, who played 11 years in the NBA, is the vice-president and general manager of the Milwaukee Bucks, the only black in sports with any real executive authority. Starting with Bill Russell in 1966, there have also been a handful of black basketball coaches, and the Detroit Pistons recently established another first when they fired one black coach and replaced him with another. But Jackie Robinson went to his grave without ever seeing a black manager in baseball or a black head coach in football. The league offices feature token blacks, but the team front offices seldom make even that effort. Probably the top black baseball executive is an Atlanta Braves functionary who just happens to be superstar Henry Aaron's brother-in-law.

Black and white players almost never mingle outside the locker rooms; most players (workers) are too much like everyone else—determinedly middle class, allegedly college educated, upwardly mobile, better paid, and less satisfied. They are obsessed with security, and their allegiance is to their players' association (union), not to the fans (consumers) or to the team (company). If the community and the family are breaking down, so is the team.

The division that has evolved in sports is more dramatic than anything the Kerner Report discussed in other areas of society. As sports become more acceptable, even fashionable, as ticket prices increase and enter the expense-account domain, athletic audiences will become more white middle class. "All you have to do is look up in the stands to tell what is happening to sports," says Tom Meschery, a published poet who played and coached professional basketball through last season. "There was a time when sports provided cheap entertainment for ordinary folks. Now they are becoming a plaything of the rich." The movement of stadia and arenas to the suburbs reduces attendance among inner-city fans, both black and white. Those who build suburban stadia tacitly concede that they are appealing only to fans who own automobiles—and all that that implies. Parking acreage, not public transportation, now determines stadium location. We are creating a pattern of de facto segregation of sports fans, just as surely as the same pattern exists for housing and schools.

But as the audience becomes more white, middle class, suburban, and affluent, more of the participants are black. Thus most spectators are being asked to identify with a racial minority they have always rejected, even feared. The question is, how long will the white American psyche tolerate this situation? Since whites have deserted their homes, neighborhoods, schools, stores, churches, cities, and city halls to escape association with black Americans, there is no reason to doubt that they will give up their sports, too.

It is indicative of things to come that the two fastest-growing sports of the Sixties—ice hockey and car racing—are also the most lily-white. They are so Caucasian that by comparison they make golf and tennis seem positively checkerboard. We are, in fact, at the point where many people think of sports in terms of race—white sports and black sports, the black sports being basketball, first, and then football and baseball.

There is evidence that this division is widening: some good, young, white athletes are already, consciously or otherwise, turning away from the big-three sports because of the competition they fear from blacks. Several of the top young tour golfers—Bob Goalby, Hale Irwin, Jim Colbert, DeWitt Weaver, Bunky Henry—were once football stars; Ray Floyd, Bob Murphy, and Fred Marti were pro-baseball prospects before making the switch; and Ken Harrelson left the major leagues to try the links. The best U.S. tennis player, Stan Smith, quit basketball, which was his favorite game, and concentrated on tennis while still in high school because he felt he had a better chance for success there.

For several years now, up-and-coming white basketball players have been required to venture into the black summer leagues—which also means the black sections of town—to develop their talents to the fullest. In our stockade society, how many white teenagers will have the drive and nerve to do that, especially when they find the competition so tough? As young white athletes—and their fathers, coaches, and neighbors—see whites thwarted in their efforts to reach the top in basketball, football, and baseball, they are inclined to feign indifference and cede the games to blacks. A magnetic arrangement is growing stronger. As more blacks go into the games they identify with, more whites will avoid these games, more blacks will take their places, and so on.

In 1971, the football draft was no different than basketball. In the first ten rounds of the NFL selections, 214 of the 260 players, 82 percent, were black. For a long time, pro football would select only the big-name black college stars on the first few rounds, holding off till the fourth or fifth round before picking the black unknowns from the small Negro colleges. Blacks themselves caught on and called these "the nigger rounds." That barrier is down, though, because once a team broke any sort of quota understandings, everybody had to follow. Similarly, pro basketball always had its own limits of black personnel. But the number kept rising because Red Auerbach, the coach (now general manager) of the Boston Celtics, would not go along. And the more blacks he played, the more games his team won. For a while in the late Sixties, some NBA teams tried to stay white by stacking the bench with Caucasian stiffs, but even that ghost has been given up. It is not uncommon for pro teams to carry only two or three whites on a 12-man roster.

Over-all, the NBA is almost two-thirds black, while major league football and baseball is approaching a 50 percent black population (counting Latin Americans as black in baseball, which is what whites always do). None of these figures, though, indicates the true black dominance of major sports—because most of the big stars, the country's glamor figures, are black. Almost all the superstars in basketball, most of the best baseball hitters, and a large majority of football running backs, receivers, and defensive aces are black.

The emphasis on the white quarterback in football has obscured the increasing presence and proficiency of blacks in almost all other positions. Similarly, the dearth of black pitchers creates a misleading impression about baseball. Because of the nature of the game, pitching tends to be emphasized just when baseball is getting its most attention, at World Series or All-Star Game time. Although blacks have long ruled the game on a day-to-day basis as hitters, the stars of most World Series games have been white pitchers. The qhite quarterbacks and pitchers have made football and baseball appear to be much more white than they are. But the success of some black pitchers—notably Bob Gibson and Vida Blue—will probably encourage more good black athletes to take up pitching. It also seems that blacks are at last getting genuine encouragement and opportunities to compete for the quarterback position on pro teams. This will accelerate the pace of black dominance, and it appears that in a few more years almost all the athletic performers—and heroes—will be black. But they will be playing in stadia and arenas in white zones before virtually all-white crowds. There is no reason to expect that the white sports fan will pay money indefinitely for the chance to watch somebody else beat him at his own game.

Assuming that America is not yet ready to cleanse its soul of racial bias, what can logically be expected? All of these projections are, of course, still far in the future, but surely declining attendance figures and TV ratings will be the first sign. (Perhaps it is unfair and hasty to read too much into scattered early returns, but pro-basketball ratings slumped last year for the first time, and tennis was up precipitously.) When the bloom is more apparently off the rose, we might then expect that the cleverest owners—often vain and uncharitable men—would quickly unload their franchises, possibly to black business interests—just as blacks have assumed financial control in areas that whites have deserted.

Basketball is especially vulnerable because, racial problems aside, it is an organic disaster as a game: the players have grown too large and proficient, and the whole sport is mocked by the incredible size and talent of two or three men. Baseball, of course, suffers from an old-fashioned image. Football is the national craze now and appears more substantial than either basketball or baseball, but it is strictly a TV game and susceptible in a flash-flood way. For one thing, pro football is a season-ticket enterprise, and while 50,000 seats may be sold out every week for a team, it is always the same 50,000 people. Most fans' commitment to football involves no more than punching on the TV set. This is hard to translate into dollars and cents for owners and advertisers who are looking for growth patterns and reasonably long-range investments.

Besides, there are always new places for the fans to go. Hockey, a rub-a-dub contest spiced with hokum brawls and goals no one can see until a light goes on, seems to have the brightest future—at least for so long as ticket-buying Americans identify more closely with white Canadians than they do with black Americans. Hockey outsells pro basketball in almost every town where the two sports compete. The only exception is Los Angeles, where the Lakers have been an outstanding team chock-full of superstars, and the Kings' level of hockey play has been an insult to good taste. On the other hand, the most vivid, representative case study involves Philadelphia, which has traditionally viewed itself as the urban cynosure of basketball. The very first season they were in existence (1967–68), the hockey Flyers, dull but all-white, outdrew the predominantly black 76ers, who were then defending world champions with the best record in basketball. A survey taken in Philadelphia in 1970 showed that hockey fans were more affluent, better educated, and lived in better areas than did basketball fans. The survey also established the fact (for whatever it may be worth) that almost three fourths of the hockey and only one fourth of the basketball fans prefer violence in sports.

In any event, hockey could easily become the major winter spectator sport, with the summer dominated by tennis, golf, and auto racing. In the spring and fall, baseball and football might ultimately be replaced by a couple of other team games—soccer and lacrosse, say—that have only been small time in the U.S. so far.

Soccer has great worldwide appeal, though, and both it and lacrosse, which is a rock-'em, sock-'em exercise not unlike hockey, have long flourished in prep schools and suburbs. A professional soccer league of sorts was formed a few years ago, and a regional "club" lacrosse league has been organized along the Eastern Seaboard. It bears a strong resemblance to what the major baseball, football, and basketball associations were in their early stages. Indeed, lacrosse is more structurally advanced today than pro basketball was 25 years ago; and the NBA had no national-TV contract until a dozen years after its creation. Once white fans and money start deserting the black sports, television will probably lead the way in the search for fresh athletic entertainment. Lacrosse and soccer are especially attractive since they are fast, virtually all-white, and can be set conveniently in already existing stadia.

Once they are established and everyone jumps on the band wagon, there could be a quick and complete turnover. Whites would flee from baseball, football, and basketball as they did from Newark, downtown shopping, and beloved old PS 100 once they tilted. If white Americans persist in maintaining the attitudes that result in two separate societies, one price they will have to pay, it seems, will be the loss of the three games that have been such a large part of 20th-Century America.

Democracy in Football

GEORGE DAVIS

Education must be a preparation for life. Of what efficacy are the measures an older generation learns through experience if they cannot be passed down to its progenitors? Our society seems to place a premium on self-reliancy and spontaneity, upon the pressures of life, upon the ability to make a valid decision with the resources which the moment, or the rules, or whatever game or endeavor provide.

Life is flux, moving steadily onward. The individual, society, or species that fails to be either lucky enough or foresighted enough to meet the challenges of this flux simply ceases to exist. Dies.

Mankind, of all else we know, seems to be the only element concerned with dominating that direction. The lion and the antelope try to control, but their efforts seen ineffective alongside our own.

I say "dominate" because quite often the rational measures implied by the word "control" slip by us into the infliction of cruelty, shortsightedness, and the totalitarian approach that we normally associate with "dominate." In our attempts to control nature, we often find ourselves exploiting it. What we like to think of as society, our means of working out a plan to live togehter, very often becomes regimentation. In our dealings with each other on an individual basis, be they economic, marital, or social, equalitarian symbiosis is almost nonexistent.

Any experienced attorney can attest to that.

Life is tough, it is competitive. People are individuals first and joiners later if they can see it serves them. To live a person needs to be alert,

SOURCE: George Davis, quoted in Neil Amdur, *The Fifth Down: Democracy and the Football Revolution* (New York: Delta, 1972), excerpts from pp. 191–198, 209–210, 216–218.

decisive, know how to project goals and how to work to achieve them. He needs to know how to adapt when situations change without worrying that such adaptation is a slur on his ego. He needs to know compassion when opportunity affords him that luxury. He needs to respect rules that have been drawn up to keep the situation he lives in from degenerating to anarchy but which allow him to prove himself and manifest what he has said or wants before he starts toward it.

As a species, we rule the planet, temporarily stalemate nature, and find ways to implement what we have found by experience to help us in these tasks.

Like most species, we respect territory most, because territory means life. Football is a game of territory: You protect your own and try to invade someone else's. Is this a crime? On an international scale, under the present circumstances, yes. But when you consider what is happening to our population, no, it is not.

We need football to keep people cognizant of which qualities are necessary to confront the exigencies of life. I'm not talking abut life as we know it. Most of us live a very artificial life. Farmers and ghetto people are closer to what life has been for most people since man first clubbed the last competing species into submission. Unfortunately, farmers and ghetto people are a minority and we're forced to pay them off from time to time to keep society going.

Football is life in microcosm. If you cannot stretch it that far, mostly due to its inability to include the female in anything but the remote fringes of its activities, then you have to admit that football is war in microcosm. Unquestionably, it has become the best laboratory for discerning what the male of the species has become—not what he ought to be. Any quarterback knows the difference between what is and what ought to be.

I remember hearing a distinguished history teacher say that all male children want to be athletes to begin with. The way athletics is set up, the child gets into it and goes as far as he can until someone knocks him down. If this is true, it stands to reason that there are going to be many males who have to decide whether to stand around and watch and enjoy the games this way or test their athletic spirit in competition.

An increasing preponderance of people have made the decision to watch. If this practice serves in some way to make their lives better, this is wonderful. Our problem is how to get the second-string right guard to feel a part of something, the player who does participate.

Let's look at the second-string right guard. It is February. He has mended, physically and mentally, from the previous season. If he is a high school student, he is thinking about next year, about being able to walk down the street in his hometown as the first-string right guard. If he is a college student, he is concerned about spring practice and the importance of impressing coaches, his girlfriend, parents, alumni. If he is a professional, he knows that the difference between being first-string and second-string is money in his pocket, bread on the table, pride in whatever town he goes home to in the winter or within his own house.

How do you motivate this athlete to go down to the gym and work on the Universal machine, or run repeat 40-yard dashes, or take part in an off-season program?

If he is a high school athlete, you can tell him that next year is it or else no scholarship. If he is a college student on scholarship, you can tell him that if he doesn't do exactly as you tell him you'll rescind his scholarship and let him figure out how to pay for tuition, books, room and board, and laundry. And don't think coaches haven't done that. If he is a pro, he knows the difference in dollar signs and the problems of being "blackballed" as a troublemaker.

You can also present it to him that the program depends on his being stronger and faster. If you do this, he will either work his ass off, and you are the winner, or he will decide that his own interests are more important. In that case, you've lost him temporarily.

Most coaches depend on the power of being able to deny their wards recognition from participation. I wonder how the physics or political science departments of a high school or college would fare if they were able to exert such a strong weapon over their students.

Instructors have grades, which ultimately might deprive a student of funds. But the problem stems from one of those vagaries of evolution: the opaque forehead. Nobody, but nobody, can accurately guess what takes place in the mind of an athlete. The coach might extrapolate from his actions, but the athlete knows this tendency and, therefore, tends to use less and less of the habits that might give some insight into what he is thinking. If an athlete is busy trying to hide how he really feels inside, he cannot produce meaningfully.

Football is more than fun and games. Today it is something that works. I pursued a lot of things in my life to try to find out what life was all about—music, philosophy, most of the social studies, with the exception of math. Sooner or later, I've found, you could question them. What you learn in sociology and psychology today is extremely troubled by theories. The reason is that if mankind is as aggressive and destructive as primate zoological studies say he is, our sociology as we know it today will not work. I've never had to question football, because if you work harder, do it faster, are more determined, and have a little more faith, you can win, trite as some of these values may sound.

I can recall a visit I took to Berkeley, California. It was during the time that the University of California was on strike and some hippie-types, you would call them that, were selling goods they had made, just squatting on the sidewalk beside ornaments, candles, and sandals they had carved out of raw materials. At the time I was with a high school sophomore, a quarterback who I had brought down to watch the Cal spring practice. The boy was intrigued by the sight of these people, but you could sense that he felt detached from this life.

"That's really bad news, isn't it?" he said to me, after we had passed the group. It was the typical remark you would have expected from a young man who had never experienced anything outside of his secure, sheltered, middle-class existence.

What he said infuriated me. I told him that I respected these people because they were selling something that was theirs, that they had made. I said, sure, I couldn't follow them in a number of respects, but they were doing what they wanted to, what they believed in. That boy's father made a living selling something someone else had made, and he sold it at a fat markup, too. What he did wasn't essential, as I see it. Yet he derives more out of it than anyone else.

That boy I was talking to is going to be a leader someday. Yet at that moment he didn't know any more about what life really was than if he had been watching it on television. People are going to depend on that boy in the future, too. Hopefully, our system will help him learn responsibility, the ability to make a decision, and the confidence to follow his decision through to the finish. Football, as well as a hippie selling his wares, depends upon one thing; what you, yourself, do. You can hold your head up only when you are among people who know you. You either get up and get going or cave in and conk out.

Another experience that relates to this came while I was shopping in San Francisco with my wife. We were up at Macy's, in the women's department, and I was putting myself in for a bad half hour, like most men. I found a chair and sat down. Across the way I could see this guy looking at me, like he knew me from somewhere. I never saw him before in my life, but I decided to take a chance. I walked over to him and said, "Where'd you play?"

"Oregon State," he said.

"When?" I asked.

"Nineteen forty-eight to forty-nine," he said.

"You must have played against SC in the Coliseum," I said.

"Hell, yes. Those were some mean games."

We sat there for an hour and talked. I told him who I was. His wife was doing the same thing my wife was. We didn't know each other when we walked in there, but we were still as close as two guys could be. The point was we knew what the other guy was; we didn't have to go through all this card-reading, birth certificates, and social formality. There was no worry about what we had to do to become friends. We knew what we could do. I've got guys I haven't seen in twenty years who I played ball with in college. I can go to them and ask them pretty important questions, personal and private. I'd never ask them for things they couldn't do. I know what they can do. I know how far they'd go. That's pretty important, because I don't think there are people in many areas of life who can do that.

Every coach is looking for answers, but not everyone knows how to achieve this goal. You can be a driver but, in the end, you'll probably destroy as many great athletes as you build. You can follow the book, and many coaches do, but one day you'll find that the answer to your problem isn't on page 96. You can be logical and try to relate; I go with logic, but logic isn't everything. You get more performance out of people with a little less logic and a little more belief.

The biggest problem is motivating your athletes to perform. It's all a matter of motivation. You know what he's going to have to do. Well, who will he do it better for? Will he do it better for an authority or will he do it better for his peer group?

People associated with sociology know the answer. It's the peer group. Most of us all our lives have been cast in roles so tight that we don't dare escape them. I think many coaches feel if they take away the threat of not playing an athlete, the athlete won't obey them. That's not true. They'll be more closely disciplined by their peer group and what they think of them than they would possibly be by what their coaches think of them. Joe Namath is a good example. He's independent, a free soul, but his commitment to his teammates is complete. He would rather hurt himself than his teammates. I believe that.

You know how it is to fool authority. You get a kick out of it. You scribble something on the blackboard when a teacher's out of the room; you sneak up to a rock festival against your parents' orders; you're Jewish and you date Gentiles; you're white and you hang around with blacks. It's tough on the authority the more you try to fool it. Authority can't win because they're too many. You're going to fool them some way—staying out late, partying, loafing in practice. But what happens if you've got the authority. Or if the guy that lets you down is your best buddy? I think you're going to stick in there pretty close, because I think you see good in him and he sees good in you, particularly if he has told you you're the best. You can't chicken out. You've got to produce.

Don't get the idea that this is some type of permissive philosophy, though. It's not. It's just that the motivation lies where it should: what's best for the athlete and the people he's interested in.

One of the major problems with athletics, and with this entire nation, is that somehow motivation has gotten away from the individual. We're trying to escape from responsibility because the responsibility isn't worthwhile or because we didn't ask for it. . . .

I've talked to athletes who've told me that democracy can't work, that team members will play favorites. It can happen. But it's also possible that these athletes have been trained to think that there is a supreme, infallible being who should make all decisions. As such, this athlete is a coach's dream. All this athlete has to do is substitute the coach for that supreme being. It should be easy for him to do this because all he need do is take another step in a direct line from his childhood.

When he was young, he placed his father in the position of being always right. He couldn't do much, and he could see that his father could do just about everything within the scope of a child's world. When he was a freshman in high school, his coach could block and tackle better than he could, so the substitution process continued.

But what happens after he graduates from college? Is he well prepared, or would it have been better if he had made some decisions along the way? Granted, stunting defenses have taken care of the necessity of a player's having to make decisions without the coach's help. But blocking rules are increasingly set to make those decisions automatic. Maybe coaches should install a chess tournament as their first practice technique to find out if anybody can still think in a fluid situation.

Chess should be required training for coaches. It teaches you to consider a direct move in the context of the entire board and all possibilities, including those outside of your control—namely, your opponent's.

That applies to coaching, because the board includes alumni, whose fragile egos are shattered by somebody down the street criticizing the performance of alma mater. It also includes the welfare of the player, in the context that he is at the university to receive an education, not to become the community whipping post for a losing coach. And it includes administrators, at whose whim many coaches are merely pawns.

Someone has to sit in the seat between the father-mother image and adjust reality. That is what teachers and coaches are for. My idea is that they should form a transitional figure between belief in a supreme being and a self-realized product.

You may have athletes who haven't learned the basic requirements of responsible decision-making from their fathers. If that happens, you are going to lose until they learn it from the football situation. It doesn't make any difference whether you vote or not, or how much you yell and scream. The indecision that will beat you is the athlete's failing to make the choice of when to release the sprint-out pass or whether, as the defensive back, to come up or stay back on the sweep.

Coaches insist football isn't the place for social experimentation. But athletes don't get practice in making decisions respecting their interests in the classroom. Kids need the experience of making their decisions; they can master the ability to make the right decision at the right time. Hell, they better. . . .

The importance of the vote is not who gets picked. In the years that I've used the vote, I've hardly ever differed with anybody. The important concept is that the players don't have to do what I want them to do. They can see we'll play anyone. They don't need me. The security blanket for most coaches is that if the athlete doesn't do it the coach's way, the coach won't play the athlete. But the athlete wants to play, even when he's being paid as a professional. He doesn't want to collect $20,000 for sitting on the bench. It's a big recognition factor in his life. He's got to have that; that's why everyone's out there.

The athlete must do what the coach says. As soon as you take authority away, the only reason the athlete has to believe the coach is that you're a better teacher. You're teaching him that your way is right, as opposed to the way he wants to do it.

One of the big misconceptions I see in life for a young man is that parents, society, and school tell him that he has to be a nice guy. Everybody has to like him. He has to be polite, he can't get into fights, he can't be a natural person, he must listen to and respect authority. Result: The athlete gets considerably confused about what winning really means, or succeeding, or how to achieve success in life. It becomes involved, whether you're in a major corporation or on a football team. You worry what the halfback or vice-president does before you worry about what you do.

This indecisiveness has produced a funny kind of guy in our society. He'd rather have someone else make the decisions, so if anything goes wrong, he can blame him. This is the syndrome. It runs all the way from blaming the President to blaming the football coach. Democracy is hard on its leaders, because the public can criticize and nobody can really change the political structure until the next election.

In many cases, democracy is probably too hard on its leaders, because it's getting so that the leaders are making strange decisions and avoiding the issues. It becomes, again, a fear of failure.

The athlete doesn't want responsibility for the same reason; he's afraid of failure. Plus the fact that there is this credibility gap, this lack of communication between what is preached by the coach and what must be practiced by the athlete. The vote eliminates a generation gap. The gap may be there, but it doesn't make any difference. The athlete has to worry about what his own peer group thinks about him, not the coach. He can't escape his friends. He can't find a place to drink without them knowing; he can't find a place to smoke without them knowing. They know if he's goofing off, if he's hitting, if he's trying as hard as he did last year. This is something the coach may not know.

The rewarding aspect about our democracy, about any democracy, is that it works. The wonderful thing that's finally happened in America is that we educated our children for democracy, we did a good job, and now that they're democratic and militant as hell, we're overreacting. Schools have been a tremendous success because they've induced students to think. The only problem now is that you can't fool the students. They won't accept everything you tell them.

Some cynics say that quarterbacks can't tell who's better at right guard, that professionals would vote only for themselves, not their teammates. Tell me one player who didn't want to win, at any price. Tell me one player who didn't want to play with the best possible eleven men. Name one pro quarterback who wants to drop back and pass when one of his bodyguards in the offensive line is sliding on his ass. Name one pro player who wouldn't love to cash a check as champion of the National Football League and another for the Super Bowl, not to mention all those endorsements that are passed around after the season.

No one likes to lose. The vote gives the players the opportunity to express their viewpoint, and not just between cliques or in polarized situations between black and white.

A coach once told me that no black football player would ever vote for a white athlete over a black brother at the same position. On a team that is polarized with racial problems, I'd agree. No team can win if it is split along these lines. That's one of the crucial areas of democracy, any democracy, on or off the field. If you have incompetent politicians or bad players who don't play it straight, you'll lose and you'll lose badly. You'll have too many divergent forces tugging in too many different directions for their own gain. They're not being fair with their constituents or their teammates.

What does the vote achieve? It takes the problems of discipline and responsibility and puts them where they belong, with the players. The coach becomes a teacher, what he is being paid to do, a resource unit. My job is to teach, to help athletes reach a level of independence. At any level this is how democracy works and why it succeeds.

■ FOR FURTHER STUDY

Brown, Gwilym S. "Jeepers! Peppers is in Charge Now." *Sports Illustrated* (October 23, 1972), pp. 40–49.

Coakley, Jay J. *Sport in Society: Issues and Controversies.* St. Louis: C. V. Mosby, 1978, chapter 12.

Crase, Darrell. "The Continuing Crisis in Athletics." *Phi Delta Kappan,* 56 (October, 1974), 99–101.

Dickinson, Vern. "Modernization and Sport." *Quest,* 24 (Summer 1975), 48–58.

Donnelly, Peter. "Vertigo in America: A Social Comment." *Quest,* 27 (Winter 1977), 106–113.

Edwards, Harry. *Sociology of Sport.* Homewood, Illinois: Dorsey, 1973, chapter 12.

Edwards, Harry. "Change and Crisis in Modern Sport." *Black Scholar*, 8 (1976), 60–65.

Elias, Norbert, and Eric Dunning. "The Quest for Excitement in Unexciting Societies." *The Cross-Cultural Analysis of Sport and Games*. Edited by Gunther Luschen. Champaign, Illinois: Stipes, 1970, pp. 31–51.

Fixx, James F. *The Complete Book of Running*. New York: Random House, 1977, chapter 23.

Furst, R. Terry. "Social Change and the Commercialization of Professional Sports." *International Review of Sport Sociology*, 6 (1971), 153–170.

"Games Big People Play," *Mother Jones* (September/October 1976).

Gammons, Peter. "A Matter of Dollars and Sense." *Sports Illustrated* (November 29, 1976), pp. 28–29.

Gilbert, Bil. "Gleanings from a Troubled Time." *Sports Illustrated* (December 25, 1972), pp. 34–46.

Gilbert, Bil. "Imagine Going to School to Learn to Play." *Sports Illustrated* (October 13, 1975), pp. 84–87.

Goodman, Cary. "Degoaling Sports." *Sport Sociology Bulletin*, 5 (Fall 1976), 11–13.

Hellison, Donald R. *Humanistic Physical Education*. Englewood Cliffs, N.J.: Prentice-Hall, 1973.

Hellison, Don. *Beyond Balls and Bats*. Washington, D.C.: AAHPER, 1978.

Heywood, Lloyd A., and Rodney B. Warnick. "Campus Recreation: The Intramural Revolution." *Journal of Physical Education and Recreation*, 47 (October 1976), 52–54.

Hjortsberg, W. "Goodby, Goodby, Goodby, Mr. Chips." *Sports Illustrated* (1976), pp. 88–96.

Hogan, Candace Lyle. "Fair Shake or Shakedown?" *WomenSports*, 3 (September 1976), 50–54.

Ingham, A.G. "Occupational Subcultures in the Work World of Sport." *Sport and Social Order*. Edited by D. W. Ball and J. W. Loy. Reading, Mass.: Addison-Wesley, 1975, pp. 333–389.

Kahn, Roger. "Jack Scott: How Radical is Radical, Anyhow?" *Esquire*, 84 (October 1975), 48–54.

Kando, Thomas M. *Leisure and Popular Culture in Transition*. St. Louis: C. V. Mosby, 1975.

Kirshenbaum, Jerry. "Assembly Line for Champions." *Sports Illustrated* (July 12, 1976), pp. 56–65.

Laughlin, N. T. "Existentialism, Education, and Sport." *Issues in Physical Education and Sport*. Edited by G. H. McGlynn. Palo Alto, Calif.: National Press Books, 1974, pp. 169–180.

Lawson, R. A. "Physical Education and Sport: Alternatives for the Future." *Quest*, 21 (January 1974), 19–29.

Leonard, George. *The Ultimate Athlete*. New York: Viking Press, 1975.

Leonard, John. "No Sweat: The Coming Leisure." *New Times*, 8 (January 7, 1977), 64–68.

Ley, Katherine. "Women in Sports: Where Do We Go From Here, Boys?" *Phi Delta Kappan*, 56 (October 1974), 129–131.

Lipsyte, Robert. *Sports World: An American Dreamland*. New York: Quadrangle/New York Times Book Company, 1975.

Miller, Stuart. "New Directions in Sport." *Intellectual Digest*, 4 (September 1973), 48–50.

Mosston, M., and R. Mueller. "Mission, Omission, and Submission in Physical Education." *Issues in Physical Education and Sport*. Edited by G. H. McGlynn. Palo Alto, Calif.: National Press Books, 1974, pp. 97–106.

Poe, Randall. "The Angry Fan." *Harper's* (November 1975), pp. 86–95.

Rosato, Frank. "The Group Process: Some Suggestions for Athletics." *The Physical Educator*, 31 (May 1974), 87–89.

Rust, Val D., and Terry Schofield. "The West German Sports Club System: A Model for Lifelong Learning." *Phi Delta Kappan*, 59 (April 1978), 543–546.

Sage, George H. "Humanistic Theory, the Counterculture, and Sport: Implications for Action and Research." *Sport and American Society*. 2nd ed. Edited by George H. Sage. Reading, Mass.: Addison-Wesley, 1974, pp. 415–429.

Scott, Jack. *The Athletic Revolution*. New York: Free Press, 1971.

Scott, Jack. "Sport and the Radical Ethic." *Quest*, 19 (January 1973), 71–77.

Stern, Barry E. "The Cultural Crisis in American Sports." *JOPER*, 43 (April 1972), 42–44.

Weiner, Jay. "Athletic Revolution at Oberlin . . ." *I.S.S.S. Newsletter*, 1 (February 1973), 1, 13.

Wilson, Wayne. "Social Discontent and the Growth of Wilderness Sport in America: 1965-1974." *Quest*, 27 (Winter 1977), 54–60.

Wolf, Gary K. *Killerbowl*. Garden City, N.Y.: Doubleday, 1975.

■ SELECTED PERIODICALS

American Journal of Sport Psychology, Professor Rainer Martens, Department of Physical Education, University of Illinois, Champaign-Urbana, Illinois 61820.

Arena. The Institute for Sport and Social Analysis. Virginia Wesleyan College, Wesleyan Drive, Norfolk, Virginia 23502.

Black Sports. Published by Black Sports, Inc., 386 Park Avenue South, New York, New York 10016.

International Journal of Sport Psychology. International Society of Sport Psychology, Edizioni Luigi Pozzi, Via Panama 68, 00198, Rome, Italy.

International Review of Sport Sociology. Committee for the Selection of Sport of the International Council of Sport and Physical Education (UNESCO) and of the International Sociological Association, Polish Scientific Publishers, Marymoncka 34, Academy of Physical Education, Warsaw, Poland.

Journal of Leisure Research. Published by the National Recreation and Park Association, 606 Clark Hall, University of Missouri, Columbia, Missouri 65201.

Journal of Physical Education and Recreation. Published by the American Association for Health, Physical Education, and Recreation, 1201 Sixteenth Street, N.W., Washington, D.C. 20036.

Journal of Sport and Social Issues. The Institute for Sport and Social Analysis, Virginia Wesleyan College, Wesleyan Drive, Norfolk, Virginia 23502.

Journal of Sport Behavior. Sponsored by the United States Sports Academy, University of South Alabama, Mobile, Alabama 36688.

Journal of Sport History. North American Society for Sport History, 101 White Building, Pennsylvania State University, University Park, Pennsylvania 16802.

LeftField. Published by The Fight to Advance the Nation's Sports, 1028 Connecticut Avenue, Suite 607, Washington, D.C. 20036.

Quest. Department of Health, Physical Education and Recreation, University of Maryland, College Park, Maryland.

The Physical Educator. Published by Phi Epsilon Kappa, 9030 Log Run Drive North, Indianapolis, Indiana 46234.

Research Quarterly. Published by the American Association for Health, Physical Education, and Recreation, 1201 Sixteenth Street, N.W., Washington, D.C. 20036.

Review of Sport and Leisure. Department of Recreation Studies, Governors State University, Park Forest South, Illinois 60466.

Sport. Published by MVP Sports, Inc., a subsidiary of Downe Communications, Inc., 641 Lexington Avenue, New York, New York 10022.

The Sporting News. 1212 N. Lindbergh Blvd., St. Louis, Missouri 63166.

Sports Illustrated. Published by Time, Inc., 541 North Fairbanks Court, Chicago, Illinois 60611.

WomenSports. Published by Charter Publishing Company, 230 Park Avenue, New York, New York 10017.